PERSONALITY DISORDERS

AND THE FIVE-FACTOR MODEL OF PERSONALITY

PERSONALITY DISORDERS
AND THE FIVE-FACTOR MODEL OF PERSONALITY

EDITED BY PAUL T. COSTA, JR. AND THOMAS A. WIDIGER

factor

AMERICAN PSYCHOLOGICAL ASSOCIATION ▪ WASHINGTON, DC

First printing December 1993
Second printing November 1994

Published by
American Psychological Association
750 First Street, NE
Washington, DC 20002-4242

Copies may be ordered from
APA Order Department
P.O. Box 2710
Hyattsville, MD 20784

In the UK and Europe, copies may be ordered from
American Psychological Association
3 Henrietta Street
Covent Garden, London
WC2E 8LU United Kingdom

Typeset in Berkeley by Impressions, Madison, WI

Printer: Edwards Brothers, Inc., Ann Arbor, MI
Dust Jacket Printer: Phoenix Color Corp., Hagerstown, MD
Cover and Jacket Designer: Grafik Communications, Ltd., Alexandria, VA
Technical/Production Editors: Mark A. Meschter and Cynthia L. Fulton

Library of Congress Cataloging-in-Publication Data
Personality disorders and the five-factor model of personality / Paul T. Costa, Jr. and Thomas A. Widiger, editors
    p.   cm.
    Includes bibliographical references and index.
    ISBN 1-55798-214-7 (acid-free paper)
    1. Personality disorders. 2. NEO Five-Factor Inventory. 3. NEO Personality Inventory. I. Costa, Paul T. II. Widiger, Thomas A. III. Title: Five-factor model of personality.
RC554.P474 1993
616.85'8—dc20
                            93-26795
                                CIP

British Library Cataloguing-in-Publication Data
A CIP record is available from the British Library

Printed in the United States of America

Contents

Contributors

Robert K. Brooner, *Department of Psychiatry and Behavioral Sciences, Johns Hopkins University School of Medicine*

Stephen Bruehl, *Department of Behavioral Science, University of Kentucky College of Medicine*

Lee Anna Clark, *Department of Psychology, University of Iowa*

John F. Clarkin, *Department of Psychiatry, Cornell University Medical Center*

Elizabeth M. Corbitt, *Department of Psychiatry, Indiana University Medical Center*

Paul T. Costa, Jr., *Gerontology Research Center, National Institute on Aging, Baltimore, Maryland*

John M. Digman, *Oregon Research Institute, Eugene, Oregon*

Cynthia G. Ellis, *Department of Psychology, University of Kentucky*

Peter J. Fagan, *Department of Psychiatry and Behavioral Sciences, Johns Hopkins Medical Institutions*

Allen J. Frances, *Department of Psychiatry and Behavioral Sciences, Duke University Medical Center*

Robert D. Hare, *Department of Psychology, University of British Columbia*

Timothy J. Harpur, *Department of Psychology, University of Illinois at Urbana–Champaign*

Stephen D. Hart, *Department of Psychology, University of British Columbia*

Jeffrey H. Herbst, *Gerontology Research Center, National Insitute on Aging, Baltimore, Maryland*

Gregory K. Lehne, *Private Practice, Baltimore, Maryland*

W. John Livesley, *Department of Psychiatry, University of British Columbia*

K. Roy MacKenzie, *Department of Psychiatry, University of British Columbia*

Robert R. McCrae, *Gerontology Research Center, National Institute on Aging, Baltimore, Maryland*

Joyce L. McEwen, *Department of Psychology, Southern Methodist University*

Theodore Millon, *Department of Psychology, University of Miami and Harvard Medical School*

Aaron L. Pincus, *Department of Psychology, Pennsylvania State University*

Cynthia Sanderson, *Department of Psychiatry, Cornell University Medical College*

Chester W. Schmidt, Jr., *Department of Psychiatry and Behavioral Sciences, Johns Hopkins University School of Medicine*

Marsha L. Schroeder, *Department of Psychology, University of British Columbia*

Glenn V. Thomas, *Department of Psychology, University of Kentucky*

Timothy J. Trull, *Department of Psychology, University of Missouri–Columbia*

Lu Vorhies, *Department of Psychology, Southern Methodist University*

Thomas A. Widiger, *Department of Psychology, University of Kentucky*

Jerry S. Wiggins, *Department of Psychology, University of British Columbia*

Janice A. Wormworth, *Department of Psychology, University of British Columbia*

INTRODUCTION: PERSONALITY DISORDERS AND THE FIVE-FACTOR MODEL OF PERSONALITY

Paul T. Costa, Jr. and Thomas A. Widiger

In the last 10 years, interest in personality disorder research has shown substantial growth. Personality disorders were, no doubt, catapulted into a prominent position by the creation of a special axis, Axis II, with its release in the third edition of the *Diagnostic and Statistical Manual of Mental Disorders* (*DSM-III*; American Psychiatric Association, 1980) multiaxial classification of mental disorders system in 1980. Research interest in personality disorders can be documented by the fact that over 750 empirical studies are abstracted in the American Psychological Association's *PsycLIT* database, covering the 5-year period from January 1987 to June 1992. The *Journal of Personality Disorders* is devoted exclusively to the area. The many national and international conferences and workshops that have been held on personality disorders also attest to this growth.

But this large and growing literature on personality disorders should not obscure the fact that there are serious theoretical and methodological problems with the whole *DSM-III* personality disorder diagnostic enterprise. Officially, the diagnostic criteria sets of *DSM-III*'s Axis II are supposed to define or diagnose patients into mutually exclusive, categorical diagnostic entities. But as many reports document, the average number of personality disorder diagnoses is often greater than 4 (Skodol, Rosnick, Kellman, Oldham, & Hyler, 1988; Widiger, Trull, Hurt, Clarkin, & Frances, 1987). This comorbidity is a serious problem because it suggests redundancy, or a lack of divergent construct validity, for the 11 diagnostic categories (see Appendix C for a listing of the 11 current and proposed personality disorder categories).

Other crucial problems concern the lack of evidence supporting the construct validity of many of the personality disorder categories, problems of excessive comorbidity among the Axis II disorders (Nurnberg et al., 1991; Widiger et al., 1991), and comorbidity of Axis I and Axis II diagnoses (Docherty, Fiester, & Shea, 1986; McGlashan, 1987; Widiger & Hyler, 1987).

Many of the problems of *DSM-III* might be resolved by using continuous dimensions instead of discrete categories. Dimensional alternatives have been frequently proposed, but until recently, there was no consensus on which personality dimensional model should be used. The *five-factor model* (FFM; Digman, 1990; McCrae, 1992) is a taxonomy of personality traits in terms of five broad dimensions (the "Big Five"): *Neuroticism* (N), *Extraversion* (E), *Openness to Experience* (O), *Agreeableness* (A), and *Conscientiousness* (C). An emergent and still-growing consensus on the FFM suggests that this is a comprehensive classification of personality dimensions that may be a conceptually useful framework for understanding personality disorders.

By the early 1990s there had been considerable research confirming the FFM and demonstrating the value of studying individual differences in personality (e.g., Digman, 1990; McCrae, 1992; Wiggins & Pincus, 1989). But one important question was whether studies using the models and methods of normal personality research could shed light on psychopathological and psychiatric problems, particularly personality disorders.

"Normal" and "abnormal" psychology have traditionally been considered separate fields, but this rigid

1

dichotomy has never made sense to trait psychologists. Trait psychologists know that individual differences in most characteristics are continuously distributed, and it seems reasonable to hypothesize that different forms of psychopathology might be related to normal variations in basic personality dispositions.

Considerable evidence in support of this hypothesis is provided by results of analyses relating measures of personality to measures of psychopathology in normal and clinical samples. A number of studies (e.g., Costa & McCrae, 1990; Morey, 1986; Trull, 1992) show general parallels between psychopathological and normal personality dimensions. Many of the chapters in this book explore ways in which normal personality dimensions can illuminate clinical constructs. We hope that the book helps promote further research and facilitates integration of research on personality disorders with decades of research on normal personality structure and measurement.

From the time this book was first contemplated, interest in and efforts to apply the FFM to a variety of different disorders and populations has moved at a rapid pace. We originally limited our focus to diagnostic issues, but the scope has now been enlarged to include treatment implications and alternative reconceptualizations.

We hope that the reader will want to read on and sample directly the fruits of the field, as it were. One aim of this book is to promote greater interest and research between the FFM and personality disorders. The book is intended to give its readers a glimpse of the application of the FFM to diagnosis and treatment of the personality disorders.

BACKGROUND OF THE FFM

The FFM is a hierarchical model of the structure of personality traits. *Personality traits* are often defined as enduring "dimensions of individual differences in tendencies to show consistent patterns of thoughts, feelings, and actions" (McCrae & Costa, 1990, p. 23). Traits reflect relatively enduring dispositions and are distinguished from *states* or *moods*, which are more transient. The FFM had its origins in analyses of trait-descriptive terms in the natural language. John, Angleitner, and Ostendorf (1988) have given

an excellent account of this important line of research, and the contributions of Tupes and Christal (1961), Norman (1963), Goldberg (1982), and Borkenau and Ostendorf (1990) are deservedly recognized.

But most research and practice of personality assessment has been based on questionnaires. As Wiggins (1968) wrote, the "Big Two" dimensions of N and E have been long associated with Hans Eysenck. Another two-dimensional model that deserves special attention is the interpersonal circle model (i.e., the *interpersonal circumplex*) associated with Kiesler (1983), Leary (1957), and Wiggins (1982).

With the addition of *Psychoticism* (P), Eysenck's P, E, N model (1975) is one of several competing three-factor models. Tellegen (1985) has advanced an alternative three-factor model that substitutes *Constraint* for P. It should be noted that in Tellegen's model both N and E are construed as the dimensions *Negative Affectivity* (NA) and *Positive Affectivity*, respectively. Cloninger (1987), a psychiatrist, has advanced a neuroadaptive-based personality model with three dimensions that is both similar to and different from Eysenck and Tellegen's three-factor models. In Cloninger's model, N (or NA) is called *Harm Avoidance*; *Novelty Seeking* is largely low C; and the third dimension, *Reward Dependence*, has no simple and direct correspondence to any of the five established dimensions of the FFM (Costa & McCrae, 1993).

Dimensional models that contain more factors than the familiar five are seen in the 10 factors of Guilford, Zimmerman, and Guilford's (1976) Guilford–Zimmerman Temperament Survey. Of course, Cattell's (Cattell, Eber, & Tatsuoka, 1970) Sixteen Personality Factor Questionnaire represents Cattell's model of 16 primary personality traits.

All of these systems are interesting, and many are valuable in understanding personality disorders, especially the interpersonal circumplex. But mounting evidence suggests that all or nearly all of these models can be either subsumed by the FFM or interpreted in terms of it. Postulated dimensions beyond the Big Five, such as the Guilford–Zimmerman and Cattell models, for example, are generally regarded as tapping trait dimensions at a lower level in the hierarchy.

The consensus currently is that at the second-order level, the five broad dimensions of N, E, O, A, and C are the basic dimensions of personality. For the sake of this text, we have adopted the position articulated by McCrae and John (1992) that it is fruitful to assume that the FFM is the correct representation of the structure of traits and move on to its application to important topics and outcomes in psychological and psychiatric practice.

The present collection of chapters, therefore, does not attempt to present a balanced view of alternative dimensional models applied to personality disorders. It specifically adopts the FFM perspective. In fact, this book is organized around the premise that the FFM is the most adequate and comprehensive taxonomy for describing personality and for understanding problems associated with personalities or personality disorders.

DESCRIPTION OF FACTORS

In this section, we briefly describe the broad or higher order dimensions of the FFM. These dimensions are defined by many more specific traits. One specification is provided by the facet scales of the Revised NEO Personality Inventory (NEO-PI-R; Costa & McCrae, 1992), an instrument designed to measure the FFM. Details on the facets are given in Appendix D.

Neuroticism

N refers to the chronic level of emotional adjustment and instability. High N identifies individuals who are prone to psychological distress. As mentioned earlier, an alternative label is NA, but N also includes unrealistic ideas, excessive cravings or difficulty in tolerating the frustration caused by not acting on one's urges, and maladaptive coping responses. As shown in Appendix D, N includes the facet scales for anxiety, angry hostility, depression, self-consciousness, impulsivity, and vulnerability.

Extraversion

E refers to the quantity and intensity of preferred interpersonal interactions, activity level, need for stimulation, and capacity for joy. People who are high in E tend to be sociable, active, talkative, person oriented, optimistic, fun loving, and affectionate; whereas people who are low in E tend to be reserved (but not necessarily unfriendly), sober, aloof, independent, and quiet. Introverts are not unhappy or pessimistic people, but they are not given to the exuberant high spirits that characterize extraverts.

Openness to Experience

O is much less well known than either N or E and, in fact, is often construed differently as the alternative label *intellect* suggests. But O differs from ability and intelligence and involves the active seeking and appreciation of experiences for their own sake. Open individuals are curious, imaginative, and willing to entertain novel ideas and unconventional values; they experience the whole gamut of emotions more vividly than do closed individuals. By contrast, closed individuals (those who are low in O) tend to be conventional in their beliefs and attitudes, conservative in their tastes, dogmatic, and rigid in their beliefs; they are behaviorally set in their ways and emotionally unresponsive.

Agreeableness

A, like E, is an interpersonal dimension and refers to the kinds of interactions a person prefers along a continuum from compassion to antagonism. People who are high in A tend to be softhearted, good-natured, trusting, helpful, forgiving, and altruistic. Eager to help others, they tend to be responsive and empathic and believe that most others want to and will behave in the same manner. Those who are low in A (called antagonistic) tend to be cynical, rude or even abrasive, suspicious, uncooperative, and irritable, and can be manipulative, vengeful, and ruthless.

Conscientiousness

C assesses the degree of organization, persistence, control, and motivation in goal-directed behavior. People who are high in C tend to be organized, reliable, hard-working, self-directed, punctual, scrupulous, ambitious, and persevering; whereas those who are low in C tend to be aimless, unreliable, lazy, careless, lax, negligent, and hedonistic.

METHODS OF ASSESSMENT

It must be pointed out that there are a number of different instruments to measure the FFM. These include various adjective-based instruments: Goldberg (1982, 1992) has developed several sets of adjective measures of the FFM including 50 transparent bipolar adjective sets and 100 unipolar adjective markers. Wiggins and Trapnell (in press) have melded the insights from the lexical tradition with the theoretical sophistication of the interpersonal circumplex with the development of the Interpersonal Adjective Scales Revised–Big Five. Q-sort procedures developed by McCrae, Costa, and Busch (1986) and Robbins, John, and Caspi (in press) are also available. In the questionnaire area, there is the Hogan Personality Inventory (Hogan, 1986), a six-factor variant of the FFM that was designed to reflect Hogan's socioanalytic theory. Many of the chapters in this book use the NEO Personality Inventory (NEO-PI; Costa & McCrae, 1985), which was designed to operationalize a hierarchical model of the FFM, and the NEO-PI-R (Costa & McCrae, 1992), which became available in 1992 after most of the empirical studies reported in this book were completed.

In addition to self-reports, there are a number of different procedures that can be used to measure the dimensions of the FFM, including observer ratings (Form R) of the NEO-PI-R for spouses and peers and clinician ratings. The FFM is not just a theoretical model but is operationalized in a number of different though converging ways. For example, Costa and McCrae (in press) recently reported convergence among a number of these measures of the FFM.

The third, revised edition of the *Diagnostic and Statistical Manual of Mental Disorders* (DSM-III-R; American Psychiatric Association, 1987) provides criteria to make the diagnosis of each personality disorder, but it does not provide any reliable and valid means of assessing individuals or their personality traits. There are several well-validated measures of the FFM, and if they were to be consistently used in personality disorder research, then they might contribute to advances in the field.

CONTENTS OF THE PRESENT BOOK

Part I: Conceptual Background

The first of the five parts that make up this book is titled Conceptual Background and contains three chapters. In chapter 1, Digman provides an insightful historical background for the FFM itself. Far from being of recent vintage, the FFM has a hoary pedigree, tracing its roots to McDougall (1932) and Thurstone (1934). But as Digman notes, the model was virtually ignored for years by mainstream personologists and has had a very tardy reception. He ably discusses several reasons and concludes on an optimistic note that there may be a paradigm shift occurring today in personality studies, and the long-ignored FFM may be the new paradigm of personality structure of the future.

In chapter 2, Widiger and Frances comprehensively review the conceptual and empirical support for dimensional and categorical representations of personality disorders. They ably discuss the advantages and disadvantages of the categorical and dimensional models of classification. Particularly useful is their evaluation of the empirical data that are relevant to the respective validity of these two perspectives. They review alternative dimensional models including Cloninger's neuroadaptive model (1987), the interpersonal circumplex, the biogenetic spectrum model of Siever and Davis (1991), and Gunderson's hierarchical model (Gunderson, Links, & Reich, 1991). As might be expected, they pay particular attention to the empirical support for the FFM as the most compelling choice for the representation of personality disorders. Interestingly, they point out important obstacles that the FFM must overcome before clinicians can be expected to use it within their practices.

Chapter 3, titled "A Description of the *DSM-III-R* and *DSM-IV* Personality Disorders With the Five-Factor Model of Personality," represents a conceptual effort by us and the prominent clinicians Clarkin, Sanderson, and Trull to translate the *DSM-III-R* and proposed *DSM-IV* personality disorders into the hierarchical model of the five factors as operationalized by the scales of the NEO-PI-R. Table 1 in this chapter (see also Appendix A) represents testable hypotheses about the maladaptively extreme facets for each of the 11 *DSM-III-R* personality disorder categories. Table 2 (see also Appendix B) lists the hypothesized facets for the 4 new personality disorder categories proposed for *DSM-IV*. We hope that these hypotheses will be tested in future clinical research.

Part II: Empirical Research

Because the FFM has only been applied to personality disorders in the last few years, there are few studies in the literature. But the few that are to be found confirm the premise that personality disorders can be understood in terms of the FFM personality dimensions. Trull and McCrae in chapter 4 review the limited evidence showing that individuals with different personality disorders differ in predictable ways on the five factors. They suggest that the FFM can aid in understanding each disorder's core symptomatology, as well as the overlap between Axis I and Axis II disorders. They also provide thoughtful analyses of the constructs for the borderline and narcissistic personality disorders and make cogent suggestions for further research.

In chapter 5, Wiggins and Pincus present a lucid and forceful account of structural conceptualizations of personality dimensions and personality disorders from the dyadic and FFM interactional perspectives. These authors demonstrate empirically that Millon's influential conceptions of personality disorders as embodied in the Millon Clinical Multiaxial Inventory (MCMI; Millon, 1982) scales correspond to the well-established dimensions of normal personality. Wiggins and Pincus also illustrate a unique approach to assessing personality pathology, called *combined-model assessment*, which uses the eight interpersonal scales of the interpersonal circumplex along with the domain scores of N, O, and C from the FFM.

The next two chapters identify the basic dimensions of personality pathology that underlie the personality disorder categories. Clark, Vorhies, and McEwen (in chapter 6) explore the boundaries of normal range personality and abnormal personality. They define the constituent components of maladaptive personality traits through a series of sophisticated conceptual and statistical analyses. Their chapter gives a clear account of the 22 personality disorder symptom clusters and a self-report inventory, the Schedule for Nonadaptive and Adaptive Per-

sonality (SNAP [formerly the Schedule for Normal and Abnormal Personality]; Clark, 1993), developed to assess personality disorders. Their results lend strong support for a dimensional approach to the assessment of personality disorders by showing that the FFM is sufficient in scope to account for most of the reliable variance in these personality disorder traits. They also present some interesting analyses that seek to determine whether the O and A dimensions of the FFM add incremental validity to the prediction of maladaptive traits beyond the three-dimensional or N, E, C dimensions of Tellegen (1985) and Cloninger (1987).

Schroeder, Wormworth, and Livesley (in chapter 7) provide an important investigation of dimensions of personality pathology different than those of the *DSM-III-R*. Livesley, Jackson, and Schroeder (1992) developed the Dimensional Assessment of Personality Pathology–Basic Questionnaire (DAPP-BQ) as an alternative to the Axis II categories of *DSM-III-R*. Although all 16 scales of the DAPP-BQ are encompassed by the five personality dimensions, not all disorder scales predicted equally or with high levels of precision. Scales with specific behavioral content or focus (e.g., intimacy and conduct problems) are not well predicted by the NEO-PI scales and raise the issue of whether additional dimensions of personality pathology are necessary to give a more comprehensive and precise specification of the personality disorder domain.

Part III: Patient Populations and Clinical Cases

The first three chapters that make up this part examine the FFM in clinical populations. In chapter 8, Brooner, Schmidt, and Herbst apply the NEO-PI to a clinical population principally defined by an Axis I disorder: substance abuse. Outpatient opioid abusers with and without comorbid Axis II diagnoses are characterized on the NEO-PI scales. Brooner et al. examine four relatively pure personality disorder groups: antisocial, avoidant, borderline, and paranoid. The respective personality profiles of these disorders generally support the hypothesized predictions of Widiger et al. of chapter 3. The authors lastly present several cases that demonstrate how personality characteristics and life history relate to personality disorder diagnoses.

The psychopathic personality has long been of gripping interest to personality psychopathologists and those interested in understanding the antisocial personality disorder. The authors of chapter 9—Harpur, Hart, and Hare—are internationally known experts on the topic, and their contribution provides a scholarly comparison of the FFM and the two-factor theory of psychopathy. The Psychopathy Check List (Hare, 1980; Hare & Frazelle, 1980) is compared with Eysenck's P, E, N model to illustrate that considerable variance is unaccounted for in Eysenck's three-dimensional model. Harpur et al. help the reader to understand that the key personality characteristics, as opposed to the chronic antisocial behaviors and lifestyle, of the psychopath—the selfishness, callousness, and remorseless use of others—is strongly related to low agreeableness or antagonism.

In chapter 10, Lehne (a practicing clinician) explores the usefulness of self-report inventories of clinical and normal personality in the forensic evaluation of sex offenders. Lehne's data and experience present a remarkable counterpoint to the often expressed concern that self-reports are inherently untrustworthy and not relevant to clinical practice. The portrait painted by Lehne's data on the MCMI and the NEO-PI is both reassuring and informative. Data from this clinical sample replicate relations between NEO-PI and MCMI scales and, furthermore, show that sex offenders are high on N (and all six of its facets) and high on excitement seeking. Lehne questions whether traditional reliance on personality disorder diagnoses to transmit information about individuals embroiled in a forensic evaluation is useful and appropriate. He suggests that future research should focus more on personality dispositions to provide information that is useful in understanding forensic clients and their rehabilitation planning.

Four clinical cases of personality disorder are presented in the next four chapters. As the reader will note, several authors move straight into the case study without providing background discussion of the personality disorder in question. This should not be problematic because the personality disorders in these chapters are well known (e.g., borderline personality disorder).

Bruehl, in chapter 11, presents the case of Betty, a 45-year-old white divorced female who is diagnosed as borderline personality disorder. This case presentation, as well as the others in this section, aptly illustrate and apply the theoretical descriptions provided in chapter 3. Bruehl discusses the clinical ratings of Betty on the traits measured by the NEO-PI-R and links both her Axis I symptoms (which include sleep problems, appetite disturbance, social withdrawal, etc.) and her borderline symptomatology to high N facets and the low E facets of warmth, gregariousness, and positive emotions. Particularly interesting is Bruehl's discussion of Betty's high values, ideas, and openness to fantasy as they relate to her history of childhood sexual abuse and the sexual identity confusion she exhibits.

Corbitt (in chapter 12) deals with narcissism in a sophisticated clinical analysis of the diagnostic construct and suggests that the FFM translation may not be as straightforward as Widiger et al. posit in chapter 3. Corbitt focuses on the ambiguity and complicated evaluation of the narcissistic patient's response to criticism by others and the reasons for seeking treatment. The patient's self-description as given by her NEO-PI-R profile illustrates the salient role of low agreeableness facets and low facet scores on self-consciousness and vulnerability as contributing to her narcissistic disorder. Other aspects of the patient's personality profile are used to highlight treatment issues.

In chapter 13, Ellis presents an illustration of the Axis I eating disorder bulimia nervosa, which is complicated by the involvement of a variety of comorbid Axis II disorders, including avoidant and borderline personality disorders and recurrent major depression. As Ellis's detailed life history and treatment history of patient Alice make clear, Alice's enduring difficulty in controlling her urges and impulses is manifested in her substance use, promiscuity, and self-destructive behavior. Ellis makes clear that although Alice meets *DSM-III-R* criteria for borderline and avoidant personality disorders, the author prefers to understand her patient's clinical pathology as stemming from her maladaptive personality traits of high N and low E. Treatment focus and progress are nicely related by Ellis to Alice's core personality features.

In chapter 14, Thomas presents the last case in Part IV, a mixed personality disorder with passive–

aggressive and avoidant features. This chapter reflects a common clinical scenario of an outpatient client who is difficult to diagnose because she displays symptoms from many personality disorders, though few if any of them are prototypical. Thomas's recounting of his patient Sarah's course of therapy nicely illustrates the central role of insight and understanding of one's own personality. Again, the descriptive comprehensiveness of the FFM helps to resolve this diagnostic uncertainty in a manner that also allows effective treatment planning.

Part IV: Treatment of Personality-Disordered Patients

Sanderson and Clarkin (in chapter 15), with their enormously rich clinical experience, provide a clinically astute examination of how the five personality dimensions of the FFM affect therapy focus, alliance, and outcome. Their chapter illustrates with clinical vignettes how patient dimensions assessed by the FFM are related to planning and applying psychological interventions. The authors discuss disorder-specific treatment approaches and the need to individually optimize therapy procedures by taking into account the patient's assets and liabilities, problem complexity, coping style, and reactance level.

Sanderson and Clarkin present an NEO-PI profile for female borderline personality disorder patients based on 64 carefully diagnosed patients who presented with impulsive acting out (and more direct suicidal behavior) and on a specific 26-year-old female borderline patient in an attempt to show how the personality profile can help in treatment planning.

K. Roy MacKenzie's chapter 16, "Using Personality Measurements in Clinical Practice," provides a practical guide to using structured instruments to assess psychotherapy candidates. Mackenzie attempts to repair what he calls the "diagnostic fragmentation" fostered by the *DSM* by the astute use of formal psychological testing, which he lucidly describes. Mac-Kenzie gives helpful information on how to introduce structured assessments to patients so as to ensure compliance and reliable results. He also gives many valuable insights into how to use structured assessments to select intervention strategies that are responsive to different treatment settings or milieus.

In chapter 17, Fagan shifts the focus from individuals to couples. The author illustrates the utility of the dimensional approach of the FFM to evaluate and treat a married couple who seek treatment for sexual dysfunction. The personal histories of the husband and wife, as well as their sexual and marital histories, provide the context for Fagan's treatment strategy. His skillful interpretation of their respective NEO-PI profiles helps set appropriate behavioral treatment goals in a behavioral treatment modality. Therapist Fagan offers the interesting insight that limited treatment goals can often be the means to successful treatment outcome.

Part V: Reconceptualization

In the course of writing this book, many of the authors came to reconceptualize their own views of personality disorders. Some of these reconceptualizations are presented in this final section. In chapter 18, Clark and Livesley collaborated to compare conceptually and empirically the two trait structures of disordered personality discussed in chapters 6 and 7. SNAP (Clark, 1993) and DAPP-BQ (Livesley et al., 1992) factors were content-matched and then correlated with NEO-PI or NEO Five-Factor Inventory (Costa & McCrae, 1989) scores to empirically validate the conceptual matchings across the Clark and Livesley systems. Overall, there were far more convergences or similarities between the SNAP and DAPP-BQ traits in terms of their correlations with the FFM. It is rare indeed to observe such high levels of productive collaboration. We express a special note of appreciation for their creative efforts.

Chapter 19, by Millon, who is arguably the most influential theorist in the field of personality disorders, is a classic consideration of the complex constructs of personality and personality disorders. Displaying the conceptual scope and scholarly erudition that are his hallmarks, Millon gives a spirited defense of the categorical or typal approach and a lengthy discussion of manifest and latent clinical taxa. It should also be observed that Millon expresses the view that the FFM, although not his own preferred model for taxonomic construction, may nevertheless contribute toward a "deeper and more penetrating vision" (p. 298).

McCrae, in chapter 20, offers a bold and provocative vision (or more accurately a revision or reformulation) of Axis II. The creators of the *DSM* nosology, as well as many of the contributors to this book, in his view, may have tacitly reified personality disorders. Noting that the empirical structure of personality disorder symptoms does not reproduce the theoretical structure of the *DSM*, McCrae rejects the notion of trying to define and assess disordered personalities. In its place, he suggests compiling a catalog of symptoms related to each pole of the five factors. A diagnosis of a personality-related problem would thus signify only the need for professional intervention as well as its likely form. Personalities are not disordered in this view and would not be the focus of treatment; therapeutic efforts would be targeted to the symptoms or personality-related problems.

In chapter 21, Widiger attempts to indicate how one would conceptualize a disorder of personality on the basis of the comprehensive description provided by a FFM assessment. The author makes explicit a key assumption of most of the chapters in this book: that maladaptive traits are extreme variants of normal personality traits. It follows, then, that the degree of elevation or deviation from the mean on any particular NEO-PI-R facet scale would suggest maladaptivity. Widiger argues that the NEO-PI-R can be used to provide a comprehensive description of traits that have different degrees of adaptivity and maladaptivity across situations/roles.

Finally, in the concluding Summary and Unsolved Issues in this book, we identify a number of unresolved issues that we judge to warrant special attention either because they are recurrent or because of their underlying importance. Some, such as whether O is related to personality disorders, will be resolved only by future research that we hope will be stimulated by this book. Other issues, such as whether clinicians will accept a FFM dimensional model, will be answered only by time and clinical practices. With this discussion as a brief guide, we urge the reader on.

References

American Psychiatric Association. (1980). *Diagnostic and statistical manual of mental disorders* (3rd ed.). Washington, DC: Author.

American Psychiatric Association. (1987). *Diagnostic and statistical manual of mental disorders* (3rd. ed., rev.). Washington, DC: Author.

Borkenau, P., & Ostendorf, F. (1990). Comparing exploratory and confirmatory factor analysis: A study on the 5-factor model of personality. *Personality and Individual Differences, 11,* 515–524.

Cattell, R. B., Eber, H. W., & Tatsuoka, M. M. (1970). *The handbook for the Sixteen Personality Factor Questionnaire.* Champaign, IL: Institute for Personality and Ability Testing.

Clark, L. A. (1993). *Manual for the Schedule for Nonadaptive and Adaptive Personality (SNAP).* Minneapolis: University of Minnesota Press.

Cloninger, C. R. (1987). A systematic method for clinical description and classification of personality variants. *Archives of General Psychiatry, 44,* 573–588.

Costa, P. T., Jr., & McCrae, R. R. (1985). *NEO Personality Inventory manual.* Odessa, FL: Psychological Assessment Resources.

Costa, P. T., Jr., & McCrae, R. R. (1988). Personality in adulthood: A six-year longitudinal study of self-reports and spouse ratings on the NEO Personality Inventory. *Journal of Personality and Social Psychology, 54,* 853–863.

Costa, P. T., Jr., & McCrae, R. R. (1989). *The NEO-PI/NEO-FFI manual supplement.* Odessa, FL: Psychological Assessment Resources.

Costa, P. T., Jr., & McCrae, R. R. (1990). Personality disorders and the five-factor model of personality. *Journal of Personality Disorders, 4,* 362–371.

Costa, P. T., Jr., & McCrae, R. R. (1992). *Revised NEO Personality Inventory (NEO-PI-R) and NEO Five-Factor Inventory (NEO-FFI) professional manual.* Odessa, FL: Psychological Assessment Resources.

Costa, P. T., Jr., & McCrae, R. R. (1993). Ego development and trait models of personality. *Psychological Inquiry, 4,* 20–23.

Costa, P. T., Jr., & McCrae, R. R. (in press). Domains and facets: Hierarchical personality assessment using the Revised NEO Personality Inventory. In J. C. Rosen (Ed.), *Advances in psychological assessment* (Vol. 9). New York: Plenum.

Digman, J. M. (1990). Personality structure: Emergence of the five-factor model. *Annual Review of Psychology, 50,* 116–123.

Docherty, J. P., Fiester, S. J., & Shea, T. (1986). Syndrome diagnosis and personality disorder. In A. Frances & R. Hales (Eds.), *Psychiatry update: The American Psychiatric Association annual review* (Vol. 5, pp. 315–355). Washington, DC: American Psychiatric Press.

Eysenck, H. J., & Eysenck, S. B. G. (1975). *Manual of the Eysenck Personality Questionnaire.* San Diego, CA: EdITS.

Goldberg, L. R. (1982). From ace to zombie: Some explorations in the language of personality. In C. D. Spielberger & J. N. Butcher (Eds.), *Advances in personality assessment* (Vol. 1, pp. 203–234). Hillsdale, NJ: Erlbaum.

Goldberg, L. R. (1992). The development of markers of the Big Five factor structure. *Psychological Assessment, 4,* 26–42.

Guilford, J. S., Zimmerman, W. S., & Guilford, J. P. (1976). *The Guilford–Zimmerman Temperament Survey handbook: Twenty-five years of research and application.* San Diego, CA: EdITS.

Gunderson, J. G., Links, P. S., & Reich, J. H. (1991). Competing models of personality disorders. *Journal of Personality Disorders, 5,* 60–68.

Hare, R. D. (1980). A research scale for the assessment of psychopathy in criminal populations. *Personality and Individual Differences, 1,* 111–117.

Hare, R. D., & Frazelle, J. (1980). *Some preliminary notes on the use of a research scale for the assessment of psychopathy in criminal populations.* Unpublished manuscript, Department of Psychology, University of British Columbia, Vancouver, Canada.

Hogan, R. (1986). *Hogan Personality Inventory manual.* Minneapolis, MN: National Computer Systems.

John, O., Angleitner, A., & Ostendorf, F. (1988). The lexical approach to personality: A historical review of trait taxonomic research. *European Journal of Personality, 2,* 171–205.

Kiesler, D. J. (1983). The 1982 interpersonal circle: A taxonomy for complementarity in human transactions. *Psychological Review, 90,* 185–214.

Leary, T. (1957). *Interpersonal diagnosis of personality.* New York: Ronald Press.

Livesley, W. J., Jackson, D. N., & Schroeder, M. L. (1992). A comparison of the factorial structure of personality disorders in a clinical and general population sample. *Journal of Abnormal Psychology, 101,* 432–440.

McCrae, R. R. (1992). The five-factor model: Issues and applications [Special issue]. *Journal of Personality, 60.*

McCrae, R. R., & Costa, P. T., Jr. (1990). *Personality in adulthood.* New York: Guilford Press.

McCrae, R. R., Costa, P. T., Jr., & Busch, C. M. (1986). Evaluating comprehensiveness in personality systems: The California Q-Set and the five-factor model. *Journal of Personality, 54,* 430–446.

McCrae. R. R., & John, O. P. (1992). An introduction to the five-factor model and its applications. *Journal of Personality, 60,* 175–215.

McDougall, W. (1932). Of the words character and personality. *Character and Personality, 1,* 3–16.

McGlashan, T. (1987). Borderline personality disorder and unipolar affective disorder: Long-term effects of comorbidity. *Journal of Nervous and Mental Disease, 175,* 467–473.

Millon, T. (1982). *Millon Clinical Multiaxial Inventory manual* (3rd ed.). Minneapolis, MN: National Computer Systems.

Morey, L. C. (1986). A comparison of three personality disorder assessment approaches. *Journal of Psychopathology and Behavioral Assessment, 8,* 25–30.

Norman, W. T. (1963). Toward an adequate taxonomy of personality attributes: Replicated factor structure in peer nomination personality ratings. *Journal of Abnormal and Social Psychology, 66,* 574–583.

Nurnberg, H. G., Raskin, M., Levine, P. E., Pollack, S., Siegel, O., & Prince, R. (1991). The comorbidity of borderline personality disorder and other DSM-III-R Axis II personality disorders. *American Journal of Psychiatry, 148,* 1371–1377.

Robbins, R. W., John, O. P., & Caspi, A. (in press). Major dimensions of personality in early adolescence: The Big Five and beyond. In C. P. Halverson, G. A. Kohnstamm, & R. P. Martin (Eds.), *The developing structure of temperament and personality from infancy to adulthood.* Hillsdale, NJ: Erlbaum.

Siever, L. J., & Davis, K. L. (1991). A psychobiological perspective on the personality disorders. *American Journal of Psychiatry, 148,* 1647–1658.

Skodol, A. E., Rosnick, L., Kellman, H. D., Oldham, J., & Hyler, S. E. (1988). Validating structured DSM-III-R personality disorder assessments with longitudinal data. *American Journal of Psychiatry, 145,* 1297–1299.

Tellegen, A. (1985). Structures of mood and personality and their relevance to assessing anxiety with an emphasis on self-report. In A. H. Tuma & J. D. Maser (Eds.), *Anxiety and the anxiety disorders* (pp. 681–706). Hillsdale, NJ: Erlbaum.

Thurstone, L. L. (1934). The vectors of the mind. *Psychological Review, 41,* 1–32.

Trull, T. J. (1992). DSM-III-R personality disorders and the five-factor model of personality: An empirical comparison. *Journal of Abnormal Psychology, 101,* 553–560.

Tupes, E. R., & Christal, R. (1961). *Recurrent personality factors based on trait ratings.* USAFD Technical Report No. 67-97. Lackland Air Force Base, TX.

Widiger, T. A., Frances, A. J., Harris, M., Jacobsberg, L., Fyer, M., & Manning, D. (1991). Comorbidity among Axis II disorders. In J. Oldham (Ed.), *Axis II: New perspectives on validity* (pp. 165–194). Washington, DC: American Psychiatric Press.

Widiger, T. A., & Hyler, S. (1987). Axis I/Axis II interactions. In J. Cavenar, R. Michels, & A. Cooper (Eds.), *Psychiatry.* Philadelphia: Lippincott.

Widiger, T. A., Trull, T. J., Hurt, S., Clarkin, J., & Frances, A. (1987). A multidimensional scaling of the DSM-III personality disorders. *Archives of General Psychiatry, 44,* 557–563.

Wiggins, J. S. (1968). Personality structure. In P. R. Farnsworth (Ed.), *Annual Review of Psychology, 19*, 293–350. Palo Alto, CA: Annual Reviews.

Wiggins, J. S. (1982). Circumplex models of interpersonal behavior in clinical psychology. In P. C. Kendall & J. N. Butcher (Eds.), *Handbook of research methods in clinical psychology* (pp. 183–221). New York: Wiley.

Wiggins, J. S., & Pincus, A. L. (1989). Conceptions of personality disorders and dimensions of personality. *Psychological Assessment: A Journal of Consulting and Clinical Psychology, 1*, 305–316.

Wiggins, J. S., & Trapnell, P. D. (in press). Personality structure: The return of the Big Five. In S. R. Briggs, R. Hogan, & W. H. Jones (Eds.), *Handbook of personality psychology*. San Diego, CA: Academic Press.

PART I

CONCEPTUAL BACKGROUND

CHAPTER 1

HISTORICAL ANTECEDENTS OF THE FIVE-FACTOR MODEL

John M. Digman

The current enthusiasm for the five-factor model (FFM; often referred to as the "Big Five") for organizing the complexities of personality could suggest to those who are unacquainted with its history that it is something quite new, an exciting "new look" at an old field. It comes as a surprise, then, to learn that it was proposed more than a half century ago and that a study demonstrating its essential validity was reported soon thereafter. Now, after many years of lying on the closet shelf of personality theory, the model has been dusted off, "as good as new," and appears to be for many researchers (e.g., Borkenau, 1988; Costa & McCrae, 1985; Digman, 1990; Goldberg, 1983; John, 1990; John, Angleitner, & Ostendorf, 1988; Peabody & Goldberg, 1989) a very meaningful theoretical structure for organizing the myriad specifics implied by the term *personality*.

AN EARLY HYPOTHESIS AND AN EARLY STUDY

It was McDougall (1932), at the time a leading theoretician, who first proposed that "personality may to advantage be broadly analyzed into five distinguishable but separable factors" (p. 5). Soon thereafter, Thurstone (1934) reported a factor analysis of 60 trait adjectives in terms of five factors and expressed his surprise at finding "that the whole list of sixty adjectives can be accounted for by postulating only five independent common factors" (p. 13).

Thus, more than 50 years ago, a model was proposed by a well-known personality theorist, McDougall, and a clear empirical demonstration of it was provided by an eminent psychometrist, Thurstone. Thurstone's article appeared on page 1 (Vol. 41) of *Psychological Review* and had previously been an essential part of his presidential address to the American Psychological Association. This was hardly an obscure introduction by an unknown, and yet almost 50 years were to pass before theorists were to take this model seriously as a worthwhile framework for their research.

There are many reasons for the failure of others to follow up on Thurstone's pioneering study. One is that a factor analysis, as carried out before the days of computers, was an incredibly difficult and time-consuming undertaking. Analysis of even a 30-variable problem was a daunting task that could suggest many weeks of clerical work filled with the possibility of errors of calculation at every turn. Thurstone's study, based on a sample of 1,300 subjects and 60 variables, stood alone, Promethean and awe inspiring, for many years. Until Cattell (1947, 1948) undertook his studies in the following decade, no one apparently had the courage to undertake a study of this magnitude.

Second, Thurstone, like so many other early pioneers of the FFM, did not follow up on his finding but turned to other pursuits, notably the field of intelligence. Quite possibly, had he devoted years of

I express my appreciation to Lewis R. Goldberg for his many thoughtful suggestions over the years.

work and writing to the implications of his finding, we would today know the model as the "Thurstone Five."

Later, other investigators would emulate Thurstone both in noting that five factors appeared to explain the variability in trait ratings and in failing to pursue the implications of their findings beyond a published report or two. Thus, Fiske (1949), Tupes and Christal (1961), and Borgatta (1964) published analyses of trait ratings that corroborated and extended Thurstone's findings, yet for one reason or another—other commitments or other interests, perhaps—none of these authors went beyond their initial reports.

A third reason for the model's tardy reception may be traced to the manner in which psychologists, including those interested in the topic, generally viewed the field of personality. As a glance at the textbooks written during the past 50 years will confirm, the field has been long on grand theory and short on systematic research. Generally, research has been undertaken to test some aspect of personality theory, such as Freud's theory of repression or Erikson's theory of personality development.

In addition, as noted by Carver and Scheier (1988), theory and research in personality have been characterized by two quite different approaches. One has been an interest in intrapersonal phenomena, as opposed to individual differences. The former is in the grand tradition, characteristic of continental European tradition, of the search for human identity; the latter, in the tradition of English and American psychometrics. These very different approaches are suggestive of Snow's (1959) distinction between the "two cultures," one with its roots in literature, philosophy, and the arts and the other with its roots in science and technology. One cannot easily imagine an Erikson, a Maslow, or their followers giving close attention to a factor analysis of a set of rating scales.

Finally, the approach to personality study that has been generally known as the "factor approach," dominated by the work of Cattell (e.g., 1943, 1947, 1948, 1957, 1965), Eysenck (e.g., 1947, 1970), and to some degree Guilford (e.g., 1959, 1975), has not been persuasive to personologists or others—and for good reason. Were there 16 or more factors—or only

3? Is Cattell's Extraversion the same as Guilford's? How could the application of a standard statistical technique, factor analysis, produce such different systems? For years, the systems of Cattell, Eysenck, and Guilford have appeared to represent the results of organizing the field of personality descriptors by use of factor analysis: two systems (Cattell's and Guilford's), both rather complex yet different from each other in many respects, and Eysenck's, either different from both in its simplicity and in its higher level of abstraction. How could three reputable investigators, using the same technique, arrive at three such different systems? Small wonder that many researchers cast a dubious eye toward factor analysis as a means of bringing order to the field.

FIVE-FACTOR SOLUTIONS FROM 1949 TO 1980

While the textbooks were devoting space to the Cattell and Eysenck systems as representative of factor theories, a series of studies was slowly building a solid, data-based reputation for the FFM. They include the work of Fiske (1949), Tupes and Christal (1961), Norman (1963), Borgatta (1964), and Norman and Goldberg (1966). An interesting aspect of this work is that although most of these studies were conducted independently, generally with no preconception as to outcome, they are in substantial agreement.

Fiske's study was done in conjunction with the Michigan Veterans Administration (VA) Selection Research Project (Kelly & Fiske, 1951). Cattell served as consultant for the project, with the result that 22 of his rating scales were used in the study. Using these scales, VA trainees were rated by peers, by evaluators, and by themselves. Fiske conducted factor analyses of the three sets of correlations and, like Thurstone 15 years before him, could find evidence for no more than five factors. Furthermore, in many respects, his interpretation of these factors was not very different from current interpretations (see Digman & Takemoto-Chock, 1981). The study, impressive for its time, was reported in a journal usually circulated among personality researchers, but it had little impact on the field.

Another consultant to the VA Project, Tupes, subsequently used 30 of Cattell's scales in a study of Air Force trainees. Analysis of the data suggested the presence of only five broad factors (Tupes & Christal, 1961). Intrigued by this, these investigators reanalyzed the correlations of Cattell and Fiske and found them to be in good agreement with their own analyses. Not only was agreement impressive with respect to the number of factors but the factors appeared to be remarkably similar in content across the three different studies. Tupes and Christal interpreted these robust five factors as Surgency (or Extraversion), Agreeableness, Conscientiousness, Emotional Stability, and Culture.

Shortly thereafter, Norman (1963), using 20 of the Tupes–Christal scales, reported a successful replication of their results. Borgatta (1964), familiar with the Tupes–Christal study, devised a set of behavior descriptors that were used by subjects in a study of interactions in small group discussion. Analysis of the scaled descriptors produced five factors very similar in content to the Tupes–Christal factors, except for the Culture factor, which Borgatta felt was better interpreted as Intelligence.

Here, then, by the middle 1960s, were all the ingredients needed for systematic research in personality: five robust trait dimensions that had been originally suggested by an insightful theorist, McDougall, and by a pioneering study by a well-known psychometrist, Thurstone, and clearly demonstrated by four independent studies, all of which were in good agreement. Yet, until very recently, few investigators knew of these studies, and the standard textbooks ignored them completely.

Why were these studies almost completely ignored? As I have noted elsewhere (Digman, 1990), the times were not right for the model to catch the attention of personality researchers. For one thing, the 1960s and 1970s witnessed an enthusiasm for behaviorism, with its disdain for anything so subjective as "personality" or ratings. Another factor was the rift between social psychologists and personality psychologists, the former seemingly demonstrating the vastly greater importance of the situation in determining behavior compared with personality traits.

THE 1980S AND THEREAFTER

In the early 1980s, three independent lines of research converged on the FFM as the most appropriate model for ordering the myriad specific constructs of personality. One line was a revival of interest in the model for the field of personality ratings; a second, studies of the structure of the language of personality descriptors; the third, analyses of personality inventories.

My own conversion to the FFM followed unsuccessful attempts to replicate a more complex model of child personality as measured by teacher ratings (Digman, 1963, 1972). A meta-analysis of several studies (Digman & Takemoto-Chock, 1981) demonstrated the robustness of the five-factor solution: "Regardless of whether teachers rate children, officer candidates rate one another, college students rate one another, or clinical staff members rate graduate trainees, the results are pretty much the same" (pp. 164–165). Other studies (Digman & Inouye, 1986; Goldberg, 1980, 1982, 1990; John, 1989; McCrae & Costa, 1985, 1989) amply confirmed this.

The second line of research to converge on the FFM as the appropriate model was the systematic work over the years of Goldberg and his associates on the structure of the everyday language of personality descriptors (Goldberg, 1980, 1981, 1982, 1990; Hampson, 1988; Hampson, John, & Goldberg, 1986). An essential aspect of this work pertaining to the FFM is its investigation of the hierarchical nature of the language of personality, extending from the most specific—and most precise—terms, such as *quiet*, to such broad terms as *Extraversion*, which like other FFM constructs subordinates a broad domain of related, lower level constructs.

Suggestions that the FFM might be noted in the structure of personality inventories as well (Amelang & Borkenau, 1982; Digman, 1979; Goldberg, 1981; Hogan, 1983) led to several studies that confirmed this (Costa & McCrae, 1988a, 1988b; McCrae & Costa, 1987, 1989). Thus, the Sixteen Personality Factor Questionnaire (Cattell, Eber, & Tatsuoka, 1970), the Guilford–Zimmerman Temperament Survey (Guilford & Zimmerman, 1949), the Personality Research Form (Jackson, 1974), the Myers–Briggs Type Indicator (Myers & McCauley, 1985), the

Eysenck Personality Inventory (Eysenck & Eysenck, 1964), and the California Q-Set (Block, 1961) represent some or all of the FFM.

The structure of the language of personality, as represented in ratings of self and of others, thus appears to be as well established as any principle coming from empirical research in psychology. Furthermore, when subjects report in inventories what they typically do and what they typically feel, the organization of such behavior and emotion into scales appears to fall into the FFM pattern as well.

LOOKING BACK

Eriksen (1957), reviewing the research efforts of a previous generation, was hopeful that the application of factor analysis to the complexities of personality traits would clarify the field. It appears that it has done just that: Five broad trait dimensions appear to encompass the common features of just about all of the more specific characteristics of personality traits.

But why did it take more than a half century to establish this principle when it was clearly suggested so long ago by McDougall and by Thurstone? The question is disturbing because it suggests that the progress of science is not as straightforward or as rational as it is generally assumed to be. I have proposed some reasons for the slow acceptance of the model. However, only one of these, the difficulty of carrying out a factor analysis in the precomputer era, seems reasonable. The others suggest that such research ran contrary to the paradigms—or fashions—of the day. Perhaps the times and paradigms are different today and a well-grounded theoretical model of personality has at last been accepted.

References

Amelang, A., & Borkenau, P. (1982). Über die faktorielle Structur und externe Validität einiger Fragebogen-skalen zur Erfassung von Dimensionen der Extraversion und emotionalen Labilität [On the factor structure and external validity of some questionnaire scales measuring dimensions of extraversion and neuroticism]. *Zeitschrift für Differentielle und Diagnostische Psychologie, 3,* 119–146.

Block, J. (1961). *The Q-Sort method in personality assessment and psychiatric research.* Springfield, IL: Charles C Thomas.

Borgatta, E. F. (1964). The structure of personality characteristics. *Behavioral Science, 12,* 8–17.

Borkenau, P. (1988). The multiple classification of acts and the Big Five factors of personality. *Journal of Research in Personality, 22,* 337–352.

Carver, C. S., & Scheier, M. F. (1988). *Perspectives on personality.* Boston: Allyn & Bacon.

Cattell, R. B. (1943). The description of personality: Basic traits resolved into clusters. *Journal of Abnormal and Social Psychology, 38,* 476–506.

Cattell, R. B. (1947). Confirmation and clarification of primary personality factors. *Psychometrika, 12,* 197–220.

Cattell, R. B. (1948). The primary personality factors in women compared with those in men. *British Journal of Psychology, 1,* 114–130.

Cattell, R. B. (1957). *Personality and motivation structure and measurement.* New York: World Book.

Cattell, R. B. (1965). *The scientific analysis of personality.* London: Penguin Books.

Cattell, R. B., Eber, H. W., & Tatsuoka, M. M. (1970). *Handbook for the Sixteen Personality Factor Questionnaire.* Champaign, IL: Institute for Personality and Ability Testing.

Costa, P. T., Jr., & McCrae, R. R. (1985). *The NEO Personality Inventory manual.* Odessa, FL: Psychological Assessment Resources.

Costa, P. T., Jr., & McCrae, R. R. (1988a). From catalog to classification: Murray's needs and the five-factor model. *Journal of Personality and Social Psychology, 55,* 258–265.

Costa, P. T., Jr., & McCrae, R. R., (1988b). Personality in adulthood: A six-year longitudinal study of self-reports and spouse ratings on the NEO Personality Inventory. *Journal of Personality and Social Psychology, 54,* 653–863.

Digman, J. M. (1963). Principal dimensions of child personality as seen in teachers' judgments. *Child Development, 34,* 43–60.

Digman, J. M. (1972). The structure of child personality as seen in behavior ratings. In R. M. Dreger (Ed.), *Multivariate personality research* (pp. 587–611). Baton Rouge, LA: Claitor's Publishing.

Digman, J. M. (1979, October). *The five major dimensions of personality variables: Analysis of personality questionnaire data in the light of the five robust factors emerging from studies of rated characteristics.* Paper presented at the annual meeting of the Society of Multivariate Experimental Psychology, Los Angeles, CA.

Digman, J. M. (1990). Personality structure: Emergence of the five-factor model. *Annual Review of Psychology, 50,* 116–123.

Digman, J. M., & Inouye, J. (1986). Further specification of the five robust factors of personality. *Journal of Personality and Social Psychology, 50,* 116–123.

Digman, J. M., & Takemoto-Chock, N. (1981). Factors in the natural language of personality: Reanalysis, comparison, and interpretation of six major studies. *Multivariate Behavioral Research, 16,* 149–170.

Eriksen, C. W. (1957). Personality. *Annual Review of Personality, 8,* 185–210.

Eysenck, H. J. (1947). *Dimensions of personality.* New York: Praeger.

Eysenck, H. J. (1970). *The structure of human personality.* (3rd ed.). London: Methuen.

Eysenck, H. J., & Eysenck, S. B. G. (1964). *Manual of the Eysenck Personality Inventory.* London: University Press.

Fiske, D. W. (1949). Consistency of the factorial structures of personality ratings from different sources. *Journal of Abnormal and Social Psychology, 44,* 329–344.

Goldberg, L. R. (1980, May). *Some ruminations about the structure of individual differences: Developing a common lexicon for the major characteristics of human personality.* Paper presented at the annual convention of the Western Psychological Association, Honolulu.

Goldberg, L. R. (1981). Language and individual differences: The search for universals in personality lexicons. In L. Wheeler (Ed.), *Review of personality and social psychology* (Vol. 2, pp. 141–165). Beverly Hills, CA: Sage Publications.

Goldberg, L. R. (1982). From ace to zombie: Some explorations in the language of personality. In C. D. Spielberger & J. N. Butcher (Eds.), *Advances in personality assessment* (Vol. 1, pp. 203–234). Hillsdale, NJ: Erlbaum.

Goldberg, L. R. (1983, June). *The magical number five, plus or minus two: Some conjectures on the dimensionality of personality descriptors.* Paper presented at a research seminar, Gerontology Research Center, Baltimore, MD.

Goldberg, L. R. (1990). An alternative "description of personality": The Big Five factor structure. *Journal of Personality and Social Psychology, 59,* 1216–1229.

Guilford, J. P. (1959). *Personality.* New York: McGraw-Hill.

Guilford, J. P. (1975). Factors and factors of personality. *Psychological Bulletin, 82,* 802–814.

Guilford, J. P., & Zimmerman, W. S. (1949). *The Guilford–Zimmerman Temperament Survey.* Beverly Hills, CA: Sheridan Supply.

Hampson, S. E. (1988). *The construction of personality: An introduction* (2nd. ed.). London: Routledge & Kegan Paul.

Hampson, S. E., John, O. P., & Goldberg, L. R. (1986). Category breadth and hierarchical structure in personality: Studies of asymmetries in judgments of trait implications. *Journal of Personality and Social Psychology, 51,* 37–54.

Hogan, P. (1983). Socioanalytic theory of personality. In M. M. Page (Ed.), *The 1982 Nebraska Symposium on Motivation: Current theory and research* (pp. 59–89). Lincoln: University of Nebraska Press.

Jackson, D. N. (1974). *Personality Research Form manual* (3rd ed.). Port Huron, MI: Research Psychologists Press.

John, O. P. (1989, November). Big Five prototypes for the Adjective Checklist using observer data. In O. P. John (Chair), *The Big Five: Historical perspective and current research.* Symposium conducted at the annual meeting of the Society of Multivariate Experimental Psychology, Honolulu.

John, O. P. (1990). The "Big Five" factor taxonomy: Dimensions of personality in the natural language and in questionnaires. In L. A. Pervin (Ed.), *Handbook of personality* (pp. 66–100). New York: Guilford Press.

John, O. P., Angleitner, A., & Ostendorf, F. (1988). The lexical approach to personality: A historical review of trait taxonomic research. *European Journal of Personality, 2,* 171–205.

Kelly, E. E., & Fiske, D. W. (1951). *The prediction of performance in clinical psychology.* Ann Arbor, MI: University of Michigan Press.

McCrae, R. R., & Costa, P. T., Jr. (1985). Updating Norman's "adequate taxonomy": Intelligence and personality dimensions in natural languages and questionnaires. *Journal of Personality and Social Psychology, 49,* 710–721.

McCrae, R. R., & Costa, P. T., Jr. (1987). Validation of the five-factor model across instruments and observers. *Journal of Personality and Social Psychology, 52,* 81–90.

McCrae, R. R., & Costa, P. T., Jr. (1989). Reinterpreting the Myers–Briggs Type Indicator from the perspective of the five-factor model of personality. *Journal of Personality, 57,* 17–40.

McDougall, W. (1932). Of the words character and personality. *Character and Personality, 1,* 3–16.

Myers, I. B., & McCauley, M. H. (1985). *Manual: A guide to the development and use of the Myers–Briggs Type Indicator.* Palo Alto, CA: Consulting Psychologists Press.

Norman, W. T. (1963). Toward an adequate taxonomy of personality attributes: Replicated factor structure in peer nomination personality ratings. *Journal of Abnormal and Social Psychology, 66,* 574–583.

Norman, W. T., & Goldberg, L. R. (1966). Raters, ratees, and randomness in personality structure. *Journal of Personality and Social Psychology, 4*, 681–691.

Peabody, D., & Goldberg, L. R. (1989). Some determinants of factor structures from personality trait descriptors. *Journal of Personality and Social Psychology, 57*, 552–567.

Snow, C. P. (1959). *The two cultures.* Cambridge, UK: Cambridge University Press.

Thurstone, L. L. (1934). The vectors of mind. *Psychological Review, 41*, 1–32.

Tupes, E. R., & Christal, R. (1961). *Recurrent personality factors based on trait ratings* (USAFD Tech. Rep. No. 67-97). Lackland, TX: Lackland Air Force Base.

CHAPTER 2

TOWARD A DIMENSIONAL MODEL FOR THE PERSONALITY DISORDERS

Thomas A. Widiger and Allen J. Frances

The purpose of this chapter is to review the conceptual and empirical support for a dimensional classification of personality disorders, focusing in particular on the five-factor model (FFM). The question of whether mental disorders are optimally classified categorically or dimensionally is an ongoing debate (Blashfield, 1984; Kendell, 1975). The issue is particularly pertinent to the topic of personality disorders given the tradition to measure personality with dimensions rather than typologies (Frances, 1982; Gangestad & Snyder, 1985; Livesley, 1985; Widiger & Frances, 1985).

The third, revised edition of the *Diagnostic and Statistical Manual of Mental Disorders* (*DSM-III-R*; American Psychiatric Association, 1987) personality disorder diagnoses are categorical. It has been suggested that because the *DSM-III-R* diagnoses involve determination of the number of personality disorder symptoms, the *DSM-III-R* uses a hybrid model that already recognizes and includes a dimensional assessment of each patient (Millon, 1991). However, in practice, the *DSM-III-R* is used and interpreted to make categorical distinctions (Carson, 1991). One does convert the number of symptoms to a categorical distinction on the basis of a cut-off point along a scale (e.g., five of eight for the borderline diagnosis), but the diagnosis that is recorded concerns the presence or absence of a personality disorder. Clinicians

thereafter refer to the presence or absence of a personality disorder, not the degree to which a personality style is maladaptive or the extent to which each personality disorder is present.

The number of symptoms possessed by each patient is assessed to indicate not the extent to which a person is borderline but the likelihood that a person has the borderline personality disorder (BDL). The BDL criteria set provides not a scale to indicate the degree to which a person is maladaptively borderline but a set of fallible indicators for determining the category (presence vs. absence of BDL) within which the patient falls. An analogy would be a set of fallible indicators (e.g., a list of interests, opinions, or attitudes) that could be used either to indicate the likelihood that one is male (a categorical classification) or to indicate the degree to which one is masculine (a dimensional classification). The *DSM-III-R* criteria sets could be used to indicate the extent to which a person is borderline, but they are currently used to indicate whether the personality disorder is either present or absent.

In this chapter, we discuss the advantages and disadvantages of the categorical and dimensional models of classification. We then discuss the empirical data that are relevant to the respective validity of these two perspectives, focusing in particular on the empirical support for the FFM.

This chapter is an extended and updated version of previously published material (Widiger, 1991, 1993).

ADVANTAGES OF THE CATEGORICAL APPROACH

Three major advantages of the categorical approach have been cited in the literature: (a) ease in conceptualization and communication, (b) familiarity, and (c) consistency with clinical decision making. We discuss each of these advantages in turn.

Ease in Conceptualization and Communication

A categorical model is simpler than a dimensional model in some respects. It is simpler to consider a person as having or not having a disorder than it is to consider various degrees to which a person might have a disorder; similarly, it is simpler to consider the presence of one, two, or three disorders than it is to consider a profile of degrees to which all of the various disorders are present. It is easier to communicate the presence of one or two categorical diagnoses than it is to recall and transmit a profile of scores along five or more dimensions. Also, one category (e.g., BDL) can communicate a great deal of vivid information (Frances, 1993).

Diagnosis within a categorical model requires only one decision: whether the person does or does not have a particular personality disorder. Diagnosis within a dimensional model requires more specific and detailed assessment, increasing the complexity of clinical diagnosis. To the extent that a dimensional model retains more information than a categorical model, it requires the obtainment and the communication of more information.

For example, it could be apparent that a patient does not have a histrionic, a dependent, a borderline, an avoidant, a narcissistic, or an antisocial personality disorder. The patient might have a few symptoms of each of these disorders but not have enough to suggest that any of these disorders is present. The clinician could then simply ignore the diagnostic criteria for all of these disorders, focusing instead on the one or two personality disorders most likely to be present. With a dimensional model, a comprehensive assessment would require consideration of all of the dimensions, even if only a few symptoms were present for any one of them.

Familiarity

The second major advantage of the categorical system is that it is more familiar to clinicians. All previous versions of the *DSM* personality disorder diagnoses and all of the other diagnoses within *DSM-III-R* are categorical. It would represent a major shift in clinical practice to convert to a dimensional system (Frances, 1990). The categorical approach is also consistent with the neo-Kraepelinian emphasis on identifying homogeneous, distinct syndromes (Guze & Helzer, 1987; Klerman, 1986). The concept of disorder implies to many clinicians the presence of a distinct syndrome that is in some respects qualitatively different from normality.

The *DSM* has always used a categorical format for clinical diagnoses, and it would be a major disruption to clinical practice to replace the Axis II personality disorders with the FFM dimensions (Frances, 1993). Such a major revision would likely result in considerable opposition by many clinicians and researchers (Zimmerman, 1988). The criteria for revisions to the American Psychiatric Association's nomenclature are much more conservative for the fourth edition of the *DSM* (*DSM-IV*; American Psychiatric Association, in press) than they were for the third edition (*DSM-III*; American Psychiatric Association, 1980) or *DSM-III-R* (Frances, Widiger, & Pincus, 1989). In the absence of clear guidance as to how the FFM would be used to guide the forensic, disability, insurance, and clinical decisions that are currently guided by the *DSM-III-R* Axis II personality disorders, it might not be practical or realistic to replace Axis II with the FFM.

Consistency With Clinical Decisions

A third argument in favor of the categorical model is that clinical decision making tends to be categorical. A primary function of diagnosis is to suggest treatment, and treatment decisions are not usually in shades of gray. One either hospitalizes or one does not; one either prescribes a medication or one does not. If treatment, insurance, forensic, and other clinically relevant decisions were along a continuum rather than being largely categorical, then the diagnostic system would likely have been more quantitative than qualitative.

Many clinicians convert a dimensional system to categories to facilitate their decision making. The Minnesota Multiphasic Personality Inventory (MMPI; Hathaway & McKinley, 1967), for example, provides the potential for making detailed assessments along a number of dimensions, yet it is often converted to typological code types. One might then question the advantage of potentially increasing the work and complexity of diagnosis by requiring ratings along a continuum that are then ignored in clinical practice.

DISADVANTAGES OF THE CATEGORICAL APPROACH

The only ambiguity that occurs within the categorical model is the decision regarding presence versus absence. If the case is not a literally borderline condition, then the diagnosis is often straightforward. With a dimensional model, there is the potential for a variety of difficult and ambiguous decisions for every patient. For example, even if a personality disorder is clearly present, a dimensional classification still requires an assessment of whether the person is moderately or severely disordered.

In practice, however, the *DSM-III-R* categorical system can be more complex and cumbersome than can a dimensional model. The current system requires the assessment of 104 diagnostic criteria. A systematic and comprehensive assessment of the 11 *DSM-III-R* personality disorders usually requires 2 hr but can take over 4 hr (e.g., Loranger, 1988; Pfohl, Blum, Zimmerman, & Stangl, 1989). Although 2 hr is substantial, even this amount of time allows for an average of only 1 min and 9 sec to assess each personality disorder criterion. A systematic and comprehensive assessment of five dimensions would require much less time and effort. The categorical system is easier to use only if one fails to conduct a comprehensive or systematic assessment (e.g., ignoring most of the categories). Clinicians, in fact, rarely provide a complete assessment of the *DSM-III-R* personality disorders because it is neither feasible nor practical (e.g., Morey & Ochoa, 1989; Pfohl, Coryell, Zimmerman, & Stangl, 1986). As a result, chart diagnoses contain substantially fewer diagnoses than would be provided by a semistructured interview. This may not be so much a failing of the clinician as perhaps a

failing of the nomenclature (Frances, Pincus, Widiger, Davis, & First, 1990).

ADVANTAGES OF THE DIMENSIONAL APPROACH

The major advantages of the dimensional system are (a) resolution of a variety of classificatory dilemmas, (b) retention of information, and (c) flexibility. We discuss each of these advantages in turn.

Classificatory Dilemmas

The ease in conceptualizing and communicating the categorical model is advantageous only if the model provides accurate information. To the extent that it involves the loss of valid information, it is likely to impair decision making and contribute to classificatory dilemmas. One difficulty with a categorical distinction is identifying a nonarbitrary boundary. In *DSM-III* and *DSM-III-R*, only the number of criteria needed to establish a diagnosis or "cut-off points" for the schizotypal disorder and BDL were based on empirical data (Spitzer, Endicott & Gibbon, 1979), and subsequent research has indicated that the cut-off points would have been different if the data had been collected in different settings (Finn, 1982; Widiger, Hurt, Frances, Clarkin, & Gilmore, 1984). The arbitrary nature of the cut-off points is not problematic for prototypical cases, but it is problematic for cases closer to the boundaries. Cases near the boundaries of a categorical distinction are not adequately characterized by the category on either side (i.e., either presence or absence of the disorder). For example, Widiger, Sanderson, and Warner (1986) indicated that, with respect to MMPI profile scores, patients with five BDL symptoms (i.e., patients with the disorder) were more like patients with four or fewer symptoms (i.e., patients without the disorder) than they were like patients with more than five symptoms (i.e., other patients with the disorder).

The cut-off points provided in the *DSM-III-R* are clearly problematic. One does not need any external validator to recognize that there are problems with the prevalence rates and with multiple diagnoses (Morey, 1988b; Widiger & Rogers, 1989). Some diagnoses occur too often (e.g., BDL), and some too infrequently (e.g., schizoid). Patients may meet the criteria for as many as 5, 6, 7, and even 11 personality disorder diagnoses. The average number of personality disorder diagnoses per patient has been reported to be 2.8 (Zanarini, Frankenburg, Chauncey, & Gunderson, 1987), 3.75 (Widiger, Trull, Hurt, Clarkin, & Frances, 1987), and 4.6 (Skodol, Rosnick, Kellman, Oldham, & Hyler, 1988).

Nurnberg et al. (1991) assessed the comorbidity of *DSM-III-R* BDL with the other Axis II personality disorders in 110 outpatients. Twenty percent (*n* = 22) met the *DSM-III-R* criteria for BDL, with 82% of these having at least one other personality disorder diagnosis. These investigators concluded that the overlap was extensive and not confined to any one of the three broad clusters in which *DSM-III-R* organizes the personality disorders. Nurnberg et al. (1991) suggested that "borderline personality disorder appears to constitute a broad, heterogeneous category with unclear boundaries" (p. 1371) and that "a better understanding of personality disorder awaits a paradigmatic shift away from discrete nosologic categories to alternative models" (p. 1376).

The arbitrariness of the categorical distinctions contributes to diagnostic dilemmas and diagnostic disagreements. To the extent that the presence-versus-absence distinction is arbitrary, clinicians are required to make major distinctions, for which is no valid or meaningful distinction. If the distinction between the presence versus absence of an avoidant personality disorder is arbitrary, then it is understandable that there has been substantial disagreement and poor reliability (Angus & Marziali, 1988; Mellsop, Varghese, Joshua, & Hicks, 1982). All studies that have compared interrater reliability of the categorical models with that of the dimensional models have found better reliability for the latter (e.g., Heumann & Morey, 1990).

A more dimensional rating (e.g., degrees of severity) will also include arbitrary distinctions—in fact, more of them. But the availability of additional options is less problematic. For example, it is less problematic or controversial to determine whether someone has four versus five symptoms of BDL than it is to determine whether the disorder is either present or absent. Four or five out of eight (borderline) symptoms is still within a literally borderline range, but presence versus absence suggests qualitatively

distinct and substantially different conditions. The distinction of four versus five symptoms is as arbitrary as is presence versus absence, but the impact of the arbitrariness is less severe.

The accepted thresholds for the *DSM-III-R* diagnoses are also somewhat misleading. Even if there is a consensus that a person has BDL when five of the eight criteria are present, there will still be considerable disagreement regarding the threshold for the presence of each individual criterion. The point at which a person has clinically significant identity disturbance, affective instability, or chronic feelings of emptiness and boredom is undefined in *DSM-III-R* and probably cannot be defined in any manner that would not be arbitrary. Research programs have obtained adequate levels of interrater reliability for the diagnosis of BDL, but this is typically the result of developing local operational criteria for each symptom that are unlikely to agree with the operationalizations that are being used at another research site or with another semistructured interview (Angus & Marziali, 1988; Kavoussi, Coccaro, Klar, Bernstein, & Siever, 1990).

Retention of Information

The second advantage of the dimensional approach is the retention of information. Members and nonmembers of a category tend not to be homogeneous with respect to the criteria that were used to make the diagnosis. There are 93 different ways to meet the *DSM-III-R* criteria for BDL (Clarkin, Widiger, Frances, Hurt, & Gilmore, 1983) and 848 different ways to meet the *DSM-III-R* criteria for antisocial personality disorder (not even counting the number of different ways to meet the criteria for the conduct disorder and parental irresponsibility items), yet only one diagnostic label (i.e., presence of the disorder) is given to characterize all of these cases. There are 162 different possible combinations of BDL symptomatology in people who do not have BDL, and all of these cases are simply labeled as *not having the disorder*.

The handicap to research (and clinical practice) of the failure of the categorical system to adequately characterize personality disorder pathology was discussed by McGlashan (1987). McGlashan was researching the comorbidity of BDL and depression and needed a comparison group of depressives without BDL. He therefore obtained a group of depressed subjects who did not meet the *DSM-III* criteria for BDL. However, these subjects had on average three of the BDL criteria.

> *In short, the "pure" . . . cohort was not pure. . . . The result is that our comparison groups, although defined to be categorically exclusive, may not have been all that different, a fact which in turn, may account for some of the similarities [between the supposedly pure depressives and the borderlines]. (p. 472)*

In other words, the subjects diagnosed as not having BDL did in fact have BDL pathology. McGlashan therefore concluded that the DSM "emerges as poorly constructed for the study of comorbidity" (p. 473).

DSM-III-R adopted a polythetic format for the categorical diagnoses (i.e., multiple, optional criteria) in recognition that patients do not fit neatly into distinct categories (Spitzer, 1987). Not all BDL, histrionic, or avoidant patients are alike with respect to the degree or manner in which they are borderline, histrionic, or avoidant (Livesley, 1985; Widiger & Frances, 1985). However, accepting this heterogeneity does not resolve the problems that arise from the heterogeneity, given that the polythetic categories tend to be inadequate for providing sufficiently precise information regarding the individual patient (Widiger & Kelso, 1983). Categories do provide vivid and clear images of each personality disorder, thereby facilitating communication, but to the extent that the patient is not a prototypical case, the communication will be misleading and stereotypical (Cantor & Genero, 1986; Schacht, 1985). The categorical format is simpler, but this simplicity can be at the expense of not recognizing the complexity that actually exists.

A dimensional model diminishes stereotyping by providing more precise information. The heterogeneity is retained and informs clinical decisions. It is, in fact, a paradox that for a diagnosis in which reliability and validity are very problematic (e.g., Mellsop et al., 1982), reliable and valid information is excluded from the classification. The ordinal-interval scales that are inherent to the dimensional model have

more statistical power, yet *DSM-III-R* currently uses nominal scales. One would expect that one would want to be as accurate as possible when diagnosing BDL pathology; describing personality symptomatology; and determining empirically the familial, treatment, or other correlates of a personality disorder (Widiger, 1993).

Flexibility

A final advantage of the dimensional approach is its flexibility. The categorical format does have advantages. Perhaps its greatest advantage is its compatibility with clinical decision making. This advantage, however, can be retained within a dimensional model by simply providing cut-off points. A conversion from the categorical to the dimensional format, on the other hand, is not possible. Once the categorical diagnosis is provided, the ability to return to a more precise classification (e.g., the number of personality disorder symptoms) cannot be recovered. Many clinicians do convert an MMPI dimensional profile to a categorical code type, but most prefer to be provided with a dimensional profile that they can then convert according to their specific clinical needs. Some coding systems will be more preferable in some situations than in others. Clinicians often use code types, but the code types that they use vary across situations and clinical decisions. The dimensional model allows the option of different cut-off points for different decisions and different clinical issues (Finn, 1982; Widiger et al., 1984).

A handicap of *DSM-III-R* is that it must respond to a variety of needs (Frances et al., 1990). It provides the nomenclature used for decisions regarding hospitalization, medication, psychotherapy, insurance coverage, scientific research, criminal responsibility, disability, and so forth. It is unlikely that the diagnostic thresholds for each of the categories in *DSM-III-R* will be optimal for all of these needs (Kendler, 1990). The points at which BDL traits likely will result in a depressive mood disorder, will be responsive to medications, will be too problematic for some forms of psychotherapy (e.g., group or gestalt), should receive insurance coverage for their treatment, will need hospitalization for their treatment, will be so disabling as to warrant governmental assistance, or will significantly impair the ability of the person to conform to the requirements of the law are not the same. All of these decisions are currently guided by one diagnostic threshold that is unlikely to be optimal for all of these needs (Widiger & Trull, 1991).

DISADVANTAGES OF THE DIMENSIONAL APPROACH

A major limitation of the dimensional approach, particularly the FFM, may be the lack of apparent clinical utility (Frances, 1993). Clinicians are much more familiar with the treatment implications of the borderline, dependent, schizotypal, and narcissistic personality disorder diagnoses than they are with the treatment implications of excessive agreeableness, conscientiousness, or extraversion. It is also unclear how one would use the FFM within clinical practice. Most clinicians rely on interviews to assess personality disorders, and most researchers currently favor the use of semistructured interviews over self-report inventories. As yet, there is no explicit guidance as to how one would assess the various levels of introversion, conscientiousness, or neuroticism with a clinical interview or the facets within any one of these broader domains.

It has been suggested that a dimensional system could impede the effort to discover and validate discrete syndromes and specific etiologies and treatment (Gunderson, Links, & Reich, 1991). A surface continuum can conceal underlying discontinuities (e.g., different viruses produce similar symptomatology that overlap on a continuum but are in fact qualitatively distinguishable on immunological grounds). The empirical question is whether there are, in fact, latent-class taxons and, more simply, whether a categorical or a dimensional model is more consistent with the research on personality disorders.

EMPIRICAL SUPPORT FOR THE DIMENSIONAL MODEL

A variety of data are relevant to the issue of empirical support, including (but not limited to) face validity, concurrent and predictive validity, factor and cluster analyses, multimodality, and a host of taxometric techniques (e.g., discontinuous regression, admixture analysis, latent-class analysis, and maximum covaria-

tion analysis). We discuss in turn each of the methods that have been applied to the personality disorders.

Face Validity

It is evident that theorists and researchers are not in agreement with respect to which model of classification is preferable. Authors of review articles that have argued in favor of the dimensional format for the personality disorders include Adamson (1989), Clarkin and Sanderson (in press), Cloninger (1987, 1989), Costa and McCrae (1992), Eysenck (1986, 1987), Gorton and Akhtar (1990), Grove and Tellegen (1991), Kato (1988), Kiesler (1991), Kroll (1988), Livesley (1991), McLemore and Brokaw (1987), McReynolds (1989), Plutchik and Conte (1985), Schacht (1985), Stone (1992), Tyrer (1988), Vaillant (1984), Widiger and Kelso (1983), and J. Wiggins (1982). Some, however, have argued for retaining the categorical approach (i.e., Frances, 1990, 1993; Gunderson, 1987; Gunderson et al., 1991; Millon, 1981; Spitzer & Williams, 1985; O. Wiggins & Schwartz, 1991). Others have been more neutral or at least unclear in their position (e.g., Akiskal, 1989; Blashfield, 1984; Frances, 1982; Kernberg, 1984; Millon, 1990; Oldham, 1987; Robins & Helzer, 1986; Rutter, 1987).

It is also unclear whether practicing clinicians prefer a categorical or a dimensional format. A variety of surveys regarding *DSM-III* and *DSM-III-R* have been conducted, but none has surveyed clinicians with respect to whether they prefer a categorical or a dimensional format for diagnosing personality disorders. Hine and Williams (1975) suggested that there would be little difficulty in obtaining acceptance of a dimensional approach within psychiatry based on their empirical study with medical students. Kass, Skodol, Charles, Spitzer, and Williams (1985) indicated that feedback from staff and trainees during their study indicated that a 4-point severity rating was both feasible and acceptable in routine clinical practice. Maser, Kaelber, and Weise (1991) surveyed 146 psychologists and psychiatrists from 42 countries not including the United States and found that 89% considered the *DSM-III-R* to be at least fairly successful in providing diagnostic categories. However, this survey question concerned all of the disorders considered together. Specifically, "the personality disorders led the list of diagnostic categories with which respondents were dissatisfied" (Maser et al., 1991, p. 275). Maser et al. did not ask whether the respondents would prefer a more dimensional classification.

Concurrent and Predictive Validity

Many studies have obtained statistically significant differences on a variety of variables between patients with a personality disorder and patients without the respective disorder on a variety of variables (Gunderson & Zanarini, 1987). These findings are consistent with and have been cited as support for the categorical model of classification (Gunderson, 1987). However, although these findings do suggest that a valid construct is measured by the diagnostic algorithm, they are not at all informative with respect to the question of whether the construct is a category or a dimension (Grove & Andreasen, 1989; Kendell, 1975). One can take any continuum, such as height or IQ, define two groups on the basis of scores along the continuum (e.g., IQ scores from 70 to 85 and from 86 to 100), and obtain statistically significant differences between the groups with respect to variables associated with the continuum (e.g., educational achievement, family history, or parental education).

A more compelling datum is whether the strength of the relationship between the diagnostic construct and an external variable is increased or decreased when it is dichotomized. A dimensional variable will show reduced relationships with external variables when it is dichotomized, whereas a truly dichotomous variable will show decreased relationships or at least no change when it is dimensionalized (Cohen & Cohen, 1975). The former occurs as a result of the loss of information; the latter occurs as a result of the inclusion of irrelevant, invalid information (Miller & Thayer, 1989).

Of the personality disorder studies that reported results with the data analyzed both categorically and dimensionally, results in all but one have favored the dimensional analyses (e.g., Hart & Hare, 1989; Heumann & Morey, 1990; Hogg, Jackson, Rudd, & Edwards, 1990; Hyler et al., 1989; Kavoussi et al., 1990; Loranger, Susman, Oldham, & Russakoff, 1987; Nazikian, Rudd, Edwards, & Jackson, 1990;

O'Boyle & Self, 1990; Reich, Noyes, & Troughton, 1987; Skodol, Oldham, Rosnick, Kellman, & Hyler, 1991; Standage & Ladha, 1988; Walton, 1986; Widiger & Sanderson, 1987; Widiger et al., 1987, 1991; Zimmerman & Coryell, 1990; Zimmerman, Pfohl, Coryell, Stangl, & Corenthal, 1988). The exception was obtained by Zimmerman and Coryell (1989) in a case in which there was a ceiling effect, with both the categorical and dimensional ratings obtaining maximal reliability values. The consistency of this finding is not a statistical artifact. Rather, it indicates that reliable and valid information is lost by converting the data to a nominal scale. If the additional information with respect to the degree to which a person has a personality disorder were not providing reliable or valid information, then including it would have decreased the reliability and validity of the diagnosis.

Factor and Cluster Analyses

Factor analysis and multidimensional scaling have been used to identify the dimensions that might underlie or explain the correlation among variables. A number of such studies have been conducted with the *DSM-III* personality disorders (e.g., Blashfield, Sprock, Pinkston, & Hodgin, 1985; Hyler & Lyons, 1988; Kass et al., 1985; Millon, 1987; Morey, Waugh, & Blashfield, 1985; Widiger et al., 1987) and with other nomenclatures (e.g., Plutchik & Platman, 1977; Presley & Walton, 1973; Tyrer & Alexander, 1979). It has been suggested that factor analytic results provide support for the dimensional approach to classification. Eysenck (1986), for example, suggested that factor analytic studies do not support a categorical model because factor scores are almost always continuous, with individuals often scoring on all of the factors. However, although these analyses can indicate the feasibility of such a model and the dimensions that might underlie a set of variables, the results have not been compelling with respect to whether the variable domain is fundamentally categorical or dimensional. The geometric model on which scaling and factor analytic techniques are based hampers their use for determining whether a categorical or a dimensional model is most appropriate (Kendell, 1975; Morey, 1988a). Factors can be derived from measures of a class variable. One can identify dimensions of masculinity and femininity that are useful and valid in the measurement of personality, but the underlying variable may still be a latent-class taxon.

A complementary limitation occurs with cluster analysis. Cluster analyses are useful in developing types or categories by which to classify subjects. Morey (1988a) demonstrated through a cluster analysis of the *DSM-III-R* personality disorder criteria sets that most of the categorical distinctions in *DSM-III-R* do have empirical support in that the clustering recreated the *DSM-III-R* categories (with only a few exceptions). However, clustering methods will create subgroups regardless of whether they actually exist (Aldenderger & Blashfield, 1984; Grove & Andreasen, 1989). Cluster analysis may then be more suitable in confirming a particular categorical system than in determining whether the categorical system is more valid than a dimensional one.

An application of factor analysis that is relevant to the appropriateness of a dimensional versus a categorical model is the comparison of factor solutions across groups that are purportedly distinct with respect to a latent-class taxon. Measures that are highly discriminating between such groups should not correlate substantially within the groups, nor should the factor solution of the intercorrelation among such measures replicate across groups (Eysenck, 1987). Tyrer and Alexander (1979), for example, reported that the factor solutions of the intercorrelations among 24 personality variables assessed by a semistructured interview replicated across 65 patients with a primary clinical diagnosis of personality disorder and 65 patients with other diagnoses. These investigators suggested that these findings support the concept of personality disorders as being extreme variants of a multidimensional continuum. Similar findings were reported by Livesley (1991) using a self-report measure of 79 dimensions of personality disorder pathology, the intercorrelations of which were factor analyzed in a sample of 274 healthy subjects and 158 patients. Livesley (1991) concluded that "a dimensional model is . . . supported by empirical evidence that the structure of traits describing the features of personality disorder pathology is the same in personality-disordered and non-personality-disordered individuals" (p. 53).

Lack of Empirical Support for Categorical Approaches: Evidence From Taxometric Analyses

Multimodality indicates a discontinuity in the distribution of a variable, thereby suggesting the existence of categories or types (Kendell, 1975; Mendelsohn, Weiss, & Feimer, 1982). Neither multimodality nor a distinct break in the distribution of scores of a personality disorder measure has ever been obtained with data on personality disorder. Frances, Clarkin, Gilmore, Hurt, and Brown (1984) obtained personality disorder ratings on 76 outpatients and concluded that "the DSM-III criteria for personality disorders do not select out mutually exclusive, categorical diagnostic entities. . . . [The] frequency of multiple diagnoses supports the argument for a dimensional—rather than a categorical—system of personality diagnosis" (p. 1083). Kass et al. (1985) obtained personality disorder ratings from a consecutive sample of 609 outpatients and concluded that "our data do not lend support to the usefulness of a categorical approach" (p. 628). "Since many more patients had some [maladaptive] personality traits or almost met DSM-III criteria than actually met the full criteria . . . the categorical judgments of DSM-III necessarily resulted in the loss of information" (p. 630). Zimmerman and Coryell (1990) obtained personality disorder ratings on 808 first-degree relatives of patients and normal controls and concluded that the "scores are continuously distributed without points of rarity to indicate where to make the distinction between normality and pathology" (p. 690). Nestadt et al. (1990) obtained histrionic ratings from a representative sample of a local community ($n = 810$) and reported that "this personality diagnosis is rather arbitrarily given individuals who extend beyond a cut-off level, . . . others less severe but similar in the nature of their dispositional features might have identical symptoms under certain life circumstances" (p. 420). Oldham et al. (1992) administered both the Structured Clinical Interview for *DSM-III-R* Personality Disorders (SCID-II; Spitzer, Williams, & Gibbon, 1987) and the Personality Disorders Examination (PDE; Loranger et al., 1987) to 106 consecutively admitted inpatients. These investigators reported substantial comorbidity among the personality disorders to the point that they questioned the validity of the categorical distinctions (particularly for the narcissistic and avoidant personality disorders and for the distinction between the borderline and the histrionic disorders). However, they did conclude that "there may be merit in maintaining the categorical diagnostic system to allow further research to be done" (p. 219). They suggested that, in the meantime, clinicians provide the categorical diagnosis when the patient meets the criteria for only one or two disorders: "For patients with more than two disorders, a single diagnosis of 'extensive personality disorder' might be made, with a dimensional description of the predominate characteristics" (Oldham et al., 1992, p. 219).

The absence of multimodality and distinct breaks, however, are not conclusive, particularly in the absence of any objective technique for interpreting the results (Gangestad & Snyder, 1985; Hicks, 1984). The assessment of multimodality should be conducted with the full range of personality disorder pathology. Such large scale, epidemiologic research has not yet been conducted, although the studies by Nestadt et al. (1990) and Zimmerman and Coryell (1990) may be close enough.

A compelling approach to the problem of identifying multimodality is admixture analysis, which examines the distribution of canonical coefficient scores derived from a discriminant function analysis for evidence of bimodality. This technique has suggested the presence of discrete breaks in the distribution of measures of somatoform and psychotic disorders (Cloninger, Martin, Guze, & Clayton, 1985). Cloninger (1989) indicated that he used admixture analysis with personality disorder data and "found that underlying [the] relatively distinct subgroups appeared to be multiple dimensions of personality that were normally distributed" (p. 140).

> *The real take-home message to me is not that we do not have methods to detect relatively discrete groups but that with psychiatric disorders the groups are not totally discrete, and this finding may be consistent with extreme syndromes that develop*

> *superimposed on top of underlying dimensional variation. (Cloninger, 1989, p. 140)*

Lenzenweger and Moldin (1990) applied admixture analysis to items from the Perceptual Aberrations Scale (PAS; Chapman, Chapman, & Raulin, 1978) and reported that the results suggested the presence of qualitative discontinuities in the distribution of schizotypal indicators. Others, however, have been somewhat skeptical regarding the power of admixture analysis to detect latent-class taxons (Grayson, 1987a, 1987b; Grove & Andreasen, 1989). It is possible that the lack of sufficiently reliable and valid measurement instruments, sampling biases (e.g., confining the analysis to a limited range along the distribution), and item biases (e.g., items with narrow or skewed levels of difficulty) can distort the findings in either direction.

Additional statistical approaches include latent-class analysis, discontinuous regression, and maximum covariation analysis (Gangestad & Snyder, 1985; Golden & Meehl, 1979; Hicks, 1984; Mendelsohn et al., 1982). Only maximum covariation analysis (MAXCOV) has been applied to the personality disorders. MAXCOV capitalizes on the fact that the covariation between any two signs of a categorical variable will be minimized in groups of subjects who share class membership and will be maximized in mixed groups, whereas no such variation in covariation will be found across levels of a dimensional variable (Meehl & Golden, 1982). MAXCOV has suggested the presence of latent-class taxons for some personality variables (Gangestad & Snyder, 1982; Strube, 1989) and for a "schizoid" taxon that would include the full spectrum of schizophrenic pathology (including the schizotypal, schizoid, and other personality disorders that might share a genetic liability for schizophrenia; Golden & Meehl, 1979). Trull, Widiger, and Guthrie (1990) applied MAXCOV to the *DSM-III-R* criteria for BDL. The charts of 409 psychiatric inpatients were systematically coded for symptoms of dysthymia (a dimensional variable), fallible indicators of biological sex (a categorical variable), and BDL. A clear peak was found for biological sex, the curve was flat for dysthymia, and no middle peak was found for BDL. Trull et al. concluded that "the results are most consistent with the hypothesis that [BDL] is optimally conceptualized as a dimensional variable" (p. 47). It should also be noted, however, that the Trull et al. findings were not unambiguous. The MAXCOV curve for BDL did not peak in the center of the distribution, although it did peak at the end, which could be inconsistent with both the dimensional and the categorical models. Lenzenweger and Korfine (1992) obtained the same results using indicators of schizotypia from the PAS and interpreted the peak at the end of the curve to be most consistent with a low base rate latent-class taxon.

EMPIRICAL SUPPORT FOR THE FIVE-FACTOR DIMENSIONAL MODEL

Overall, the empirical research does appear to be more consistent with a dimensional than with a categorical model of classification. The research indicates that reliable and valid information is lost by the use of the categorical model and that more reliable and valid data are obtained with the dimensional model. Studies using more sophisticated statistical techniques, such as admixture analysis and MAXCOV, also give more support to the dimensional model than to the categorical model, with perhaps the exception of the schizotypal personality disorder (Lenzenweger & Korfine, 1992).

However, this research does not suggest which dimensional model is preferable. A variety of dimensional models have been proposed for personality and personality disorders (Clark, 1990; Cloninger, 1987; Eysenck, 1987; Frances, 1982; Hyler & Lyons, 1988; Kiesler, 1986; Tyrer, 1988; Widiger & Frances, 1985). Many studies have also attempted to identify empirically the dimensions that underlie the personality disorders (Blashfield et al., 1985; Clark, 1989, 1990; Costa & McCrae, 1990; Hyler & Lyons, 1988; Hyler et al., 1990; Kass et al., 1985; Livesley & Jackson, 1986; Livesley, Jackson, & Schroeder, 1989; Lyons, Merla, Ozer, & Hyler, 1990; Millon, 1987; Morey, 1985, 1986; Morey et al., 1985; Plutchik & Platman, 1977; Presley & Walton, 1973; Romney & Bynner, 1989; Schroeder, Wormworth, & Livesley, 1992; Strack & Lorr, 1990; Trull, 1992; Tyrer & Alexander, 1979; Widiger et al., 1987,

1991; J. Wiggins & Pincus, 1989), but there is no obvious consistency in the findings (Morey, 1986) due in part to the substantial variability in the methodologies that have been used and the unreliability of personality disorder assessment. The studies have varied in the analyses used (e.g., multidimensional scaling versus factor analysis), the methods of data collection (e.g., clinical interview, self-report inventories, and ratings of analogue case studies), the populations sampled (e.g., inpatients, outpatients, and college students), and the variables analyzed (e.g., trait scales and diagnostic ratings). Even when consistent factor solutions have been obtained across studies, the interpretation of these factors has varied substantially (Widiger et al., 1991).

Romney and Bynner (1989) subjected the factor analytic solutions of Livesley and Jackson (1986), Kass et al. (1985), and Hyler and Lyons (1988) to a confirmatory covariance-structure analysis to assess the extent to which the results were consistent with the interpersonal circumplex (Benjamin, 1993; Kiesler, 1986; Widiger & Kelso, 1983; J. Wiggins, 1982). The results indicated that the narcissistic, paranoid, schizoid, dependent, and histrionic personality disorders could be adequately described with respect to the interpersonal circumplex dimensions but that additional dimensions were needed to account for the other personality disorders. The investigators suggested, for example, that a cognitive dimension was needed to represent the compulsive personality disorder.

Widiger et al. (1987) averaged the correlations among the personality disorders provided in or obtained from nine studies (Dahl, 1986; Kass et al., 1985; Livesley & Jackson, 1986; Millon, 1987; Morey, 1988b; Morey et al., 1985; Pfohl et al., 1986; Widiger et al., 1987; Zanarini et al., 1987). The averaged correlations were then submitted to both a multidimensional scaling (MDS) and a factor analysis (FA). A four-factor solution was optimal for the FA, a three-dimensional solution for the MDS. The three MDS dimensions were identical to the second through fourth dimensions of the FA. Widiger et al. interpreted the first FA dimension as representing the five-factor dimension of Neuroticism. The third MDS and the fourth FA dimensions contrasted the compulsive personality disorder with other diagnoses, replicating the findings of Kass et al. (1985) and Hyler and Lyons (1988). Neither Kass et al. nor Hyler and Lyons, however, offered a substantive interpretation for this dimension, dismissing it simply as a methodological artifact and therefore concluding that the findings supported a three-dimensional model (i.e., the three clusters of odd–eccentric, dramatic–emotional, and anxious–fearful). Widiger et al. indicated that this factor clearly represented the five-factor dimension of Conscientiousness. The remaining two dimensions obtained by Widiger et al. were interpreted as representing the interpersonal dimensions of introversion–extraversion and dominance–submission, which are rotated variants of the five-factor dimensions of Extraversion and Agreeableness (McCrae & Costa, 1989). Widiger et al., however, did not identify an Openness to Experience dimension.

A consistent difficulty with the FA and MDS research, however, is the failure to provide an independent measure of the dimensions that are used to interpret the FA and MDS solutions. The interpretations by the investigators are subjective, inconsistent, and readily debatable in the absence of any independent, objective measure. Only seven studies have assessed empirically the relationship between an independent, objective measure of a dimensional model and the personality disorders. Two concerned the interpersonal circumplex (DeJong, Brink, Jansen, & Schippers, 1989; Morey, 1985), one concerned the interpersonal circumplex and the FFM (J. Wiggins & Pincus, 1989), and four concerned the FFM (Costa & McCrae, 1990; Lyons et al., 1990; Schroeder et al., 1992; Trull, 1992).

Morey (1985) administered the Millon Clinical Multiaxial Inventory (MCMI; Millon, 1977) and the Interpersonal Check List (ICL) to 66 psychiatric inpatients. Canonical correlation analyses indicated that 36% of the variance among the ICL variables was accounted for by the MCMI scales, and 47% of the MCMI was accounted for by the ICL. A plotting of the MCMI scales with respect to the circumplex indicated substantial differentiation among the MCMI scales with respect to the power (or control) axis but very little differentiation with respect to affiliation (extraversion–introversion). This finding is somewhat surprising given the apparent ease with which one

can conceptually distinguish the personality disorders with respect to their degree of extraversion–introversion. A limitation of their study is that most of their subjects would have been diagnosed with major Axis I disorders, such as schizophrenia, bipolar disorder, or major depression. The effect of these disorders on the self-report personality scores could be substantial. However, DeJong et al. (1989) obtained quite similar findings using the ICL and the SIDP (Pfohl et al., 1986). There was again substantial differentiation with respect to the power (control) dimension and little differentiation with respect to affiliation. In fact, all of the personality disorders were placed on the hate half of the love–hate dimension, including the dependent personality disorder.

J. Wiggins and Pincus (1989) administered a variety of personality disorder and five-factor measures to 581 college students. They found that the interpersonal circumplex dimensions were useful in differentiating among and accounting for the variance for some of the personality disorders but that the additional dimensions of Neuroticism, Openness, and Conscientiousness were necessary to account for all of the personality disorders. For example, Conscientiousness was particularly useful in differentiating compulsive (maladaptively extreme conscientiousness) from passive–aggressive and antisocial disorders. BDL was defined largely by excessive and global neuroticism. The schizotypal personality disorder was the only personality disorder to load on Openness, but additional predictions regarding Openness were confirmed by the bivariate correlations of Openness with the compulsive, schizoid, and avoidant (low openness) and the schizotypal and histrionic (high openness) scales.

Costa and McCrae (1990) obtained self-report, spouse, and peer ratings of the five factors and self-report measures of the personality disorders with the MMPI (Morey et al., 1985), the MCMI, and the MCMI-II (Millon, 1987). The results were largely consistent with the findings of J. Wiggins and Pincus (1989). The FFM accounted for a substantial proportion of the variance in personality disorder pathology, with each of the five dimensions providing substantial contributions. The Conscientiousness dimension, for example, was again useful in characterizing and differentiating the compulsive personality disorder, as well as being negatively correlated with the antisocial, passive–aggressive, and histrionic disorders. Narcissism was positively correlated with antagonism and negatively correlated with neuroticism. The avoidant and dependent disorders were both characterized by neuroticism, but the avoidant was also characterized by introversion (on the MCMI). The avoidant and schizoid disorders were both characterized by introversion, but the avoidant was also characterized by neuroticism. The weakest findings occurred for the Openness to Experience dimension.

Schroeder, Wormworth, and Livesley (1992) factor analyzed the Dimensional Assessment of Personality Pathology–Basic Questionnaire (DAPP-BQ; Livesley, Jackson, & Schroeder, 1989) along with the NEO Personality Inventory (NEO-PI; Costa & McCrae, 1985) in a sample of 300 normal subjects. The DAPP-BQ contains 18 dimensions of personality pathology, such as affective lability, interpersonal disesteem, narcissism, and stimulus seeking (Livesley et al., 1989). A five-factor solution was obtained, four factors of which corresponded to the five-factor domains (Neuroticism, Extraversion, Agreeableness, and Conscientiousness). The third factor was defined jointly by introversion and closedness to experience. Most of the DAPP-BQ scales involve some aspect of neuroticism; compulsivity was associated primarily with conscientiousness; passive oppositionalism was associated with low conscientiousness; lack of interpersonal esteem, suspiciousness, conduct problems, and rejection were associated with antagonism; diffidence was associated with agreeableness; intimacy problems, social avoidance, and restricted expression were associated with introversion; and conduct problems, stimulus seeking, and insecure attachment were associated with extraversion. Schroeder et al. suggested that the "dimension of Openness to Experience appears to play a relatively minor role in explicating personality disorder" (p. 52). However, although openness was not of primary importance with respect to any of the 18 DAPP-BQ scales, it did provide unique and important contributions with respect to accounting for variance in compulsivity, diffidence, identity problems, restricted expression (low openness), and affective lability (high openness). These latter findings are consistent with those

obtained by J. Wiggins and Pincus (1989). Overall, Schroeder et al. concluded that "the evidence suggests that personality disorders are not characterized by functioning that differs in quality from normal functioning; rather, personality disorders can be described with traits or dimensions that are descriptive of personality, both disordered and normal" (p. 52) and that "the domain of personality pathology can be explained reasonably well within the five-factor model" (p. 51).

In an extensive study, Trull (1992) administered the NEO-PI (Costa & McCrae, 1985), the MMPI personality disorders scales developed by Morey et al. (1985), the Personality Diagnostic Questionnaire–Revised (PDQ-R; Hyler & Rieder, 1987), and the Structured Interview for *DSM-III-R* Personality Disorders–Revised (SIDP-R; Pfohl et al., 1989) to 54 outpatients. This is the only published study to date to assess the relationship of the FFM to the personality disorders in a clinical sample assessed with a multimethod design, including both a semistructured interview as well as a self-report inventory. Trull found extensive support for the FFM interpretation of the personality disorders. For example, antisocial personality disorder was negatively correlated with agreeableness and conscientiousness, BDL was defined essentially by excessive neuroticism and antagonism, avoidant by introversion and neuroticism (whereas schizoid personality disorder correlated negatively with neuroticism), and histrionic personality disorder was characterized by excessive extraversion. Trull, however, did not replicate the previously reported findings of a correlation of dependency with agreeableness or compulsive personality disorder with conscientiousness.

ALTERNATIVE MODELS

To the extent that the *DSM-III-R* personality disorders involve maladaptive variants of normal personality traits, a model that provides the fundamental dimensions of personality should also provide the fundamental dimensions of abnormal personality (Widiger & Kelso, 1983). The FFM of personality is thus a compelling choice for use with the personality disorders in part because of the substantial empirical support it has received as a model of personality

(Digman, 1990). Prior research has also indicated how the five factors subsume the variance and constructs provided in alternative personality disorder dimensional models, including the interpersonal circumplex model (McCrae & Costa, 1989) and the dimensional model proposed by Eysenck (1987). Although research concerning the empirical relationship between the five factors and the personality disorders has only just begun, the findings are encouraging. Even the most vocal critics of the FFM acknowledge that it provides the point of departure for a dimensional formulation of the personality disorders. Grove and Tellegen (1991) asserted that their "view is that the Big Five . . . provides a good starting point for describing normal and disordered personality" (p. 36).

There are other compelling alternatives, including (a) the dimensions of reward dependence, harm avoidance, and novelty seeking proposed by Cloninger (1987); (b) the interpersonal circumplex models proposed by Kiesler (1986) and Benjamin (1993); (c) the seven-factor model proposed by Tellegen and Waller (in press); (d) the three clusters by which the *DSM-III-R* categorical diagnoses are arranged (i.e., odd–eccentric, dramatic–emotional, and anxious–fearful); (d) the four spectra of Axis I/II pathology of anxiety/inhibition, impulsivity/aggression, affective instability, and cognitive/perceptual disorganization proposed by Siever and Davis (1991); and (e) the hierarchical model proposed by Gunderson (1984, 1992). None, however, appears to have compelling empirical support as a model for all of the personality disorders.

We indicated earlier that the interpersonal circumplex is unable to account for all of the personality disorder pathology and is subsumed by the two factors of Extraversion and Agreeableness (McCrae & Costa, 1989; Dejong et al., 1989; J. Wiggins & Pincus, 1989). Kass et al. (1985) and Hyler and Lyons (1988) obtained factor analytic solutions that they suggested provided substantial support for the three clusters presented in the *DSM-III-R*. Both studies obtained three factors that were consistent with the dramatic–emotional, odd–eccentric, and anxious–fearful clusters. However, the results may have been compelled in part by the implicit diagnostic theory of the clinicians who provided the personality disorder

ratings (Widiger et al., 1987). More important, both studies obtained a fourth factor that the investigators dismissed as a methodological artifact. The fourth factor was in each case consistent with the Conscientiousness dimension, as suggested by J. Wiggins and Pincus (1989).

Fabrega, Ulrich, Pilkonis, and Mezzich (1991) reported a variety of demographic and clinical differences among 2,344 patients who were classified within the three *DSM-III* clusters of odd–eccentric, dramatic–emotional, or anxious–fearful. For example, the odd–eccentric patients were more likely to be male (72%) than were the dramatic–emotional (48%) or the anxious–fearful (43%) patients. Odd–eccentric patients were least likely to have a comorbid Axis I disorder, and dramatic–emotional patients were the most likely to have substance abuse disorders. Fabrega et al. suggested that the results supported the validity of the three clusters. It is likely, however, that a variety of other cluster arrangements would have obtained similarly substantial findings. Morey (1988a) provided a more direct test of the three-cluster arrangement. Morey cluster analyzed the *DSM-III-R* personality disorder diagnostic criteria on the basis of data obtained from 291 patients. The cluster analysis did recover most of the personality disorder diagnoses, but Morey acknowledged a "failure to confirm the existence of three superordinate classes of personality disorder . . . [as] suggested both in DSM-III and DSM-III-R" (p. 320).

Cloninger's (1987) model is appealing from a biogenetic perspective, given that it is derived from theory and research on the neurobiology of motivation and learning (Cloninger & Gilligan, 1987). Cloninger related each dimension to a relatively specific but interactive neurotransmitter system. Harm avoidance is thought to reflect variation in the behavioral inhibition system. Its principle monamine neuromodulator is serotonin, with the locus of activity primarily within the septohippocampal system. Reward dependence is said to involve the behavioral maintenance system, mediated by noradrenergic projections to the neocortex, with norepinephrine being the major neuromodulator. Novelty seeking is thought to reflect variation in the brain's incentive system involving mesolimbic dopaminergic pathways. The model is intriguing, but the neural pathways and neuromodulators that underlie motivation and learning may be only indirectly and often remotely related to the phenotypic variation in personality traits. In addition, there has not yet been any published study that relates empirically Cloninger's dimensions to the personality disorders.

The biogenetic spectrum model proposed by Siever and Davis (1991) is a compelling alternative to the model suggested by Cloninger (1987). There is substantial empirical support for a biogenetic association for many of the personality disorders with near-neighbor Axis I mental disorders (Siever, Klar, & Coccaro, 1985). For example, schizotypal personality disorder may represent a characterologic variant of schizophrenic pathology, avoidant personality disorder a variant of anxiety pathology, BDL a variant of mood and impulsivity pathology, antisocial a variant of impulsivity pathology, compulsive a variant of anxiety pathology, and schizoid a variant of schizophrenic pathology. From this perspective, the personality disorders would represent not extreme variants of normal traits but characterologic variants of Axis I mental disorders. The dimensions that define the personality disorders would be not the same as those that define normal personality but the dimensions that underlie most Axis I psychopathology. However, Widiger and Trull (1992) indicated that the anxiety, impulsivity/hostility, and mood spectra of Siever and Davis are already facets of Neuroticism, a dimension that is involved in almost all of the personality disorders. Widiger and Trull suggested that the cognitive–perceptual spectrum may also represent an additional facet of Neuroticism. It would be of interest in future research to assess whether the phenomenological and biogenetic association of the personality disorders with Axis I disorders is consistent with this extension of the FFM. No study, however, has yet assessed directly the Siever and Davis model, in part because of the absence of a measure of their proposed dimensions. Although it is the case that Neuroticism and its facets are integral to an understanding of personality disorder pathology, it is possible that a complete and comprehensive understanding would also need to consider the dimensions of Introversion, Antagonism, Conscientiousness, and perhaps even Openness.

Tellegen and Waller (in press) suggested that a limitation in the development of the FFM is its exclu-sion of state and evaluative terms from the original analyses of the English language by Norman (1963) and Goldberg (1981). Evaluative terms may be particularly important when characterizing abnormal personality, and Tellegen and Waller suggested that the inclusion of these terms results in seven rather than five factors. Five of the factors are equivalent to the FFM, but a few provide a more explicit representation of abnormal variants due to the inclusion of the evaluative terms. For example, the Openness to Experience dimension contrasts being traditional, conventional, conservative, and unimaginative with being unconventional, progressive, radical, unusual, surprising, uncanny, odd, and strange. This formulation of openness (which Tellegen and Waller referred to as *conventionality*) might be better suited than openness for characterizing the peculiar ideation, speech, and behavior of the schizotypal personality disorder. The two additional dimensions are identified as *positive evaluation* and *negative evaluation*. Positive evaluation contrasts being excellent, first-rate, outstanding, exceptional, special, lofty, and refined with being run-of-the-mill. Negative evaluation contrasts being depraved, evil, immoral, deceitful, detestable, lousy, cruel, destructive, stupid, and mentally imbalanced with being fair and decent. Positive evaluation may be better at characterizing the narcissistic personality disorder and negative evaluation better at characterizing the sadistic (and perhaps the antisocial) disorder than may the FFM.

However, Tellegen and Waller (in press) have not yet published their research concerning the seven-factor model, and it is difficult to evaluate its cogency. It is readily conceivable, for example, that the evaluative terms could be subsumed by the FFM if the respective dimensions were extended to include the more extreme, aberrant manifestations of these dimensions. The original emphasis by Costa and McCrae (1985) on characterizing normal personality with the NEO-PI could have resulted in an inadequate representation of the more extreme and abnormal variants of these traits. The results of Tellegen and Waller do suggest that odd, peculiar, and eccentric behaviors represent extreme variants of openness to experience, and the same may be true for the terms contained within the positive and negative evaluation dimensions. The positive evaluation dimension may represent an extreme variant of low neuroticism (i.e., an excessive absence of insecurity, anxiety, doubts, and vulnerabilities), consistent with the negative correlation of narcissism and psychopathy with neuroticism (Costa & McCrae, 1990; J. Wiggins & Pincus, 1989). The negative evaluation dimension might represent in large part an extreme variant of antagonism. This dimension already includes socially undesirable traits such as rude, suspicious, vengeful, ruthless, irritable, and manipulative behavior, and it is possible that the traits of evil, depraved, immoral, deceitful, cruel, and detestable are simply more extreme variants of these traits. It will be of interest in future research to explore the relationship between the five factors and the evaluative terms identified by Tellegen and Waller.

Gunderson (1987) has been one of the more outspoken opponents of a dimensional model for classifying personality disorders. However, he has also suggested that only a subset of the personality disorders involve a qualitatively distinct mental disorder (Gunderson, 1984, 1992; Gunderson et al., 1991). Gunderson suggested, for example, that the borderline, schizotypal, paranoid, antisocial, narcissistic, and schizoid personality disorders involve pathologies that are deeper, more severe, and/or earlier in their origins than the pathologies of the compulsive, avoidant, histrionic, and dependent disorders. Their etiologies and pathologies may, then, be more discrete and distinctive.

> *The dimensional model deals with the observable surface characteristics and is most applicable to the less severe personality disorders that move imperceptibly into normally occurring traits. The categorical model assumes primary, nonobservable defining characteristics.* (Gunderson et al., 1991, p. 65)

As yet, however, there are no data to suggest that the paranoid, schizotypal, borderline, antisocial, narcissistic, and schizoid personality disorders are more consistent with a categorical model than are the compulsive, avoidant, histrionic, and dependent disorders.

Gunderson's model is similar to that proposed by Meehl (1986). Meehl suggested that a subset of the personality disorders (e.g., antisocial and schizotypal) could be taxonomic in nature (i.e., categorical), although most would be more appropriately classified dimensionally. To the extent that there is a specific etiology and pathology for a particular personality disorder, a categorical model could prove to be optimal for its diagnosis and classification. Underlying the phenotypic distribution of masculine and feminine personality traits is a qualitative genotypic distinction. However, it may still be more accurate and informative to characterize people with respect to their overt personality traits of masculinity and femininity than to lump and stereotype people as being simply men or women. There is likely to be a genetic predisposition for most, if not all, personality traits, but the interaction of these apparently specific etiologies with social, cultural, and other environmental experiences can alter these originally black/white distinctions into more complex and idiosyncratic shades of gray. It is useful to know that schizotypal personality traits are due in part to a genetic predisposition that is associated with schizophrenia (Siever & Davis, 1991), but characterizing the personalities of individuals with the schizotaxic genotype by one diagnostic label can be as stereotyping and misleading as can characterizing the personalities of biogenetically female patients as being simply feminine.

CONCLUSIONS

Our review of the literature suggests that it is difficult to dismiss the arguments and data favoring a dimensional model of classification for the personality disorders. The only studies to provide data supporting the categorical model have been confined to the schizotypal personality disorder or have concerned simply group (mean or frequency) differences. The latter results are the least informative with respect to determining which model offers the best fit to the data. Data with respect to bimodality, admixture analysis, maximum covariation analysis, and predictive validity have been most consistent with the dimensional model. Research has consistently indicated that reliable and valid information is lost by the failure to use the dimensional approach. A dimensional model resolves the major classificatory dilemmas, provides a more specific and precise description of the traits of the individual patient, and is flexible enough to allow categorical distinctions when they are desirable.

The major limitation of the dimensional model appears to be familiarity, and it is hoped that this book will contribute to an increased appreciation, understanding, and acquaintance with the dimensional perspective. The FFM provides a particularly compelling alternative to the *DSM-III-R* categorical diagnoses. Clinicians who use the FFM will be able to provide a reasonably comprehensive description of their patients' personalities with respect to their adaptive as well as maladaptive traits. The empirical support for the FFM is substantial with respect to normal personality and encouraging with respect to the personality disorders. It is suggested that future research assess whether the alternative models offer any incremental (concurrent or predictive) validity that is not provided by the FFM or whether the alternative models can in fact be subsumed by one or more of the dimensions and their facets. We also suggest further research with clinical populations to assess whether the findings from the relatively normal populations generalize to a personality-disordered sample and to consider the issue of how maladaptivity would be defined and assessed by the FFM.

References

Adamson, J. (1989). An appraisal of the DSM-III system. *Canadian Journal of Psychiatry, 34*, 300–310.

Akiskal, H. (1989). The classification of mental disorders. In H. Kaplan & B. Sadock (Eds.), *Comprehensive textbook of psychiatry* (Vol. 1, 5th ed., pp. 583–598). Baltimore: Williams & Wilkins.

Aldenderger, M., & Blashfield, R. (1984). *Cluster analysis.* Beverly Hills, CA: Sage.

American Psychiatric Association. (1980). *Diagnostic and statistical manual of mental disorders* (3rd ed.). Washington, DC: Author.

American Psychiatric Association. (1987). *Diagnostic and statistical manual of mental disorders* (3rd ed., rev.). Washington, DC: Author.

American Psychiatric Association. (in press). *Diagnostic and statistical manual for mental disorders.* (4th ed.). Washington, DC: Author.

Angus, L., & Marziali, E. (1988). A comparison of three measures for the diagnosis of borderline personality disorder. *American Journal of Psychiatry, 145*, 1453–1454.

Benjamin, L. (1993). *Interpersonal diagnosis and treatment of personality disorders: A structural approach.* New York: Guilford Press.

Blashfield, R. (1984). *The classification of psychopathology.* New York: Plenum.

Blashfield, R., Sprock, J., Pinkston, K., & Hodgin, J. (1985). Exemplar prototypes of personality disorder diagnoses. *Comprehensive Psychiatry, 26*, 11–21.

Cantor, N., & Genero, N. (1986). Psychiatric diagnosis and natural categorization: A close analogy. In T. Millon & G. Klerman (Eds.), *Contemporary directions in psychopathology* (pp. 233–256). New York: Guilford Press.

Carson, R. C. (1991). Dilemmas in the pathway of DSM-IV. *Journal of Abnormal Psychology, 100*, 302–307.

Chapman, L. J., Chapman, J. P., & Raulin, M. L. (1978). Body-image aberration in schizophrenia. *Journal of Abnormal Psychology, 87*, 399–407.

Clark, L. (1989, August). *The basic traits of personality disorder: Primary and higher-order dimensions.* In R. R. McCrae (Chair), *Personality disorders from the perspective of the five factor model.* Symposium conducted at the 97th annual meeting of the American Psychological Association, New Orleans, LA.

Clark, L. (1990). Towards a consensual set of symptom clusters for assessment of personality disorder. In J. Butcher & C. Spielberger (Eds.), *Advances in personality assessment* (Vol. 8, pp. 243–266). Hillsdale, NJ: Erlbaum.

Clarkin, J. F., & Sanderson, C. (in press). The personality disorders. In A. Bellack & M. Hersen (Eds.), *Psychopathology in adulthood: An advanced text.* New York: Guilford Press.

Clarkin, J. F., Widiger, T. A., Frances, A. J., Hurt, S., & Gilmore, M. (1983). Prototypic typology and the borderline personality disorder. *Journal of Abnormal Psychology, 92*, 263–275.

Cloninger, C. R. (1987). A systematic method for clinical description and classification of personality variants. *Archives of General Psychiatry, 44*, 573–588.

Cloninger, C. R. (1989). Establishment of diagnostic validity in psychiatric illness: Robins and Guze's method revisited. In L. Robins & J. Barrett (Eds.), *The validity of psychiatric diagnosis* (pp. 9–18). New York: Raven Press.

Cloninger, C. R., & Gilligan, S. (1987). Neurogenic mechanisms of learning: A phylogenetic perspective. *Journal of Psychiatry Research, 21*, 457–472.

Cloninger, C. R., Martin, R., Guze, S., & Clayton, P. (1985). Diagnosis and prognosis in schizophrenia. *Archives of General Psychiatry, 42,* 15–25.

Cohen, J., & Cohen, P. (1975). *Applied multiple regression/correlation analysis for the behavioral sciences.* Hillsdale, NJ: Erlbaum.

Costa, P. T., Jr., & McCrae, R. R. (1985). *The NEO Personality Inventory manual.* Odessa, FL: Psychological Assessment Resources.

Costa, P. T., Jr., & McCrae, R. R. (1990). Personality disorders and the five-factor model of personality. *Journal of Personality Disorders, 4,* 362–371.

Costa, P. T., Jr., & McCrae, R. R. (1992). The five-factor model of personality and its relevance to personality disorders. *Journal of Personality Disorders, 6,* 343–359.

Dahl, A. (1986). Some aspects of the DSM-III personality disorders illustrated by a consecutive sample of hospitalized patients. *Acta Psychiatrica Scandinavica, 73,* 61–66.

DeJong, C., Brink, W., Jansen, J., & Schippers, G. (1989). Interpersonal aspects of DSM-III Axis II: Theoretical hypotheses and empirical findings. *Journal of Personality Disorders, 3,* 135–146.

Digman, J. (1990). Personality structure: Emergence of the five factor model. *Annual Review of Psychology, 41,* 417–440.

Eysenck, H. (1986). A critique of contemporary classification and diagnosis. In T. Millon & G. Klerman (Eds.), *Contemporary directions in psychopathology* (pp. 73–98). New York: Guilford Press.

Eysenck, H. (1987). The definition of personality disorders and the criteria appropriate for their description. *Journal of Personality Disorders, 1,* 211–219.

Fabrega, H., Ulrich, R., Pilkonis, P., & Mezzich, J. (1991). On the homogeneity of personality disorder clusters. *Comprehensive Psychiatry, 32,* 373–386.

Finn, S. (1982). Base rates, utilities, and DSM-III: Shortcomings of fixed-rule systems of psychodiagnosis. *Journal of Abnormal Psychology, 91,* 294–302.

Frances, A. J. (1982). Categorical and dimensional systems of personality diagnosis: A comparison. *Comprehensive Psychiatry, 23,* 516–527.

Frances, A. J. (1990, May). *Conceptual problems of psychiatric classification.* Paper presented at the 143rd annual meeting of the American Psychiatric Association, New York.

Frances, A. J. (1993). Dimensional diagnosis of personality—Not whether, but when and which. *Psychological Inquiry, 4,* 110–111.

Frances, A. J., Clarkin, J., Gilmore, M., Hurt, S., & Brown, S. (1984). Reliability of criteria for borderline personality disorder: A comparison of DSM-III and the Diagnostic Interview for Borderline Patients. *American Journal of Psychiatry, 42,* 591–596.

Frances, A. J., Pincus, H. A., Widiger, T. A., Davis, W. W., & First, M. B. (1990). DSM-IV: Work in progress. *American Journal of Psychiatry, 147,* 1439–1448.

Frances, A. J., Widiger, T. A., & Pincus, H. A. (1989). The development of DSM-IV. *Archives of General Psychiatry, 46,* 373–375.

Gangestad, S., & Snyder, M. (1985). "To carve nature at its joints": On the existence of discrete classes in personality. *Psychological Review, 92,* 317–349.

Goldberg, L. (1981). Language and individual differences: The search for universals in personality lexicons. In L. Wheeler (Ed.), *Review of personality and social psychology* (Vol. 2, pp. 141–165). Beverly Hills, CA: Sage.

Golden, R., & Meehl, P. (1979). Detection of the schizoid taxon with MMPI indicators. *Journal of Abnormal Psychology, 88,* 217–233.

Gorton, G., & Akhtar, S. (1990). The literature on personality disorders, 1985–1988: Trends, issues, and controversies. *Hospital and Community Psychiatry, 41,* 39–51.

Grayson, J. (1987a). Can categorical and dimensional views of psychiatric illness be distinguished? *British Journal of Psychiatry, 151,* 355–361.

Grayson, J. (1987b). Discussion. *Psychiatric Developments, 4,* 377–385.

Grove, W. M., & Andreasen, N. (1989). Quantitative and qualitative distinctions between psychiatric disorders. In L. Robins & J. Barett (Eds.), *The validity of psychiatric diagnosis* (pp. 127–141). New York: Raven Press.

Grove, W. M., & Tellegen, A. (1991). Problems in the classification of personality disorders. *Journal of Personality Disorders, 5,* 31–41.

Gunderson, J. G. (1984). *Borderline personality disorder.* Washington, DC: American Psychiatric Press.

Gunderson, J. G. (1987, May). Competing models of personality disorders. In H. Klar (Chair), *Current controversies in personality disorders.* Symposium conducted at the 140th annual meeting of the American Psychiatric Association, Chicago.

Gunderson, J. G. (1992). Diagnostic controversies. In A. Tasman & M. Riba (Eds.), *Review of psychiatry* (Vol. 11, pp. 9–24). Washington, DC: American Psychiatric Press.

Gunderson, J. G., Links, P. S., & Reich, J. H. (1991). Competing models of personality disorders. *Journal of Personality Disorders, 5,* 60–68.

Gunderson, J. G., & Zanarini, M. (1987). Current overview of the borderline diagnosis. *Journal of Clinical Psychiatry, 48,* 5–11.

Guze, R., & Helzer, J. (1987). The medical model and psychiatric disorders. In J. Cavenar, R. Michels, & A. Cooper (Eds.), *Psychiatry* (Vol. 1, pp. 1–12). Philadelphia: Lippincott.

Hart, S., & Hare, R. (1989). Discriminant validity of the psychopathy checklist in a forensic psychiatric population. *Psychological Assessment: A Journal of Consulting and Clinical Psychology, 1,* 211–218.

Hathaway, S. R., & McKinley, J. C. (1967). *Minnesota Multiphasic Personality Inventory manual.* New York: Psychological Corporation.

Heumann, K., & Morey, L. (1990). Reliability of categorical and dimensional judgments of personality disorder. *American Journal of Psychiatry, 147,* 498–500.

Hicks, L. (1984). Conceptual and empirical analysis of some assumptions of an explicitly typological theory. *Journal of Personality and Social Psychology, 46,* 1118–1131.

Hine, F., & Williams, R. (1975). Dimensional diagnosis and the medical student's grasp of psychiatry. *Archives of General Psychiatry, 32,* 525–528.

Hogg, B., Jackson, H., Rudd, R., & Edwards, J. (1990). Diagnosing personality disorders in recent-onset schizophrenia. *Journal of Nervous and Mental Disease, 178,* 194–199.

Hyler, S. E., & Lyons, M. (1988). Factor analysis of the DSM-III personality disorder clusters: A replication. *Comprehensive Psychiatry, 29,* 304–308.

Hyler, S. E., Lyons, M., Rieder, R. O., Young, L., Williams, J. B. W., & Spitzer, R. L. (1990). The factor structure of self-report DSM-III Axis II symptoms and their relationship to clinicians' ratings. *American Journal of Psychiatry, 147,* 751–757.

Hyler, S. E., & Rieder, R. O. (1987). *Personality Diagnostic Questionnaire–Revised.* New York: Author.

Hyler, S. E., Rieder, R., Spitzer, R., & Williams, J. (1983). *Personality Diagnostic Questionnaire.* Unpublished manuscript, New York State Psychiatric Institute, New York.

Hyler, S. E., Rieder, R., Williams, J., Spitzer, R., Lyons, M., & Hendler, J. (1989). A comparison of clinical and self-report diagnoses of DSM-III personality disorders in 552 patients. *Comprehensive Psychiatry, 30,* 170–178.

Kass, F., Skodol, A. E., Charles, E., Spitzer, R. L., & Williams, J. B. W. (1985). Scaled ratings of DSM-III personality disorders. *American Journal of Psychiatry, 142,* 627–630.

Kato, M. (1988). Issues on diagnosing and classifying personality disorders. In J. Mezzich & M. von Cranach (Eds.), *International classification in psychiatry* (pp. 166–172). Cambridge, UK: Cambridge University Press.

Kavoussi, R., Coccaro, E., Klar, H., Bernstein, D., & Siever, L. (1990). Structured interviews for borderline personality disorder. *American Journal of Psychiatry, 147,* 1522–1525.

Kendell, R. (1975). *The role of diagnosis in psychiatry.* Oxford, UK: Blackwell Scientific.

Kendler, K. S. (1990). Towards a scientific psychiatric nosology: Strengths and limitations. *Archives of General Psychiatry, 47,* 969–973.

Kernberg, O. F. (1984). *Severe personality disorders.* New Haven, CT: Yale University Press.

Kiesler, D. (1986). The 1982 Interpersonal Circle: An analysis of DSM-III personality disorders. In T. Millon & G. Klerman (Eds.), *Contemporary directions in psychopathology* (pp. 571–597). New York: Guilford Press.

Kiesler, D. (1991). Interpersonal methods of assessment and diagnosis. In C. R. Snyder & D. R. Forsyth (Eds.), *Handbook of social and clinical psychology: The health perspective* (pp. 438–468). Elmsford, NY: Pergamon Press.

Klerman, G. (1986). Historical perspectives on contemporary schools of psychopathology. In T. Millon & G. Klerman (Eds.), *Contemporary directions in psychopathology* (pp. 3–28). New York: Guilford Press.

Kroll, J. (1988). *The challenge of the borderline patient.* New York: Norton.

Lenzenweger, M. F., & Korfine, L. (1992). Confirming the latent structure and base rate of schizotypy: A taxometric analysis. *Journal of Abnormal Psychology, 101,* 567–571.

Lenzenweger, M. F., & Moldin, S. O. (1990). Discerning the latent structure of hypothetical psychosis proneness through admixture analysis. *Psychiatry Research, 33,* 243–257.

Livesley, W. J. (1985). The classification of personality disorder: I. The choice of category concept. *Canadian Journal of Psychiatry, 30,* 353–358.

Livesley, W. J. (1991). Classifying personality disorders: Ideal types, prototypes, or dimensions? *Journal of Personality Disorders, 5,* 52–59.

Livesley, W. J., & Jackson, D. (1986). The internal consistency and factorial structure of behaviors judged to be associated with DSM-III personality disorders. *American Journal of Psychiatry, 139,* 1360–1361.

Livesley, W. J., Jackson, D., & Schroeder, M. (1989). A study of the factorial structure of personality pathology. *Journal of Personality Disorders, 3,* 292–306.

Loranger, A. (1988). *Personality Disorder Examination (PDE) manual.* New York: DV Communications.

Loranger, A., Susman, V., Oldham, J., & Russakoff, L. (1987). The personality disorder examination: A preliminary report. *Journal of Personality Disorders, 1,* 1–13.

Lyons, M., Merla, M., Ozer, D., & Hyler, S. (1990, August). *Relationship of the "Big Five" factors to DSM-III personality disorders.* Paper presented at the 98th annual meeting of the American Psychological Association, Boston, MA.

Maser, J. D., Kaelber, C., & Weise, R. E. (1991). International use and attitudes toward DSM-III and DSM-III-R: Growing consensus in psychiatric classification. *Journal of Personality Disorders, 100,* 271–279.

McCrae, R. R., & Costa, P. T., Jr. (1989). The structure of interpersonal traits: Wiggins's circumplex and the five-factor model. *Journal of Personality and Social Psychology, 56,* 586–595.

McGlashan, T. (1987). Borderline personality disorder and unipolar affective disorder: Long-term effects of comorbidity. *Journal of Nervous and Mental Disease, 175,* 467–473.

McLemore, C. W., & Brokaw, D. (1987). Personality disorders as dysfunctional interpersonal behavior. *Journal of Personality Disorders, 1,* 270–285.

McReynolds, P. (1989). Diagnosis and clinical assessment: Current status and major issues. *Annual Review of Psychology, 40,* 83–108.

Meehl, P. E. (1986). Diagnostic taxa as open concepts: Meta-theoretical and statistical questions about reliability and construct validity in the grand strategy of nosological revision. In T. Millon & G. Klerman (Eds.), *Contemporary directions in psychopathology* (pp. 215–231). New York: Guilford Press.

Meehl, P. E., & Golden, R. (1982). Taxometric methods. In P. Kendall & J. Butcher (Eds.), *Handbook of research methods in clinical psychology* (pp. 127–181). New York: Wiley.

Mellsop, G., Varghese, F., Joshua, S., & Hicks, A. (1982). The reliability of Axis II of DSM-III. *American Journal of Psychiatry, 139,* 1360–1361.

Mendelsohn, G., Weiss, D., & Feimer, N. (1982). Conceptual and empirical analysis of the typological implications of patterns of socialization and femininity. *Journal of Personality and Social Psychology, 42,* 1157–1170.

Miller, M., & Thayer, J. (1989). On the existence of discrete classes in personality: Is self-monitoring the correct joint to carve? *Journal of Personality and Social Psychology, 57,* 143–155.

Millon, T. (1977). *Millon Clinical Multiaxial Inventory.* Minneapolis, MN: National Computer Systems.

Millon, T. (1981). *Disorders of personality: DSM-III. Axis II.* New York: Wiley.

Millon, T. (1987). *Manual for the MCMI-II.* Minneapolis, MN: National Computer Systems.

Millon, T. (1990). The disorders of personality. In L. A. Pervin (Ed.), *Handbook of personality: Theory and research* (pp. 339–370). New York: Guilford Press.

Millon, T. (1991). Classification in psychopathology: Rationale, alternatives, and standards. *Journal of Abnormal Psychology, 100,* 245–261.

Morey, L. C. (1985). An empirical comparison of interpersonal and DSM-III approaches to classification of personality disorders. *Psychiatry, 48,* 358–364.

Morey, L. C. (1986). A comparison of three personality disorder assessment approaches. *Journal of Psychopathology and Behavioral Assessment, 8,* 25–30.

Morey, L. C. (1988a). The categorical representations of personality disorder: A cluster analysis of DSM-III-R personality disorders. *Journal of Abnormal Psychology, 97,* 314–321.

Morey, L. C. (1988b). Personality disorders in DSM-III and DSM-III-R: Convergence, coverge, and internal consistency. *American Journal of Psychiatry, 145,* 573–577.

Morey, L. C., & Ochoa, E. (1989). An investigation of adherence to diagnostic criteria: Clinical diagnosis of the DSM-III personality disorders. *Journal of Personality Disorders, 3,* 180–192.

Morey, L. C., Waugh, M., & Blashfield, R. (1985). MMPI scales for DSM-III personality disorders: Their derivation and correlates. *Journal of Personality Assessment, 49,* 245–251.

Nazikian, H., Rudd, R., Edwards, J., & Jackson, H. (1990). Personality disorder assessment for psychiatric inpatients. *Australian and New Zealand Journal of Psychiatry, 24,* 37–46.

Nestadt, G., Romanoski, A., Chahal, R., Merchant, A., Folstein, M., Gruenberg, E., & McHugh, P. (1990). An epidemiological study of histrionic personality disorder. *Psychological Medicine, 20,* 413–422.

Norman, W. (1963). Toward an adequate taxonomy of personality attributes: Replicated factor structure in peer nomination personality ratings. *Journal of Abnormal and Social Psychology, 66,* 574–583.

Nurnberg, H. G., Raskin, M., Levine, P. E., Pollack, S., Siegel, O., & Prince, R. (1991). The comorbidity of borderline personality disorder and other DSM-III-R Axis II personality disorders. *American Journal of Psychiatry, 148,* 1371–1377.

O'Boyle, M., & Self, D. (1990). A comparison of two interviews for DSM-III-R personality disorders. *Psychiatry Research, 32,* 85–92.

Oldham, J. M. (1987). DSM-III personality disorders: Assessment problems. *Journal of Personality Disorders, 1,* 241–247.

Oldham, J. M., Skodol, A. E., Kellman, H. D., Hyler, S. E., Rosnick, L., & Davies, M. (1992). Diagnosis of DSM-III-R personality disorders by two structured interviews: Patterns of comorbidity. *American Journal of Psychiatry, 149,* 213–220.

Pfohl, B., Blum, N., Zimmerman, M., & Stangl, D. (1989). *Structured Interview for DSM-III-R Personality Disorders–Revised (SIDP-R).* Iowa City: University of Iowa, Department of Psychiatry.

Pfohl, B., Coryell, W., Zimmerman, M., & Stangl, D. (1986). DSM-III personality disorders: Diagnostic overlap and internal consistency of individual DSM-III criteria. *Comprehensive Psychiatry, 27,* 21–34.

Plutchik, R., & Conte, H. R. (1985). Quantitative assessment of personality disorders. In R. Michels & J. O. Cavenar (Eds.), *Psychiatry* (Vol. 1, pp. 1–13). Philadelphia: Lippincott.

Plutchik, R., & Platman, S. (1977). Personality connotations of psychiatric diagnoses. *Journal of Nervous and Mental Disease, 165,* 418–422.

Presley, A., & Walton, H. (1973). Dimensions of abnormal personality. *British Journal of Psychiatry, 122,* 269–276.

Reich, J., Noyes, R., & Troughton, E. (1987). Lack of agreement between instruments assessing DSM-III personality disorders. In C. Green (Ed.), *Conference on the Millon clinical inventories* (pp. 223–234). Minnetonka, MN: National Computer Systems.

Robins, L., & Helzer, J. (1986). Diagnosis and clinical assessment: The current state of psychiatric diagnosis. *Annual Review of Psychology, 37,* 409–432.

Romney, D., & Bynner, J. (1989). Evaluation of a circumplex model of DSM-III personality disorders. *Journal of Research in Personality, 23,* 525–538.

Rutter, M. (1987). Temperament, personality and personality disorder. *British Journal of Psychiatry, 150,* 443–458.

Schacht, T. (1985). DSM-III and the politics of truth. *American Psychologist, 40,* 513–521.

Schroeder, M. L., Wormworth, J. A., & Livesley, W. J. (1992). Dimensions of personality disorder and their relationships to the Big Five dimensions of personality. *Psychological Assessment, 4,* 47–53.

Siever, L. J., & Davis, K. L. (1991). A psychobiological perspective on the personality disorders. *American Journal of Psychiatry, 148,* 1647–1658.

Siever, L., Klar, H., & Coccaro, E. (1985). Psychobiologic substrates of personality. In H. Klar & L. Siever (Eds.), *Biologic response styles: Clinical implications* (pp. 37–66). Washington, DC: American Psychiatric Press.

Skodol, A. E., Oldham, J. M., Rosnick, L., Kellman, H. D., & Hyler, S. E. (1991). Diagnosis of DSM-III-R personality disorders: A comparison of two structured interviews. *International Journal of Methods in Psychiatric Research, 1,* 13–26.

Skodol, A. E., Rosnick, L., Kellman, H. D., Oldham, J., & Hyler, S. E. (1988). Validating structured DSM-III-R

personality disorder assessments with longitudinal data. *American Journal of Psychiatry, 145,* 1297–1299.

Spitzer, R. L. (1987). Nosology. In A. Skodol & R. Spitzer (Eds.), *An annotated bibliography of DSM-III* (pp. 3–11). Washington, DC: American Psychiatric Press.

Spitzer, R. L., Endicott, J., & Gibbon, M. (1979). Crossing the border into borderline personality and borderline schizophrenia. *Archives of General Psychiatry, 36,* 17–24.

Spitzer, R. L., & Williams, J. B. W. (1985). Classification of mental disorders. In H. I. Kaplan & B. J. Sadock (Eds.), *Comprehensive textbook of psychiatry* (pp. 591–613). Baltimore: Williams & Wilkins.

Spitzer, R. W., Williams, J. B. W., & Gibbon, M. (1987). *Structured Clinical Interview for DSM-III-R Personality Disorders (SCID-II).* New York: New York State Psychiatric Institute, Biometric Research Unit.

Standage, K., & Ladha, N. (1988). An examination of the reliability of the Personality Disorder Examination and a comparison with other methods of identifying personality disorders in a clinical sample. *Journal of Personality Disorders, 2,* 267–271.

Stone, M. (1992). The treatment of severe personality disorders. In A. Tasman & M. Riba (Eds.), *Review of psychiatry* (Vol. 11, pp. 98–115). Washington, DC: American Psychiatric Press.

Strack, S., & Lorr, M. (1990). Item factor structure of the Personality Adjective Check List. *Journal of Personality Assessment, 55,* 86–94.

Strube, M. (1989). Evidence for the type in type A behavior: A taxometric analysis. *Journal of Personality and Social Psychology, 56,* 972–987.

Tellegen, A., & Waller, N. (in press). Exploring personality through test construction: Development of the Multidimensional Personality Questionnaire. In S. Briggs & J. Cheek (Eds.), *Personality measures: Development and evaluation* (Vol. 1). Greenwich, CT: JAI Press.

Trull, T. J. (1992). DSM-III-R personality disorders and the five-factor model of personality: An empirical comparison. *Journal of Abnormal Psychology, 101,* 553–560.

Trull, T. J., Widiger, T. A., & Guthrie, P. (1990). The categorical versus dimensional status of borderline personality disorder. *Journal of Abnormal Psychology, 99,* 40–48.

Tyrer, P. (1988). What's wrong with DSM-III personality disorders? *Journal of Personality Disorders, 2,* 281–291.

Tyrer, P., & Alexander, J. (1979). Classification of personality disorder. *British Journal of Psychiatry, 135,* 163–167.

Vaillant, G. (1984). The disadvantages of DSM-III outweigh its advantages. *American Journal of Psychiatry, 141,* 542–545.

Walton, H. (1986). The relationship between personality disorder and psychiatric illness. In T. Millon & G. Klerman (Eds.), *Contemporary directions in psychopathology* (pp. 553–569). New York: Guilford Press.

Widiger, T. A. (1991). Personality disorder dimensional models proposed for DSM-IV. *Journal of Personality Disorders, 5,* 386–398.

Widiger, T. A. (1993). The DSM-III-R categorical personality disorder diagnoses: A critique and an alternative. *Psychological Inquiry, 4,* 75–90.

Widiger, T. A., & Frances, A. J. (1985). The DSM-III personality disorders: Perspectives from psychology. *Archives of General Psychiatry, 42,* 615–623.

Widiger, T. A., Frances, A. J., Harris, M., Jacobsberg, L. B., Fyer, M., & Manning, D. (1991). Comorbidity among Axis II disorders. In J. Oldham (Ed.), *Axis II: New perspectives on diagnostic validity* (pp. 163–194). Washington, DC: American Psychiatric Press.

Widiger, T. A., Hurt, S., Frances, A. J., Clarkin, J., & Gilmore, M. (1984). Diagnostic efficiency and DSM-III. *Archives of General Psychiatry, 41,* 1005–1012.

Widiger, T. A., & Kelso, K. (1983). Psychodiagnosis of Axis II. *Clinical Psychology Review, 3,* 491–510.

Widiger, T. A., & Rogers, J. (1989). Prevalence and comorbidity of personality disorders. *Psychiatric Annals, 19,* 132–136.

Widiger, T. A., & Sanderson, C. (1987). The convergent and discriminant validity of the MCMI as a measure of the DSM-III personality disorders. *Journal of Personality Assessment, 51,* 228–242.

Widiger, T. A., Sanderson, C., & Warner, L. (1986). The MMPI, prototypal typology, and borderline personality disorder. *Journal of Personality Assessment, 50,* 540–553.

Widiger, T. A., & Trull, T. J. (1991). Diagnosis and clinical assessment. *Annual Review of Psychology, 42,* 109–133.

Widiger, T. A., & Trull, T. J. (1992). Personality and psychopathology: An application of the five-factor model. *Journal of Personality, 60,* 363–395.

Widiger, T. A., Trull, T. J., Hurt, S., Clarkin, J., & Frances, A. (1987). A multidimensional scaling of the DSM-III personality disorders. *Archives of General Psychiatry, 44,* 557–563.

Wiggins, J. (1982). Circumplex models of interpersonal behavior in clinical psychology. In P. Kendall & J. Butcher (Eds.), *Handbook of research methods in clinical psychology* (pp. 183–221). New York: Wiley.

Wiggins, J., & Pincus, A. (1989). Conceptions of personality disorders and dimensions of personality. *Psychological Assessment: A Journal of Consulting and Clinical Psychology, 1,* 305–316.

Wiggins, O. P., & Schwartz, M. A. (1991). Research into personality disorders: The alternatives of dimensions and ideal types. *Journal of Personality Disorders, 5,* 69–81.

Zanarini, M., Frankenburg, F., Chauncey, D., & Gunderson, J. (1987). The Diagnostic Interview for Personality Disorders: Interrater and test–retest reliability. *Comprehensive Psychiatry, 28,* 467–480.

Zimmerman, M. (1988). Why are we rushing to publish DSM-IV? *Archives of General Psychiatry, 45,* 1135–1138.

Zimmerman, M., & Coryell, W. H. (1989). The reliability of personality disorder diagnoses in a nonpatient sample. *Journal of Personality Disorders, 3,* 53–57.

Zimmerman, M., & Coryell, W. H. (1990). DSM-III personality disorder dimensions. *Journal of Nervous and Mental Disease, 178,* 686–692.

Zimmerman, M., Pfohl, B., Coryell, W., Stangl, D., & Corenthal, C. (1988). Diagnosing personality disorder in depressed patients. *General Psychiatry, 45,* 733–737.

CHAPTER 3

A DESCRIPTION OF THE *DSM-III-R* AND *DSM-IV* PERSONALITY DISORDERS WITH THE FIVE-FACTOR MODEL OF PERSONALITY

Thomas A. Widiger, Timothy J. Trull, John F. Clarkin,
Cynthia Sanderson, and Paul T. Costa, Jr.

In this chapter, we provide a five-factor translation of the personality disorders provided within and proposed for the American Psychiatric Association's *Diagnostic and Statistical Manual of Mental Disorders* (*DSM*). Widiger, in chapter 21 of this book, discusses how one would diagnose a personality disorder solely from the perspective of the five-factor model (FFM) of personality. Many clinicians, however, are more familiar with the personality disorder diagnoses presented in the third, revised edition of the *DSM* (*DSM-III-R*; American Psychiatric Association, 1987). In this chapter, we indicate how each of the *DSM-III-R* (as well as fourth edition *DSM* [*DSM-IV*; American Psychiatric Press, in press]) personality disorders can be translated as maladaptively extreme variants of the five basic factors of personality. After describing each of the 11 *DSM-III-R* personality disorder categories, we then consider three new diagnostic categories under review: negativistic (NEG), self-defeating (SDF), and depressive (DPS) personality disorders. We end the chapter with a discussion of the sadistic disorder, which is a personality disorder category that, like the passive–aggressive disorder (PAG), is likely to be dropped from the *DSM-III-R*'s set of 11 in the *DSM-IV*.

We propose that extreme or excessive personality traits characterize the personality disorders. However, we do not suggest that having an extreme score on a personality scale is equivalent to having a personality disorder diagnosis. We merely state that extreme scores place individuals at risk for certain personality disorders.

Table 1 presents a summary of our descriptions of each of the *DSM-III-R* personality disorders. These descriptions are based on the diagnostic criteria and associated features presented in *DSM-III-R* (American Psychiatric Association, 1987) and in the published literature on the respective personality disorders.

PARANOID PERSONALITY DISORDER

The paranoid personality disorder (PAR) involves the tendency to interpret the actions of others as deliberately demeaning or threatening (American Psychiatric Association, 1987). Paranoid individuals tend to be suspicious, mistrustful, hypervigilant, and argumentative (Millon, 1981). PAR is therefore characterized primarily by excessively low agreeableness (antagonism), particularly on the facet of suspiciousness (low trust), which provides an explicit representation of the core feature of this personality disorder. However, PAR also includes the low agreeableness (Costa, McCrae, & Dye, 1991) facets of excessively low straightforwardness, which represents the paranoid tendencies to be secretive, devious, and scheming, and excessively low compliance, which represents the paranoid tendency of antagonistic oppositionalism (American Psychiatric Association, 1987). PAR is also characterized in part by the neuroticism facet of angry hostility (e.g., quick to react with anger) as

TABLE 1

DSM-III-R Personality Disorders and the Five-Factor Model

Diagnostic criteria	PAR	SZD	SZT	ATS	BDL	HST	NAR	AVD	DEP	OBC	PAG
Neuroticism											
Anxiety	h		h	**h/L**	H			H	H		
Hostility	H	L		H	H	H	H			h	H
Depression			h	h	H		**h/L**	h	H	h	
Self-Consciousness		L	H	**L**	**H**	H	H	H	h	h	
Impulsiveness				H	H						
Vulnerability			h		H	h	**H**	H	H		
Extraversion											
Warmth	l	L	L	l		H		**L/H**	**h**	L	
Gregariousness	l	L	L		**h**	h		L			
Assertiveness					**h**		H	**L**	L	H	
Activity						h		L			
Excitement Seeking		**L**		H		h		L		**l**	
Positive Emotions	l	L			**h**	H				l	
Openness											
Fantasy			H			h	H				
Aesthetics	l										
Feelings	l	L	L			H				L	
Actions	**L**					h		L			
Ideas			H			l					
Values			h							L	
Agreeableness											
Trust	L		L			h					
Straightforwardness	L			L	**L**	l	l				L
Altruism				L		L	L		H	L	
Compliance	L	h		L	L				H	L	L
Modesty	l			**L**			L		H		
Tendermindedness	l			L			L		**h**		
Conscientiousness											
Competence	h					l	**h**				L
Order										H	
Dutifulness				L						H	L
Achievement Striving		l			L		**h**		L	H	
Self-Discipline				L	L						L
Deliberation				L						H	

Note. H, L = high, low, respectively, based on *DSM-III-R* (American Psychiatric Association, 1987) diagnostic criteria; h, l = high, low, respectively, based on associated features provided in *DSM-III-R* (American Psychiatric Association, 1987); **H/h, L/l** = high, low, respectively, based on clinical literature. Personality disorders: PAR = paranoid; SZD = schizoid; SZT = schizotypal; ATS = antisocial; BDL = borderline; HST = histrionic; NAR = narcissistic; AVD = avoidant; DEP = dependent; OBC = obsessive–compulsive; PAG = passive–aggressive.

well as the associated features of low extraversion (cold, no sense of humor, and avoids participation in groups; American Psychiatric Association, 1987) and low openness to aesthetics, feelings, and actions (constricted affect, generally uninterested in art or aesthetics, and sticks to a rigid routine; American Psychiatric Association, 1987; Millon, 1981).

Other *DSM-III-R* personality disorders also involve low agreeableness, particularly the narcissistic (NAR) and antisocial/psychopathic (ATS) personality disorders (see Table 1 and later discussion), which explains the comorbidity of these *DSM-III-R* categorical diagnoses. NAR, for example, is also characterized by low agreeableness, but NAR emphasizes primarily the facets of low modesty (arrogance, conceit, and grandiosity), low altruism (entitlement, self-centered stinginess, and exploitation), and low tendermindedness (lack of empathy) rather than low trust or low straightforwardness.

ATS involves the antagonism facets of excessively low straightforwardness (deceptive manipulation) and low compliance (failure to conform to social norms with respect to lawful behaviors), but it can be distinguished from prototypical PAR by the lack of emphasis on low trust (suspiciousness) and the greater emphasis on low altruism (exploitation). ATS is also characterized by the extraversion facet of excitement seeking, whereas PAR is characterized by the introversion facets of low gregariousness (prefers to be alone; American Psychiatric Association, 1987), low positive emotions, and low warmth (e.g., appears cold to others; American Psychiatric Association, 1987).

From the perspective of the FFM, PAR is most similar to PAG, with both involving the same facets of low agreeableness and neuroticism (see Table 1). This is consistent with the empirical finding that PAR is most often comorbid with PAG (Widiger & Rogers, 1989). However, once again, prototypical cases can be readily distinguished, with PAG involving low conscientiousness and with PAR involving low openness and high introversion (see Table 1). To the extent that a patient who obtains a high score on hostility, a low score on straightforwardness, and a low score on compliance also obtains a low score on various facets of conscientiousness (as well as a normal score on the antagonistic facet of trust), the more likely the diagnosis will be PAG rather than PAR.

It is evident that the dimension and facets of low agreeableness (or antagonism) are helpful in explaining the overlap, as well as the distinctions, among PAR, PAG, ATS, and NAR. However, it is also evident that the categorical distinction among these personality disorders will often be arbitrary. Some patients will be more paranoid (low trust) than narcissistic (low modesty), but the diagnosis of many patients will involve varying degrees and shades of the respective facets of agreeableness. Rather than arbitrarily placing a patient within an overly simplified diagnostic category that ignores the particular constellation of the facets of antagonism (as well as the other dimensions of personality), it would be more descriptive and precise to indicate the extent to which the patient is characterized by the respective facets of antagonism.

SCHIZOID PERSONALITY DISORDER

The essential features of the schizoid personality disorder (SZD) are an indifference to social relationships and a restricted range of emotional experience and expression (American Psychiatric Association, 1987). Schizoid individuals have a profound defect in the ability to form social relationships (Millon, 1981). They are typically loners, isolated and withdrawn from others. They may live as hermits, but more often they are within society but emotionally and socially detached. They are usually employed at jobs that require little or no social interaction. They prefer to keep to themselves, declining most every opportunity to socialize. They rarely marry because the emotional intensity of a romantic or sexual relationship is foreign and of little interest.

In other words, SZD involves excessive introversion, particularly the facets of excessively low warmth (indifference to social relationships and neither desires nor enjoys close relationships; American Psychiatric Association, 1987), low gregariousness (almost always chooses solitary activities), and low positive emotions (rarely experiences joy). Clinically, one would also expect the prototypical schizoid person to exhibit excessively low excitement seeking (i.e., overly staid, cautious, and reserved; Costa & McCrae, 1985), but this facet of introversion is not explicitly represented in the *DSM-III-R* diagnostic criteria or associated features. *DSM-IV* provides a somewhat greater emphasis on low positive emotions as a result of providing more indicators of anhedonia (Kalus, Bernstein, & Siever, 1993). For example, the item "rarely experiencing joy" will become a more general trait of "few, if any, activities that provide pleasure" (Task Force on DSM-IV, 1991). Other anhedonic traits of appearing indifferent to the praise or criticism of others, emotional coldness, detachment, and flattened affectivity will also suggest low self-consciousness and low openness to feelings (as well as low positive emotions). However, because schizoid (introverted) individuals are not necessarily closed to all aspects of experience, they may not be elevated on the dimension of low openness to experience. They may in fact have substantial interests in areas of life that involve little social involvement (e.g., ideas, theories, or aesthetics). To the extent that the introverted person displays an excessive openness to ideas and fantasy, the more likely the person is to be schizotypal rather than schizoid (as we discuss later).

SCHIZOTYPAL PERSONALITY DISORDER

The essential features of the schizotypal personality disorder (SZT) are said to be "a pervasive pattern of peculiarities of ideation, appearance, and behavior and deficits in interpersonal relatedness" (American Psychiatric Association, 1987, p. 340). SZT and SZD are quite similar (Siever & Klar, 1986). Both are largely characterized by excessive introversion (see Table 1), but they are differentiated by the relative emphasis on social and physical anhedonia in SZD and by the relative emphasis on cognitive–perceptual aberrations in SZT (Siever, Bernstein, & Silverman, 1991; Widiger, Frances, Spitzer, & Williams, 1988). SZT cognitive–perceptual aberrations are involved in the *DSM-III-R* items of (a) ideas of reference, (b) odd beliefs and magical thinking, (c) unusual perceptual experiences, (d) odd or eccentric behavior or appearance, and (e) odd speech.

Many of these cognitive–perceptual aberrations do not have an obvious representation in the FFM. Widiger and Trull (1992) speculated that they may represent an additional (seventh) facet of neuroticism. Neuroticism is said to involve a disposition to unrealistic and irrational beliefs, in addition to anxiety, depression, impulsivity, hostility, vulnerability, and self-consciousness (Costa & McCrae, 1985; McCrae, Costa, & Busch, 1986). Prototypical schizoid and schizotypal patients are largely differentiated by their respective degree of neuroticism: The prototypical schizoid person displays low hostility and low self-consciousness, whereas the prototypical schizotypal displays excessively high self-consciousness (social anxiety and pervasive discomfort with others; American Psychiatric Association, 1987; Task Force on DSM-IV, 1991) and has the associated features of excessive anxiety, depression (prone to dysphoric moods), and vulnerability (prone to transient psychotic episodes).

SZT and SZD may also be differentiated with respect to their relative degree of openness to fantasy and ideas. The cognitive aberrations of the schizotypal person can reflect, in part, an excessive maladaptive openness to unusual fantasy and ideation. This conceptualization of schizotypic ideation is somewhat controversial (Widiger, 1993) and is discussed in more detail in the summary chapter by Costa and Widiger. Nevertheless, to the extent that an excessively introverted person also displays excessive neuroticism and openness to fantasy and ideas, the *DSM-III-R/DSM-IV* personality disorder diagnosis will more likely be SZT rather than SZD. It should again be emphasized, however, that this categorical distinction is often arbitrary and distorting. It would be more informative to simply describe the extent to which an introverted person is anxious, vulnerable, and open to aberrant fantasies and ideas than to impose an arbitrary, black-or-white categorical distinction.

SZT and SZD share the *DSM-III-R* criterion of suspiciousness and paranoid ideation (American Psychiatric Association, 1987). Schizotypal individuals may, then, have low scores on the trust facet of agreeableness. However, these scores would in most cases be confined to this single facet. Prototypical schizotypal individuals lack the additional traits of being vengeful, cynical, and irritable that are characteristic of PAR. In addition, the schizotypal person may display an excessive openness to aberrant fantasies and ideas, whereas the prototypical paranoid person will display an excessively low openness to aesthetics and actions. Both paranoid and schizotypal individuals, however, are introverted, anxious, and closed to feelings. In sum, to the extent that a person who is high on introversion tends to be low on agreeableness, elevated on hostility, and closed to experience, the more likely the *DSM-III-R/DSM-IV* diagnosis will be PAR rather than SZT.

ANTISOCIAL/PSYCHOPATHIC PERSONALITY DISORDER

ATS is defined in *DSM-III-R* as "a pattern of irresponsible and antisocial behavior" (American Psychiatric Association, 1987, p. 342). The diagnostic criteria are essentially a set of irresponsible, delinquent, and criminal acts and events, including, for example, (a) inability to sustain consistent work behavior; (b) failure to honor financial obligations; (c) fights and assaults; (d) lying and conning; (e) reckless regard for the safety of others and one's self; (f) failure to act as a responsible parent; (g) failure to conform to the law; (h) failure to sustain a monogamous relationship; and (i) a variety of delinquent acts in childhood, such as truancy, running away, vandalism, and thefts (American Psychiatric Association, 1987).

The diagnostic criteria essentially provide a set of behavioral examples of excessively low conscientiousness and low agreeableness. The parental irresponsibility and failure to sustain a monogamous relationship items will be deleted in *DSM-IV*. This revision will not have an appreciable effect on the five-factor description of ATS because there will still remain substantial representation of low conscientiousness. Persons who are low in conscientiousness tend to be aimless, unreliable, lax, negligent, and hedonistic (Costa & McCrae, 1985); the most extreme variants of these tendencies describe the indulgent and irresponsible antisocial individual. The antisocial person, however, is also manipulative, exploitative, vengeful, criminal, and ruthless, which are aspects of antagonism (particularly the facets of excessively low straightforwardness, altruism, compliance, and tendermindedness). Hare's (1990) Revised Psychopathy Checklist (PCL-R) formulation of psychopathy includes an additional facet of antagonism: a tendency to display a grandiose sense of self-worth in such behaviors as being overly opinionated, cocky, and boastful (low modesty). This antagonistic arrogance was described by Cleckley (1941) in his original formulations of psychopathy, but it is not represented in the *DSM-III-R* (or *DSM-IV*) description of ATS.

The *DSM-III-R* text description of ATS also includes a variety of indicators of high neuroticism, including hostility and associated features of anxiety (complaints of tension), depression (dysphoric mood), and impulsivity (inability to tolerate boredom). These facets of neuroticism are particularly evident in antisocial individuals who seek clinical treatment. They may be less evident in the more successful psychopath, who may even be characterized by unusually low levels of anxiety and self-consciousness (Sutker, Bugg, & West, 1993). The PCL-R again

provides somewhat more representation of this aspect of psychopathy (e.g., glib, verbally facile, and smooth) than does *DSM-III-R*.

The combination of low conscientiousness and low agreeableness is also characteristic of PAG. PAG and ATS can be distinguished, in part, by the different facets of agreeableness and conscientiousness that are emphasized in each case. The passive–aggressive person tends to be more sloppy and careless (low in competence), whereas the antisocial person is more reckless, unreliable, and hedonistic (low in self-discipline and deliberation). More important, perhaps, is the fact that the antisocial/psychopath displays more of the facets of low agreeableness, particularly the tendencies to be tough-minded, arrogant, and ruthlessly exploitative. The excitement-seeking facet of extraversion is also very useful in distinguishing ATS from PAG.

BORDERLINE PERSONALITY DISORDER

Borderline personality disorder (BDL) is defined in *DSM-III-R* as a "pervasive pattern of instability in self-image, interpersonal relationships, and mood" (American Psychiatric Association, 1987, p. 346). The diagnostic criteria provide a variety of examples of this instability, including (a) unstable and intense interpersonal relationships; (b) impulsivity; (c) affective instability; (d) inappropriate or intense anger; (e) recurrent self-mutilation and/or suicidal threats, gestures, or behaviors; (f) identity disturbance (e.g., uncertainty regarding self-image, long-term goals, and preferred values); (g) chronic feelings of emptiness or boredom; and (h) frantic efforts to avoid real or imagined abandonment (American Psychiatric Association, 1987). These features correspond closely to the five neuroticism facets of hostility, impulsivity, vulnerability, depression, and anxiety. A person who is elevated on neuroticism tends to be hot-tempered, angry, and easily frustrated (hostility); unable to resist impulses and transient urges (impulsivity); easily rattled, panicked, and unable to deal with stress (vulnerable); tense, fearful, worried, and apprehensive (anxiety); hopeless, guilty, and blue (depressed); and is stricken by feelings of shame, inferiority, and embarrassment (self-consciousness) (Costa & McCrae, 1985). These traits provide a very good description of the borderline patient.

There is, in fact, an isomorphic correspondence to most of the BDL criteria. Affective instability, for example, is a central feature of BDL (Gunderson, 1984), and the tendency to experience negative affect is almost synonymous with neuroticism (Watson & Clark, 1984). The tendency to experience negative affect is represented directly by the neuroticism facets of anxiety, depression, and angry hostility.

Hostility is also a core feature of BDL (Kernberg, 1984) that is represented by the *DSM-III-R* items of irritability and inappropriate or intense anger and the hostility facet of neuroticism. The hostility of neuroticism and BDL is evident in explosive outbursts of anger, temper tantrums, intense rage, and hatred. It is important to emphasize, however, that the hostility of neither BDL nor neuroticism necessarily involves aggression. The hostility of the borderline person and the person who is characterized by excessive neuroticism is not for the purpose of inflicting pain and suffering on others. Borderlines will at times get into fights, but these fights will often represent an expression of their inability to suppress or control their intense feelings of anger and rage rather than a more calculated effort to dominate, exploit, or harm others. The latter, more aggressive behavior is indicative of antagonism, which is relatively more characteristic of ATS and the sadistic personality disorder than BDL.

The borderline patient tends to engage in a wide variety of impulsive acts that are directly or at least indirectly self-destructive, including overspending, sexual involvement, substance abuse, reckless driving, binge eating, and shoplifting (American Psychiatric Association, 1987). This impulsivity corresponds to the neuroticism facet of impulsivity. These impulsive acts are not an expression of a thrill-seeking spontaneity (i.e., extraverted excitement seeking). They are instead a reflection of the borderline's inability to tolerate frustration, tension, and dysphoria. Excitement-seeking recklessness is a facet of extraversion. This form of reckless behavior can be easily confused with the impulsivity of borderlines, particularly if the assessment is at the level of overt acts, which contributes in part to the substantial overlap of the BDL diagnosis with those of ATS and the histrionic personality disorder (HST) (Widiger & Rogers, 1989). From the perspective of the FFM, however, the borderline, histrionic, and antisocial

behavior patterns are readily distinguished, with BDL involving substantial and widespread elevations on neuroticism, with HST being characterized primarily by excessive extraversion, and with ATS being characterized by low agreeableness or antagonism.

Antagonism, however, is characteristic of BDL, particularly the facets of low compliance (i.e., oppositionalism) and low straightforwardness (manipulative). Most borderline patients have elevations on antagonism as well as on neuroticism, whereas the antisocial person has substantial elevations on low altruism (exploitation), the narcissistic person has elevations on low modesty (arrogance), and the paranoid person has elevations on low trust (suspiciousness).

The emphasis in *DSM-III-R* on the use of specific and explicit behaviors to increase the reliability of diagnosis has at times resulted in the inclusion of behaviors that are only indirect manifestations of underlying personality traits (Widiger & Frances, 1985). This is most clearly evident in the case of ATS (discussed by Harpur, Hart, & Hare in chapter 9), but it is also evident in the diagnosis of BDL. Unstable, intense relations, recurrent suicidal threats, chronic feelings of emptiness, frantic efforts to avoid abandonment, self-mutilation, and the new *DSM-IV* criterion of transient, stress-related, severe dissociative symptoms or paranoid ideation are more indirect manifestations of the neuroticism facets of impulsiveness, vulnerability, self-consciousness, anxiety, and depression, or what Kernberg (1984) referred to as nonspecific manifestations of ego weakness. Frantic effort to avoid abandonment is an expression of panicked, helpless, and desperate vulnerability; and unstable, intense relationships result from the tendency to be impulsive, vulnerable, hostile, anxious, and depressed.

Conceptualizing BDL as extreme neuroticism is consistent with the psychoanalytic construct of *borderline personality organization*. Borderline personality organization refers to a level of personality functioning that cuts across the *DSM-III-R* diagnostic categories (Kernberg, 1984). Each of the other *DSM-III-R* personality disorders may or may not be at a borderline level of personality organization. It would not be meaningful from this perspective to attempt to differentiate BDL from HST, ATS, or SZT because it is likely that inpatients with these personality disorders would also be at a borderline level of personality organization (Kernberg, 1984). Neuroticism is also a characteristic level of personality dysfunction that cuts across other important individual differences (e.g., degree of extraversion and conscientiousness). Kernberg preferred to use a more inferential means by which to assess a patient's level of personality organization (e.g., assess the degree of identity diffusion, reliance on primitive defenses, and reality testing within object relations), but there is likely to be a substantial correlation between five-factor neuroticism and the level of personality organization. The nonspecific manifestations of borderline personality functioning that was identified by Kernberg (e.g., anxiety tolerance, impulse control, and vulnerability to stress) are consistent with the facets of neuroticism identified by Costa and McCrae (1985).

Conceptualizing BDL as extreme neuroticism is also helpful in addressing the problematic heterogeneity of patients who meet the *DSM-III-R* criteria for the diagnosis (Clarkin, Widiger, Frances, Hurt, & Gilmore, 1983). Few cases are prototypical, with some being characterized primarily by affective instability, some by impulsivity, and others by intense anger and hostility (Hurt et al., 1990). The dimensional nature of the five-factor formulation of neuroticism recognizes that not all individuals share the same facets of neuroticism to the same degree. Clinicians need not lump together all of the diverse presentations of borderline symptomatology within one undifferentiated category but can instead provide a more detailed and specific description of the individual patient with respect to the various facets of neuroticism. Some patients may be characterized primarily by the facet of hostility, some by impulsivity, and others by anxiety, vulnerability, depression, and/or self-consciousness.

Conceptualizing BDL as extreme neuroticism also helps to explain the excessive prevalence and comorbidity of this popular but controversial diagnosis (Widiger & Frances, 1989b). Neuroticism, as a characteristic level of personality dysfunction (i.e., vulnerability to stress, impulse dyscontrol, and negative emotionality) is almost ubiquitous within clinical populations (Eysenck & Eysenck, 1985). Personality dysfunction to the point of needing inpatient hospitalization usually involves excessive neuroticism. A diagnostic category that consists essentially of excessive neuroticism should be very prevalent and should be the most common personality disorder within inpatient settings. To the extent that the other personality disorders involve some degree of neuroticism (see Table 1) one would also expect considerable overlap and comorbidity with BDL, particularly within inpatient settings. The excessive prevalence and comorbidity of borderline personality that is so problematic to its validity as a distinct personality disorder (Cloninger, 1989; Gunderson & Zanarini, 1987; Widiger & Frances, 1989b) is then readily understandable from the perspective of the FFM.

HISTRIONIC PERSONALITY DISORDER

HST is described by Millon (1981) as the "gregarious pattern" (p. 131), and HST largely represents an extreme variant of extraversion. Extraversion involves the tendency to be outgoing, talkative, and affectionate (high warmth); to be convivial; to have many friends; and to actively seek social contact (high gregariousness); to be assertive and dominant (high assertiveness); to be energetic, fast-paced, and vigorous (high activity); to be flashy; to seek strong stimulation; to take risks (high excitement seeking); and to be high-spirited, buoyant, optimistic, and joyful (high positive emotions). These facets of extraversion provide a vivid description of the prototypical histrionic person. Being outgoing, optimistic, and gregarious is not inherently maladaptive, but being extremely extraverted means being at a high risk for HST. Histrionic individuals express emotions with an inappropriate exaggeration (excessively high positive emotions); they crave excitement and stimulation (high excitement seeking); they are quick to form numerous, generally superficial, relationships (high gregariousness); and they display inappropriate affection, intimacy, and seductiveness (high warmth).

HST is most often comorbid with BDL (Widiger & Rogers, 1989). This is due, in part, to the excessive neuroticism (hostility and vulnerability for the histrionic) and antagonism (in particular a manipulative, deceptive, and exploitative low straightforwardness and low altruism) that are characteristic of both disorders. However, the comorbidity is also due to the borderline's associated features of extraversion that are not included in the *DSM-III-R* description of BDL but that are described in the clinical literature (e.g., excessive seeking of social contacts, assertive dominance, and excessive positive emotionality; Kernberg, 1984).

BDL and HST may be distinguished, in part, by the level of openness to experience that is characteristically excessive in the histrionic person (e.g., flights into romantic fantasy, creative imagination, craving of novelty, and bored with routine; American Psychiatric Association, 1987). The histrionic person may also tend to be lower in self-discipline (needs immediate gratification and has no tolerance for frustration; American Psychiatric Association, 1987). To the extent that a patient's personality description is largely confined to most of the facets of neuroticism (i.e., an absence of excessive extraversion and openness), the *DSM-III-R/DSM-IV* diagnosis is more likely to be confined to BDL. However, as we emphasized before, most patients do not provide prototypical, pure cases of BDL or HST and, therefore, fall somewhere in between the prototypical profiles. For example, most inpatients with HST function at least at a moderate level of neuroticism (i.e., a borderline level of personality organization; Kernberg, 1984).

NARCISSISTIC PERSONALITY DISORDER

NAR is characterized primarily by traits of grandiosity, entitlement, arrogance, and exploitation (American Psychiatric Association, 1987) and is evident from the perspective of the FFM primarily by low agreeableness. The narcissist is not particularly hostile (which is a facet of neuroticism) or even physically aggressive. Facets of low agreeableness include exploitation, conceit, self-centeredness, and arrogance, which clearly describe the narcissistic person. The *DSM-III-R* and *DSM-IV* criteria of interpersonal exploitation, entitlement, low empathy, arrogance, and grandiose sense of self-importance (American Psychiatric Association, 1987) involve these facets of low agreeableness.

Low agreeableness or antagonism is also characteristic of PAR, ATS, BDL, and PAG, but as we indicated earlier, prototypical cases of these personality disorders are largely differentiated by the facets of

antagonism that are emphasized in each case. For example, the excessive suspiciousness (low trust) of PAR is not characteristic of NAR, and the oppositionalism and manipulativeness of ATS, BDL, and PAG (low compliance and low straightforwardness) are not as characteristic of NAR. The narcissistic person also tends to display relatively higher levels of conscientiousness than do antisocial, borderline, histrionic, and passive–aggressive individuals. These personality disorders are characterized, in part, by low conscientiousness, whereas NAR involves more normal and often high levels of competence and achievement striving. These features of narcissism are not included in the *DSM-III-R* criteria for NAR, but they are described within the clinical literature (Kernberg, 1984; Ronningstam & Gunderson, 1988).

An ambiguity in the five-factor description of NAR is the characteristic level of neuroticism. Individuals who are grandiose, overly self-confident, arrogant, and have an inflated self-esteem often describe themselves as being excessively low in neuroticism, particularly with respect to the facets of self-consciousness, anxiety, and vulnerability. Most people have some degree of self-consciousness and vulnerability, but it is characteristic of the narcissist to deny the presence of any substantial faults, fallibilities, or foibles (Watson & Clark, 1984). Excessively low scores on self-report measures of neuroticism may then be indicative of narcissism, particularly when these scores are not confirmed by ratings provided by a peer or spouse (Costa & McCrae, 1990). Close associates are often more aware of the narcissist's flaws and insecurities, and a substantial discrepancy between peer and self-ratings of vulnerability can be useful in suggesting an inflated self-esteem.

Narcissists, however, often experience cracks in their armor of grandiosity. They can, in fact, be quite vulnerable to threats to self-esteem (Kernberg, 1984). This vulnerability is particularly evident in narcissists who seek treatment. *DSM-III-R* does not explicitly include a criterion that represents this vulnerability. However, *DSM-III-R* does include other indicators of neuroticism, particularly self-consciousness (hypersensitivity to criticism), hostility (rage and envy), and depression (feelings of unworthiness). The *DSM-IV* criteria for NAR place somewhat less emphasis on high neuroticism (e.g., by deleting the hypersensitivity to criticism item) and place somewhat more emphasis on arrogant antagonism (by adding the items of arrogance, haughty attitudes, and the belief that others are envious of one's self).

AVOIDANT PERSONALITY DISORDER

The third edition of the *DSM* (*DSM-III*; American Psychiatric Association, 1980) formulation of the avoidant personality disorder (AVD) was based primarily on the construct of an active–detached personality syndrome developed by Millon (1981). Avoidant individuals are introverted because of a "hypersensitivity to potential rejection, humiliation, or shame" (Millon, 1981, p. 298). They are socially withdrawn in spite of a strong desire for affection and acceptance. They are alone and lonely but intensely shy and insecure (Pilkonis, 1984). In *DSM-III-R*, more emphasis was given to the features of insecurity, inhibition, and timidity, as emphasized in the psychoanalytic construct of the phobic character (Widiger et al., 1988). The essential features of the disorder are now described as "a pervasive pattern of social discomfort, fear of negative evaluation, and timidity" (American Psychiatric Association, 1987, p. 351).

From the perspective of the FFM, AVD involves (a) introversion, particularly the facets of low gregariousness (no close friends, avoids significant interpersonal contact, and unwilling to get involved with others; American Psychiatric Association, 1987); low excitement seeking (exaggerates potential dangers, difficulties, or risks in doing anything outside of normal routine); low activity (avoidance of social and occupational activities, and canceling of social plans); and low assertiveness (not represented in the *DSM-III-R* criteria but present within the clinical literature; Millon, 1981; Pilkonis, 1984); and (b) neuroticism, particularly the facets of vulnerability, self-consciousness, and anxiety (e.g., easily hurt by criticism and disapproval, reticent in social situations because of fear of saying something foolish, fears being embarrassed, and afraid of not being liked). Avoidant individuals are anxious, timid, and insecure in their introversion. They are easily rattled, panicked, and unable to deal with stress (vulnerable); tense, fearful, worried, and apprehensive (anxious); and prone to

feelings of embarrassment and inferiority (self-consciousness) (Costa & McCrae, 1985).

The differentiation of AVD and SZD has been controversial (Livesley, West, & Tanney, 1985; Trull, Widiger, & Frances, 1987), but the comorbidity and differentiation of AVD and SZD are understandable from the perspective of the FFM. Both involve introversion and (to a lesser extent) low openness to experience. The avoidant person may at times be less open to experience than is the schizoid, given the phobic avoidance of many activities (Frances & Widiger, 1987). However, the prototypical SZD and AVD are readily distinguished with respect to neuroticism. SZD is characterized by low neuroticism, whereas AVD is characterized by high neuroticism. To the extent that an introverted patient is elevated on neuroticism (particularly the facets of vulnerability, anxiety, and self-consciousness), the more likely will be a diagnosis of AVD rather than one of SZD.

AVD and SZD can also be distinguished to some extent by facets of introversion. AVD introversion tends to emphasize the facets of low activity (passivity), low assertiveness (retiring and unassuming), and low excitement seeking (cautious and inhibited), whereas SZD introversion involves primarily the facets of low warmth (cold and distant), low positive emotions (anhedonia), and low gregariousness (preference to be alone and solitary), as well as low excitement seeking. Prototypical avoidant individuals may, in fact, be characterized by high warmth because they are fully capable of expressing strong feelings of affection. Avoidant individuals may sometimes appear to be low in warmth, given their tendency to avoid social situations, but they desire and will seek social contact (although in an awkward, self-conscious, and inhibited manner).

DSM-III had, in fact, included a criterion of a desire for the affection and acceptance of others to differentiate AVD from SZD (American Psychiatric Association, 1980). It was deleted in *DSM-III-R* because a desire for affection and acceptance is normative (i.e., nonpathological) and because it is characteristic of people without AVD. Nevertheless, this criterion was useful in distinguishing AVD from SZD (Trull et al., 1987; Widiger, 1991) and in representing the capacity of the avoidant person to be warm and affectionate, a trait commonly seen in clinical experience (Frances & Widiger, 1987). A proposal for *DSM-IV* was to revise the "no-close-friends" item to again include a clause that it occurs despite a desire to relate to others (Millon, 1991; Task Force on *DSM-IV*, 1991). The final decision was to delete the no-close-friends item altogether. There were many revisions to other AVD items, most of which will have the effect of placing more emphasis on the neuroticism facet of self-consciousness (e.g., belief that one is socially inept, restraint due to fear of being shamed or ridiculed).

It is useful to emphasize again, however, that the avoidant and schizoid behavior patterns tend to shade into one another. Most patients will not provide prototypical cases but will instead involve shades of gray of avoidant and schizoid traits. Some will have low gregariousness and low assertiveness or low warmth and low assertiveness with moderate neuroticism. It would then be more precise and informative to indicate the respective levels on the relevant facets of introversion and neuroticism than to characterize the patient as either avoidant or schizoid (or both).

DEPENDENT PERSONALITY DISORDER

The essential feature of the dependent personality disorder (DEP) "is a pervasive pattern of dependent and submissive behavior" (American Psychiatric Association, 1987, p. 354). DEP represents primarily an extreme variant of agreeableness with high levels of neuroticism and low assertiveness (see Table 1). Dependent individuals are characterized by a marked need for social approval and affection and will sacrifice many of their own needs, values, options, pleasures, and other goals to live in accord with the desires of others (Millon, 1981). They are self-effacing, docile, submissive, and sacrificial. Agreeableness is often adaptive and desirable, involving such traits as being trusting, good-natured, helpful, forgiving, and accommodating; but "agreeableness can also assume a pathological form, in which it is usually seen as dependency" (Costa & McCrae, 1985, p. 12).

The *DSM-III-R* criteria set includes many explicit examples of pathological agreeableness, including excessive compliance (does not make everyday decisions without excessive advice or reassurance and

allows others to make most of the important decisions; American Psychiatric Association, 1987), excessive modesty (agrees with others even when the person believes they are wrong), and excessive altruism (volunteers to do things that are unpleasant or demeaning). The other *DSM-III-R* criteria mostly represent facets of neuroticism, particularly vulnerability, anxiety, depression, and self-consciousness (e.g., is preoccupied with fears of being abandoned, feels devastated or helpless when close relationships end, belittles one's self, and is easily hurt by criticism or disapproval).

One minor note with respect to the five-factor description of *DSM-III-R* DEP is the low achievement striving. Dependent individuals have difficulty initiating and completing projects (American Psychiatric Association, 1987). It is not that they are not motivated to be conscientious but that they fail to be conscientious, and therefore, they may not consider themselves to be competent even when they are being competent. In *DSM-IV*, this item is clarified to indicate that the failure to complete projects is due to a lack of self-confidence rather than to a lack of motivation, energy, or ability (Hirschfeld, Shea, & Talbot, 1991). Dependent individuals may then describe themselves as being low in competence and dutifulness (and may at times fail to be competent), but their self-description of low conscientiousness can also reflect their high levels of neuroticism (low self-esteem).

The diagnoses of AVD and DEP often co-occur, more so perhaps than the comorbidity of AVD with SZD (Trull et al., 1987; Widiger & Rogers, 1989). This is somewhat odd on the surface, given that social withdrawal and aloneness would appear to be mutually exclusive with dependency. However, their comorbidity is due primarily to their sharing of similar facets of neuroticism (vulnerability, anxiety, depression, and self-consciousness). Prototypical cases are readily distinguished with respect to the dimensions of introversion and agreeableness. The dependent person exhibits low assertiveness, whereas the avoidant person may at times display high warmth; but the prototypical avoidant person is particularly characterized by the introversion facet of low gregariousness, which is not evident in a dependent person. *DSM-IV* will increase their differentiation by revising the item "feels devastated and helpless when a close relationship ends" to "urgently seeks another relationship to provide care and support" (i.e., a revision from neuroticism to extraversion).

Prototypical cases of AVD and DEP are also distinguished with respect to the domain of agreeableness. To the extent that a person who is moderately anxious, self-conscious, vulnerable, and depressed is also excessively trustworthy, gullible, compliant, modest, and tenderminded, the person will more likely be diagnosed as DEP rather than AVD. Once again, however, it is important to emphasize that the categorical distinction between DEP and AVD is arbitrary at their boundaries. It would not be surprising, for example, for some patients to be characterized by high agreeableness and high introversion (as well as neuroticism). These individuals would provide a problematic differential diagnosis to the clinician who uses the categorical *DSM-III-R/DSM-IV* taxonomy because the patient would appear to be both avoidant and dependent. However, from the perspective of the FFM, the patient would simply be described as being elevated on (the respective facets of) neuroticism, introversion, and agreeableness.

OBSESSIVE–COMPULSIVE PERSONALITY DISORDER

The essential feature of the obsessive–compulsive personality disorder (OBC) "is a pervasive pattern of perfectionism and inflexibility" (American Psychiatric Association, 1987, p. 354). The diagnostic criteria include (a) overconscientiousness, scrupulousness, and inflexibility; (b) perfectionism that interferes with task completion; (c) preoccupation with details, rules, lists, order, organization, or schedules; and (d) excessive devotion to work and productivity. All of these features are clearly maladaptive, extreme variants of conscientiousness. Conscientiousness involves a person's degree of organization, persistence, and motivation in goal-directed behavior. Conscientious individuals tend to be organized, reliable, hard-working, self-disciplined, businesslike, and punctual (Costa & McCrae, 1985). People who are overly conscientious are excessively devoted to work, perfectionistic to the point that tasks are not completed

(e.g., unable to complete projects because their own strict standards are not met), and preoccupied with organization, rules, and details.

The additional items of inability to discard objects, lack of generosity, and indecisiveness will at times reflect indirect expressions of extreme conscientiousness. Obsessive–compulsive individuals are indecisive "because of ruminating about priorities" (American Psychiatric Association, 1987, p. 356) or "because of an inordinate fear of making a mistake" (American Psychiatric Association, 1987, p. 355). The overly conscientious person abhors making a mistake and not being maximally efficient. As a result, they are at times their own worst enemy, becoming stalled and derailed by their own severe standards and expectations. Even when the decision is trivial (e.g., which movie to attend, where to have dinner, or what apparently worthless objects to throw away) they may ruminate endlessly. Trivial, everyday decisions can sometimes be the most problematic because they lack a clearly optimal solution (e.g., in chosing between two restaurants at which to dine when neither restaurant is clearly preferable, or in deciding, quite regretfully, to throw away old shirts, records, or pictures because someday someone might need or want them). Obsessive–compulsive individuals want to make the correct decision, and when the criteria for making a decision are ambiguous, obsessive–compulsive individuals are easily frustrated and stalled.

The prototypical obsessive–compulsive patient, however, is also somewhat antagonistic. The tendency to be stingy and withholding (both with respect to emotions and possessions), to insist that others conform, and to resist the authority of others can reflect antagonistic low compliance and low altruism. A new item included in the *DSM-IV* diagnosis of OBC is rigidity and stubbornness (Task Force on DSM-IV, 1991), which will further increase the extent to which antagonism is reflected in the diagnosis.

The obsessive–compulsive person is also closed to values (inflexible in matters of morality, ethics, or values; American Psychiatric Association, 1987), closed to feelings (restricted expression of affection), low in warmth (formal and serious in relationships), and high in assertiveness (insistence that others submit). Associated features may include low positive emotions, low excitement seeking, hostility, depression, and self-consciousness (particularly in the more maladaptive cases of OBC).

PASSIVE–AGGRESSIVE AND NEGATIVISTIC PERSONALITY DISORDERS

PAG involves a pervasive pattern of passive resistance to reasonable demands for adequate social and occupational performance (American Psychiatric Association, 1987). The resistance is typically expressed indirectly rather than openly and directly. The *DSM-III-R* diagnostic criteria emphasize the ways in which the person avoids responsibilities and demands by (a) procrastinating, (b) working slowly or doing a poor job, (c) forgetting, and (d) obstructing the efforts of others. Millon (1981), however, used the term *negativistic* to describe the behavior pattern and provided more general traits such as sullen, complaining, stubborn, irritable, and disgruntled. These traits are evident in the other *DSM-III-R* criteria of (a) becoming sulky, irritable, or argumentative when asked to do something; (b) protesting against demands perceived to be unreasonable; (c) expressing resentment in response to useful suggestions; and (d) critical or scornful of people in positions of authority.

It is evident that PAG involves primarily low agreeableness (low compliance and low straightforwardness) and excessively low conscientiousness (low competence, low dutifulness, and low self-discipline). The passive–aggressive person may also be high in the neuroticism facet of hostility (resents demands, sulky, and irritable; American Psychiatric Association, 1987). Earlier, we indicated how PAG is differentiated from the other personality disorders with respect to the five factors.

A new diagnosis proposed for *DSM-IV* was NEG (Task Force on DSM-IV, 1991). This proposal was developed by Millon (1981, 1993) as an alternative to PAG because PAG is being deleted from *DSM-IV* (Gunderson, 1992; Widiger, 1991). Our description of this proposed diagnosis from the perspective of the FFM is presented in Table 2. The diagnostic criteria for NEG (Task Force on DSM-IV, 1991) do not differ substantially from those for PAG with respect to the dimensions of the FFM. In *DSM-IV*, the criteria set for NEG was given the name of passive–

aggressive (with Millon's term of negativistic placed in parenthesis) and placed in the appendix for diagnoses needing further study. The emphasis remains on low agreeableness and low conscientiousness. The diagnosis of NEG may place somewhat more empha-

TABLE 2

Personality Disorders Proposed for *DSM-IV*

Diagnostic criteria	NEG	SDF	DPS	SDS
Neuroticism				
Anxiety			H	
Hostility	H			h
Depression		H	H	l
Self-Consciousness			H	
Impulsiveness				
Vulnerability		H		
Extraversion				
Warmth				
Gregariousness				
Assertiveness	H			H
Activity				
Excitement Seeking				
Positive Emotions		L		
Openness				
Fantasy				
Aesthetics				
Feelings				
Actions				
Ideas				
Values				
Agreeableness				
Trust				
Straightforwardness		L		
Altruism		H		**L**
Compliance	L	L		L
Modesty				
Tender-mindedness			L	L
Conscientiousness				
Competence	L			
Order				
Dutifulness				
Achievement Striving			L	
Self-Discipline			L	
Deliberation				

Note. H/h, L/l = high, low, respectively, based on proposed *DSM-IV* diagnostic criteria (Task Force on DSM-IV, 1991); **H, L** = high, low, based on clinical literature. Personality disorders: NEG = negativistic; SDF = self-defeating; DPS = depressive; SDS = sadistic.

sis on low agreeableness with the variety of items that tap this dimension: critical, complaining, sullen, argumentative, scornful, resentful, envious, discontented, whining, and grumbling (Task Force on DSM-IV, 1991).

SELF-DEFEATING AND DEPRESSIVE PERSONALITY DISORDERS

One of the more persistent criticisms of *DSM-III* personality disorder taxonomy was the failure to include a depressive–masochistic personality disorder diagnosis (Frances & Cooper, 1981; Gunderson, 1983; Kernberg, 1984; Simons, 1987). The major opposition to the diagnosis at that time was from the Mood Disorder Advisory Committee, which argued that individuals with chronic feelings of pessimism, dysphoria, and self-blame should be diagnosed with a mood disorder (dysthymia) rather than with a personality disorder (Frances, 1980). The *DSM-III-R* Personality Disorders Advisory Committee responded to this concern by proposing a masochistic personality disorder diagnosis for *DSM-III-R* that placed more emphasis on the psychodynamic construct of masochism than on the traits of a depressive personality disorder (Widiger & Frances, 1989a). However, this proposal then met with substantial opposition from people who were concerned about a potential sex bias and an overdiagnosis of personality disorders in victims of abuse (Caplan, 1987; Kass, Spitzer, Williams, & Widiger, 1989; Walker, 1987). The emphasis given to the psychodynamic construct of masochism raised the understandable concern of a regressive return to archaic and sex-biased constructs of feminine masochism. The diagnosis (with the name changed to self-defeating) was therefore placed in an appendix to *DSM-III-R* for diagnoses needing further research (Widiger et al., 1988). However, the other side of the depressive–masochistic coin has resurfaced with the proposal to include a depressive personality disorder diagnosis in *DSM-IV* (Phillips, Gunderson, Hirschfeld, & Smith, 1990; Phillips, Hirschfeld, Shea, & Gunderson, 1993).

The criteria for SDF include feelings of inadequacy, worthlessness, and pessimism. These individuals tend to have chronic feelings of dysphoria, dejection, and gloom. They are self-blaming, self-crit-

ical, and brooding. They tend to choose people and situations that lead to disappointment, they respond to positive events with feelings of guilt and depression, they reject opportunities for pleasure (feeling undeserving), and they engage in excessive self-sacrifice. These are all representative of facets of neuroticism, particularly depression (e.g., hopeless, guilty, and depressed) and vulnerability (e.g., easily rattled, panicked, and unable to deal with stress).

The self-defeating person is also characterized by low conscientiousness (e.g., fails to accomplish tasks despite an ability to do so and chooses situations that lead to failure) and low agreeableness (incites angry responses from others, rejects people who treat them well, and rejects or renders ineffective the help of others). The combination of low conscientiousness, low agreeableness, and neuroticism also suggests PAG, which is not particularly surprising because these diagnostic constructs are themselves overlapping and difficult to distinguish (Millon, 1981; Widiger & Frances, 1989a). However, the respective facets of neuroticism and conscientiousness that are involved are different, and prototypical cases can be distinguished. PAG involves the neuroticism facet of hostility, whereas SDF involves self-consciousness and vulnerability; PAG involves low competence and low dutifulness, whereas SDF involves low achievement striving. The *DSM-III-R* criteria for SDF also include an item that involves the agreeableness facet of excessive altruism (engages in excessive self-sacrifice) that would not be seen in a passive–aggressive person. This latter item was proposed for deletion if SDF remained in *DSM-IV* (Fiester, 1991). However, the final decision was to delete SDF entirely from the manual.

The DPS proposal is quite similar to that for SDF, but it does involve an elimination of the features of low conscientiousness and most of the features of agreeableness (see Table 2). Only one of the diagnostic criteria for DPS involves low agreeableness (negativistic, critical, and judgmental of others; Task Force, 1991). The DPS criteria are then largely confined to neuroticism and in particular to the one facet of trait depression (dejection, gloomy, cheerless, low self-esteem, feelings of inadequacy, self-blaming, brooding, pessimistic, and guilty; Task Force on DSM-IV, 1991). The criteria for DPS, however, do involve to some extent the neuroticism facets of anxiety (e.g., worrying) and self-consciousness (e.g., self-critical). DPS will appear in the appendix to *DSM-IV* for diagnoses needing further study.

SADISTIC PERSONALITY DISORDER

The sadistic personality disorder diagnosis was developed during the process of reviewing the proposal for SDF (Kass et al., 1989; Widiger et al., 1988). It was considered in some respects to be complementary to SDF because the person who is prone to abusing others is likely to be sadistic and because the person who is repeatedly abused is likely to be self-defeating (or masochistic; Simons, 1987). The diagnosis had substantial precedent within the psychodynamic and psychological literature (Widiger et al., 1988), but the proposed criteria lacked empirical support and critical review. The diagnosis was, therefore, placed in an appendix to *DSM-III-R* for diagnoses needing further research. It will be deleted entirely from the manual in *DSM-IV* (Pincus, Francis, Davis, First, & Widiger, 1992; Widiger, 1991).

The proposed criteria in *DSM-III-R* included (a) use of physical cruelty or violence for the purpose of establishing dominance; (b) humiliation of others; (c) harsh punishment of others; (d) amusement or pleasure in the suffering of animals and people; (e) lying for the purpose of inflicting pain; (f) intimidating and terrorizing others; and (g) fascination with weapons, injury, and torture (American Psychiatric Association, 1987). These are all extreme variants of antagonism. The only other dimension of personality that is involved in the diagnostic criteria for this disorder is the extraversion facet of assertiveness (dominance and control). Sadistic individuals are not only extremely antagonistic to the point of being ruthless and brutal, but they are also domineering (e.g., the restriction of the autonomy of others). The sadistic person is not characterized by the other facets of extraversion, such as warmth, gregariousness, or positive emotions.

The major distinction for the sadistic personality disorder diagnosis is with ATS. The sadistic person may, in fact, simply represent an aggressive (antagonistic) subtype of psychopathy (Widiger et al., 1988). Making a distinction between ATS and the sadistic personality disorder may then be as meaningless as

trying to determine whether a person is psychopathic or antisocial. However, the dimensions along which these categories can at times be distinguished are informative, in that the prototypical sadistic person would not be characterized by low conscientiousness and the typical sadistic person would probably be more highly elevated on antagonism than would the average psychopathic/antisocial person. To the extent that the elevations on antagonism are extreme and largely confined to this domain, the more likely the diagnosis will be sadistic personality disorder rather than ATS.

References

American Psychiatric Association. (1980). *Diagnostic and statistical manual of mental disorders* (3rd ed.). Washington, DC: Author.

American Psychiatric Association. (1987). *Diagnostic and statistical manual of mental disorders* (3rd ed., rev.). Washington, DC: Author.

American Psychiatric Association. (in press). *Diagnostic and statistical manual of mental disorders* (4th ed.). Washington, DC: Author.

Caplan, P. (1987). The psychiatric association's failure to meet its own standards: The dangers of self-defeating personality disorder as a category. *Journal of Personality Disorders, 1,* 178–182.

Clarkin, J. F., Widiger, T. A., Frances, A. J., Hurt, S. W., & Gilmore, M. (1983). Prototypic typology and the borderline personality disorder. *Journal of Abnormal Psychology, 92,* 263–275.

Cleckley, H. (1941). *The mask of sanity.* St. Louis, MO: Mosby.

Cloninger, C. R. (1989). Establishment of diagnostic validity in psychiatric illness: Robins and Guze's method revisited. In L. Robins & J. Barrett (Eds.), *The validity of psychiatric diagnosis* (pp. 9–18). New York: Raven Press.

Costa, P. T., Jr., & McCrae, R. R. (1985). *The NEO Personality Inventory manual.* Odessa, FL: Psychological Assessment Resources.

Costa, P. T., Jr., & McCrae, R. R. (1990). Personality disorders and the five-factor model of personality. *Journal of Personality Disorders, 4,* 362–371.

Costa, P. T., Jr., McCrae, R. R., & Dye, D. A. (1991). Facet scales for agreeableness and conscientiousness: A revision of the NEO Personality Inventory. *Personality and Individual Differences, 12,* 887–898.

Eysenck, H., & Eysenck, M. (1985). *Personality and individual differences: A natural science approach.* New York: Plenum.

Fiester, S. J. (1991). Self-defeating personality disorder: A review of data and recommendations for DSM-IV. *Journal of Personality Disorders, 5,* 194–209.

Frances, A. J. (1980). The DSM-III personality disorders: A commentary. *American Journal of Psychiatry, 137,* 1050–1054.

Frances, A. J., & Cooper, A. (1981). Descriptive and dynamic psychiatry: A perspective on DSM-III. *American Journal of Psychiatry, 138,* 1198–1202.

Frances, A. J., & Widiger, T. A. (1987). A critical review of four DSM-III personality disorders: Borderline, avoidant, dependent, and passive–aggressive. In G. Tischler (Ed.), *Diagnosis and classification in psychiatry* (pp. 269–289). New York: Cambridge University Press.

Gunderson, J. G. (1983). DSM-III diagnosis of personality disorders. In J. Frosch (Ed.), *Current perspectives on personality disorders* (pp. 20–39). Washington, DC: American Psychiatric Press.

Gunderson, J. G. (1984). *Borderline personality disorder.* Washington, DC: American Psychiatric Press.

Gunderson, J. G. (1992). Diagnostic controversies. In A. Tasman & M. B. Riba (Eds.), *Review of Psychiatry* (Vol. 11, pp. 9–24). Washington, DC: American Psychiatric Press.

Gunderson, J. G., & Zanarini, M. (1987). Current overview of the borderline diagnosis. *Journal of Clinical Psychiatry, 48*(suppl.), 5–11.

Hare, R. D. (1990). *Manual for the Revised Psychopathy Checklist.* Unpublished manuscript, University of British Columbia, Vancouver, Canada.

Hirschfeld, R. M. A., Shea, M. T., & Talbot, K. (1991). Dependent personality disorder: Perspectives for DSM-IV. *Journal of Personality Disorders, 5,* 135–149.

Hurt, S. W., Clarkin, J. F., Widiger, T. A., Fyer, M. R., Sullivan, T., Stone, M. H., & Frances, A. J. (1990). Evaluation of DSM-III decision rules for case detection using joint conditional probability structures. *Journal of Personality Disorders, 4,* 121–130.

Kalus, O., Bernstein, D. P., & Siever, L. J. (1993). Schizoid personality disorder: A review of its current status. *Journal of Personality Disorders, 7,* 43–52.

Kass, D., Spitzer, R. L., Williams, J. B. W., & Widiger, T. A. (1989). Self-defeating personality disorder and DSM-III-R: Development of diagnostic criteria. *American Journal of Psychiatry, 146,* 1022–1026.

Kernberg, O. F. (1984). *Severe personality disorders.* New Haven, CT: Yale University Press.

Livesley, W. J., West, M., & Tanney, A. (1985). Historical comment on the DSM-III schizoid and avoidant personality disorders. *American Journal of Psychiatry, 142,* 1344–1347.

McCrae, R. R., Costa, P. T., Jr., & Busch, C. M. (1986). Evaluating comprehensiveness in personality systems: The California Q-Set and the five-factor model. *Journal of Personality, 54,* 430–446.

Millon, T. (1981). *Disorders of personality: DSM-III. Axis II.* New York: Wiley.

Millon, T. (1991). Avoidant personality disorder: A brief review of issues and data. *Journal of Personality Disorders, 5,* 353–362.

Millon, T. (1993). Negativistic (passive–aggressive) personality disorder. *Journal of Personality Disorders, 7,* 78–85.

Phillips, K. A., Gunderson, J. G., Hirschfeld, R. M. A., & Smith, L. E. (1990). A review of the depressive personality. *American Journal of Psychiatry, 147,* 830–837.

Phillips, K. A., Hirschfeld, R. M. A., Shea, M. T., & Gunderson, J. G. (1993). Depressive personality disorder: Perspectives for DSM-IV. *Journal of Personality Disorders, 7,* 30–42.

Pilkonis, P. A. (1984). Avoidant and schizoid personality disorders. In H. E. Adams & P. B. Sutker (Eds.), *Comprehensive handbook of psychopathology* (pp. 479–494). New York: Plenum.

Pincus, H. A., Frances, A. J., Davis, W. W., First, M. B., & Widiger, T. A. (1992). DSM-IV and new diagnostic categories: Holding the line on proliferation. *American Journal of Psychiatry. 149,* 112–117.

Ronningstam, E., & Gunderson, J. (1988). Narcissistic traits in psychiatric patients. *Comprehensive Psychiatry, 29,* 545–549.

Siever, L. J., Bernstein, D. P., & Silverman, J. M. (1991). Schizotypal personality disorder: A review of its current status. *Journal of Personality Disorders, 5,* 178–193.

Siever, L. J., & Klar, H. (1986). A review of DSM-III criteria for the personality disorders. In A. J. Frances & R. E. Hales (Eds.), *Psychiatry update* (Vol. 5, pp. 279–314). Washington, DC: American Psychiatric Press.

Simons, R. (1987). Self-defeating and sadistic personality disorders: Needed additions to the diagnostic nomenclature. *Journal of Personality Disorders, 1,* 161–167.

Sutker, P. B., Bugg, F., & West, J. A. (1993). Antisocial personality disorder. In P. B. Sutker & H. E. Adams (Eds.), *Comprehensive handbook of psychopathology* (2nd ed., pp. 337–369). New York: Plenum.

Task Force on DSM-IV. (1991). *DSM-IV options book: Work in progress (9/1/91).* Washington, DC: American Psychiatric Association.

Trull, T. J., Widiger, T. A., & Frances, A. J. (1987). Covariation of criteria sets for avoidant, schizoid, and dependent personality disorders. *American Journal of Psychiatry, 144,* 767–771.

Walker, L. (1987). Inadequacies of the masochistic personality disorder diagnosis for women. *Journal of Personality Disorders, 1,* 183–189.

Watson, D., & Clark, L. (1984). Negative affectivity: The disposition to experience aversive emotional states. *Psychological Bulletin, 96,* 465–490.

Widiger, T. A. (1991). Critical issues in the design of DSM-IV, Axis II. In R. Michels (Ed.), *Psychiatry* (Vol. 1, chap. 14.1, pp. 1–10). Philadelphia: Lippincott.

Widiger, T. A. (1993). The DSM-III-R categorical personality disorder diagnoses: A critique and an alternative. *Psychological Inquiry, 4,* 75–90.

Widiger, T. A., & Frances, A. J. (1985). The DSM-III personality disorders: Perspectives from psychology. *Archives of General Psychiatry, 42,* 615–623.

Widiger, T. A., & Frances, A. J. (1989a). Controversies concerning the self-defeating personality disorder. In R. C. Curtis (Ed.), *Self-defeating behaviors: Experimental research, clinical impressions, and practical implications* (pp. 289–309). New York: Plenum.

Widiger, T. A., & Frances, A. J. (1989b). Epidemiology, diagnosis, and comorbidity of borderline personality disorder. In A. Tasman, R. E. Hales, & A. J. Frances (Eds.), *Review of psychiatry* (Vol. 8, pp. 8–24). Washington, DC: American Psychiatric Press.

Widiger, T. A., Frances, A. J., Spitzer, R. L., & Williams, J. B. W. (1988). The DSM-III-R personality disorders: An overview. *American Journal of Psychiatry, 145,* 786–795.

Widiger, T. A., & Rogers, J. H. (1989). Prevalence and comorbidity of personality disorders. *Psychiatric Annals, 19,* 132–136.

Widiger, T. A., & Trull, T. J. (1992). Personality and psychopathology: An application of the five-factor model. *Journal of Personality, 60,* 363–394.

PART II

EMPIRICAL RESEARCH

CHAPTER 4

A FIVE-FACTOR PERSPECTIVE ON PERSONALITY DISORDER RESEARCH

Timothy J. Trull and Robert R. McCrae

The premise of this book is that personality disorders can be understood in terms of the dimensions of personality identified in the five-factor model (FFM). Perhaps the most obvious question, then, is whether there is good empirical evidence that individuals with different personality disorders can in fact be characterized by distinctive and appropriate personality profiles across the five factors, or dimensions, of the FFM. The answer is "not yet." In one respect this is not surprising: It is only in the past few years that the FFM has commanded any attention from psychiatric researchers, and there has simply not been sufficient time to accumulate a body of data on personality-disordered patients using measures of this model.

In this chapter, we review some recent research on personality disorders from the perspective of the FFM. We believe this can aid in the understanding of a disorder's core symptomatology, its overlap with other personality disorders, and its overlap with syndromes described in Axis I of the third, revised edition of the *Diagnostic and Statistical Manual of Mental Disorders* (*DSM-III-R*; American Psychiatric Association, 1987). Many of the controversies that plague personality disorder research can be illuminated from this perspective. In particular, we focus on the overlap between Axis I and Axis II disorders, heterogeneity within the borderline personality disorder (BDL) category, and the nature of the narcissistic personality disorder (NAR) construct.

One might suppose that there would be much literature on the personality traits that characterize various disorders using older instruments like the Eysenck Personality Inventory (Eysenck & Eysenck, 1964), the Sixteen Personality Factor Questionnaire (Cattell, Eber, & Tatsuoka, 1970), or the Guilford-Zimmerman Temperament Survey (Guilford, Zimmerman, & Guilford, 1976). Because the FFM is comprehensive, it is usually possible to interpret scales from other instruments such as these in its terms. Thus, it might be possible to organize a literature review in terms of the five factors even if they were never measured directly.

Somewhat surprisingly, there is relatively little information to organize in this way. A great deal of research (for a review see Widiger & Frances, 1987) has focused on the reliability and comparability of different instruments designed specifically for assessing the personality disorders, such as the Minnesota Multiphasic Personality Inventory (MMPI; Hathaway & McKinley, 1967) Personality Disorder Scales (Morey, Waugh, & Blashfield, 1985) and the Millon Clinical Multiaxial Inventory (MCMI; Millon, 1983), and studies have linked the scales of these instruments to measures of normal personality in normal samples (e.g., Wiggins & Pincus, 1989). But the strategy of administering normal personality measures to characterize individuals diagnosed with specific disorders has only rarely been followed.

We thank Thomas A. Widiger for his comments and suggestions regarding earlier versions of this chapter. The research described in this chapter was supported, in part, by a Summer Research Fellowship from the Research Council of the University of Missouri–Columbia to Timothy J. Trull.

Two recent studies, however, merit special attention as steps in this direction. Lyons, Merla, Ozer, and Hyler (1990) administered a self-report personality disorder inventory, the Personality Diagnostic Questionnaire (PDQ; Hyler et al., 1989), to a clinical sample for which clinicians' ratings of personality disorders were available; over half of the subjects met diagnostic criteria for at least one personality disorder. Although the initial intent was to examine correspondence between the PDQ scales and clinician ratings, interest in the FFM led to a secondary analysis. By administering the PDQ and Goldberg's (1990) adjective scales to a second sample, Lyons et al. were able to select PDQ items that approximated four of the five factors (an Openness scale could not be created from PDQ items). When these new PDQ scales were compared with clinicians' ratings in the original sample, several significant relations were found. Specifically, Extraversion (E) was positively related to clinicians' ratings of histrionic personality disorder (HST) and negatively related to schizoid (SZD), avoidant (AVD), and several other personality disorders. Agreeableness (A) was positively related to dependent personality disorder (DEP) and negatively related to paranoid (PAR), NAR, and antisocial (ATS) personality disorders. Conscientiousness (C) was positively related to obsessive–compulsive personality disorder (OBC) and negatively related to ATS and BDL. All of these findings replicate associations found between personality disorder scales and measures of the five factors in normal samples (Costa & McCrae, 1990). However, Neuroticism (N) was only weakly related to clinicians' ratings, and the pattern of findings did not resemble that found in normal samples.

Trull (1992) has provided more direct evidence on this question by administering the NEO Personality Inventory (NEO-PI; Costa & McCrae, 1985)—a standard measure of the FFM—to 54 psychiatric outpatients. The patients were rated for the presence of personality disorder symptoms on the basis of a semistructured interview; in addition, patients completed two self-report personality disorder inventories. Results were generally consistent across the three assessments of personality disorders and replicated most findings previously reported for nonpsychiatric samples. In contrast to the Lyons et al. results, the NEO-PI's measure of N proved to be a powerful predictor of several personality disorders, especially BDL. Both these studies provide evidence that individuals with diagnosable personality disorders do differ in predictable ways on the five factors.

PERSONALITY, PERSONALITY DISORDERS, AND CLINICAL SYNDROMES

The multiaxial system of the *DSM-III-R* (American Psychiatric Association, 1987) is based on the premise that mental disorders in adults can be categorized as clinical syndromes (Axis I) or personality disorders (Axis II). The latter are inflexible and maladaptive forms of enduring personality traits; the former are typically more florid conditions that may be intermittent or have a late-life onset. How should these two kinds of disorders be related? Certainly they are not mutually exclusive—the whole notion of providing diagnoses on both axes was intended to underscore the possibility that patients might have personality disorders in addition to clinical syndromes. But the degree of comorbidity might be considered surprising.

Docherty, Fiester, and Shea (1986) reviewed studies that presented comorbidity rates for personality disorders and affective disorders as well as for personality disorders and anxiety. Studies varied as to whether they reported on Axis I syndromes in individuals with personality disorders or, conversely, the rate of personality disorder in individuals with Axis I syndromes. Axis I comorbidity rates with BDL diagnosis were reported most frequently; only a few studies reported comorbidity rates in non-BDL personality-disordered patients. Across studies, the prevalence rates for a comorbid affective disorder in BDL patients fell in the 25–60% range. In patients with major depression, a comorbid BDL disorder was frequently found as well. In one study that examined other (non-BDL) personality disorder diagnoses in a sample of depressed patients (Pfohl, Stangl, & Zimmerman, 1984), relatively high rates of HST, DEP, and AVD were found. Docherty et al. also reviewed the few studies that examined the comorbidity of personality disorders and anxiety disorders. For example, Akiskal (1981) reported that 10% of the 100 BDL patients in his sample met criteria for agoraphobia and/or phobic disorders and that 8% met criteria for OBC.

Other investigators have also noted the high comorbidity rates of depressive disorders and personality disorders (Gunderson & Elliot, 1985; Millon & Kotik, 1985; Widiger & Hyler, 1987). For example, Millon and Kotik discussed each third edition *Diagnostic and Statistical Manual of Mental Disorders* (*DSM-III*; American Psychiatric Association, 1980) personality disorder with respect to the likelihood that this personality style increased vulnerability to depressive episodes. They reported that those patients with DEP, HST, AVD, BDL, OBC, and passive–aggressive personality disorder (PAG) were particularly prone to depression. In addition, Millon and Kotik reported that acute anxiety states are likely in these patients as well.

If personality disorders are understood as variants of normal personality dimensions, then these comorbidity data suggest that personality traits may themselves be linked to the Axis I syndromes of depression and anxiety—a suggestion that has been made for a number of years (Eysenck, 1970). In particular, the relation between personality and depression has been the subject of a great deal of attention (e.g., Hirschfeld & Klerman, 1979; Hirschfeld, Klerman, Clayton, & Keller, 1983). There are four basic ways in which maladaptive personality traits can interact with depression: (a) personality can be a predisposition to the development of depression; (b) personality can result from depression; (c) personality and depression can be independent yet affect the manifestation, course, and treatment of each other; or (d) personality and depression can both be manifestations of a common underlying etiology (Hirschfeld et al., 1983; Widiger & Trull, 1992).

Because of these different possibilities, early studies that measured personality in individuals who were clinically depressed or in remission from an episode of depression were difficult to interpret. Some recent studies have suggested that personality traits are indeed a predisposing factor. Hirschfeld et al. (1989) reported a true prospective study of the first onset of major depression that showed elevated N scores in individuals who subsequently developed clinical depression. Zonderman, Stone, and Costa (1989) have also shown that a brief measure of N was a significant risk factor for subsequent hospital diagnoses of depression and other psychiatric disorders in a national sample.

These findings are understandable in view of the fact that N (or *negative affectivity*, as Watson & Clark, 1984, call it) predisposes individuals to experience negative affect. At moderate levels, N is associated with unhappiness and lowered life satisfaction (Costa & McCrae, 1980). At very high levels, it can lead to clinically significant depression or anxiety.

From the perspective of the FFM, comorbidity of these Axis I syndromes and Axis II disorders might therefore be interpreted in terms of shared links to N. This view leads to the hypothesis that personality disorders that are associated with N should also show comorbidity with anxiety and depression. Millon and Kotik (1985) noted links between these Axis I syndromes and DEP, HST, AVD, PAG, BDL, and OBC. With the exception of HST, scales that measured all of these were positively and substantially correlated with the NEO-PI's measure of N (Costa & McCrae, 1985, 1990). By contrast, the scales for NAR, PAR, and ATS showed little relation to N, and these personality disorders typically show little comorbidity with depression or anxiety.

DSM-III-R tends to treat personality traits and affects as different phenomena. Research on personality, however, has shown that these two are intimately linked and that one of the five major factors of personality—N—is chiefly defined by the tendency to experience a variety of negative affects. Any diagnostic system that attempts to separate personality traits from affective predispositions is liable to be arbitrary and ambiguous. Akiskal (1981), for example, has been a strong proponent of conceptualizing BDL as a subtype of affective disorder, a view that would transfer that diagnosis to Axis I. Conversely, recent arguments have been made that some of the Axis I disorders—notably dysthymia and social phobia—should be construed as personality disorders and transferred to Axis II (Keller, 1989; Turner & Biedel, 1989).

There is a meaningful distinction between predisposing factors and the phenomena to which they predispose. After all, many individuals who are high in N never suffer from a diagnosable mental disorder. But comorbidity is inevitable when both are present, and much of this can be understood as the operation of underlying personality traits. It would be of substantial interest in future research on the comorbidity of depression (or anxiety) with DEP, AVD, OBC, HST, and other personality disorders to assess whether the comorbidity still occurs when variance due to N is controlled or, conversely, whether personality disorder diagnoses have some incremental validity in predicting episodes of depression or anxiety over and above the predictions that can be made from measures of N. It may be that comorbidity with anxiety and depression for most of the personality disorders is simply due to their shared variance with N.

BORDERLINE PERSONALITY DISORDER

BDL is a popular, yet controversial, diagnosis. More literature has been published on BDL than on any other personality disorder. Blashfield and McElroy (1987) estimated that BDL accounted for 40% of all personality disorder articles in 1985, and in their estimation, ATS was a distant second, accounting for 25%. BDL is also by far the most commonly diagnosed personality disorder (Widiger & Trull, 1993). The variety of definitions (American Psychiatric Association, 1987; Gunderson & Zanarini, 1987; Kernberg, 1984) and uses of the term *borderline* has made integration of the research literature difficult, and the label continues to be used to describe a wide variety of patients.

Clinical Heterogeneity

A number of researchers have noted the clinical heterogeneity of patients within the BDL category (e.g., Clarkin, Widiger, Frances, Hurt, & Gilmore, 1983). With *DSM-III-R*'s polythetic format for diagnosing BDL, there are literally 93 ways to be a borderline (eight items taken five or more at a time). Because any five of the eight criteria can satisfy the BDL diagnostic decision rule, BDL patients are heterogeneous with respect to clinical symptomatology. For example, a patient can meet the criteria for BDL by exhibiting symptoms of inappropriate/intense anger, recurrent suicidal threats/behavior, identity disturbance, chronic feelings of emptiness/boredom, and frantic efforts to avoid real/imagined abandonment, without showing the unstable/intense interpersonal relations, impulsivity, and affective instability that many clinicians would consider to be hallmarks of

the BDL diagnosis. On the other hand, another BDL patient might manifest the latter three symptoms, as well as inappropriate/intense anger and chronic feelings of emptiness/boredom, but not suicidal threats/ behavior, identity disturbance, or frantic attempts to avoid abandonment. A comparison of these two hypothetical BDL patients reveals markedly different clinical pictures and may suggest different treatment approaches. Clearly, the polythetic system for diagnosing BDL is a breeding ground for clinical heterogeneity.

Several investigators have reported distinct clusters of symptoms within the BDL criteria set. For example, Hurt et al. (1990) examined the interrelations among the eight BDL criteria in a sample of 465 *DSM-III* BDLs and 114 patients with other personality disorders (OPD). A single linkage-clustering algorithm was used to determine the homogeneity of the entire BDL criteria set. It was found that the BDL criteria varied in their correlation with each other. On the basis of similarity ratings, three subsets of criteria were identified: an identity cluster (chronic feelings of emptiness/boredom, identity disturbance, and intolerance of being alone), an affective cluster (intense/inappropriate anger, instability of affect, and unstable interpersonal relationships), and an impulse cluster (self-damaging acts and impulsive behavior). When BDL patients were sorted according to symptom cluster membership, further evidence for heterogeneity within the BDL category was found. All three clusters were represented by a substantial number of BDL cases, although most cases manifested symptoms from the affective and impulse criteria clusters. These results point to the substantial heterogeneity within the BDL criteria set as well as among patients diagnosed with BDL.

Nurnberg, Hurt, Feldman, and Shu (1988) also found heterogeneity within the BDL criteria set. In an investigation that compared borderline symptomatology of a narrowly defined BDL group and a nonpatient control group, various combinations of two, three, four, and five BDL symptoms all resulted in high sensitivity and high positive predictive power rates for the BDL diagnosis. Nurnberg et al. concluded that the *DSM-III* BDL criteria set is not homogeneous and that these criteria do not appear to identify a distinct, categorical diagnostic entity. Bor-

TABLE 1

Mean Minnesota Multiphasic Personality Inventory (MMPI) Scales *T* Scores of Patients Diagnosed With Borderline Personality Disorder

Study	*n*	MMPI scale												
		L	F	K	1	2	3	4	5	6	7	8	9	0
Evans et al. (1984)	45	48	76	50	67	80	71	84	57	75	77	85	68	64
Gustin et al. (1983)	29	44	85	46	78	89	70	84	68	78	89	98	70	68
Hurt et al. (1985)														
Inpatient	21	46	71	48	68	79	70	77	—	72	77	80	64	63
Outpatient	21	46	83	42	67	81	67	80	—	78	81	91	75	67
Kroll et al. (1981)	21	48	84	47	62	82	70	84	60	78	74	85	65	63
Loyd et al. (1983)	27	48	73	46	70	75	73	81	60	64	78	64	70	65
Patrick (1984)	27	44	77	46	64	78	65	80	55	74	68	87	61	60
Resnick et al. (1988)	37	45	66	47	56	73	63	76	54	70	71	71	61	61
Snyder et al. (1982)	26	46	86	45	75	86	68	85	68	79	88	98	72	65
Trull (1991)	61	48	73	49	64	80	70	80	50	73	72	79	64	63
Widiger et al. (1986)	44	47	78	46	70	81	67	82	60	80	80	91	68	65
Mdn		46	77	46	67	80	70	81	60	75	77	85	68	64

Note. Loyd et al. (1983) used the MMPI-168 short form of the MMPI; *T* scores from this study were reported in Evans et al. (1984). Borderline group in Kroll et al. (1981) was defined by a score of >7 on the Diagnostic Interview for Borderlines (Kolb & Gunderson, 1980). Evans et al. (1984), Gustin et al. (1983), Loyd et al. (1983), Snyder et al. (1982), Trull (1991), and Widiger et al. (1986) all indicated that MMPI scores were *K*-corrected. *n* = sample size.

derline patients exhibited a wide variety of BDL symptom combinations, and no prototypical pattern was found.

MMPI Profiles of BDL Patients

Another example of the heterogeneity within the BDL category comes from the literature reporting MMPI clinical scale scores of *DSM-III* and *DSM-III-R* BDLs. We reviewed 10 published studies that reported mean MMPI *T* scores for adult BDL patients or presented figures from which mean *T* scores could be estimated. Most of these studies sampled inpatient borderlines, and two of the studies (Hurt, Clarkin, Francis, Abrams, & Hunt, 1985; Resnick et al., 1988) sampled outpatient borderlines. Four of the studies (Hurt et al., 1985; Kroll et al., 1981; Resnick et al., 1988; Widiger, Sanderson, & Warner, 1986) established the BDL diagnosis via a semistructured inter-

view; the remaining studies relied on clinical diagnoses.

Table 1 presents the mean MMPI *T* scores reported in each respective study. As indicated, at least one study reported mean MMPI *T* scores at or above 70 on all scales except on the L, K, 5, and O scales. There is clearly no definitive BDL MMPI code type (Morey & Smith, 1988). BDL appears instead to be represented by a nonspecific elevation across most scales, and substantial variability occurs with respect to the MMPI code types obtained by borderline patients.

The lack of specificity for an MMPI code type (and the heterogeneity among individual subjects) can be understood when BDL is reinterpreted from the perspective of the FFM. Elevations on the MMPI Scales 1–4 and 6–9 indicate the presence of anxiety, dysphoria, hostility, feelings of inadequacy, difficulty concentrating, suspiciousness, feelings of alienation, rumination, and the possibility of brief psychotic episodes. This range of symptoms is very similar to the group of traits that covary to define N in normal individuals. For example, in studies of the NEO-PI, N is defined by scales that measure anxiety, hostility, depression, self-consciousness, impulsiveness, and vulnerability. With the possible exception of self-consciousness, a strong case can be made that a patient with BDL would score high on all of these scales. The findings of studies that used the MMPI in clinical samples thus parallel the findings from studies that used normal samples: Measures of BDL are correlated with measures of N (Costa & McCrae, 1990; Wiggins & Pincus, 1989).

We do not suggest that BDL is equivalent to and indistinguishable from extreme N. The diagnostic criteria in *DSM-III-R* include not only some N traits (e.g., constant anger) but also some specific symptoms or behaviors (e.g., suicide attempts) that do not characterize all high-N individuals. A better formulation would be that BDL reflects a set of behaviors and symptoms to which high-N individuals are particularly prone. Interpretation of BDL as a result of extreme N would explain the prevalence of this diagnosis. N is related to a wide variety of psychiatric diagnoses (Zonderman et al., 1989), and the psychological distress it creates is probably the reason most patients seek psychological or psychiatric help. It is, therefore, not surprising that clinical populations show consistently elevated means on measures of N (e.g., Miller, 1991; Mutén, 1991). Within this population of high-N individuals, a large proportion would likely meet the criteria for BDL.

N can be considered a cluster of covarying traits, but individuals differ in the extent to which these specific traits characterize them. Some will be characterized primarily by hostility and depression; some by hostility and anxiety; some by depression, vulnerability, and impulsivity; and so forth. In extreme form, any of these patterns might lead to the symptoms of BDL, but they would also lead to differences that could explain in part the heterogeneity of BDL patients.

A high total score on N can be reached in many different ways, just as the diagnosis of BDL can be reached by different patterns of symptoms. Although this heterogeneity is an embarrassment in categorical models that attempt to define a qualitatively distinct entity, it is understandable in terms of factor models of personality, for which factors are defined by covarying but distinct traits. As an alternative to the single diagnostic category of BDL, it would be considerably more informative to describe each individual patient on measures of several traits in the domain of N. By including multifaceted measures of N in studies of BDL patients, more detailed information could be obtained, and the comparability of different samples of BDL patients could be ascertained.

The covariation of facets of N is well established; by contrast, the criterial symptoms of BDL do not covary as neatly. This can be seen in factor analyses of personality disorder symptoms, which do not recover a single BDL factor (Clark, 1989), and in research by Hurt et al. (1990) showing that it is possible to identify BDL subtypes. One important question for future research will be the relation of BDL criterial elements to measures of N and its facets. Correlation with N might be used as a basis for selecting a more coherent subset of BDL symptoms.

Comorbidity

It is an implicit assumption of the categorical model of psychiatric diagnoses that disorders refer to distinct conditions (e.g., Trull, Widiger, & Guthrie, 1990). BDL, from this perspective, is a distinct personality disorder that can be distinguished from HST, DEP, AVD, and other mental disorder diagnoses. This assumption was the impetus for revising the criteria for HST and NAR in *DSM-III-R*; an attempt was made to increase or improve the differentiation of these two disorders from BDL (Widiger, Frances, Spitzer, & Williams, 1988). Gunderson (1982, 1987) explicitly argued that BDL is a discrete mental disorder that can be distinguished from other personality disorders, and he has presented empirical data (Gunderson, 1982) to support the validity of this distinction.

In fact, however, BDL shows extensive comorbidity with other diagnoses. We have already reviewed evidence on the co-occurrence of BDL with Axis I affective and anxiety disorders. Swartz, Blazer, George, and Winfield (1990), using a new diagnostic algorithm derived from the Diagnostic Interview Schedule (Robins, Helzer, Croughan, & Ratcliff,

1981) to identity cases of BDL in a community sample, also reported frequent comorbid alcohol abuse/dependence and noted that 98% of BDL subjects met criteria for at least one additional psychiatric disorder in the past year. Viewing BDL as an expression of extreme N can explain these high rates of comorbidity because mood disorders, anxiety disorders, substance use disorders, and somatic disorders are themselves all associated with N.

With regard to other personality disorders, Widiger et al. (1991) recently examined the comorbidity rates of BDL and other personality disorders averaged across 13 studies that provided relevant data. They noted that at least one comorbid personality diagnosis occurred in 96% of all BDL patients. A factor analysis of averaged covariation showed that BDL, along with PAG, defined "a non-specific factor and/or a general factor of Neuroticism" (p. 187).

If one assumes that personality disorders are pathological expressions of the five basic personality factors, then the comorbidity of disorders should be predictable. Disorders that are related to the same dimensions should covary, those that are oppositely related to the same factor (as OBC and ATS are oppositely related to C) should be mutually exclusive, and those that are related to different factors should co-occur in proportion to their mutual base rates.

The data reviewed and reanalyzed by Widiger et al. (1991) are roughly consistent with this premise. In addition to the general or N factor, a second factor contrasts SZD and AVD with HST and NAR; this factor can be interpreted as E. A third factor contrasts PAR, SZD, and NAR with DEP and has some resemblance to (reversed) A. A final factor is defined solely by OBC, with small negative loadings on ATS and BDL; this factor might be interpreted as C.

The disorders that show low levels of comorbidity with BDL ought themselves to be unrelated to N. In the Widiger et al. (1991) review, BDL showed the lowest covariation with SZD and OBC, which appear to be more closely related to low E and C, respectively, than to N (Wiggins & Pincus, 1989). However, it must be noted that the highest levels of comorbidity with BDL are with HST, AST, and PAG. Only one of these—PAG—is chiefly related to N in studies of normal samples using personality disorder questionnaires (Costa & McCrae, 1990).

There are several possible explanations for this anomaly. Perhaps individuals who are diagnosed as having HST and ATS are, in fact, higher in N than it would appear from studies of instruments like the MMPI and MCMI—recall that Millon and Kotik (1985) found comorbidity of HST with depression and anxiety. Perhaps BDL contains other features besides N that it shares with these two disorders—the dramatic, emotional, or erratic features that led *DSM-III-R* to class them together in Cluster B. Perhaps this clustering itself led to bias in diagnosis: Individuals with BDL were presumed to be more likely to have HST or ATS. Only assessment of the five factors in individuals who are diagnosed as having personality disorders can resolve these questions.

Borderline Personality Organization

The view of BDL as extreme N is consistent with analytic formulations of *borderline personality organization* (BPO), a level of personality dysfunction that cuts across diagnostic categories (Kernberg, 1975, 1984). According to Kernberg, at a descriptive level patients with BPO exhibit a number of symptoms that are considered to be characteristic of N, including free-floating anxiety, "polysymptomatic neurosis," impulsivity, and proneness to addiction. Kernberg also proposes that those with BPO may exhibit any number of phobic, obsessive–compulsive, dissociative, hypochondriacal, or conversion symptoms. Most important, Kernberg considers the borderline construct as defining a level of personality organization that cuts across other domains or styles of personality functioning. Kernberg does not consider BDL a distinct personality disorder but rather a level of personality functioning that distinguishes among persons with, for example, a histrionic, dependent, or compulsive personality style. Thus, Kernberg would not attempt to determine whether a patient who is diagnosed as being BDL is instead actually histrionic (a differential diagnosis that would be important to Gunderson, 1987), but whether a patient who is diagnosed as being HST is functioning at a borderline level of personality organization.

This conception is structurally and substantively consistent with the interpretation of BDL as a manifestation of extreme N. Structurally, the FFM recognizes that individuals must be characterized on all five dimensions and differ only in their level on each of these. For example, an HST patient who is functioning at a borderline level might correspond to an extravert with a high level of N. Substantively, the nonspecific manifestations of ego-weakness that Kernberg lists essentially describe the various facets of N. As a descriptive dimension, the origin and dynamics of N are unspecified; Kernberg provides a psychoanalytically oriented theory of BPO that is based on internal structural factors (e.g., ego-weakness, variability in reality testing, use of primitive defenses, quality of object relations). At the phenomenological level, however, BPO shares much with the FFM conceptualization of N.

NARCISSISTIC PERSONALITY DISORDER

The widespread interest in BDL may be attributed to the frequency with which borderline patients are encountered in clinical practice. Interest in the NAR must have another basis, because NAR is one of the less frequently diagnosed of personality disorders (Cooper, 1987). Although there are relatively few cases of NAR, there are many theories and descriptions. The narcissistic personality has been of interest to clinicians for almost a century (Millon, 1981), and narcissism has been included in the taxonomies of personality theorists such as Murray (1938) and Leary (1957). Freud's description of this construct has influenced many contemporary psychoanalytic theorists (e.g., Kernberg, Mahler, Kohut).

Interpreting the Narcissistic Personality Inventory

Because of continued clinical interest in narcissism, a number of scales have been developed to assess this construct, including the Narcissistic Personality Inventory (NPI; Raskin & Hall, 1979), the Narcissistic Personality Disorder Scale (Ashby, Lee, & Duke, 1979), and scales from the MMPI and MCMI. Of these, the NPI has received the most empirical attention. The NPI was developed through a rational/empirical strategy of test construction in which items that assessed the *DSM-III* criteria for NAR were generated and subjected to a series of internal consistency and item–total correlational analyses (Raskin & Hall, 1979).

A conceptual analysis of the content of the NPI suggests that it measures chiefly high E and low A. Raskin and Terry (1988) reported a factor analysis of NPI items, which yielded seven factors. The Authority and Exhibition factors include such items as "I am assertive" and "I would do almost anything on a dare," which appear to tap the dominance and excitement-seeking facets of E; the Superiority, Exploitation, and Entitlement factors appear to reflect the opposites of such defining traits of A as modesty, straightforwardness, and compliance.

These interpretations are supported by studies of the correlates of the NPI. Raskin and Terry (1988) reported correlations between NPI scores and both observational and self-report personality scores. Correlations were found with the observational ratings of sensation seeking, dominance, extraversion, energy level, exhibitionism, assertiveness, leadership, extent of participation in a group, and self-confidence—all traits associated with E—and with criticality, aggressiveness, autocracy, and self-centeredness versus submissiveness, patience, modesty, gentleness, peaceableness, and sensitivity—contrasting definers of A. Positive correlations were found with the California Personality Inventory (CPI; Gough, 1956) scales for dominance, sociability, social presence, and capacity for status, which are related to E; and negative correlations were found with CPI scales for femininity, self-control, and tolerance, which are related to A (McCrae, Costa, & Piedmont, 1993).

Raskin and Novacek (1989) subsequently reported a number of significant correlations between the NPI and MMPI scales. The NPI correlated positively with MMPI Scale 9 (Ma) and negatively with MMPI Scales 2 (D), 7 (Pt), and 0 (Si) as well as the scales for repression, anxiety, and ego control. These correlates suggest that the NPI scores are negatively related to N, that is, that narcissistic individuals are well adjusted. This association is not as easily seen from an examination of NPI items or factors, which do not directly tap chronic negative affect. However, it is well known that N is inversely related to self-esteem (e.g., Costa, McCrae, & Dye, 1991), and high NPI scorers certainly seem to have high self-esteem.

Problems in Conceptualization and Measurement of NAR

The associations between narcissism and high E, low A, and low N are not unique to the NPI. Both the

MMPI NAR scale and the MCMI NAR scale show the same pattern when correlated with NEO-PI factors (Costa & McCrae, 1990). The negative association of NAR with N could account for its relative rarity in clinical samples, just as the positive association of BDL with N accounts for its high prevalence. Thus, there is a good deal of empirical evidence to support the conceptualization of NAR as a combination of high E, low A, and low N.

We might, therefore, suggest that there is no need for a separate narcissistic construct or for separate scales to measure narcissism: Combinations of scores on any measure of the FFM could be used more parsimoniously. Proponents of the construct would probably object to this proposal. Raskin and Shaw (1988), for example, showed that associations between NPI scores and the use of first person pronouns remained significant even after controlling for Eysenck Personality Questionnaire (Eysenck & Eysenck, 1975) E, P, and N scales and a measure of locus of control. Whether the association would have remained after controlling for measures of A remains to be tested. The basic issue—one that recurs for all the personality disorders—is whether measures of NAR have incremental validity over measures of the five factors themselves.

It is also possible to argue that the elements of the NAR—high E, low A, and low N—in combination represent a uniquely important configuration of traits. For example, there may be a specific etiology associated with this constellation of traits, or there may be something about the combination that is pathological, even though the elements themselves are not. In general, it would be of interest in future studies to determine whether some constellations of the five-factor dimensions are, in fact, more common than others or are more clearly associated with personal, social, or occupational dysfunction (Widiger & Trull, 1992).

Psychometrically, however, summary scores on multidimensional measures are ambiguous (Briggs & Cheek, 1986). Well-adjusted and highly extraverted individuals might score high on the NPI even if they were somewhat agreeable—a combination we would hardly characterize as narcissistic. Raskin and Terry (1988) also noted this problem and suggested analyses at the level of the more homogeneous NPI fac-

tors. The same criticism, of course, applies to the MMPI and MCMI NAR scales. The appropriate way to assess a true configuration of traits is by measuring each component separately and requiring that all be present to meet diagnostic criteria.

Interpreting narcissism as high E, low A, and low N succinctly summarizes the correlates of narcissistic scales and makes conceptual analysis easier. From this formulation, it is easy to see that most narcissistic scales do not square well with *DSM-III-R* criteria for NAR. The diagnostic criteria certainly suggest low A: NAR patients are envious, lack empathy, have a sense of entitlement, and are interpersonally exploitative. But nothing in the *DSM-III-R* definition suggests high E: Sociability, leadership, and excitement seeking are not mentioned at all. Worse yet, *DSM-III-R* suggests that narcissists should score high, not low, on N. They are hypersensitive to criticism, painfully self-conscious, and frequently depressed (Trull, 1992). Concordance between narcissistic scales and NAR diagnoses might well be low.

Of course, it is possible that the *DSM-III-R* definition of NAR is incorrect and should be amended to emphasize high E and low N as well as low A. But such a redefinition does not specify why narcissism should be considered a disorder. Well-adjusted, sociable, albeit somewhat egotistical individuals do not have obvious pathology. Personal vanity may be a vice, but it is also an accepted part of contemporary culture. Those who wish to operationalize narcissism by scales that correlate with extraversion and adjustment must provide a rationale for claiming that high scorers—even extremely high scorers—are suffering from a personality disorder. Analyses of narcissistic scales in terms of the FFM cannot resolve this issue, but they may quickly force clinicians and researchers to face it.

One final issue in the assessment of narcissism should be noted. Psychoanalytically oriented theorists—and to some extent *DSM-III-R*—emphasize the illusory nature of the narcissist's self-esteem and the disparity between overt grandiosity and covert fragility and insecurity (Cooper, 1987). Self-reports on personality instruments always reflect the self-concept; and if there are truly distortions in the self-concept, then the validity of self-reports is questionable. One of the chief merits of the FFM is the fact that its factors can be validly assessed from observer ratings as well as from self-reports. Future research on individuals with NAR should certainly include ratings made by knowledgeable informants as well as self-reports; indeed, the discrepancies between these two may prove to be the most useful indicators of NAR.

CONCLUSION

We have attempted to show that a consideration of the *DSM-III-R* Axis II disorders from the perspective of the FFM can be useful in understanding previous research on personality disorders. The FFM appears to provide a comprehensive model of normal personality traits; to the extent that personality disorders involve maladaptive or extreme variants of these personality traits, the model should be relevant. We believe that reconceptualizing the personality disorders in these terms helps to resolve many of the controversies in personality disorder research.

The FFM helps to explain the high comorbidity rates of certain personality disorders and mood disorders. Consideration of the FFM reveals why the controversy over BDL as a personality disorder versus a subaffective disorder has developed and suggests that *DSM-III-R*'s distinction between mood disorder and personality disorder may be artificial.

Heterogeneity within the BDL category can be explained by recognizing that the BDL diagnosis applies to those who are extreme on the traits that define the dimension of N. These traits are ubiquitous within clinical populations, which explains why BDL is so prevalent and diagnostically nonspecific. Conceptualizing BDL as extreme N is also consistent with Kernberg's (1984) formulation of BPO.

From the perspective of the FFM, scales that measure narcissism (especially the NPI) can be seen as measures of high E, low A, and low N. This formulation points out difficulties with multidimensional scales, highlights differences between scales that measure narcissism and diagnostic criteria for NAR, and directs attention to the question of why certain combinations of traits should be considered pathological.

We encourage personality disorder researchers to include measures of the FFM in their studies. The chosen instruments would ideally include measures of specific traits, as well as the global dimensions, to specify in detail the personality characteristics of individuals with Axis II diagnoses. In many cases, it would be wise to supplement self-reports with ratings from knowledgeable informants. The routine inclusion of such measures in studies of personality disorders would help refine the definition of particular disorders, assess the incremental validity of personality disorder scales, examine the role of N and other personality factors in accounting for comorbidity among mental disorders, and develop hypotheses about tailoring treatment to the personality profile of the individual patient.

References

Akiskal, H. S. (1981). Subaffective disorders: Dysthymic, cyclothymic, and bipolar II disorders in the "borderline" realm. *Psychiatric Clinics of North America, 4,* 25–46.

American Psychiatric Association. (1980). *Diagnostic and statistical manual of mental disorders* (3rd ed.). Washington, DC: Author.

American Psychiatric Association. (1987). *Diagnostic and statistical manual of mental disorders* (3rd ed., rev.). Washington, DC: Author.

Ashby, H. V., Lee, R. R., & Duke, E. H. (1979, August). *A narcissistic personality disorder MMPI scale.* Paper presented at the 87th annual meeting of the American Psychological Association, New York.

Blashfield, R., & McElroy, R. (1987). The 1985 journal literature on personality disorders. *Comprehensive Psychiatry, 28,* 536–546.

Briggs, S. R., & Cheek, J. M. (1986). The role of factor analysis in the development and evaluation of personality scales. *Journal of Personality, 54,* 106–148.

Cattell, R. B., Eber, H. W., & Tatsuoka, M. M. (1970). *The handbook for the Sixteen Personality Factor Questionnaire.* Champaign, IL: Institute for Personality and Ability Testing.

Clark, L. A. (1989, August). The basic traits of personality disorder: Primary and higher-order dimensions. In R. R. McCrae (Chair), *Personality disorders from the perspective of the five-factor model.* Symposium conducted at the 97th annual meeting of the American Psychological Association, New Orleans, LA.

Clarkin, J. F., Widiger, T. A., Frances, A., Hurt, S., & Gilmore, M. (1983). Prototypic typology and the borderline personality disorder. *Journal of Abnormal Psychology, 92,* 263–275.

Cooper, A. M (1987). Histrionic, narcissistic, and compulsive personality disorders. In G. L. Tischler (Ed.),

Diagnosis and classification in psychiatry: A critical appraisal of DSM-III (pp. 290–299). New York: Cambridge University Press.

Costa, P. T., Jr., & McCrae, R. R. (1980). Influence of extraversion and neuroticism on subjective well-being: Happy and unhappy people. *Journal of Personality and Social Psychology, 38,* 668–678.

Costa, P. T., Jr., & McCrae, R. R. (1985). *The NEO Personality Inventory manual.* Odessa, FL: Psychological Assessment Resources.

Costa, P. T., Jr., & McCrae, R. R. (1990). Personality disorders and the five-factor model of personality. *Journal of Personality Disorders, 4,* 362–371.

Costa, P. T., Jr., McCrae, R. R., & Dye, D. A. (1991). Facet scales for Agreeableness and Conscientiousness: A revision of the NEO Personality Inventory. *Personality and Individual Differences, 12,* 887–898.

Docherty, J. P., Fiester, S. J., & Shea, T. (1986). Syndrome diagnosis and personality disorder. In A. Frances & R. Hales (Eds.), *Psychiatry update: The American Psychiatric Association annual review* (Vol. 5, pp. 315–355). Washington, DC: American Psychiatric Press.

Evans, R., Ruff, R., Braff, D., & Ainsworth, T. (1984). MMPI characteristics of borderline personality inpatients. *Journal of Nervous and Mental Disease, 172,* 742–748.

Eysenck, H. J. (1970). A dimensional system of psychodiagnosis. In A. R. Mahrer (Ed.), *New approaches to personality classification* (pp. 169–208). New York: Columbia University Press.

Eysenck, H. J., & Eysenck, S. B. G. (1964). *Manual of the Eysenck Personality Inventory.* London: University Press.

Eysenck, H. J., & Eysenck, S. B. G. (1975). *Eysenck Personality Questionnaire manual.* San Diego, CA: EdITS.

Goldberg, L. R. (1990). An alternative "description of personality": The Big-Five factor structure. *Journal of Personality and Social Psychology, 59,* 1216–1229.

Gough, H. G. (1956). *California Psychological Inventory.* Palo Alto, CA: Consulting Psychologists Press.

Guilford, J. S., Zimmerman, W. S., & Guilford, J. P. (1976). *The Guilford–Zimmerman Temperament Survey handbook: Twenty-five years of research and application.* San Diego, CA: EdITS.

Gunderson, J. G. (1982). Empirical studies of the borderline diagnosis. In L. Grinspoon (Ed.), *Psychiatry 1982 annual review* (pp. 415–437). Washington, DC: American Psychiatric Press.

Gunderson, J. G. (1987, May). *Competing models of personality disorders.* Paper presented at the annual meeting of the American Psychiatric Association, Chicago, IL.

Gunderson, J. G., & Elliot, G. R. (1985). The interface between borderline personality disorder and affective disorder. *American Journal of Psychiatry, 142,* 277–288.

Gunderson, J. G., & Zanarini, M. C. (1987). Current overview of the borderline diagnosis. *Journal of Clinical Psychiatry, 48*(Suppl. 8), 5–11.

Gustin, Q., Goodpaster, W., Sajadi, C., Pitts, W., LaBasse, D., & Snyder, S. (1983). MMPI characteristics of the DSM-III borderline personality disorder. *Journal of Personality Assessment, 47,* 50–59.

Hathaway, S. R., & McKinley, J. C. (1967). *Minnesota Multiphasic Personality Inventory manual.* New York: Psychological Corporation.

Hirschfeld, R. M., & Klerman, G. (1979). Personality attributes and affective disorders. *American Journal of Psychiatry, 136,* 67–70.

Hirschfeld, R. M., Klerman, G., Clayton, P. J., & Keller, M. B. (1983). Personality and depression: Empirical findings. *Archives of General Psychiatry, 40,* 993–998.

Hirschfeld, R. M., Klerman, G., Lavoni, P., Keller, M. B., Griffith, P., & Coryell, W. (1989). Premorbid personality assessments of first onset of major depression. *Archives of General Psychiatry, 46,* 345–350.

Hurt, S., Clarkin, J., Frances, A., Abrams, R., & Hunt, H. (1985). Discriminant validity of the MMPI for borderline personality disorder. *Journal of Personality Assessment, 49,* 56–61.

Hurt, S., Clarkin, J., Widiger, T., Fyer, M., Sullivan, T., Stone, M., & Frances, A. (1990). Evaluation of DSM-III decision rules for case detection using joint conditional probability structures. *Journal of Personality Disorders, 4,* 121–130.

Hyler, S. E., Rieder, R. O., Williams, J. B. W., Spitzer, R. L., Hendler, J., & Lyons, M. (1989). A comparison of self-report and clinical diagnosis of DSM-III personality disorders in 552 patients. *Comprehensive Psychiatry, 30,* 170–178.

Keller, M. (1989). Current concepts in affective disorders. *Journal of Clinical Psychiatry, 50,* 157–162.

Kernberg, O. (1975). *Borderline conditions and pathological narcissism.* Northvale, NJ: Jason Aronson.

Kernberg, O. (1984). *Severe personality disorders.* New Haven, CT: Yale University Press.

Kolb, J. E., & Gunderson, J. G. (1980). Diagnosing borderlines with a semi-structured interview. *Archives of General Psychiatry, 37,* 37–41.

Kroll, J., Sines, L., Martin, K., Lari, L., Pyle, R., & Zander, J. (1981). Borderline personality disorder: Construct validity of the concept. *Archives of General Psychiatry, 38,* 1021–1026.

Leary, T. (1957). *Interpersonal diagnosis of personality.* New York: Ronald Press.

Loyd, C., Overall, J., & Click, M. (1983). Screening for borderline personality disorders with the MMPI-168. *Journal of Clinical Psychology, 39*, 722–726.

Lyons, M. J., Merla, M. E., Ozer, D. J., & Hyler, S. E. (1990, August). *Relationship of the "Big-Five" factors to DSM-III personality disorders.* Paper presented at the 98th annual meeting of the American Psychological Association, Boston, MA.

McCrae, R. R., Costa, P. T., Jr., & Piedmont, R. L. (1993). Folk concepts, natural language, and psychological constructs: The California Psychological Inventory and the five-factor model. *Journal of Personality, 61*, 1–26.

Miller, T. (1991). The psychotherapeutic utility of the five-factor model of personality. *Journal of Personality Assessment, 57*, 415–433.

Millon, T. (1981). *Disorders of personality: DSM-III, Axis II.* New York: Wiley.

Millon, T. (1983). *Millon Clinical Multiaxial Inventory manual* (3rd ed.). Minneapolis, MN: Interpretive Scoring Systems.

Millon, T., & Kotik, D. (1985). The relationship of depression to disorders of personality. In E. Beckham & W. Leber (Eds.), *Handbook of depression* (pp. 700–744). Homewood, IL: Dorsey Press.

Morey, L. C., & Smith, M. (1988). Personality disorders. In R. Greene (Ed.), *The MMPI: Use with specific populations* (pp. 110–158). Philadelphia: Grune & Stratton.

Morey, L. C., Waugh, M. H., & Blashfield, R. K. (1985). MMPI scales for DSM-III personality disorders: Their derivation and correlates. *Journal of Personality Assessment, 49*, 245–251.

Murray, H. A. (1938). *Explorations in personality.* New York: Oxford University Press.

Mutén, E. (1991). Self-reports, spouse ratings, and psychophysiological assessment in a behavioral medicine program: An application of the five-factor model. *Journal of Personality Assessment, 57*, 449–464.

Nurnberg, H. G., Hurt, S. W., Feldman, A., & Shu, R. (1988). Evaluation of diagnostic criteria for borderline personality disorder. *American Journal of Psychiatry, 145*, 1280–1284.

Patrick, J. (1984). Characteristics of DSM-III borderline MMPI profiles. *Journal of Clinical Psychology, 40*, 655–658.

Pfohl, B., Stangl, D., & Zimmerman, M. (1984). The implications of DSM-III personality disorders for patients with major depression. *Journal of Affective Disorders, 7*, 309–318.

Raskin, R., & Hall, C. S. (1979). A narcissistic personality inventory. *Psychological Reports, 45*, 590.

Raskin, R., & Novacek, J. (1989). An MMPI description of the narcissistic personality. *Journal of Personality Assessment, 53*, 66–80.

Raskin, R., & Shaw, R. (1988). Narcissism and the use of personal pronouns. *Journal of Personality, 56*, 393–404.

Raskin, R., & Terry, H. (1988). A principal-components analysis of the Narcissistic Personality Inventory and further evidence of its construct validity. *Journal of Personality and Social Psychology, 54*, 890–902.

Resnick, R. J., Goldberg, S., Schulz, S. C., Schulz, P. M., Hamer, R., & Friedel, R. (1988). Borderline personality disorder: Replication of MMPI profiles. *Journal of Clinical Psychology, 44*, 354–360.

Robins, L. N., Helzer, J. E., Croughan, J., & Ratcliff, K. S. (1981). National Institute of Mental Health diagnostic interview schedule: Its history, characteristics, and validity. *Archives of General Psychiatry, 38*, 381–389.

Snyder, S., Pitts, W., Goodpaster, W., Sajadi, C., & Gustin, Q. (1982). MMPI profile of DSM-III borderline personality disorder. *American Journal of Psychiatry, 139*, 1046–1048.

Swartz, M., Blazer, D., George, L., & Winfield, I. (1990). Estimating the prevalence of borderline personality disorder in the community. *Journal of Personality Disorders, 4*, 257–272.

Trull, T. J. (1991). Discriminant validity of the MMPI-Borderline Personality Disorder Scale. *Psychological Assessment: A Journal of Consulting and Clinical Psychology, 3*, 232–238.

Trull, T. J. (1992). DSM-III-R personality disorders and the five-factor model of personality: An empirical comparison. *Journal of Abnormal Psychology, 101*, 553–560.

Trull, T. J., Widiger, T. A., & Guthrie, P. (1990). The categorical versus dimensional status of borderline personality disorder. *Journal of Abnormal Psychology, 99*, 40–48.

Turner, S., & Biedel, D. (1989). Social phobia: Clinical syndrome, diagnosis and comorbidity. *Clinical Psychology Review, 9*, 3–18.

Watson, D., & Clark, L. A. (1984). Negative affectivity: The disposition to experience aversive emotional states. *Psychological Bulletin, 96*, 465–490.

Widiger, T. A., & Frances, A. J. (1987). Interviews and inventories for the measurement of personality disorders. *Clinical Psychology Review, 7*, 49–75.

Widiger, T. A., Frances, A. J., Harris, M., Jacobsberg, L., Fyer, M., & Manning, D. (1991). Comorbidity among Axis II disorders. In J. Oldham (Ed.), *Axis II: New perspectives on validity* (pp. 165–194). Washington, DC: American Psychiatric Press.

Widiger, T. A., Frances, A. J., Spitzer, R., & Williams, J. (1988). The DSM-III-R personality disorders: An overview. *American Journal of Psychiatry, 145*, 786–795.

Widiger, T. A., & Hyler, S. (1987). Axis I/Axis II interactions. In J. Cavenar, R. Michels, & A. Cooper (Eds.), *Psychiatry* (pp. 1–10). Philadelphia: Lippincott.

Widiger, T. A., Sanderson, C., & Warner, L. (1986). The MMPI, prototypal typology, and borderline personality disorder. *Journal of Personality Assessment, 50,* 540–553.

Widiger, T. A., & Trull, T. J. (1992). Personality and psychopathology: An application of the five-factor model. *Journal of Personality, 60,* 363–394.

Widiger, T. A., & Trull, T. J. (1993). Borderline and narcissistic personality disorders. In H. Adams & P. Sut-

ker (Eds.), *Comprehensive handbook of psychopathology* (2nd ed., pp. 371–394). New York: Plenum.

Wiggins, J. W., & Pincus, A. (1989). Conceptions of personality disorders and dimensions of personality. *Psychological Assessment: A Journal of Consulting and Clinical Psychology, 1,* 305–316.

Zonderman, A. B., Stone, S. V., & Costa, P. T., Jr. (1989, August). *Age and neuroticism as risk factors for the incidence of diagnoses of psychotic and neurotic disorders.* Paper presented at the 97th annual meeting of the American Psychological Association, New Orleans, LA.

CHAPTER 5

PERSONALITY STRUCTURE AND THE STRUCTURE OF PERSONALITY DISORDERS

Jerry S. Wiggins and Aaron L. Pincus

In this chapter, we advocate the use of operationalized structural models of personality in the interpretation of dimensions that underlie the interrelations among conceptions of personality disorders. We begin with an overview of empirical studies of the structure of personality disorders and consider two major perspectives on the nature of these disorders. We then provide an overview of dimensional approaches to personality and consider four theoretical perspectives on the five-factor model (FFM) of personality. Next, we consider, in detail, the relations between personality structure and the structure of personality disorders. Finally, we illustrate the advantages of a combined five-factor and interpersonal circumplex model in the assessment of personality disorders. Throughout the chapter we present reanalyses of our previously published data that illustrate the specific points of our discussion.

STRUCTURE OF PERSONALITY DISORDERS

Empirical Studies

Current conceptualizations of personality disorders are products of a brief, but intensive, 10 years of theoretical development and empirical investigation. Only in the latter half of this period has research focused on the "structure" underlying conceptions of personality disorders. In Tables 1 and 2, we present a summary of these empirical investigations of personality disorder structure. As Widiger (1989) pointed out, one clear distinction among these studies is the presence or absence of an independently operationalized dimensional model that is used to evaluate empirical findings concerning the structure of personality disorders. Studies conducted in the absence of a dimensional model may nonetheless be important if they reveal a consistent empirical pattern of results. However, such studies are vulnerable to a subjectivity of interpretation of dimensions that may contribute to an apparent lack of consistency of results across studies. Studies that include an operationalized dimensional model have selected models that have emerged from a 50-year history of investigations into personality structure (Wiggins & Trapnell, in press). From Tables 1 and 2, it is clear that such studies have provided a more coherent pattern of results than studies that do not relate the structure of personality disorders to validated taxonomies of personality traits.

A second distinction that influences the structural study of personality disorders involves the assumption that is made about the relation between normal and disordered personality. If one assumes that disordered personality is qualitatively different from normal personality, then the inclusion of a dimensional model of personality may be insufficient or inappropriate for investigation. If one assumes that

The preparation of this chapter was greatly facilitated by Social Sciences and Humanities Research Council of Canada grant 410-90-1374 awarded to Jerry S. Wiggins and by a University of British Columbia Killam Predoctoral Fellowship awarded to Aaron L. Pincus. We thank Anita DeLongis, Dimitri Papageorgis, Paul Trapnell, and Candace Taylor Wiggins for their helpful comments on an earlier version of this chapter.

TABLE 1

Methods and Dimensions Identified in Structural Investigations of Personality Disorders (PDs): Studies Lacking Independent Operationalization of Dimensions[a]

Study	Method	Dimension
Blashfield, Sprock, Pinkston, & Hodgin, 1985	MDS of case diagnosis across clinicians	Acting out Interpersonal involvement
Clark, 1989	Factor analysis of *DSM-III* Axis II & some Axis I criteria	Negative emotionality Positive emotionality Impulsivity
Hyler & Lyons, 1988	Factor analysis of PD severity ratings on a nationwide sample	Asocial Unstable Anxious Compulsive
Kass, Skodal, Charles, Spitzer, & Williams, 1985	Factor analysis of PD severity ratings on a clinical sample	Odd/eccentric Dramatic/erratic Anxious/fearful Compulsive
Livesley & Jackson, 1986	Factor analysis of "prototypical" PD behavioral acts	Interpersonal/cognitive dysfunction Impulsivity Compulsive
Livesley, Jackson, & Schroeder, 1989	Factor analysis of 100 scales that assess PD behavioral dimensions	15 primary dimensions
Livesley & Schroeder, 1990	Factor analysis of *DSM* Cluster A–associated behavioral dimensions	Paranoid behaviors Sensitivity Social avoidance Perceptual/cognitive distortion
Morey, 1988	Cluster analysis of *DSM* PD criteria rated on diagnosed PD patients	11 clusters corresponding to DS PD categories 2 higher order clusters: acting out & anxious rumination
Morey, Waugh, & Blashfield, 1985	Factor analysis of MMPI PD scales	Odd/eccentric Dramatic/erratic Anxious/fearful
Strack, 1987	Factor analysis of the PACL in normals	Affective neuroticism vs. affective control Assertion vs. submission Extraversion vs. intraversion
Widiger, Trull, Hurt, Clarkin, & Francis, 1987	MDS of *DSM* criteria rated on inpatient PD sample	Social involvement Dominance Anxious rumination vs. acting out

Note. DSM = *Diagnostic and Statistical Manual of Mental Disorders;* DSM-III = DSM, 3rd ed.; MDS = Multidimensional Scaling; MMPI = Minnesota Multiphasic Personality Inventory; PACL = Personality Adjective Check List.
[a]Excluding studies that used the full Millon Clinical Multiaxial Inventory.

disordered personality reflects quantitative differences in the manifestation or severity of normal personality traits (i.e., a dimensional approach), then the adoption of a personality taxonomy for use as a structural referent becomes a necessary or even fundamental conceptual task.

The dimensions underlying the personality disorders identified in studies lacking an operationalized

TABLE 2

Methods and Dimensions Identified in Structural Investigations of Personality Disorders (PDs): Studies Operationalizing a Dimensional Model

Study	*Model*/Method	Dimensions
Costa & McCrae, 1990	*Five-factor model* Factor analysis of MCMI, MCMI-II, & NEO-PI combined	Neuroticism Extraversion Openness Agreeableness Conscientiousness
DeJong, van den Brink, Jansen, & Schippers, 1989	*Interpersonal circumplex*[a] Correlated SIDP scales with ICL octant scales	Power (control) vs. submission
Morey, 1985	*Interpersonal circumplex* Correlated MCMI scales with ICL octant scales	Power (control) vs. submission
Pincus & Wiggins, 1990a	*Interpersonal circumplex* Correlated PACL and MMPI PD scales with IIP-C octant scales; projected scales onto IIP-C circumplex	Dominance vs. submission Nurturance vs. coldness
Plutchik & Conte, 1986	*Interpersonal circumplex* Factor analysis of clinician's trait ratings for *DSM-III* PDs	Dominance vs. submission Nurturance vs. coldness
Plutchik & Platman, 1977	*Interpersonal circumplex* Factor analysis of clinician's trait ratings for *DSM-II* PDs	Dominance vs. submission Nurturance vs. coldness
Romney & Bynner, 1989	*Interpersonal circumplex* Confirmatory factor analysis of data sets to test the goodness of fit for circular model	Dominance vs. submission Nurturance vs. coldness
Strack, Lorr, & Campbell, 1990	*Interpersonal circumplex* Evaluated circular ordering of PACL & MCMI-II scales	PACL: Extraversion vs. introversion; resistance vs. conformity MCMI-II: Expressive vs. impassive; compulsive vs. impulsive
Wiggins & Pincus, 1989	*Interpersonal circumplex* Projected PACL & MMPI PD scales onto IAS-R circumplex	Dominance vs. submission Nurturance vs. coldness

Note. DSM-II = *Diagnostic and Statistical Manual for Mental Disorders,* 2nd ed.; DSM-III = *DSM,* 3rd ed.; IAS-R = Revised Interpersonal Adjective Scales; IASR-B5 = Extended Interpersonal Adjective Scales; ICL = Interpersonal Check List; IIP-C = Inventory of Interpersonal Problems Circumplex Scales; MCMI = Millon Clinical Multiaxial Inventory; MCMI-II = revised MCMI; MMPI = Minnesota Multiphasic Personality Inventory; NEO-PI = NEO Personality Inventory; PACL = Personality Adjective Check List; SIDP = Structured Interview for *DSM-III* Personality Disorders.
[a]Empirical results have consistently demonstrated that the interpersonal circumplex is related to a subset of PDs.

model of personality reflect solutions extracted at different levels within the hierarchy of personality constructs (Comrey, 1988). These levels range from first order, narrow-band factors (e.g., 15 primary dimensions identified by Livesley, Jackson, & Schroeder, 1989; Livesley & Schroeder, 1990) to superordinate, broad-band factors such as "acting out" and "interpersonal involvement" (Blashfield, Sprock, Pinkston, & Hodgin, 1985). The varying levels of extraction, in combination with subjective interpretation of factors, are likely the greatest sources of confusion in interpreting results. Another challenge to the investigation of structural relations between personality disorders and personality traits is the operationalization of personality disorder constructs. Attempts to investigate the relations between dimensions of personality and clinically diagnosed personality disorders are embroiled in a "criterion problem" due to the low reliability of clinical diagnoses (Wiggins & Pincus, 1989). Furthermore, the various interview schedules and self-report measures of personality disorders have not been empirically evaluated in a systematic manner (Widiger & Frances, 1987). There are also conceptual divergences among the different methods of assessment. For these reasons, we have chosen to operationalize the personality disorders by using self-report instruments that reflect two major perspectives on the disorders.

Two Perspectives on Personality Disorders

Millon Millon (1981, 1986, 1990) proposed a dimensional model of personality based on three basic polarities from which one can derive the personality disorder categories. The three polarities are (a) the nature of reinforcement (whether the person generally experiences positive reinforcement, negative reinforcement, both, or neither), (b) the source of reinforcement (self, other, or ambivalent), and (c) the instrumental coping style of the individual (actively initiating or passively accommodating). Millon (1990) articulated the personality disorders with reference to how these polarities combine to give rise to individual differences in eight clinical domains: Expressive Acts, Interpersonal Conduct, Cognitive Style, Object Representations, Self-Image, Regulatory Mechanisms, Morphologic Organization, and Mood/Temperament.

Millon (1990) reported that an instrument to assess these personality polarities was under development. Two other instruments are currently available that assess Millon's conception of personality disorders as syndrome derivations from the three basic polarities: The Millon Clinical Multiaxial Inventory–II (MCMI-II; Millon, 1987) and the Personality Adjective Check List (PACL; Strack, 1987).

The DSM The publication of the third edition of the *Diagnostic and Statistical Manual of Mental Disorders*

(*DSM-III*; American Psychiatric Association, 1980) and the third, revised edition of the *DSM* (*DSM-III-R*; American Psychiatric Association, 1987) marked major conceptual changes in classification of personality disorders. Along with developmental disorders, personality disorders were placed on a separate axis (Axis II) in this multiaxial diagnostic system. This ensures that in the evaluation of adults, these disorders are not overlooked when attention is directed to the usually more florid Axis I disorders (Widiger, Frances, Spitzer, & Williams, 1988).

For a number of reasons, the construct validity of the *DSM* personality disorders requires continued investigation. Most diagnoses are currently based on limited empirical data. The *DSM* groups personality disorders into three clusters: (a) odd/eccentric (paranoid, schizoid, and schizotypal), (b) dramatic/erratic (histrionic, narcissistic, antisocial, and borderline), and (c) anxious/fearful (avoidant, dependent, compulsive, and passive–aggressive). This clustering is not based on any explicit assumptions or hypotheses regarding the personality disorders (Widiger, 1989). Instead, the placement is based on presumably similar phenomenologies, analogous to the organization of the Axis I syndromes (Frances, 1980; Spitzer, Williams, & Skodal, 1980). It is clear from Tables 1 and 2 that structural investigations of personality disorders have provided only limited support for the *DSM* clusters. A number of self-report measures and interviews have been developed to assess the *DSM* personality disorders (Reich, 1987, 1989; Widiger & Frances, 1987). Two selected examples are considered in the following section.

Assessment Instruments

PACL The PACL (Strack, 1987) was derived under a combined rational/empirical scale construction strategy to yield self-report measures of the 11 personality styles described in Millon's (1981, 1986) theory of psychopathology. Reliable adjective scales were constructed for 8 of Millon's 11 personality styles. It was not possible to construct reliable scales for the 3 "severe" personality styles of borderline, schizotypal, and paranoid. Validity studies of the PACL scales include studies of their convergence with other self-report measures (Strack, 1987; Strack, Lorr, & Campbell, 1990) and their relations to the major dimensions of personality

(Pincus & Wiggins, 1990a; Wiggins & Pincus, 1989). In results to be presented later, our analyses are based on a set of nonoverlapping PACL scales constructed by Wiggins and Pincus (1989). Representative items for each PACL scale can be seen in Table 3.

MMPI Personality Disorder Scales The Minnesota Multiphasic Personality Inventory (MMPI; Hathaway & McKinley, 1967) personality disorder scales (Morey, Waugh, & Blashfield, 1985) were derived under a combined rational/empirical strategy to yield self-report measures of the 11 personality disorders described in *DSM-III*. Both overlapping and nonoverlapping scale sets are available, and the results presented later are restricted to the set with nonoverlapping items. The results of validity studies suggest that the scales have meaningful relations to major dimensions of personality (Pincus & Wiggins, 1990a; Wiggins & Pincus, 1989) and that they warrant further investigation (Dubro, Wetzler, & Kahn, 1988; Greene, 1987; Trull, 1991). Representative items for each MMPI scale can be seen in Table 3.

Principal Components of Personality Disorders

Because the MMPI and PACL personality disorder scales were generated from different conceptual perspectives, it is important to examine their similarities and differences with reference to the structural dimensions that underlie them. With this in mind, we administered the two sets of self-report measures to 581 undergraduate psychology students at the University of British Columbia (Wiggins & Pincus, 1989). We computed the correlations among all 19 scales and subjected the resultant intercorrelation matrix to a principal components analysis. The retention of five components was clearly indicated by both Kaiser-Guttman and Scree test criteria. These five components were analytically rotated to a varimax criterion of simple structure. The resultant component matrix is provided in Table 4.

As shown in Table 4, conjoint factor analysis of personality disorder scales from the MMPI and PACL yields a relatively clear simple structure solution of five orthogonal components. It is also apparent that there are a number of clear-cut structural conver-

gences between corresponding scale pairs from the two instruments. In contrast, there are several instances in which corresponding scale pairs show clearly divergent structural patterns from one another; and finally, for the first four components at least, it is evident that the factors that underlie the scale intercorrelations are bipolar in nature. Thus, we have established a clear factorial structure that suggests both convergences and divergences among the conceptions of personality disorders reflected in two promising self-report measures. The next, and more important, question is, "How should we interpret this solution?"

One approach would be to compare the present factor solution with those obtained in the studies listed in Table 1. For example, how does the present five-factor structure compare with the four-factor structure obtained by Kass, Skodal, Charles, Spitzer, and Williams (1985)? As we have already emphasized, the problem with such a comparison, and with comparisons of our findings with any of the studies listed in Table 1, is one of subjectivity. We would, in effect, be comparing our own implicit theory of personality disorders with those of other investigators. Such differences are not easily resolved in the absence of an explicit and operationalized model of personality structure.

The structural convergences and divergences among the corresponding pairs of personality disorder scales from the MMPI and PACL might be interpreted with respect to judged similarities and differences in item content, as suggested by the examples in Table 3. The strong factorial convergence of the two schizoid scales might be interpreted as reflecting the common item theme of "detachment" in the PACL and MMPI scales. The two antisocial scales are just as clearly different in their factorial composition, and this might be attributed to the "domineering" content of the PACL items in contrast to the "rule infraction" theme of the MMPI items.

Content analytic rating procedures can sometimes illuminate the similarity and differences among personality scales. However, in the absence of an explicit and operationalized model, such procedures are inherently subjective and thus do not lend themselves to interpretations of the underlying dimensionality of sets of scales (McCrae, Costa, & Piedmont,

TABLE 3

Characteristic Items of the PACL and MMPI Personality Disorder Scales

Scale	PACL items	MMPI items
Schizoid	detached distant remote	I like parties and socials. (False) I enjoy social gatherings just to be with people. (False) I am a good mixer. (False)
Avoidant	ignored excluded insecure	I am easily embarrassed. I am certainly lacking in self-confidence. Criticism or scolding hurts me terribly.
Dependent	sweet warm-hearted respectful	At times I think I am no good at all. I am entirely self-confident. (False) I have several times given up doing a thing because I thought too little of my ability.
Histrionic	outgoing lively talkative	I find it hard to make small talk when I meet new people. (False) While in trains, buses, etc., I often talk to strangers. I like to go to parties and other affairs where there is lots of loud fun.
Narcissistic	egoistic conceited arrogant	When in a group of people I have trouble thinking of the right things to talk about. (False) If given the chance I would make a good leader of people. I have no dread of going into a room by myself where other people have already gathered and started talking.
Antisocial	domineering forceful aggressive	In school I was sometimes sent to the principal for cutting up. As a youngster I was suspended from school one or more times for cutting up. If I could get into a movie without paying and be sure I would not be seen, I would probably do it.
Compulsive	organized orderly neat	I frequently find myself worrying about something. I must admit that I have at times been worried beyond reason over something that did not matter. I have met problems so full of possibilities that I have been unable to make up my mind about them.
Passive–Aggressive	moody annoyed temperamental	I find it hard to keep my mind on a task or job. I have more trouble concentrating than others seem to have. I have difficulty in starting to do things.
(Schizotypal)	No PACL scale	I have strange and peculiar thoughts. I have had very strange and peculiar experiences. I often feel as if things were not real.
(Borderline)	No PACL scale	I am not easily angered. (False) I get mad easily and then get over it soon. I sometimes feel that I am about to go to pieces.
(Paranoid)	No PACL scale	There are persons who are trying to steal my thoughts and ideas. I have often felt that strangers were looking at me critically. I feel that I have often been punished without cause.

Note. MMPI = Minnesota Multiphasic Personality Inventory personality disorder scales; PACL = Personality Adjective Check List. From "Conceptions of Personality Disorders and Dimensions of Personality; by J. S. Wiggins and A. L. Pincus, 1989, *Psychological Assessment, 1,* p. 307. Copyright 1989 by the American Psychological Association.

1993). For that reason, we now turn to a consideration of personality structure and an examination of operationalized models that may illuminate the nature of the structure presented in Table 4.

PERSONALITY STRUCTURE

Dimensional Approaches

In dimensional approaches to personality, the term

TABLE 4

Principal Components of Personality Disorder Scales

Scale	I	II	III	IV	V
Dependent (MMPI)	.75				
Avoidant (PACL)	.70	.42			
Avoidant (MMPI)	.61	.45			
Narcissistic (PACL)	−.53				
Narcissistic (MMPI)	−.66				
Antisocial (PACL)	−.81				
Schizoid (PACL)		.81			
Schizoid (MMPI)		.80			
Histrionic (MMPI)	−.36	−.74			
Histrionic (PACL)		−.77			
Passive–Aggressive (PACL)			.80		
Passive–Aggressive (MMPI)			.58		
Borderline (MMPI)[a]			.68		
Dependent (PACL)	.57		−.61		
Compulsive (MMPI)				.69	
Compulsive (PACL)			−.47	.63	
Antisocial (MMPI)				−.63	
Schizotypal (MMPI)[a]					.81
Paranoid (MMPI)[a]					.61

Note. $N = 581$; loadings $< .33$ omitted. MMPI = Minnesota Multiphasic Personality Inventory personality disorder scales; PACL = Personality Adjective Check List.
[a]No PACL scales for these disorders.

structure had its origins in the classical distinction between personality structures and personality dynamics (Rapaport, 1960); the present-day meaning however is more delimited (Wiggins, 1968). The literature of personality structure encompasses investigators' efforts, over the last half century, to provide a structural representation of the interrelations among what they believed to be comprehensive sets of variables reflecting individual differences in human dispositions. Perhaps more than any other area of personality study, personality structure research has been dependent on, inspired by, and even subordinated to the development of mathematical/statistical procedures for data analysis. Computers and their associated software have dramatically transformed this field from one in which conceptualizations exceeded possibilities of data analysis to one in which software capabilities now exceed both the quality of data and the scope of conceptualization (Wiggins, 1986).

The interdependence between theory and method in personality structure research is due to the fact that most attempts to provide multivariate representations of personality structure have been based on the method of factor analysis. The latter is a set of procedures for reducing a matrix of intercorrelations among observed personality variables to a matrix of smaller rank for the purpose of identifying the latent variables (factors) that gave rise to the original matrix of intercorrelations. The logic underlying this procedure is precisely that which led Spearman (1927) and Thurstone (1934) to seek the factor(s) underlying correlations among performances judged to reflect "intelligence."

There are many different computational procedures whereby intercorrelations among personality variables may be reduced to factors, and unfortunately, there is substantial disagreement as to which set of procedures is optimal (see *Multivariate Behavioral Research*, Vol. 25, No. 1, whole issue [Society of Multivariate Experimental Psychology, 1990]). As a consequence, theories of personality structure may differ not only in substance but in preferred method, and it is often difficult to determine the extent to which apparent substantive differences are due to differences in computational procedures. To further complicate matters, there are theories of personality structure that use multivariate models, such as the circumplex, which depart in significant ways from the factor-analytic tradition.

The field of personality structure as we know it today began with the comprehensive, cumulative, and systematic research programs of Cattell (1943), Eysenck (1947), and Guilford (1948). The programs of Cattell and Eysenck and their many followers are still pursued actively. By the 1980s, use of well-validated structural models of personality for purposes of integrating the huge variety of operationalized personality constructs became the central task of a number of investigators (e.g., Costa & McCrae, 1988; Wiggins & Broughton, 1985). A "third force" as it were that promises possible consolidations among these and other schools of thought may be found in the work of those investigators who advocate an FFM personality structure (see Digman, chapter 1 in this book). One of the reasons for the current widespread interest in the FFM is that it has been found to be a highly robust structure that is invariant across many different computational procedures for deriving factors (Goldberg, 1980). Another reason is that the model may be interpreted from a number of different theoretical perspectives (Wiggins & Trapnell, in press). As we discuss later, the FFM has been interpreted from such perspectives as the *enduring–dispositional* (McCrae & Costa, 1990), the *dyadic–interactional* (Trapnell & Wiggins, 1990), the *social–competency* (Hogan, 1983), and the *lexical* (Goldberg, 1981).

Theoretical Perspectives on the FFM

In Table 5, we provide examples of some of the ways in which the major theoretical perspectives on the FFM differ from one another. The *focus of convenience* (Kelly, 1955) of a perspective refers to the research problem or goal the theorists had in mind when they developed their version of the FFM. In general, five-factor representations perform best in areas of their original focus of convenience. The *theoretical orientation* of each perspective influences the overall research strategy adopted, the substantive choices that are made in scale development, and the generalizability claimed for the five-factor representation. The *universe of content* from which items and scales are sampled is largely determined by the focus of convenience and theoretical orientation of the perspective and is itself an important determinant of existing substantive differences among the theoretical perspectives of the FFM.

In addition to substantive differences, the *assessment instruments* that are used to implement the various perspectives differ from one another in terms of item format, scale construction strategies, and psychometric characteristics. Any of the instruments listed may be used to investigate the FFM, but their *representative applications* tend to reflect the focus of convenience and theoretical orientation of the perspective that gave rise to a given measure. Further discussion of the four theoretical perspectives and the differences among them may be found in Wiggins and Trapnell (in press).

Assessment Instruments

As shown in Table 5, each of the four theoretical perspectives on the FFM is associated with a particular assessment instrument that serves as an operational definition of that perspective. In later sections, we present empirical data relevant to three of these instruments: the NEO Personality Inventory (NEO-PI; Costa & McCrae, 1985), the extended, revised Interpersonal Adjective Scales (IASR-B5; Trapnell & Wiggins, 1990), and the Hogan Personality Inventory (HPI; Hogan, 1986).[1] In the following subsections, we briefly describe the manner in which these instruments were constructed.

NEO-PI The NEO-PI (Costa & McCrae, 1985) evolved from a series of studies of the stability of trait dimensions across age groups (e.g., Costa & McCrae, 1976). Three age-invariant factors were identified in instruments such as the Sixteen Personality Factor Questionnaire (Cattell, Eber, & Tatsuoka, 1970), the Eysenck Personality Inventory (Eysenck & Eysenck, 1964), the EASI Temperament Survey (Buss & Plomin, 1975), and the Experience Inventory (Coan, 1974). The five broad domains (or dimensions) of Neuroticism (N), Extraversion (E), Openness to Experience (O), Agreeableness (A), and Conscientiousness (C) are represented in the NEO-PI. The domains of N, E, and O are represented in the NEO-PI by six original facets that reflect previously identified substantive components; and facet scales for A and C have subsequently been developed (Costa, McCrae, & Dye, 1991). Representative items for each of the NEO-PI factors may be found in Table 6.

IASR-B5 The IAS evolved from a program of research initiated by Goldberg (1977). On the basis of a priori distinctions among different domains of trait categories, Wiggins (1979) provided a conceptually based definition of the universe of content of the interpersonal domain that distinguished that domain from others (e.g., temperamental, characterological, cognitive). This definition of the interpersonal domain was influenced by the earlier conceptual and empirical work of others in the dyadic–interactional tradition (e.g., Carson, 1969; Foa, 1961; Leary, 1957; Lorr & McNair, 1963).

---

[1] Goldberg's (1992) Standard Markers were not available to us at the time of data collection.

TABLE 5

Characteristics of Four Theoretical Perspectives on the Five-Factor Model

Characteristic	Enduring–Dispositional (Costa & McCrae, 1989)	Dyadic–Interactional (Trapnell & Wiggins, 1990)	Social–Competency (Hogan, 1983)	Lexical (Goldberg, 1981)
Focus of convenience	Longitudinal studies of personality and aging	Dyadic interactions in psycho-therapeutic settings	Prediction of effective performance in work and social settings	Development of compelling taxonomy of personality-descriptive terms in the natural language
Theoretical orientation	Traditional multivariate trait theory of individual differences is a legitimate alternative to other theories of personality	Agency and communion are propaedutic to the study of characterological, emotional, and cognitive dispositions	Actors have needs for social approval, status and predictability; observers use trait terms to evaluate social usefulness of actors	Those individual differences that are of the most significance in the daily transactions of persons will eventually become encoded in their language
Universe of content	Literature review of earlier scales with reference to study of aging	Theoretically based taxonomy of trait terms derived from Goldberg's earlier taxonomy	Review of earlier five-factor studies from a social–competency perspective	Semantic relations among trait terms selected from dictionary searches
Assessment instruments	NEO-PI: domains of neuroticism, extraversion, openness, agreeableness, and conscientiousness; each measured by six facets	IASR-B5: domains of dominance and nurturance form eight circumplex scales; domain scores for neuroticism, openness, and conscientiousness	HPI: primary scales of ambition, likability, sociability, adjustment, prudence, and intellectance; each measured by subsets of homogeneous item clusters	Standard Markers: domain scores for surgency, agreeableness, conscientiousness, emotional stability, and intellect; each marked by 20 adjectives
Representative application	Relations between NEO-PI and instruments from major research traditions in personality assessment	Relations between IASR-B5 and conceptions of personality disorders	Prediction of organizational and occupational performance	Investigations of generalizability of English taxonomy to Dutch and German languages

Note. HPI = Hogan Personality Inventory; IASR-B5 = extended Interpersonal Adjective Scales; NEO-PI = NEO Personality Inventory.

Theoretically guided circumplex methodology was used in the construction of eight adjective scales that were arrayed in a circular order around the principal axes of dominance and nurturance (Wiggins, 1979).

A short form of the IAS was subsequently developed (the IAS-R) that more clearly distinguished the dominance axis from the presumably orthogonal domain of C (Wiggins, Trapnell, & Phillips, 1988). The IAS-

---

TABLE 6

Characteristic Five-Factor Items From the NEO Personality Inventory (NEO-PI), the Hogan Personality Inventory (HPI), and the Extended Interpersonal Adjective Scale (IASR-B5)

NEO-PI	HPI	IASR-B5
Extraversion	**Sociability**	**Dominance**
(+) I like to have a lot of people around me.	(+) I like parties and socials.	(+) Dominant
(+) I am a very active person.	(+) I like to be the center of attention.	(+) Assertive
(−) I usually prefer to do things alone.	(−) I don't care for large, noisy crowds.	(−) Unauthoritative
(−) I don't consider myself especially "high-spirited."	(−) In a group, I never attract attention to myself.	(−) Unaggressive
	Ambition	
	(+) In a group, I like to take charge of things.	
	(+) I have a natural talent for influencing people.	
	(−) I am a follower, not a leader.	
	(−) I am not a competitive person.	
Agreeableness	**Likability**	**Love**
(+) I would rather cooperate with others than compete with them.	(+) I work well with other people.	(+) Gentlehearted
(+) Most people I know like me.	(+) I'm good at cheering people up.	(+) Kind
(−) If I don't like people, I let them know it.	(−) I would rather work with facts than people.	(−) Coldhearted
(−) I often get into arguments with my family and co-workers.	(−) When people are nice to me I wonder what they want.	(−) Unsympathetic
Conscientiousness	**Prudence**	**Conscientiousness**
(+) When I make a commitment, I can always be counted on to follow through.	(+) It bothers me when my daily routine is interrupted.	(+) Organized
(+) I am a productive person who always gets the job done.	(+) I am a hard and steady worker.	(+) Orderly
(−) Sometimes I'm not as dependable or reliable as I should be.	(−) I am often careless about my appearance.	(−) Disorganized
(−) I never seem to be able to get organized.	(−) Life is no fun when you play it safe.	(−) Unorderly
Neuroticism	**Adjustment**	**Neuroticism**
(+) I often feel helpless and want someone else to solve my problems.	(+) I am a happy person.	(+) Worrying
(+) I often feel tense and jittery.	(+) Most of the time I am proud of myself.	(+) Tense
(−) I am seldom sad or depressed.	(−) I get depressed a lot.	(−) Unnervous
(−) I am not a worrier.	(−) I'm uncertain about what to do with my life.	(−) Unworrying
Openness	**Intellectance**	**Openness**
(+) I often enjoy playing with theories or abstract ideas.	(+) I enjoy solving riddles.	(+) Philosophical
(+) I am intrigued by the patterns I find in art and nature.	(+) I read at least ten books a year.	(+) Imaginative
(−) I seldom notice the moods or feelings that different environments produce.	(−) In school I didn't like math.	(−) Unphilosophical
(−) I don't like to waste my time daydreaming.	(−) I hate opera singing.	(−) Uninquisitive

Note. Plus sign indicates a positive response; minus sign indicates a negative response.

R was also found to meet the strong geometric and substantive assumptions involved in assessment from the dyadic–interactional perspective (Wiggins, Phillips, & Trapnell, 1989). The IAS-R was recently extended to include adjectival scales that index the remaining three domains of the FFM: C, N, and O (Trapnell & Wiggins, 1990). This extended instrument—the IASR-B5—was used in the empirical work that is discussed later in this chapter. Representative IASR-B5 items are listed in Table 6.

HPI The HPI operationalizes the social–competency perspective with a six-factor variant of the FFM (Hogan, 1986). The first factor of the FFM was originally designated as the *Surgency/Extraversion* (E) dimension (Norman, 1963; Tupes & Christal, 1961). Subsequent formulations have emphasized the assertive component of this factor (e.g., Trapnell & Wiggins, 1990), the sociability component (e.g., Costa & McCrae, 1985), or both (e.g., Goldberg, 1992). Hogan (1983) felt that assertiveness and sociability were sufficiently conceptually distinct to warrant their representation by the two global domains of Ambition and Sociability, respectively. These two global domains of the HPI, as well as the other four (Likability, Prudence, Adjustment, and Intellectance) clearly reflect Hogan's (1986) intention to measure dimensions that have "broad, general importance for personal and social effectiveness" (p. 5). Items were generated for each of these dimensions by considering what a person might say to convince others that he or she was leaderlike, sociable, likable, self-controlled, well-adjusted, or intelligent (Hogan, 1986, p. 9). These items were grouped into homogeneous item clusters (HICs) within the appropriate global domains. Thus, for more fine-grained analyses, the global domains can be decomposed into 5–10 HICs. Representative HPI items are listed in Table 6.

Principal Components of Five-Factor Domain Scales

As should be evident by now, the three instruments just described were generated from different theoretical perspectives but were developed with reference to a common FFM structure. To the extent that the instruments can be demonstrated to share a common underlying factor structure, it is possible to interpret variations in patterns of factor loadings among the three instruments as differences in substantive emphasis that arise from differences in theoretical perspectives. To provide a simplified illustration of this point, we return to the data gathered on the 581 undergraduate psychology students, which included complete NEO-PI, IASR-B5, and HPI protocols.

We computed the intercorrelations among the 16 domain scales from the three instruments and subjected the intercorrelation matrix to a principal-components analysis. Both Kaiser-Guttman and Scree test criteria clearly indicated retention of five components, and these were rotated to a varimax solution. As can be seen from Table 7, the rotated component matrix of the five-factor domain scales is highly compatible with the hypothesis that the NEO-PI, IASR-B5, and HPI domain scales share a common underlying factor structure.

The pattern of factor loadings in Table 7 suggests that the NEO-PI and IASR-B5 are more similar to one another than they are to the HPI. The former two instruments provide the "defining" loadings on all five factors. The NEO-PI and IASR-B5 have similar conceptions of the nature of neuroticism, openness, and conscientiousness; and both were developed in part with reference to Goldberg's work on trait-descriptive adjectives. Table 7 also suggests that "dominant" and "sociable" interpretations of the first factor of the model converge on a common E factor, similar to that identified in earlier studies. Similarly, "openness" and "intellect" interpretations converge on a common factor, which suggests that the ultimate nature of this presently controversial dimension must be settled on other than psychometric grounds.

Overall, there are only three instances of "significant" (>.33) scale factor loadings occurring on more than one factor, and these may be interpreted in light of substantive emphases that arise from the different theoretical perspectives. The results of a more fine-grained analysis of these data suggest that the loading of HPI Ambition on both the E and O factors was primarily due to the Ambition HIC of "generates ideas" (e.g., "I'm known for coming up with good ideas"). The loading of NEO O on both the O and A factors was primarily due to the O facet of "openness to feelings" (e.g., "I find it easy to empathize—to feel myself what others are doing"); and finally, the loading of HPI Likability on both the E and A factors was mainly due to the Likability HIC of "likes people" (e.g., "I enjoy meeting new people").

We noted earlier that the present empirical analysis is a simplified illustration, and we would like to reemphasize that the scientific case for the robustness of the FFM does not stand or fall on this particular example. A more definitive design would be one in which the dimensionality of the five trait domains is assessed by the multiple methods of questionnaires, self-ratings, and ratings by knowledgeable others and evaluated by the confirmatory procedures of structural equation models. This is precisely what Borkenau and Ostendorf (1990) did, and their findings provide rigorous support for the FFM on the global level of domain scores. Other less elaborate but equally convincing studies could just as easily be cited (e.g., Goldberg, 1980; McCrae & Costa, 1987). The point we are perhaps beating to death is that despite differences in substantive emphasis that stem from the different theoretical perspectives, the FFM of personality structure provides a meaningful, representative, and robust framework within which it is possible to interpret the structure of personality disorders as represented in Table 4. The converse is not, in our opinion, true.

PERSONALITY STRUCTURE AND THE STRUCTURE OF PERSONALITY DISORDERS

Correlations Among Components

What is the relation between the five factors that we found to underlie the two sets of personality disorder scales and the five factors that we found to underlie the three sets of personality domain scales? A preliminary, and again highly limited, answer to this question may be obtained by examining the zero-order correlations among the five component scores for personality disorders and the five component scores for personality dimensions in our university sample. These correlations are presented in Table 8. Until quite recently, the five-factor tradition in normal personality assessment and the quest for a satisfactory taxonomy of disordered personalities have developed in relative isolation from each other. Because of this, we would certainly not expect a complete isomorphism between the two factorial solutions, as would be indicated by a diagonal matrix of correlations with only five elements.

The considerable number of moderate and substantial correlations in Table 8 is compatible with our general hypothesis that conceptions of personality disorders reflect the well-established five dimensions of personality. Different personality disorders would

TABLE 7

Principal Components of Five-Factor Domain Scales

Scale	I	II	III	IV	V
Extraversion (NEO)	.84				
Dominance (IAS)	.82				
Sociability (HPI)	.81				
Ambition (HPI)	.71		.38		
Neuroticism (NEO)		.92			
Neuroticism (IAS)		.89			
Adjustment (HPI)		−.84			
Openness (IAS)			.85		
Openness (NEO)			.80	.35	
Intellectance (HPI)			.72		
Love (IAS)				.83	
Agreeableness (NEO)				.81	
Likability (HPI)	.45			.68	
Conscientiousness (IAS)					.84
Conscientiousness (NEO)					.83
Prudence (HPI)					.65

Note. $N = 581$; loadings < .33 omitted. NEO = NEO Personality Inventory; IAS = Extended Interpersonal Adjective Scales; HPI = Hogan Personality Inventory.

be expected to reflect different numbers and different combinations of these personality dimensions in ways that can only be understood through conjoint factor analysis. The results of a conjoint factor analysis of personality disorder and five-factor inventories can be interpreted as an identification of the salient personality dimensions underlying conceptions of specific personality disorders.

TABLE 8

Correlations Among Personality Disorder Components and Five-Factor Components

Five-factor components	Personality disorder components				
	I	II	III	IV	V
Neuroticism	**0.57**		0.53	−0.19	0.27
Extraversion	0.14	**−0.71**	−0.40		
Agreeableness	−0.33	−0.46	**−0.47**		−0.20
Conscientiousness	−0.27			**0.63**	
Openness			−0.20		0.12

Note. $N = 581$; $r = 0.10$ is significant at $p < .01$.

Conjoint Principal Component Analysis

Having established that the personality disorder scales and the personality domain scales share dimensions in common, we now consider the joint factor space shared by the scale sets. From the intercorrelation matrix formed by the 35 scales, we extracted five components that were clearly indicated by both the Scree test and eigenvalues-greater-than-unity criteria. The varimax-rotated five-factor solution is presented in Table 9. It is clear from that table that the five factors are the familiar ones of N, E, O, A, and C. Within each factor, corresponding MMPI and PACL disorder scales have been paired, where possible, followed by the highest loading personality domain scales with labels in italics.

Because of the clarity with which the FFM appears in Table 9, it is now possible to interpret the principal components of personality disorder scales alone (Table 4) with reference to an operationalized model of personality structure. Earlier, we cautioned against optimistic expectations of an isomorphism between the five components of personality disorder scales and the five components of personality scales. However, in comparing Table 4 with Table 9, it is evident that almost complete convergence occurs on four of the five components and that only 4 of the 19 personality disorder scales in Table 4 do not load most highly on a corresponding component in Table 9.

The first component in Table 4 provides a bipolar contrast between avoidant (+) and narcissistic (−) personality disorders and is loaded positively by the MMPI dependent scale. As shown in Table 9, it is the global dimension of N (Component II) on which avoidant and dependent personality disorders are similar to each other and in contrast to narcissistic personality disorders. The second bipolar component in Table 4 contrasts histrionic and schizoid personality disorders along the dimension of E found in the first component of Table 9. The third bipolar component in Table 4 contrasts passive–aggressive and borderline personality disorders with the PACL dependent scale. Although only the latter scale loads on Component III of Table 9, components in both tables reflect A (and its opposite pole, antagonistic hostility). In Table 9, the MMPI borderline and PACL

TABLE 9

Principal Components for Combined Analysis of Five-Factor and Personality Disorder Scales

Scale	I	II	III	IV	V
Histrionic (MMPI)	.79				
Histrionic (PACL)	.73				
Schizoid (PACL)	− .77				
Schizoid (MMPI)	− .81				
Extraversion (NEO)	.86				
Sociability (HPI)	.80				
Dominance (IAS)	.73		− .34		
Likability (HPI)	.61		.50		
Ambition (HPI)	.55		− .38		.40
Borderline (MMPI)[a]		.69			
Passive–Aggressive (PACL)		.67			
Avoidant (PACL)	− .51	.65			
Avoidant (MMPI)	− .53	.64			
Dependent (MMPI)		.63			
Narcissistic (PACL)		− .37	− .36		
Narcissistic (MMPI)	.47	− .52	− .34		
Neuroticism (NEO)		.91			
Neuroticism (IAS)		.81			
Adjustment (HPI)		− .81			
Dependent (PACL)			.73		
Antisocial (PACL)	.36	− .37	− .60		
Paranoid (MMPI)[a]			− .41		
Agreeableness (NEO)			.77		
Love (IAS)			.72		
Compulsive (PACL)		− .35		.76	
Compulsive (MMPI)		.36		.47	
Passive–Aggressive (MMPI)		.34		− .35	
Antisocial (MMPI)				− .49	
Conscientiousness (IAS)				.76	
Conscientiousness (NEO)				.74	
Prudence (HPI)				.66	
Schizotypal (MMPI)[a]					.38
Openness (IAS)					.83
Openness (NEO)					.78
Intellectance (HPI)					.38

Note. N = 581; loadings < .33 omitted. MMPI = Minnesota Multiphasic Personality Inventory Personality Disorder Scales; PACL = Personality Adjective Check List; NEO = NEO Personality Inventory; HPI = Hogan Personality Inventory; IAS = Extended Interpersonal Adjective Scales.
[a]No PACL scales for these disorders.

passive–aggressive scales load strongly on Component II (N), reflecting the emotional elements of these disorders. The fourth bipolar component of Table 4 contrasts the conceptions of compulsive disorders with the MMPI conception of antisocial disorder along the dimension of C (Component IV of Table 9). Finally, the fifth component of Table 4 is positively loaded by schizotypal and paranoid disorder scales, with the former being related to O on the fifth component of Table 9.

The striking, and admittedly somewhat unexpected, convergences between the component solutions in Tables 4 and 9 serve to forestall the possible criticism that the inclusion of so many markers of the FFM in the conjoint analysis might have "swamped" the variance of personality disorder scales and forced them into a five-component solution. The original structure of the personality disorder scales was only slightly changed in the conjoint analysis; and these changes, in our opinion, are substantively understandable from the perspective of the FFM.

From a clinical perspective, the secondary loadings of the personality disorder scales on the five interpretable factors of Table 9 are perhaps of even greater interest than the primary loadings. These secondary loadings serve to characterize the multidimensional nature of some disorders (e.g., avoidant personality disorders are both neurotic and introverted), to distinguish one disorder from another (e.g., in contrast to avoidant disorders, schizoid disorders are mainly introverted), and to distinguish between alternative conceptions of personality disorders (e.g., the PACL antisocial disorder scale reflects hostility, surgency, and lack of neuroticism; whereas the MMPI antisocial disorder scale reflects mainly low conscientiousness).

We have previously provided more extended interpretations of the results of this conjoint component analysis, which are buttressed by regression analyses of the NEO-PI facets onto the component-specific personality disorder scales and by examination of the item content of the personality disorder scales (Wiggins & Pincus, 1989).[2] Widiger and Trull (1992) have also provided interpretations of the same component matrix within the broader context of the personality disorder literature.

DYADIC–INTERACTIONAL PERSPECTIVE

The Interpersonal Domain

Some of the more salient characteristics of the dyadic–interactional perspective were presented in Table 3. Our particular operationalization of this perspective is in the eight interpersonal circumplex scales of the IAS-R (Wiggins et al., 1988) that are embedded within the five-factor measures of the IASR-B5 (Trapnell & Wiggins, 1990). The structural model underlying the IAS-R is presented at the top of Figure 1, where it can be seen that the underlying dimensions of dominance and nurturance (DOM and LOV, respectively, in the figure) form a circumplex of eight interpersonal octants. The theoretical location of these octants is indicated by two-letter codes that preserve the 40-year tradition of circumplex representations of interpersonal behavior (Freedman, Leary, Ossorio, & Coffey, 1951). The eight octant labels that correspond to the alphabetic designations in Figure 1 are assured–dominant (PA), arrogant–calculating (BC), cold-hearted (DE), aloof–introverted (FG), unassured–submissive (HI), unassuming–ingenuous (JK), warm–agreeable (LM), and gregarious–extraverted (NO).

Although the interpersonal circumplex and the FFM were developed independently, personality taxonomists have recognized for some time that the dominance and nurturance axes of the circumplex are conceptually similar to the E and A dimensions of the FFM (e.g., Goldberg, 1981). It is only recently, however, that empirical correspondences between the two models have been examined in detail (e.g., McCrae & Costa, 1989; Trapnell & Wiggins, 1990). At the level of domain scores, the IASR-B5 and NEO-PI are essentially interchangeable, as can be seen in Table 7. However, within the plane defined by the bipolar, orthogonal components of dominance and nurturance, there are differences in emphasis between the two models.

The eight octants that constitute the circumplex model have been defined with reference to a formal

---

[2] The data set analyzed by Wiggins and Pincus did not include the HPI. Their results were highly similar and, if anything, clearer because the NEO-PI and IASR-B5 domain scales provided substantial and univocal markers of each of the five factors.

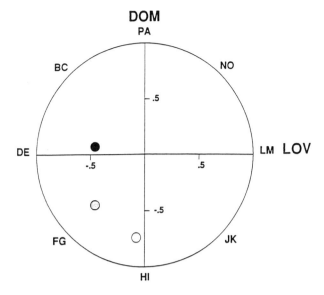

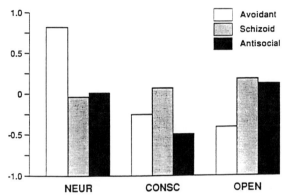

FIGURE 1. **Combined-model assessment of three personality disorder groups. From "Extension of the Interpersonal Adjective Scales to Include the Big Five Dimensions of Personality" by P. D. Trapnell and J. S. Wiggins, 1990,** *Journal of Personality and Social Psychology,* **59, p. 789. Copyright 1990 by the American Psychological Association. DOM = dominance; LOV = nurturance; PA = assured–dominant; NO = gregarious–extraverted; LM = warm–agreeable; JK = unassuming–ingenuous; HI = unassured–submissive; FG = aloof–introverted; DE = cold-hearted; BC = arrogant–calculating; NEUR = neuroticism; CONSC = conscientiousness; OPEN = openness.**

geometric model of personality structure (Wiggins et al., 1989). Consequently, when persons (or scales) are projected onto this plane, there are concrete substantive implications associated with different locations on the circle (e.g., Gurtman, 1991; Kiesler, 1983; Wiggins et al., 1989). Even small differences in

angular displacement between two clinical groups may have clear behavioral implications (e.g., Alden & Capreol, 1993).

The octants of the interpersonal circumplex are, to some extent, analogous to the NEO-PI facets for E and A and to the HPI HICs for Ambition and Likability. The principal difference is that the IAS-R octants are defined structurally, whereas the NEO-PI facets and HPI HICs are not. From the perspective of the FFM, this difference is of no great consequence; from a circumplex perspective, however, it may be important. To demonstrate this point, we projected NEO-PI and HPI domain scores onto the IAS-R circumplex that was obtained from our university sample. As can be seen in Figure 2, the sets of orthogonal coordinates for the three instruments represent alternative theoretical views on the optimal positioning of the first two axes of the FFM (McCrae & Costa, 1989). These differences span an arc of 135°, which encompasses most of the substantive distinctions among the bipolar variables of the interpersonal circumplex. Such differences in emphasis within IAS-R circumplex space have implications for the interpersonal diagnosis of personality. Although there are good arguments for orienting the two NEO-PI domain scales through extraversion and deference (e.g., McCrae & Costa, 1989), interpersonal theory is strongly committed to the proposition that agency (dominance) and communion (nurturance) are more fundamental conceptual coordinates for the measurement and understanding of interpersonal behavior (Wiggins, 1991).

Interpretation of the personality disorders from the structural perspective of the interpersonal circumplex considerably antedates the more recent applications of the five-factor perspective. Circumplex interpretations have been made of the personality disorders of first edition *DSM* (American Psychiatric Association, 1952) (e.g., Leary, 1957), second edition *DSM* (American Psychiatric Association, 1968) (e.g., Plutchik & Platman, 1977), and *DSM-III* (e.g., Kiesler, 1986; Wiggins, 1982). The nine studies listed in Table 2 continue this tradition. We have conducted a circumplex analysis of the conceptions of personality disorders represented by the MMPI and PACL disorder scales in our university

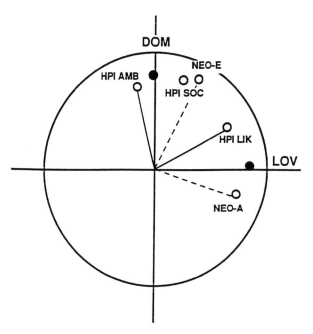

FIGURE 2. Projections of NEO Personality Inventory and Hogan Personality Inventory domain scales onto the circumplex of the revised Interpersonal Adjective Scales (*N* = 581). HPI AMB = ambition; HPI SOC = sociability; HPI LIK = likability; NEO-E = extraversion; NEO-A = agreeableness; DOM = dominance; LOV = nurturance.

sample. Two principal components were extracted from the intercorrelations among the IAS-R octant scales, and these components were rotated in such a way as to minimize least-squared differences between the theoretical angular locations of the octants and their empirical locations. The MMPI and PACL disorder scales were then projected onto the rotated circumplex by trigonometric procedures (Wiggins & Pincus, 1989). Six sets of the 11 disorder scales had sufficiently high communality values (distance from the center of the circle) to warrant interpretation of their locations on the circumplex. These scale sets were distributed around the entire circle and were located in the following quadrants: Histrionic in Quadrant I; narcissistic and antisocial in Quadrant II; schizoid and avoidant in Quadrant III; and dependent in Quadrant IV. These locations, as well as the similarities and differences in locations of MMPI and PACL scales with the same labels, were interpreted with reference to previous circumplex studies and related conceptions of personality disorders (Wiggins & Pincus, 1989).

Here, we focus on the finding, similar to that reported by others (e.g., Romney & Bynner, 1989), that significant projections on the circumplex were found for 6 of the 11 personality disorders. This finding has been described as indicating the "inadequate" nature of the circumplex for capturing the full range of personality disorders (e.g., Widiger & Trull, 1992). One could, with equal justification, characterize the FFM as inadequate for capturing the distinctions among 6 personality disorders within the domain of the circumplex model. It is more appropriate to recognize that the two models are complementary and that they operate at different levels of analysis (McCrae & Costa, 1989, p. 593). For that reason, we advocate combined five-factor and interpersonal circumplex assessment.

Combined-Model Assessment

We return, for the final time, to the data provided by our 581 university students to illustrate what we mean by *combined assessment*. In evaluating the discriminant validity of the MMPI personality disorder scales, we determined the location on the interpersonal circumplex of three groups of subjects who had received high scores on the MMPI disorder scales of avoidant, schizoid, and antisocial, respectively (Trapnell & Wiggins, 1990). As is evident from the top of Figure 1, the often difficult differentiation between avoidant and schizoid subjects is achieved by distinguishing the unassured–submissive (HI) tendency of the former from the aloof–introverted (FG) tendency of the latter. The cold-hearted (DE) tendency of subjects who scored high on the antisocial scale clearly distinguishes them from the other two groups. The bar graphs at the bottom of Figure 1 contrast the three groups on the remaining N, C, and O domain scales from the IASR-B5. Here, the critical role of neuroticism in further distinguishing avoidant from schizoid groups is quite evident. Avoidant subjects are also relatively closed to experience in relation to the other two groups; and, as expected, the antisocial group is low on conscientiousness.

The combined-model profile analysis illustrated in Figure 1 is a useful method for representing similarities and differences among groups for six of the personality disorders of *DSM-III*. Differences among the remaining five personality disorder groups would be

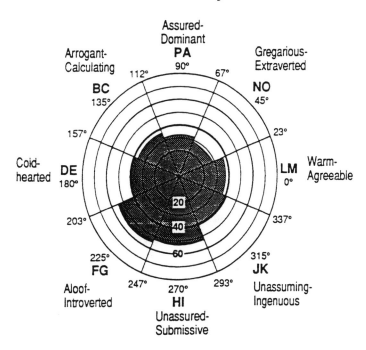

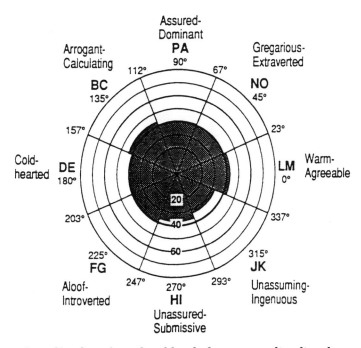

FIGURE 3. Interpersonal profiles for schizoid and borderline personality disorder groups.

expected to occur mainly in the bar graph portion of the profile. This is because the communality values of the interpersonal profiles for these groups were low, and hence, their location on the circumplex would be close to the center of the circle. Does this mean that the circumplex model is inadequate for representing these groups? No. It simply means that these groups did not have significant loadings on the interpersonal factors of the FFM (Factors I and III in Table 9).

The lack of significant factor loadings on dominance and nurturance for five of the personality disorder groups may be puzzling on first consideration. Does this mean that these subjects did not have coherent patterns of interpersonal dispositions? This question is best answered with reference to the full interpersonal circumplex profiles presented in Figure 3. The profile at the top of the figure is based on subjects who had elevations on the MMPI schizoid personality scale (which loads on the E factor). Note that the shape of this profile is the characteristic configuration we refer to as the "interpersonal spaceship" (Wiggins et al., 1989). The highest elevation is on the defining octant (aloof–introverted [FG]), which is followed by moderate elevations on adjacent octants (DE and HI) and then diminishes to a highly truncated opposite octant (gregarious–extraverted [NO]). This group profile suggests that there is a coherent pattern of interpersonal dispositions associated with elevations on the schizoid personality scale—namely, the aloof–introverted personality.

The profile at the bottom of Figure 3 is based on a group of subjects who had elevations on the MMPI borderline personality disorder scale (which loads mainly on the N factor). This profile does not have the distinctive shape we would expect from the semantic constraints of the circumplex (Wiggins et al., 1989): It is essentially circular in shape. If this were an individual profile of one of our subjects, then it would be considered unusual. However, it is a group profile, which is based on subjects whose individual profiles tend to have characteristic spaceship configurations but that differ from one another in their defining octants to the extent that they tend to cancel each other out (Pincus & Wiggins, 1990b). The group profile suggests that there is no single pattern of interpersonal dispositions associated with ele-

vations on the borderline personality disorder scale. A global disposition toward neuroticism may be associated with different interpersonal styles in different individuals (Shapiro, 1989). (In the rather special case of the borderline personality, different interpersonal styles might be observed in the same individual over time [American Psychiatric Association, 1987]). Thus, within the framework of the combined model, circumplex assessment of individuals who are classified as falling within any taxonomic category of personality disorder may be useful, regardless of whether the first two factors of the FFM are implicated in the definition of that category.

References

Alden, L. E., & Capreol, M. (1993). Interpersonal treatment of avoidant personality disorder. *Behavior Therapy, 24,* 357–376.

American Psychiatric Association. (1952). *Diagnostic and statistical manual of mental disorders* (1st ed.). Washington, DC: Author.

American Psychiatric Association. (1968). *Diagnostic and statistical manual of mental disorders* (2nd ed.) Washington, DC: Author.

American Psychiatric Association. (1980). *Diagnostic and statistical manual of mental disorders* (3rd ed.). Washington, DC: Author.

American Psychiatric Association. (1987). *Diagnostic and statistical manual of mental disorders* (3rd ed., rev.). Washington, DC: Author.

Blashfield, R. K., Sprock, J., Pinkston, K., & Hodgin, J. (1985). Exemplar prototypes of personality disorder diagnosis. *Comprehensive Psychiatry, 26,* 11–21.

Borkenau, P., & Ostendorf, F. (1990). Comparing exploratory and confirmatory factor analysis: A study on the 5-factor model of personality. *Personality and Individual Differences, 11,* 515–524.

Buss, A. H., & Plomin, R. (1975). *A temperament theory of personality development.* New York: Wiley-Interscience.

Carson, R. C. (1969). *Interaction concepts of personality.* Chicago: Aldine.

Cattell, R. B. (1943). The description of personality: II. Basic traits resolved into clusters. *Journal of Abnormal and Social Psychology, 38,* 476–507.

Cattell, R. B., Eber, H. W., & Tatsuoka, M. (1970). *Handbook for the Sixteen Personality Factor Questionnaire.* Champaign, IL: Institute for Personality and Ability Testing.

Clark, L. A. (1989, August). The basic traits of personality disorder: Primary and higher order dimensions. In

R. R. McCrae (chair), *Personality disorders from the perspective of the five-factor model.* Symposium conducted at the 97th annual meeting of the American Psychological Association, New Orleans, LA.

Coan, R. W. (1974). *The optimal personality.* New York: Columbia University Press.

Comrey, A. L. (1988). Factor-analytic methods of scale development in personality and clinical psychology. *Journal of Consulting and Clinical Psychology, 56,* 754–761.

Costa, P. T., Jr., & McCrae, R. R. (1976). Age differences in personality structure: A cluster analytic approach. *Journal of Gerontology, 31,* 564–560.

Costa, P. T., Jr., & McCrae, R. R. (1985). *The NEO Personality Inventory manual.* Odessa, FL: Psychological Assessment Resources.

Costa, P. T., Jr., & McCrae, R. R. (1988). From catalogue to classification: Murray's needs and the five-factor model. *Journal of Personality and Social Psychology, 55,* 258–265.

Costa, P. T., Jr., & McCrae, R. R. (1990). Personality disorders and the five-factor model of personality. *Journal of Personality Disorders, 4,* 362–371.

Costa, P. T., Jr., McCrae, R. R., & Dye, D. A. (1991). Facet scales for agreeableness and conscientiousness: A revision of the NEO Personality Inventory. *Personality and Individual Differences, 12,* 887–898.

DeJong, C. A. J., van den Brink, W., Jansen, J. A. M., & Schippers, G. M. (1989). Interpersonal aspects of DSM-III axis II: Theoretical hypotheses and empirical findings. *Journal of Personality Disorders, 3,* 135–146.

Dubro, A. F., Wetzler, S., & Kahn, M. W. (1988). A comparison of three self-report questionnaires for the diagnosis of DSM-III personality disorders. *Journal of Personality Disorders, 2,* 256-266.

Eysenck, H. J. (1947). *Dimensions of personality.* London: Routledge & Kegan Paul.

Eysenck, H. J., & Eysenck, S. B. G. (1964). *The manual of the Eysenck Personality Inventory.* London: University of London Press.

Foa, U. G. (1961). Convergences in the analysis of the structure of interpersonal behavior. *Psychological Review, 68,* 341–353.

Frances, A. J. (1980). The DSM-III personality disorders section: A commentary. *American Journal of Psychiatry, 137,* 1050–1054.

Freedman, M. B., Leary, T. F., Ossorio, A. G., & Coffey, H. S. (1951). The interpersonal dimension of personality. *Journal of Personality, 20,* 143–161.

Goldberg, L. R. (1977, August). *Developing a taxonomy of trait-descriptive terms.* Invited address at the 86th annual meeting of the American Psychological Association, San Francisco, CA.

Goldberg, L. R. (1980, May). *Some ruminations about the structure of individual differences: Developing a common lexicon for the major characteristics of human personality.* Paper presented at the annual meeting of the Western Psychological Association, Honolulu, HI.

Goldberg, L. R. (1981). Language and individual differences: The search for universals in personality lexicons. In L. Wheeler (Ed.), *Review of personality and social psychology* (Vol. 2, pp. 141–165). Beverly Hills, CA: Sage.

Goldberg, L. R. (1992). The development of markers of the big-five factor structure. *Psychological Assessment, 4,* 26–42.

Greene, R. L. (Chair). (1987, September). *Current research on MMPI personality disorder scales.* Symposium conducted at the 95th annual meeting of the American Psychological Association, New York.

Guilford, J. P. (1948). Factor analysis in a test development program. *Psychological Review, 55,* 79–94.

Gurtman, M. B. (1991). Evaluating the interpersonalness of personality scales. *Personality and Social Psychology Bulletin, 17,* 670–677.

Hathaway, S. R., & McKinley, J. C. (1967). *Minnesota Multiphasic Personality Inventory manual.* New York: Psychological Corporation.

Hogan, R. (1983). A socioanalytic theory of personality. In M. Page (Ed.), *1982 Nebraska Symposium on Motivation: Personality—current theory and research* (pp. 55–89). Lincoln: University of Nebraska Press.

Hogan, R. (1986). *Hogan Personality Inventory manual.* Minneapolis, MN: National Computer Systems.

Hyler, S., & Lyons, M. (1988). Factor analysis of the DSM-III personality disorder clusters: A replication. *Comprehensive Psychiatry, 29,* 304–308.

Kass, F., Skodal, A. E., Charles, E., Spitzer, R. L., & Williams, J. B. W. (1985). Scaled ratings of DSM-III personality disorders. *American Journal of Psychiatry, 142,* 627–630.

Kelly, G. A. (1955). *The psychology of personal constructs* (Vol. 1). New York: Norton.

Kiesler, D. J. (1983). The 1982 Interpersonal Circle: A taxonomy for complementarity in human transactions. *Psychological Review, 90,* 185–214.

Kiesler, D. J. (1986). The 1982 Interpersonal Circle: An analysis of DSM-III personality disorders. In T. Millon & G. L. Klerman (Eds.), *Contemporary directions in psychopathology: Toward the DSM-IV* (pp. 571–597). New York: Ronald Press.

Leary, T. (1957). *Interpersonal diagnosis of personality.* New York: Ronald Press.

Livesley, W. J., & Jackson, D. N. (1986). The internal consistency and factorial structure of behaviors judged to be associated with DSM-III personality disorders. *American Journal of Psychiatry*, 143, 1473–1474.

Livesley, W. J., Jackson, D. N., & Schroeder, M. L. (1989). A study of the factorial structure of personality pathology. *Journal of Personality Disorders*, 3, 292–306.

Livesley, W. J., & Schroeder, M. L. (1990). Dimensions of personality disorder: The DSM-III-R cluster A diagnosis. *Journal of Nervous and Mental Disease*, 178, 627–635.

Lorr, M., & McNair, D. M. (1963). An interpersonal behavior circle. *Journal of Abnormal and Social Psychology*, 67, 68–75.

McCrae, R. R., & Costa, P. T., Jr. (1987). Validation of the five-factor model of personality across instruments and observers. *Journal of Personality and Social Psychology*, 52, 81–90.

McCrae, R. R., & Costa, P. T., Jr. (1989). The structure of interpersonal traits: Wiggins' circumplex and the five-factor model. *Journal of Personality and Social Psychology*, 56, 586–595.

McCrae, R. R., & Costa, P. T., Jr. (1990). *Personality in adulthood: Emerging lives, enduring dispositions.* New York: Guilford Press.

McCrae, R. R., Costa, P. T., Jr., & Piedmont, R. L. (1993). Folk concepts, natural language, and psychological constructs: The California Psychological Inventory and the five-factor model. *Journal of Personality*, 61, 1–26.

Millon, T. (1981). *Disorders of personality.* New York: Wiley.

Millon, T. (1986). A theoretical derivation of pathological personalities. In T. Millon & G. L. Klerman (Eds.), *Contemporary directions in psychopathology: Towards the DSM-IV* (pp. 639–669). New York: Guilford Press.

Millon, T. (1987). *Millon Clinical Multiaxial Inventory–II: Manual for the MCMI-II.* Minneapolis, MN: National Computer Systems.

Millon, T. (1990). *Toward a new personology: An evolutionary model.* New York: Wiley.

Morey, L. (1985). An empirical comparison of interpersonal and DSM-III approaches to the classification of personality disorders. *Psychiatry*, 48, 358–364.

Morey, L. C. (1988). The categorical representation of personality disorder: A cluster analysis of DSM-III-R personality features. *Journal of Abnormal Psychology*, 97, 314–321.

Morey, L. C., Waugh, M. H., & Blashfield, R. K. (1985). MMPI scales for DSM-III personality disorders: Their derivation and correlates. *Journal of Personality Assessment*, 49, 245–251.

Norman, W. T. (1963). Toward an adequate taxonomy of personality attributes: Replicated factor structure in peer nomination personality ratings. *Journal of Abnormal and Social Psychology*, 66, 574–583.

Pincus, A. L., & Wiggins, J. S. (1990a). Interpersonal problems and conceptions of personality disorders. *Journal of Personality Disorders*, 4, 342–352.

Pincus, A. L., & Wiggins, J. S. (1990b, August). *Interpersonal traits, interpersonal problems, and personality disorders: Dual circumplex analyses.* Paper presented at the 98th annual meeting of the American Psychological Association, Boston, MA.

Plutchik, R., & Conte, H. R. (1986). Quantitative assessment of personality disorders. In J. O. Cavenar, Jr. (Ed.), *Psychiatry* (Vol. 1, chap. 15, 1–15). Philadelphia: Lippincott.

Plutchik, R., & Platman, S. R. (1977). Personality connotations of psychiatric diagnosis: Implications for a similarity model. *Journal of Nervous and Mental Disease*, 165, 418–422.

Rapaport, D. (1960). The structure of psychoanalytic theory: A systematizing attempt. *Psychological Issues*, 2, Monograph 6.

Reich, J. H. (1987). Instruments measuring DSM-III and DSM-III-R personality disorders. *Journal of Personality Disorders*, 1, 220–240.

Reich, J. H. (1989). Update on instruments to measure DSM-III and DSM-III-R personality disorders. *Journal of Nervous and Mental Disease*, 177, 366–370.

Romney, D. M., & Bynner, J. M. (1989). Evaluation of a circumplex model of DSM-III personality disorders. *Journal of Research in Personality*, 23, 525–538.

Shapiro, D. (1989). *Psychotherapy of neurotic character.* New York: Basic Books.

Society of Multivariate Experimental Psychology. (1990, January). *Multivariate Behavioral Research*, 25(1). [Whole issue]

Spearman, C. (1927). *The abilities of man.* London: Macmillan.

Spitzer, R., Williams, J. B. W., & Skodal, A. (1980). DSM-III: The major achievements and an overview. *American Journal of Psychiatry*, 137, 151–164.

Strack, S. (1987). Development and validation of an adjective check list to assess the Millon personality types in a normal population. *Journal of Personality Assessment*, 51, 572–587.

Strack, S., Lorr, M., & Campbell, L. (1990). An evaluation of Millon's circular model of personality disorders. *Journal of Personality Disorders*, 4, 353–361.

Thurstone, L. L. (1934). The vectors of mind. *Psychological Review*, 41, 1–32.

Trapnell, P. D., & Wiggins, J. S. (1990). Extension of the Interpersonal Adjective Scales to include the Big Five dimensions of personality. *Journal of Personality and Social Psychology*, 59, 781–790.

Trull, T. J. (1991). Discriminant validity of the MMPI-Borderline Personality Disorder Scale. *Psychological Assessment: A Journal of Consulting and Clinical Psychology, 3,* 232–238.

Tupes, E. C., & Christal, R. E. (1961). Recurrent personality factors based on trait ratings. (U.S. Air Force ASD Technical Report No. 61-97). Washington, DC: U.S. Government Printing Office.

Widiger, T. A. (1989). *Personality disorder dimensional models for DSM-IV.* Unpublished manuscript written for the DSM-IV Workgroup on Personality Disorders.

Widiger, T. A., & Frances, A. J. (1987). Interviews and inventories for the measurement of personality disorders. *Clinical Psychology Review, 7,* 49–75.

Widiger, T. A., Frances, A. J., Spitzer, R. L., & Williams, J. B. W. (1988). The DSM-III-R personality disorders: An overview. *American Journal of Psychiatry, 145,* 786–795.

Widiger, T. A., & Trull, T. J. (1992). Personality and psychopathology: An application of the five-factor model. *Journal of Personality, 60,* 363–393.

Widiger, T., Trull, T., Hurt, S., Clarkin, J., & Frances, A. (1987). A multidimensional scaling of the DSM-III personality disorders. *Archives of General Psychiatry, 44,* 557–563.

Wiggins, J. S. (1968). Personality structure. In P. R. Farnsworth (Ed.), *Annual Review of Psychology, 19,* 293–350.

Wiggins, J. S. (1979). A psychological taxonomy of trait-descriptive terms: The interpersonal domain. *Journal of Personality and Social Psychology, 37,* 395–412.

Wiggins, J. S. (1982). Circumplex models of interpersonal behavior in clinical psychology. In P. S. Kendall & J. N. Butcher (Eds.), *Handbook of research methods in clinical psychology* (pp. 183–221). New York: Wiley.

Wiggins, J. S. (1986). Preface. In J. S. Wiggins (Guest Ed.), Personality assessment in the 80s: Issues and advances [Special issue]. *Clinical Psychology Review, 6,* 357–361.

Wiggins, J. S. (1991). Agency and communion as conceptual coordinates for the understanding and measurement of interpersonal behavior. In W. Grove & D. Cicchetti (Eds.), *Thinking clearly about psychology: Essays in honor of Paul E. Meehl* (Vol. 2, pp. 89–113). Minneapolis: University of Minnesota Press.

Wiggins, J. S., & Broughton, R. (1985). The interpersonal circle: A structural model for the integration of personality research. In R. Hogan & W. H. Jones (Eds.), *Perspectives in personality* (Vol. 1, pp. 1–47). Greenwich, CT: JAI Press.

Wiggins, J. S., Phillips, N., & Trapnell, P. (1989). Circular reasoning about interpersonal behavior: Evidence concerning some untested assumptions underlying diagnostic classification. *Journal of Personality and Social Psychology, 56,* 296–305.

Wiggins, J. S., & Pincus, A. L. (1989). Conceptions of personality disorders and dimensions of personality. *Psychological Assessment: A Journal of Consulting and Clinical Psychology, 1,* 305–316.

Wiggins, J. S., & Trapnell, P. D. (in press). Personality structure: The return of the Big Five. In R. Hogan, J. A. Johnson, & S. R. Briggs (Eds.), *Handbook of personality psychology.* San Diego, CA: Academic Press.

Wiggins, J. S., Trapnell, P., & Phillips, N. (1988). Psychometric and geometric characteristics of the revised Interpersonal Adjective Scales (IAS-R). *Multivariate Behavioral Research, 23,* 517–530.

CHAPTER 6

PERSONALITY DISORDER SYMPTOMATOLOGY FROM THE FIVE-FACTOR MODEL PERSPECTIVE

Lee Anna Clark, Lu Vorhies, and Joyce L. McEwen

As is now well known, beginning with its third edition of the *Diagnostic and Statistical Manual of Mental Disorders* (*DSM-III*; American Psychiatric Association, 1980), the American Psychiatric Association created a multiaxial system for the diagnosis of psychopathology. Although the general impact of the new system has been substantial, the creation of Axis II for personality disorders has had especially broad and far-reaching effects for several reasons. First, the recognition that personality dysfunction represents a domain of psychopathology separate from the clinical syndromes of Axis I has responded particularly to a perceived need on the part of the therapeutic community. Even without a formal nomenclature to support their distinction, clinicians have long made a general differentiation between the chronic affective–cognitive–behavioral patterns that characterize personality and the more episodic manifestations of psychopathology that define clinical syndromes. Thus, the introduction of a separate axis for personality disorders made official a distinction that was already used informally in clinical settings. Nevertheless, it is important to emphasize that the boundary between the two types of psychopathology often is not distinct, and many disagreements remain regarding the appropriate placement of certain disorders on Axis I versus Axis II. We encounter this issue again later in this chapter.

Second, since the inception of Axis II, the number of research reports addressing issues relevant to personality dysfunction has increased dramatically, and many studies have confirmed the high prevalence of

these disorders (see Widiger & Rogers, 1989), although again many disagreements remain regarding the exact number and nature of specific disorders. Third, the profound impact of personality dysfunction on many other areas of psychopathology—from poorer psychosocial functioning in community samples (e.g., Drake & Vaillant, 1985) to poorer prognosis for those with various Axis I conditions (e.g., Pfohl, Stangl, & Zimmerman, 1984)—has also been well documented.

Apart from its impact on the clinical world, however, the creation of Axis II is important for another reason. *DSM-III* and its revision (*DSM-III-R*; American Psychiatric Association, 1987) explicitly define *personality disorders* in terms of personality traits that "are inflexible and maladaptive and cause either significant functional impairment or subjective distress" and define *personality traits* as "enduring patterns of perceiving, relating to, and thinking about the environment and oneself, [that] are exhibited in a wide range of important social and personal contexts" (American Psychiatric Association, 1987, p. 335). Significantly, this definition of traits—and its extension into abnormality—is congruent with both classical and prevailing views of normal-range personality traits (e.g., Allport, 1937; Janis, Mahl, Kagan, & Holt, 1969; Pervin, 1989), thus creating a theoretical bridge between disordered and normal-range personality. Traditionally, personality research has been carried out quite separately from research into personality-related pathology, but this new *DSM* view of personality disorders as sets of maladaptive traits provides a basis for integration of the two domains.

AN INTEGRATIVE VIEW OF PERSONALITY AND PERSONALITY DISORDER

A discussion of the many implications that a trait-based definition of personality dysfunction has for personality theory (and vice versa) goes beyond the scope of this chapter, but two points are particularly important in the present context. First, personality theorists generally view traits as continuously distributed and as exhibiting broad individual differences, such that some individuals may exhibit a trait very strongly whereas others may exhibit a trait very weakly, if at all. In other words, traits are dimensional in nature. Putting this view together with a trait-based conceptualization of personality disorders, we propose that there is a common set of personality traits with both normal-range and extreme variants. Taking the trait dimension of aggression as an example, extremely aggressive behavior and extremely unaggressive (i.e., very passive or unassertive) behaviors are both likely to be considered abnormal, whereas various expressions of moderately aggressive or assertive behavior—or extreme behaviors that appear only in response to highly unusual situations—generally represent normal-range phenomena.

A second important point is that personality theorists view traits not as fixed behavioral responses but as reflecting adaptations to the environment that are consistent within a certain range for each individual (Pervin, 1989). According to the *DSM* definition, a personality-disordered person's traits have lost this adaptive aspect and so have become dysfunctional. Thus, normal-range personality may also be differentiated from abnormal personality on the basis of the flexibility and environmental responsivity of the person's traits.

Integrating these two points leads to the notions that (a) there is a single trait structure encompassing both normal and abnormal personality; (b) within the normal range, personality traits exhibit broad individual differences that represent a person's characteristic and adaptive style of thinking, feeling, and behaving; whereas (c) personality dysfunction is characterized by extreme and inflexible expressions of these personality traits that represent dysfunctional ways of thinking, feeling, and behaving. This integrative view suggests that it should be possible to develop a single system for the assessment of normal and abnormal personality and to study personality variation across the full range of trait expression and adaptability. In this chapter, we describe the development of such an integrated system of assessment and explore its implications for a descriptive understanding of personality dysfunction.

Unfortunately, despite its explicit definition of personality disorders as maladaptive traits, the diagnostic formulation of Axis II personality disorders in the *DSM* was not based on personality theory. Rather, it reflected the prevailing psychiatric approach to diagnosis and thus was categorical, rather than dimensional, in nature. Originally, criteria for 11 diagnostic categories were developed. Two provisional diagnoses were then added in *DSM-III-R*, and the criteria for the primary 11 diagnoses were also revised.

This system has had tremendous impact on the study of dysfunctional personality. One direct result is that the vast majority of recent research has been based on a categorical model of personality dysfunction; more specifically, most research has focused on one or more of the 13 *DSM* categories. For example, in the most recent issue of the *Journal of Personality Disorders* at the time of this writing (Vol. 4, No. 2, summer 1990), only 1 of 10 articles directly assessed the subjects' personality traits (Livesley, Schroeder, & Jackson, 1990), and this assessment focused only on those traits relevant to the dependent personality disorder.

At the same time, however, recognition is growing that the current categorical system—indeed any categorical system—may not optimally describe the domain (e.g., Eysenck, Wakefield, & Friedman, 1983; Frances & Widiger, 1986; Gunderson, 1983; Widiger & Frances, 1985). One of the most severe problems with the current system is the high degree of comorbidity among the personality disorders. A recent review of four studies (Widiger & Rogers, 1989) indicated that, on average, 85% of patients with a personality disorder received multiple Axis II diagnoses. Furthermore, the average degree of overlap between any two pairs of personality disorders was 10%, ranging from 0% (between obsessive–compulsive personality disorder and antisocial personality disorder) to 46% (between borderline personality disorder and histrionic personality disorder). It is very difficult to reconcile these data with the ideal that classification of psychopathology into separate diagnoses requires that the disorders be distinct and that the number of cases that fall into the boundaries between disorder be relatively few (Kendell, 1975). Some have argued that these criteria should be applied only to classical classification systems because they are too stringent for the prototypical model used for the Axis II disorders (e.g., Cantor, Smith, French, & Mezzich, 1980). Yet even prototypical models are supposed to exhibit distinctiveness at the "basic" or most optimal level for categorization (Cantor et al., 1980), and it would be hard to argue that the personality disorders exhibit this feature.

A second problem with the current system stems directly from its use of a prototypical classification model for diagnosis. To receive a personality disorder diagnosis using the *DSM*, patients must exhibit the required number of symptoms (from a longer list) for that diagnosis. For example, they must have five of nine symptoms to meet criteria for borderline personality disorder or four of eight for avoidant personality disorder. Thus, with this system, two patients who share only a single symptom could both receive the borderline personality disorder diagnosis. On the other hand, if two patients had four borderline personality disorder symptoms in common, but one of them further exhibited a fifth symptom, then only the latter would receive the diagnosis. This system leads to tremendous potential heterogeneity within diagnoses and also to unrecognized similarity between subjects who do not share a diagnosis.

THE TRAIT APPROACH TO PERSONALITY DISORDER

As a result of such difficulties, a number of researchers have proposed that a trait-based dimensional system may be more appropriate for the assessment of personality dysfunction (e.g., Eysenck et al., 1983; Tyrer, 1988; Widiger & Kelso, 1983). However, there is relatively little research on personality-related pathology from a trait-dimensional point of view (see Clark, 1990). One reason for this has been mentioned: The categorical model of *DSM* is a powerful force in directing research. Regrettably, the existence

of an official categorical system that focuses on defining *personality disorders* (i.e., specific diagnostic entities) has impeded direct investigation of the maladaptive traits that characterize *personality disorder* (i.e., the domain of personality dysfunction). Another is simply historical: Because personality disorders have been defined categorically, trait theorists have generally not become involved in personality disorder research. A third important reason for the paucity of trait-based research in personality disorders is that adopting a trait point of view cannot be done in a piecemeal fashion. Although it is certainly possible to research specific personality traits— indeed, personality researchers have done so for years—such research is maximally useful to the extent that it can be fit into a larger context and thus contribute to the understanding of the overall structure of personality. Accordingly, before the trait approach can be extended to Axis II, one must first explore the boundaries of the domain and its constituent components. The considerable time and resources required by such research may have inhibited the application of this approach to personality disorders.

However, if—as we hypothesized earlier—normal and abnormal personality represent aspects of an integrated single domain, then it should not be necessary for personality disorder researchers to start de novo in defining the structure of abnormal personality. Theorists such as Cattell and Eysenck have spent years delineating the fundamental parameters that underlie the manifest differences among individuals. They—and many others—have developed sophisticated methodologies that have led to major advances in understanding personality and its structure.

More specifically, during their early development, the fields of personality and personality assessment were characterized by multiple and conflicting views, and personality itself was viewed by many as a hodge-podge of ever-proliferating trait constructs. However, a broad consensus has recently emerged that there are a limited number of basic personality dimensions. Although several competing models remain—and many specifics are still being hotly debated and researched—the five-factor model (FFM) of personality has gained wide acceptance as a framework for the global classification of personality traits (e.g., Digman & Takemoto-Chock, 1981; McCrae & Costa, 1987; Wiggins & Trapnell, in press). Moreover, as the existence of this book attests, the relevance of this model for clinical psychology, and especially personality disorders, is gaining recognition as well (see also McCrae & Costa, 1986). We hope that this book will help lead to (a) a broader awareness of the importance of trait research to the understanding of Axis II phenomena; (b) a realization that research on personality disorders can and should be informed by the theoretical, methodological, and empirical advances made in normal personality research; (c) an interest in Axis II on the part of normal-range personality researchers; and finally (d) a fruitful integration of these historically separate fields of inquiry.

In our own research applying a trait approach to personality dysfunction, we have built on earlier efforts by investigating three basic questions: (a) What are the basic maladaptive traits that comprise the personality disorders, as defined by current conceptualizations? (b) How can personality researchers assess these maladaptive traits—both clinically and through self-report—and what is the relation between these two methods of assessment? and (c) What is the relation between these traits and those already identified in normal-range personality? In investigating these questions, we adapted various methods—which were developed by Cattell, Tellegen, and others—for defining trait structure. Moreover, we were strongly guided by their theoretical and empirical research.

In the remainder of this chapter, we address the first of these questions by describing research that led to the identification of 22 personality disorder symptom clusters (Clark, 1990). To answer the second question, we then discuss the development of a self-report inventory that was designed to assess traits relevant to personality dysfunction (Clark, 1993) and present evidence—using this inventory in conjunction with clinical ratings of the personality disorder symptom clusters—that supports a trait-based approach to the assessment of personality-related pathology. Finally, we relate in some detail our investigations into the final question, that is, the relation between normal and abnormal personality. In

particular, through a series of analyses, we demonstrate that the FFM, which has provided a useful framework for understanding the structure of normal personality traits, is also highly relevant to the traits underlying Axis II. Although some five-factor instruments that were designed for normal personality may need to be adapted for optimal assessment of personality dysfunction, we conclude that the model itself is well suited for exploring the entire domain of adaptive and maladaptive personality.

SYMPTOM CLUSTERS IN PERSONALITY DISORDERS

Our initial approach to identifying the basic maladaptive traits that comprise the domain started with the personality disorder criteria by examining whether the criteria could be grouped into meaningful symptom clusters that reflect underlying trait dimensions (Clark, 1990). We began with all of the *DSM* personality disorder criteria and also included criteria from non-*DSM* conceptualizations of personality disorder (e.g., Cleckley, 1964; Liebowitz & Klein, 1981; Perry & Klerman, 1978) and from selected Axis I disorders (dysthymia, cyclothymia, and generalized anxiety disorder) that have been noted to resemble personality disorders in important respects (Akiskal, Hirschfeld, & Yerevanian, 1983; Frances, 1980). Twenty-nine clinical psychologists and psychology graduate students sorted these criteria into synonym groups, and a consensual set of 22 symptom clusters were identified through factor analysis (Clark, 1990). Two detailed examples of these clusters are shown in Table 1, and a list of all 22 clusters is given in the first column of Table 2 (for a complete listing of the criteria see Clark, 1990).

The clusters showed several important characteristics. First, the symptoms for a diagnosis never formed a single cluster; that is, every personality disorder was represented by a set of traits. Second, each of the symptom clusters contained criteria from more than one diagnosis. This result, of course, reflects the well-known problem of symptom overlap among personality disorders (e.g., Frances & Widiger, 1986) and simply confirms the fact that the various maladaptive traits comprising the domain are shared across diagnoses rather than being peculiar to one.

TABLE 1

Two Examples of Consensually Defined Personality Disorder Symptom Clusters

Diagnosis	Symptoms
	Social isolation
Schizoid	Almost always chooses solitary activities
	Neither desires nor enjoys close relationships
Schizoid/avoidant/-schizotypal	Has no close friends or confidants (or only one) other than first-degree relatives
Avoidant	Avoids social activities or occupations that involve significant interpersonal contact
	Reticent in social situations because of a fear of saying something inappropriate or foolish
	Impulsivity
Antisocial	Fails to plan ahead, or is impulsive
	Reckless regarding his or her own or others' personal safety
	Unable to sustain consistent work behavior
	Lacks life plan[a]
	Fails to learn from experience[a]
	Poor judgment[a]
Borderline	Impulsiveness in at least two areas that are potentially self-damaging

Note. Adapted from *Advances in Personality Assessment* (p. 253–254), edited by J. N Butcher and C. D. Spielberger, 1990, Hillsdale, NJ: Erlbaum. Copyright 1990 by Erlbaum. See Clark (1990) for a complete listing of the symptom clusters.
[a]From Cleckley's (1964) primary symptoms of psychopathy.

Third, many of the Axis I and non-*DSM* personality disorder criteria combined with the *DSM*-based symptoms in the clusters that emerged. This result can be interpreted in several ways. It may reflect simply a methodological artifact; that is, because the symptoms were included in the factor analysis, they had to load on some factor. However, these symptoms could have had low loadings on all factors, which would indicate independence from personality dysfunction; but this did not happen. Also, it was possible for these symptoms to form factors of their own, without any interrelation to the Axis II symptoms; and indeed, three factors (anhedonia, high energy, and negativism–pessimism) were composed primarily of symptoms from current Axis I disorders. Another interpretation is that the domain of personality disorders is somewhat broader than is defined currently by the *DSM*; that is, the same maladaptive traits that define the Axis II disorders may also play an important role in some syndromes that are currently defined as belonging on Axis I or that are not recognized currently in the *DSM*. In particular, some researchers have noted the overlap of certain anxiety disorders (especially generalized anxiety disorder and social phobia, generalized type) with avoidant personality disorder (e.g., Brooks, Baltazar, & Munjack, 1989; Turner & Beidel, 1989). Similarly, the construct of depressive personality disorder and its relation to dysthymia (especially primary early onset dysthymia) is a topic of current debate (e.g., Klein, 1990). Still others have proposed personality disorders for which affective symptomatology is central (e.g., hysteroid dysphoria; Liebowitz & Klein, 1981). As noted earlier, the boundary between Axis I and Axis II pathology remains in need of clarification.

Once these symptom clusters were identified conceptually, it was important to establish that they were also clinically meaningful and could be rated reliably on actual patients. On the basis of their state hospital charts, 56 inpatients were rated on each of the 22 symptom clusters by two independent judges (for a complete description of the sample and methods see Clark, McEwen, Collard, & Hickok, 1993). Ratings on 18 Axis I symptom clusters were also made to provide a basis for comparing the results. For both sets of symptoms, ratings were made on a 3-point scale: $1 =$ not present or of minor clinical significance; $2 =$ present but of moderate significance; $3 =$ a prominent clinical symptom.

The personality disorder symptom clusters proved to be quite prevalent in the sample: The median base rate for at least subclinical expression of the clusters (a rating of 2) was 44.7%, and several traits were highly prevalent. For example, impulsivity and dependency were judged to be present, at least subclinically, in over 85% of the sample. Only two symptom clusters—rigidity and high energy—had a very low prevalence (<10%). In contrast, the base rate for the Axis I symptoms was considerably lower ($Mdn = 14.3\%$; range $= 1.8\%$ for phobias to 76.8%

TABLE 2

Conceptual Correspondences Among Personality Disorder Symptom Clusters and 15 Personality Trait Scales From the Schedule for Nonadaptive and Adaptative Personality (SNAP)

Symptom cluster	Personality trait scale
Suspiciousness Hypersensitivity	Mistrust
Self-centered exploitation Passive–aggression	Manipulativeness
Anger/aggression	Aggression
Eccentric thought	Eccentric Perceptions
Antisocial behavior	Disinhibition
Suicide proneness Self-derogation	Self-Harm
Negative affect Negativism/pessimism	Negative Temperament
Dramatic exhibitionism Grandiose egocentrism	Exhibitionism Entitlement
Emotional coldness Social isolation	Detachment
Dependency	Dependency
Anhedonia (−) High energy	Positive Temperament
Impulsivity	Impulsivity
Conventionality	Propriety Workaholism

Note. Adapted from *Manual for the Schedule for Nonadaptive and Adaptive Personality (SNAP)* (p. 16) by L. A. Clark, 1993, Minneapolis: University of Minnesota Press. Copyright 1993 by the University of Minnesota Press.

for drug abuse or dependence). Thus, there was ample evidence of the existence of personality-related pathology in the hospital charts.

Moreover, the ratings of the symptom clusters proved to be reliable. When the two clusters with very low base rates were omitted, the average interrater reliability for the personality disorder symptom clusters was 0.73 (range = 0.57 for passive–aggression and exploitation to 0.96 for eccentric thoughts). (Intraclass coefficients, rather than Pearson correlations, were used to compute these reliabilities because the two raters were not always the same people.) This value indicates adequate reliability and is broadly comparable to the value of 0.88 that was obtained for the Axis I symptoms (range = 0.40 for obsessions–compulsions to 0.98 for eating disturbance, omitting low base-rate symptoms), which are usually thought to be considerably more reliable.

Although the rated clusters represent conceptual categories of broadly synonymous symptoms, they also appeared to have certain traitlike properties. Recall that the judges rated each symptom on a 1–3 scale. All three rating levels were used with some frequency: On average, approximately half (46%) of the patients were rated as showing symptoms of a given cluster, either fully (21%) or at a subclinical level (25%). These data suggest that the clusters were seen as having varying degrees of expression and were not simply present or absent. These data contrast sharply with the Axis I symptoms, which were rated, on the average, as subclinically present only 11% of the time, with a mean of 18% of the patients per cluster clearly showing the symptoms and 71% of the patients per cluster rated as symptom free. Thus, subclinical manifestations were more rare for the Axis I symptoms compared with the Axis II symptoms, which suggests that the latter were viewed somewhat more dimensionally by the raters. In future research, it will be interesting to replicate these findings with a longer rating scale to establish more conclusively whether personality disorder symptom clusters are indeed distributed more continuously (i.e., dimensionally) than bimodally (i.e., categorically).

A second traitlike property of the symptom clusters was their apparent stability. The judges rated each set of symptoms twice: first for current manifestations of each cluster and then again to reflect the patients' lifetime status. It is noteworthy that, with one exception (suicide proneness; $r = 0.48$), these two sets of ratings were highly correlated: The median r was 0.95, with a range of 0.75 (hypersexuality) to 1.00 (rigidity) (Clark et al., 1993). This may have resulted because the chart information was not sufficiently detailed to permit differentiation of the two types of ratings; however, an alternative explanation is that the patients' standing on the various clusters was, in fact, rather stable. That is, it is likely that those who showed evidence of aggressiveness, for example, in their lifetime histories also exhibited aggressive tendencies during their current hospital stay. In support of this interpretation, the corresponding correlations for the Axis I symptoms were somewhat lower, ranging from 0.33 (hallucinations) to 1.0 (phobias and obsessions–compulsions), with a median *r* of 0.84. Although this figure still suggests considerable stability, it nevertheless is consistent with the notion that many Axis I symptoms are episodic in nature.

These results demonstrate that conceptually identified personality disorder symptom clusters also have an empirical basis: The clusters were rated as moderately-to-highly prevalent in a patient sample, they have acceptable interrater reliability coefficients, and they exhibit certain traitlike properties such as dimensionality and stability. Although these results are encouraging, it may be premature to identify these personality disorder symptom clusters as traits. Before they could be called traits, for example, personality researchers would need to establish more firmly that they exhibit certain psychometric properties, that they are identifiable in nonpatient samples, that they can also be assessed through other methods (e.g., self-report), and that they are systematically (and appropriately) related to other personality-relevant variables. We address these issues in the following sections. Also, the relations between these clusters and another set of traits that were also designed to assess personality dysfunction are discussed by Clark and Livesley in chapter 18 of this book.

MALADAPTIVE TRAITS OF PERSONALITY DISORDER

Scale Development

Although the identified symptom clusters appear to have certain traitlike properties, the extent to which they represent personality trait dimensions is not yet clear. For example, the stabilities (i.e., retest reliabilities) of the clusters are unknown. Examining these reliabilities would require rating the individual personality disorder symptoms on multiple occasions, which is clearly a major undertaking, especially because relatively large samples would be needed. Nevertheless, such research would help to illuminate the structure and psychometric properties of person-

ality disorder symptoms. At the same time, however, it is important to investigate the trait structure of personality disorders using more than one method or approach to assess the convergent/discriminant validity of the emergent structure.

Clark (1993) has pursued one such alternative method. Specifically, using the symptom clusters as the basis for potential trait dimensions, Clark (1993) developed a self-report inventory (the Schedule for Nonadaptive and Adaptive Personality [SNAP]) that assesses 12 primary traits and three broad temperament dimensions. Because this instrument plays a central role in the results we present later, we briefly describe its development here. A broad range of items were written to assess 16 of the 22 identified symptom clusters, which were then administered to a large sample of university students. The content of the remaining 6 clusters appeared to be tapped by three broad temperament scales that were developed by Clark and Watson (1990), so independent scale development was not undertaken (a description of these scales follows shortly). Broadly following the method described by Tellegen (1982; Tellegen & Waller, in press), factor-analytic techniques were used to evaluate both items and constructs. That is, factor analyses indicated (a) the ways in which scales measuring a target construct could be improved (e.g., by eliminating poor items and adding relevant items to enhance internal consistency), and (b) the ways in which constructs could be developed (e.g., through the addition of items that would expand their scope or alter their focus). The independence of the scales from each other was also a consideration. This process was repeated through several rounds of data gathering and scale revision/cross-validation using university, outpatient clinic, and inpatient samples.

The primary scales just described encompass 16 of the 22 symptom clusters; the remaining clusters were assessed with three broad temperament scales that were developed by Clark and Watson (1990): negative temperament, positive temperament, and disinhibition (vs. constraint). These scales have been incorporated into the SNAP, but they are also available separately as the General Temperament Survey (Clark & Watson, 1990). These scales correspond broadly to three factors of the FFM: negative temperament with Neuroticism, positive temperament with

Extraversion, and disinhibition with (low) Conscientiousness.[1] However, it should be noted that two of the temperament scales were specifically designed to assess the affective cores of their respective dimensions rather than to sample their entire content domains (Watson & Clark, 1992, in press). The relevance of this point is noted in a subsequent analysis.

It is important to note that the symptom clusters themselves were considered directly at only two times: first, when they guided the initial compilation of the item pool and, second, with the publication of *DSM-III-R*, when the symptom clusters were expanded—and new items were written—to incorporate the revisions. Otherwise, scale construction was driven by the data, in terms of both developing the constructs that emerged from the analyses and making the psychometric refinements that these required. As a result, in several cases, clusters that were distinguishable conceptually did not yield independent self-report scales (e.g., the suspiciousness and hypersensitivity clusters combined to form a single self-report scale, mistrust). In other cases, two self-report scales were required to assess the content of a single conceptual cluster (e.g., the conventionality cluster contained content related to both conservative values and willingness to work hard, which split into separate self-report scales). Thus, although having their conceptual basis in the symptoms of personality disorder, the scales were ultimately not constrained by them.

To summarize, on the basis of the initial results, additional items were written to either solidify and refine the assessed constructs or expand them in directions suggested by the factor analyses. This process resulted in 12 primary trait scales that are each homogeneous in item content and that are maximally distinctive within the broad constraints imposed by the trait domain of personality disorders.[2] The scales are listed in the second column of Table 2 in such a way as to indicate their conceptual correspondences with the symptom clusters (shown in the first column). (Hypersexuality and instability have been omitted because of their lack of convergence with any SNAP scale; Clark, 1993.)

Clark (1993) reported extensive data regarding the psychometric properties of the scales. Briefly, the scales are internally consistent in both college and patient samples. Median alpha coefficients for the scales were 0.81, 0.83, and 0.76 in college, mixed-patient, and Veterans Affairs hospital samples, respectively. The scales were also stable ($r = 0.81$) over a short (1-week) interval in a patient sample and over moderate (1- and 2-month) time periods (median retest $r = 0.81$ and 0.79, respectively) in a college sample. Moreover, only one scale intercorrelation exceeded 0.50 in either the college or mixed-patient sample. This is especially noteworthy given the high degree of overlap that is typically found for self-reported psychopathology (e.g., Gotlib, 1984). Thus, the scales exhibit the psychometric properties that are appropriate to measures of trait dimensions.

Factor Structure

Although the primary SNAP scales are largely independent, an examination of the scale intercorrelation matrix nonetheless revealed notable clusters of interrelated scales (Clark, 1993). Moreover, all but 3 of 12 primary scales (eccentric perceptions, exhibitionism, and entitlement) are substantially correlated with one of the temperament scales. These data suggest a hierarchical arrangement, in which the 12 primary scales represent a lower order level of analyses and in which the temperament scales (each reflecting a group of primaries) comprise the higher order level.

To investigate this issue, separate principal factor analyses of all 15 SNAP scales were performed on each of the three samples mentioned earlier: normal college students ($n = 476$), a mixed-inpatient sample ($n = 55$), and a sample of Veterans Affairs hospital substance abuse patients ($n = 135$). As is typical

---

[1] Various labels have been used for the five factors: (a) *Extraversion*, surgency, positive affectivity; (b) *Agreeableness*; (c) *Conscientiousness*, will to achieve, constraint versus disinhibition; (d) *Neuroticism*, negative affectivity versus emotional stability; and (e) *Openness (to Experience)*, culture, intellectance. In this chapter, we primarily use the (italicized) labels of Costa and McCrae (1985) when referring to the FFM model but also use our own terminology when referring to three-factor models.

[2] Diagnostic and validity scales have also been developed but are not relevant in this context and so are not discussed here (for details see Clark, 1993; see also Clark & Watson, 1990, for more information regarding the General Temperament Survey scales and their development).

in analyses of normal-range personality scales, a few higher order dimensions exhausted the common scale variance, regardless of sample type. Specifically, the first three factors accounted for 94%, 89%, and 93% of the common variance (46%, 55%, and 51% of the total variance) in the three samples, respectively. Therefore, the three-factor solution was subjected to varimax rotation in all samples.

The structure proved to be quite robust, with highly similar factors emerging in the three samples, although some sample variation was noted with regard to secondary loadings. In only two cases, however, did these differences also suggest a possible divergence between the normal and patient samples. Thus, it is most likely that they simply represent random sample variation rather than evidence of different structures for normal and abnormal personality. Furthermore, the observed structure clearly replicated that found in analyses of many normal-range personality inventories, such as the Eysenck Personality Questionnaire (Eysenck & Eysenck, 1975), the California Psychological Inventory (Gough, 1987), and the Multidimensional Personality Questionnaire (Tellegen, 1982, in press; Tellegen & Waller, in press). Specifically, the factors were clearly identifiable as Neuroticism or negative affectivity, Extraversion or positive affectivity, and disinhibition versus Conscientiousness.

Neuroticism (negative affectivity) was defined by mistrust, aggression, eccentric perceptions, self-harm, negative temperament, and detachment; manipulativeness also marked this factor in the college sample. Extraversion (positive affectivity) was marked by exhibitionism and entitlement on the high end, with detachment and dependency loading on the low end. Finally, disinhibition versus conscientiousness was associated with impulsivity and manipulativeness on the high (disinhibited) end and with propriety and workaholism on the low (conscientious) end. Aggression also marked this factor in the patient samples.

In one sense, given the inclusion of temperament scales that were specifically designed to represent these three higher order factors, the emergence of this structure is not surprising. On the other hand, the origin and conceptual basis for the primary SNAP scales is rather different from that of most personality assessment instruments; that is, the items were based

on clusters of symptoms of personality disorder, not on trait adjectives or concepts per se. From this point of view, the high degree of similarity between the observed factors and those that have emerged in other instruments is striking, and it adds to the growing body of evidence indicating that the basic structure of personality is quite robust. Furthermore, it supports our hypothesis that there is a common trait structure that encompasses both the adaptive and maladaptive variants of personality.

There remains the question of why the remaining two factors of the FFM (Agreeableness and Openness) did not emerge in these analyses. One possibility is that their content is not sufficiently represented in personality disorder symptomatology to emerge as higher order factors. The chapters in this book, however, attest to the improbability of this hypothesis (see also Wiggins & Pincus, 1989). Another explanation is more methodological: Three of the higher order factors were directly represented by scales in these analyses, which would facilitate their emergence. In contrast, higher order scales that were specifically designed to assess Agreeableness and Openness were not included, which would likely hinder the expression of these factors. To test this hypothesis, it would be necessary to factor analyze the SNAP together with one or more measures of all of the five factors. We present such analyses later in this chapter.

Relations Between Self-Report and Clinical Assessments

Symptom Clusters We demonstrated earlier that the personality disorder symptom clusters have both a conceptual and an empirical basis. We have also shown that psychometrically sound self-report scales can be derived from these clusters and that they yield a factor structure very similar to that found using other instruments with diverse conceptual histories. It is now important to investigate whether the symptom clusters are related systematically to the trait measures that were developed from them. That is, what is the relation between the patients' self-views of their (maladaptive) personality traits and clinical ratings of criteria that are intended to represent behavioral expressions of these traits?

Clark et al. (1993) examined this issue and presented correlations between SNAP scale scores and the chart-based symptom ratings described earlier. Their results demonstrated that there are broad-based relations between the two types of measures: 17 of 22 symptom clusters were significantly correlated with one or more SNAP scale. Moreover, the observed relations were quite systematic. For example, clinically rated social isolation was related to self-reported detachment, whereas rated dependency correlated with both self-reported dependence and (negatively) aggression. Axis I symptomatology was also related to the SNAP scales, but the correlations tended to be weaker and, therefore, less easily interpreted. Thus, these results suggested that self-reported personality traits are more specifically related to personality disorder symptoms than to other types of psychopathology.

However, Clark et al. (1993) only examined these relations at the lower order level of individual scales. It is also illuminating to examine how the higher order factors are related to personality disorder symptom ratings. Therefore, we computed factor scores based on the three-factor solution that was described earlier and correlated these factor scores with the symptom cluster ratings, including symptoms from both Axis I and Axis II. All significant correlations ($p < .05$) are presented in Table 3.

Several aspects of the table are noteworthy. First, as was shown with the lower order scales, the observed correlations are, for the most part, straightforward and easily interpretable. For example, subjects who are low in self-reported extraversion (positive affectivity) are likely to be rated as self-derogatory and chronically depressed, whereas disinhibited subjects (i.e., low Conscientiousness) are rated as having prominent antisocial behavior and as being prone to alcohol abuse or dependence. Second—in contrast to the lower order scale level, at which the SNAP scales were somewhat more strongly correlated with the Axis II symptoms—the higher order factors are as broadly and as strongly correlated with Axis I symptoms as with personality disorder symptoms. The reason for this is unclear, but it may be that the higher order factors tap very broad-based dimensions of psychopathology that are equally reflected in Axis I and Axis II symptomatology. In

contrast, at the lower order level, specific relations between the SNAP scales and rated personality disorder symptomatology can emerge more strongly. This hypothesis is supported by the fact that fewer personality disorder symptom clusters were correlated with the higher order factors than with the lower order scales.

To summarize, the observed relations between higher order factors of self-report and clinically rated symptomatology were systematic and easily interpretable. At the same time, however, it appears that personality-related pathology may be understood more precisely by examining relations at the lower order level. Thus, with regard to the FFM, it may prove important to investigate the lower order or "facet" level rather than simply examining the five higher order factors. This is an interesting area for future research.

Correlations With Diagnoses Although our focus in this chapter is on personality disorder symptomatology, it is also interesting to examine relations at the diagnostic level. In addition to symptom ratings, hospital chart diagnoses were recorded for all 56 subjects in the inpatient sample (for details see Clark et al., 1993). An overall frequency count of the patients' most recent hospital diagnoses was made, and 13 diagnostic groups (8 for Axis I and 7 for Axis II) were created such that no group was either overly broad or too specific. For example, a large number of subjects received substance abuse diagnoses, so these were subdivided into three groups: alcohol, single drug, and polydrug abuse/dependence. In contrast, patients with adjustment disorder with depressed mood were grouped together with those having major depression because there were too few with adjustment disorder to form a separate category.

Each diagnosis was scored dichotomously as either absent (0) or present (1), and Clark et al. (1993) reported correlations between these scores and the SNAP scales. As was shown with the symptom ratings, the self-reports and diagnoses were broadly and systematically related. For example, a diagnosis of borderline personality disorder correlated significantly with self-reported dependency, self-harm, negative temperament, and (negatively) with entitlement. Correlations with Axis I diagnoses

TABLE 3

Correlations of Three Factor Scales From the Schedule for Nonadaptive and Adaptive Personality (SNAP) With Ratings of Axis I and Axis II Symptom Clusters in a State Hospital Sample

Scale	Axis II			Axis I	
	Symptom	r		Symptom	r
Negative affectivity (Neuroticism)	Suicide proneness	0.33*		Eating disturbance	−0.27*
	Aggression	0.28*			
	High energy	0.27*			
Positive affectivity (Extraversion)	Hypersensitivity	−0.27*		Chronic depression	−0.44***
	Self-derogation	−0.37**		Cognitive impairment	0.32*
				Inappropriate affect	0.31*
Disinhibition (vs. Conscientiousness)	Antisocial behavior	0.34*		Somatic complaints	−0.35**
	Anhedonia	−0.29*		Alcohol dependence	0.32*
				Vegetative signs	−0.31*
				Acute depression	−0.27*

Note. N = 56; all significant correlations are shown.
*p < .05; **p < .01; ***p < .001.

were equally strong and systematic. For example, subjects who received a diagnosis of polydrug abuse/dependence obtained higher scores on manipulativeness, disinhibition, impulsivity, and exhibitionism and lower scores on propriety and workaholism.

As with symptomatology, however, correlations with the higher order factors were not previously reported, so we report on those relations here. Table 4 presents all significant correlations, together with the sample prevalence for each diagnosis. In each case, scale means and standard deviations are also given for the subgroups of patients with and without each disorder, respectively.[3]

The higher order personality traits proved to be systematically related to both Axis I and Axis II disorders (although some of the data must be interpreted cautiously because of the low prevalence of certain diagnoses in this relatively small sample). One noteworthy finding is that correlates of the disinhibition (vs. the conscientiousness) factor were stronger than at the symptom level. The rather different self-characterizations of subjects who abused or were dependent on a single drug versus multiple drugs is particularly interesting. Those with a single-drug diagnosis portrayed themselves as higher in Neuroti-

cism and Conscientiousness, whereas polydrug users were (not surprisingly) low in Conscientiousness. This difference may have arisen because the single-drug abusers included a number of dysphoric subjects who had become addicted to prescription drugs, which they (over)used in order to cope with stress, whereas the polydrug abusers were more likely to be addicted to street drugs, to come from dysfunctional families, and to have a poor employment record and a history of antisocial behavior.

It should be noted that—due to substantial comorbidity—the reported correlations are not independent of one another. For example, both of the subjects who were diagnosed with antisocial personality disorder were also polydrug users, and slightly over half (55%) of those with borderline personality disorder also received a depressive diagnosis. It may be that the presence of a personality disorder diagnosis is a predisposing factor (either genetically or for psychosocial reasons) for development of the Axis I syndrome in these cases. (Of course, the reverse could also be true; but because the manifestations of personality disorders are often seen as early as adolescence and are long-standing features of the person's functioning, this seems less compelling.)

[3] Because the p value of the correlation between a dichotomous and continuous variable is the same as that for the t statistic comparing the means of the two groups, all mean differences are also statistically significant.

TABLE 4

Correlations of Three Factor Scales From the Schedule for Nonadaptive and Adaptive Personality With Chart Diagnoses in a State Hospital Sample

Factor	Diagnostic group (n)	r	Present (M ± SD)	Absent (M ± SD)
Negative affectivity (Neuroticism)	Bipolar disorder (2)	0.28*	1.26 ± 0.17	−0.05 ± 0.87
	Single-drug abuse (7)	0.27*	0.62 ± 0.94	−0.09 ± 0.85
	Eating disorder (4)	−0.38**	−1.18 ± 0.32	0.09 ± 0.85
Positive affectivity (Extraversion)	Borderline PD (22)	−0.40**	0.45 ± 1.01	−0.30 ± 0.75
	Unipolar depression (14)	−0.36**	0.57 ± 0.96	−0.19 ± 0.85
Disinhibition (vs. Conscientiousness)	Antisocial PD (2)	0.42**	2.07 ± 0.64	0.08 ± 0.89
	Polydrug abuse (28)	0.59***	0.55 ± 0.93	−0.57 ± 0.63
	Single-drug abuse (7)	−0.41**	−1.04 ± 0.74	0.15 ± 0.91

Note. Total $N = 56$; PD = personality disorder; n = number of subjects receiving each diagnosis. Means and standard deviations are standard scores. All significant correlations are shown. p values apply to both correlations and comparisons of mean differences (t tests).
*$p < .05$; **$p < .01$; ***$p < .001$.

However, another plausible interpretation of these data is that personality trait factors reflect common substrates that underlie the overlapping diagnoses and that contribute directly to their comorbidity. For example, being extremely low in Conscientiousness may itself represent a feature of antisocial personality disorder that also predisposes one to drug abuse. These are important questions for future research.

Finally, it is also important to emphasize that these correlations represent diagnostic covariations with personality factors within a patient sample. That is, they provide important information regarding differential diagnosis. For example, the data in Table 4 indicate that patients with borderline personality disorder score lower on the Extraversion factor than do other patients in the sample; this is a fairly strong diagnostic statement. This fact may also explain the paucity of correlations with the Neuroticism factor. Inpatient samples tend to have a restricted range on this factor because the majority yield highly elevated scores (Clark et al., 1993). Further research is needed to examine this issue.

Summary

Beginning with analyses of personality disorder symptomatology, we have examined the broad domain of maladaptive personality traits and have presented data that explicate the internal structure of this domain. First, we showed that clusters of personality disorder symptoms have several traitlike properties, such as dimensionality and temporal stability. We then described the development of self-report scales that were derived from these clusters of personality disorder symptoms. The trait structure that emerged from factor analyses of these scales closely resembled that identified in analyses of many normal-range personality inventories. Moreover, these higher order personality factors were shown to be systematically related to both the clinical ratings of symptomatology and diagnoses. Interestingly, these relations were not limited to the personality disorders but included strong Axis I correlates as well, which suggests that these higher order personality factors have broad implications for pathology.

In sum, we have shown that trait-based measures of personality disorder are related to aspects of both normal and abnormal personality, which thereby supports the hypothesis that a single personality trait structure underlies both domains. However, because our analyses examined only personality disorder symptoms and their associated traits and diagnoses, they leave several questions unanswered. First, we have not yet explored directly the relation between abnormal and normal personality traits, nor have we determined whether all factors of the FFM have maladaptive variants that are related to Axis II symptomatology. We now examine these issues.

RELATIONS BETWEEN NORMAL AND ABNORMAL PERSONALITY TRAITS

In this section, we report on a study in which subjects completed two measures of the FFM, which was designed to assess normal personality, in addition to completing the SNAP, which (as noted earlier) was developed to assess maladaptive traits. Through a series of correlational, factor analytic, and multiple regression analyses, we explored (a) the basic correlations between normal-range and maladaptive traits, (b) the structure of personality traits when both normal and pathological traits are considered together, (c) the ability of the FFM to predict traits of personality disorder, and (d) the relative effectiveness of the three- and five-factor models for predicting these maladaptive traits. Given that Neuroticism, Extraversion, and Conscientiousness have previously been shown to be related to personality-relevant pathology, we are particularly interested here in the extent to which the dimensions of Agreeableness and Openness are related to this domain.

Method

Subjects and Procedures Students who were enrolled in an introductory psychology course at Southern Methodist University (a private southwestern college) completed a packet of self-report questionnaires at the beginning of the 1989 fall semester. Two months later, 225 subjects from these same classes completed a second round of testing. The data we present here are on 194 subjects (68 men and 126 women) who completed both sets of measures. The mean age of the sample was 18.7 years (SD = 0.99; range = 17–23); 94% were White.

Measures *Goldberg Scales* The Goldberg scales (Goldberg, 1983) originally consisted of 40 bipolar pairs of adjectives, with each of the five factors represented by 8 adjectival pairs. However, McCrae and Costa (1985, 1987) expanded this instrument by adding 8 additional pairs that were intended to assess each factor. They were concerned with increasing the reliability of the factors and also broadening the content of the Openness factor. Subjects completed this 80-item version during the first round of testing.

They rated which adjective best characterized their personality on a 1–5 scale: 1 = very much like trait A; 3 = about average on this dimension; 5 = very much like trait B. Following McCrae and Costa (1987), a principal factor analysis of the items was performed for the entire initial sample (N = 603), and five varimax-rotated factors were extracted. Factor scores were computed for each of these factors and were used in the analyses that follow.

NEO Personality Inventory The NEO Personality Inventory (NEO-PI; Costa & McCrae, 1985) is a 181-item measure that was designed to assess the FFM. Items are rated on a 0–4 scale on the basis of whether (and how strongly) the subject agrees or disagrees with each statement. The domains of Neuroticism, Extraversion, and Openness are each composed of six 8-item facets, whereas Agreeableness and Conscientiousness are assessed simply with 18-item scales. Facets have been recently developed for these factors also but were not available for this study. Costa and McCrae (1985) presented extensive psychometric and validational data for the NEO-PI, and the psychometric analyses of our data (e.g., descriptive statistics, internal consistency reliabilities) yielded comparable results (Vorhies, 1990). Subjects completed the NEO-PI during the second round of testing.

SNAP Subjects completed the SNAP (Clark, 1993) in the second round of testing. The development, content, and psychometric properties of this inventory have already been described. It should be noted that much of the normative data presented earlier (e.g., regarding internal consistency, reliability, and factor structure) included these subjects' data.

Results

Correlational Analyses *Correlations Between Two Sets of FFM Scales* The two measures of the FFM (i.e., the NEO-PI and the Goldberg scales) were first intercorrelated to determine whether corresponding scales were actually tapping the same dimensions. Convergent correlations ranged from 0.42 for Openness–culture to 0.62 for Conscientiousness, which confirms the general correspondence of the two sets of scales, especially considering that these coefficients also reflect a 2-month retest interval. Discriminant correlations were all quite low, ranging from 0.23 (NEO-PI

Extraversion with Goldberg Agreeableness) to
−0.17 (NEO-PI Neuroticism with Goldberg Conscientiousness), with a median absolute value of
0.13.

Correlations between these five-factor measures
and the three SNAP temperament scales were also
computed, and they again confirmed the convergence of these measures: Convergence coefficients
of the SNAP temperament scales with the NEO-PI
and Goldberg scales, respectively, were 0.74 and
0.55 for Neuroticism–negative temperament, 0.61
and 0.46 for Extraversion–positive temperament,
and −0.59 and −0.50 for Conscientiousness versus disinhibition. Once again, it should be noted
that the SNAP and NEO-PI were assessed at the
same time, whereas the Goldberg scales were completed 2 months earlier. This explains, in part, why
the SNAP temperament scales converged better
with the NEO-PI than with the Goldberg scales. In
addition, because the SNAP and NEO-PI are both
questionnaires—whereas the Goldberg scores are
based on bipolar adjective ratings scales—it is
likely that methodological factors also contributed
to this pattern.

Discriminant correlations were again notably
lower, ranging from −0.28 (negative temperament
with NEO-PI Agreeableness) to 0.35 (positive temperament and NEO-PI Agreeableness), with a
median absolute value of 0.15. These results suggest that the scales possess substantial convergent
and discriminant validity. That is, although these
measures are not entirely interchangeable, the bulk
of their systematic variance appears to reflect the
same respective underlying constructs; therefore,
they should yield highly similar results in most
analyses.

*Correlations of the FFM Scales With Personality
Disorder Trait Scales*   Next, the two sets of five-factor
scales were correlated with the primary SNAP scales
(a) to replicate the relations observed earlier between
the primary trait and higher order temperament
scales of the SNAP, using the corresponding NEO-PI
and Goldberg measures of Neuroticism, Extraversion,
and Conscientiousness; and (b) to examine whether
any of the SNAP scales show significant correlations
with the other two higher order scales: Agreeableness
and Openness. Every SNAP scale proved to be significantly correlated with at least one of five-factor
marker pairs, which thereby supports the hypothesis
that there is substantial overlap between measures of
normal and abnormal personality. SNAP scales that
were significantly correlated ($p < .01$) with a particular five-factor scale in each of the two instruments are
given in Table 5; a stringent p value was used in this
case because of the large number of correlations (12
SNAP Scales × 10 Five-Factor Scales) that were
computed.

Looking first at Neuroticism, Extraversion, and
Conscientiousness, the five-factor scales yielded correlations similar to those found with the corresponding SNAP temperament scales, with few exceptions.
For example, three of the four scales significantly
related to Neuroticism in this analysis (self-harm,
mistrust, and aggression) also marked the Neuroticism/negative affectivity factor in the previously
described analyses. Similarly, three of the four scales
that correlated in this sample with Extraversion, and
four of the five that were related to Conscientiousness, marked their respective factors in the earlier
analyses. The most notable discrepancy involved
dependency, which correlated with Neuroticism and
(negatively) with Conscientiousness in these analyses
but which previously marked the low end of the
Extraversion factor. Nevertheless, it must be said that
overall the NEO-PI, Goldberg, and SNAP temperament scales yielded very comparable results, which
further demonstrates the convergent validity of these
instruments.

As can also be seen in Table 5, several SNAP
scales were strongly and significantly correlated with
Agreeableness and—to a lesser extent—Openness,
which indicates that these factors do indeed play a
role in personality-related pathology. It is interesting
to note that each of the scales that correlated significantly with Agreeableness was also related to another
of the five factors. Specifically, aggression was also
related to Neuroticism, manipulativeness (negatively)
was related to Conscientiousness, and detachment
(negatively) was related to Extraversion. This may
suggest that (dis)agreeableness is an important modifying element of personality, such that certain traits
become maladaptive only to the extent that they have
an additional, disagreeable quality. For example, it
may be that "pure" introversion can be adaptive,

TABLE 5

Replicated Correlations Between the Schedule for Nonadaptive and Adaptive Personality (SNAP) Primary Scales and Two Sets of Scales Measuring the Five-Factor Model

Factor	SNAP scale	NEO-PI	Goldberg
Neuroticism	Self-Harm	0.57	0.32
	Dependency	0.48	0.25
	Mistrust	0.47	0.28
	Aggression	0.35	0.25
Extraversion	Exhibitionism	0.64	0.52
	Detachment	−0.66	−0.54
	Entitlement	0.28	0.20
	Impulsivity	0.19	0.31
Openness	Eccentric Perceptions	0.26	0.30
	Propriety	−0.23	−0.30
	Impulsivity	0.22	0.23
Agreeableness	Aggression	−0.58	−0.48
	Manipulativeness	−0.49	−0.32
	Detachment	−0.38	−0.35
Conscientiousness	Workaholism	0.54	0.49
	Impulsivity	−0.51	−0.52
	Manipulativeness	−0.44	−0.30
	Dependency	−0.41	−0.34
	Propriety	0.26	0.24

Note. $N = 194$ university students. NEO-PI = NEO Personality Inventory; Goldberg = Goldberg scales.

whereas disagreeable introversion is maladaptive and expresses itself as detachment. Similarly, pure low Conscientiousness may simply reflect adaptively care-free, nondirected behavior; whereas disagreeable, unconscientious behavior may emerge as manipulativeness. This is an interesting hypothesis for further research.

It is important to note that Openness was significantly correlated with several SNAP scales. Although these correlations were not as strong as those with the other factors, they were nevertheless quite systematic. Eccentric perceptions appears to represent a cognitive pattern that is too open, that is, so open that it begins to lose its reality base. Similarly, being too open to experience may lead to impulsive and disinhibited behavior. Proprietous people, on the other hand, are characteristically rigid and closed to new ideas and experiences.

To summarize, separate measures of the five factors yielded a clear convergent and discriminant pat-

tern. More important, scales that assess maladaptive personality traits were shown to be related to measures of all five factors, which indicates the general relevance of the FFM for Axis II phenomena. However, several SNAP scales were correlated with more than one of the five factors, so it should be illuminating to examine the overall structure of these maladaptive traits in relation to the FFM. Therefore, in the next section, we describe a factor analysis of these measures.

Factor Analyses To investigate the combined structure of normal and abnormal personality traits, we first performed a principal factor analysis of the Goldberg, NEO-PI, and SNAP scales. The SNAP temperament scales were omitted from these analyses to avoid overrepresenting three of the five factors. Examination of the eigenvalues revealed that the first five factors (all with eigenvalues > 1) accounted for all of the common variance (55% of the total variance) and that successive factors each contributed an additional 5% or less. Therefore, we extracted five varimax-rotated factors; these results are presented in Table 6. For clarity of presentation, the FFM scales are given in boldface, and all loadings below 0.30 are omitted (for the complete matrix see Vorhies, 1990).

Several things are evident in the table. First, the five factors of the model emerge cleanly in these data: The corresponding Goldberg and NEO-PI scales each mark one—and only one—of the extracted five factors. Second, each of the factors is also clearly marked by one or more SNAP scales, and conversely, every SNAP scale loads strongly on at least one of the five factors (SNAP marker scale loadings range = 0.43–0.79). These results clearly indicate that the SNAP scales contain content relevant to all five factors and, furthermore, that the dimensions of the FFM account for much of the variance in traits of personality disorder. Third, seven of the SNAP scales have substantial loadings on more than one factor, which indicates—as was also suggested by the correlational analyses—that certain (lower order) traits in the domain of personality disorder are factorially complex. For example, as noted earlier, detachment loads negatively on both Extraversion and Agreeableness. Although the split loadings seem quite interpretable in every case, nevertheless, it will be

TABLE 6

Principal Factor Analysis With Varimax Rotation of the Schedule for Nonadaptive and Adaptive Personality Primary Scales and Two Sets of Scales Measuring the Five-Factor Model

Scale	N	E	O	A	C
NEO-PI Neuroticism	**0.79**				
Self-harm	**0.66**				
Mistrust	**0.62**			−0.36	
Goldberg Neuroticism	**0.57**				
Dependency	**0.50**				−0.39
NEO-PI Extraversion		**0.84**			
Exhibitionism		**0.79**			
Goldberg Extraversion		**0.69**			
Entitlement		**0.44**			
Detachment		**−0.68**		−0.34	
Goldberg Openness			**0.69**		
NEO-PI Openness			**0.60**		
Eccentric perceptions	0.41		**0.43**		
Propriety			**−0.43**		0.38
NEO-PI Agreeableness				**0.75**	
Goldberg Agreeableness				**0.68**	
Manipulativeness				**−0.62**	−0.33
Aggression				**−0.68**	
NEO-PI Conscientiousness					**0.77**
Goldberg Conscientiousness					**0.74**
Workaholism					**0.69**
Impulsivity				0.31	**−0.66**

Note. N = 194 university students. NEO-PI = NEO Personality Inventory. Goldberg = Goldberg scales. N = Neuroticism; E = Extraversion; O = Openness; A = Agreeableness; C = Conscientiousness. Highest loading for each scale is in boldface. Names of NEO-PI and Goldberg marker scales are also in boldface. Loadings below 0.30 are omitted.

important to replicate these findings in a patient sample. We are currently collecting such data using the SNAP and a five-factor measure.

To summarize, the factor-analytic results lend considerable support to two related hypotheses. First, the same underlying personality trait structure has been shown to emerge from analyses of normal and maladaptive personality traits. Once again, these data provide evidence of structural continuity across normal and abnormal personality. Second—and more specifically—a comprehensive (although perhaps not exhaustive) set of maladaptive traits has been shown

to correlate significantly with all of the dimensions of the FFM, which supports the notion that this particular model of personality has relevance for understanding personality disorder. As already mentioned, it will be important to replicate these findings in a patient sample, and the necessary data collection is already in progress.

Several interesting issues remain unresolved by these analyses. Needless to say, the FFM is not without its critics and rivals; most notably, three-factor models also currently have a number of prominent proponents (e.g., Eysenck, Gough, Tellegen, Cloninger). Although we have seen evidence of substantial overlap between the five-factor dimensions of Neuroticism, Extraversion, and Conscientiousness and the three higher order dimensions proposed by these theorists, each personality researcher has his or her own view of the basic composition and nature of these constructs; moreover, the scope of corresponding dimensions varies from researcher to researcher. For example, Eysenck's third dimension (labeled *psychoticism*)—although strongly related to (low) Conscientiousness—also clearly encompasses some of the variance accounted for by (dis)Agreeableness in the FFM. However, it is currently unclear whether one or the other model is generally more comprehensive and essentially incorporates the other, or whether each model assesses some portion of the personality trait domain that the other misses.

Therefore, it is interesting to investigate (a) the extent to which the additional dimensions of Agreeableness and Openness contribute to the prediction of maladaptive traits beyond that accounted for by Neuroticism, Extraversion, and Conscientiousness; (b) how well the FFM, as a whole, can predict scores on maladaptive traits; and (c) whether scales that were developed within the three-factor tradition can contribute information to the prediction of these traits beyond that attributable to the FFM as a whole. To answer these questions, we turned to multiple regression analyses.

Multiple Regression Analyses *Predicting Maladaptive Personality Traits From the FFM* To focus on the contribution of the FFM per se, rather than on a particular set of marker scales, we first created a single composite measure for each five-factor dimension by combining the two corresponding scores from the NEO-PI and Goldberg scales. To adjust for scaling differences in the measures, the scores for each scale were standardized before they were added. We then performed a series of hierarchical multiple regression analyses in which each of the primary SNAP scales was predicted from the five-factor dimensions using the following procedure. First, the dimensions of Neuroticism, Extraversion, and Conscientiousness were entered into the equation (Step 1). For each SNAP scale, the percentage of variance that is accounted for (R^2) at this step is presented in the first column of Table 7; the second column of Table 7 lists the specific dimensions that made a significant contribution at this step ($p < .05$), with the stronger predictor listed first. Openness and Agreeableness were then entered in Steps 2 and 3, with the stronger predictor entered first at Step 2. These R^2 changes are also shown in Columns 3 (for Openness) and 4 (for Agreeableness). Finally, the overall R^2 is shown in the last column; these values include the contributions of all five dimensions, regardless of significance of their contribution.

Several aspects of the results deserve comment. First, as can be seen in the table, the three dimensions of Neuroticism, Extraversion, and Conscientiousness account for a substantial portion of the variance in some—but not all—of the SNAP scales. Specifically, the multiple correlations (Rs) for impulsivity, exhibitionism, and detachment were all greater than 0.60, whereas those for several other scales (mistrust, self-harm, dependency, and workaholism) fell between 0.35 and 0.60. However, the multiple Rs for the remaining SNAP scales (eccentric perceptions, entitlement, propriety, and aggression) ranged from 0.26 to 0.35.

Second, for the most part, these findings parallel the results of the factor analysis (see Table 6); for example, manipulativeness split across the Agreeableness and Conscientiousness factors in the factor analysis and was also significantly predicted by both Agreeableness and Conscientiousness in the regression analysis. However, results for a few scales yielded discrepant results. For example, impulsivity was strongly related to Conscientiousness in both

analyses but had a secondary loading on Openness in the factor analysis. In contrast, Extraversion and Agreeableness were better predictors than Openness in the regression analysis. The fact that Neuroticism, Extraversion, and Conscientiousness were entered first into the regression equation may account for some of the observed discrepancies, but it is also possible that some of the SNAP scales are more sensitive to different analytic approaches, perhaps because they are more factorially complex.

Third, even when controlling for Neuroticism, Extraversion, and Conscientiousness, the dimensions of Agreeableness and Openness account for a significant portion of the variance in every scale, and their contribution is quite substantial in several cases. Specifically, Openness contributed most strongly to eccentric perceptions and propriety, whereas Agreeableness proved to be the strongest predictor for aggression and manipulativeness. It is noteworthy that these findings all support the factor-analytic results. Finally, when all five dimensions are taken together, they produce multiple Rs that are quite impressive, ranging from 0.40 to 0.70 across the 12 SNAP scales (mean multiple $R = 0.59$). Thus, in most cases, the majority of the reliable variance in these traits of personality disorder is explained by the FFM.

On the other hand, entitlement, eccentric perceptions, and propriety appear to fall somewhat outside the domain assessed by the FFM. These scales may assess traits that are rare in normal-range personality. Alternatively, they may represent pathologically extreme forms of normal traits, so they are not well captured by scales that assess the FFM, which were designed for use with normal subjects. We subsequently investigated this latter possibility.

To summarize, the dimensions of the FFM, as a whole, account for a large portion of the variance in most maladaptive personality traits. Moreover, the higher order factors of Neuroticism, Extraversion, and Conscientiousness do not exhaust the predictable variance; rather, the dimensions of Agreeableness and Openness are also important in understanding this domain. Finally, several traits appear to contain specific variance that is not well represented within the FFM. These may represent types of pathology

TABLE 7

Multiple Regression Analyses Predicting Schedule for Nonadaptive and Adaptive Personality (SNAP) Primary Scales From Three and Five Higher Order Dimensions

SNAP scale[a]	Step 1 R^2	Significant dimensions[b]	Step 2 R^2 change due to: O	A	Final R^2
Detachment	0.46***	E	0.01	0.05***	0.51
Exhibitionism	0.42***	E	0.01	0.04***	0.47
Impulsivity	0.40***	C, E	0.03**	0.06***	0.48
Aggression	0.12***	N	0.00	0.33***	0.45
Dependency	0.29***	N, C	0.04**	0.06***	0.39
Manipulativeness	0.17***	C	0.00	0.23***	0.39
Workaholism	0.35***	C	0.01	0.02*	0.37
Self-harm	0.28***	N, E	0.00	0.02*	0.31
Mistrust	0.21***	N, E	0.00	0.05***	0.26
Propriety	0.10***	C	0.10***	0.02	0.21
Entitlement	0.09***	E, C	0.03**	0.05**	0.17
Eccentric Perceptions	0.07***	N	0.09***	0.00	0.17
M	0.25		0.03	0.08	0.35

Note. $N = 194$ university students. N = Neuroticism; E = Extraversion; O = Openness; A = Agreeableness; C = Conscientiousness. N, E, and C were entered as a block, followed by O and A in a stepwise hierarchical regression.
[a]Scales are listed in order of decreasing final squared multiple correlation (R^2). [b]$p < .05$; predictors are listed in order of strength.
*$p < .05$; **$p < .01$; ***$p < .001$.

Additional Contributions of the Three-Factor Model in Predicting Maladaptive Personality Traits We now turn to an investigation of the third issue raised earlier; that is, to what extent do scales that have been developed within the three-factor tradition contribute variance to the prediction of maladaptive traits beyond the variance captured by the FFM as a whole? Similar to the FFM, three-factor models have largely focused on normal-range personality variation. Nevertheless, abnormal behavior has played a more prominent role in the conceptualization of these three-factor models from their inception. Thus, one might expect that scales developed within this tradition would assess some trait variance relevant to psychopathology (and particularly personality disorders) that is not well represented in measures of the FFM. To investigate this issue, we again performed a series of hierarchical regression analyses to predict the primary SNAP scales. In these analyses, we first entered all of the five-factor scores as a block in Step 1. These results (given in the first column of Table 8) correspond to the last column in Table 7; Column 2 in Table 8 lists the specific dimensions that made significant contributions at this step (results differ slightly in some cases from those presented in Table 7 because of differences in the order of entry). We then entered the three SNAP temperament scales, with the predictors entered in order of strength at each step.[4] These changes in the squared multiple

[4] The disinhibition scale shares items with several primary SNAP scales; for the regressions involving these scales, the respective overlapping items were removed from the disinhibition scale.

TABLE 8

Multiple Regression Analyses Assessing the Additional Contribution of the Three-Factor Model Over the Five-Factor Model in Predicting Schedule for Nonadaptive and Adaptive Personality (SNAP) Primary Scales

SNAP scale[a]	Step 1 R^2	Significant dimensions[b]	R^2 Change, Steps 2–4			
			NT	PT	D	Total
Detachment	0.51***	E, A	0.01*	0.02**	0.00	0.03
Impulsivity	0.48***	C, E, A, O	0.00	0.00	0.08***	0.08
Exhibitionism	0.47***	E, A	0.02**	0.02**	0.00	0.04
Aggression	0.45***	A, N, E	0.02**	0.00	0.08***	0.10
Dependency	0.39***	N, C, O, A	0.00	0.02*	0.00	0.02
Manipulativeness	0.39***	A, C, E	0.02*	0.00	0.06***	0.08
Workaholism	0.37***	C, A	0.03***	0.09***	0.02**	0.14
Self-harm	0.31***	N, A, E	0.01	0.01	0.02*	0.04
Mistrust	0.26***	N, A	0.04**	0.00	0.01	0.05
Propriety	0.21***	O, C, N	0.01	0.03*	0.01	0.04
Entitlement	0.17***	E, A, O, C	0.00	0.09***	0.00	0.09
Eccentric perceptions	0.17***	O, N	0.09***	0.02*	0.01	0.12
M	0.35		0.02	0.03	0.02	0.07

Note. $N = 194$ university students. N = Neuroticism; E = Extraversion; O = Openness; A = Agreeableness; C = Conscientiousness; NT = negative temperament; PT = positive temperament; D = disinhibition. N, E, O, A, and C were entered as a block, followed by NT, PT, and D in a stepwise hierarchical regression.
[a]Scales are listed in order of decreasing Step 1 squared multiple correlation (R^2). [b]$p < .05$; predictors are listed in order of strength.
*$p < .05$; **$p < .01$; ***$p < .001$.

correlation (R^2) are also shown in Table 8, in Column 3 for negative temperament, in Column 4 for positive temperament, and in Column 5 for disinhibition. Finally, the overall R^2 change across Steps 2–4 is given in the last column; these figures again include all three temperament dimensions, regardless of the significance of their contribution.

First, it is noteworthy that each of the temperament scales contributes significantly to the prediction of five to seven SNAP scales, and in several cases, this contribution is substantial. For example, negative temperament adds an additional 9% to the prediction of eccentric perceptions, whereas positive temperament contributes an additional 9% to both entitlement and workaholism. Because these scales were specifically designed to assess the affective cores of Neuroticism and Extraversion, respectively, these data suggest that some of the emotion-related vari-

ance in these maladaptive traits may not be accounted for by the FFM. Disinhibition, on the other hand, was designed to assess a broad higher order factor, similar to that described by Tellegen and Waller (in press). In five-factor terms, we have shown that disinhibition is largely strongly related to (low) Conscientiousness, but it is also correlated significantly (-0.32) with Agreeableness. In this regard, it is interesting that two of the scales to which disinhibition contributed substantially—aggression and manipulativeness—were strong markers of the Agreeableness factor (see Table 6). It may be that these SNAP scales represent such extreme forms of disagreeableness that the FFM scales, which were designed to assess traits within normal range, fail to capture some of this (dis)agreeableness variance. If so, then disinhibition, which was developed with somewhat more concern for the assessment of psychopathology, may tap some of this remaining variance. As mentioned earlier, the role of (dis)agreeableness in personality disorder is an important area for further research.

A second noteworthy point is that the two SNAP scales that were least well predicted by the FFM—entitlement and eccentric perceptions—showed the greatest R^2 change with the addition of the temperament scales, so that a multiple R of 0.50 or greater is now obtained for all of the primary SNAP scales. This leads us to our final point: By combining the predictive power of the five-factor scales and the SNAP temperament scales, the average percentage of variance accounted for reaches a remarkable 0.42 (range = 0.25 for propriety to 0.56 for impulsivity). In several cases, the R^2 values approach the scale reliabilities (i.e., alpha coefficients), which suggests that—taken together—these models nearly exhaust the reliable variance of certain maladaptive traits. Thus, these results strongly support the claim that basic models of personality are broadly relevant to personality disorder and that these models are valuable in understanding the structure of maladaptive as well as normal-range personality traits.

TOWARD A DIMENSIONAL APPROACH TO THE ASSESSMENT OF PERSONALITY DISORDER

We have presented evidence to demonstrate that a dimensional approach has a great deal to offer to the assessment of personality disorder. For example, we have shown that self-report measures of maladaptive traits are systematically related to clinical ratings of personality disorder symptom clusters. These data suggest that self-ratings can play as important a role in screening for personality disorder as they do currently in the assessment of Axis I symptomatology such as depression, anxiety, somatic complaints, hallucinations, and delusions. Moreover, we have shown that the concepts and structures of normal-range personality are highly relevant to personality-related pathology. Specifically, we have presented evidence that the domains of normal and abnormal personality share a common trait structure, and we have hypothesized that what differentiates the ordered from the disordered personality is not its component traits per

se but whether the trait expression is moderate or extreme, flexible or rigid, and adaptive or maladaptive.

Although these results may technically represent new information, they will come as no surprise to many readers. Indeed, the theoretical merits of a dimensional system for understanding personality disorder have been touted for some time now. Nevertheless, empirical research in this area has not proceeded very far, in part, because of the lack of assessment instruments for investigating personality disorder dimensionally. However, our results suggest that it may not be necessary to develop entirely new instruments to assess the traits underlying personality disorder. Rather, if normal and abnormal personality share a common trait structure, then the development of instruments for assessing maladaptive traits can build upon the extensive knowledge base of personality psychology that has been accumulating since the 1930s. Moreover, many existing personality tests (such as those we have considered here) may prove useful with personality-disordered populations, although some adaptation may be needed to maximize their utility in clinical settings. In addition, we have shown that the SNAP (the scales of which were based conceptually on personality disorder symptom clusters) provides reliable and reasonably independent measures of maladaptive personality traits. Its scales have been shown to be systematically related both to personality disorder symptoms and to measures of normal-range personality; therefore, we believe it will prove to be a useful tool in exploring the interface between normal and abnormal personality.

In conclusion, the findings reported here have significant implications for both normal personality and personality disorder. Demonstration of the relevance of normal personality structure for personality disorder gives Axis II researchers access to sophisticated research methodologies, a rich knowledge base, and well-developed theoretical structures. On the other hand, for the traditional field of personality, awareness of its importance to personality disorders opens up a new arena in which to expand its knowledge, apply its methods, and test its theories. We hope that recognition of the structural unity of personality will foster research and promote integration of the fields of normal and abnormal personality. Clearly, the understanding of personality and its pathology will be greatly enhanced as researchers in both domains recognize and develop their common interest.

References

Akiskal, H. S., Hirschfeld, R. M., & Yerevanian, B. I. (1983). The relationship of personality to affective disorder. *Archives of General Psychiatry, 40,* 801–810.

Allport, G. W. (1937). *Personality: A psychological interpretation.* New York: Holt, Rinehart & Winston.

American Psychiatric Association. (1980). *Diagnostic and statistical manual of mental disorders* (3rd ed.). Washington, DC: Author.

American Psychiatric Association. (1987). *Diagnostic and statistical manual of mental disorders* (3rd ed., rev.). Washington, DC: Author.

Brooks, R. B., Baltazar, P. L., & Munjack, D. J. (1989). Co-occurrence of personality disorders with panic disorder, social phobia, and generalized anxiety disorder: A review of the literature. *Journal of Anxiety Disorders, 29,* 259–285.

Butcher, J. N., & Spielberger, C. D. (Eds.). (1990). *Advances in personality assessment* (Vol. 8). Hillsdale, NJ: Erlbaum.

Cantor, N., Smith, E. E., French, R. de S., & Mezzich, J. (1980). Psychiatric diagnosis as prototype categorization. *Journal of Abnormal Psychology, 89,* 181–193.

Clark, L. A. (1990). Toward a consensual set of symptom clusters for assessment of personality disorder. In J. N. Butcher & C. D. Spielberger (Eds.), *Advances in personality assessment* (Vol. 8, pp. 243–266). Hillsdale, NJ: Erlbaum.

Clark, L. A. (1993). *Manual for the Schedule for Nonadaptive and Adaptive Personality (SNAP).* Minneapolis: University of Minnesota Press.

Clark, L. A., McEwen, J., Collard, L. M., & Hickok, L. G. (1993). Symptoms and traits of personality disorder: Two new methods for their assessment. *Psychological Assessment, 5,* 81–91.

Clark, L. A., & Watson, D. W. (1990). *General Temperament Survey (GTS).* Unpublished manuscript, Southern Methodist University.

Cleckley, H. (1964). *The mask of sanity* (4th ed.). St. Louis, MO: Mosby.

Costa, P. T., Jr., & McCrae, R. R. (1985). *The NEO Personality Inventory manual.* Odessa, FL: Psychological Assessment Resources.

Digman, J., & Takemoto-Chock, N. K. (1981). Factors in the natural language of personality: Re-analysis and comparison of six major studies. *Multivariate Behavioral Research, 16,* 149–170.

Drake, R. E., & Vaillant, G. E. (1985). A validity study of Axis II of DSM-III. *American Journal of Psychiatry, 142,* 553–558.

Eysenck, H. J., & Eysenck, S. B. G. (1975). *Eysenck Personality Questionnaire manual.* San Diego, CA: EdITS.

Eysenck, H. J., Wakefield, J. A., & Friedman, A. F. (1983). Diagnosis and clinical assessment: The DSM-III. *Annual Review of Psychology, 34,* 167–193.

Frances, A. J. (1980). The DSM-III personality disorders section: A commentary. *American Journal of Psychiatry, 137,* 1050–1054.

Frances, A. J., & Widiger, T. (1986). The classification of personality disorders: An overview of problems and solutions. In A. J. Frances & R. E. Hales (Eds.), *Psychiatry update: The American Psychiatric Association Annual Review.* (Vol. 5, pp. 240–257). Washington, DC: American Psychiatric Press.

Goldberg, L. R. (1983, June). *The magical number five, plus or minus two: Some conjectures on the dimensionality of personality.* Paper presented at Gerontology Research Center research seminar, Baltimore, MD.

Gotlib, I. H. (1984). Depression and general psychopathology in university students. *Journal of Abnormal Psychology, 93,* 19–30.

Gough, H. G. (1987). *California Psychological Inventory administrator's guide.* Palo Alto, CA: Consulting Psychologist Press.

Gunderson, J. G. (1983). DSM-III diagnoses of personality disorders. In J. P. Frosch (Ed.), *Current perspectives on personality disorders* (pp. 20–39). Washington DC: American Psychiatric Press.

Janis, I. L., Mahl, G. F., Kagan, J., & Holt, R. R. (1969). *Personality: Dynamics, development, and assessment.* New York: Harcourt, Brace & World.

Kendell, R. (1975). *The role of diagnosis in psychiatry.* Oxford, UK: Blackwell Scientific.

Klein, D. N. (1990). The depressive personality: Reliability, validity, and relationship to dysthymia. *Journal of Abnormal Psychology, 99,* 412–421.

Liebowitz, M. R., & Klein, D. F. (1981). Interrelationship of hysteroid dysphoria and borderline personality disorder. *Psychiatric Clinics of North America, 4,* 67–87.

Livesley, W. J., Schroeder, M. L., & Jackson, D. N. (1990). Dependent personality disorder and attachment problems. *Journal of Personality Disorders, 4,* 131–140.

McCrae, R. R., & Costa, P. T., Jr. (1985). Updating Norman's "Adequate Taxonomy": Intelligence and personality dimensions in natural language and in questionnaires. *Journal of Personality and Social Psychology, 49,* 710–721.

McCrae, R. R., & Costa, P. T., Jr. (1986). Clinical assessment can benefit from recent advances in personality psychology. *American Psychologist, 41,* 1001–1002.

McCrae, R. R., & Costa, P. T., Jr. (1987). Validation of a five-factor model of personality across instruments and observers. *Journal of Personality and Social Psychology, 52,* 81–90.

Perry, J. C., & Klerman, G. L. (1978). The borderline patient: A comparative analysis of four sets of diagnostic criteria. *Archives of General Psychiatry, 35,* 141–150.

Pervin, L. A. (1989). *Personality: Theory and research.* New York: Wiley.

Pfohl, B., Stangl, D., & Zimmerman, M. (1984). The implications of DSM-III personality disorders for patients with major depression. *Journal of Affective Disorders, 7,* 309–318.

Tellegen, A. (1982). *A brief manual for the Differential Personality Questionnaire.* Unpublished manuscript, University of Minnesota.

Tellegen, A. (in press). *Multidimensional Personality Questionnaire.* Minneapolis: University of Minnesota Press.

Tellegen, A., & Waller, N. (in press). Exploring personality through test construction: Development of the Multidimensional Personality Questionnaire. In S. R. Briggs & J. M. Cheek (Eds.), *Personality measures: Development and evaluation* (Vol. 1). Greenwich, CT: JAI Press.

Turner, S. M., & Beidel, D. C. (1989). Social phobia: Clinical syndrome, diagnosis, and comorbidity. *Clinical Psychology Review, 9,* 3–18.

Tyrer, P. (1988). What's wrong with DSM-III personality disorders? *Journal of Personality Disorders, 2,* 281–291.

Vorhies, L. (1990). *The factor structure of personality dimensions: Three factors or five?* Unpublished master's thesis, Southern Methodist University.

Watson, D., & Clark, L. A. (1992). On traits and temperament: General and specific factors of emotional experience and their relations to the five-factor model. *Journal of Personality, 60,* 443–476.

Watson, D., & Clark, L. A. (in press). The positive emotional core of extraversion. In R. T. Hogan, J. Johnson, & S. R. Briggs (Eds.), *Handbook of personality psychology.* San Diego, CA: Academic Press.

Widiger, T. A., & Frances, A. (1985). The DSM-III personality disorders: Perspectives from psychology. *Archives of General Psychiatry, 42,* 615–623.

Widiger, T. A., & Kelso, K. (1983). Psychodiagnosis of Axis II. *Clinical Psychology Review, 2,* 115–135.

Widiger, T. A., & Rogers, J. H. (1989). Prevalence and comorbidity of personality disorders. *Psychiatric Annals, 19,* 132–136.

Wiggins, J. S., & Pincus, A. L. (1989). Conceptions of personality disorders and dimensions of personality. *Psychological Assessment, 1,* 305–316.

Wiggins, J. S., & Trapnell, P. D. (in press). Personality structure: The return of the Big Five. In R. T. Hogan, J. Johnson, & S. R. Briggs (Eds.), *Handbook of personality psychology.* San Diego, CA: Academic Press.

CHAPTER 7

DIMENSIONS OF PERSONALITY DISORDER AND THE FIVE-FACTOR MODEL OF PERSONALITY

Marsha L. Schroeder, Janice A. Wormworth, and W. John Livesley

The relation between the contemporary classification of personality disorder and the structure of normal personality has only recently received attention (Costa & McCrae, 1990; Wiggins & Pincus, 1989). In many ways, the classification of personality disorders and the study of personality structure have proceeded along independent paths using different approaches and methods. Conceptions of normal personality structure have emerged from extensive empirical studies, whereas conceptions of personality disorders are largely the consensus of experts who base their decisions on traditional clinical concepts and accumulated clinical experience. Consequently, classifications of personality disorders consist of relatively unstructured lists of diagnoses that reflect multiple theoretical perspectives within the clinical tradition. They do not incorporate, to any significant degree, accumulated empirical knowledge of normal personality structure. The consequence of these developments is that current classifications tend to lack explicit structure and clear conceptual underpinnings.

Several proposals have been advanced to anchor diagnostic concepts to more satisfactory theoretical bases. Millon (1981), for example, suggested that diagnoses and diagnostic criteria could be derived from three basic dimensions based on social cognitive theory: the nature of reinforcement, the source of reinforcement, and the instrumental coping style. Cloninger (1987) proposed anchoring diagnoses in neurotransmitter systems. The merit of these approaches is that they provide an explicit rationale for determining the number of personality disorder diagnoses to be included in the classification and for selecting diagnostic criteria. A problem is the lack of an extensive theoretical rationale for basing the classification on a given set of dimensions. An alternative would be to relate diagnostic concepts to a general model of personality structure. This approach is particularly appealing given the emerging body of evidence in support of the five-factor model (FFM) of personality (Digman, 1990). With this approach, personality disorders would be conceptualized as extremes of normal personality variants rather than as discrete classes of behaviors, as is the case with the classification of the third, revised edition of the *Diagnostic and Statistical Manual of Mental Disorders* (*DSM-III-R*; American Psychiatric Association, 1987).

Initially, empirical investigations of the relation between personality disorders and personality examined the relation between personality disorder diagnoses and the interpersonal circumplex (Kiesler, 1986; Wiggins, 1968, 1982). Although many diagnostic concepts could be adequately accounted for by a two-factor model, an observation noted by Plutchik and Platman (1977), the circumplex does not represent all aspects of personality disorder. Cognitive traits, in particular, do not fit within this model.

More recently, studies have investigated the relations between personality disorders and the FFM.

The research reported in this chapter was supported by Medical Research Council of Canada grant MA-99424 and by a National Health and Welfare Canada Research Scholar Award to W. John Livesley.

Wiggins and Pincus (1989; see also Wiggins & Pincus, chapter 5) reported that personality disorders, assessed using the Minnesota Multiphasic Personality Inventory (MMPI; Hathaway & McKinley, 1967) personality disorder scales (Morey, Waugh, & Blashfield, 1985), could be adequately accommodated by the FFM when assessed using the NEO Personality Inventory (NEO-PI; Costa & McCrae, 1985). Costa and McCrae (1990) also presented evidence that the FFM could adequately account for personality diagnoses. When the five factors were measured by self-report, peer ratings, and spouse ratings, they were found to correlate with personality disorder diagnoses measured by MMPI scales. Significant correlations were also found with the Millon Clinical Multiaxial Inventory (Millon, 1982). These studies provide convincing preliminary evidence that *DSM-III-R* diagnostic concepts, as measured by the MMPI and Millon scales, can be adequately accounted for by the FFM.

In the study discussed here, we investigated the extent to which these observations generalize when personality disorders are conceptualized using an approach different from that of *DSM-III-R*. In earlier studies (Livesley, 1986, 1987), we attempted to identify the basic dimensions underlying the overall domain of personality disorders by investigating the structure of the traits defining each diagnosis. The resulting dimensions provide a representative description of the domain at a primary or ungeneralized level. Investigation of the relation between these dimensions and the five major factors provides alternative ways to test the generality of the relation between personality structure and personality disorders. In the following section, we describe the steps taken to identify the underlying dimensions of personality disorder. We then report on their relation to the NEO-PI dimensions.

DIMENSIONS OF PERSONALITY DISORDER

Those attempting to identify the underlying dimensions of the domain of personality disorders have adopted two research approaches. Hyler et al. (1990) factor analyzed responses to the Personality Diagnostic Questionnaire, a self-report instrument that assesses each *DSM-III* diagnostic criterion with a single item. The authors reported an 11-factor solution that they believed to underlie the diagnostic criteria. The value of this approach is that it suggests a structure underlying the domain defined by *DSM-III-R* diagnostic concepts and criterion sets. The method relies, however, on the use of single items to assess criteria that differ considerably in generality, tapping content ranging from specific behaviors to general traits. It also assumes that *DSM-III-R* diagnoses provide a representative sample of the overall domain. Several *DSM-III-R* diagnoses have, however, been criticized for poor content validity. For example, antisocial personality disorder does not include many of the features that clinicians consider important aspects of the diagnosis, particularly the interpersonal features associated with the traditional concept of psychopathy (Frances, 1980; Hare, 1983; Millon, 1981). Similarly, histrionic personality disorder omits many of the traditional analytic concepts of hysterical personality (Kernberg, 1984).

A second research approach attempts to specify the domain of personality disorders more comprehensively than does *DSM-III-R* before attempting to identify the underlying structure. Clark (1990), for example, used clinicians' judgments to identify the structural relations among descriptors selected to provide an overall representation of the domain. We used a similar starting point for our investigations.

From an extensive literature review, we compiled a list of descriptors for each *DSM-III-R* diagnosis (Livesley, 1986). Consensual judgments of panels of clinicians were used to identify the most prototypical features of each diagnosis (Livesley, 1987). We were able to order the features of each *DSM-III-R* diagnosis based on its prototypicality ratings. The list of highly prototypical features for a given diagnosis invariably contained several items that referred to the same characteristic. For example, features highly prototypical of paranoid personality disorder included "mistrustful," "feels persecuted," and "expects trickery or harm." All refer to behaviors that are indicative of "suspiciousness." Therefore, the list of features describing each diagnosis was reduced to fewer traits by grouping together those referring to the same behavior. We proceeded by using the most highly rated feature for a given diagnosis to define a trait category. The next most highly rated feature was placed in this category if appropriate. If not, an additional trait category was used. This process was repeated until all features were categorized. Each trait category was then defined on the basis of features from which it was derived; the greatest weight was placed on the most prototypical feature. This procedure was repeated for all categories. Trait categories were then examined across all disorders; definitions were revised until a relatively mutually exclusive set of trait categories was established. Thus, each disorder is defined by a cluster of traits. For example, schizoid personality disorder consists of low affiliation, avoidant attachment, defective social skills, generalized hypersensitivity, lack of empathy, restricted affective expression, self-absorption, and social apprehensiveness. Initially, 79 traits were required to define all 11 diagnoses in *DSM-III-R*. These traits provided a representative depiction of the domain of personality disorder.

The next step was to develop self-report scales to assess each trait. This was accomplished using the structured approach to scale development described by Jackson (1971). The scales were administered to two general population samples. During the course of scale development, some proposed scales were found to have low internal consistency; consequently, these scales were subdivided into homogeneous item sets. We developed new scales to assess additional criteria proposed in *DSM-III-R*. As a result of this process, the number of scales increased to 100. The final scales were administered to two independent samples: a general population sample of 274 subjects and a clinical sample of 158 patients with a primary diagnosis of personality disorder. The structure of the two data sets was analyzed independently using exploratory factor analysis. Fifteen-factor obliquely rotated solutions provided the closest approximation to simple structure for data from both the general population sample (Livesley, Jackson, & Schroeder, 1989) and the clinical sample (Livesley & Schroeder, 1990, 1991). Like other investigators (e.g., Clark, 1990; Hyler et al., 1990), we identified factors with only superficial resemblance to *DSM-III-R* diagnostic concepts. The factor structures were similar across the general population and clinical samples (Livesley

& Schroeder, 1990), an observation lending substantial support to a dimensional model for representing personality disorders (Eysenck, 1987).

INSTRUMENT DEVELOPMENT

We developed the Dimensional Assessment of Personality Pathology–Basic Questionnaire (DAPP-BQ) because the 100-scale questionnaire is too long for practical research application. Furthermore, 100 scales provide too much information to be easily interpreted and synthesized. Even though efforts were made during scale development to construct relatively distinct measures, substantial intercorrelations were observed among some scales. Thus, it seemed likely that a more parsimonious set of descriptors could be derived from the 100 scales without great loss of descriptive detail. In this section, the term *components* refers to the 100 scales developed previously; the term *scales* refers to the 18 DAPP-BQ scales; the term *factor* refers to the previously described factor analytic results. On the basis of the factor analytic studies described earlier, we formed clusters of components that loaded together in both analyses. These clusters provided construct definitions. Thus, the scale content generally is narrower in scope than was the factor content in either analysis. This strategy was used to form the pool of potential items for 14 of the 18 DAPP-BQ scales. A strong factor that we previously labeled *Identity Disturbance*, which emerged in both factor analyses, was divided into two separate, but correlated, clusters because of its breadth of content. The scales Identity Problems and Anxiousness were developed from this factor. Two additional clusters of components were formed that resulted in the scales Suspiciousness and Self-Harming Behaviors. These did not emerge clearly as factors in both analyses, but we believe that they are of sufficient importance to be included as scales in the DAPP-BQ.

Scale items were chosen from the components in the cluster formed on the basis of the factor analytic results. Each scale has content from multiple components. For example, the Identity Problems scale comprises anhedonia, chronic feelings of emptiness and boredom, labile self-concept, and pessimism. We attempted to ensure satisfactory domain sampling by selecting items in approximately equal numbers from each component. DAPP-BQ scale content was also guided by item analysis. Items with highly skewed distributions were eliminated as were those that had a low correlation with their total scale score. The scales have 16 items each, except Suspiciousness, which has 14, and Self-Harming Behaviors, which has 12. The scales demonstrated good levels of internal consistency in the general population and clinical samples. Scales and their constituent components are listed in Table 1 along with reliability estimates from the two samples on which the DAPP-BQ was developed.

METHOD

Instruments

Dimensions of personality disorder were assessed with the DAPP-BQ. Two DAPP-BQ scales, Self-Harming Behaviors and Perceptual Cognitive Distortion, were not included in the questionnaire used in the present study because of low item endorsement rates in the general population subjects. The second measure used was the NEO-PI (Costa & McCrae, 1985), a 181-item inventory that yields measures of the Big Five factors of normal personality.

Subjects and Procedures

The subjects were 300 general population members recruited with posters and newspaper advertisements to participate in a study of personality. The sample included students and staff of the University of British Columbia as well as community members. The mean age of participants was 34.4 years ($SD = 11.8$). Half of the participants were male. A general population rather than a clinical sample was used to permit the collection of sufficient data for multivariate analyses. Consistent with other studies (Jackson & Messick, 1962; Tyrer & Alexander, 1977), our past research has shown similar patterns of responses from the two groups (Livesley & Schroeder, 1990; Livesley, Schroeder, & Jackson, 1990). Subjects completed the test materials in small groups supervised by a research assistant. A subgroup of 59 participants completed the questionnaire a second time approximately 6 weeks after initial testing to permit the evaluation of the stability of responses over time.

RESULTS

We examined the psychometric properties of the 16 DAPP-BQ scales. Coefficient alpha values were acceptable for all scales. These ranged from 0.80 (Conduct Problems) to 0.93 (Anxiousness). We also calculated coefficients of generalizability (CGs; Cronbach, Gleser, Nanda, & Rajaratnam, 1972) for the 59 cases with retest data. A Design VII CG was calculated for each DAPP-BQ scale. This design corresponds to a three-way fully crossed random effects Persons × Items × Occasions analysis of variance design; it yields seven independent variance components. Estimates of the variance components are calculated from the observed mean square values. For the calculation of the CG, the variance component estimate corresponding to the Persons main effect is wanted variance. The variance component estimates corresponding to the Persons × Items, the Persons × Occasions, and the Persons × Items × Occasions interactions represent error variance in this application. We were interested in the extent to which we could differentiate among individuals (i.e., reliably rank order them), generalizing over the Item and Occasion facets of the design (see Schroeder, Schroeder, & Hare, 1983, for a detailed example of the technique). CGs ranged from 0.86 (Rejection) to 0.95 (Anxiousness). Because respondents usually completed the questionnaire only once, we also estimated the CG values for a single occasion. These were only slightly lower, ranging from 0.82 (Rejection and Social Avoidance) to 0.93 (Anxiousness). These CG values attest to the stability of the responses.

Principal Component Analyses

To determine the extent to which five personality factors would emerge when the NEO-PI and DAPP-BQ scales are intercorrelated, we performed a principal component analysis on the 21 × 21 matrix of scale intercorrelations. Decomposition of the correlation matrix yielded five eigenvalues greater than unity. The five-factor solution accounted for 70.6% of the total variance. The Harris-Kaiser obliquely rotated factor pattern matrix is presented in Table 2. The rotated factors were nearly orthogonal; the largest factor intercorrelation was 0.12.

The first factor, which was marked by the NEO-PI Neuroticism dimension, captured aspects of the

TABLE 1

Dimensional Assessment of Personality Pathology–Basic Questionnaire (DAPP-BQ) Dimension Reliabilities and Constituent Scales

	Coefficient alpha	
Dimension	General population sample	Clinical sample
Compulsivity Orderliness, precision, conscientiousness	0.88	0.86
Conduct problems Interpersonal violence, juvenile antisocial behavior, addictive behaviors, failure to adopt social norms	0.87	0.84
Diffidence Submissiveness, suggestibility, need for advice	0.89	0.85
Identity problems Anhedonia, chronic feelings of emptiness and boredom, labile self-concept, pessimisism	0.94	0.92
Insecure attachment Separation protest, secure base, proximity seeking, feared loss, intolerance of aloneness	0.93	0.90
Intimacy problems Desire for improved attachment relationships, inhibited sexuality, avoidant attachment	0.88	0.85
Narcissism Need for adulation, attention seeking, grandiosity, need for approval	0.91	0.87
Suspiciousness Hypervigilance, suspiciousness	0.89	0.89
Affective lability Affective lability, affective over-reactivity, generalized hypersensitivity, labile anger, irritability	0.91	0.86
Passive oppositionality Passivity, oppositional, lack of organization	0.90	0.90
Perceptual cognitive distortion Depersonalization, schizotypal cognition, brief stress psychosis	0.89	0.89
Rejection Rigid cognitive style, judgmental, interpersonal hostility, dominance	0.87	0.85
Self-harming behaviors Ideas of self-harm, self-damaging acts	0.92	0.94
Restricted expression Reluctant self-disclosure, restricted expression of anger, restricted expression of positive sentiments, self-reliance	0.90	0.91
Social avoidance Low affiliation, defective social skills, social apprehensiveness, fearfulness of interpersonal hurt, desire for improved affiliative relationships	0.93	0.88
Stimulus seeking Sensation seeking, recklessness, impulsivity	0.89	0.89
Interpersonal disesteem Contemptuousness, egocentrism, exploitation, interpersonal irresponsibility, lack of empathy, remorselessness, sadism	0.87	0.80
Anxiousness Guilt proneness, indecisiveness, rumination, trait anxiety	0.94	0.93

Note. Suspiciousness scale has 14 items; self-harming behaviors scale has 12. $N = 274$ for the general population sample; $N = 158$ for the clinical sample.

TABLE 2

Obliquely Rotated Factor Pattern for Combined Analysis of the NEO Personality Inventory (NEO-PI) Factors and Dimensional Assessment of Personality Pathology–Basic Questionnaire (DAPP-BQ) Dimensions

Factor/dimension	Factors				
	I	II	III	IV	V
NEO-PI					
Neuroticism	**0.84**	−0.21	0.02	−0.16	−0.13
Extraversion	−0.18	**0.72**	**−0.42**	−0.05	0.08
Openness to Experience	−0.05	0.06	**−0.41**	0.09	−0.16
Agreeableness	−0.06	0.11	−0.09	**0.86**	0.01
Conscientiousness	−0.14	0.04	−0.05	0.08	**0.94**
DAPP-BQ					
Anxiousness	**0.83**	−0.19	0.09	−0.11	0.06
Affective lability	**0.68**	−0.01	−0.17	−0.35	0.00
Diffidence	**0.64**	0.08	0.32	0.25	−0.07
Insecure attachment	**0.61**	0.22	−0.02	−0.10	0.04
Social avoidance	**0.59**	−0.15	**0.42**	−0.07	−0.09
Identity problems	**0.58**	−0.04	**0.53**	−0.14	−0.11
Narcissism	**0.58**	0.32	0.00	−0.29	−0.06
Stimulus seeking	−0.01	**0.64**	−0.03	−0.27	0.00
Restricted expression	0.15	0.01	**0.81**	0.03	−0.03
Intimacy problems	−0.11	−0.16	**0.58**	−0.12	−0.08
Interpersonal disesteem	0.11	0.09	0.19	**−0.76**	0.01
Rejection	0.11	0.32	−0.03	**−0.62**	0.05
Suspiciousness	0.30	0.10	0.32	**−0.58**	0.13
Conduct problems	0.12	0.16	−0.08	**−0.48**	−0.18
Compulsivity	0.12	0.06	0.13	−0.05	**0.72**
Passive–oppositionality	**0.51**	0.09	0.22	−0.06	**−0.55**

Note. N = 300; loadings greater than .40 are in boldface.

DAPP-BQ reflecting distress and dissatisfaction with self; notable were the high loadings by the DAPP Anxiousness and Affective Lability dimensions. This strong first factor appears to represent core features of personality disorder. The second factor, marked by the NEO-PI Extraversion dimension, had one other salient loading, the DAPP-BQ Stimulus Seeking scale. This dimension is similar to Zuckerman's (1971) Sensation Seeking construct, which measures the need for high levels of excitement, stimulation, and novelty. On the third factor, the scale with the highest loading was DAPP-BQ Restricted Expression, which measures difficulties with self-disclosure and the overt expression of emotion. The NEO-PI Openness to Experience and Extraversion scales had negative loadings. The other DAPP-BQ scales loading on

this factor (Intimacy Problems, Identity Problems, and Social Avoidance) tap dissatisfaction with self and difficulties with interpersonal relationships. The scale with the largest loading on the fourth factor was the NEO-PI Agreeableness dimension. The remaining salient loadings (Interpersonal Disesteem, Rejection, Suspiciousness, and Conduct Problems) were all negative. These scales reflect aspects of interpersonal behavior emphasizing distrust and lack of regard and concern for others. The scale with the largest loading on the fifth factor was the NEO-PI Conscientiousness dimension. Not surprisingly, the DAPP-BQ Compulsivity dimension loaded highly on this factor along with Passive Oppositionality (negatively). The latter scale measures difficulties planning, organizing, and completing tasks.

We also performed a principal component analysis on the intercorrelations among the 16 DAPP-BQ scales by themselves to evaluate the extent to which factors resembling those of the FFM would emerge on their own. Decomposition of the correlation matrix yielded four eigenvalues greater than unity; the scree plot also strongly indicated a four-factor solution. The four factors accounted for 67.3% of the total variance. The obliquely rotated pattern matrix is presented in Table 3.

The large first factor contained content suggesting the label *Neuroticism*. The high salient loadings by Insecure Attachment, Anxiousness, Diffidence, and Affective Lability are consistent with this label. The content of the factor is highly similar to the DAPP-BQ content of the first factor in the combined DAPP-BQ/NEO-PI analysis. The second factor in the DAPP-BQ analysis is similar to the fifth factor from the combined analysis. We propose the label *Disagreeableness*. Interestingly, the Stimulus-Seeking scale also loaded highly on this factor, whereas in the combined analysis it loaded on a separate factor marked by NEO-PI Extraversion. The DAPP-BQ very likely does not contain sufficient content tapping extraversion for this factor to emerge clearly by itself. The third DAPP-BQ factor had salient loadings by the DAPP-BQ dimensions that loaded on the third factor in the combined analysis. The factor in the combined analysis also had negative salient loadings by NEO-PI Extraversion and Openness to Experience. The third DAPP-BQ factor appears largely to tap Introversion. The fourth factor clearly represents Compulsivity.

TABLE 3

Obliquely Rotated Factor Pattern for Dimensional Assessment of Personality Pathology–Basic Questionnaire Scales

Dimension	Factor			
	I	II	III	IV
Insecure attachment	**0.82**	0.08	−0.28	0.05
Anxiousness	**0.81**	−0.08	0.16	0.09
Diffidence	**0.71**	−0.32	0.21	−0.08
Affective lability	**0.65**	0.30	−0.10	−0.01
Narcissism	**0.60**	0.38	−0.08	−0.06
Social avoidance	**0.57**	−0.09	**0.44**	0.11
Passive–oppositionality	**0.54**	0.00	0.16	**−0.47**
Rejection	0.06	**0.80**	−0.06	0.09
Interpersonal disesteem	0.02	**0.74**	0.26	0.00
Conduct problems	−0.02	**0.67**	−0.04	−0.38
Stimulus seeking	−0.07	**0.66**	−0.18	−0.04
Suspiciousness	0.24	**0.57**	0.35	0.21
Intimacy problems	−0.38	0.09	**0.91**	−0.04
Restricted expression	0.05	−0.06	**0.84**	0.05
Identity problems	**0.52**	0.04	**0.54**	−0.07
Compulsivity	0.19	0.09	0.04	**0.92**

Note. $N = 300$; loadings greater than .40 are in boldface.

This analysis also suggests that four of the FFM factors are important in describing personality pathology. Factors corresponding to Neuroticism, Conscientiousness, (low) Extraversion, and (low) Agreeableness are apparent in this analysis. Again, a factor resembling Openness to Experience did not emerge.

Canonical Correlation Analysis

We also examined the relations among the NEO-PI and DAPP-BQ scales using canonical correlation analysis. This technique describes dependencies between two sets of variables by forming successive pairs of linear combinations, called *canonical variates*, that correlate maximally. The second pair of canonical variates correlates maximally, subject to the constraint that they are orthogonal to the first pair, and so forth, until all possible pairs of variates have been formed. The maximum number of pairs of canonical variates is equal to the number of variables in the smaller set. In the present application, the 5 NEO-PI scales can be thought of as predictor or independent variables and the 16 DAPP-BQ scales as criterion or

dependent variables. The canonical correlation analysis demonstrated considerable linkage between the two sets of variables. All five canonical correlations attained statistical significance. Table 4 shows the canonical correlations and structure coefficients. The latter are the correlations between the original variables and the derived canonical variables; these indicate which variables had the greatest weight in forming the linear composite and thus are useful for interpreting the meaning of the canonical variate.

The large first canonical correlation indicates strong linkage between the two sets of variables. A high score on the first predictor canonical variate resulted from a combination of high Neuroticism, low Extraversion, and low Conscientiousness. The corresponding criterion variate correlated highly with a number of scales, suggesting a pattern that is pervasive in personality pathology. A high scorer on this variate would tend to be passive, anxious, and lacking in self-confidence and to have a diffuse self-concept. The content is similar to that of the first factor from both principal component analyses, except that Narcissism and Insecure Attachment did not correlate substantially with the first criterion canonical variate.

The second canonical correlation essentially represents the linkage between NEO-PI Conscientiousness and DAPP-BQ Compulsivity. For the third correlation, a high score on the predictor variate indicates a low level of Agreeableness coupled with high Extraversion and Neuroticism. The criterion variate correlates with several DAPP-BQ dimensions, including Affective Lability, Conduct Problems, Stimulus Seeking, and measures indicating low regard for others. This pattern suggests a proactive personal style, in contrast with the more passive style seen in conjunction with the first canonical correlation. The predictor variate for the fourth canonical correlation had a high correlation with Agreeableness and a moderate correlation with Extraversion. The criterion variate had high negative correlations with Interpersonal Disesteem and Suspiciousness, suggesting that a high scorer would be mistrustful of others. The fifth canonical correlation was considerably lower than the other four. The predictor variate correlated highly with Openness to Experience, whereas the criterion variate did not correlate highly with any DAPP-BQ scale. The largest correlation was with Diffidence

TABLE 4

Canonical Correlation Analysis of Dimensional
Assessment of Personality Pathology–Basic
Questionnaire (DAPP-BQ) and NEO Personality
Inventory (NEO-PI) Scales

Variable	Canonical variates				
	I	II	III	IV	V
R	0.91	0.86	0.84	0.74	0.48
DAPP-BQ					
Anxiousness	0.75	0.39	0.38	0.12	−0.02
Passive-oppositionality	0.74	−0.39	0.18	−0.18	−0.22
Identity problems	0.71	0.26	0.18	−0.16	−0.39
Social avoidance	0.71	0.35	0.02	−0.21	0.03
Diffidence	0.61	0.20	0.06	0.27	−0.46
Restricted expression	0.38	0.24	−0.21	−0.26	−0.30
Compulsivity	−0.30	0.74	0.09	0.06	−0.14
Narcissism	0.33	0.04	0.67	0.12	−0.10
Affective lability	0.51	0.21	0.66	0.11	0.23
Interpersonal disesteem	0.06	0.16	0.66	−0.63	−0.17
Rejection	−0.13	−0.00	0.66	−0.31	−0.12
Stimulus seeking	−0.33	−0.24	0.57	0.10	−0.15
Conduct problems	0.10	−0.11	0.54	−0.24	0.14
Insecure attachment	0.32	0.16	0.43	0.12	−0.33
Suspiciousness	0.19	0.29	0.49	−0.51	−0.16
Intimacy problems	0.23	0.14	−0.18	−0.34	−0.25
NEO-PI					
Neuroticism	0.84	0.27	0.45	0.11	−0.04
Extraversion	−0.62	−0.36	0.53	0.43	−0.15
Openness to Experience	−0.08	−0.25	0.10	0.27	0.89
Conscientiousness	−0.62	0.74	−0.05	0.23	0.12
Agreeableness	−0.07	−0.16	−0.64	0.75	0.03

Note. N = 300.

(negative). This finding again suggests that Openness
to Experience is not strongly related to personality
pathology. Wiggins and Pincus's (1989) canonical
correlation analysis similarly indicated only modest
relations between Openness to Experience and self-
report measures of *DSM-III-R* diagnoses.

Multiple Regression Analyses

To examine further the relation between the NEO-PI
scales and the DAPP-BQ dimensions, we performed a
series of multiple regression analyses. The multiple
correlations and standard regression coefficients (beta
weights) greater than 0.15 are presented in Table 5.
We note again the prominent role that Neuroticism
plays in the prediction of several DAPP-BQ scales. As
was seen from the combined principal component

analysis of the two sets of scales, however, the other
NEO-PI scales also play a role in the description of
personality pathology.

Agreeableness was negatively related to several
scales that measure problematic interpersonal behavior; Agreeableness was positively related to Diffidence, a scale measuring the willingness to acquiesce
to others' wishes. The NEO-PI Extraversion dimension showed a strong relation to Stimulus Seeking
and played a lesser role in the prediction of nine
other DAPP-BQ scales. Conscientiousness was related
to the DAPP-BQ Compulsivity and Passive Oppositionality (negatively). Openness to Experience did
not play a major role in predicting any DAPP-BQ
scales. Nevertheless, Openness to Experience does
appear to play a lesser role in a number of DAPP-BQ
dimensions; the regression coefficients in Table 5
suggest an inverse relation between Openness to
Experience and personality disorder.

The values of the multiple correlations indicate
that a number of DAPP-BQ scales share a substantial
proportion of variance with the NEO-PI factors. The
lowest multiple correlation was found with Intimacy
Problems. This DAPP-BQ scale measures difficulties
with the formation and maintenance of close personal relationships and difficulties with the expression of sexuality. Three other DAPP-BQ scales
(Conduct Problems, Restricted Expression, and Insecure Attachment) showed only modest relations with
the NEO-PI dimensions; each demonstrated less than
30% shared variance. Thus, not all aspects of personality disorder can be predicted by the NEO-PI
dimensions with a high level of precision. The Intimacy Problems and Conduct Problems scales have
largely behavioral content, which may help to
explain their relatively low multiple correlations; the
NEO-PI scales do not tap this content. The Restricted
Expression and Insecure Attachment scales describe
problems with interpersonal relationships; again, this
content is not strongly represented in the NEO-PI.
The former scale measures difficulties with the
expression of both positive and negative emotions.
The Insecure Attachment scale taps content similar to
Bowlby's (1969, 1977) concept of anxious attachment. Those with a high score on the scale would be
expected to have difficulties functioning independently of an attachment figure and to be preoccupied
with fears of losing those closest to them.

TABLE 5

Multiple Regression Analyses Predicting Dimensional Assessment of Personality Pathology–Basic Questionnaire (DAPP-BQ) Dimensions With the NEO Personality Inventory (NEO-PI) Scales

DAPP-BQ dimension	R	Standardized regression coefficients
Affective lability	0.75	0.74 N − 0.19 A + 0.18 O + 0.17 E
Anxiousness	0.83	0.84 N
Compulsivity	0.70	0.69 C − 0.16 O + 0.15 N
Conduct problems	0.51	0.21 E − 0.39 A
Diffidence	0.66	0.60 N + 0.29 A − 0.23 O
Identity problems	0.73	0.54 N − 0.20 O − 0.18 E
Insecure attachment	0.52	0.52 N + 0.22 E
Interpersonal disesteem	0.74	− 0.70 A
Intimacy problems	0.40	− 0.31 E − 0.17 O
Narcissism	0.65	0.59 N + 0.35 E − 0.18 A
Passive–oppositionality	0.78	− 0.60 C + 0.32 N
Rejection	0.61	− 0.52 A + 0.34 E
Restricted expression	0.50	− 0.36 E − 0.21 O
Social avoidance	0.73	0.47 N − 0.41 E
Stimulus seeking	0.61	0.59 E − 0.24 A
Suspiciousness	0.64	− 0.52 A + 0.22 N

Note. $N = 300$. For NEO-PI scales, N = Neuroticism, E = Extraversion, O = Openness to Experience, A = Agreeableness, and C = Conscientiousness. Coefficients less than 0.15 are omitted.

DISCUSSION

We developed the DAPP-BQ self-report scales as reliable measures of important features of personality pathology. The results of the present study indicate that many of these measures are strongly related to the five factors of normal personality. These results are consistent with those obtained by Costa and McCrae (1990) and Wiggins and Pincus (1989). The fact that we used a different conceptualization of personality pathology provides evidence of the robustness of the relation between the domains of normal personality and personality disorder. Because little information is available about the structure of the domain of personality disorder, it is desirable to relate the DAPP-BQ scales to well-established personality factors like the NEO-PI dimensions.

The 18 DAPP-BQ scales provide an alternative to the *DSM-III-R* Axis II categories for describing personality disorder. The latter system was developed largely on the basis of clinical impressions in the absence of sound theoretical underpinnings. In developing the DAPP-BQ, we attempted to examine the domain of personality pathology in a comprehensive and systematic manner, using both rational and empirical considerations. We believe that the DAPP-BQ can prove useful in research because it provides more detailed and precise information than can be obtained from knowledge of category membership.

From the relations between the two tests, it is clear that the NEO Neuroticism factor plays a prominent role in the explication of several aspects of personality disorder. In contrast, the Openness to Experience factor appears to be of lesser importance. To a great extent, our research and that of others suggest that personality pathology can be described with the same traits that underlie normal personality functioning. The relation between the two domains is not, however, uniformly high. Some DAPP-BQ scales with behavioral content demonstrated only modest relation with the NEO-PI factors. Although not included in the present study, we believe that the Self-Harming Behaviors and Perceptual Cognitive Distortion scales from the DAPP-BQ also would not be highly related to the NEO-PI. These latter features of personality disorder also may not represent continua.

Future research is needed to investigate the generalizability of the results presented here. It would be desirable to replicate the study with a sample of personality-disordered individuals. It also seems important to generalize the findings beyond self-reports. Some aspects of personality disorder may be more readily apparent to a skilled observer or a knowledgeable informant than to an individual making a self-rating. Further research is needed to develop a more precise specification of the domain of personality pathology. Personality disorders are described with terms that vary in specificity. It would be desirable to develop a comprehensive set of trait-level descriptors that map out the domain of personality pathology similar to the way the NEO-PI factors describe normal personality.

References

American Psychiatric Association. (1987). *Diagnostic and statistical manual of mental disorders* (3rd ed., rev.). Washington, DC: Author.

Bowlby, J. (1969). *Attachment and loss* (Vol. 1). London: Hogarth Press.

Bowlby, J. (1977). The making and breaking of affectional bonds. *British Journal of Psychiatry, 130*, 201–210, 421–431.

Clark, L. A. (1990). Toward a consensual set of symptom clusters for assessment of personality disorder. In J. N. Butcher & C. D. Spielberger (Eds.), *Advances in personality assessment* (Vol. 9, pp. 243–266). Hillsdale, NJ: Erlbaum.

Cloninger, C. R. (1987). A systematic method for clinical description and classification personality variants. *Archives of General Psychiatry, 44*, 573–588.

Costa, P. T., Jr., & McCrae, R. R. (1985). *The NEO Personality Inventory manual*. Odessa, FL: Psychological Assessment Resources.

Costa, P. T., Jr., & McCrae, R. R. (1990). Personality disorders and the five-factor model of personality. *Journal of Personality Disorders, 4*, 362–371.

Cronbach, L. J., Gleser, G. C., Nanda, H., & Rajaratnam, N. (1972). *The dependability of behavioral measurements*. New York: Wiley.

Digman, J. M. (1990). Personality structure: Emergence of the five-factor model. *Annual Review of Psychology, 41*, 417–440.

Eysenck, H. J. (1987). The definition of personality disorders and the criteria appropriate to their description. *Journal of Personality Disorders, 1*, 211–219.

Frances, A. J. (1980). The DSM-III personality disorders section: A commentary. *American Journal of Psychiatry, 137*, 1050–1054.

Hare, R. D. (1983). Diagnosis of antisocial personality disorder in two prison populations. *American Journal of Psychiatry, 140*, 887–890.

Hathaway, S. R., & McKinley, J. C. (1967). *Minnesota Multiphasic Personalityy Inventory manual*. New York: Psychological Corporation.

Hyler, S. E., Lyons, M., Rieder, R. O., Young, L., Williams, J. B., & Spitzer, R. L. (1990). The factor structure of self-report DSM-III Axis II symptoms and their relationship to clinicians' ratings. *American Journal of Psychiatry, 147*, 751–757.

Jackson, D. N. (1971). The dynamics of structured personality tests. *Psychological Review, 78*, 229–248.

Jackson, D. N., & Messick, S. (1962). Response styles of the MMPI: Comparison of clinical and normal samples. *Journal of Abnormal Psychology, 65*, 285–299.

Kernberg, O. (1984). *Severe personality disorders*. New Haven, CT: Yale University Press.

Kiesler, D. J. (1986). The 1982 interpersonal circle: An analysis of DSM-III personality disorders. In T. Millon & G. L. Klerman (Eds.), *Contemporary directions in psychopathology: Towards DSM-IV* (pp. 571–597). New York: Guilford Press.

Livesley, W. J. (1986). Trait and behavioral prototypes of personality disorder. *American Journal of Psychiatry, 143*, 728–732.

Livesley, W. J. (1987). A systematic approach to the delineation of personality disorders. *American Journal of Psychiatry, 144*, 772–777.

Livesley, W. J., Jackson, D. N., & Schroeder, M. L. (1989). A study of the factorial structure of personality pathology. *Journal of Personality Disorders, 3*, 292–306.

Livesley, W. J., & Schroeder, M. L. (1990). Dimensions of personality disorder. The DSM-III-R cluster A diagnoses. *Journal of Nervous and Mental Disease, 178*, 627–635.

Livesley, W. J., & Schroeder, M. L. (1991). Dimensions of personality disorder. The DSM-III-R cluster B diagnoses. *Journal of Nervous and Mental Disease, 179*, 320–328.

Livesley, W. J., Schroeder, M. L., & Jackson, D. N. (1990). Dependent personality disorder. *Journal of Personality Disorders, 4*, 131–140.

Millon, T. (1981). *Disorders of personality: DSM-III Axis II.* New York: Wiley.

Millon, T. (1982). *Millon Clinical Multiaxial Inventory manual* (3rd ed.). Minneapolis, MN: National Computer Systems.

Morey, L. C., Waugh, M. H., & Blashfield, R. K. (1985). MMPI scales for DSM-III personality disorders: Their derivation and correlates. *Journal of Personality Assessment, 49,* 245–251.

Plutchik, R., & Platman, S. R. (1977). Personality connotations of psychiatric diagnosis. *Journal of Nervous and Mental Disease, 165,* 418–422.

Schroeder, M. L., Schroeder, K. G., & Hare, R. D. (1983). Generalizability of a checklist for assessment of psychopathy. *Journal of Consulting and Clinical Psychology, 51,* 511–516.

Tyrer, P., & Alexander, M. S. (1977). Classification of personality disorder. *British Journal of Psychiatry, 135,* 163–167.

Wiggins, J. S. (1968). Personality structure. *Annual Review of Psychology, 19,* 293–350.

Wiggins, J. S. (1982). Circumplex model of interpersonal behavior in clinical psychology. In P. C. Kendall & J. N. Butcher (Eds.), *Offprints from the handbook of research methods in clinical psychology* (pp. 183–221). New York: Wiley.

Wiggins, J. S., & Pincus, A. L. (1989). Conceptions of personality disorders and dimensions of personality. *Psychological Assessment: A Journal of Consulting and Clinical Psychology, 1,* 305–316.

Zuckerman, M. (1971). Dimensions of sensation seeking. *Journal of Consulting and Clinical Psychology, 36,* 45–52.

PART III

PATIENT POPULATIONS AND CLINICAL CASES

PERSONALITY TRAIT CHARACTERISTICS OF OPIOID ABUSERS WITH AND WITHOUT COMORBID PERSONALITY DISORDERS

Robert K. Brooner, Chester W. Schmidt, Jr., and Jeffrey H. Herbst

This chapter examines the relation between normal personality traits and specific Axis II personality diagnoses obtained in a sample of opioid abusers. We describe several personality diagnostic categories of the revised third edition of the *Diagnostic and Statistical Manual of Mental Disorders* (*DSM-III-R*; American Psychiatric Association, 1987) from the perspective of the five-factor model (FFM) of personality. First, we compare the personality traits of drug abusers with and without comorbid personality disorder. Second, we examine the personality traits of drug abusers with specific Axis II diagnoses in relation to empirically derived hypotheses regarding the personality traits of these conditions (see Widiger et al., chapter 3 in this book).

Drug abusers typically have higher rates of personality disorder compared with the normal population (Blume, 1989). The prevalence of personality disorder among drug abusers has ranged from 65% to 90%, with antisocial personality disorder (ATS) representing the most frequent diagnosis (Khantzian & Treece, 1985; Kosten, Kosten, & Rounsaville, 1989; Kosten, Rounsaville, & Kleber, 1982; Rounsaville, Weissman, Kleber, & Wilber, 1982). In addition, many drug abusers satisfy criteria for multiple personality diagnoses. For instance, Kosten et al. (1982) found that 68% of 384 opiate abusers met *DSM-III-R* criteria for an Axis II disorder, with 24% meeting criteria for two or more disorders. Khantzian and Treece (1985) reported similar findings in their study of 133 narcotic abusers. Of these patients, 65%

($n = 86$) satisfied *DSM-III-R* criteria for at least one personality disorder diagnosis.

Previous studies have assessed the personality traits of drug abusers from a dimensional perspective. For example, three studies used the Adjective Check List (ACL) to describe the personality trait characteristics of drug abusers (Craig, 1988; Kilmann, 1974; Sutker, Patsiokas, & Allain, 1981). These studies characterized drug abusers as headstrong, impulsive, competitive, aggressive, and markedly indifferent to the concerns of others. Reith, Crockett, and Craig (1975) used the Edwards Personal Preference Schedule to compare the personality traits of drug-abusing criminal offenders with those of non–drug-abusing offenders. The drug-abusing offenders were significantly more impulsive and aggressive and less persistent in tasks compared with the non–drug-abusing offenders. These studies identified several personality trait dimensions common among drug abusers (e.g., impulsiveness, aggressiveness). However, they provide no information on the relation of drug abuse and Axis II comorbidity to a comprehensive taxonomic framework of normal personality traits.

Brooner, Herbst, Schmidt, Bigelow, and Costa (1993) used the NEO Personality Inventory (NEO-PI; Costa & McCrae, 1985, 1989) to comprehensively examine the normal personality traits of 203 opioid abusers. Patients were diagnostically categorized according to the *DSM-III-R* Axis II conditions into four groups: (a) pure antisocial group (ATS with no additional Axis II diagnosis), (b) mixed antisocial group (ATS plus another Axis II diagnosis), (c) other Axis II group (Axis II diagnosis other than ATS), and (d) non–Axis II group (no personality disorder). The mixed ATS group had a significantly higher level of Neuroticism compared with the pure ATS group. As suggested in a review article by Alterman and Cacciola (1991), ATS drug abusers with other personality diagnoses were significantly more prone to emotional distress and instability compared with drug abusers with ATS only. Not surprisingly, the mixed ATS group and the other Axis II group both scored higher in neuroticism than did the non–Axis II group. The mixed ATS group also reported lower levels of agreeableness (i.e., more interpersonal antagonism) than did the non–Axis II and the other Axis II groups. Finally, no significant group differences were found on the Conscientiousness, Extraversion, or Openness to Experience personality domains.

In this chapter, we further examine the NEO-PI profiles of opioid drug abusers to determine the personality characteristics of several diagnostic subgroups not described in the earlier report (Brooner et al., 1993). First, the mean NEO-PI personality profile of the 203 drug abusers is compared with the NEO-PI normative sample. Second, the personality profiles of drug abusers with no personality disorder diagnosis (non–Axis II group) are compared with those of drug abusers with any Axis II disorder (Axis II group) and with those of the NEO-PI normative sample. Third, the NEO-PI personality profiles of pure ATS, pure avoidant (AVD), pure borderline (BDL), and pure paranoid (PAR) drug abusers are examined in relation to empirically derived hypotheses regarding the personality traits of these conditions (see Widiger et al., chapter 3). Finally, the case history and treatment performance of three drug abusers with either ATS, AVD, or BDL are discussed with respect to their standing on normal personality trait dimensions.

As noted earlier, Widiger and colleagues (chapter 3) have characterized the *DSM-III-R* personality disorders from the perspective of the FFM. They describe the defining (i.e., core) features and associated features of the Axis II diagnoses in terms of domains and facet scales of the five basic dimensions of normal personality as operationalized by the NEO-

PI. Table 1 presents an adaptation of this translation of NEO-PI facet scales for Neuroticism, Extraversion, and Openness to Experience and domain scales for Agreeableness and Conscientiousness for specific personality diagnoses that are individually examined in this chapter (i.e., pure ATS, pure AVD, pure BDL, and pure PAR).

The following hypotheses were examined. First, ATS drug abusers would have elevated levels of Hostility, Impulsiveness, and Excitement Seeking and low levels of Agreeableness and Conscientiousness. Associated features of ATS would include high levels of Anxiety and Depression and low levels of Warmth. Second, AVD drug abusers would have high levels of Anxiety, Self-Consciousness, and Vulnerability and low levels of Warmth, Gregariousness, Activity, Excitement Seeking, and Openness to Actions. An associated feature of this disorder would include a high level of depression. Third, BDL drug abusers would have high levels of Anxiety, Hostility, Depression, Impulsiveness, and Vulnerability. Finally, PAR drug abusers would have high levels of Hostility and low levels of Agreeableness (i.e., high interpersonal antagonism). Associated features of PAR would include high levels of Anxiety and low levels of Warmth, Gregariousness, Positive Emotions, Aesthetics, and Feelings.

The data presented are from 203 drug abusers who participated in a longitudinal study of the relation between personality and psychopathology to drug-abuse treatment outcome. A detailed description of the study method was presented in an earlier report (Brooner et al., 1993). Briefly, all patients were opioid abusers admitted to an outpatient drug treatment program that incorporated methadone hydrochloride as one component of care. Their mean age was 33.75 years, 46% were male, 67% were White, 26% were employed, and 15% were married and living with a spouse. Information for making *DSM-III-R* Axis II personality diagnoses was derived from the Structured Clinical Interview for *DSM-III-R* (Spitzer, Williams, Gibbon, & First, 1988); personality traits were assessed by the NEO-PI. To minimize the possible effects of drug intoxication and withdrawal on patient symptom reports, both instruments were administered between 22 and 28 days after admission.

TABLE 1

Conceptual Relationships Among the *DSM-III-R* Diagnostic Criteria for Antisocial (ATS), Avoidant (AVD), Borderline (BDL), and Paranoid (PAR) Disorders and the Five-Factor Model[a]

NEO-PI scales	ATS	AVD	BDL	PAR
Neuroticism facets				
Anxiety	h	H[b]	H	h
Hostility	H[b]		H[b]	H[b]
Depression	h[b]	h[b]	H[b]	
Self-Consciousness		H[b]		
Impulsiveness	H[b]		H[b]	
Vulnerability		H[b]	H[b]	
Extraversion facets				
Warmth	l[b]	L[b]		l[b]
Gregariousness		L[b]		l
Assertiveness				
Activity		L		
Excitement Seeking	H[b]	L		
Positive Emotions				l
Openness to Experience facets				
Fantasy				
Aesthetics				
Feelings				l
Actions		l		l
Ideas				
Values				
Agreeableness domain	L[b]			L[b]
Conscientiousness domain	L[b]			

Note. Upper-case letters relate to the defining features of the disorder in the third, revised edition of the *Diagnostic and Statistical Manual of Mental Disorders* (*DSM-III-R*; American Psychiatric Association, 1987), and lower-case letters relate to associated features in the *DSM-III-R*. H or h indicate high on the trait, and L or l indicate low on the trait.
[a]Adapted from Widiger, Trull, Clarkin, Sanderson, and Costa (chapter 3, this book).   [b]Empirical support for the relationship.

PERSONALITY CHARACTERISTICS OF THE 203 OPIOID ABUSERS

The total sample of 203 opioid abusers differed from the NEO-PI normative sample (Costa & McCrae, 1989) on three of the five personality domains. Drug abusers reported high levels (*T* score range = 55–65) of Neuroticism and low levels (*T* score range = 35–45) of Agreeableness and Conscientiousness com-

pared with the normative sample. They also scored within the high range on three of the six Neuroticism facets (Hostility, Depression, and Vulnerability). Although no group differences were found for the Extraversion domain, drug abusers did score within the low range of the Warmth facet and within the high range of the Excitement Seeking facet. Finally, drug abusers scored within the low range on Openness to Actions. All other NEO-PI domain and facet scales for drug abusers were comparable to those of the NEO-PI normative sample.

Viewed from this perspective, the FFM of personality characterizes opioid drug abusers as prone to high levels of emotional distress, interpersonal antagonism, and excitement seeking and low levels of conscientiousness. It is important to note that the personality profile obtained in this study is consistent with data reported from other studies of drug abusers despite the use of different self-report personality instruments.

OVERALL AND SPECIFIC PREVALENCE RATES OF PERSONALITY DISORDER

Personality disorder was present in 37% (76 of 203) of the patients included in this report. This overall rate of personality disorder is obviously lower than reported in other studies (e.g., Khantzian & Treece, 1985). The reason for the relatively low rate of personality disorder obtained in the present study is unclear but may be related to methodological and/or patient differences. First, previous studies have typically examined patients at the time of admission to treatment, a period when the acute effects of intoxication and withdrawal from brain depressants and brain stimulants may result in greater symptom reporting (including symptoms required for many of the Axis II conditions). Methods for determining Axis II comorbidity among drug abusers have also varied across studies. For example, Khantzian and Treece relied on a standard, nonstructured clinical interview to detect personality disorder. In contrast, the data presented here were obtained following the patient's initial stabilization in the treatment program (i.e., 3–4 weeks after admission), and all Axis II diagnoses were based on information derived from a structured clinical interview.

Among the 76 drug abusers who met criteria for a personality disorder, 32% (24 of 76) met the criteria for two or more diagnoses. Among those with only one Axis II disorder, 28 received a sole diagnosis of (pure) ATS, 8 received a sole diagnosis of (pure) AVD, 5 received a sole diagnosis of (pure) BDL, and 5 received a sole diagnosis of (pure) PAR.

PERSONALITY CHARACTERISTICS OF DRUG ABUSERS WITHOUT AN AXIS II DISORDER COMPARED WITH THOSE OF SUBJECTS IN THE NEO-PI NORMATIVE SAMPLE

The profile of the 127 non–personality-disordered opioid abusers was compared with those of subjects in the NEO-PI normative sample (Costa & McCrae, 1989). As shown in Figure 1, drug abusers without an Axis II diagnosis (solid line) differed from subjects in the normative sample on both the Agreeableness and Conscientiousness domains. With respect to the NEO-PI facet scales, the only prominent elevation occurred on the Excitement Seeking facet of Extraversion. In terms of experiential style, drug abusers appeared somewhat set in their ways (low Openness to Actions). Interestingly, drug abusers without a personality disorder obtained Neuroticism domain and facet scores that were quite similar to those found in the NEO-PI normative sample. Thus, drug abusers without a personality diagnosis were not highly prone to emotional distress or instability.

PERSONALITY CHARACTERISTICS OF DRUG ABUSERS WITH VERSUS WITHOUT AN AXIS II DIAGNOSIS

Table 2 compares the mean NEO-PI domain and facet T scores of the drug abusers without an Axis II disorder (i.e., non–Axis II group; $n = 127$) with those of the drug abusers with at least one Axis II disorder (i.e., Axis II group; $n = 76$). The personality profiles of the two groups are shown in Figure 1.

A two-group multivariate analysis of variance (MANOVA) including the five NEO-PI domains indicated significant group differences, $T^2 = 0.213$, $F(5, 197) = 8.38$, $p < .001$. Examination of the univar-

iate effects indicated that the Axis II group scored significantly higher on Neuroticism, $F(1, 201) = 25.47$, $p < .001$, and lower on Agreeableness, $F(1, 201) = 21.93$, $p < .001$, and Conscientiousness, $F(1, 201) = 9.72$, $p < .01$, than did the non–Axis II group. In fact, the Axis II group scored within the very low range of the Agreeableness domain ($T = 32.4$). Thus, Axis II comorbidity in drug abusers was generally related to having a strong disposition toward emotional distress and instability, high interpersonal antagonism and mistrust, and low motivation and cooperativeness.

A two-group MANOVA including the six facet scales of Neuroticism also revealed significant group differences, $T^2 = 0.17$, $F(6, 196) = 5.58$, $p < .001$. Univariate analyses showed that the Axis II group scored significantly higher than did the non–Axis II group on all six facet scales of Neuroticism: Anxiety, $F(1, 201) = 8.08$, $p < .01$; Hostility, $F(1, 201) = 18.3$, $p < .01$; Depression, $F(1, 201) = 10.74$, $p < .01$; Self-Consciousness, $F(1, 201) = 13.80$, $p < .01$; Impulsiveness, $F(1, 201) = 7.24$, $p < .01$; and Vulnerability, $F(1, 201) = 19.48$, $p < .01$.

A two-group MANOVA including the six facet scales of Extraversion also indicated significant group differences, $T^2 = 0.12$, $F(6, 196) = 3.81$, $p < .01$. The Axis II group scored higher on Excitement Seeking, $F(1, 201) = 4.29$, $p < .05$, and lower on Warmth, $F(1, 201) = 10.63$, $p < .01$, and Positive Emotions, $F(1, 201) = 3.90$, $p < .05$, than did the non–Axis II group. Finally, a two-group MANOVA, $T^2 = 0.07$, $F(6, 196) = 2.27$, $p < .05$, including the six facet scales of Openness to Experience also showed significant group differences. The Axis II group scored higher on Openness to Fantasy, $F(1, 201) = 4.04$, $p < .05$, than did the non–Axis II group.

In short, these data provide further information concerning the impact of Axis II comorbidity on normal personality traits in drug abusers. The pattern of group differences on the NEO-PI facet scales of Neuroticism, Extraversion, and Openness to Experience show clearly that having both a drug-abuse and a personality disorder diagnosis is associated with a pervasive tendency toward marked emotional distress and instability, very low interpersonal warmth, and low positive emotions compared with drug abusers

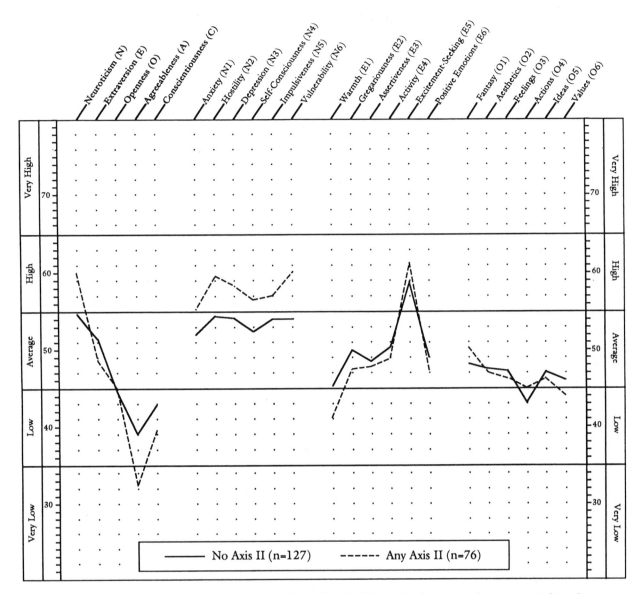

FIGURE 1. NEO Personality Inventory (NEO-PI) profile of 127 opioid abusers with no Axis II disorder (solid line) and 76 opioid abusers with any Axis II disorder (broken line). Profile form from *The NEO Personality Inventory Manual* by P. T. Costa, Jr. and R. R. McCrae, 1985, Odessa, FL: Psychological Assessment Resources. Copyright 1985 by Psychological Assessment Resources.

in the non–Axis II group. High distress among drug abusers in this study was characteristic only of those who received a personality disorder diagnosis. Both the non–Axis II and the Axis II groups were prone to high excitement seeking, high interpersonal antagonism and mistrust (i.e., low Agreeableness), and high disregard for established social rules and conventions (i.e., low Conscientiousness). In general, this finding indicates that high excitement seeking, low agreea-

bleness, and low conscientiousness are FFM personality traits characteristic of opioid drug abusers.

PERSONALITY CHARACTERISTICS OF DRUG ABUSERS WITH ATS, AVD, BDL, AND PAR DIAGNOSES

We subsequently examined the hypotheses generated from Widiger et al.'s (chapter 3) translation of the

TABLE 2

NEO Personality Inventory (NEO-PI) Domain and Facet *T* Scores (*M* ± *SD*) for Opioid Abusers With and Without Personality Disorder Diagnoses

Domain/facet	No Axis II disorder (*N* = 127)		Any Axis II disorder (*N* = 76)	
	M	*SD*	*M*	*SD*
NEO-PI domains				
Neuroticism	54.6	7.8	60.3	7.5
Extraversion	50.7	6.9	48.6	8.8
Openness to Experience	44.9	8.1	45.0	7.7
Agreeableness	39.2	9.7	32.4	10.2
Conscientiousness	42.8	8.3	38.9	8.8
Neuroticism facets				
Anxiety	52.1	7.3	55.2	7.6
Hostility	54.4	8.2	59.6	8.7
Depression	54.2	9.1	58.4	8.4
Self-Consciousness	52.6	7.4	56.6	7.7
Impulsiveness	54.0	8.2	57.1	7.4
Vulnerability	54.1	8.9	60.3	11.0
Extraversion facets				
Warmth	45.4	8.6	40.9	10.9
Gregariousness	49.7	8.8	47.4	9.5
Assertiveness	48.6	7.6	47.7	8.3
Activity	50.3	6.7	48.9	8.0
Excitement Seeking	58.6	8.7	61.1	7.9
Positive Emotions	49.3	7.5	47.0	8.4
Openness facets				
Fantasy	48.2	6.7	50.3	7.3
Aesthetics	47.5	9.1	47.2	9.4
Feelings	47.3	9.2	46.5	8.3
Actions	43.2	7.5	45.0	8.3
Ideas	47.0	7.6	46.6	8.7
Values	46.0	8.2	43.9	7.0

DSM-III-R criteria using the FFM (see Table 1). Specifically, the mean *T* scores for the NEO-PI domains and facets were determined for the 28 pure ATS drug abusers, 8 pure AVD drug abusers, 5 pure BDL drug abusers, and 5 pure PAR drug abusers drawn from the original sample of 203 patients (see Figure 2); statistical comparisons were not made given the small sample size in each of the groups.

The personality profiles presented in Figure 2 illustrate some of the similarities and differences in the personality characteristics among the four Axis II groups. For example, the ATS, AVD, and BDL groups

scored in the high range on the Neuroticism domain, whereas PAR patients scored within the average range of the domain. On the Extraversion domain, the BDL group scored higher than did the ATS and PAR groups, and each of these groups scored higher than did the AVD group. There were no apparent group differences on the Openness to Experience domain; each scored in the low-average to low range. Finally, all four groups scored within the low to very low range of Agreeableness and within the low range of Conscientiousness. These findings indicate that the interpersonal style of the drug abusers with an Axis II disorder, regardless of the specific diagnosis, was highly antagonistic with a tendency to be suspicious, uncooperative, and manipulative. They also had strong patterns of unconscientiousness, irresponsibility, and disorganized behavior. The personality traits of each group are discussed in the following sections in relation to the expected findings generated by the FFM translation of these Axis II diagnoses (see Table 1).

Pure ATS Drug Abusers

As noted earlier, the "defining" personality features of the ATS diagnosis were predicted to include high scores on Hostility, Impulsiveness, and Excitement-Seeking facets and low scores on Agreeableness and Conscientiousness domains. Associated features of the diagnosis were expected to include high scores on Anxiety and Depression and low scores on Warmth. In contrast to these expected associated features, the clinical literature indicates that ATS patients would score low on both the Anxiety and Depression facets (Brooner et al., 1993; chapter 3 in this book).

Consistent with these predictions, the ATS group obtained high scores on the Hostility and Impulsiveness facets of Neuroticism, high scores on the Excitement Seeking facet of Extraversion, very low scores on the Agreeableness domain, and low scores on the Conscientiousness domain. Each of the defining features of this disorder was present among the group. They also showed slight elevations on the Depression and Vulnerability facets of Neuroticism, a pattern of scores that was somewhat consistent with the associated features of ATS. In fact, Widiger et al. (chapter 3) reported that the profile obtained by this group

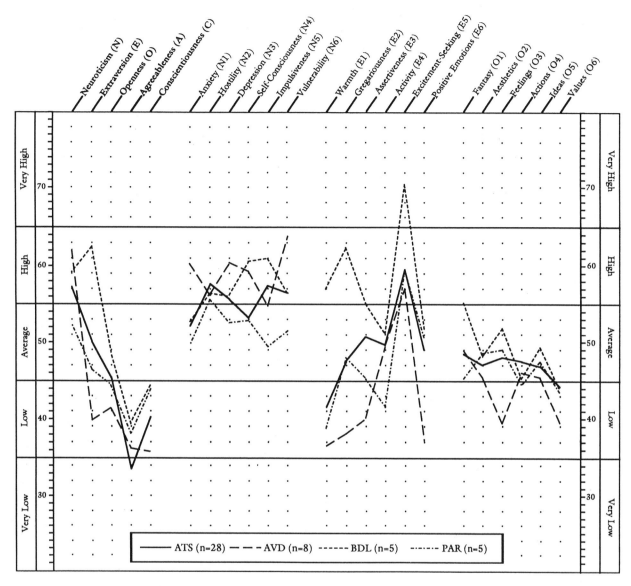

FIGURE 2. NEO Personality Inventory (NEO-PI) profiles of ATS, AVD, BDL, and PAR opioid abusers. Profile form from *The NEO Personality Inventory Manual* by P. T. Costa, Jr. and R. R. McCrae, 1985, Odessa, FL: Psychological Assessment Resources. Copyright 1985 by Psychological Assessment Resources.

was especially evident among ATS patients seeking treatment.

In contrast to the expected personality profile, the ATS group reported levels of Anxiety, which were consistent with the clinical literature. Also, their high scores on Vulnerability were unexpected. Nonetheless, the basic profile of this group was remarkably similar to the hypothesized findings despite the fact that all ATS patients also had a chronic drug-abuse disorder that had a clear impact on personality. In fact, the ATS group obtained the lowest Agreeableness score of any group. This finding is likely to

reflect the combined contribution of the personality disorder and the drug dependence on this aspect of normal personality.

Pure AVD Drug Abusers

Briefly, the defining features of AVD were expected to include high Anxiety, Self-Consciousness, and Vulnerability and low Warmth, Gregariousness, Activity, Excitement Seeking, and Openness to Actions. In addition, AVD patients were expected to score high on Depression as an associated feature of the disorder.

This group also produced a NEO-PI profile that was consistent with both the predicted defining and associated features of the disorder. With respect to the defining features, they obtained high scores on the Neuroticism facets of Anxiety, Self-Consciousness, and Vulnerability and low scores on the Extraversion facets of Warmth and Gregariousness. In addition, they had the associated characteristic of high Depression in their personality profiles and low Assertiveness consistent with clinical impression.

The high Hostility and Excitement Seeking and low Agreeableness and Conscientiousness scores were not predicted for the AVD diagnosis. As noted earlier, the high scores on these traits may reflect the independent contribution of chronic drug abuse on personality style.

Pure BDL Drug Abusers

The defining features of this group were expected to include high scores on each of the Neuroticism facets except Self-Consciousness. Associated features of the disorder were expected to include high scores on Gregariousness, Assertiveness, and Excitement Seeking. In fact, the BDL group scored within the high range on each of the six facets of Neuroticism, except Anxiety. They also had high scores on the associated features of Gregariousness and Excitement Seeking.

Although a high level of Self-Consciousness among BDL patients was not predicted, clinical impression indicates that these patients are prone to experience strong feelings of inferiority and embarrassment (see chapter 3 in this book). Finally, low Agreeableness and Conscientiousness scores of these patients were consistent with having a chronic drug-use disorder.

Pure PAR Drug Abusers

The PAR group was predicted to score high on Hostility and low on Agreeableness. Associated features of the diagnosis were expected to include high scores on Anxiety and low scores on Warmth, Gregariousness, Positive Emotions, and Openness to Aesthetics and Feelings.

This group also produced a personality profile consistent with the defining features of the PAR diagnosis. Specifically, they scored high on Hostility and low on Agreeableness. They also scored low on

Warmth and Activity and high on Excitement Seeking. Based on this profile, PAR drug abusers are easily frustrated and prone to react with anger. They do not have close emotional ties and are typically mistrusting of others. They are slow and deliberate in their actions and crave excitement, stimulation, and thrills. Although high Excitement Seeking and low Conscientiousness were not predicted for those with a PAR diagnosis, both are characteristic of this drug-abusing population.

TREATMENT IMPLICATIONS

All of the drug abusers in the study, including those with an Axis II diagnosis, obtained low scores on the Agreeableness and Conscientiousness personality domains. According to Miller (1991), patients who are disagreeable and unconscientious pose a major challenge for the therapist. Disagreeable or antagonistic patients tend to be skeptical of the therapist and have problems forging an effective therapeutic alliance. Thus, patients who are extremely disagreeable may be at the greatest risk of treatment drop-out or premature discharge. Similarly, unconscientious patients are likely to resist treatment plans that are highly structured, particularly if intensive in nature. Recognition of these personality dynamics is important in predicting the patient's general reaction to treatment and in improving the therapist's understanding of the problem and response to the patient's disruptive behaviors. Clinical impression has led many to argue that clear and consistent limit setting is an essential aspect to treating drug abusers. The data reviewed here clearly support that impression. Furthermore, some drug abusers are more antagonistic and disorganized than others. Identification of the highly antagonistic and disorganized patient can assist treatment providers in quickly establishing reasonable therapeutic goals and an appropriate level of limit setting within the treatment plan. The failure to recognize these aspects of personality in the treatment of drug abusers may reduce treatment effectiveness and may increase the likelihood of premature discharge.

Drug abusers with a personality disorder clearly pose a special challenge for both research and clinical practice. Not only do these patients experience the severe and pervasive problems associated with a drug-use disorder, but many of these problems are exacerbated by the presence of a personality disorder (Kosten et al., 1989). Recognition of the special problems associated with the care of the dually diagnosed drug abuser is important. It is especially critical to establish reasonable therapeutic goals and target dates for their achievement that will support treatment retention and enhance clinical outcomes. For example, cessation of drug use is a primary and early goal of drug-abuse treatment. In fact, the success of this goal is generally seen as essential to addressing the employment, relationship, emotional, and legal problems common among drug-abusing patients. Cessation of drug use early in the course of treatment may be an appropriate clinical expectation for many drug abusers who are not challenged further by a personality disorder. However, applying the same expectation to patients with a personality disorder may result in multiple failures early in treatment that may negatively affect the therapeutic process and contribute to lower rates of retention.

It has also been shown that patients with high levels of emotional distress are more motivated to enter and remain in treatment compared with those with little or no distress (Miller, 1991; Woody, McLellan, Luborsky, & O'Brien, 1985). This may be particularly critical in the care of personality-disordered drug abusers. In the present study, the AVD, BDL, and ATS groups scored within the high range of Neuroticism.

Although high Neuroticism may improve motivation for treatment, Miller (1991) labeled the combination of high Neuroticism, low Extraversion, and low Conscientiousness the *misery triad*, often associated with a poor treatment prognosis in non–drug-abusing clinical populations. The combination of these traits is especially evident in the personality profile of the AVD group. The AVD abusers were characterized by high Neuroticism and low Extraversion, Openness, Agreeableness, and Conscientiousness scores. Their low level of extraversion may be especially detrimental to treatment outcome. Many therapies require active involvement in the therapeutic process and the patients' hope that the therapist can help them. Introversion may negatively affect

both of these dimensions in therapy. In addition, the low Openness characteristic of the AVD drug abusers suggests a rigid experiential style associated with low levels of curiosity.

Although standard drug-abuse counseling provides some benefits to personality-disordered drug abusers, specialized interventions may improve their treatment outcomes. In fact, knowledge about the personality dynamics of drug abusers with AVD or other personality disorder diagnoses may be useful in selecting specialized forms of treatment. For example, Miller (1991) suggested that behavioral interventions or cognitive–behavioral therapy may be particularly useful for patients with the misery triad. Previous research with drug abusers provides some support for this therapeutic approach. Woody et al. (1985) showed that drug abusers with high levels of psychiatric distress had better clinical outcomes when they received both standard counseling and cognitive–behavioral therapy compared with a group that received standard counseling only. They also found significant differences in the treatment outcomes of ATS drug abusers with or without a diagnosis (lifetime or current) of major depression. The depressed ATS drug abusers had better outcomes than did the nondepressed group when cognitive therapy was added to standard counseling. Similarly, Kadden, Cooney, Getter, and Litt (1989) reported that "sociopathic" alcoholics who received behavioral coping skills training had lower rates of relapse to alcohol use over a 26-week period than did those who received interactional therapy.

In summary, each of the personality-disordered groups considered in this chapter experienced low levels of Agreeableness and Conscientiousness. As noted earlier, patients with these traits may have better clinical outcomes when the treatment plan is clear and consistent and incorporates firm behavioral controls. The recognition of the special problems of these patients should also be reflected in the development of treatment goals that enhance rather than reduce retention in therapy. Finally, existing data suggest that enhancing the standard care of these patients by adding specialized forms of behavioral treatment may also improve both retention and clinical outcomes.

CLINICAL CASE REPORTS

In concluding this chapter, we present three case histories to illustrate the usefulness of the FFM in delineating the personality trait characteristics of drug abusers with specific personality diagnoses. One case was selected from each of the ATS, BDL, and AVD groups after reviewing the personality profiles of all patients in each group. The selected cases were chosen because they represented strong examples of the personality profile predicted for the diagnosis.

Each clinical report reviews the relevant case history, the NEO-PI personality profile, and two measures of 3-month treatment performance. The first treatment outcome measure is the Addiction Severity Index (ASI; McLellan, Luborsky, Woody, & O'Brien, 1980). The ASI is a semistructured interview designed to assess problem severity in seven areas commonly associated with alcohol and drug dependence: medical, legal, drug, alcohol, employment, family, and psychiatric. Scores can range from 0.00 to 1.00, with higher scores reflecting greater problem severity. A comparison of scores obtained at Month 1 and Month 3 of treatment is made to assess changes in problem severity across each of the ASI domains. The second measure involves urinalysis drug test records. All urine specimens were collected on a random basis using direct observation techniques to minimize falsified urine samples. The percentage of urine samples positive for drug and alcohol is shown.

Case Report: ATS Opioid Abuser

Rick was a 41-year-old married White male who was admitted for treatment of opioid dependence. Rick's family history was remarkable for alcohol and drug problems in his father and two of four brothers. He described his childhood as being "very" traumatic. Rick's father reportedly murdered his mother when he was "very young" and also physically abused him. He was separated from his brothers and placed in foster care following his mother's death. Over the years, he was moved to several foster care homes because of severe behavior problems. He was frequently truant from school, was suspended on several occasions for truancy and fighting, and finally quit school after completing the eighth grade. He began working at age 14 as a bricklayer and had had numerous jobs lasting for less than 1 year. Although employed as a bricklayer for the past 5 months, he reported missing "lots" of work because of his drug use.

Rick was married twice, first at age 17. His first marriage ended in divorce after 2 years. He had had multiple extramarital relationships and stated that the marriage had failed because both he and his wife were "too young." At age 26, he married a nurse, who provided the majority of financial support. Although he reported repeated extramarital relationships over the past 15 years, he described his marriage as stable and sexually satisfying.

His legal history included four arrests and numerous illegal behaviors that escaped detection (i.e., robbery and sale of drugs). He was first arrested at age 17 for robbing a bar. Each of his subsequent arrests involved possession of illegal substances. He served a 1-year prison sentence for possession of speed and marijuana and an 18-month prison sentence for possession of heroin. At the time of his admission to the outpatient drug treatment program, Rick was on a 1-year unsupervised probation for possession of marijuana.

Rick denied any significant medical history and chose not to be HIV-1 tested despite frequent sharing of needles and a history of unprotected sex with multiple partners. His admission history and physical (H&P) was unremarkable. His social life was relatively barren; he denied having any close friends, hobbies, or recreational interests. In fact, he described himself as "selfish" in his interpersonal relationships and "unmotivated" to set any goals except to "try and stay alive." He began using alcohol on a daily basis at age 16, marijuana at age 18, and stimulants and sedatives at age 20. At age 21, he began intravenous heroin use and by age 30 was using cocaine intravenously. His first treatment for drug abuse occurred at age 20. Since then, he reported having more than 10 episodes of treatment, usually at different programs, and viewed all of them as unsuccessful. He denied other psychiatric problems or treatment. On mental-state examination, he was fully oriented, and his talk was both logical and directed. His mood was euthymic, and he was negative for delusions, hallucinations, true obsessions or compulsions, and phobias.

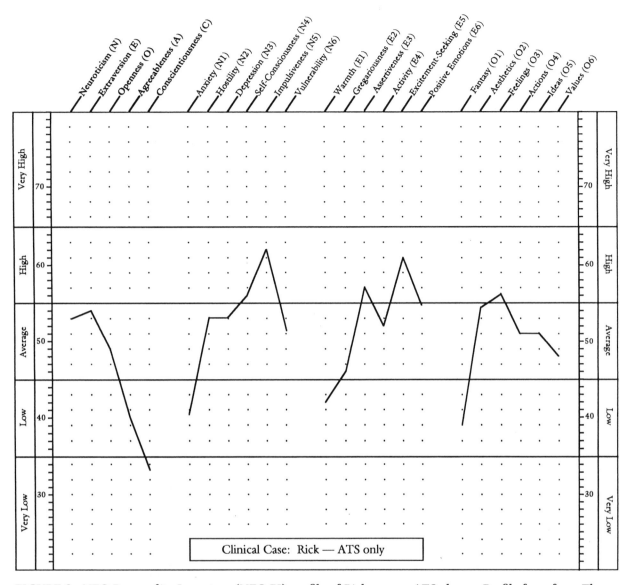

FIGURE 3. NEO Personality Inventory (NEO-PI) profile of Rick, a pure ATS abuser. Profile form from *The NEO Personality Inventory Manual* by P. T. Costa, Jr. and R. R. McCrae, 1985, Odessa, FL: Psychological Assessment Resources. Copyright 1985 by Psychological Assessment Resources.

Rick's personality profile is presented in Figure 3. Compared with the NEO-PI normative sample, Rick scored in the average ranges of Neuroticism, Extraversion, and Openness. He scored in the low range of Agreeableness and in the very low range of Conscientiousness.

Rick's low level of Agreeableness indicated marked interpersonal antagonism and a egocentric, critical, and mistrusting view of others. His extremely low standing on the Conscientiousness domain indicated very little concern about day-to-day responsibilities and little self-discipline. Both the low

Agreeableness and very low Conscientiousness are consistent with a diagnosis of ATS and of a drug-abuse disorder. These traits were also consistent with many aspects of his early history (e.g., frequent truancy and fighting, school suspensions, and multiple foster care placements) and his adult behaviors (frequent marital infidelity, unstable work history, criminal activities, lack of friends, and no life goals). He reported using any means possible to obtain drugs (e.g., "dealing" and forging prescriptions). His poor drug-abuse treatment history may also have been associated with his low Agreeableness and extremely low Conscientiousness.

More detailed information on Rick's personality characteristics was provided by an examination of his NEO-PI facet scores. Specifically, he scored in the high range on the Self-Consciousness and Impulsiveness facets of Neuroticism and in the low range on the Anxiety facet. We can speculate that his elevated concern over how others perceive him was associated with an effort to present himself well. This is somewhat consistent with his demonstrated ability to attract numerous female sexual partners despite his infidelity and antagonism, obtain multiple jobs despite a very poor work history, and receive unsupervised probation despite an extensive arrest history. His high impulsiveness almost certainly contributed to his continued drug use and poor responses to treatment and many life problems (e.g., employment problems). Regardless of the nature or severity of his life problems, his average score on the Anxiety facet indicated very little concern or worry.

Rick's scores on the Extraversion facets also provide details that help in understanding the relation of personality disorder diagnosis to personality characteristics and life history. His low interpersonal warmth clearly contributed to his lack of close friends and may have been associated with his poor treatment history. It is interesting that, although he clearly preferred to remain formal and distant in his emotional relationships with others, he had maintained a 15-year relationship with his wife. However, he acknowledged chronic problems in the relationship and multiple episodes of extramarital affairs. In light of this, one could speculate that his wife provided the stability and support (including financial) to sustain the marriage. His high level of Excitement Seeking was consistent with both his ATS and drug dependence diagnoses and with his criminal behaviors and extramarital relationships. Finally, on the facets of Openness to Experience, he scored low on Fantasy and high on Feelings. This pattern of scores indicated a very limited imagination and a strong belief in the value of his emotional experience.

Given Rick's personality profile, we expected a poor treatment prognosis, particularly given only standard drug-abuse counseling. This prognosis was supported by the results of his first 3 months of treatment. On the ASI, Rick reported increased drug use and family and social problems compared with baseline scores. Although he also reported less legal and employment problems, these changes were probably related to his being on unsupervised probation and having slightly improved work attendance. He reported no changes in medical problems, alcohol use, or psychiatric problems. The results of urine drug tests during the first 3 months of treatment clarified his self-reported increase in drug use. Of the eight urine specimens that were provided, six (75%) were positive for drug use. Specifically, five of the six specimens were positive for morphine and two were positive for cocaine.

Case Report: AVD Opioid Abuser

Persephone was a 22-year-old single White female who was admitted for treatment of opioid dependence. At the time of admission, she was 4 months pregnant with her third child. Persephone's family history was significant for alcohol and drug problems in both parents and in each of her two siblings. In fact, her parents had both been treated for substance abuse, with her father having multiple treatment episodes. Persephone was born prematurely, only weighing 3 pounds at birth. The first 3 months of her life were spent in the hospital for treatment of bronchial pneumonia and other medical complications. She reported an otherwise healthy childhood but attained developmental milestones later than expected. For example, she began walking at 3 years of age. The family had chronic, severe financial problems and moved frequently during her childhood. The parents separated when Persephone was 11 years old. A maternal uncle began living with them but was removed after attempting to rape her. The mother was married a second time to an opioid drug abuser who had been in several different treatment programs.

Persephone's school history was remarkable for frequent truancy, several failed years, and drop-out after she completed the seventh grade. She reported "good" relationships with teachers but was "a loner" and had frequent fights with peers. She had a very limited work history. Her only job had been that of a house painter at age 19. She quit this job after several months because of "child care problems" and no "motivation." She had relied on social services and her boyfriend for financial support. Her legal history was negative for any arrests.

Persephone had become sexually active at age 14 and reported having had a total of three sexual partners, including her present boyfriend with whom she had been for 8 years. In fact, this boyfriend was also the father of her two children (4 and 6 years old) and her unborn baby. She had her first child at age 16 and her second child at age 18. The boyfriend was a truck driver who abused heroin and other drugs and had one brief unsuccessful treatment episode. Although she reported that their relationship was "good," they argued frequently, and he had physically abused her on several occasions.

Persephone's medical history was unremarkable, and her admission H&P was normal. Her social life had been extremely limited. She denied having friends with the exception of her boyfriend, had no "social life," and had no specific life goals. In fact, she reported being unable to "imagine" what goals to even set. She began using heroin at the age of 20 when her boyfriend "talked me into doing it with him." The drug-abuse history was otherwise negative with the exception of "social drinking." Prior to admission, she reported 1 year of continuous heroin use, ranging from three times a day to "as much as I could get." This was her first drug-abuse treatment episode. She denied a history of other psychiatric treatment. On mental-state examination, she was fully oriented, and her talk was both logical and directed. She reported recurrent brief periods of anxiety, irritability, and depression but denied problems with self-attitude or vital sense and was negative for thoughts of self-harm. She was also negative for delusions, hallucinations, obsessions or compulsions, or phobias.

Persephone's personality profile is presented in Figure 4. Compared with the NEO-PI normative sample, Persephone scored in the high range of Neuroticism; the low ranges of Extraversion, Openness, and Conscientiousness; and the very low range of Agreeableness.

Her high Neuroticism and low Extraversion scores indicated a tendency toward emotional distress and instability combined with considerable introversion. The low Openness to Experience score indicated that she was extremely closed to new experiences. Her

very low Agreeableness and low Conscientiousness scores pointed to a great deal of interpersonal antagonism and mistrust and an absence of structure, direction, or life goals. The high Neuroticism and low Extraversion scores were both consistent with the conceptual formulation of the AVD diagnosis. These personality traits were also consistent with several aspects of her life (e.g., recurring dysphoria, lack of friends, and lack of social interest). The low Openness to Experience score was somewhat surprising but was perhaps generally related to her lack of formal education. It was certainly consistent with her poor academic performance and her inability to imagine what she might "do in life." In fact, she reported being very content with her status as an untrained, unemployed mother on social assistance. Very low Agreeableness and low Conscientiousness scores are not conceptually related to AVD but are characteristic of a drug-use disorder. These traits were also consistent with prominent aspects of her behavior (e.g., frequent fights in school and with her boyfriend, poor school attendance, poor interpersonal relationships, and lack of direction or life goals).

More detailed information on the personality characteristics of Persephone was provided by an examination of her NEO-PI facet scores. Specifically, her Neuroticism facet scores indicated a marked tendency toward anxiety, anger, depression, vulnerability to stress, and self-consciousness. These traits are strongly associated with AVD, with the exception of high hostility, and correlated with her complaints of periodic intense dysphoria. We speculated that the high hostility was related to her interpersonal antagonism, frequent arguments, and fights with others.

Persephone's scores on the Extraversion facets were also interesting. Her low scores on the Warmth, Gregariousness, and Activity scales were all consistent with AVD. She was extremely distant from others, preferred to be left alone, and was slow and deliberate in her actions. Consistent with these traits, she had no close personal friends or confidants other than her boyfriend. Although low Assertiveness and Positive Emotions scores are not conceptually related to AVD, these traits were consistent with her lack of autonomy and her tendency toward dysphoria. The high Excitement Seeking was characteristic of her

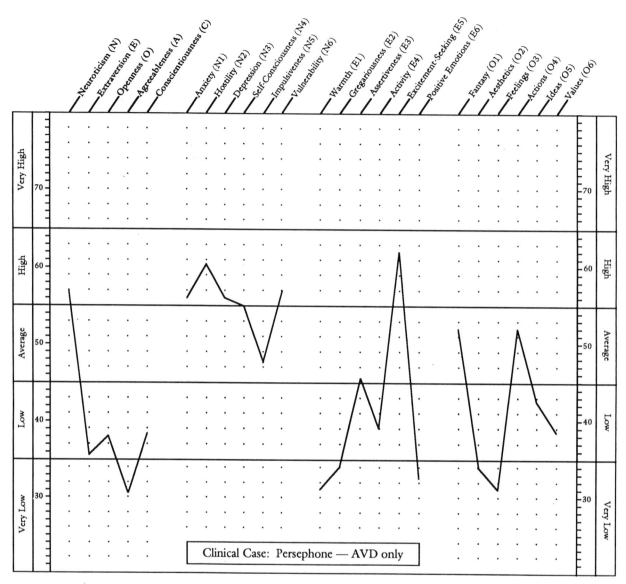

FIGURE 4. NEO Personality Inventory (NEO-PI) profile of Persephone, a pure AVD abuser. Profile form from *The NEO Personality Inventory Manual* by P. T. Costa, Jr. and R. R. McCrae, 1985, Odessa, FL: Psychological Assessment Resources. Copyright 1985 by Psychological Assessment Resources.

drug-abuse disorder. Finally, her scores on facets of the Openness to Experience domain indicated an experiential style that was generally closed to new ideas, with a rather narrow-minded and rigid set of moral beliefs.

Given this personality profile, her treatment prognosis was guarded. Although Persephone's marked tendency toward emotional distress and instability could have motivated treatment involvement, her extremely low level of introversion and interpersonal antagonism and her low conscientiousness were mitigating features. This prognosis was supported by the

mixed results of her first 3 months of treatment. At baseline, she obtained a high ASI severity score (i.e., 1.00) for employment problems and a relatively low severity score (i.e., 0.07) for drug problems; all other ASI problem domains were rated as nonproblematic (i.e., 0.00). There were no changes in any of the ASI domain scores at Month 3 with the exception of a slight increase in problem alcohol use (i.e., 0.01). Thus, she appeared to have derived little benefit from treatment. However, it should be noted that the ASI's failure to detect more of her problems at baseline (e.g., lack of friends, social interests or activities, occupational skills, or life goals) reflects the instrument's inability to adequately assess psychosocial functioning. It is possible that a more sensitive psychosocial measure may have shown greater change.

In contrast to the ASI data, only 2 of 13 (15%) urine specimens were positive for drugs or alcohol. The first positive sample was obtained shortly following admission, the second 1 week after the birth of her child. Thus, the rate of drug and alcohol use was relatively low over the initial 3 months of treatment. Of course, it is possible that being pregnant helped her exert greater control over her drug abuse. Regardless of the reason for her reduced drug abuse, these data indicated a positive response to treatment despite the lack of change in other life areas.

Case Report: BDL Opioid Abuser

Nancy was a 40-year-old single White female who was admitted for treatment of opioid dependence. Her family history was positive for alcohol problems in both of her parents and in one of her two brothers. She reported having a "bad experience" growing up and marked conflict with both parents and one of her brothers. In fact, she "ran away" from home on several occasions beginning at age 16 and was finally placed in reform school were she remained until her 18th year.

Nancy provided limited information about her school attendance or academic performance. She had completed the 10th grade and denied frequent truancy or school suspensions. In reform school, she had studied cosmetology. Between the ages of 18 and 30, she had more than 20 different jobs including assistant commercial artist, cocktail waitress, telephone solicitor, cosmetologist, and cashier. Since age 30, her main sources of income had included frequent prostitution, sale of illicit drugs, and social service support.

Nancy became sexually active at age 16 and denied a history of sexual abuse. Although never married, she reported having five "serious" relationships, each to a chronic drug abuser. She had been with her current boyfriend for 10 years, and they had a 3-year-old daughter. Her boyfriend was unemployed and abused heroin and other drugs. She described the relationship as chronically unstable and "unhealthy." In fact, she reported that each of her

"important" relationships had been "intense and abusive," describing them as "codependent drug relationships." She reported having sexual relations with other men during each of her "long-term" relationships. Aside from frequent "one-night stands," she had been engaged in prostitution for more than 10 years. As a result of these practices, she estimated having had sexual relations with more than 200 different people. She denied condom use throughout much of this activity and had only recently begun to use them consistently. Despite a history of high-risk sexual behavior and intravenous drug use, she reported two consecutive (over a 6-month period), recent negative HIV-1 test results.

Her legal history was remarkable for multiple arrests on a variety of charges and frequent activities that escaped detection (e.g., prostitution, drug sales, theft, and shoplifting). At age 16, she was arrested three times for running away from home. She was sent to reform school for 3 months following the second occasion and was returned there until 18 years of age after the third episode. At age 20, she was arrested for selling LSD and was placed on unsupervised probation. Between the ages of 29 and 37, she was arrested six times for shoplifting and was fined for each offense. At age 37, she was arrested for prostitution and was court ordered to a long-term residential treatment program where she stayed for 2 years.

Her medical history was also remarkable. At age 21, she contracted hepatitis from intravenous drug use, and at age 23 she contracted gonorrhea for the first time. She was hospitalized at age 24 for treatment of a skull fracture sustained in a fall, had three hospitalizations for treatment of "seizures" during sedative withdrawal, and at age 31 had three fingers amputated due to gangrene resulting from multiple drug injections. Finally, she had four abortions between the ages of 23 and 39. Nancy first began abusing substances at age 15, starting with solvents (e.g., sniffing glue) and followed by alcohol and intravenous use of heroin by age 16. At age 19, she began using marijuana, stimulants, and sedatives on a regular basis. On admission, she reported using heroin intravenously up to four times per day. Her treatment history was remarkable for multiple inpatient and outpatient admissions, representing more

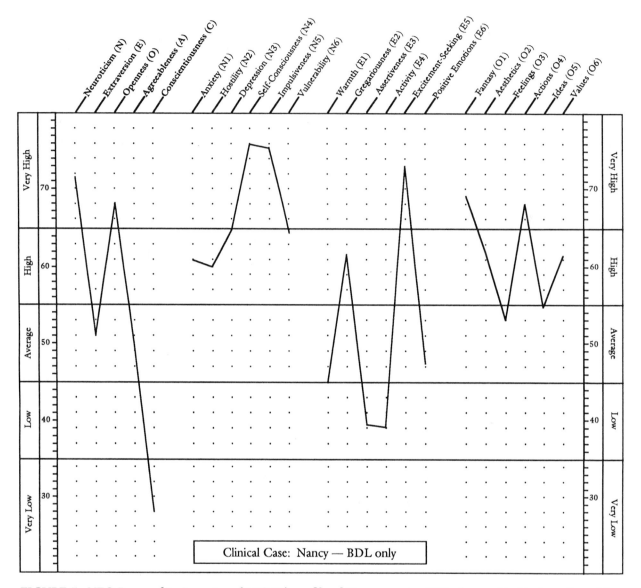

FIGURE 5. NEO Personality Inventory (NEO-PI) profile of Nancy, a pure BDL abuser. Profile form from *The NEO Personality Inventory Manual* by P. T. Costa, Jr. and R. R. McCrae, 1985, Odessa, FL: Psychological Assessment Resources. Copyright 1985 by Psychological Assessment Resources.

than 14 episodes of care. She denied treatment for other psychiatric problems. On mental-state examination, she was fully oriented, and her talk was both logical and directed. Although she complained of brief periods of intense anxiety, depression, and anger, she denied a change in self-attitude or vital sense. She was also negative for delusions, hallucinations, true obsessions or compulsions, or phobias.

Nancy's personality profile is presented in Figure 5. Compared with the NEO-PI normative sample, she scored in the very high range of Neuroticism and Openness to Experience, in the average range of Extraversion and Agreeableness, and in the very low range of Conscientiousness.

The very high Neuroticism and Openness to Experience scores indicated a strong tendency toward extreme emotional distress and instability combined with a marked interest in new experiences. Her remarkably low Conscientiousness score indicated a lack of consistent structure, direction, or life plan. The extremely high score on Neuroticism was consistent with both the conceptual formulation of the BDL diagnosis and with much of her life history (e.g., intense periods of dysphoria and extreme affective instability, chronically unstable relationships, and self-damaging behaviors).

Although her high score on the Openness domain was not predicted, it was consistent with major aspects of her life history (e.g., varied employment positions, sexual relations with many people, and use of hallucinogens). Her extremely low standing on the Conscientiousness domain was also not predicted but was consistent with prominent aspects of her behavior and with the clinical impression of a large number of similar patients (e.g., running away from home, reform school, frequent shoplifting, chronic prostitution, severe drug abuse, multiple failed treatment episodes, lack of direction and marked opposition to structure, and no consistent life goals). Many of her medical problems may also have been associated with her low standing on Conscientiousness. For example, she reported only limited condom use despite having had over 200 sexual partners and a good knowledge of the risks associated with her behavior. In addition, her score on Conscientiousness was certainly consistent with the drug-abuse disorder.

More detailed information on Nancy's personality characteristics was provided by an examination of her NEO-PI facet scores. Specifically, she obtained high scores on each of the facets of the Neuroticism domain. Thus, she was highly prone to pervasive emotional distress. She scored especially high on the Self-Consciousness and Impulsiveness facet scales. Thus, embarrassment or shyness was a problem for her when dealing with strangers and was consistent with her life history. She had great difficulty controlling her impulses and desires.

In terms of the Extraversion facets, she scored high on Gregariousness and Excitement Seeking and low on Assertiveness and Activity. Thus, she tended to seek out people and enjoyed excitement, stimulation, and thrills (e.g., her sexual contacts). Both of these personality traits are consistent with the repeated behavior of many BDL patients to avoid being alone or to avoid experiencing boredom. Her high score on Excitement Seeking is also characteristic of a drug-abuse disorder. Her low Assertiveness may have been related to a fear of abandonment and marked vulnerability to stress common among BDL patients. Her low level of activity may have been

associated with her strong tendency toward dysphoria. In terms of experiential style, she was remarkably open to new experiences. She had a vivid imagination and active fantasy life, enjoyed new and different activities, and was quite liberal in her social and moral beliefs.

Given her personality profile, Nancy's treatment prognosis was guarded, particularly because she was receiving only standard counseling. Although her marked tendency toward emotional distress and general Openness would have suggested a good prognosis, her very low standing on Conscientiousness clearly represented a major problem. This prognosis was generally supported by the results of her first 3 months of treatment. Her baseline ASI scores indicated severe employment problems (i.e., chronic unemployment), moderate family and social problems (i.e., unstable relationship with current boyfriend and strained family relations), and a modest problem with drugs and alcohol. There were few changes in any of these problem areas at follow-up, and she had developed a moderate medical problem (0.49). A very similar picture emerged from her drug test records. First, although eight tests were scheduled, she provided urine specimens for only five. Three (60%) of the five urine specimens were positive, primarily for sedative drugs (e.g., alprazolam).

CONCLUSION

The data presented in this chapter are useful for understanding the relation of opioid drug abuse and personality disorder to the FFM of normal personality. First, all patients obtained low scores on the NEO-PI domains of Agreeableness and Conscientiousness and high scores on the Excitement Seeking facet of Extraversion. In fact, the high interpersonal antagonism (i.e., low Agreeableness), high disregard for established social rules and conventions (i.e., low Conscientiousness), and high excitement seeking reported by these patients were remarkably consistent with clinical impressions and provide additional insight into many of the therapeutic problems common in the treatment of opioid abusers. Second, the NEO-PI also showed clear differences in the personality traits of opioid abusers. For example, high Neuroticism was characteristic only of those patients who also had a personality disorder. Third, support was obtained in the study for several hypotheses regarding the relations between the FFM and specific personality diagnoses discussed in chapter 3 by Widiger et al. Specifically, most of the defining personality features predicted for patients with ATS, AVD, and BDL were confirmed. Finally, the case histories showed the potential benefit of the FFM in predicting response to drug-abuse treatment. Taken together, these data provide new information about the relation of the FFM of normal personality to opioid abuse with and without comorbid personality disorder and support new research on the implications of the FFM for improving patient–treatment matching.

References

Alterman, A. I., & Cacciola, J. S. (1991). The antisocial personality disorder diagnosis in substance abusers: Problems and issues. *Journal of Nervous and Mental Disease, 179*, 401–409.

American Psychiatric Association. (1987). *Diagnostic and statistical manual of mental disorders* (3rd ed., rev.). Washington, DC: Author.

Blume, S. B. (1989). Dual diagnosis: Psychoactive substance dependence and the personality disorders. *Journal of Psychoactive Drugs, 21*, 139–144.

Brooner, R. K., Herbst, J. H., Schmidt, C. W., Bigelow, G. E., & Costa, P. T., Jr. (1993). Antisocial personality disorder among drug abusers: Relations to other personality diagnoses and the five-factor model of personality. *Journal of Nervous and Mental Disease, 181*, 313–319.

Costa, P. T., Jr., & McCrae, R. R. (1985). *The NEO Personality Inventory manual.* Odessa, FL: Psychological Assessment Resources.

Costa, P. T., Jr., & McCrae, R. R. (1989). *The NEO-PI/NEO-FFI manual supplement.* Odessa, FL: Psychological Assessment Resources.

Craig, R. J. (1988). Psychological functioning of cocaine free-basers derived from objective psychological tests. *Journal of Clinical Psychology, 44*, 599–606.

Kadden, R. M., Cooney, N. L., Getter, H., & Litt, M. D. (1989). Matching alcoholics to coping skills or interactional therapies: Posttreatment results. *Journal of Consulting and Clinical Psychology, 57*, 698–704.

Khantzian, E. J., & Treece, C. (1985). DSM-III psychiatric diagnosis of narcotic addicts: Recent findings. *Archives of General Psychiatry, 42*, 1067–1071.

Kilmann, P. R. (1974). Personality characteristics of female narcotic addicts. *Psychological Reports, 35*, 485–486.

Kosten, T. A., Kosten, T. R., & Rounsaville, B. J. (1989). Personality disorders in opiate addicts show prognostic specificity. *Journal of Substance Abuse Treatment, 6*, 163–168.

Kosten, T. R., Rounsaville, B. J., & Kleber, H. D. (1982). DSM-III personality disorders in opiate addicts. *Comprehensive Psychiatry, 23*, 572–581.

McLellan, A. T., Luborsky, L., Woody, G. E., & O'Brien, C. P. (1980). An improved evaluation instrument for substance abuse patients. *Journal of Nervous and Mental Disease, 168*, 26–33.

Miller, T. R. (1991). The psychotherapeutic utility of the five-factor model of personality: A clinician's experience. *Journal of Personality Assessment, 57*, 415–433.

Reith, G., Crockett, D., & Craig, K. (1975). Personality characteristics in heroin addicts and nonaddicted prisoners using the Edwards Personality Preference Schedule. *International Journal of the Addictions, 10*, 97–112.

Rounsaville, B. J., Weissman, M. M., Kleber, H. D., & Wilber, C. H. (1982). The heterogeneity of psychiatric diagnosis in treated opiate addicts. *Archives of General Psychiatry, 39*, 161–166.

Spitzer, R. L., Williams, J. B. W., Gibbon, M., & First, M. B. (1988). *Instruction manual for the Structured Clinical Interview for DSM-III-R (SCID).* New York: Biometrics Research Department, New York State Psychiatric Institute.

Sutker, P. B., Patsiokas, A. T., & Allain, A. N. (1981). Chronic illicit drug abusers: Gender comparisons. *Psychological Reports, 49*, 383–390.

Woody, G. E., McLellan, A. T., Luborsky, L., & O'Brien, C. P. (1985). Sociopathy and psychotherapy outcome. *Archives of General Psychiatry, 42*, 1081–1086.

CHAPTER 9

PERSONALITY OF THE PSYCHOPATH

Timothy J. Harpur, Stephen D. Hart, and Robert D. Hare

In contemplating the five-factor model of personality (FFM) along side the two-factor model of psychopathy described here, it is worth highlighting some arresting contrasts and similarities. The FFM and psychopathy share venerable histories, the former traced to the 1930s (Wiggins & Trapnell, in press) and the latter to the early 1800s (Pichot, 1978). However, they provide contrasting historical trajectories: The former is now presented as the most comprehensive system in the sphere of personality theory (Digman, 1990; John, 1990), whereas the latter is the distillate of a once far-ranging category that "at some time or other and by some reputable authority . . . has been used to designate every conceivable type of abnormal character" (Curran & Mallinson, 1944, p. 278). We might stretch the analogy a little further and suggest that both share an interrupted history, the former because of the vagaries of publication sources (Wiggins & Trapnell, in press) and the latter because of the emergence of the third edition of the *Diagnostic and Statistical Manual of Mental Disorders* (*DSM-III*; American Psychiatric Association, 1980) and its criminally oriented approach to psychopathy. Regardless of whether these comparisons are appropriate, we are left today with two structural models, one comprehensive, the other highly specific; each may help to clarify and organize thinking in its respective field. This chapter considers what we know, or might guess, about the relations between these models.

We first examine some historical views of the psychopathic personality as well as more recent conceptualizations represented by the *DSM-III*'s antisocial personality disorder (APD) and an alternative set of criteria for assessing psychopathy: the Psychopathy Checklist (PCL). We then review research on psychopathy using two structural models of normal personality: Eysenck's three-factor model and the FFM. Finally, we discuss how the two-factor PCL relates to the FFM and explore some implications for the use of the FFM in the field of personality disorders.

THE PSYCHOPATHIC PERSONALITY

Historically, the psychopathic personality represented an all-encompassing category of mental disorder that was distinct from, but on the same level of specificity as, psychosis and neurosis. Thus, Schneider (1958) referred to psychopathic personalities in much the same way that we now refer to personality disorders. He identified ten varieties of psychopathy, only one of which bears much resemblance to the term as it is currently used in North America. A similar use is apparent in the first edition of the *Diagnostic and Statistical Manual of Mental Disorders* (*DSM*; American Psychiatric Association, 1952). Here, the term *personality disorder* was used for the most general classification of personality disturbances, of which four types were identified: *personality pattern disturbances, personality trait disturbances, sociopathic personality disturbances,* and *special symptom reactions.* Sociopathic

We thank Stephan Ahadi, Jerry Clore, Ed Diener, Aaron Pincus, and Paul Trapnell, as well as the editors of this book, for their helpful comments on an earlier version of this chapter.

personality disturbances were further divided into four subtypes: the *antisocial reaction*, the *dyssocial reaction*, the *sexual deviation*, and the *addictions*. In the second edition of the *DSM* (*DSM-II*; American Psychiatric Association, 1968), the category *sociopathic personality, antisocial reaction* was retained to describe a personality type that would be recognizable to most clinicians today. The prominent features included failure to profit from experience and punishment; a lack of loyalty to any person, group, or code; callousness, hedonism, and emotional immaturity; a lack of responsibility and judgment; and an ability to rationalize behavior so that it appears warranted, reasonable, and justified.

From this brief summary, one might discern at least two types of confusion (see Pichot, 1978, for a discussion of some other sources of confusion). The first is that the term *psychopathic* has been applied to personality disturbances at different levels of generality. This has ceased to be an issue in North American nosology, although it continues to present a problem in England (Pichot, 1978). The second source of confusion concerns the descriptive content of the specific category that is termed either APD (American Psychiatric Association, 1980, 1987) or *psychopathy*.

Nevertheless, more recent writings have been remarkably consistent in the description of the personality characteristics of the psychopath. Beginning with Cleckley (1941) and continuing with Buss (1966), Craft (1965), Hare (1970), Karpman (1961), McCord and McCord (1964), and Millon (1981), among others, clinicians and researchers appear to have agreed in general about the personality and behavioral attributes that are relevant to the construct. These have typically included, with varying emphases and orders of importance, impulsivity; a lack of guilt, loyalty, or empathy; an incapacity to form deep or meaningful interpersonal relationships; a failure to learn from experience or punishment; profound egocentricity and superficial charm; persistent antisocial and criminal behavior without any evidence of remorse for the harm done to others; and a predisposition to aggression, particularly under the influence of alcohol.

Although different writers have argued about specific criteria, there has been general agreement about the breadth and content of the category for nearly 50

years (see Curran & Mallinson, 1944; Davies & Feldman, 1981; Gray & Hutchison, 1964; Livesley & Jackson, 1986). This conception of the disorder, by whatever name it is known, has been reflected in the definitions of the corresponding categories designated by the American Psychiatric Association and the World Health Organization in the *DSM* and *DSM-II* and the International Classification of Diseases-9 and -10, respectively.

Antisocial Personality Disorder

The definition of APD included in *DSM-III* departs quite markedly from this consensus. In keeping with the policy of creating fixed and explicit criteria for the identification of psychopathology, a definition of APD was created that consisted largely of determining whether the subject had participated in a number of criminal or antisocial acts in childhood and in adulthood (American Psychiatric Association, 1980). Although the advent of *DSM-III* undeniably boosted the reliability of psychiatric diagnosis in general, in the case of APD, it is widely believed that this increase in reliability has been at the expense of validity (Frances & Widiger, 1986; Gerstley, Alterman, McLellan, & Woody, 1990; Hare, 1983; Hare, Hart, & Harpur, 1991; Harpur, Hare, & Hakstian, 1989; Millon, 1981; Morey, 1988a; Widiger, Frances, Spitzer, & Williams, 1988). Robins (1978), whose research had a profound influence on the *DSM-III* definition, justified the reliance on solely behavioral criteria as follows:

> *We can get reasonably good agreement on behaviours typifying the disorder, but little agreement on why they occur. There are many who feel that the essence of antisocial personality is inability to love, lack of anxiety, or inability to feel guilt. Yet there are people whom these same diagnosticians would agree are psychopaths who claim to love someone (particularly their mothers), who say they feel nervous and fearful, and who say that they are sorry for their behaviour. To maintain a conviction about the nature of the psychological substrate in these cases requires believing that these psychopaths do not really feel the way they*

claim to feel . . . Yet the grounds for discounting the psychopath's claim to love, anxiety, and guilt, is always his behaviour . . . Since we rely on behaviour to infer the psychological substrate anyhow, I find it more parsimonious to stick to behaviour and skip the inferences until such time as we have a way to validate them independently of behaviour. (p. 256)

Although the logic of Robins's (1978) claim is valid, reliance on the specific behaviors listed in *DSM-III* (or its revision, *DSM-III-R* [American Psychiatric Association, 1987]) is problematic. In the first place, it is not clear that the behaviors chosen are the most appropriate for assessing the traits that even Robins acknowledged underlie the disorder. For instance, impulsivity is assessed by determining whether the individual travels from place to place without a pre-arranged job or plan or lacks a fixed address for at least a month. Although these behaviors are relevant to impulsivity, they are clearly not the only behaviors relevant to the trait and are probably not the most prototypical. Recent theoretical advances in the use of behavioral acts in the assessment of dispositional constructs (e.g., Buss & Craik, 1983) could be brought to bear on this issue (Buss & Craik, 1986; but see also Block, 1989). As yet, however, they have not been.

In the second place, without a more sophisticated use of behavioral indicators, it will not be possible to measure accurately the subtleties of which Robins (1978) spoke (e.g., the inability to form meaningful relationships despite verbal claims of the opposite). The inability to maintain a totally monogamous relationship for more than one year (APD Criterion C9) is presumably intended, in part, to tap this characteristic.

The criteria for APD (and its revision) are out of step not only with historical conceptions of the disorder but also with the other sets of criteria included in Axis II of *DSM-III*. No other personality disorder is defined by a closed-ended checklist of behaviors that must be used to infer the characteristics or symptoms

in question. For other disorders, both personality traits and specific characteristics are elaborated in general terms, using typical, but not necessary, examples. Histrionic Personality Disorder Criterion B2, for example, reads "egocentric, self-indulgent, and inconsiderate of others." Schizotypal Personality Disorder Criterion A5 reads "odd speech (without loosening of associations or incoherence), e.g., speech that is digressive, vague, overelaborate, circumstantial, metaphorical" (American Psychiatric Association, 1980). In *DSM-III-R*, this difference between these two criteria remains marked and is best illustrated by the language used to describe the adult APD criteria: Eight of the ten criteria contain the phrase "as indicated by," followed by a list of specific behaviors. Every other criterion listed on Axis II is a general descriptive phrase, sometimes followed by "e.g., . . ."

One might view the specificity of the APD criteria as a sign of sophistication, suggesting a better understanding of this disorder than of the others. We think that a more accurate assessment of this difference is given by Lilienfeld (1990), who suggested that *DSM-III's* definition treats psychopathic traits as closed concepts, allowing the diagnostician to consider only a fixed and limited set of indicators of a trait. As a result, many other behaviors or attributes that may be highly relevant to the trait in question are considered inadmissible as diagnostic information. Conceptualizing traits as closed concepts ignores the fact that traits are dispositions to act in a variety of trait-relevant ways across a variety of situations and that any one behavior is likely to be multiply determined.

The Psychopathy Checklist

At approximately the same time that the criteria for APD were being finalized, Hare (1980; Hare & Frazelle, 1980) developed an alternative criterion set for assessing psychopathy in male criminal populations. The instrument was aimed at assessing the construct as defined by Cleckley (1976), incorporating many of the trait concepts omitted from *DSM-III*. In addition, the PCL[1] treated most of the constructs it measured as open concepts, giving typical examples of the kinds of behaviors indicative of, say, a lack of empa-

---

[1] The PCL was recently revised in relatively minor ways (see Hare et al., 1990). The properties of the scale and the constructs measured are essentially unchanged by this revision, so for the purposes of this chapter, we do not distinguish between the two versions.

thy, but not strictly circumscribing the behaviors that could be considered in making a judgment regarding each trait.

A detailed review of the PCL is beyond the scope of this chapter, but recent reviews of its development and scoring are available in Hare (1991) and Hart, Hare, and Harpur (1992). The PCL consists of the 20 items shown in Table 1, each scored on a 0–2 scale according to the extent to which the item applies to the individual. Subjects are interviewed, and a source of collateral information, usually a prison or forensic psychiatric file, is reviewed. Items are scored after considering both sources of information. Although the item titles are representative, more specific operationalizations given in the scoring manual are followed when rating each one. The scale is highly reliable, as demonstrated by its use in several different laboratories (Hare et al., 1990; Harpur, Hakstian, & Hare, 1988; Kosson, Smith, & Newman, 1990; Ogloff, Wong, & Greenwood, 1990; Schroeder, Schroeder, & Hare, 1983; Smith & Newman, 1990; Wong, 1988) and is readily administered by anyone familiar with the construct of psychopathy and experienced with the populations in which it is to be assessed.

Considerable evidence has accrued attesting to the construct validity of the PCL. That is, the expected pattern of relations has been obtained with diagnoses of APD and psychopathy-related self-report scales (Hare, 1985; Harpur et al., 1989; Harpur & Hare, 1991a; Hart, Forth, & Hare, 1991; Hart & Hare, 1989; Kosson et al., 1990; Newman & Kosson 1986), as well as with a wide variety of demographic, behavioral, and experimental variables (for reviews, see Hare, 1991; Hare, Williamson, & Harpur, 1988; Harpur & Hare, 1990; Harpur et al., 1989; Hart et al., 1992; Newman & Wallace, in press; Wong, 1984). Moreover, the PCL appears to be superior to APD criteria in predicting criminal behaviors and accounting for the results of laboratory research (Hare et al., 1991; Hart et al., 1992).

Factor analysis has revealed two highly replicable factors underlying the PCL items (Hare et al., 1990; Harpur et al., 1988; see Table 1). Factor 1 measures a selfish, callous, and remorseless use of others and contains most of the personality characteristics considered central to the traditional clinical conception

TABLE 1

Items in the Revised Psychopathy Checklist

Factor 1
1. Glibness/superficial charm
2. Grandiose sense of self-worth
4. Pathological lying
5. Conning/manipulative
6. Lack of remorse or guilt
7. Shallow affect
8. Callous/lack of empathy
16. Failure to accept responsibility for actions

Factor 2
3. Need for stimulation/proneness to boredom
9. Parasitic lifestyle
10. Poor behavioral controls
12. Early behavior problems
13. Lack of realistic, long-term goals
14. Impulsivity
15. Irresponsibility
18. Juvenile delinquency
19. Revocation of conditional release

Items not included in factor scales
11. Promiscuous sexual behavior
17. Many short-term marital relationships
20. Criminal versatility

of the disorder. Factor 2 measures social deviance, as manifested in a chronically unstable and antisocial lifestyle. The items defining this factor tend to be scored more on the basis of explicit behaviors than inferred traits. In the eleven samples examined to date, these two factors have shown consistent correlation of 0.50, indicating a strong relation, but by no means an identity, between these two constructs.

A variety of evidence is available attesting to the discriminant validity of these two factors. Factor 1 is more strongly related to global ratings of psychopathy and to Cleckley's (1976) criteria than is Factor 2, whereas the reverse is true for diagnoses of APD (Harpur et al., 1989). A variety of self-report instruments commonly used to assess psychopathy are moderately related to Factor 2 but fail to measure the egocentric, callous, and manipulative traits captured by Factor 1. An exception to this trend are assessments of narcissism, which share with Factor 1 features of egocentricity, grandiosity, and a lack of empathy (Harpur et al., 1989; Harpur & Hare, 1991a; Hart et al., 1991; Hart & Hare, 1989). Evidence that the two factors may be distinguished in terms of their relations with age, social class, cognitive abilities, alcohol and drug abuse or dependence, violent behavior, and recidivism may be found in Harpur and Hare (1991b, 1991c), Harpur et al. (1989), Hart and Hare (1989), and Smith and Newman (1990).

The identification of two factors underlying our assessments of psychopathy has helped to clarify the relation between the PCL and APD criteria. Correlations between the two are shown in Table 2. It is apparent from these correlations that the strong relation between the PCL and APD criteria reported by Hare (1985) is mediated largely by Factor 2. Conversely, one could say that the PCL conception of psychopathy differs from the *DSM-III*'s conception of APD by virtue of the former's inclusion of Factor 1. In fact, Factor 1 is more related to current conceptions of narcissism (or narcissistic personality disorder) than to APD (see Table 2). Our contention is that those pathological characteristics of narcissism measured by Factor 1 in fact covary with a more general trait of social deviance and that together they form the higher order construct of psychopathy. Arguments and evidence for this position, in addition to that provided by structural analyses of the PCL, can be found in Gerstley et al. (1990); Harpur, Hare, Zimmerman, and Coryell (1990); and Morey (1988a, 1988b).

This research places psychopathy in a unique position among the personality disorders as a construct for which there exist both a highly reliable assessment procedure and substantial evidence for its construct validity. In addition, detailed knowledge of the structure of this disorder provides a firm criterion with which to compare dimensional models of normal personality. Unfortunately, the data currently available are meager. This is largely because adequate assessments of psychopathy, as we conceptualize it, require the application of detailed and time-consuming procedures. The use of available self-report questionnaires or 10-minute interviews will not provide an adequate basis for assessing the personality characteristics that are crucial in the psychopath. In addition, the inclusion of APD in the official diagnostic taxonomy of the American Psychiatric Association directs many research efforts toward use of this category, despite its lesser homogeneity and predictive power.

TABLE 2

Correlations Between the Psychopathy Checklist (PCL) and Assessments of Antisocial Personality Disorder (APD) and Narcissism (NAR)

Assessment	N	PCL	Factor 1	Factor 2
Diagnoses				
APD	319	0.56	0.42	0.55
	180[a]	0.55	0.37	0.61
	387	0.63	0.49	0.58
	114	0.58	0.39	0.57
	80[b]	0.45	0.21[c]	0.59
APD-R	176[a]	0.54	0.32	0.63
Prototypicality ratings				
APD	80[b]	0.71	0.40	0.83
NAR	80[b]	0.39	0.49	0.24

Note. Adapted from *The Hare Psychopathy Checklist–Revised* by R. D. Hare, 1991, Toronto, Ontario: Multi-Health Systems. Copyright 1991 by Multi-Health Systems. APD-R = antisocial personality disorder–revised. Similar superscripts indicate identical or overlapping samples. All *p*s < .05 except [c].

PSYCHOPATHY AND MODELS OF NORMAL PERSONALITY

Given the long history of this disorder, it is not surprising that the relation between psychopathy and dimensions of normal personality has been the subject of research (and speculation) for many years. Here, we review research using two structural models of normal personality: Eysenck's three-dimensional model and the FFM as assessed by Wiggins' interpersonal adjective scales and the NEO Personality Inventory (NEO-PI).

Eysenck's Three-Factor Model

Eysenck produced not only a seminal body of theory on the structure of personality (Eysenck, 1967, 1970; Eysenck & Eysenck, 1976) but an extension of that theory to account for criminal behavior (Eysenck, 1977; Eysenck & Gudjonsson, 1989). Although his research represents a major contribution to the literature on crime and personality, it is not entirely clear how applicable his theory is to the understanding of the psychopathic personality. In its original formulations (Eysenck, 1964, 1977; Eysenck & Eysenck, 1978), the distinction between the psychopath and the criminal was ignored on the grounds that considerable overlap was assumed to exist between them. Although such an assumption may be justified when using APD as a diagnostic category, it is clearly not appropriate when psychopathy is defined using the PCL. Base rates for APD may be as high as 75% in Canadian correctional facilities, but base rates for PCL-defined psychopathy are about 30% (Correctional Service of Canada, 1990; Hare, 1983; Harpur & Hare, 1991b; Hart & Hare, 1989; Wong, 1984).

More recently, Eysenck and Gudjonsson (1989) acknowledged the need to distinguish criminality in general from psychopathy:

> *Psychopathy and criminality are not to be identified, although both are characterized by antisocial behavior; psychopaths are not necessarily criminals in the legal sense, and criminals may not be psychopathic in their behavior. Nevertheless, both share the trait of antisocial behavior, and it seems likely that they will also share personality traits related to this type of behavior. (p. 48)*

Eysenck's theory predicts that psychopaths should be characterized by high scores on all three of his personality dimensions, Extraversion (E), Neuroticism (N), and Psychoticism (P), with "primary" psychopaths characterized chiefly by high P scores and "secondary" psychopaths characterized by high E and N scores. Although there is considerable evidence for the relation between these dimensions and criminal behavior (for a review see Eysenck & Gudjonsson, 1989), the studies that have compared PCL-defined psychopathy with the Eysenck Personality Questionnaire (EPQ) have found only partial support for the predicted relations. Hare (1982) reported moderate correlations between these scales and the PCL in a sample of 173 inmates from a medium-security Canadian institution. Statistically significant but marginal correlations were reported with scores on P ($r = 0.16$) and L (lie) ($r = -0.14$). Furthermore, zone analysis using median splits on E, N, and P revealed no significant differences in the level of psychopathy for subjects classified within any of the eight personality octants. Kosson et al. (1990) reported a somewhat higher correlation between the

PCL and P ($r = 0.34$) but only for White inmates. The correlations with E and N, however, were negligible. A different pattern of correlations was reported for Black inmates, psychopathy being correlated with E but not with P or N. This difference must be interpreted with caution, however, in light of the limited information available on the use of the PCL with Black inmates (see Kosson et al., 1990).

Harpur et al. (1989) examined the relation between E, N, and P and the PCL factors using the sample described by Hare (1982) plus an additional 49 subjects. The correlations, with total PCL scores, shown in Table 3, remained very small. However, it was apparent that Psychoticism was solely related to Factor 2 and was completely orthogonal to the cluster of personality attributes measured by Factor 1. A second theoretically interesting result emerged: Neuroticism was positively correlated with Factor 2 but negatively correlated with Factor 1. A similar divergent pattern of correlations between the PCL factors and anxiety was replicated using a variety of other measures of trait anxiety (mean $r = -0.21$ and 0.03 for Factors 1 and 2, respectively; Harpur et al., 1989).

A number of artifactual explanations for these modest correlations must be considered before examining more substantive explanations. Most obviously, either limitations in the range of scores or dissimulation might have contributed to attenuating the correlations. The first possibility can be discounted by comparison of the standard deviations obtained in our samples with published norms. Only P showed a slight reduction (12%) compared with normal subjects (Hare, 1982).

Although one defining feature of the psychopath is pathological lying, several arguments can be made against the possibility that dissimulation plays a role in this correlation. In the first place, the kind of information that the inmates are asked to reveal, even when completing scales for psychoticism and socialization, is far less probing than is the interview that the inmate has already completed, usually on videotape, as part of the PCL assessment. It seems unlikely that an inmate would be unwilling to admit to the kinds of behaviors examined by the P scale having very likely already discussed far more serious criminal and antisocial acts on tape. Furthermore, the

TABLE 3

Correlations Between the Psychopathy
Checklist (PCL) and Eysenck Personality
Questionnaire (EPQ) Scales

EPQ scale	PCL	Factor 1	Factor 2
Extraversion	0.11	0.08	0.10
Neuroticism	0.02	−0.17*	0.16*
Psychoticism	0.14*	0.01	0.22*
Lie	−0.17*	−0.03	−0.22*

Note. Adapted from "Two-Factor Conceptualization of
Psychopathy: Construct Validity and Assessment
Inplications" by T. J. Harpur, R. D. Hare, and A. R.
Hakistan, 1989, *Psychological Assessment: A Journal of
Consulting and Clinical Psychology*, 5. Copyright 1989 by
the American Psychological Association. $N = 222$.
*$p < .05$.

questionnaires are always administered as part of a
research project for which there is no strong or obvious benefit to the inmate for impression management. In situations with significant outcomes for the
inmate (e.g., parole hearings), psychopaths might be
expected to display considerable care in their self-disclosure, although it cannot be assumed that this is
generally the case. Finally, several scales designed to
measure impression management (e.g., faking good
or bad, dissimulation) have been administered to
inmates over the years, and their relation with psychopathy has always been zero or negative. In our
data, the EPQ Lie scale was as highly correlated with
Factor 2 as was P but in the direction opposite to
that predicted if psychopaths were dissimulating.

Assuming, then, that these results are not artifactual, what implications do they have for our understanding of the personality of the psychopath? In a
large sample of carefully assessed inmates, the relations between psychopathy and Eysenck's dimensions
were small. If we examine separately the two factors
measured by the PCL, the picture is clarified somewhat. Factor 2, a measure of extreme social deviance
and antisocial behavior, did show the expected pattern of positive correlations with all three EPQ
dimensions, although the size of the correlations was
modest at best. Factor 1 of the PCL shows a relation
only with anxiety, and in this case, it was in the
direction opposite to that predicted by Eysenck.

To provide as comprehensive a test of Eysenck's
hypothesis as possible, and in light of the hypothesis
discussed later in this chapter, a further analysis was
undertaken using the sample described by Harpur et
al. (1989). We examined whether the interaction of
the E, N, and P dimensions might provide a stronger
link with psychopathy than had been found for the
zero-order correlations. Although to our knowledge
such an interactive model has not been explicitly
endorsed by Eysenck, it is implicit in his use of
quadrant or octant analysis. In a hierarchical multiple
regression, the main effects of the three dimensions,
the three two-way interactions between pairs of
dimensions, and the three-way interaction term were
regressed on each of the PCL factor scores. In each
case, the analysis proceeded by entering all main
effects, then testing the change in R^2 when the block
of two-way effects was added, and finally testing for
the three-way term (see Cohen & Cohen, 1983).

The results did not support the hypothesis that an
interactive combination of E, N, and P would
improve upon the main effects of these dimensions.
For Factor 1, the multiple correlation after entry of
the main effects failed to reach significance ($R^2 =
0.03$, $p < .07$), and addition of the two- or three-way
interaction terms failed to produce a significant incre-
ment in this value. The squared multiple correlation
with all terms entered reached 0.05.

Not surprisingly, the main effects for E, N, and P
were significantly related to PCL Factor 2 scores ($R^2
= 0.08$, $p < .001$), with all three variables contribut-
ing to the relationship. Inclusion of the interaction
terms did not boost this relationship significantly,
producing a squared multiple correlation of 0.09 for
the full model.

Having attempted to relate psychopathy to
Eysenck's model of personality in a variety of ways,
we see no reason to alter the opinion expressed by
Hare (1982) that "high scores on the P scale may be
more a reflection of criminal and antisocial tendencies and behavior than of the inferred psychological
constructs . . . that are essential for the diagnosis of
psychopathy" (p. 41), these psychological constructs
being largely measured by PCL Factor 1. It must be
acknowledged that E, N, and P do share the predicted relations with the trait of social deviance
measured by Factor 2, and somewhat less clearly by

APD criteria, but in combination, they accounted for less than 10% of the variance of Factor 2 scores and none of the variance of Factor 1 scores. Even allowing for unreliability and the different measurement methods, considerable variance in psychopathy is unaccounted for within this three-dimensional model.

The Five-Factor Model

Although Eysenck's measurement of E and N is largely congruent with conceptions of five-factor theorists, his dimension of Psychoticism combines elements of low conscientiousness and low agreeableness, traits considered orthogonal within the five-dimensional system (Costa, McCrae, & Dye, 1991). In addition, although he acknowledged the importance of intelligence as an aspect of personality relevant to behavior (Eysenck & Gudjonsson, 1989), he did not measure it in any form in the EPQ. In view of the inadequacy of three factors in predicting our assessments of psychopathy, and particularly because the controversial P dimension is the dimension most strongly related to the PCL, it is clearly necessary to determine whether the separation of agreeableness and conscientiousness and the measurement of openness can provide a more comprehensive characterization of the nature of the two psychopathy constructs.

Most of the dimensions of personality measured to date have been selected for their theoretical relevance to psychopathy rather than for their interpretability within a comprehensive structural model of personality. In particular, scales from clinical assessment instruments such as the Minnesota Multiphasic Personality Inventory (MMPI; Hathaway & McKinley, 1967) and the Millon Clinical Multiaxial Inventory (MCMI; Millon, 1983, 1987), Zuckerman's Sensation Seeking Scale (Zuckerman, 1978), the Socialization scale of the California Psychological Inventory (Gough, 1969), as well as scales relating to Machiavellianism, empathy, and impulsiveness, have been administered. Although interpretively ambiguous with respect to the FFM, these scales have often

shown the most robust correlations with psychopathy. In addition, there are myriad clinical descriptions of the psychopath that provide a rich source of information allowing us to develop a more detailed picture of the personality profile of the psychopath. In this section, we discuss these findings and present new data using instruments designed more specifically to measure the FFM.

Psychopaths are prototypically thrill seeking, impulsive, lacking in anxiety, unable to sustain long-term plans or relationships, cynical, egocentric, manipulative, Machiavellian, cold-hearted, and callous. A rough translation of these characteristics within the organizing framework of the FFM produces a descriptive profile of the psychopath: high on Extraversion and low on Neuroticism, Openness, Agreeableness, and Conscientiousness (relative to a normative sample).[2] In fact, this characterization may hide as much as it reveals. In the first place, there is strong evidence for the existence of two distinct constructs underlying our conception of psychopathy. Second, the mapping of these characteristic traits onto the framework of the FFM is not straightforward, given that a single, consensual description of the five factors has yet to emerge (John, 1990). Third, the specific traits listed earlier and expanded on in the clinical literature tend to be at a lower level of generality than are the broad dimensions that form the framework for the FFM. Finally, in many cases, the traits that are characteristic of psychopathy are the very same traits that have generated the greatest disagreement concerning their place within this organizing framework. Bearing these difficulties in mind, we now examine the available data.

We have several sources of data pertinent to recent conceptions of the FFM. Although the sample sizes are in some cases small and the data derive from diverse samples, we present them here as a spur to future, more comprehensive data collection efforts and as a structure on which to hang our (sometimes speculative) thinking. We rely on the reader to weigh the relative importance of different results based on the nature and size of each sample.

---

[2] There is no consensus as to the most appropriate names for the five factors (John, 1990). We have chosen to use the terms *Extraversion, Agreeableness, Neuroticism, Conscientiousness,* and *Openness* solely because these derive from the NEO-PI, which we have used in our research. This choice of convenience is not intended to imply endorsement of these labels over any other.

Samples Research using the PCL has been conducted almost exclusively in criminal populations. Most of the results reported here follow this pattern, both because of the higher prevalence of the disorder among incarcerated criminals and because the PCL was developed (and validated) on a male forensic population.

Nevertheless, the need to extend the applicability of the PCL to other populations is widely recognized. For this reason, we have begun to examine how the PCL performs in nonforensic populations. Data from one of these samples, 50 undergraduate volunteers (25 men, 25 women), included self-report personality measures as well as PCL assessments.

Psychopathy assessments on criminal samples were performed as described in an earlier section. Several important differences should be noted about the assessments carried out on the students. For obvious reasons, no historical records were readily available for these subjects, so PCL items were completed entirely on the basis of an interview. Also, because none of the subjects admitted to having a criminal record, several of the items on the PCL, mostly from Factor 2, could not be scored because they are based largely or wholly on criminal activity. When necessary, such items were omitted, and the PCL total and factor scores were prorated. The absence of overt antisocial behavior among students may have made it more difficult to score Factor 2 for this group, leading perhaps to lower reliabilities for coding this factor (unfortunately, reliabilities are not available yet for this sample). Alternatively, because these items had to be scored on the basis of different information, the construct actually measured by the PCL Factor 2 in noncriminal samples may have differed slightly from that measured in criminal samples.

Most important, of course, the students scored on average far lower (and in a narrower range) on the total PCL and both factors than did the prison inmates. The mean scores (and standard deviations) for the 50 students for the total PCL, Factor 1, and Factor 2 were 6.7 (5.5), 1.7 (2.0), and 4.3 (3.7),

respectively.[3] This compares with mean scores for prison inmates of 23.6 (7.0), 8.7 (4.0), and 11.4 (4.0), respectively (Hare, 1991). In fact, of the 50 students assessed, only 1 scored above the mean score obtained for prison populations, and none would have been diagnosed as a psychopath by our usual cut-off, a total score of 30 or above. The range of scores on the PCL for the student and inmate samples used for the present study were almost entirely different: Only 3 inmates scored below 17 on the total PCL, and only 2 students out of 50 scored above this value.

Because of these differences, it would not be appropriate to consider the two samples to be equivalent. Although we would hope that strong relations between personality variables would hold across the range of PCL scores, it is quite possible that the relations between the PCL and external criteria are nonlinear. These are largely speculations, but they emphasize the fact that dissimilarity between pairs of nominally comparable correlations in the two samples should be interpreted with caution and should not be assumed to constitute a replication failure.

Measures In the student sample and in the inmate samples, we and other investigators have made use of a variety of assessment devices. The two with the clearest relation to the FFM are the revised Interpersonal Adjective Scales (IAS-R; Wiggins, Trapnell, & Phillips, 1988), and its more recent extension to the FFM (IASR-B5; Trapnell & Wiggins, 1991), and the NEO-PI (Costa & McCrae, 1985).

We obtained self-report data on the IAS-R for 113 inmates from a study by Foreman (1988) and for 47 student subjects. The students also completed the NEO-PI, as did 28 of the inmates. Finally, we obtained a set of ratings on each of the FFM dimensions made by observers watching videotaped PCL assessment interviews. Tapes from 12 inmates and 12 students were rated independently by two research assistants using the adjective scales of the IASR-B5. The raters were blind to the subjects' PCL scores and had, in fact, never been trained in the assessment of

---

[3] There were marked sex differences in scores on the PCL. Means for the total PCL, Factor 1, and Factor 2 were 8.5, 2.6, and 5.3, respectively, for males and 4.8, 0.7, and 3.4, respectively, for females. Differences for the total PCL and Factor 1 scores were significant. The only personality measure significantly differentiating the sexes was the dimension of Love, on which females scored higher than males.

psychopathy. These ratings, made on an 8-point scale, were then averaged and converted to scores on each dimension (see Trapnell & Wiggins, 1991).

The Interpersonal Circumplex The IAS-R assesses interpersonal dispositions within a circumplex spanned by the major dimensions of Love and Dominance. These dimensions correspond closely to Extraversion and Agreeableness as measured, for instance, by the NEO-PI, although the precise alignment of these pairs of dimensions within the circumplex differs (McCrae & Costa, 1989; Wiggins & Pincus, chapter 5; Wiggins & Trapnell, in press). Unlike data from the EPQ, these data can provide a measure of Agreeableness independent of Conscientiousness.

Harpur et al. (1989) reanalyzed part of Foreman's (1988) data to examine the location of the two PCL factors in relation to self-reported interpersonal style. The correlations between the PCL and these dimensions are shown in Table 4. A strong negative relation between both factors and Love was apparent, as was a positive relation between Dominance and Factor 1. Factor 2 was unrelated to Dominance as measured by the IAS-R. These data provide strong reason to think that Agreeableness is a dimension relevant to psychopathy independent of Conscientiousness.

The data for the student sample are also presented in Table 4. A strong convergence is apparent for the dimension of Love, although the relation appears to be dominated by PCL Factor 1 in the student data. The relation between the PCL and Dominance was negligible in this sample, however. Perhaps in the low range of PCL scores present in the student sample, the importance of Dominance in scoring the PCL items is lessened. In any case, the data for both samples confirm the long-standing view that psychopathy is characterized, above all, by a cold, callous, and antagonistic personality, but they

once again present a slightly mixed message with respect to Extraversion/Dominance.

The NEO-PI For a more detailed understanding of the relation between psychopathy and the FFM, we have begun to administer the NEO-PI to inmates assessed on the PCL. The NEO-PI provides domain scales with excellent psychometric properties for measuring each of the five dimensions, as well as six facet scales underlying the dimensions of Neuroticism, Extraversion, and Openness. Unfortunately, data are currently available for only 28 subjects.

Means and standard deviations for psychopathic and nonpsychopathic inmates (PCL total scores > 30 and < 30, respectively) are shown in Table 5. Mean values for the domain and facet scales are also presented in Figure 1, plotted as T-score profiles based on a normal adult sample (Costa & McCrae, 1989). These profiles reveal that the nonpsychopathic inmates showed relatively little deviation from the normative sample. A moderate elevation in Neuroticism, attributable mostly to increased depression and feelings of inferiority and shame (measured by the Self-Consciousness facet), is apparent.

Psychopaths, on the other hand, showed a distinctive personality profile, with a moderate elevation on Neuroticism, a moderate depression on Conscientiousness, and an extreme depression on Agreeableness.[4] It should be emphasized that these values are group means. Based on these data, about 50% of psychopaths would receive a T score of 35 or lower, and few, if any, would score over 50 on this dimension.

Correlations between the PCL, its factors, and the five domain scales for this sample are shown in Table 6. The correlations mirror the mean differences observed for the two groups: Those for Extraversion

---

[4] The personality profile for psychopaths shown in Figure 1 probably underestimates their low scores on Agreeableness and Conscientiousness. Current norms for the NEO-PI are based on subjects from the Baltimore Longitudinal Study on Aging (BLSA; see McCrae & Costa, 1987). This sample was drawn largely from managerial, professional, and scientific occupations, and it overrepresents subjects from higher educational and socioeconomic levels. Differences between the normative sample and the criminals considered here would be quite marked.

Psychological Assessment Resources, Inc., has recently circulated revised norms for the Five-Factor Inventory (FFI; a short form of the NEO-PI domain scales) based on a new normative sample that matches more closely the age and race (and presumably education and socioeconomic status, although this is not stated explicitly) of the U.S. population. Comparison of these norms with those for the BLSA sample provide some estimate of the bias that might be present in the profiles in Figure 1. Mean FFI scores for adult males on Neuroticism, Extraversion, and Conscientiousness were approximately 0.1 to 0.2 standard deviations higher in the newly collected normative sample. Both criminal groups' corresponding T scores would be expected to be slightly lower if based on these more representative norms. The mean level of Agreeableness in the new sample was approximately 0.75 standard deviations higher. This substantial difference means that the T score for psychopaths in Figure 1, already very low, would be lowered even further, probably by a substantial amount.

TABLE 4

Correlations Between the Psychopathy Checklist (PCL) and the Revised Interpersonal Adjective Scales (IAS-R)

IAS-R scale	PCL		Factor 1		Factor 2	
	In	St	In	St	In	St
Dominance	0.19*	−0.03	0.35*	0.08	−0.01	−0.17
Love	−0.30*	−0.32*	−0.26*	−0.42*	−0.29*	−0.25

Note. In = Inmate sample, $N = 113$; St = student sample, $N = 47$.
*$p < .05$.

and Neuroticism were in line with results obtained using the EPQ, although the broader domain encompassed by the NEO-PI Neuroticism dimension eliminated the negative correlation with Factor 1. As expected, Agreeableness, Conscientiousness, and Openness were all negatively correlated with the PCL, but only the negative correlation with Agreeableness reached statistical significance. It is interesting to note that both factors correlated about equally with Agreeableness, a result that is consistent with the projection of the PCL factors and the NEO-PI Agreeableness scale on the interpersonal circumplex (Harpur et al., 1989; McCrae & Costa, 1989).

Also included in Tables 5 and 6 are comparable statistics for the student sample. The students' mean scores on the NEO-PI domain scales were similar to those reported for a normative college sample (Costa & McCrae, 1989). The relations between the PCL and the five factors were broadly consistent with those for the inmate sample. The correlation between psychopathy and Conscientiousness was stronger for the student sample than for the inmate sample, perhaps because of the greater range of scores on this dimension (SDs = 10.3 and 8.1 for students and inmates, respectively).[5] In addition, Openness related positively to the PCL for the students but negatively for the inmates.

The breadth of the domain tapped by three of the five dimensions of the NEO-PI is ensured by the inclusion of six facet scales. A more detailed picture of the relation between the PCL factors and the domains of Extraversion, Neuroticism, and Openness may be obtained by examining these more specific traits. Although the numbers of subjects are small, we include these correlations in Table 7. We now turn to each of the five major dimensions in more detail.

Neuroticism The trait of neuroticism has historically provoked the greatest debate in relation to psychopathy. On the one hand, an absence of anxiety has been considered a necessary component of the disorder (see Spielberger, Kling, & O'Hagan, 1978). On the other hand, Robins (1966) reported a positive correlation between the number of psychopathic and neurotic symptoms. This conflicting picture has been clarified by the realization that the two PCL factors differ in their relation to anxiety and that the definitions of psychopathy used by theorists on either side of this debate have emphasized one or the other of these components of the disorder (Harpur et al., 1989). The clinical prototype of the psychopath represented by Factor 1 is moderately related to low anxiety, whereas the trait of social deviance tapped by Factor 2, APD, and Robins's (1966) earlier defini-

---

[5] As noted in Footnote 3, there were reliable sex differences in scores on the PCL. Although the gender differences for mean scores on Neuroticism, Extraversion, and Conscientiousness were not statistically significant, they were nevertheless substantial. These differences might have artifactually obscured the relations between the PCL and the personality measures. However, analyzing the data separately for the two sexes would have reduced the sample sizes substantially. For this reason, results will be reported for the whole sample. Nevertheless, separate-sex analyses were run, with results that were mostly consistent with those reported. For the male students, correlations of the PCL with the NEO-PI domain scales were larger than those reported in Table 6 for Neuroticism, Agreeableness, and Conscientiousness (0.34, −0.44, and −0.40, respectively). Similar increases were seen for correlations with the PCL factors. The very limited range of PCL scores obtained for the female students makes interpretation of these correlations difficult, although they were generally similar to those reported for the combined sample.

TABLE 5

Means and Standard Deviations for NEO Personality Inventory (NEO-PI) Domain Scales for Psychopaths, Nonpsychopaths, and Students

NEO domain scale	Psychopaths		Nonpsychopaths		Male students		Female students		Adult males[a]	
	M	*SD*	*M*	*SD*	*M*	*SD*	*M*	*SD*	*M*	*SD*
Neuroticism	83.8	17.3	80.9	22.6	83.9	24.7	91.1	24.7	73.0	19.3
Extraversion	106.3	19.9	98.1	20.0	113.7	17.6	112.4	15.2	102.6	18.0
Openness	110.5	12.1	110.8	18.3	127.8	20.0	125.3	19.7	109.2	17.4
Agreeableness	39.8	5.7	47.1	10.2	43.8	9.1	47.0	7.7	48.4	6.1
Conscientiousness	46.2	10.0	48.4	6.7	43.2	12.4	48.0	6.9	49.8	8.2

Note. Psychopaths, $N = 12$; nonpsychopaths, $N = 16$; male students, $N = 24$; female students, $N = 23$; adult males, $N = 502$.
[a]From *NEO-PI/FFI Manual Supplement* (p. 3) by P. T. Costa, Jr. and R. R. McCrae, 1989, Odessa, FL: Psychological Assessment Resources. Copyright 1989 by Psychological Assessment Resources.

tion of the psychopath is largely uncorrelated with anxiety. Furthermore, the relation between somatic complaints and chronic negative affect in the general population is probably mediated by alcoholism, drug abuse, and other behaviors that increase health risks (Costa & McCrae, 1987). The fact that psychopaths use drugs and alcohol to an excessive degree and that this use is related solely to PCL Factor 2 (Smith & Newman, 1990) may account entirely for reports that they demonstrate many somatic symptoms, regardless of their level of anxiety.

A second source of confusion may stem from varied conceptions of anxiety. The consistent relation between the PCL factors and anxiety just described has been found for many different instruments (Harpur et al., 1989). However, these instruments all had in common a relatively narrow conception of the trait. The Neuroticism dimension of the NEO-PI, on the other hand, incorporates both a Hostility scale that emphasizes short-temperedness and an Impulsiveness scale oriented toward a lack of control over cravings and temptation, both traits that would be expected to show positive relations with psychopathy. In fact, these two traits show strong relations with the PCL: Psychopaths' profiles for Neuroticism facets show peaks in the high range for these scales, whereas their scores on the remaining four facets are equal to or lower than those for nonpsychopaths (see Figure 1). As expected, both impulsivity and hostility related most strongly to Factor 2.

Because of the inclusion of Impulsiveness and Hostility, a negative correlation between Factor 1 and the NEO-PI domain scale could hardly be expected. However, the more specific facet of Anxiety also failed to show the expected negative correlation. Whether this was attributable to sampling error or the nature of the NEO-PI Anxiety facet is unclear at present.

Extraversion As discussed in relation to Eysenck's theory, Extraversion should be positively related to psychopathy. The data, however, failed to confirm prediction. A substantial relation was visible with only a single facet, Excitement Seeking, and this correlation was considerably weaker in the student sample than in the inmate sample. This relation is consistent with the empirical and theoretical link between Sensation Seeking (Zuckerman, 1978) and psychopathy (Hare & Jutai, 1986; Harpur et al., 1989; Zuckerman, 1978), and its specific nature may help explain why the broad domain scale was only marginally related to the PCL.

In addition to Sensation Seeking, the trait of impulsivity is one of the dimensions that shows a robust relation with the PCL and its factors (Hare & Jutai, 1986; Harpur & Hare, 1991a; Harpur et al., 1989; Kosson et al., 1990; Newman & Kosson, 1986). However, the position of impulsivity within the FFM is controversial. Eysenck initially identified impulsivity as a component of Extraversion but later incorporated it, along with elements of Sensation

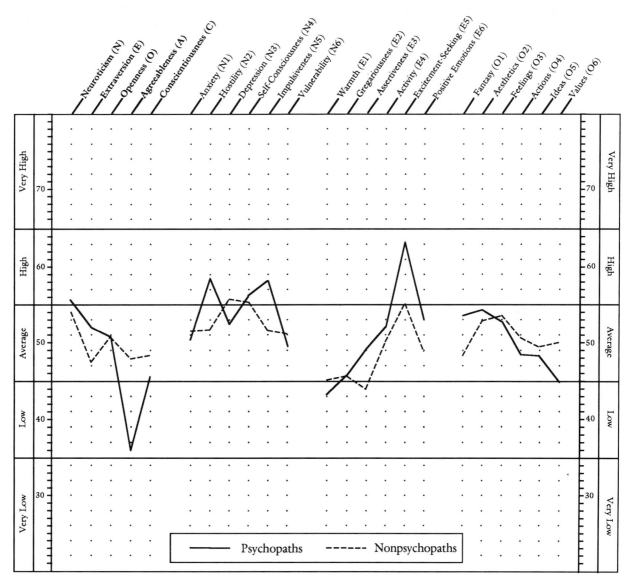

FIGURE 1. **Mean NEO Personality Inventory profiles for psychopathic (solid line) and nonpsychopathic (broken line) inmates. Profile form from *The NEO Personality Inventory Manual* by P. T. Costa, Jr. and R. R. McCrae, 1985, Odessa, FL: Psychological Assessment Resources. Copyright 1985 by Psychological Assessment Resources.**

Seeking, into his Psychoticism dimension. Costa and McCrae (1985), as noted, considered Impulsiveness (a failure to inhibit urges and impulses) to be a facet of Neuroticism, Excitement Seeking to be a facet of Extraversion, and the more cognitive dimensions of Self-Discipline ("the ability to continue with a task despite boredom"; p. 888) and Deliberation ("caution, planning, and thoughtfulness" and quick decision making; p. 889) to be facets of Conscientiousness (Costa, McCrae, & Dye, 1991; McCrae & Costa, 1985). John's (1990) consensual

adjectival markers for the five dimensions place "assertive" and "adventurous" at the pole of Surgency and "planful" and "painstaking" at the pole of Conscientious but identify no clear place for cognitive or behavioral impulsivity.

Despite conceptual arguments in favor of the taxonomic distinctions included in the NEO-PI (e.g., Costa, McCrae, & Dembroski, 1989; Costa et al., 1991), empirical results are less clear-cut. For instance, Excitement Seeking, Impulsiveness, and Hostility, the facet scales correlating substantially

TABLE 6

Correlations of the Psychopathy Checklist (PCL) and NEO Personality Inventory (NEO-PI) Domain Scales

NEO domain scale	PCL		Factor 1		Factor 2	
	In	St	In	St	In	St
Neuroticism	0.14	0.10	0.06	0.05	0.15	0.11
Extraversion	0.07	0.05	−0.10	0.17	0.16	−0.17
Openness	−0.13	0.19	−0.17	0.20	0.01	0.05
Agreeableness	−0.47*	−0.26	−0.35	−0.41*	−0.36	−0.18
Conscientiousness	−0.12	−0.38*	−0.07	−0.33*	−0.15	−0.38*

Note. In = inmate sample, N = 28; St = student sample, N = 47.
*p < .05.

TABLE 7

Correlations of the Psychopathy Checklist (PCL) and NEO Personality Inventory (NEO-PI) Facet Scales

NEO facet scale	PCL		Factor 1		Factor 2	
	In	St	In	St	In	St
N1: Anxiety	0.00	−0.14	0.07	−0.14	−0.05	−0.13
N2: Hostility	0.41*	0.12	0.14	0.17	0.48*	0.09
N3: Depression	−0.11	0.14	−0.05	0.07	−0.14	0.14
N4: Self-Consciousness	0.02	0.06	0.15	0.02	0.00	0.09
N5: Impulsiveness	0.33	0.25	0.05	0.15	0.44*	0.21
N6: Vulnerability	0.02	0.12	−0.06	0.01	0.03	0.19
E1: Warmth	−0.15	−0.08	−0.14	−0.07	−0.08	−0.12
E2: Gregariousness	0.03	0.09	0.02	0.22	−0.03	0.02
E3: Assertiveness	0.15	0.08	−0.02	0.27	0.21	−0.14
E4: Activity	−0.07	−0.02	−0.18	−0.05	0.00	−0.16
E5: Excitement Seeking	0.42*	0.17	0.22	0.24	0.38	0.00
E6: Positive Emotions	−0.05	−0.05	−0.28	−0.03	0.20	−0.15
O1: Fantasy	0.25	0.16	0.15	0.22	0.27	0.06
O2: Aesthetics	−0.03	0.23	−0.18	0.15	0.21	0.13
O3: Feelings	−0.08	−0.03	−0.10	0.04	0.01	−0.17
O4: Actions	−0.21	0.14	−0.26	0.04	−0.14	0.14
O5: Ideas	−0.15	0.20	−0.13	0.29*	−0.05	0.06
O6: Values	−0.29	0.01	−0.07	0.00	−0.46*	−0.05

Note. In = inmate sample, N = 28; St = student sample, N = 47.
*p < .05.

with the PCL, all show complex loadings (0.30) in a factor analysis of the NEO-PI (Costa et al., 1991). Both Impulsiveness and Excitement Seeking share strong negative loadings on Conscientiousness, whereas Hostility loads as highly on the Agreeableness dimension as it does on Neuroticism. In the revision of the NEO-PI, the facet scales of Self-Discipline and Deliberation also share with Impulsiveness substantial loadings on both Neuroticism and Conscientiousness (Costa & McCrae, 1992).

However this controversy is resolved, the fact remains that psychopathy is consistently related to these various aspects of impulsivity, broadly defined. We leave it to others to decide whether it is more parsimonious to consider these as individual facets of several dimensions within the FFM or as elements of a unitary, biologically based dimension of temperament (e.g., Zuckerman, 1989).

One further, interesting relation was suggested by the opposite correlations of the PCL factors with Positive Emotions in the inmate sample. Factor 1 includes an item measuring lack of empathy, but no formal measure of positive (or negative) affectivity has been used with psychopaths. The failure of psychopaths (or of subjects scoring high on Factor 1) to experience positive emotions would be an interesting extension of the growing literature linking psychopathy and affective insensitivity (see Williamson, Harpur, & Hare, 1991). Although the effect was absent in the student sample, this may not rule out its relevance in the inmate sample (as discussed earlier).

Openness to Experience The dimension of Openness to Experience has the most limited research base of the five factors. The most important component of the dimension with respect to psychopathy is that of openness of attitudes and values. Its converse has been characterized by McCrae and Costa (1985) as authoritarianism and dogmatism, both characteristics one should not be surprised to see in a psychopath. This impression is supported by the negative correlation seen for inmates with the NEO-PI Openness domain scale, particularly with the Values facet (see Tables 6 and 7). The strong negative correlation with the Values scale, which includes items measuring dogmatic moralism and intolerance, confirms the clinical impression that psychopaths are capable of verbalizing dogmatic ethical and moral views despite their flagrant failure to abide by these same precepts.

The marked divergence of results between the inmate and student samples is probably related to the vast differences in socioeconomic status, education, and background that separates the undergraduates from the criminals in general. These differences might be expected to show up in this domain more than others because exposure to artistic, literary, and culinary diversity is undoubtedly greater at a university than in a prison (of course, these differences would be present for these two populations long before they had contact with either prison or higher education). In this domain at least, it would seem likely that the inmate data should be given precedence.

The Openness facet scales also suggest some detailed differences among the scales. In particular, a positive relation was apparent with Fantasy (daydreaming, active imagination, etc.) despite a negative relation with the remaining scales.

Agreeableness Perhaps the greatest consensus would be found for the contention that psychopaths are prototypically low on the trait of Agreeableness. All of our data confirm that the PCL identifies individuals who are extremely hostile, aggressive, antagonistic, cynical, and manipulative. As we have shown, this places them at one pole of the IAS-R measure of this dimension, and this is confirmed by the correlations of the PCL with the NEO-PI Agreeableness domain for both students and inmates. Historical characterizations of the psychopath (e.g., Leary, 1957; Wiggins, 1982), as well as recent conceptions of the negative pole of the dimension of Agreeableness, fit well with this finding. Adjectives defining the negative pole of Agreeableness include *ruthless, selfish, callous, antagonistic, manipulative,* and *proud* (Costa et al., 1989; but see John, 1990, for an alternative list), all of them likely to appear in anyone's description of the prototypical psychopath. Other aspects of this dimension emphasized by Costa et al. (1989) are its similarity to Machiavellianism, the accompanying cognitive attitude of mistrust and cynicism, and the affective components of contemptuousness and callousness. It is important to note that some of these negative traits are potentially adaptive in certain circumstances.

Further empirical evidence for the link between the PCL and low Agreeableness comes from studies using the MMPI. Although attempts have been made to recover the FFM dimensions using the MMPI item content (e.g., Costa, Busch, Zonderman, & McCrae, 1986), studies of psychopathy have only reported correlations of the PCL with the MMPI clinical scales.[6] These studies have consistently reported moderate correlations between the PCL and the MMPI Psychopathic Deviate and Hypomania scales (Hare, 1985; Harpur et al., 1989). Of the MMPI clinical scales, these are the two with the strongest (inverse) relation with self-reported and peer-rated Agreeableness (Costa et al., 1989).

In the same manner, the MCMI-II (Millon, 1987) can be used to "triangulate" the PCL. The largest correlation is, not surprisingly, between the PCL and MCMI-II Antisocial personality scale ($r = 0.45$; Hart et al., 1991). This scale, in turn, correlates substantially with both Agreeableness ($r = -0.42$) and Conscientiousness ($r = -0.40$) as measured by the NEO-PI. The MCMI-II Aggressive/Sadistic scale, which correlates negatively (-0.46) with Agreeableness but negligibly with the remaining four NEO-PI dimensions, also correlates positively (0.36) with the PCL. Other studies pertinent to Agreeableness/Antagonism collected measures of Machiavellianism (Christie & Geis, 1970) and empathy (Davis, 1983). Moderate correlations were found between the PCL and both measures (Harpur & Hare, 1991a).

Although these findings are consistent, they disguise several more subtle relations. Other scales in the MCMI-II correlated moderately with the PCL. In addition, the two PCL factors were differentially related to these scales. The highest correlation of Factor 1 with any MCMI-II scale (in an inmate sample) was only 0.28. Factor 2 correlated 0.30 or above with Passive–Aggressive, Schizotypal, Borderline, and Paranoid scales, as well as with Antisocial and Aggressive/Sadistic scales. Whereas the Antisocial and Aggressive scales primarily share a negative relation with Agreeableness and Conscientiousness, the Passive–Aggressive, Schizotypal, and Borderline scales have in common a robust positive relation with Neuroticism (Costa & McCrae, 1990; see also Wiggins & Pincus, chapter 5). This pattern confirms the earlier

contention that psychopathy represents a pattern of deviation across several of the FFM dimensions. Again, however, the presence of the two factors in the PCL complicates the picture. Although the correlations were small, Factor 1 showed a consistently negative relation with Anxiety, correlating with Narcissism, that in turn is negatively related to NEO Neuroticism (Costa & McCrae, 1990), as well as with MCMI-II Anxiety ($r = -0.22$ and -0.07 for Factors 1 and 2, respectively; Hart et al., 1991).

This picture will undoubtedly be clarified with the introduction of the NEO-PI facet scales for Agreeableness, permitting finer discriminations to be made within this domain. The domain will be differentiated with respect to Trust (vs. suspicion), Straightforwardness (vs. Machiavellianism), Altruism (vs. selfish egocentricity), Compliance (vs. quarrelsomeness or anger expression), Modesty (vs. arrogance), and Tendermindedness (vs. toughmindedness or callousness). Given their extremely low standing on the broad dimension, psychopaths would be expected to score at the antagonistic pole of each of these facets. However, some differences, particularly with respect to the PCL factors might emerge. Manipulativeness, egocentricity, and grandiosity are prominent features of PCL Factor 1, leading us to predict the strongest relation between this factor and the facets of Trust, Straightforwardness, Altruism, and Modesty. Factor 2, characterized by anger and toughmindedness, should correlate most strongly with Compliance and Tendermindedness.

Conscientiousness Conscientiousness must also rank as a dimension on which all practitioners would agree that psychopaths should score low. Few self-report data, other than those already reviewed, are available to confirm this hypothesis, but a careful examination of the scoring criteria for the PCL (Hare, 1985, 1991) and for DSM-III-R criteria for APD (American Psychiatric Association, 1987) reveals that behaviors characteristic of irresponsibility, undependability, a lack of deliberation, and a lack of persistence are prominent features of the disorder. On the other hand, examination of the breadth of traits subsumed under the dimension of Conscientiousness

---

[6] Of course, many studies have simply used these scales to classify subjects as psychopathic, a procedure that clearly fails to identify the same subjects assessed as psychopaths using the PCL.

also reveals characteristics that are less central to psychopathy. John (1990) reported that disorderliness, frivolousness, and forgetfulness are considered prototypical of low Conscientiousness, and Costa et al. (1991) included Competence ("the sense that one is capable"; p. 889) and Order ("the tendency to keep one's environment tidy"; p. 889) in their six facets of Conscientiousness. Our impression is that neither Competence nor Order is inherently related to psychopathy. If anything, psychopaths might consider themselves to be exceptionally competent, in line with other inflated and unrealistic views of their own abilities, resulting in a positive correlation with this facet.

On the other hand, Self-Discipline and Deliberation, which we have already discussed in relation to impulsivity, are both characteristics that are lacking in the psychopath. In scoring the PCL, behaviors indicative of this deficit throughout the subject's life (e.g., being bored by schoolwork, quitting jobs out of boredom after 1 or 2 days, having inadequate or unrealistic plans after release from prison) are used to score PCL Items 3 (Need for Stimulation/Proneness to Boredom) and 13 (Lack of Realistic Long-Term Plans). Both of these items load on Factor 2, suggesting that these facets, and perhaps the Conscientiousness domain in general, relate most strongly to psychopaths' impulsive and antisocial characteristics.

The correlations in Table 6 seem to support the suggestion that psychopathy is negatively related only to certain facets of Conscientiousness. The correlations with the domain scale are generally small, consistent with there being a strong relation with only a few subtraits within the domain. In addition, the magnitude of the correlation is slightly larger for Factor 2 than for Factor 1. It is unclear why, in this instance, the students demonstrated a correlation of larger magnitude than that of the inmates.

Data concerning the psychopathy–conscientiousness relation are also available from a variety of studies making use of the Socialization scale (Gough, 1969). This scale has a proven empirical relation with PCL assessments (Hare, 1985; Newman & Kosson, 1986), although it is much more strongly related to Factor 2 of the PCL and does little to measure Factor 1.

FFM Ratings A final source of data is available that may be useful as a counterbalance to the preponderance of self-report measures already discussed. Ratings of the five factors, based on videotapes of the interview used to assess psychopathy, were completed using the IASR-B5 (Trapnell & Wiggins, 1991). Ratings were obtained for 12 students and 12 inmates assessed on the PCL. Because the inclusion of both students and inmates resulted in a very high correlation between the PCL factors ($r = 0.93$), we present only analyses of the total PCL score.

Strong relations between the PCL and each of the FFM dimensions were obtained. These correlations are presented in Table 8 for the entire sample and for the 12 criminal and 12 noncriminal subjects separately. Despite the small numbers, the pattern of results for the entire sample was largely duplicated in each group. This is important because combining criminal and noncriminal subjects introduces a confound between level of psychopathy and a number of other variables (e.g., criminality, social class, education) that differentiate criminals from college students. For example, the IASR-B5 adjectives for Openness emphasize artistic, literary, and philosophical dispositions, with relatively little emphasis on some other facets of this domain such as dogmatic values and openness to feelings. These are aspects of Openness that might particularly characterize students (who score low on the PCL) but not criminals (who score higher).

The pattern of results confirmed the profile of relations we expect between psychopathy and the five factors. However, several features of this study should be noted before the results are taken at face value. The ratings were performed on interviews gathered for other reasons and were not specifically designed to elicit behavior relevant to the dimensions subsequently rated. This procedure could lead to the underestimation of certain characteristics because of lack of data or to the undesirable sharing of method variance between FFM and PCL ratings (for which the interviews were specifically designed). The latter possibility would seem to be more likely in view of the fact that four of the five correlations for the entire sample exceeded the estimated reliability of the averaged FFM ratings (ranging from 0.54 to 0.77 based on the intraclass correlation coefficient and use of the Spearman-Brown Prophecy formula). Nevertheless, whatever the magnitude of the correlations, the pattern conformed closely to the expected profile.

TABLE 8

Correlations Between the Psychopathy Checklist (PCL) Total Scores and the Shortened Revised Interpersonal Adjective Scale (IASR-B5) Scale Ratings

IASR-B5 scale	PCL		
	Inmates	Students	All
Dominance	0.55	0.67*	0.66*
Love	−0.73*	0.27	−0.82*
Neuroticism	−0.52	−0.59*	−0.44*
Openness	−0.52	0.35	−0.76*
Conscientiousness	−0.77*	−0.49	−0.83*

Note. Inmates, $N = 12$; students, $N = 12$; all, $N = 24$.
*$p < .05$.

PSYCHOPATHY, FIVE-FACTOR PROFILES, AND INTERACTIONS

From the results reviewed here, it is possible to get a reasonable picture of how the two-factor model of psychopathy embodied in the PCL relates to the FFM of personality. The factor of social deviance (PCL Factor 2) is related in predictable ways to four of the five dimensions: positively to Extraversion and Neuroticism and negatively to Agreeableness and Conscientiousness. If one thinks of Psychoticism as the converse of the latter two dimensions combined, this accords well with Eysenck's theoretical treatment of criminality in general. It must be said, however, that the magnitude of these relations is not large and that a multiple correlation accounting for less than 10% of the variance of Factor 2 (based on Eysenck's scales) leaves much variance unaccounted for.

The construct measured by Factor 1 of the PCL showed a substantial relation with the Agreeableness facet of the NEO-PI, as it does with the related scales of Dominance, Machiavellianism and Empathy. A modest but consistently negative correlation has been found with various measures of anxiety other than the NEO-PI. However, for the most part, self-report questionnaires seem to measure quite poorly the characteristics identified by the interview-based assessments using the PCL.

What are the implications of these observations and findings for either psychopathy or the FFM? We think there are several. First, it is worth considering again the fact that the personality scales that are most

strongly related to the PCL have frequently been those that bear a complex relation to the FFM. In several instances, the prototypical characteristics of the psychopath combine several dimensions of the FFM. As an example, psychopaths are typically hostile and aggressive, as manifested in their violent and abusive behavior, their cold and callous affective reactions, and their contemptuous and cynical attitudes. These characteristics form a unified whole when seen in a psychopathic inmate but are represented by distinct dimensions in the FFM. The facet of Neuroticism termed *Hostility* measures anger and low frustration tolerance ("hot-blooded" hostility; Costa et al., 1989), and not surprisingly, this scale correlates substantially with the PCL (Factor 2). "Cold-blooded" hostility is hypothesized, however, to appear as an antagonistic orientation to other people and to be measured best as a facet of Agreeableness. Similar arguments can be made about the various manifestations of impulsiveness, which form a coherent cluster when considered as elements of psychopathy but are represented in the domains of Extraversion, Neuroticism, and Conscientiousness in the FFM framework.

This raises a major question facing FFM theorists: What are the developmental origins of the factors, and what kind of causal model can be developed to explain them (John, 1990; see also Buss, 1991)? With respect to psychopathy, an unbiased observer might conclude that the most likely lines of causal influence do not lie along the five dimensions to which this book is devoted but along dimensions of hostility, impulsiveness, and sensation seeking that bear a complex relation with the major domains. Needless to say, the resolution of this issue will have to accommodate a far broader range of data than is considered here (e.g., Buss, 1991; John, 1990; Zuckerman, 1991).

These observations also have implications for how the FFM may be used as an organizing framework for examining personality disorders in general, as advocated by, for instance, Costa and McCrae (1990) and Wiggins and Pincus (chapter 5). To date, these approaches have used self-report measures of personality disorder dimensions administered to nonclinical populations. One rationale for this has been that the poor empirical basis for current operationalizations of personality disorders and the unreliability inherent in their assessment lead to a "criterion problem" when measures of personality dimensions, based on far more extensive bodies of empirical research, are used as predictors (Wiggins & Pincus, 1989). Although this is true, it makes moot the question of whether the empirical relations uncovered by these analog studies mirror those that would be seen in a clinically disordered population. Psychopathy represents perhaps the single exception to this criterion problem.

It is troubling, then, that none of the self-report measures demonstrates very strong empirical relation to the PCL. Given the evidence attesting to the PCL's reliability and validity, this failure cannot simply be ascribed to the use of a poor criterion. Other than for Agreeableness, the relations are also too small to be accounted for solely on the grounds of nonshared method variance between the measures.

The FFM profile of the psychopath is considerably more complex than that envisaged for several other personality disorders. The simplest relation proposed is one in which an extreme position on a single major dimension places one at risk for a specific disorder (e.g., extreme Openness may characterize schizotypal personality disorder). More complex linear relations have also been considered (e.g., the profile for psychopathy given in Figure 1). However, the traits that make up our description of psychopathy appear to be more than this linear combination in two distinct ways. First, perhaps with the exception of Agreeableness/Antagonism, the broad level description of the five factors does not represent the most appropriate level at which to describe traits that define the psychopath. In each instance, one subtrait or facet may relate to the disorder, but another facet of the same dimension may manifest an opposite relation. Indeed, the present data indicate that discrimination of psychopathic from nonpsychopathic inmates is best achieved using specific facets, not general domain scales.

Second, the prototypical characteristics of the psychopath appear, both phenomenologically and possibly statistically, to be more than mere linear combinations of the five dimensions. Someone extremely low on Conscientiousness and Openness to Values is not, we contend, very close to being a psychopath. Even the addition of a low score on

Agreeableness does not, it seems to us, push the person much closer to the diagnosis. In the absence of, say, Dominance, Excitement Seeking, and Impulsivity as well, the syndrome fails to take on its distinctive form: One might see a shiftless authoritarian person but not a psychopath.

These speculations are open to empirical testing in at least two ways. The most obvious is that an interactive combination of the five factors (or perhaps of a subset of facet scales) should be able to predict clinical assessments. This interactive model was tested earlier using Eysenck's dimensions, with little success. However, the addition of the remaining dimensions, or measurement of the less broad-band facet scales, may provide a combination of normal traits that produces the clinical picture. Although the data we have are not adequate in terms of sample sizes, we decided to try a partial test of this hypothesis using the data from students and inmates on the NEO-PI domain scales.

Psychopathy and Five-Factor Interactions

The primary data for examining the interaction hypothesis were the NEO-PI domain scores gathered on 47 students. As was done for the EPQ scales, the main effects and interaction terms for the five scales were entered into a hierarchical multiple regression equation predicting subjects' PCL and Factor 1 and Factor 2 scores. Because of the small sample size, it was not possible to test anything more than the two-way interactions between the scales. The five main effects were entered first to test the magnitude of the combined linear relations between the five factors and the PCL. Next, the 10 two-way interactions were entered, and the increase in multiple correlation was tested.

The main effects of the five factors significantly predicted the PCL total scores, $R^2 = 0.26$, $F(5, 41) = 2.82$, $p < .03$, and Factor 1 scores, $R^2 = 0.38$, $F(5, 41) = 4.95$, $p < .01$, but not Factor 2 scores, ($R^2 = .20$, $.08 < p < .09$). In both instances, the beta weights for Conscientiousness and Agreeableness were negative and significant. The addition of the two-way terms increased the multiple correlations to 0.52 for the PCL total, to 0.60 for Factor 1, and to 0.49 for Factor 2, although none of these increases reached significance (all $ps > .10$), largely because of the reduction in the degrees of freedom resulting from the addition of the 10 two-way terms. Nevertheless, the introduction of the interaction terms increased the multiple correlations considerably, accounting for between 49% and 60% of the variance of PCL ratings. Inspection of the beta weights for the full models revealed an interesting consistency: Beta weights for two interaction terms were significantly related to the total PCL and to both factors, and no other interaction terms even approached significance. The two interactions were Agreeableness $\times$ Neuroticism ($A \times N$) and Agreeableness $\times$ Conscientiousness ($A \times C$); in each case, the resulting beta was large and negative.

On the basis of this observation, the regression was run once more, entering the five main effects at Step 1, followed by the two two-way interactions of $A \times N$ and $A \times C$ at Step 2. Using these seven terms produced multiple correlations of 0.42, 0.50, and 0.37, respectively, for the full model (all *ps* < .01). The standardized regression equations for these models are shown in Table 9, where the nature of the interaction becomes apparent. In every case, the beta weights indicated a substantial positive contribution made to the prediction of psychopathy by the main effects of Neuroticism, Conscientiousness, and Agreeableness, but an even stronger negative contribution was made by the interaction of $A \times N$ and $A \times C$. Because these latter terms were made simply by the multiplication of the component scales, we are led to the interpretation that the role of Agreeableness in predicting psychopathy ratings is moderated by a subject's score on both Neuroticism and Conscientiousness. Furthermore, an extreme score on the PCL would only be expected if someone scored particularly low on all three traits.

Because the preceding analyses were based on a student sample with a small sample size and seven independent variables, they of course cannot be trusted very far. In addition, the possibility of capitalizing on chance findings by selecting only these two interactions is great (Cohen & Cohen, 1983). Nevertheless, the theoretical importance of these two interactions is apparent from the literature reviewed in this chapter, suggesting that something more than chance is at work.

It seemed worthwhile, therefore, to explore this finding further using the remaining data on the NEO-PI gathered on 28 inmates. A cross-validation using this sample would seem to provide as challenging a test as possible of the validity of these findings, given that the new sample was from an entirely different population, was entirely male, and scored in a completely different range on the dependent variables. Despite this, we computed predicted PCL, Factor 1, and Factor 2 scores based on the regression equations given in Table 9 and on NEO-PI scores standardized within the prison sample. Correlations between the predicted PCL total and Factor 1 and Factor 2 scores and the inmates' actual ratings were 0.52, 0.47, and 0.29, respectively, the first two significant at *p* < .02 even with only 28 subjects.

The interactive model developed on students apparently did a remarkable job of predicting PCL scores on carefully assessed inmates. The cross-validated correlation of 0.52 is as high as has been obtained with any self-report scales designed specifically to assess this disorder. Whether this value would be maintained with a larger sample remains to be seen, but it seems likely that more accurate prediction could be achieved by developing the regression weights on a similar criminal sample.

PSYCHOPATHY AND THE FFM: SOME IMPLICATIONS

The data reviewed in this chapter have a number of implications for use of the FFM in the field of personality disorders. Clinical lore and empirical literature present a fairly clear picture of where psychopathy should fit in the FFM, and some of the additional data we have presented contribute further to this picture. The question of the relation between personality disorders and dimensions of personality being presently debated continues to be framed in terms of the most straightforward linear relations possible: Extremity on one dimension puts one at risk for pathology, or at best, several dimensions contribute to that risk. There is good reason for maintaining this simplicity. Nonlinear effects frequently fail to cross-validate, and when combined with criteria of dubious reliability (and perhaps even more dubious validity), the likelihood of capitalizing on sample-specific findings is great. Nevertheless, it would be foolish not to consider the possibility that

TABLE 9

Standardized Regression Equations Relating the Five-Factor Model to the Psychopathy Checklist (PCL) Total and Factor Scores

$$\text{PCL Total} = 0.13\text{*E} + 1.89\text{*N} + 1.62\text{*C} + 0.18\text{*O} + (2.46 - 1.93\text{*N} - 2.55\text{*C})\text{*A}$$

$$\text{Factor 1} = 0.24\text{*E} + 1.69\text{*N} + 0.84\text{*C} + 0.19\text{*O} + (1.55 - 1.80\text{*N} - 2.48\text{*C})\text{*A}$$

$$\text{Factor 2} = -0.08\text{*E} + 1.79\text{*N} + 1.89\text{*C} + 0.08\text{*O} + (2.75 - 1.87\text{*N} - 2.91\text{*C})\text{*A}$$

Note. N = Neuroticism; E = Extraversion; O = Openness; A = Agreeableness; C = Conscientiousness.

more complex relations may be necessary to model the complexity of the real world.

Psychopathy as assessed by the PCL is perhaps the most reliable and well-validated diagnostic category in the field of personality disorders. Our data suggest that it is also a good candidate for demonstrating a possible interactive relation between dimensions of normal personality and personality disorder.

A second implication concerns the strategy for creating a taxonomy suitable for classification of personality disorders. A clinical approach to this advocates operationalizing clinical knowledge, developing adequate assessment procedures, and performing research using clinically diagnosed individuals as the main database. A more parsimonious strategy might be to begin with a well-developed taxonomy of normal functioning and to search for extreme variants of these normal dimensions, namely, individuals likely to display pathology of some kind. Both strategies are likely to provide some useful information, but if psychopathy is to serve as an example, one would have to conclude that it would take a great many years using the latter strategy to arrive at a pathological variant of the FFM combined in the profile that is apparent in psychopathy. It would take even longer if the disorder turns out to be a truly interactive combination of traits.

Third, the question remains whether the five broad-band factors are, in fact, sufficient (in whatever linear or nonlinear combination) to "produce" the personality of the psychopath. Although the linear relation between the five broad-band dimensions and the PCL are not large, the interactive model cross-validated on a small sample, accounted for 27% of the PCL variance. Even with method variance

removed and optimal weights developed on a comparable criminal sample, there still may remain unexplained variance in the assessment of psychopathy.

What kinds of characteristics might be left out? One possibility is that the FFM is not, in fact, comprehensive. Grove and Tellegen (1991), for instance, suggested that the dimensions of Excellence (feeling oneself remarkable or unique) and Evilness (feeling oneself fundamentally bad) have been omitted from previous taxonomies because of the exclusion of evaluative adjectives from earlier word lists. The former dimension would most certainly be relevant to the psychopath's seemingly indestructible self-esteem. The latter dimension might reveal an interesting discrepancy between self- and peer-report.

It may also be unreasonable to expect the five broad-band factors to be the best predictors of this disorder. In general, predictive power is greater using traits measured at the more specific facet levels, and, as we have emphasized throughout, it is mostly specific facet scales, not the broad domain scales, that demonstrate strong relations with the PCL. Although we could not test this with the present data, we expect that a combination of selected facet scales would provide a stronger relation with the PCL than the domain scales examined here.

Our concentration on the domain scales may also account for the relative lack of differentiation of the two PCL factors in our data. At the level of the facet scales, however, several of the correlations were far stronger with Factor 2 than with Factor 1. Despite ample evidence attesting to the discriminant validity of these two components of psychopathy, few self-report measures successfully assess the egocentric, manipulative, and callous characteristics assessed by Factor 1. Those that do so most successfully are scales measuring dominance, narcissism, Machiavellianism, and a lack of empathy (Harpur & Hare, 1991c; Hart et al. 1991). These traits were not well represented by the NEO-PI data, but they should be better captured by the forthcoming facet scales for Agreeableness and Conscientiousness.

Another possibility is the emergence of a new or distinct type of personality organization that is qualitatively different from that seen in nonpathological subjects. A specific five-factor profile might certainly represent a risk factor for developing this type of personality organization, but it may require additional experiences or attributes that lie outside the traditional sphere of personality research for its full emergence. This speculation need not be entirely abstract, however. Current conceptions of personality organization make frequent use of cognitive concepts and processes as mediating factors in the expression of personal dispositions in behavior. Psychopaths, as a group, display a puzzling set of abnormalities in several basic cognitive functions involved in attention (Harpur, 1991; Harpur & Hare, 1990; Kosson & Newman, 1986), impulse control (Newman & Wallace, in press), and the processing of affect and language (Hare et al., 1988; Williamson et al., 1991). These may represent critical additional risk factors for the development of the disorder in addition to, or in combination with, the underlying personality structure.

References

American Psychiatric Association. (1952). *Diagnostic and statistical manual of mental disorders.* Washington, DC: Author.

American Psychiatric Association. (1968). *Diagnostic and statistical manual of mental disorders* (2nd ed.). Washington, DC: Author.

American Psychiatric Association. (1980). *Diagnostic and statistical manual of mental disorders* (3rd ed.). Washington, DC: Author.

American Psychiatric Association. (1987). *Diagnostic and statistical manual of mental disorders* (3rd ed., rev.). Washington, DC: Author.

Block, J. (1989). Critique of the act frequency approach to personality. *Journal of Personality and Social Psychology, 56,* 234–245.

Buss, A. H. (1966). *Psychopathology.* New York: Wiley.

Buss, D. M. (1991). Evolutionary personality psychology. *Annual Review of Psychology, 42,* 459–491.

Buss, D. M., & Craik, K. H. (1983). The act frequency approach to personality. *Psychological Review, 90,* 105–126.

Buss, D. M., & Craik, K. H. (1986). Acts, dispositions, and clinical assessment: The psychopathology of everyday conduct. *Clinical Psychology Review, 6,* 387–406.

Christie, R., & Geis, F. L. (1970). *Studies in Machiavellianism.* New York: Academic Press.

Cleckley, H. (1941). *The mask of sanity.* St. Louis, MO: Mosby.

Cleckley, H. (1976). *The mask of sanity* (5th ed.). St. Louis, MO: Mosby.

Cohen, J., & Cohen, P. (1983). *Applied multiple regression/ correlation analysis for the behavioral sciences* (2nd ed.). Hillsdale, NJ: Erlbaum.

Correctional Service of Canada. (1990). *Forum on corrections research, 2*(No. 1). Ottawa, Canada: Author.

Costa, P. T., Jr., Busch, C. M., Zonderman, A. B., & McCrae, R. R. (1986). Correlations of MMPI factor scales with measures of the five factor model of personality. *Journal of Personality Assessment, 50,* 640–650.

Costa, P. T., Jr., & McCrae, R. R. (1985). *The NEO Personality Inventory manual.* Odessa, FL: Psychological Assessment Resources.

Costa, P. T., Jr., & McCrae, R. R. (1987). Neuroticism, somatic complaints, and disease: Is the bark worse than the bite? *Journal of Personality, 55,* 301–316.

Costa, P. T., Jr., & McCrae, R. R. (1989). *NEO-PI/FFI manual supplement.* Odessa, FL: Psychological Assessment Resources.

Costa, P. T., Jr., & McCrae, R. R. (1990). Personality disorders and the five-factor model of personality. *Journal of Personality Disorders, 4,* 362–371.

Costa, P. T., Jr., & McCrae, R. R. (1992). *Revised NEO Personality Inventory (NEO-PI-R) and NEO Five-Factor Inventory (NEO-FFI) professional manual.* Odessa, FL: Psychological Assessment Resources.

Costa, P. T., Jr., McCrae, R. R., & Dembroski, T. M. (1989). Agreeableness versus antagonism: Explication of a potential risk factor for CHD. In A. W. Siegman & T. M. Dembroski (Eds.), *In search of coronary-prone behavior: Beyond Type A* (pp. 41–63). Hillsdale, NJ: Erlbaum.

Costa, P. T., Jr., McCrae, R. R., & Dye, D. A. (1991). Facet scales for agreeableness and conscientiousness: A revision of the NEO Personality Inventory. *Personality and Individual Differences, 12,* 887–898.

Craft, M. J. (1965). *Ten studies into psychopathic personality.* Bristol, UK: John Wright.

Curran, D., & Mallinson, P. (1944). Psychopathic personality. *Journal of Mental Science, 90,* 266–286.

Davis, M. H. (1983). Measuring individual differences in empathy: Evidence for a multidimensional approach. *Journal of Personality and Social Psychology, 44,* 113–126.

Davies, W., & Feldman, P. (1981). The diagnosis of psychopathy by forensic specialists. *British Journal of Psychiatry, 138,* 329–331.

Digman, J. M. (1990). Personality structure: Emergence of the five-factor model. *Annual Review of Psychology, 41,* 417–440.

Eysenck, H. J. (1964). *Crime and personality.* London: Routledge & Kegan Paul.

Eysenck, H. J. (1967). *The biological basis of personality.* Springfield, IL: Charles C Thomas.

Eysenck, H. J. (1970). *The structure of human personality.* London: Methuen.

Eysenck, H. J. (1977). *Crime and personality* (3rd ed.). London: Routledge & Kegan Paul.

Eysenck, H. J., & Eysenck, S. B. G. (1976). *Psychoticism as a dimension of personality.* London: Hodder & Stoughton.

Eysenck, H. J., & Eysenck, S. B. G. (1978). Psychopathy, personality and genetics. In R. D. Hare & D. Schalling (Eds.), *Psychopathic behavior: Approaches to research* (pp. 197–223). New York: Wiley.

Eysenck, H. J., & Gudjonsson, G. H. (1989). *The causes and cures of criminality.* New York: Plenum.

Foreman, M. (1988). *Psychopathy and interpersonal behavior.* Unpublished doctoral dissertation, University of British Columbia, Vancouver, Canada.

Frances, A. J., & Widiger, T. (1986). The classification of personality disorders: An overview of problems and solutions. In A. J. Frances & R. E. Hales (Eds.), *American Psychiatric Association Annual Review* (Vol. 5, pp. 244–257). Washington, DC: American Psychiatric Press.

Gerstley, L. J., Alterman, A. I., McLellan, A. T., & Woody, G. E. (1990). Antisocial personality disorder in substance abusers: A problematic diagnosis? *American Journal of Psychiatry, 147,* 173–178.

Gough, H. G. (1969). *Manual for the California Psychological Inventory.* Palo Alto, CA: Consulting Psychologists Press.

Gray, K. C., & Hutchison, H. C. (1964). The psychopathic personality: A survey of Canadian psychiatrists' opinions. *Canadian Psychiatric Association Journal, 9,* 452–461.

Grove, W. M., & Tellegen, A. (1991). Problems in the classification of personality disorders. *Journal of Personality Disorders, 5,* 31–41.

Hare, R. D. (1970). *Psychopathy: Theory and research.* New York: Wiley.

Hare, R. D. (1980). A research scale for the assessment of psychopathy in criminal populations. *Personality and Individual Differences, 1,* 111–117.

Hare, R. D. (1982). Psychopathy and the personality dimensions of psychoticism, extraversion and neuroticism. *Personality and Individual Differences, 3,* 35–42.

Hare, R. D. (1983). Diagnosis of antisocial personality disorder in two prison populations. *American Journal of Psychiatry, 140,* 887–890.

Hare, R. D. (1985). Comparison of procedures for the assessment of psychopathy. *Journal of Consulting and Clinical Psychology, 53,* 7–16.

Hare, R. D. (1991). *The Hare Psychopathy Checklist–Revised.* Toronto, Ontario: Multi-Health Systems.

Hare, R. D., & Frazelle, J. (1980). *Some preliminary notes on the use of a research scale for the assessment of psychopathy in criminal populations.* Unpublished manuscript, Department of Psychology, University of British Columbia, Vancouver, Canada.

Hare, R. D., Harpur, T. J., Hakstian, A. R., Forth, A. E., Hart, S. D., & Newman, J. P. (1990). The Revised Psychopathy Checklist: Reliability and factor structure. *Psychological Assessment: A Journal of Consulting and Clinical Psychology, 2,* 338–341.

Hare, R. D., Hart, S. D., & Harpur, T. J. (1991). Psychopathy and the proposed *DSM-IV* criteria for antisocial personality disorder. *Journal of Abnormal Psychology, 100,* 391–398.

Hare, R. D., & Jutai, J. W. (1986). Psychopathy, stimulation seeking, and stress. In J. Strelau, F. H. Farley, & A. Gale (Eds.), *The biological bases of personality and behavior* (Vol. 2, pp. 175–184). Washington, DC: Hemisphere.

Hare, R. D., Williamson, S. E., & Harpur, T. J. (1988). Psychopathy and language. In T. E. Moffitt & S. A. Mednick (Eds.), *Biological contributions to crime causation* (pp. 68–92). Dordrecht, The Netherlands: Martinus Nijhoff.

Harpur, T. J. (1991). *Visual attention in psychopathic criminals.* Unpublished doctoral dissertation, University of British Columbia, Vancouver, Canada.

Harpur, T. J., Hakstian, A. R., & Hare, R. D. (1988). Factor structure of the Psychopathy Checklist. *Journal of Consulting and Clinical Psychology, 56,* 741–747.

Harpur, T. J., & Hare, R. D. (1990). Psychopathy and attention. In J. Enns (Ed.), *The development of attention: Research and theory* (pp. 429–444). Amsterdam: North-Holland.

Harpur, T. J., & Hare, R. D. (1991a). *Self-report correlates of psychopathy: Narcissism, Machiavellianism, and empathy.* Unpublished manuscript.

Harpur, T. J., & Hare, R. D. (1991b). *The assessment of psychopathy as a function of age.* Manuscript submitted for publication.

Harpur, T. J., & Hare, R. D. (1991c, August). *Psychopathy and violent behavior: Two factors are better than one.* Paper presented at the 99th annual meeting of the American Psychological Association, San Francisco, CA.

Harpur, T. J., Hare, R. D., & Hakstian, A. R. (1989). Two-factor conceptualization of psychopathy: Construct validity and assessment implications. *Psychological Assessment: A Journal of Consulting and Clinical Psychology, 1,* 6–17.

Harpur, T. J., Hare, R. D., Zimmerman, M., & Coryell, W. (1990, August). *Dimensions underlying DSM-III personality disorders: Cluster 2.* Paper presented at the 98th annual convention of the American Psychological Association, Boston, MA.

Hart, S. D., Forth, A. E., & Hare, R. D. (1991). The MCMI-II and psychopathy. *Journal of Personality Disorders, 5,* 318–327.

Hart, S. D., & Hare, R. D. (1989). Discriminant validity of the Psychopathy Checklist in a forensic psychiatric population. *Psychological Assessment: A Journal of Consulting and Clinical Psychology, 1,* 211–218.

Hart, S. D., Hare, R. D., & Harpur, T. J. (1992). The Psychopathy Checklist: An overview for researchers and clinicians. In P. McReynolds & J. Rosen (Eds.), *Advances in psychological assessment* (Vol. 8, pp. 103–130). New York: Plenum.

Hathaway, S. R., & McKinley, J. C. (1967). *Manual for the Minnesota Multiphasic Personality Inventory.* New York: Psychological Corporation.

John, O. P. (1990). The "Big Five" factor taxonomy: Dimensions of personality in the natural language and in questionnaires. In L. A. Pervin (Ed.), *Handbook of personality: Theory and research* (pp. 66–100). New York: Guilford Press.

Karpman, B. (1961). The structure of neurosis: With special differentials between neurosis, psychosis, homosexuality, alcoholism, psychopathy, and criminality. *Archives of Criminal Psychodynamics, 4,* 599–646.

Kosson, D. S., & Newman, J. P. (1986). Psychopathy and allocation of attentional capacity in a divided-attention situation. *Journal of Abnormal Psychology, 95,* 257–263.

Kosson, D. S., Smith, S. S., & Newman, J. P. (1990). Evaluation of the construct validity of psychopathy in Black and White male inmates: Three preliminary studies. *Journal of Abnormal Psychology, 99,* 250–259.

Leary, T. (1957). *Interpersonal diagnosis of personality.* New York: Ronald Press.

Lilienfeld, S. O. (1990). *Conceptual and empirical issues in the assessment of psychopathy.* Unpublished manuscript.

Livesley, W. J., & Jackson, D. N. (1986). The internal consistency and factorial structure of behaviors judged to be associated with *DSM-III* personality disorders. *American Journal of Psychiatry, 143,* 1473–1474.

McCord, W., & McCord, J. (1964). *The psychopath: An essay on the criminal mind.* Princeton, NJ: Van Nostrand.

McCrae, R. R., & Costa, P. T., Jr. (1985). Openness to experience. In R. Hogan & W. H. Jones (Eds.), *Perspectives in personality* (Vol. 1, pp. 145–172). Greenwich, CT: JAI Press.

McCrae, R. R., & Costa, P. T., Jr. (1987). Validation of the five-factor model of personality across instruments and observers. *Journal of Personality and Social Psychology, 52,* 81–90.

McCrae, R. R., & Costa, P. T., Jr. (1989). The structure of interpersonal traits: Wiggin's circumplex and the five-factor model. *Journal of Personality and Social Psychology, 56,* 586–595.

Millon, T. (1981). *Disorders of personality: DSM-III. Axis II.* New York: Wiley.

Millon, T. (1983). *Millon Clinical Multiaxial Inventory manual* (3rd ed.). Minneapolis, MN: National Computer Systems.

Millon, T. (1987). *Millon Clinical Multiaxial Inventory–II manual.* Minneapolis, MN: National Computer Systems.

Morey, L. C. (1988a). The categorical representation of personality disorder: A cluster analysis of *DSM-III* personality features. *Journal of Abnormal Psychology, 97,* 314–321.

Morey, L. C. (1988b). A psychometric analysis of the *DSM–III–R* personality disorder criteria. *Journal of Personality Disorders, 2,* 109–124.

Newman, J. P., & Kosson, D. S. (1986). Passive avoidance learning in psychopathic and nonpsychopathic offenders. *Journal of Abnormal Psychology, 95,* 252–256.

Newman, J. P., & Wallace, J. (in press). Psychopathy and cognition. In K. S. Dobson & P. C. Kendall (Eds.), *Psychopathology and cognition.* San Diego, CA: Academic Press.

Ogloff, J. P. R., Wong, S., & Greenwood, A. (1990). Treating criminal psychopaths in a therapeutic community program. *Behavioral Sciences and the Law, 8,* 81–90.

Pichot, P. (1978). Psychopathic behaviour: A historical overview. In R. D. Hare & D. Schalling (Eds.), *Psychopathic behavior: Approaches to research* (pp. 55–70). New York: Wiley.

Robins, L. N. (1966). *Deviant children grown up.* Baltimore: Williams & Wilkins.

Robins, L. N. (1978). Aetiological implications in studies of childhood histories relating to antisocial personality. In R. D. Hare & D. Schalling (Eds.), *Psychopathic behavior: Approaches to research* (pp. 255–271). New York: Wiley.

Schneider, K. (1958). *Psychopathic personalities.* Springfield, IL: Charles C Thomas.

Schroeder, M. L., Schroeder, K. G., & Hare, R. D. (1983). Generalizability of a checklist for the assessment of psychopathy. *Journal of Consulting and Clinical Psychology, 51,* 511–516.

Smith, S. S., & Newman, J. P. (1990). Alcohol and drug abuse/dependence disorders in psychopathic and nonpsychopathic criminal offenders. *Journal of Abnormal Psychology, 99,* 430–439.

Spielberger, C. D., Kling, J. K., & O'Hagan, S. E. J. (1978). Dimensions of psychopathic personality: Antisocial behaviour and anxiety. In R. D. Hare & D. Schalling (Eds.), *Psychopathic behavior: Approaches to research* (pp. 23–46). New York: Wiley.

Trapnell, P. D., & Wiggins, J. S. (1991). Extension of the Interpersonal Adjective Scales to the Big Five dimensions of personality. *Journal of Personality and Social Psychology, 59,* 781–790.

Widiger, T. A., Frances, A. J., Spitzer, R. L., & Williams, J. B. W. (1988). The *DSM-III-R* personality disorders: An overview. *American Journal of Psychiatry, 145,* 786–795.

Wiggins, J. S. (1982). Circumplex models of interpersonal behavior in clinical psychology. In P. C. Kendall & J. N. Butcher (Eds.), *Handbook of research methods in clinical psychology* (pp. 183–221). New York: Wiley.

Wiggins, J. S., & Pincus, A. L. (1989). Conceptions of personality disorders and dimensions of personality. *Psychological Assessment: A Journal of Consulting and Clinical Psychology, 1,* 305–316.

Wiggins, J. S., & Trapnell, P. D. (in press). Personality structure: The return of the Big Five. In S. R. Briggs, R. Hogan, & W. H. Jones (Eds.), *Handbook of personality psychology.* San Diego, CA: Academic Press.

Wiggins, J. S., Trapnell, P., & Phillips, N. (1988). Psychometric and geometric characteristics of the revised Interpersonal Adjective Scales (IAS-R). *Multivariate Behavioral Research, 23,* 517–530.

Williamson, S., Harpur, T. J., & Hare, R. D. (1991). Abnormal processing of affective words by psychopaths. *Psychophysiology, 28,* 260–273.

Wong, S. (1984). *Criminal and institutional behaviors of psychopaths: Programs Branch Users Report.* Ottawa, Ontario, Canada: Ministry of the Solicitor-General of Canada.

Wong, S. (1988). Is Hare's Psychopathy Checklist reliable without an interview? *Psychological Reports, 62,* 931–934.

Zuckerman, M. (1978). Sensation seeking and psychopathy. In R. D. Hare & D. Schalling (Eds.), *Psychopathic behavior: Approaches to research* (pp. 165–185). New York: Wiley.

Zuckerman, M. (1989). Personality in the third dimension: A psychobiological approach. *Personality and Individual Differences, 10,* 391–418.

Zuckerman, M. (1991). *Psychobiology of personality.* New York: Cambridge University Press.

CHAPTER 10

THE NEO-PI AND THE MCMI IN THE FORENSIC EVALUATION OF SEX OFFENDERS

Gregory K. Lehne

Forensic evaluations are conducted in a variety of different settings using psychological instruments that are oriented toward diagnosing psychopathology or personality disorders or describing personality factors. The personality characteristics of sex offenders have been investigated using many different instruments (see Levin & Stava, 1987). Sex offenders are an appropriate population in which to empirically investigate the nature of the relationship between personality disorders and personality factors, as measured by the Millon Clinical Multiaxial Inventory (MCMI; Millon, 1983) and the NEO Personality Inventory (NEO-PI; Costa & McCrae, 1985). The relationship between personality disorders and personality factors has previously been studied only in nonclinical samples, from which significant and sensible patterns of correlations were found (Costa & McCrae, 1990; Wiggins & Pincus, 1989).

Sex offenders who were undergoing forensic evaluation at the Johns Hopkins Hospital (Baltimore, MD) Sexual Disorders Clinic were tested with the MCMI and NEO-PI. The correlations between their scores on these two inventories were determined. In this clinical sample, personality disorders and personality factors were related in ways similar to those found in previous research with nonclinical samples (Costa & McCrae, 1990). An actual case history illustrates the types of information provided by the MCMI and NEO-PI in an initial evaluation and

retesting 4 months later. Consistencies between the two testings with the NEO-PI, and differences in results from the testings with the MCMI, raise issues for forensic evaluations and the conceptualization of personality disorders and personality factors. I conclude this chapter with a discussion of my personal experience in evaluating personality disorders and related traits among forensic populations..

PERSONALITY EVALUATION OF SEX OFFENDERS

The research literature on personality variables and sex offenders has most frequently used the Minnesota Multiphasic Personality Inventory (MMPI; Hathaway & McKinley, 1967) (Dahlstrom, Welsh, & Dahlstrom, 1972), or occasionally the MCMI, to assess personality disorders. Other studies have used inventories like the Edwards Personal Preference Schedule (EPPS; Edwards, 1959), the Eysenck Personality Questionnaire (EPQ; Eysenck & Eysenck, 1975), or the Sixteen Personality Factor Questionnaire (16PF; Cattell, Eber, & Tatsuoka, 1970) to examine the personality traits of sex offenders. Much of this literature is reviewed by Levin and Stava (1987).

In general, the literature fails to confirm any direct or clear association between personality disorders and sex offenders. With reference to 27 studies that they reviewed using the MMPI, Levin and Stava

I express my appreciation to Paul T. Costa, Jr., Robert R. McCrae, and Alan Zonderman of the Gerontology Research Center (National Institute on Aging, Baltimore, MD) and to Fred Berlin and Sharon Dean of the Sexual Disorders Clinic (Johns Hopkins Hospital, Baltimore, MD) for their assistance in collecting and analyzing the data in this chapter.

(1987) concluded that the resultant knowledge was sparse and that "negative or inconsistent findings outweigh those of a positive nature" (p. 69). They reported that the most consistent findings are that sex offenders who use force may be more likely to show elevations on the MMPI Schizophrenia scale or show a 48/84 highpoint pairs profile characterized by social alienation, chronic hostility, and peculiarities of thought. No tests were able to differentiate particular groups of sex offenders from other populations. Some groups of sex offenders, such as exhibitionists, produced normal MMPI results in most studies, despite predictions from the literature that they would be passive or schizoid.

The MCMI is available with a special computer-generated forensic clinical interpretation, but the scoring is the same with forensic subjects as with other clinical populations. The MCMI was used in several studies to categorize personality disorders among sex offenders. Unlike the MMPI, the MCMI is specifically normalized to provide a typology of personality disorders in categories that roughly correspond to disorders of the third, revised edition of the *Diagnostic and Statistical Manual of Mental Disorders* (*DSM-III-R*; American Psychiatric Association, 1987). The MCMI uses a base-rate (BR) scale score cut-off point of 85 or greater to indicate the probable presence of a disorder, with a score of 75–84 indicating the presence of a related trait. Only high scores are interpreted, not low scores or scores in the average range, so the test does not provide a measure of normal personality factors in nonclinical samples.

In one study, 101 men who had been incarcerated as "sexually dangerous persons," primarily rapists and child molesters, were administered the MCMI (Bard & Knight, 1987). Despite the pathological nature of the sample, none of the sample means were greater than 75 (which would have indicated the prevalence of a personality trait or disorder). In fact, 25% of the men had no elevations on any of the scales of the MCMI. The remaining men could be clustered into three groups.

The first group, called the *detached type*, included both rapists and child molesters who had elevated scores on the Avoidant scale ($M = 87$), with lesser mean elevations on the Schizoid (Asocial) ($M = 76$) and Dependent (Submissive) ($M = 74$) scales. The

second group showed the most typical criminal sample characteristics, with elevations on the following scales: Narcissistic ($M = 90$), Antisocial (aggressive; $M = 85$), and Histrionic (gregarious; $M = 78$). This group included mostly (82%) rapists. The third group had MCMI elevations on the Antisocial (aggressive) ($M = 81$) and Passive–Aggressive (negativistic) ($M = 76$) scales. This group seemed to be more generally dangerous, in ways that were not only sexual.

Thus, in this study, sex offenders could not be defined by any one personality type or by any combination of sex offense and personality type. However, individual sex offenders showed elevations on a variety of clinical scales designed to assess the presence of personality disorders. They could be classified into groups with similar personality patterns but not with the same sex offenses.

Another study that compared rapists and child molesters on the MCMI found some differences but no clear profile for either group (Neuman, 1981). Rapists were scored as more extraverted, gregarious, and active than child molesters. Rapists were also found to have a more active ambivalent personality style compared with a more passive, ambivalent style for child molesters. But in general, it was difficult to find results with the MCMI (or the MMPI, which was also used in this study) that supported predictions from the literature about the personality characteristics of sex offenders.

Because sex offenders showed a variety of personality disorders in both studies that used the MCMI, they were deemed to be an appropriate clinical sample in which to examine the relationship between personality disorders and personality factors. Sex offenders are not characterized by any single pattern of personality disorders that would tend to bias the results of a correlational study.

Personality factors have been studied in sex offenders using the EPPS (Fisher, 1969; Fisher & Howell, 1970; Fisher & Rivlin, 1971; Langevin, Paitich, Freeman, Mann, & Handy, 1978; Scott, 1982), the 16PF (Langevin et al., 1978), the EPQ (Wilson & Cox, 1983), the Comrey Personality Scale (Smukler & Schiebel, 1975), and the California Psychological Inventory (Forgac & Michaels, 1982). Findings from assessments that used personality factor inventories showed differences among types of offenders on personality characteristics such as introversion, abasement, aggression, deference, succorance and nurturance (Levin & Stava, 1987). The difficulty in interpreting the results of these studies is that the personality factors that have been derived vary among the different instruments, and the research studies have been performed within different populations. Nevertheless, the studies do suggest that research on the personality factors of sex offenders is appropriate and likely to show significant differences.

RELATIONSHIP BETWEEN PERSONALITY DISORDERS AND PERSONALITY FACTORS

The relationship between personality disorders and the five-factor model (FFM) of personality has been studied by Costa and McCrae (1990) and also by Wiggins and Pincus (1989). Costa and McCrae (1985) correlated results from the MCMI and the NEO-PI in two separate normal populations with no noted propensities toward personality disorders. Their analysis of the results suggested that personality factors, as measured by the NEO-PI, were related in fairly clear and specific ways to the personality disorders as defined by the MCMI. For example, the MCMI Schizoid scale scores were negatively correlated with scores on the NEO-PI Extraversion scale, and the MCMI Avoidant scale scores were correlated negatively with Extraversion and positively with Neuroticism scores on the NEO-PI. Both MCMI Histrionic and Narcissistic scales were positively correlated with Extraversion and Openness on the NEO-PI but differed in their correlations with other factors. The results of Wiggins and Pincus's (1989) study, which used a different methodology but also used a normal population, are generally consistent with the findings from Costa and McCrae (1990).

Costa and McCrae (1990) interpreted the overall pattern of findings as indicating that the NEO-PI is measuring underlying factors that are part of personality disorders as assessed by the MCMI. Thus, personality disorders could be conceptualized as extreme and/or dysfunctional combinations of normal personality factors. However, the empirical findings can be faulted for the use of a nonclinical sample, for which the MCMI was not strictly appropriate and which probably had a low frequency of personality disorders.

The conceptual relationship among personality factors and disorders has not been studied in forensic or sex-offending populations. In general, clinical tests of personality disorders, like the MCMI, are used with clinical populations and are not normalized in a way that makes them valid with nonclinical populations. So Costa and McCrae's (1990) findings of correlations between the NEO-PI and the MCMI may not hold up in a clinical population. However, tests of normal personality factors, like the NEO-PI, can be used with clinical populations without compromising their validity. There is little data available to relate the results of such testing to possible personality disorders or pathology.

Thus, it is not known whether a clinical forensic population, such as sex offenders, would show a similar pattern of correlations on the personality disorder scales of the MCMI and the five factors of personality as measured by the NEO-PI. Also unexplored is the relative usefulness of evaluating sex offenders using clinical tests of personality disorders compared with more normative inventories of personality factors. These are the issues that are examined in the present study that tested a clinical forensic group of sex offenders with the MCMI and the NEO-PI.

PRESENT STUDY

Procedures

Men who were undergoing evaluation or treatment at the Sexual Disorders Clinic of the Johns Hopkins Hospital were the subjects for the study of the correlation between MCMI and NEO-PI test scores. The population of the Sexual Disorders Clinic tends to be sexually compulsive with multiple offenses and has typically offended against victims outside the family. Thus, this group is a primary forensic population, as well as a clinical population. All of the men had admitted to engaging in inappropriate sexual behavior and were charged with or convicted of at least one sex offense. Mentally retarded men and men with reading difficulties were excluded from the study.

Each man underwent a complete psychiatric evaluation and was diagnosed according to *DSM-III-R* criteria. The Axis I psychiatric diagnosis judged most directly related to the sexual offense was designated as the primary diagnosis. Ninety-nine men completed the evaluation process and produced valid test results on both the MCMI and the NEO-PI. In most cases (*n* = 81), the primary diagnosis was a sexual disorder or paraphilia (pedophilia, *n* = 44; exhibitionism, *n* = 8; other paraphilias, involving adolescent or adult-oriented behavior, *n* = 29). In 18 cases, the inappropriate sexual behavior was not associated with a sexual disorder. There were 9 cases of transitory adjustment disorders, 4 cases related to alcohol or substance abuse or conduct disturbance, 1 case with an atypical psychotic episode, and 4 cases with no psychiatric diagnoses.

The evaluated sex offenders were tested with both the MCMI and the NEO-PI, either at the time of their initial evaluation or at the time of a group psychotherapy session. Testing was done using the paper-and-pencil versions of the MCMI and the NEO-PI. Tests were scored according to the published manuals, with no deviations from standard procedures, and using the appropriate adjustments and normative tables (Costa & McCrae, 1985; Millon, 1983). The results of the testing were not used in making diagnoses of the patients or clinical recommendations.

Results

On the MCMI, a score of 85 or greater was taken as evidence for the presence of a personality disorder. Among the 99 men, 33% had no MCMI scores greater than 85, 28% had one scale score above 84, 23% had two or three scale scores above 84, and 15% had four to six scale scores above 84. Scale scores of 75–84 indicate the presence of a personality trait related to the more extreme disorder. Scores below 75 should not be interpreted in individual cases. Table 1 shows the frequency of scores in this population of sex offenders. All of the means are below a score of 75. Thus, no individual trait or combination of personality traits and/or disorders is characteristically descriptive of this population of sex offenders. Dependent (50% of sample) and passive–aggressive (36%) are the most common personality disorder scale elevations, and anxiety (47%) and dys-

TABLE 1

Descriptive Statistics for Millon Clinical Multiaxial Inventory (MCMI) Personality Disorder Scales in a Sex Offender Sample

MCMI scale	Disorder (%)	Trait (%)
Schizoid (asocial)	18	12
Avoidant	23	8
Dependent (submissive)	34	16
Histrionic (gregarious)	9	10
Narcissistic	9	17
Antisocial (aggressive)	11	8
Compulsive (conforming)	3	9
Passive–Aggressive (negativistic)	27	9
Schizotypal (schizoid)	2	5
Borderline (cycloid)	5	10
Paranoid	7	6
Anxiety	30	17
Somatoform	5	14
Hypomanic	2	2
Dysthymic	28	16
Alcohol Abuse	3	8
Drug Abuse	6	12
Psychotic Thinking	1	4
Psychotic Depression	1	5
Psychotic Delusions	4	3
None	33	13

Note. N = 99 men; base-rate scale scores for disorders ≥ 85; base-rate scale scores for traits (in parentheses) = 75–84.

thymia (44%) are the most prevalent clinical symptom syndromes.

With reference to the NEO-PI, Table 2 shows the means and standard deviations for the sample. Unlike the MCMI, which uses BR cut-off scores, all scores on the NEO-PI can be interpreted. Thus the NEO-PI means of the sample can be interpreted as providing a descriptive profile of this group of sex offenders, in comparison to a normal, nonclinical population. A higher mean score would indicate a greater presence of that personality factor in the sex offender sample, and a lower score would correspond to a smaller presence of that factor. Whether significant deviations in either direction correspond in a meaningful way to psychopathology is a question which is examined empirically in the correlational analysis of the NEO-PI and the MCMI.

This sex offender sample's mean scores were at least one-half a standard deviation higher than the normal population on all facets of the Neuroticism

TABLE 2

Descriptive Statistics for NEO Personality Inventory (NEO-PI) Scales in a Sex Offender Sample

NEO-PI scale	*M*	Range
Domain		
Neuroticism	60.9	High
Extraversion	53.0	Average
Openness to Experience	49.0	Average
Agreeableness	45.2	Average
Conscientiousness	46.3	Average
Neuroticism facet		
Anxiety	57.2	High
Hostility	55.7	High
Depression	62.0	High
Self-Consciousness	57.6	High
Impulsiveness	56.5	High
Vulnerability	58.5	High
Extraversion facet		
Warmth	49.1	Average
Gregariousness	52.8	Average
Assertiveness	48.2	Average
Activity	52.8	Average
Excitement Seeking	57.1	High
Positive Emotions	51.5	Average
Openness facet		
Fantasy	50.0	Average
Aesthetics	50.8	Average
Feelings	52.3	Average
Actions	49.0	Average
Ideas	48.0	Average
Values	46.3	Average

Note. N = 99 men.

domain—Anxiety and Depression (which were also elevated on the MCMI), as well as Hostility, Self-Consciousness, Impulsiveness, and Vulnerability. The mean score on the Excitement Seeking facet of Extraversion was also higher than in the general population. All other scores were within the average range, corresponding to a typical normal population sample.

The group means are consistent with apparently honest and candid responding to the inventory questions. There was no evidence that suggested that responses were distorted in a socially desirable direction, for example producing artificially low scores on the facets of Hostility, Impulsiveness, or Excitement Seeking or high scores on the Agreeableness or Conscientiousness domains.

The results of testing sex offenders in this sample with the MCMI and the NEO-PI show that it is a population that produces results in the clinically significant range. The sample population shows a high level of neuroticism, which would be expected for clinical samples, and a variety of personality traits and disorders. Yet there is no homogeneous pattern in the findings because the sample is not characterized by the prevalence of any one particular personality trait, disorder, or cluster of traits.

Correlations between the BR scores on the MCMI and the scale scores for the five factors on the NEO-PI are provided in Table 3. The pattern of these correlations is compared, in Table 4, with the correlations reported in Costa and McCrae (1990) for a normal sample of 207 men and women. This comparison is not strictly equivalent because Costa and McCrae (1990) included both men and women, whereas the present sample involved only men. Also, Costa and McCrae (1990) used raw scores for the MCMI, whereas the present sample used BR scores. Nevertheless, the patterns of correlations are remarkably similar. Of the 55 correlational cells (11 MCMI Disorders × 5 NEO-PI Factors), there is agreement in the direction of significant correlations or the absence of a correlation in 36 cells (65%). There were no cases of disagreement in the direction of a correlation. In 10 cells (18%), there are significant correlations only for the sex offender sample. In 9 cells (16%), there are significant correlations only for the normal sample; with only three exceptions, these noncorresponding correlations were lower than 0.5.

The correlations in the sample of sex offenders also replicate the basic pattern of findings from normal populations found by Wiggins and Pincus (1989), which was also replicated by Costa and McCrae (1990). In all of these studies, extraversion was strongly and negatively correlated with schizoid and avoidant personality disorders and positively correlated with histrionic and narcissistic disorders. In addition, negative correlations were found in all of the studies between agreeableness and antisocial and paranoid personality disorders. Conscientiousness was positively correlated with compulsive personality disorder in all the studies. Neuroticism was positively correlated with avoidant and borderline disorders in all three studies. A negative correlation between

TABLE 3

Correlations of Millon Clinical Multiaxial Inventory (MCMI) and NEO Personality Inventory (NEO-PI) Scale Scores in a Sex Offender Sample

MCMI scale	NEO-PI domains				
	N	E	O	A	C
Schizoid	0.54**	−0.56**	−0.33**	−0.47**	−0.28**
Avoidant	0.63**	−0.57**	−0.26*	−0.43**	−0.23*
Dependent	0.20*	−0.19	−0.21*	0.19	−0.10
Histrionic	−0.18	0.63**	0.42**	0.04	0.02
Narcissistic	−0.30**	0.57**	0.25*	−0.05	0.28**
Antisocial	0.09	0.13	−0.05	−0.49**	−0.01
Compulsive	−0.63**	0.21*	−0.09	0.58**	0.36**
Passive–Aggressive	0.69**	−0.32**	−0.01	−0.50**	−0.31**
Schizotypal	0.44**	−0.63**	−0.30**	−0.18	−0.22*
Borderline	0.49**	−0.29**	0.00	−0.16	0.13
Paranoid	0.02	0.09	−0.08	−0.31**	0.18
Anxiety	0.45**	−0.46**	−0.07	−0.21*	−0.26**
Somatoform	0.12	−0.22*	−0.05	0.10	0.04
Hypomanic	0.26**	0.33**	0.26**	−0.29**	0.03
Dysthymic	0.50**	−0.49**	−0.04	−0.14	−0.28**
Alcohol Abuse	0.48**	−0.06	−0.01	−0.35**	−0.19
Drug Abuse	0.16	0.43**	0.21*	−0.32**	0.03
Psychotic Thinking	0.56**	−0.41**	−0.24*	−0.49**	−0.18
Psychotic Depression	0.64**	−0.38**	−0.16	−0.41**	−0.19
Psychotic Delusions	0.14	−0.08	−0.20*	−0.27**	0.17

Note. N = 99 men. N = Neuroticism; E = Extraversion; O = Openness to Experience; A = Agreeableness; C = Conscientiousness.
*p < .05; **p < .01.

openness and schizotypal disorder was also replicated in these studies. A positive correlation between openness and histrionic disorder was also replicated.

In addition, the sex offender sample replicates the findings from Costa and McCrae's (1990) normal sample for much of the pattern for both the neuroticism and extraversion factors. In both studies, neuroticism is positively correlated with avoidant, passive–aggressive, schizotypal, and borderline disorders and negatively correlated with narcissistic and compulsive personality disorders. For the extraversion factor, there is replication of negative correlations with schizoid, avoidant, schizotypal, and borderline personality disorders and positive correlations with histrionic and narcissistic disorders.

Neuroticism and extraversion are the factors that have the most consistent correlational relationships with personality disorders in the different samples. Except as previously mentioned, the openness, agreeableness, and conscientiousness factors had less consistent agreements in correlations between the two studies.

In the sex offender sample, not all of the personality disorders as measured by the MCMI could be uniquely differentiated on the basis of the patterns of correlations with the NEO-PI. For example, scores

TABLE 4

Comparison of Significant Correlations of Millon Clinical Multiaxial Inventory (MCMI) Personality Disorder Scales With NEO Personality Inventory (NEO-PI) Factors in Normal[a] and Sex Offender[b] Samples

MCMI scale/sample	N	E	O	A	C
Schizoid					
Normal		− −			
Sex offenders	+ +	− −	−	−	−
Avoidant					
Normal	+	− −			
Sex offenders	+ +	− −	−		
Dependent					
Normal	+		−	+	
Sex offenders					
Histrionic					
Normal		+ +	+		−
Sex offenders		+ +	+		
Narcissistic					
Normal	−	+	+	−	
Sex offenders	−	+ +			+
Antisocial					
Normal	−		+	−	
Sex offenders				−	
Compulsive					
Normal	−		−		+
Sex offenders	− −			+ +	+
Passive–Aggressive					
Normal	+ +				
Sex offenders	+ +		−	− −	−
Schizotypal					
Normal	+	−	−		
Sex offenders	+	− −	−		
Borderline					
Normal	+ +	−			
Sex offenders	+	−			
Paranoid					
Normal				−	
Sex offenders				−	

Note. N = Neuroticism; E = Extraversion; O = Openness to Experience; A = Agreeableness; C = Conscientiousness. All correlations at $p < .01$ level of significance. + + and − − indicate positive and negative correlations, respectively, that are $\geq .5$; + and − indicate positive or negative correlations, respectively, that are $< .5$.
[a]$N = 207$ men and women from Costa and McCrae (1990), correlations based on raw scores. [b]$N = 99$ men, present study sample, correlations based on base-rate scores.

for the MCMI Antisocial and Paranoid scales had negative correlations with NEO-PI agreeableness scores and no other significant correlations. Essentially, both of these personality disorders share an interpersonal antagonism, which is an essential part of low agreeableness. It is important to remember that the sex offender population had a diversity of scores and evidence of few clinical traits or disorders on the MCMI Antisocial ($19\% > 75$ BR) and Paranoid ($13\% > 75$ BR) scales.

In the sex offender sample, there were no correlations between dependent personality characteristics and any NEO-PI factors. This is remarkable because the dependent personality disorder was the most frequently elevated scale on the MCMI in the sex offender sample ($50\% > 75$ BR).

Discussion

The MCMI and the NEO-PI were developed from different theoretical perspectives. The MCMI was developed using Millon's theory of personality and pathology, which ultimately goes back to a conceptualization of people's sources of reinforcements and activity levels in pursuing those reinforcements (Millon, 1981). Pathology results from extremes in personality styles and personality decompensation under situations of marked stress. The MCMI is loosely related to *DSM-III-R* categories, which also incorporate a historical psychiatric typology of personality disorders. The NEO-PI is based on factor analytic research on personality in both the natural language and theory-based personality inventories.

The correlation of the results from testing a sample of sex offenders with the MCMI and the NEO-PI shows that the two tests produced findings that generally could be interpreted in mutually consistent ways. Neuroticism and extraversion are the two factors most consistently linked in theory, research, and common parlance to personality disorders. Both positive and negative correlations between these factors and different personality disorders have been shown in several studies.

Neuroticism, as a general indicator of distress and negative affectivity, is positively correlated with borderline, passive–aggressive, schizotypal (and possibly schizoid), and avoidant personality disorders. Individuals with these types of disorders are commonly perceived by others as negative and discontented. A negative correlation with Neuroticism was found for the narcissistic and compulsive personality disorders; these types of individuals do not typically describe themselves as discontented, which is consistent with low neuroticism.

Similarly, the correlations between extraversion and various personality disorders closely correspond to the definitional qualities of the disorders. For example, histrionic and narcissistic individuals are by definition outgoing and oriented toward influencing others with their personality styles. Avoidant, schizoid, schizotypal, and borderline personality disorders involve deficiencies in the ability to relate interpersonally. The other disorders do not present such defining characteristics with reference to extraversion.

Thus, the correlation of the results from the MCMI and NEO-PI provides support for the idea that there are common personality factors that underlie the personality disorders. But the tests do not say the same things. The magnitude of the correlation or agreement between the different studies and tests decreases for factors such as openness, agreeableness, and conscientiousness.

There is no clear formula or pattern that allows the direct translation of findings on one test to be translated into the language of the other. In the present study, it was not possible to identify each or all of the different personality disorders in terms of specific NEO-PI profiles. Nor do the results of either of the tests directly translate into *DSM-III-R* categories of personality disorders. Despite the typology of MCMI scale names that appear to correspond to the discrete personality disorders in *DSM-III-R*, the actual results of testing with the MCMI tend to produce patterns of scores with two or three scale elevations as often as they produce a single scale elevation. This implies that the MCMI personality disorders are not mutually exclusive syndromes. Thus, interpreting the results of testing on the MCMI and/or the diagnosis of personality disorders according to *DSM-III-R* criteria requires skilled, professional clinical expertise.

It may be that discriminability of personality disorders can be improved in the future with new versions of tests (such as the MCMI-II; Millon, 1987) or by more analysis of facets of specific personality factors, such as the facets of the NEO-PI. The MCMI-II

was not available at the time of the testing of sex offenders, and the sample size was too small to allow for a reliable correlational analysis of NEO-PI facet scores.

But it also may be that the present conceptualization of personality disorders is part of the problem of discriminability. Personality disorders may be historical artifacts of the intellectual-domain bias of psychiatry, clinical psychology, and social work. Many other fields of human services, such as industrial and occupational psychology, career consulting and guidance, and pastoral counseling typically use models of personality other than *DSM-III-R* personality disorders.

The criminal justice and forensic fields are presently split between using personality disorder models and other approaches to analyzing the personality characteristics of individuals in their purview. Thus, forensic evaluators are caught in the middle in their attempts to evaluate individuals in terms that are mutually understandable to clinically trained personnel and others who are involved in the criminal justice system (such as attorneys, judges, juries, and probation officers) with no background in clinical psychology. The case example that follows illustrates some of the issues of forensic evaluation in using concepts of personality disorders on the basis of assessment with the MCMI compared with using the NEO-PI factors.

CASE EXAMPLE

Ron was a 35-year-old man who was referred by his doctor for evaluation after he was legally charged with exposing himself to a young adolescent girl in the food mall of a public shopping center. He was first seen 4 days after his arrest and was then seen a week later, at which time he was tested with the MCMI and the NEO-PI. After 4 months of weekly, individual psychotherapy he was retested. He was not a subject in the previously described research sample.

Ron reported an extensive history of exposing himself to teenage and adult females, and he reported one prior arrest. He also had been frequently involved with prostitutes and had frequently attended strip bars, either alone or with friends, at which times he drank prodigious quantities of alcohol. He drank only rarely otherwise in social situations and never to excess. He had no other history of inappropriate sexual behavior. His legal history also included arrests for shoplifting. He had previously undergone psychiatric treatment for his sexual behavior and depression. His first suicide attempt was at age 12. He was suicidally depressed following his previous arrest for indecent behavior.

He was morbidly obese, with medical complications of diabetes and high blood pressure, and had no prior success in losing weight. He was happily married to a Vietnamese woman whom he met while he was in the U.S. armed services, and they had a 10-year-old son. He and his wife reported some difficulties in communication, but no other marital or sexual problems. He was well regarded in his career, and was socially popular among his peers at work. Outside of work, he reported no social friendships or hobbies.

At the time of the initial evaluation, Ron was significantly depressed with suicidal plans and feared the loss of his marriage and job as a consequence of his arrest. He had almost no appetite, had lost 25 pounds, and also had problems sleeping. His physical hygiene was appropriate. His speech was clear, coherent, and task-oriented. Despite being intermittently overcome with tears, he repeatedly made jokes during the evaluation session, some of which were self-deprecating. He had a dramatic storytelling style and seemed prone to exaggeration or overstatement. He reported a history of being class clown and office joker.

The initial diagnoses were exhibitionism and major depression (recurrent). The diagnosis of a personality disorder was deferred. The impression was that he suffered from some personality disorder but that he did not meet a sufficient number of criteria for any one *DSM-III-R* diagnosis.

Ron's history of adolescent shoplifting, illicit sexual behavior that continued during his marriage, and recklessness in drinking and driving, along with his self-justification and disregard for the effects of his illegal behavior on others, suggested antisocial personality disorder features. Borderline personality disorder features included his instability of mood accompanied with suicidal plans and poor self-

esteem; his excessive impulsiveness in sexuality, shoplifting, and drinking; and concerns about abandonment by his wife and family. His personality style seemed excessively emotional and attention-seeking in a clowning way, which is suggestive of histrionic characteristics. Dependent personality disorder features were also present in his seeking affirmation from others and his hypersensitivity to possible disapproval, his preoccupation and imagined devastation if his wife and son abandoned him, and a tendency to allow his wife to make all the major decisions for the family. One of the difficulties in the diagnosis of possible personality disorder was that many of these characteristics might be more related to his other diagnoses of depression or exhibitionism rather than indicative of an independent personality disorder.

Initial testing with the MCMI showed significant elevations on the scales measuring passive–aggressive (96) and dependent (88) personality disorders, with scores in the trait range on the scales measuring borderline (82) and avoidant (77) personality disorders. The MCMI Anxiety and Depression scales each had scores over 100, but no other scales were elevated. The complete scores for the MCMI scales are provided in the first column of Table 5. The MCMI computer-generated interpretative report suggested the following diagnoses: generalized anxiety disorder, dysthymic disorder, alcohol abuse, and borderline personality disorder (with prominent dependent and passive–aggressive traits).

The text of the MCMI interpretive report did not correspond to Ron's initial presentation. He depicted himself as much more disturbed and emotionally unstable and likely to act out in hostile ways than he appeared. Nor did the elevated personality disorder scales and suggested diagnoses correspond to the clinical impressions of the patient. For example, he did not either meet any of the *DSM-III-R* criteria or give the impression of a passive–aggressive personality disorder, although his highest MCMI scale score was for this disorder.

This pattern of scores on the MCMI is not unusual among sex offenders. In the previously described research sample, as in Ron's results, the two most frequently occurring scale scores over 85 were for the Dependent (34% of the sample) and Passive–Aggres-

TABLE 5

Case Example: Millon Clinical Multiaxial Inventory (MCMI) Base-Rate Scores

MCMI scale	1st test	Retest
Schizoid	60	51
Avoidant	77	46
Dependent	88	80
Histrionic	71	85
Narcissistic	47	67
Antisocial	45	45
Compulsive	54	63
Passive–Aggressive	93	47
Schizotypal	53	68
Borderline	81	69
Paranoid	49	69
Anxiety	102	76
Somatoform	66	72
Hypomanic	52	60
Dysthymic	99	84
Alcohol Abuse	79	55
Drug Abuse	67	64
Psychotic Thinking	60	60
Psychotic Depression	71	43
Psychotic Delusions	62	57

Note. The MCMI was administered to the patient in the first evaluation session (1st test) and then readministered 4 months later (retest).

sive (27%) scales, along with similarly high frequencies for elevations on the scales for anxiety (30%) and dysthymia (28%).

Incorporating the results of the MCMI testing into the diagnostic process, it was decided that Ron probably suffered from a mixed personality disorder, with dependent, passive–aggressive, and histrionic features. The results of the NEO-PI were not used to make a clinical diagnosis but were included in the forensic evaluation report to describe his "premorbid" personality.

Ron's results on the NEO-PI are given in Table 6. He scored in the very high range on Neuroticism, in the very low range on Conscientiousness, and in the low range on Agreeableness. He obtained average scores on Extraversion and Openness. This pattern is more extreme and varied than the group means for sex offenders in the previously described research sample, for which the Neuroticism domain was in the high range and the other domains were in the average range.

Other than the very high Neuroticism score, the domain scores and text of the computer-generated NEO-PI report did not appear to be consistent with Ron's initial presentation and history. He appeared more extraverted and socially agreeable, with his joking style, than most patients. He had a solid record of achievement in his career as well as a stable family life, which did not appear to be consistent with his very low level of conscientiousness.

Interpretation of Ron's test scores must consider that at the time of testing, Ron was experiencing extreme depression as a result of being arrested. Thus, both the MCMI and the NEO-PI showed high scores for depression and anxiety, some of which may be associated with a transitory adjustment reaction but which may also reflect aspects of Ron's general personality style. The MCMI is designed to be used on individuals who are experiencing difficulties, and it is particularly designed to be used during the early phases of assessment and treatment. The NEO-PI was not designed to be used in times of distress or to identify transitory stress-induced reactions.

Ron's depression decreased significantly after his legal problems were satisfactorily resolved. Although he continued to report feeling depressed, his depression was masked by a jovial style, and there was no fearfulness or reports of suicidal intentions. He was retested on the MCMI and the NEO-PI 4 months after the initial testing (see Tables 5 and 6).

The pattern of results on the MCMI was quite different from that of the initial testing. The only two significant personality scale elevations were on the Histrionic (85) and Dependent (80) scales. The score on the Passive–Aggressive scale dropped from 96 to 47. Anxiety and depression scores dropped significantly, although Ron continued to be depressed and still scored in the clinical range (84, down from 101). The suggested diagnoses were dysthymic disorders, generalized anxiety disorder, and dependent personality disorder with prominent histrionic traits. The computer-generated MCMI clinical interpretive report depicted Ron in totally different, and generally positive, terms as a passive and dependent individual who strived to be socially accommodating.

The change from a dangerous, social menace to a socially conforming person did not appear to be related to any personality changes produced in psy-

TABLE 6

Case Example: NEO Presonality Inventory (NEO-PI) Scores

NEO-PI scale	1st test		Retest	
	T Score	Range	*T* Score	Range
Domains				
Neuroticism	70	Very high	70	Very high
Extraversion	46	Average	55	Average
Openness to Experience	47	Average	51	Average
Agreeableness	40	Low	44	Low
Conscientiousness	25	Very low	32	Very low
Neuroticism facet				
Anxiety	72	Very high	64	High
Hostility	55	Average	48	Average
Depression	65	Very high	75	Very high
Self-Consciousness	56	High	66	Very high
Impulsiveness	57	High	69	Very high
Vulnerability	86	Very high	60	High
Extraversion facet				
Warmth	57	High	55	Average
Gregariousness	46	Average	48	Average
Assertiveness	46	Average	53	Average
Activity	41	Low	56	High
Excitement Seeking	61	High	61	High
Positive Emotions	33	Very low	48	Average
Openness Facet Scales				
Fantasy	61	High	63	High
Aesthetics	43	Low	47	Average
Feelings	54	Average	49	Average
Actions	45	Average	45	Average
Ideas	41	Low	51	Average
Values	45	Average	45	Average

Note. The NEO-PI was administered to the patient in the first evaluation session (1st test) and then readministered 4 months later (retest).

chotherapy. Instead, an analysis of changes in item responses between the two testings showed that most of the changes were on items measuring state depression, which were also incorporated into the MCMI personality disorder scales such as the Passive–Aggressive and Borderline scales.

Retesting Ron with the NEO-PI resulted in essentially the same pattern of scores as the previous test results from the initial assessment (see Table 6). After 4 months of therapy, which predominantly addressed the depression and anxiety and some aspects of the sexual disorder, it was not evident that Ron's personality had changed. However, the therapist's impressions of Ron came to correspond to the description

of his personality, as described in the computer-generated NEO-PI report, which had not seemed particularly accurate at the time of the initial assessment.

For example, Ron had initially appeared to be highly agreeable because of his joking style, his expressions of gratitude, and his willingness to do whatever was recommended to help his situation. But later in the therapy process, it was clear that he was not actually an agreeable person. It was hard for him to feel or express concern for his wife or son, although earlier he had cried with gratitude because they had not rejected him. Later, he seemed to be generally unable to initiate positive behaviors toward them and, in fact, offended them in thoughtless ways. He became critical of professionals involved with his care, expressing (often unjustified) negative or hostile evaluations. For example, he antagonistically stated that his previous therapy was mostly "b–s–" and boasted how he had lied to his doctors in the past. By implication, he was expressing similar beliefs about his present therapy. The issues of low agreeableness and low concern for others became important in therapy to help him understand the effects of his inappropriate behavior on others. He never expressed concern about this and thus lacked one of the tools for helping control his behavior.

As his mood improved during treatment, his low conscientiousness became evident. He had created the impression of conscientiousness through his unblemished work record. Although tardiness and irresponsibility did not appear to be work issues, the nature of his job did not make it a good test of conscientiousness. He became more lax about appointments, rescheduling or canceling them or arriving late. He was also less conscientious in bringing forth relevant material in sessions—he became compliant rather than being conscientious or responsible in examining himself and his situation. He came to carelessly disregard rules that he had observed earlier in therapy (such as avoiding situations in which he might have exposed himself). Earlier he had brought up subjects for discussion, whereas later he only presented less favorable material in response to direct inquiries.

These changes in my conceptualization of him might appear to be related to changing issues in the course of therapy such as transference and so forth. But the similar results of the two testings with the NEO-PI indicate that these personality factors were present at the start of therapy and did not change. So the NEO-PI testing actually provided information that was not readily apparent in all of the dramatics of the initial presentation—aspects of Ron's "normal" personality that were somewhat masked by the presenting problems of depression, compulsive sexual behavior, and all of the stresses associated with the arrest and forensic processes.

PERSONAL EXPERIENCE

The purpose of a forensic psychological evaluation is to provide an accurate and understandable description of relatively enduring characteristics of an individual that can then be used by criminal justice personnel. The forensic evaluation is written primarily to determine the disposition of a case or to develop sentencing recommendations, including making predictions about future behavior and rehabilitation planning. Except in cases that involve criminal responsibility or insanity, psychiatric diagnoses, particularly of personality disorders, are not critical. Presentence investigation reports, for example, are the most common type of forensic evaluation, and they rarely attempt to incorporate psychiatric diagnoses.

My experience in clinical services, including work within the medical model in a hospital setting, has led me to put an emphasis on personality disorders and related traits in conducting evaluations. As such, I might incorporate into an evaluation the results of testing with instruments such as the MMPI or the MCMI, both of which have special interpretations available for forensic settings. When the test results show clinical elevations that are consistent with my understanding of a patient, I feel comfortable incorporating this information into my reports. Diagnosing a discrete personality disorder is difficult, even with *DSM-III-R* explicit criteria, and forensic patients tend not to fit neatly into the diagnostic categories.

The resultant descriptions of personality disorders and related traits often require elaborate explanations and interpretations for criminal justice personnel, who sometimes have little patience with clinical nuances of the diagnosis. The clinical disorders also sound very judgmental and negativistic. The diagnostic labels are often subjected to even more negative reinterpretations by criminal justice personnel who have associations that are different from *DSM-III-R* psychopathological criteria. In court, there is often little interest in personality disorder labels, and in trials, there might be disagreements with other professionals about the specific diagnosis of personality disorder. (Diagnosing personality disorders is, after all, part clinical skill and part art.) I justify the continued use of personality disorder diagnostics because it makes sense to me and appears to have prognostic utility in predicting future adjustment as well as the effectiveness of different types of therapy.

When one does psychological testing as part of a forensic evaluation, one is ethically obligated to report the results of all testing. Although I might choose to reinterpret the results, I cannot pretend that the results from any given test do not exist. In the case example of Ron, the diagnosis of exhibitionism instead of pedophilia was an important factor in the sentencing. Also important, however, was the unstable and negative characterization of Ron as a result of personality disorder testing with the MCMI. As it turned out, much of the negativism was derived from his more transitional and extreme depressive state following his arrest rather than being a characteristic personality disorder or trait.

In my role as an academic psychologist and researcher, I am aware of the limitations of the concepts of personality disorders, particularly as applied to forensic populations like sex offenders. The concepts of personality traits or factors, without the baggage of clinical disorders, are interesting because they are so generalizable. But they do not seem appropriate for clinical or forensic evaluations, despite their stability and prognostic utility. Somehow, they seem to predict more normal behavior, not psychopathology. I have found it hard to use the concepts of personality factors in conceptualizing treatment plans other than in a straightforward, somewhat common-sense cognitive–behavioral plan.

When I first started using the NEO-PI with sex offenders for research purposes and in my clinical practice, I was initially surprised to find that the offenders usually seemed to understand and agree with the resultant descriptions of their personality. Some of the NEO-PI reports are quite negative sounding, particularly for persons who are low in agreeableness or conscientiousness, yet the subjects rarely disagree or object to the characterization. When I incorporate the resultant analyses into evaluation reports (as premorbid or general description of personality), the persons reading them generally do not have difficulty understanding the material, nor do they tend to question or disagree with it. Typical feedback is that they feel it is useful in giving an impression of what the person was like. There are usually some implications that it is not "real" psychology, in that they share the same impression of the individual as a result of their own interactions and interviews.

The case example only raises issues, and one must be cautious not to overgeneralize. However, I was very surprised at the differences between the retesting in the case example with the MCMI and the NEO-PI. I rarely retest patients because I tend to assume that the results of testing remain stable. I had not expected so much change on the MCMI, and I did not really believe that the NEO-PI would be so consistent. To be fair to the MCMI, the manual does not hide the dual loading of depression and other state factors with personality disorder scales (Millon, 1983). Also, Millon's theory (1981) predicts that in situations of moderate to severe stress, personality disorders will decompensate into other personality disorders of greater severity (such as borderline personality disorder in the case example). But this type of knowledge is, frankly, a little esoteric for the typical forensic consumers of the concepts of personality disorders and the results of testing.

Perhaps the whole concept of personality disorders is too esoteric for use in forensic evaluations. Unlike other types of psychological evaluations, which are written to transmit information to professional clinicians, forensic evaluations are primarily prepared for nonclinicians. I wonder whether pathologizing personalities as disorders appropriately describes and respects our clients and provides useful information for the readers of our forensic reports. Descriptions of personality factors, which have consensual validity and reliability, may turn out to be more fair and useful. Personality factors, as described on inventories like the NEO-PI, at least have a basis in natural language that makes them more easily understood by nonclinicians.

What is needed is more research looking at personality factors in forensic populations. Are certain patterns of personality factors more associated with certain problems in living or more likely to change as a result of different types of rehabilitative experiences? Research examining personality disorders in sex offending populations (or in forensic populations) has not been particularly productive. Perhaps future research on personality factors may provide information that is useful in understanding forensic clients and rehabilitation planning.

References

American Psychiatric Association. (1987). *Diagnostic and statistical manual of mental disorders* (3rd ed., rev.). Washington, DC: Author.

Bard, L. A., & Knight, R. A. (1987). Sex offender subtyping and the MCMI. In C. Green (Ed.), *Conference on the Millon Clinical Inventories* (pp. 133–137). Minneapolis, MN: National Computer Systems.

Cattell, R. B., Eber, H. W., & Tatsuoka, M. M. (1970). *The handbook for the Sixteen Personality Factor Questionnaire*. Champaign, IL: Institute for Personality and Ability Testing.

Costa, P. T., Jr., & McCrae, R. R. (1985). *The NEO Personality Inventory manual*. Odessa, FL: Psychological Assessment Resources.

Costa, P. T., Jr., & McCrae, R. R. (1990). Personality disorders and the five-factor model of personality. *Journal of Personality Disorders, 4,* 262–371.

Dahlstrom, W. G., Welsh, G. S., & Dahlstrom, L. E. (1972). *An MMPI handbook: Vol. 1. Clinical interpretation* (rev. ed.). Minneapolis: University of Minnesota Press.

Edwards, A. L. (1959). *Edwards Personal Preference Schedule manual*. New York: Psychological Corporation.

Eysenck, H. J., & Eysenck, S. B. G. (1975). *Manual of the Eysenck Personality Questionnaire*. London: Hodder & Stoughton.

Fisher, G. (1969). Psychological needs of heterosexual pedophiles. *Disease of the Nervous System, 30,* 419–421.

Fisher, G., & Howell, L. M. (1970). Psychological needs of homosexual pedophiliacs. *Disease of the Nervous System, 31,* 623–625.

Fisher, G., & Rivlin, E. (1971). Psychological needs of rapists. *British Journal of Criminology, 11,* 182–185.

Forgac, G. F., & Michaels, E. J. (1982). Personality characteristics of two types of male exhibitionists. *Journal of Abnormal Psychology, 91,* 287–293.

Hathaway, S. R., & McKinley, J. C (1967). *Minnesota Multiphasic Personality Inventory manual*. New York: Psychological Corporation.

Langevin, R., Paitich, D., Freeman, R., Mann, K., & Handy, L. (1978). Personality characteristics and sexual anomalies in males. *Canadian Journal of Behavioral Sciences, 10,* 222–238.

Levin, S. L., & Stava, L. (1987). Personality characteristics of sex offenders: A review. *Archives of Sexual Behavior, 16,* 57–79.

Millon, T. (1981). *Disorders of personality: DSM-III. Axis II.* New York: Wiley.

Millon, T. (1983). *Millon Clinical Multiaxial Inventory manual* (3rd ed.). Minneapolis, MN: Interpretive Scoring Systems.

Millon, T. (1987). *Manual for the MCMI-II* (2nd ed.). Minneapolis, MN: National Computer Systems.

Neuman, C. J. (1981). *Differentiation between personality characteristics of rapists and child molesters: A validation study of the Millon Clinical Multiaxial Inventory*. Unpublished doctoral dissertation, University of Miami.

Scott, R. L. (1982). Analysis of the needs systems of twenty male rapists. *Psychological Reports, 51,* 1119–1125.

Smukler, A. J., & Schiebel, D. (1975). Personality characteristics of exhibitionists. *Diseases of the Nervous System, 36,* 600–603.

Wiggins, J. S., & Pincus, A. L. (1989). Conceptions of personality disorders and dimensions of personality. *Psychological Assessment: A Journal of Consulting and Clinical Psychology, 1,* 305–316.

Wilson, G. D., & Cox, D. N. (1983). Personality of pedophile club members. *Personality and Individual Differences, 4,* 323–329.

CHAPTER 11

A CASE OF BORDERLINE PERSONALITY DISORDER

Stephen Bruehl

Betty was a 45-year-old White, divorced female. Her original complaint when she entered therapy 4 years earlier was that she was experiencing discipline problems with her daughter and difficulties in adjusting to her recent divorce. She had been married three times and had divorced her most recent husband shortly before entering therapy. She had two children from her first marriage, a 24-year-old son and a 20-year-old daughter. Two months before Betty began her therapy, her daughter was arrested on drug possession charges and was suspended from high school. Betty was quite distraught about her inability to control her daughter's behavior. She also felt somewhat responsible for her daughter's problems, believing that her marriage to her second husband had been a selfish decision that had irreparably damaged her relationship with her daughter. Her daughter entered into court-ordered therapy concurrently with Betty's therapy. Betty had participated in predominately insight-oriented psychotherapy weekly for the next 4 years.

Betty presented as a moderately overweight woman, well-groomed and dressed neatly on most occasions. Her speech was grammatically precise, clearly enunciated, and reflected a high level of intelligence. She often spoke rapidly and intensely, exhibiting clearly her predominate affect at the time. Her body language was frequently theatrical, and she punctuated her words with elaborate arm gestures and facial expressions (e.g., clenched teeth, exagger-

ated smiles). When experiencing high levels of anxiety or anger, she wrung her hands and, on occasion, would get out of her chair and pace the room. Her affect was quite intense and variable, ranging from near-manic excitement to sobbing and screaming. Her emotions could change rapidly during the course of a session, and she sometimes appeared unable to modulate her affect.

Betty was the second of four children, with one older brother and two younger brothers. Her parents and her siblings were all currently living. Betty's relationship with her parents had been strained for a number of years. This strain had increased in the past year following Betty's telling her parents of sexual abuse by a relative when she was a child. Betty reported that her mother's response was denial that the abuse could have happened. As indicated by this incident, Betty felt that her mother had not always been supportive of her. She stated that despite this perceived lack of support, she had always respected and looked up to her mother, although her mother had always been quite domineering. She described her father in somewhat more positive terms, noting a warm relationship, but also indicated that she resented the fact that he allowed her mother to dominate him. Betty described her relationships with her siblings as moderately close, and these relationships appeared to be less filled with tension than her relationship with her mother. She had contact with her parents and her siblings approximately every 2 months.

The preparation of this chapter was supported, in part, by National Institute of Mental Health Training Grant MH15730-12.

Betty initially described her childhood as ideal. However, over the course of 2 years of therapy, she gradually revealed evidence of childhood sexual abuse perpetrated by an uncle who had lived next door. She initially had few specific memories of this abuse other than an incident at age 11 in which her uncle put his hand on her buttocks in a suggestive way. At that time, she recalled telling her uncle to stop. During the course of therapy, Betty began recovering additional memories of abuse by this uncle dating back to approximately age 2. Her earliest memory of abuse was of looking out of her crib at a bloody penis near her face. She remembered later incidents of being forced to perform oral sex, which were associated with intense nausea.

Not surprisingly, given her history, Betty's relationships with men had been problematic. She dated in high school but had no steady relationships. Her first experience of sexual intercourse was in college and resulted in intense feelings of disgust toward herself. She reported one incident of attempted date rape in college, which she successfully repelled.

Each of her marriages had been characterized by intense emotionality and a high level of conflict. Betty's first marriage occurred when she was age 20 to an East Indian man with very conservative views. Betty attempted to adopt a traditional role, allowing her husband to hold the power in the relationship. However, she later began to assert herself, which contributed to increased conflict. Betty had extramarital affairs during this marriage, and it ended after 5 years, primarily because of the power struggles that could not be resolved. Four years later, she married her second husband, who was emotionally abusive to her and sexually abused her daughter. Again, Betty experienced ongoing conflict regarding who would control the marriage. This marriage ended 4 years later. Six years after the termination of her second marriage, she remarried a third time. This marriage ended after 2 years, shortly before Betty entered therapy. She was not currently involved in a close relationship with a man, although she had dated over the past 4 years.

Betty had always had few close friends, most of them women. These relationships had tended to be emotionally intense but transient and superficial and had often ended abruptly as a result of interpersonal conflict. For example, a roommate stated, "You may be able to control your kids' lives, but not mine," and then proceeded to ask Betty to move out. Her closest relationships appeared to be with immediate family members.

Betty attended 2 years of college at age 18 but withdrew as a result of motivational problems associated with depression. Despite a long history of depressed mood, she reported no previous psychological care prior to her current therapy. She returned to college after 1 year of therapy and had recently graduated. Betty had been employed throughout much of the past 10 years. At one time, she was trained as an emergency medical technician (EMT) but worked in this job for only a short time. She had most frequently worked in retail business settings. She was currently employed full-time in retail sales.

Betty's Axis I symptoms at the time of entering therapy indicated a diagnosis of major depression, reflected in sleep problems, appetite disturbance, anhedonia, social withdrawal, concentration problems, and depressed mood. The most appropriate Axis II diagnosis was borderline personality disorder (BDL). The criteria set included a pattern of unstable and intense relationships, impulsive behavior, affective instability, marked and persistent identity disturbance, and chronic feelings of emptiness and boredom.

PERSONALITY DESCRIPTION

The clinician's evaluation of Betty's personality traits as measured by the revised NEO Personality Inventory (NEO-PI-R; Costa & McCrae, 1992) are presented in Table 1. Betty scored high on Neuroticism and Openness, average on Conscientiousness, and low on Extraversion and Agreeableness. Analysis of the facets of each of these factors provided a more detailed description of her personality.

Neuroticism

Within the Neuroticism domain, Betty scored high on every facet. She exhibited high levels of Anxiety, expressing ongoing worries regarding her relationship with her daughter, her finances, her dissatisfaction with her career, her problems in relationships with

TABLE 1

Revised NEO Personality Inventory Personality Profile

Scale	Range	Clinical implications
Neuroticism	Very high	
Anxiety	High	Nervous/ruminative
Angry Hostility	Very high	Rageful/bitter
Depression	Very high	Gloomy/despondent
Self-Consciousness	High	Insecure/ashamed
Impulsiveness	High	Spontaneous/unpredictable
Vulnerability	High	Overwhelmed/defenseless
Extraversion	Low	
Warmth	Low	Cold
Gregariousness	Low	Shy/withdrawn
Assertiveness	Average	
Activity	Average	
Excitement Seeking	High	Adventurous
Positive Emotions	Low	Placid/disinterested
Openness	High	
Fantasy	Very high	Imaginative/dissociative
Aesthetics	Average	
Feelings	Average	
Actions	Average	
Ideas	High	Cognitively flexible
Values	High	Open-minded
Agreeableness	Low	
Trust	Low	Cynical/suspicious
Straightforwardness	Low	Deceptive/manipulative
Altruism	Average	
Compliance	Low	Aggressive/oppositional
Modesty	Average	
Tendermindedness	Average	
Conscientiousness	Average	
Competence	High	Perfectionistic
Order	Average	
Dutifulness	Low	Unreliable/irresponsible
Achievement Striving	High	Driven
Self-Discipline	Average	
Deliberation	Low	Hasty

men, and her perceived personal deficits. These were her anxious thoughts at the time, but she described herself as always having been anxious and ruminative. She noted high levels of tension resulting in painful muscular "trigger points" in her back. She was also quite apprehensive regarding the intentions of men with whom she had interpersonal contact, reflecting not only her general level of anxiety but

also her self-consciousness and antagonistic suspiciousness.

Betty's very high score on the Angry Hostility facet was seen in her frequent experience of and readiness to experience anger and bitterness, especially as provoked by sexually aggressive men. For example, on a date with a man with whom she had gone out only several times, she experienced extreme irritation to the point of anger and rage in response to his inadvertently touching her buttocks. Her antagonistic aggressiveness then contributed to the threatening manner in which she expressed this anger, warning him that "the last man who did that I ripped his ear off!" This extreme verbal response reflected her low threshold for both experiencing and expressing anger. Certainly, unwelcome sexual advances would elicit rebuke from almost anyone, but the extreme nature of her response reflected as well her particularly high level of hostility and antagonism.

Her proclivity to experience and express anger was reflected in her fantasies as well. Once when Betty was swimming in a creek, men in a passing truck made comments about her appearance. This prompted a variety of "Thelma and Louise" fantasies of running to get a gun and waiting for the men to return so that she could shoot them when they reappeared (these fantasies were generated prior to the appearance of the movie). Clearly, this fantasy also reflected her antagonism.

Betty also scored high on the Depression facet of Neuroticism. She had always felt generally hopeless that she could ever improve her life situation. She described herself as having enjoyed little in her life. She indicated that her choices of husbands and boyfriends had been in part a resignation to what was available rather than a real attraction. Her mood was frequently blue, with only temporary positive moods that attempted to mask an underlying negative affect. Betty felt guilty that she had let down herself and her family by not being engaged in a high-prestige career. She also displayed a sense of low self-esteem that was inconsistent with her actual abilities. Even though she had done well in college, she felt that that had been a fluke and was not attributable to her intelligence. This low self-esteem was also noted during an intellectual evaluation. Despite the fact that her performance was in the very superior range, she displayed an extreme lack of confidence about her intellectual abilities, repeatedly stating "I'm no good at this" during testing. Although the Depression and Anxiety facets of Neuroticism do not correspond to criteria of the third, revised edition of the *Diagnostic and Statistical Manual of Mental Disorders* (*DSM-III-R*; American Psychiatric Association, 1987) for Axis I mood disorders, her standing on these two facets might suggest a personality predisposition to experience major depression and various anxiety disorders.

Betty's profile showed a high score on the Self-Consciousness facet of Neuroticism, indicating a sense of insecurity around others. Betty had been intensely ashamed of her abuse history. Although she possessed some clear memories of abuse on entering therapy, she did not reveal this to anyone for 2 more years, nor did she reveal these experiences to her therapist until 1 year ago. She was also ashamed of the fact that she frequently felt depressed and consistently attempted to "put on a smiling face" when having contact with others, despite her negative mood. Betty reported that she felt that if others knew she was depressed, they would realize her weakness.

She also scored high on the Impulsiveness facet of Neuroticism. This level of Impulsiveness reflected an inability to control her urges. When Betty's chronically elevated levels of depression and anxiety become exacerbated by situational factors, she attempted to reduce these feelings through overuse of alcohol. This, along with her low tolerance for frustration and inability to resist cravings (high Impulsiveness), resulted in a tendency toward alcohol binges. For example, in the past 2 years, she had experienced situational stressors including being forced out of two living arrangements she enjoyed because of conflict with female roommates and conflict with her parents regarding her informing them of her childhood abuse. Betty began her binge drinking on weekends. She had also used food as a means of trying to regulate her mood and, as with alcohol, tended to binge rather than eat moderately. Because of her concern about her weight, a pattern of bingeing and purging had developed, at times reaching clinically significant levels (i.e., meeting the *DSM-III-R* criteria for bulimia nervosa).

In addition to impulsive drinking and eating, she had also engaged in impulsive sex. For example, after experiencing a high level of anger toward her abuser during a therapy session, she impulsively had unprotected sex with a bisexual man with whom she had previously been a platonic friend. Betty described this friend as a person who jokingly made passes at her on a regular basis that she always turned down. On this particular occasion, when he made a pass, she "resisted" by grabbing him and wrestling him to the floor. After gaining control of him, they proceeded to have sex. This sexual impulsiveness was perhaps an attempt to manage her feelings of anger by reenacting a situation of sexual powerlessness in which, unlike her childhood abuse, she was able to get control. Despite her concerns following this event that she may have been exposed to the AIDS virus, she impulsively had unprotected sex with this same individual on later occasions when she was experiencing intense emotional dysphoria.

Because of chronically overwhelmed coping resources, she had difficulties dealing with high stress levels (i.e., the facet of Vulnerability). For example, each time examinations approached in college, Betty expressed increased feelings that "I just don't know whether I can handle it" and would become so disrupted that she would have great difficulty completing her work. High levels of stress either at work or at school consistently resulted in increasing social withdrawal and an expressed desire to "hole up and rest." Her feelings of depression and anxiety also increased dramatically during these periods.

Extraversion

Betty's personality with respect to Extraversion was interesting because she had traits of both extraversion and introversion. This complexity of her personality was evident from scores on the Extraversion facets. For example, she was elevated on Excitement Seeking, a facet evident in her bungee jumping, sky diving, and other life choices. Several years ago, Betty entered training to become an EMT. She actually worked as an EMT for only a short time. Although she found it exciting, she also found it too stressful, possibly reflecting her high Vulnerability. Despite her tendency to seek out excitement, Betty's level of Positive Emotions was low. When involved in exciting activities, she experienced temporary increases in positive mood. However, as a personality disposition, the dysphoria reflected in the facets of Neuroticism was more characteristic.

She scored in the average range on the facets of Assertiveness and Activity but in the low range of the facet of Warmth. Although in public Betty often made an effort to smile and act warmly toward others, her interpersonal warmth was quite shallow. Betty was too absorbed in her own difficulties to extend herself and make deeper contact with others. It is interesting that although Betty described herself as high on Warmth in her self-report NEO-PI-R, a more objective rating placed her as low on Warmth. This discrepancy appeared attributable to Betty considering her ability to put on a front of friendliness as an ability to be genuinely warm. This example is indicative of important discrepancies that may be observed between the self-perceptions of certain patient types and the evaluations of independent observers.

Consistent with Betty's low level of Warmth was her low level of Gregariousness. Betty made little effort to get to know individuals with whom she had regular contact, such as co-workers. Her low levels of Warmth and Gregariousness, combined with high levels of Hostility, clearly contributed to her lack of close friends, as well as her chronic difficulties in intimate relationships.

Openness to Experience

Within the Openness domain, Betty scored highest on the facet of Fantasy. Betty described herself as always having a "very active fantasy life." Because of the emotional impact of ongoing sexual abuse as a child, Betty felt a great need to escape and used fantasy as a way of doing this. As a child, she remembered frequently looking out the windows of her house, "spacing out," and imagining that she was somewhere else. This pattern of withdrawal into fantasy as an escape from stress continued into adulthood. For example, she stated that she sometimes imagined that she was a hermit in a cave, isolated from all the problems of interpersonal relationships. Betty found her tendency to withdraw into fantasy a problem, noting that this dissociation from reality had resulted in difficulty attending to and remembering emotionally aversive incidents in her life. She complained of having very few memories of actual childhood events and remembered instead frequently staring off into space and imagining being in a safer situation.

Although most of the characteristics of the *DSM-III-R* diagnosis of BDL are reflected in the facets of Neuroticism (Costa & McCrae, 1990), one particular characteristic of BDL may be reflected in high scores on the Openness to Ideas facet. Individuals who score high on Openness to Ideas possess a variety of ways of seeing themselves. At pathological levels, this "flexibility" may reflect a lack of certainty or clarity regarding identity (i.e., identity diffusion). In Betty's case, a maladaptive flexibility of ideas may have been exhibited in her sexual identity confusion. She identified herself as heterosexual but had often questioned this identity and had engaged in sexual relations with a woman on at least one occasion. Her most clear statement was that she was just uncertain regarding her sexual orientation. In addition to uncertainty about sexual identity, Betty was also uncertain about her career goals. As mentioned earlier, she had worked in a variety of sales jobs and as an EMT and had contemplated careers in medicine and social work. In general, she tended to be dissatisfied with all of her jobs and seemed uncertain regarding the direction of her future life. Betty scored high on the facet of Values. She was generally open-minded regarding what behavior she felt was acceptable, as evidenced by her close friendship and sexual relations with a bisexual man and her first marriage to an East Indian man. Betty scored in the average range on the remaining Openness facets of Aesthetics, Feelings, and Actions.

Agreeableness

Betty scored in the low range of the Agreeableness domain (i.e., antagonism). This was reflected in her low levels of Trust, Straightforwardness, and Compliance. Betty stated that she had always had her "guard up" to protect herself from others, especially men. For example, when an old male friend who wanted to develop an intimate relationship with Betty visited her at her workplace, she put him off, stating that she was busy but that he could come back when she got off work. Betty accidentally "forgot" that the man was coming back and left, leaving the friend alone. A similar incident happened shortly thereafter, and consequently, the man did not attempt to see her again. Betty felt that this forgetting was purposeful and protective. She generally appeared to be suspicious of the motives of any men who were interested in developing an intimate relationship with her. Her low level of Trust could be seen even more vividly in her perceptual distortions and misinterpretations. Betty had on a number of occasions reported seeing men behind her (e.g., through peripheral vision or while looking in the rear-view mirror of a car), only to turn around and find no one there. She also had noted irrational fears at night that someone was outside of her home trying to get in. This typically caused her to turn on all of the lights inside and outside of the house. The source of this characteristic level of mistrust and suspicion from her childhood experiences of abuse was self-evident.

Betty also scored low on the Straightforwardness facet of Argreeableness. Rather than discussing her concerns about living arrangements with her roommates, she surreptitiously manipulated the situation, prompting one of her roommates to state that "you may be able to control your kids' lives, but not mine." When Betty became concerned about her impulsive sex with her bisexual friend (who was also a co-worker), she intentionally short-changed him on a commission on a sale with the hope that he would become angry and refuse any further contact with her. Thus, she attempted to manipulate the situation rather than openly discuss her difficulties with her friend. Her manipulations and power struggles had also been interpreted in therapy as an effort to avoid being abused and exploited again by others. She felt she needed to outmaneuver others to avoid being taken advantage of.

Betty scored low on the Compliance facet of Agreeableness. She displayed a tendency to be somewhat oppositional in interactions with authority figures. For example, her first marriage to an East Indian man reflected not only flexibility of values but also opposition to her mother's expressed dislike of the man. Her consistent marital difficulties were also related to her low Compliance. Betty initially acted in a way that suggested that she wanted her husbands to take responsibility for making decisions related to finances, discipline of children, and division of labor. However, when each husband attempted to do this,

Betty covertly resisted by taking actions to undercut the husband's decisions. This behavior led to chronic but covert power struggles within the marriage. She received average scores on the Altruism, Modesty, and Tendermindedness facets of Agreeableness.

Conscientiousness

Betty's overall scores on Conscientiousness were in the low range. However, inspection of the various facets of this factor revealed a more complex picture. Betty scored in the average range on the facets of Order and Self-Discipline but in the high range on the facets of Competence and Achievement Striving. Betty's desire for competence was reflected subtly in her very precise speech patterns, as well as in her strong desire to do well in college despite her fears that she was incapable of doing so. In Betty's case, her desire to do well and appear competent seemed to be motivated by her perception of her family members as quite competent and accomplished individuals whom she continually must struggle to equal. This perception also seemed to motivate her high need for achievement. In college, she set her goals quite high, for example seeking a 4.0 grade point average. Since graduating, she had expressed a desire to become a physician, in large part because of the prestige this would bring to herself and her family. Thus, she set high expectations for herself, striving to achieve to gain acceptance from her family.

Despite her high level of intelligence and striving, Betty had failed to achieve what she desired in terms of her career because of changeable goals and a low level of Dutifulness. She perceived herself as quite committed to her responsibilities at work and school. However, throughout her college career she had consistent problems with procrastination. These problems were severe enough that she often had to stay up throughout an entire night to complete assignments on time. Although she procrastinated, she was still able to do well in school because of her high level of intelligence. Betty's low level of Dutifulness was also exhibited at work. For example, she had on a number of occasions called in sick to obtain a day off from work when she was not actually ill. Her low level of Dutifulness conflicted with her ability to achieve. On the one hand, she wanted to achieve and be competent to gain respect, but on the other hand, she did not follow through on the responsibilities required to gain that respect. Thus, she became quite angry at herself for "sabotaging" her own goals. During the course of therapy, Betty complained that her tendency to sabotage herself was one of the things she would most like to change about herself.

Betty also scored low on the Deliberation facet of Conscientiousness. In conjunction with her high Impulsiveness, her low level of Deliberation had caused problems in her life. During her second year of therapy, Betty was living alone and feeling quite lonely and depressed. When an opportunity arose to share a house with her two children, she immediately agreed, without considering the likelihood of problems as a result of her enmeshment with them. Rather than taking the time to consider possible outcomes, Betty grasped a chance to decrease her loneliness. As might have been predicted, this living arrangement did not work out, and several months later, just as hastily as she moved in, Betty moved out.

In summary, Betty's personality was characterized primarily by very high levels of Neuroticism, high levels on particular facets of Extraversion and Openness, and low levels of the facets of Agreeableness and Conscientiousness. Betty's elevated Neuroticism and low Agreeableness were consistent with what would be expected based on the *DSM-III-R* criteria for BDL. Her elevated Neuroticism was characterized by elevations on each of the six facet scales of Neuroticism, with negative affect prominent. Although Betty exhibited many of the profile characteristics that would be expected of BDL based on both *DSM-III-R* criteria and the clinical literature, her profile was not entirely prototypic. Perhaps, like most cases of BDL, Betty was not prototypic. Her low Warmth, Gregariousness, Deliberation, and Dutifulness scores were also very important in understanding the difficulties she had had in life and in therapy.

PERSONALITY IMPLICATIONS FOR TREATMENT

The strength of the psychotherapeutic relationship was slow to develop because of Betty's low levels of Warmth and Trust. Betty was quite wary initially, and for several months she attempted to minimize

the seriousness and impact of her difficulties. During this period, she presented consistently with a happy face, but as described earlier, this happy face appeared to be a "false face," masking her underlying dysphoria. Her hesitation in trusting the therapist was evident in the fact that what emerged as a central issue of therapy, namely her sexual abuse as a child, was not mentioned until 2 years into the therapy despite a powerful memory of abuse of which she was aware at the onset of therapy.

The transference issues observed in therapy related primarily to Betty's low Trust and high Hostility. As might be expected given her low Straightforwardness, she expressed her anger and lack of trust passively. During the first 2 years of therapy, there were few problems regarding scheduling issues and missed appointments. However, as the therapeutic relationship became closer and more emotionally laden, her underlying hostility toward men and her lack of trust resulted in problems in maintaining the structure of therapy. Over the past 6 months of therapy, there had been ongoing issues related to the scheduling of sessions. Betty had moved to a new job and stated that the previous appointment time would no longer work. When given several scheduling options, Betty insisted that her new schedule would not allow her to have a set appointment, and therefore, she requested that she schedule her appointments on a week-to-week basis. Given her previously good history of scheduling, this new arrangement was attempted. However, Betty began missing appointments or simply not calling to set up appointments. Betty insisted that her manager was refusing to keep her on a regular schedule and that, therefore, it was quite difficult for her to set up appointments. There was some truth to her explanations, but they were also reminiscent of the barriers she had placed in all of her past adult relationships. It was therefore important to interpret her scheduling problems as an expression of resistance and fears of trusting the therapist.

Finally, Betty was given the option of either accepting a standing appointment time or suspending treatment. Although she then chose to remain in treatment, she manipulated the therapist to accept a time she knew was inconvenient for him, and she expressed her anger by being 20 minutes late for the next two sessions, each time calling at the scheduled time to let the therapist know she would be coming (i.e., low Straightforwardness). The following session, the therapist told Betty that she would have to choose a different time. Betty complained that there were no other possible times because of her schedule but later admitted that she had never discussed the possibility of schedule changes with her manager for fear that it would make her look bad in the eyes of her employer (high Self-Consciousness). Eventually, these scheduling issues were resolved, and therapy continued to become more intense and focused on issues related to the past abuse.

Betty's low Compliance suggested that it was important to watch for control issues in therapy. On the few occasions when therapeutic "homework" assignments were attempted and agreed on, Betty failed to complete them. The effects of low Compliance could also be seen within a single session. On several occasions when therapy became unfocused and bogged down, the therapist attempted to direct therapy to issues in which Betty had expressed an interest in addressing, but each time Betty resisted by changing the direction of treatment to tangential issues. Her low Compliance seemed to interact with her low Trust and high Hostility to cause interpersonal difficulties in therapy. These same issues were responsible for her problems in previous intimate relationships with close friends, family members, and husbands.

As Betty's scheduling problems were resolved and the affective intensity of sessions increased, her high level of Vulnerability became an important issue. Her susceptibility to stress combined with her history of perceptual distortions suggested the possibility of decompensation when her work in therapy became too intense. Betty's vulnerability to stress was reflected dramatically in an incident that occurred in her ongoing therapy. While vividly experiencing the affect associated with her childhood abuse that had been repressed, Betty began stuttering and eventually was totally unable to talk. She also began shaking physically and appeared to squeeze her hands together tightly as if attempting to hold herself together. These symptoms lasted approximately 1 hour, but Betty felt quite fragile for the next several weeks. Betty later expressed the feeling that she was

splitting apart into different parts of herself as she was experiencing these symptoms.

Each of these examples focuses on the negative implications for therapy of particular personality characteristics. However, information provided by the NEO-PI-R also suggested strengths that improved treatment prognosis. Betty's high level of Openness to Ideas did reflect in part pathological aspects, but it also reflected an ability to be more cognitively flexible, encouraging the use of insight-oriented treatment. Although she had difficulty addressing and confronting her conflicts (high Vulnerability), she was very open to looking at her problems in different ways and considering alternative ways for understanding and addressing these problems. For example, Betty's initial focus in therapy was on her problems in her relationship with her daughter. Much of this early therapeutic work focused on increasing Betty's understanding of the dynamics of their relationship and working on better ways of handling her interactions with her daughter. Betty was able to engage in these tasks quite effectively, in part, because of her openness to self-insight and problem-solving alternatives.

Information from her personality profile also suggested a potential effectiveness for other particular therapeutic techniques. In Betty's case, her openness to fantasy enhanced her responsiveness to Gestalt techniques that were used to address her anger. For example, encouraging Betty to confront her deceased uncle using the empty chair technique resulted in a vivid cathartic experience. Betty immediately began talking to her uncle, engaging in an increasingly heated dialogue with him, eventually kicking and hitting the floor (where his image lay). She then suddenly stopped her activity, stating "he's gone."

Betty continued therapy, and her progress was significant. Her symptoms of depression lifted, and she reported feeling more stable. Her wide variations in emotion became less extreme, and instances of impulsive behavior became more rare. Although changes in her manner of relating interpersonally were subtle, she reported feeling more positive emotionally when interacting with others. She was not involved in an intimate relationship with a man, reflecting continued distrust, although in therapy her level of trust currently appeared moderately high.

Betty made progress in therapy, and with continued therapy, prognosis for further progress was good.

References

American Psychiatric Association. (1987). *Diagnostic and statistical manual of mental disorders* (3rd ed., rev.). Washington, DC: Author.

Costa, P. T., Jr., & McCrae, R. R. (1990). Personality disorders and the five-factor model of personality. *Journal of Personality Disorders, 4,* 362–371.

Costa, P. T., Jr., & McCrae, R. R. (1992). *Revised NEO Personality Inventory (NEO-PI-R) and the NEO Five-Factor Inventory (NEO-FFI) professional manual.* Odessa, FL: Psychological Assessment Resources.

CHAPTER 12

NARCISSISM FROM THE PERSPECTIVE OF THE FIVE-FACTOR MODEL

Elizabeth M. Corbitt

Narcissistic personality disorder (NAR) is defined in the third, revised edition of the *Diagnostic and Statistical Manual of Mental Disorders* (*DSM-III-R*; American Psychiatric Association, 1987) as "a pervasive pattern of grandiosity (in fantasy and behavior), lack of empathy, and hypersensitivity to the evaluation of others, beginning by early adulthood and present in a variety of contexts" (p. 351) and is diagnosed on the basis of the presence of at least five of nine criteria indicating these traits. Such attributes may also be conceptualized as extreme, dysfunctional variants of certain personality traits described by the five-factor model (FFM) of normal personality, such as conceit, toughmindedness, and self-consciousness. This chapter outlines the principles just described and uses a case study to illustrate the utility of the FFM in describing and conceptualizing narcissism.

The primary dimension of normal personality (as defined by the FFM) that relates to narcissism is antagonism (the polar opposite of agreeableness). Widiger, Trull, Clarkin, Sanderson, and Costa (see Table 1 in chapter 3 of this book) suggest that NAR criteria primarily involve extremely low variants of the Agreeableness facets of Modesty (indicating arrogance and conceit), Altruism (indicating self-centeredness, selfishness, and exploitation), and Tendermindedness (indicating lack of empathy), with the clinical literature also suggesting low Straightforwardness (e.g., manipulativeness). Furthermore, these investigators determined that the criteria also suggest high variants of Openness to Fantasy (e.g., "fantasies of unlimited success, power, brilliance, beauty, or ideal love"; American Psychiatric Associa-

tion, 1987, p. 351) and the Neuroticism facets of Self-Consciousness (hypersensitivity to evaluations) and Hostility (rage).

However, such predictions of the narcissistic patient's presentation on an inventory of normal personality may not be as straightforward as direct extrapolations from the *DSM-III-R* criteria suggest. A complication that is likely to arise in the evaluation of narcissistic patients is suggested by the criterion "reacts to criticism with feelings of rage, shame, or humiliation (*even if not expressed*)" (American Psychiatric Association, 1987, p. 351; italics added). The ambiguity of the narcissistic patient's response to criticism is even more explicit in the third edition of *DSM* (*DSM-III*), in which it was stated that these individuals may display a "cool indifference" to criticism, rejection, or defeat by others (American Psychiatric Association, 1980, p. 317). In fact, it has been proposed to delete this item in the fourth edition of the *DSM* (*DSM-IV*) (American Psychiatric Association, in press), in part because of the ambiguity and complexity of its assessment (Gunderson, Ronningstam, & Smith, 1991). Narcissistic patients are very vulnerable and self-conscious, but they at times express this through a complete denial of any faults or insecurities (Kernberg, 1984). Thus, narcissistic patients may deny the existence of their own vulnerability, self-consciousness, and hostility. On the sole basis of the *DSM-III-R* criteria for NAR, it may be predicted that narcissistic patients will score high on the Neuroticism facets of Self-Consciousness and/or Vulnerability. However, narcissistic patients may deny feelings of shame and inferiority and thereby produce average or even low scores on these facet scales.

Costa and McCrae (1990) supported this supposition, finding significant negative correlations between the Minnesota Multiphasic Personality Inventory (MMPI) and the Millon Clinical Multiaxial Inventory (MCMI) scales for NAR and the NEO Personality Inventory (NEO-PI; Costa & McCrae, 1985) Neuroticism scale. Similarly, in a combined factor analysis of the five factors and several personality disorder scales, Wiggins and Pincus (1989) found that both the MMPI and the Personality Adjective Check List (PACL) Narcissistic scales loaded negatively on Neuroticism. Trull (1992) likewise found a significant negative relation between the MMPI Narcissistic scale and NEO-PI Neuroticism in a clinical population of personality-disordered individuals, further supporting the contention that narcissistic patients tend to present themselves as psychologically healthy rather than as vulnerable to emotional weakness.

An additional complication of this issue involves the narcissistic patient's reasons for seeking treatment. Although theoretically one would predict a lack (or at least a denial) of depression and anxiety in patients with NAR, clinical experience suggests that they seek treatment in response to overwhelming discomfort brought about by the failure of their typical modes of defense against precisely these feelings of depression and/or anxiety. In such cases, it is likely that elevations will then occur on these facets of Neuroticism, at least in the early stages of treatment. In other words, a poorly defended narcissist may produce elevations on Neuroticism (an accurate portrayal of his or her vulnerability), whereas a rigidly defended narcissist may produce extremely low scores (reflecting a defensive denial of vulnerability).

The following case illustration further clarifies both the expected relation between NAR and the FFM and the additional issues that may ensue from both the patient's denial of traits evident to others and his or her temporary state-related symptoms.

CASE ILLUSTRATION: PATRICIA

Presenting Complaint

Patricia was a 41-year-old married woman who presented at an outpatient mental health clinic com-

plaining of interpersonal difficulties at work and recurring bouts of depression. She described a series of jobs in which she had experienced considerable friction with co-workers, stating that people generally did not treat her with the respect she deserved. She attributed her depression to the recent suspicion that perhaps people did not like her because of her behavior; she indicated that she wished to explore this possibility further in therapy so as to discover how to act with others so that they would not continue to be hostile toward her. The immediate reason for her entrance into treatment was her recent failure to succeed in a supervisory position at the bank at which she was employed—a failure that she said was very damaging to her self-esteem.

History and Clinical Description

Patricia was an only child. She described her parents as reserved to the point of coldness, stating that both were busy with their jobs and disapproved of displays of affection. Patricia said that she always felt that she was not appreciated for herself but only for what she accomplished. As an adult, Patricia had few friendships and had had only three romantic relationships, including her marriage at the age of 35. At the time she entered treatment, she reported having little time for friendships because of her long hours at work. She described her marriage as unsatisfying, stating for example that her husband was very childish (e.g., referring to his sentimentality on anniversaries as "adolescent").

Patricia reported a long history of banking jobs in which she had experienced interpersonal discord. Shortly before her entrance into treatment, Patricia was demoted from a supervisory capacity at her current job because of her inability to effectively interact with those she was supposed to supervise. She described herself as always feeling out of place with her co-workers and indicated that most of them failed to adequately appreciate her skill or the amount of time she put in at work. She reported that she was beginning to think that perhaps she had something to do with their apparent dislike of her. However, even during the initial treatment sessions, her descriptions of her past and current job situations quickly and inevitably reverted to defensive statements concerning others' mistreatment and lack of appreciation of her. Despite her stated goal of changing her own behavior so as to be better liked, it quickly became clear that her actual wish was to cause her co-workers and supervisors to realize her superiority and to treat her accordingly. Patricia stated several times, for example, that the tellers at the bank were jealous of her status and abilities as a loan officer and that this made them dislike her.

Five-Factor Description

Figure 1 provides Patricia's description of herself in terms of the domain and facet scales of the Revised NEO Personality Inventory (NEO-PI-R; Costa & McCrae, 1992b). This section describes the salient features of Patricia's self-description, especially those pertaining to narcissism, and gives examples of situations or statements that illustrate each extreme score.

As stated earlier, Agreeableness is the dimension most central to narcissism. Patricia described herself as low on five of the six facets of the Agreeableness domain. Her very low score on the facet of Modesty suggested grandiosity and arrogance about her own abilities compared with others'. Patricia often made condescending remarks about co-workers working under her, indicating that they were inferior to her in intelligence and abilities and thus had little or nothing to offer her. For example, she described one incident in which she was assigned an assistant whom she was expected to train but who could also help her with her duties. Instead of accepting such help, Patricia told her boss and the assistant that she did not see how someone so much younger and less skilled than herself could be anything but a drain on her time and energy.

Her low level of Altruism, indicating perhaps selfishness and exploitation, was evidenced in her manipulation of her work situation so that others were required to do tasks she considered beneath her while leaving more desirable tasks for herself. In one such situation, Patricia pretended to have a back injury as an excuse to avoid sales work, thus forcing the other employees to do this less pleasant job while she was given more prestigious loan accounts. Lack of empathy was suggested by Patricia's low score on the Tendermindedness facet scale. For example, she reported one incident in which a friend had agreed to meet her for dinner but was late because her child

was ill; Patricia was highly offended and irritated by what she referred to as her friend's "lack of consideration" in being late. She felt no compassion for her friend or the child.

The remaining facets of Agreeableness are less central to the construct of narcissism but were additional aspects of Patricia's personality. Her tendency toward suspiciousness, as indicated by her low Trust score, was exemplified by her belief that others did not like her and conspired against her to make her job harder (e.g., by "purposely" failing to get necessary paperwork to her on time). Finally, her low score on the Compliance scale suggested uncooperativeness; this was perhaps illustrated by her tendency not to follow instructions at work and to refuse to cooperate with her husband at home. For example, although her boss had asked Patricia not to stay at the bank after hours because of security considerations, she often stayed late to work, saying that the boss's request was "stupid and restrictive." Furthermore, she regularly ignored her husband's requests that she do at least some of the housework, for which he did in fact take most of the responsibility despite also pursuing a career in law.

On the Neuroticism domain, Patricia described herself as both depressed and anxious. As mentioned earlier, this pattern may be expected in narcissistic patients when their defensive systems are poor, particularly on first entering treatment. Although mood states do not generally affect the assessment of normal personality, clinical depression is often manifested on personality inventories in the area of Neuroticism (Costa & McCrae, 1992a). More specifically, elevations on Neuroticism tend to occur when patients are depressed and tend to decrease on their recovery from depression. This was the case with Patricia.

Patricia also exhibited an elevation on the Angry Hostility facet scale, which was apparent in her tendency to become enraged when criticized or "treated badly." On the other hand, she described herself as low on Vulnerability and Self-Consciousness, the former indicating an ability to deal well with stress and the latter suggesting feelings of security, poise, and an absence of feelings of inferiority or embarrassment. As noted earlier, this issue is complicated by the distinction between the patient's self-report and

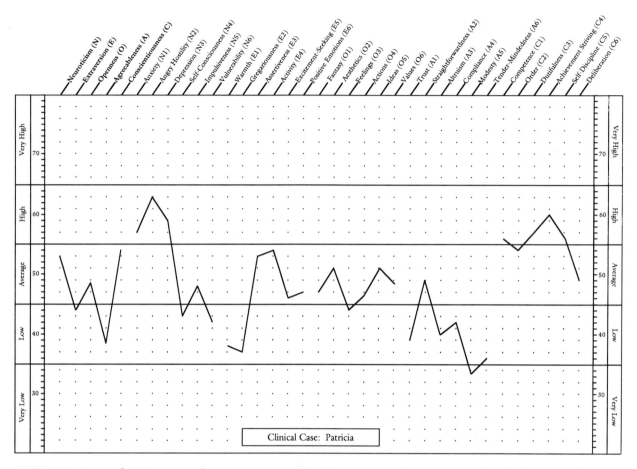

FIGURE 1. Revised NEO Personality Inventory profile of Patricia. Profile form from *The NEO Personality Inventory Manual* by P. T. Costa, Jr. and R. R. McCrae, 1985, Odessa, FL: Psychological Assessment Resources. Copyright 1985 by Psychological Assessment Resources.

others' view of him or her. Although Patricia denied feelings of humiliation and insecurity, such feelings were evident in her behavior and reactions toward others. For example, when criticized, Patricia would blush and either defensively make excuses for her behavior ("They can't expect me to work any harder than I already work!") or negate the criticism through a narcissistic stance ("She's just envious of me because I'm smarter than she is"). This behavior would be interpreted by many clinicians as a defensive reaction to deep-seated insecurity, regardless of the denial of such feelings.

Patricia described herself as low on Extraversion, specifically on the facets of Warmth and Gregariousness. Although the Extraversion domain is not theoretically central to narcissism, in Patricia's case her low scores on these facets seemed to be almost secondary to her narcissistic qualities. For example, low

Warmth implies coldness and distance from others. This was exemplified in Patricia by the infrequency with which others called her or visited with her to talk about their problems; when they did, she responded with intellectual advice usually delivered in a condescending manner, such as "When you're older, you'll understand better how things are." Furthermore, her solitary nature in having few friends, not seeking out social groups, and keeping to herself at work was indicative of low Gregariousness but may in fact have resulted in part from actual rebuffs from others in response to her antagonistic behavior.

A final interesting aspect of Patricia's self-description involved her elevations on several facets of the Conscientiousness domain. She perceived herself as accomplished, persistent, strongly committed to standards of conduct, and tending to strive for excellence. These elevations may indicate a classic narcissistic inflation of self-image, especially given that she was, even by her own report, having considerable difficulties at work.

TREATMENT

Knowledge of Patricia's levels on the five broad domains of the FFM and their facets was an aid to the conceptualization of her case in terms of personality pathology. Certain aspects of such pathology may either contribute to or constitute difficulties in treatment. Awareness of these aspects can be invaluable to the clinician in formulating treatment issues. In Patricia's case, her long-standing pattern of antagonism made the formation of a therapeutic relationship difficult. Patricia was often condescending toward and critical of her therapist, refusing at times to believe that anyone could understand her problems or help her in any way. Her lack of trust interfered with treatment as well; she was slow to develop confidence in her therapist's benevolent intent. Patricia's low compliance was also evident in treatment, as might be expected, through lateness or missed sessions as well as noncompliance with payment.

However, Patricia's depression and anxiety were motivating factors in entering and continuing treatment. Her low levels of vulnerability and self-consciousness alerted the clinician to a potential tendency toward a defensive denial. As treatment progressed, the feelings of depression and anxiety decreased, whereas her awareness of her vulnerability and self-consciousness increased. Patricia gradually came to realize that she often felt unable to deal with stresses at work and that she reacted to possibly imagined criticism and lack of respect with rage and shame, perhaps because of her feeling as a child that nothing she did was "good enough" for her parents.

References

American Psychiatric Association. (1980). *Diagnostic and statistical manual of mental disorders* (3rd ed.). Washington, DC: Author.

American Psychiatric Association. (1987). *Diagnostic and statistical manual of mental disorders* (3rd ed., rev.). Washington, DC: Author.

American Psychiatric Association. (in press). *Diagnostic and statistical manual of mental disorders* (4th ed.). Washington, DC: Author.

Costa, P. T., Jr., & McCrae, R. R. (1985). *The NEO Personality Inventory manual.* Odessa, FL: Psychological Assessment Resources.

Costa, P. T., Jr., & McCrae, R. R. (1990). Personality disorders and the five-factor model of personality. *Journal of Personality Disorders, 4,* 362–371.

Costa, P. T., Jr., & McCrae, R. R. (1992a). Normal personality assessment in clinical practice: The NEO Personality Inventory. *Psychological Assessment, 4,* 5–13.

Costa, P. T., Jr., & McCrae, R. R. (1992b). *Revised NEO Personality Inventory (NEO-PI-R) and the NEO Five-Factor Inventory (NEO-FFI) professional manual.* Odessa, FL: Psychological Assessment Resources.

Gunderson, J. G., Ronningstam, E., & Smith, L. E. (1991). Narcissistic personality disorder: A review of data on DSM-III-R descriptions. Special Series: DSM-IV and personality disorders. *Journal of Personality Disorders, 5,* 167–177.

Kernberg, O. F. (1984). *Severe personality disorders.* New Haven, CT: Yale University Press.

Trull, T. J. (1992). DSM-III-R personality disorders and the five-factor model of personality: An empirical comparison. *Journal of Abnormal Psychology, 101,* 553–560.

Wiggins, J. S., & Pincus, A. L. (1989). Conceptions of personality disorders and dimensions of personality. *Psychological Assessment: A Journal of Consulting and Clinical Psychology, 1,* 305–316.

CHAPTER 13

BULIMIA NERVOSA WITHIN THE CONTEXT OF MALADAPTIVE PERSONALITY TRAITS

Cynthia G. Ellis

This chapter discusses bulimia nervosa within the context of maladaptive personality traits. The case chosen to illustrate this is somewhat complicated by the involvement of a variety of diagnoses from the third, revised edition of the *Diagnostic and Statistical Manual of Mental Disorders* (*DSM-III-R*; American Psychiatric Association, 1987), including avoidant personality disorder (AVD), borderline personality disorder (BDL), and recurrent major depression (DPS).

Alice was a 27-year-old White, single female. She described first "turning to food" in high school when she was angry at her brother but unable to express it. The onset of regular bingeing and purging, however, did not occur until she was about 21, a time during which she also was sexually promiscuous, drank heavily, and used a variety of illicit drugs. If she was ever unsatisfied sexually, she recalled that she would go home and binge.

Table 1 presents a five-factor description of Alice's personality. Alice's Neuroticism facets were among the highest within her profile. She often stated that she expected people to perceive her as "fat and dependent" (Self-Consciousness and Vulnerability). She described herself as being weak and unassured. Throughout her life, she avoided social situations that she perceived as potentially humiliating, such as eating or crying in front of others (Self-Consciousness). Alice often considered smashing her mirror with her fist because of all that she hated in herself (her weight, chronic depression, and physical appearance), which she saw as signs of weakness and vulnerability (Depression, Vulnerability, and Self-

Consciousness). Alice seemed to project much of her hostility and negative feelings about herself onto others while harboring a pervasive expectation that all others would be disgusted by her. Her impulsiveness was expressed in a variety of ways, including her more recent bingeing patterns as well as her past drug use, promiscuous sexual behavior, and self-destructive gestures.

Alice's introversion, however, was also noteworthy. Alice had had very few close interpersonal relationships throughout her life (low Gregariousness) and reported having no positive feelings about or memories of her childhood (lack of Positive Emotions). Alice remembered being called "the quiet and sensitive one" and "suffering in silence" (Passivity) while feeling like the black sheep of the family. It seemed that Alice learned at an early age that sharing her emotions caused others to feel anxious and thus that intimacy caused problems.

LIFE HISTORY

Alice was the 8th of 11 children. Her father, who was a prominent lawyer, had a heart attack and died unexpectedly during Alice's early childhood. Alice reported only vague, emotionally neutral memories of him mixed with anger at his having died.

When Alice was a child, her mother worked part-time as an interior decorator and was at the time of Alice's assessment a full-time beautician and owner of a salon. Alice described her mother as "always trying to paint a rosy picture of everything" and felt that, because of this, her mother never allowed her to

TABLE 1

Five-Factor Description of Alice

Domain and facet scales	Range
Neuroticism	
Anxiety	Very high
Angry Hostility	Average
Depression	High
Self-Consciousness	Very high
Impulsiveness	Very high
Vulnerability	Very high
Extraversion	
Warmth	Very low
Gregariousness	Very low
Assertiveness	Very low
Activity	Low
Excitement Seeking	Low
Positive Emotions	Very low
Openness to Experience	
Fantasy	High
Aesthetics	Average
Feelings	Low
Actions	Low
Ideas	Average
Values	Average
Agreeableness	
Trust	Very low
Straightforwardness	Low
Altruism	Average
Compliance	Average
Modesty	High
Tendermindedness	Average
Conscientiousness	
Competence	Average
Order	High
Dutifulness	Average
Achievement Striving	Very high
Self-Discipline	Low
Deliberation	Average

grieve her father's death. Alice described feeling as a child that she could never have her own successes and that her mother was always comparing her with her brothers and sisters. The fact that there were so many children within a one-parent home contributed to Alice's feeling lost and alone. She reported being unable to compete for her mother's attention in ways that the other children could. For example, her mother placed great emphasis on physical attractiveness and worked aggressively to get Alice's two oldest sisters into modeling at an early age. Alice was never overweight as a child but always perceived herself as being "pudgy." She always felt that her appearance never measured up to that of her sisters. Alice considered herself to be the unwanted and neglected "ugly duckling."

The family also emphasized academic achievement. Some of Alice's siblings became lawyers or doctors. Although Alice tried hard in school, she was unable to achieve at their level. Alice recalled her mother's tendency to give her at best only back-handed praise while comparing her to one sister in particular. She would say things such as "Well, I know you tried hard, and I guess not all of my children can be like Betty." Alice had harbored considerable resentment toward her mother for being critical of her weight and appearance, devaluing her emotions, and appearing disinterested in her career, yet she had also incorporated her mother's apparent devaluation into her own self-image.

Alice stated that she had always been quite dependent on her family although she resented their competitiveness, their tendency to judge her by her physical appearance, and their continued criticism of her for being "too sensitive." She felt that some of her brothers and sisters were embarrassed to be around her because she was not as successful by their mother's standards (i.e., beautiful, thin, or brilliant). She was often left behind when the sisters closest to her age went to a party, despite the likely presence of a variety of mutual friends. Alice described that she was "taught not to feel or express emotions" because she felt people would only ridicule her if she showed how she felt. She felt she had to make herself "invisible" or she would be in the way of or would somehow embarrass her family.

Alice's description of her past included few friendships, perhaps in large part due to her intense self-consciousness. She did mention a few "friends" at work who turned to her for emotional support but whom she avoided because she did not want to be in a situation in which she "accidentally" showed her feelings and thus risked appearing incompetent and unstable. She described the cats she had had over the years as her best friends. She stated that they were the only "people" who were capable of unconditional love and who would not criticize her for her weight or emotional sensitivity. Alice stated that her cats had always been the most important people in her life, and she felt that they would be the only ones to miss her if she were to die. They were what kept her from hurting herself when she was filled with self-disgust. She often expressed a sense of impending doom and an overwhelming fear that her present two cats would die and wondered if she could handle the associated emotions (i.e., those indicated by her very high Vulnerability score). Alice believed that no one understood her deep attachment to her cats and expected people to be critical and impatient with her if and when the cats did die (Self-Consciousness).

Alice began her first serious relationship with a young man named Peter when she was 25 years old. She rarely discussed him in treatment, however, except to focus on how poorly he understood her because he came from a "healthy family in which there were only three children." Alice assumed that her boyfriend perceived her as disgustingly over-weight (Alice's weight did fluctuate as an adult, but she was never outside the average range for her height) and that it would be her fault if he were una-ble to advance in his job (i.e., his boss would not hire someone with a "fat girlfriend"). Alice rarely went to social events with Peter because of her weight. She often expected Peter to become repulsed and stop loving her.

She first met Peter during the period in her life in which she was promiscuous and drank heavily. She initially tried to avoid any emotional involvement and to use Peter only to satisfy herself sexually. Alice reported that once during lovemaking with Peter she was overcome by an intense wave of emotion that scared her. She ran to the bathroom to be alone where the anxiety slowly dissipated. Alice had experi-enced a sudden, vivid image of herself as a child with her family, including her father, picnicking in a field near a lake. She was unable to share this experience with Peter nor was she able to explain to him why she left the room. Alice could not understand at first why she had this memory; all she knew was that it was frightening and that she could not continue making love. Alice developed vaginismus soon after this experience. She later realized this was related to the fact that she had begun to allow herself to develop feelings of love for Peter. It was during treat-ment that she began to understand these experiences as reflecting her fears of intimacy.

TREATMENT HISTORY

Alice had a history of ending therapy against the advice of her therapists. She entered treatment for the first time after leaving college during the first few weeks of classes. She had become severely depressed and was unable to function. One year into her treat-ment, Alice attempted suicide. Her attempt was pre-cipitated by the return of her therapist from a week-long absence. At first she was relieved that he was gone, but on his return she realized how close she was allowing herself to feel to him and how involved she had become in therapy. She overdosed with Val-ium at the time of her next appointment. She woke up late the next morning and immediately felt embarrassed, as if she had "failed again." She was upset that no one had even noticed her suicide attempt (she did not report it to her therapist). On her third scheduled session after this episode, she refused to return to treatment. It was in the past few years that she suggested that her first therapist's absence may have awakened issues related to the loss of her father.

She entered treatment again at age 19 for depres-sion but ended it prematurely after only 1 year. At the age of 20, Alice was seen at an outpatient eating disorders clinic but did not trust the psychologist and terminated after 6 months. At age 24, Alice again sought treatment at a different outpatient psychother-apy clinic (where she saw the current author) to work on issues related to both bulimia and depres-sion. She was seen in weekly treatment for a total of 2½ years.

Throughout this course of therapy, Alice was frequently late to sessions, consistently avoiding eye contact and self-consciously fiddled with her fingers. She routinely began sessions by stating "I have nothing important to talk about," followed by a long silence. In each session, she initially spoke very softly and in monotone. She usually pre-sented with flat affect but on occasion would briefly cry while struggling to inhibit her sobs. Toward the middle of the sessions, however, Alice would begin to actively work on relevant issues and would then find it difficult to accept that the session had to end on time. Her discussions of issues would also be tentative and avoidant at first.

Once she was able to get close to an issue, she would suddenly become vague in her descriptions, state that "it is not important," and change the topic. After a productive session, she would often begin the next session with the comment that she had felt depressed after the previous session and did not want to "go through that for nothing."

Alice also developed a pattern of missing the second (and sometimes the third and fourth) session after the therapist had initiated a temporary interruption in treatment (e.g., vacation by the therapist). During the subsequent sessions, Alice would appear like a child waiting to be scolded. She would hang her head, sit on her hands, and look as if she wanted to be invisible. When asked what she was feeling, she would report that she expected to be criticized and scolded for missing sessions. It was noteworthy that she would not miss the session immediately following the break. She eventually was able to explain this as needing to be sure the therapist had returned before canceling the subsequent sessions.

After a session in which she atypically openly expressed intense grief over the ill health of one of her cats (rather than "suffering in silence"), Alice called with her decision to end treatment abruptly. She refused to discuss this decision in person, and treatment ended.

SUMMARY AND FIVE-FACTOR CONCEPTUALIZATION

Although it was bulimia that initially motivated Alice to seek treatment, it quickly became apparent that it was her introversion and neuroticism (particularly her self-consciousness, vulnerability, and depression as well as her impulsivity) that were most problematic to her life.

Alice met the *DSM-III-R* criteria for bulimia nervosa, and she did in fact have a clinically significant eating disorder. However, her bulimia was only one among a variety of manifestations of her impulsivity. It was clearly the most troublesome to her and the one for which she sought treatment, but her substance abuse, promiscuity, and self-destructive gestures were additional expressions of her difficulty in controlling her urges and impulses. Successful treat-

ment of her bulimia alone would have still left her with substantial problems. Her Axis I clinical disorder would be resolved, but the underlying personality traits that resulted in this disorder would have remained.

A comparable issue pervades the literature on the relation of bulimia to BDL (Jonas & Pope, 1992; Widiger & Shea, 1991). To some, the co-occurrence of bulimia and BDL suggests a comorbidity of two distinct, independent disorders. To others, the bulimia is a symptom or expression of the BDL psychopathology. Just as substance abuse can be an expression or manifestation of antisocial personality traits, anxiety can be an expression of avoidant personality traits, achievement can be an expression of narcissistic and compulsive personality traits, and tearful crying can be an expression of histrionic personality traits, so too can bulimia be an expression of borderline personality traits. In such cases, the fundamental or primary pathology is the personality disorder that gives rise to the bulimia (Kernberg, 1984).

Alice did in fact meet the *DSM-III-R* criteria for BDL, but she also met the *DSM-III-R* criteria for AVD. It was more parsimonious and direct to simply describe her as having excessive neuroticism and introversion. Alice was not seen as having two comorbid personality disorders, each with its own distinct etiology, pathology, and course. She simply had one personality disorder characterized by excessive neuroticism and introversion. It was the same neuroticism that was involved in both her borderline and avoidant personality traits.

Alice was also not a prototypical borderline. She did not display the substantial hostility (rage) that is evident in so many BDL patients (Kernberg, 1984). She did meet the *DSM-III-R* criteria for BDL (e.g., identity disturbance, affective instability, overidealization and devaluation of others, chronic feelings of emptiness and boredom, and recurrent suicidal threats), but her BDL symptomatology was primarily evident in her neuroticism (i.e., impulsivity, anxiety, self-consciousness, depression, vulnerability). The traits of low extraversion also contributed to her atypical BDL presentation. Many BDL patients display moderately high levels of assertiveness, gregariousness, and excitement seeking; Alice instead displayed many of the features of an AVD patient (i.e., shy, inhibited, withdrawn, passive). One could then also describe Alice as an AVD patient at a borderline level of personality organization using Kernberg's (1984) terminology or simply as an "avoidant borderline."

The implications of the personality traits of neuroticism and introversion also became quickly evident in psychotherapy. Treatment initially focused on Alice's bulimia because this was her incoming complaint. However, little progress could be made until Alice felt more secure and comfortable with the intimacy and closeness of psychotherapy. In one respect, Alice would have preferred that the therapist simply cure her bulimia without the cost, stress, and risk of her having to open up to another person. Her anxious, vulnerable, and self-conscious withdrawal significantly impaired her ability to discuss issues with her therapist or to even return for subsequent sessions. She acknowledged that her premature termination from the outpatient eating disorders clinic was attributable in large part to her fears of getting too close and involved. Alice, however, would herself turn the therapeutic focus away from her bulimia toward her more general feelings of vulnerability and self-consciousness. Whenever the issue of bulimia was discussed, she emphasized its relation to her low self-esteem and insecurity within relationships (e.g., the feelings of inferiority stemming from her family's emphasis on intelligence and beauty and her fear and anxiety that her boyfriend would be repulsed by her weight and would stop loving her). As therapy progressed, treatment focused more directly on her conflicts regarding attachment and separation. One of Alice's key insights came after reporting being intensely scared by the soothing and unbidden image of her childhood during lovemaking with Peter. She was able to see the meaning of this experience as reflecting fears of intimacy that arose when she began to acknowledge feelings of love for and involvement with Peter. Alice also eventually saw the development of her vaginismus as another expression of her problems with intimacy.

When Alice terminated treatment, she was no longer bingeing and purging, the impulse to do so had dissipated, and she had not been depressed for quite some time. She was no longer experiencing vaginismus, and she and Peter were planning to get married. Treatment, however, was clearly not entirely successful. The termination was premature, reflecting in large part the difficulties she was having with both the impending loss of one of her "closest friends" (her cat) and the increasing involvement with Peter. A follow-up contact, however, did indicate that she had successfully dealt with the eventual loss of her cat (which she did not replace with another pet), and she had in fact married Peter. Her report of her relationship with Peter was that it was at times difficult for her, but she was finding it to be very supportive and nurturing.

References

American Psychiatric Association. (1987). *Diagnostic and statistical manual of mental disorders* (3rd ed., rev.). Washington, DC: Author.

Jonas, J. M., & Pope, H. G. (1992). Axis I comorbidity of borderline personality disorder: Clinical implications. In J. Clarkin, E. Marziali, & H. Munroe-Blum (Eds.), *Borderline personality disorder: Clinical and empirical perspectives* (pp. 149–160). New York: Guilford Press.

Kernberg, O. F. (1984). *Severe personality disorders.* New Haven, CT: Yale University Press.

Widiger, T. A., & Shea, T. (1991). Differentiation of Axis I and Axis II disorders. *Journal of Abnormal Psychology, 100,* 399–406.

CHAPTER 14

MIXED PERSONALITY DISORDER WITH PASSIVE–AGGRESSIVE AND AVOIDANT FEATURES

Glenn V. Thomas

Sarah, a 39-year-old single female, originally requested therapy at the Jesse G. Harris, Jr., Psychological Services Center (at the University of Kentucky, Lexington), an outpatient clinic, to help her deal with chronic depression and inability to maintain employment. She had been unemployed for over a year and had been surviving on her rapidly dwindling savings. She was becoming increasingly despondent and apprehensive about her future. She acknowledged during the intake interview that her attitude toward work was negative and that she had easily become bored and resentful in all of her previous jobs. She believed that she might somehow be conveying her negative work attitudes to prospective employers and that this was preventing them from hiring her. She also volunteered that she detested dealing with people in general. Sarah paid little attention to her physical appearance, dressing in plain, conservative, and outdated clothes that were generally ill-fitting and unflattering. She was also significantly obese, with her dark hair cut in a short and severe style.

Sarah had a checkered employment history. She had been a journalist, a computer technician, a night watch person, and a receptionist. In all of these jobs she had experienced her supervisors as being overly critical and demanding, which she felt caused her to become resentful and inefficient. The end result was always her dismissal or her departure in anger. Sarah generally perceived her co-workers as being hostile, unfair, and rejecting. However, she would herself actively avoid them, complaining that they were

being unreasonable and coercive when they tried to persuade her to join them for activities outside of work. For example, she would believe that she was being asked to go for drinks purely because her co-workers wanted her to get drunk and act foolishly. Sarah would eventually begin to take "mental health" days off from work simply to avoid her supervisors and colleagues.

At the time she initiated therapy, Sarah suffered from significant weight gain, subjective feelings of depression and fatigue, and thoughts of suicide. She also complained of waking every few hours throughout the night and only being able to doze fitfully in the early hours of the morning. She met the criteria for major depression from the revised, third edition of the *Diagnostic and Statistical Manual of Mental Disorders* (*DSM-III-R*; American Psychiatric Association, 1987) although a diagnosis of "double depression" may have been more appropriate given that the current major depression was superimposed on a chronic, long-standing depressed mood (Keller, 1989).

Of the *DSM-III-R* Axis II disorders, she was diagnosed as having a passive–aggressive personality disorder (PAG) with paranoid and avoidant traits. From the perspective of the five-factor model of personality (Table 1), Sarah was described as being high on Neuroticism (particularly the facets of depression, vulnerability, and self-consciousness), low on Extraversion (especially gregariousness, warmth, and positive emotions), low on Agreeableness (especially trust, straightforwardness, and compliance), and low on

TABLE 1

Five-Factor Description of Sarah

Domain and facet scales	Range
Neuroticism	
Anxiety	Average
Angry Hostility	Average
Depression	High
Self-Consciousness	High
Impulsiveness	Average
Vulnerability	High
Extraversion	
Warmth	Low
Gregariousness	Low
Assertiveness	Average
Activity	Average
Excitement Seeking	Average
Positive Emotions	Low
Openness to Experience	
Fantasy	Average
Aesthetics	Average
Feelings	Average
Actions	Average
Ideas	Average
Values	Average
Agreeableness	
Trust	Low
Straightforwardness	Low
Altruism	Average
Compliance	Low
Modesty	Average
Tendermindedness	Average
Conscientiousness	
Competence	Average
Order	Average
Dutifulness	Low
Achievement Striving	Average
Self-Discipline	Low
Deliberation	Average

Conscientiousness (especially dutifulness and self-discipline). From the perspective of the criteria proposed for the fourth edition of the *DSM* (*DSM-IV*; American Psychiatric Association, in press), Sarah also met the criteria for the depressive and negativistic personality disorders (Task Force on DSM-IV, 1991).

Sarah's mood was neither something that came on her (e.g., an endogenous depression) nor a reaction to some event or occurrence in her life (e.g., an exog-

enous depression). She had been pessimistic, dejected, despondent, and gloomy throughout much of her life. She simply felt that this was the right and normal way to be. She was as critical and punitive toward others as she was toward herself. She was rarely intensely angry or enraged (i.e., average level of hostility). She was instead chronically irritable, argumentative, sarcastic, scornful, disdainful, and critical (i.e., low Agreeableness or high antagonism). She was quite mistrustful and suspicious (low trust), as well as being deceptive and manipulative herself (low straightforwardness). Sarah's low Conscientiousness was also important in understanding her personality and adjustment difficulties. Her antagonism and introversion might have been almost tolerable if she were in fact a responsible, diligent, and dutiful employee; but she was not. She was, in fact, overtly irresponsible and unreliable to the point that she would at times be fired.

It was difficult to diagnose Sarah with a *DSM-III-R* Axis II disorder because, in addition to her PAG symptoms, she displayed symptoms of a variety of other personality disorders, particularly the avoidant (AVD), schizoid (SZD), and paranoid (PAR) disorders. However, unlike the prototypical AVD patient, she did not exaggerate the potential difficulties of everyday life, she was not embarrassed by blushing or showing signs of anxiety in front of other people, she was not reticent about saying something out of a fear of sounding foolish, nor was she unwilling to get involved with people unless certain of being liked. She was easily hurt by criticism, but this pain was often expressed by disdain, irritability, and scorn. She did avoid social contacts and had no close friends (low gregariousness). Like the prototypical SZD patient, she almost always chose solitary activities, rarely experienced strong emotions (low positive emotions), and did not seem to enjoy close relationships. However, she certainly was not indifferent to criticism, did not display constricted affect, and did desire to have sexual relationships. Like the prototypical PAR patient, she was suspicious and irritable (low Agreeableness); but the paranoia, suspiciousness, and mistrust were not central or dominant in her everyday functioning. She was often suspicious and mistrustful, but more predominant were her complaints, irritability, and disdain.

PSYCHOSOCIAL HISTORY

Sarah was born in Oregon and lived there until the age of 8. She described the early period of her childhood there as being largely uneventful and for the most part pleasant and enjoyable. However, at the age of 8, Sarah's family moved to California. The move was somewhat of a surprise to the family, and Sarah thought that her father pressured the family to move to separate her mother from the rest of her family of origin.

In California, Sarah became aware of a tension between her parents. Her father was very unsociable, and the family rarely had guests. When her mother did occasionally invite friends over, her father would be largely quiet and passive. He never formed any friendships in the community. At the same time, her mother did not like to have other children in the house and would not allow Sarah to have any friends visit.

Sarah could only remember a single time in which she was allowed to have a friend to the house. The occasion was Sarah's 12th birthday, and her mother asked her how she would like to celebrate the anniversary. Sarah chose to have a friend over, but her mother made such a formal and stilted production of the event ("like a picture from *Better Homes and Gardens*") that Sarah felt uncomfortable and never wanted to repeat the experience. Her mother also rarely allowed her to visit the homes of peers, and consequently, she only socialized with others at school. Ultimately, her friends stopped inviting her to functions outside of school because they knew her mother would never let her go. In junior high and high school, she occasionally had a close friend, but she and the friend would eventually drift apart.

As a child, she tried to convince herself that she did not need friends or even her parents. She would alternate among feelings of resentment, bored indifference toward others, and loneliness. For most of her childhood, she was not quite sure how she felt toward others; but as she grew older, the bitterness and resentment increased, with infrequent but quite painful feelings of loneliness. She felt despondent, pessimistic, and depressed much of the time following to the move to California.

Sarah was also lonely within the confines of her family. Her relationship with her brother Edward, her only sibling, was very conflicted. She believed that her mother gave Edward preferential treatment. Her mother and Edward would often do things together and exclude Sarah; she believed that they shared "secret" jokes. Sarah felt that neither her father nor her mother ever expressed a genuine interest in her. As an adult, she once expressed her dissatisfaction to her mother about the way she had been treated as a child. Her mother responded with a stiff, obligatory hug, but only after her brother had left the room.

Sarah went to college in a town substantially far from home. She did not want to attend college, perceiving it as a rejection and punishment for being "bad." She eventually dropped out of college and attended vocational school, qualifying as a computer technician in 1970. However, in 1974 she went back to college to study journalism and creative writing, graduating in 1976. Her mother died of cancer while Sarah was in college. Sarah made one attempt to resolve her differences with her mother on her mother's deathbed, but she felt rebuffed and did not try again.

At the time of the assessment, Sarah lived alone. She had telephone contact with her father approximately once every 6 months and only rarely spoke with her brother. She had one friend in California, whom she described as close, but they had drifted apart over the past few years. Sarah rarely socialized, finding it difficult to create small talk and feeling awkward in groups. She tended to expect others to show interest in her, rather than vice versa, and was hurt and bitter when this did not occur.

COURSE OF THERAPY

Sarah's motivation for treatment was quite strong. She was very intelligent and displayed a strong propensity for insight and critical self-reflection (at times overly critical). Given her interpersonal history, it was important for the therapist to build a strong rapport and trusting relationship with her to prevent a possible premature termination. At the same time, Sarah clearly desired warm and meaningful interpersonal contact to the extent that an abrupt premature termination was probably unlikely.

Therapy initially proceeded smoothly, with a healthy rapport being developed fairly quickly. Sarah's inability to obtain employment was the immediate focus of concern, given her rapidly dwindling financial resources. In a relatively short period of time, she obtained employment as a receptionist. She initially felt that she was fitting in well, proudly displaying her first evaluation to her therapist. Her severe depressive symptoms gradually remitted. However, she soon began to perceive her boss as critical and was suspicious of his motives for having her in the office. She even voiced the opinion that they might be keeping her simply to have a handy scapegoat. Many of her boss's requests that seemed innocuous to her therapist were interpreted by Sarah as unreasonable, and she spent large portions of her sessions complaining about the demands and responsibilities at work and within all aspects of her life (e.g., complaints regarding her auto mechanic, her landlord, and others).

Once again, she began taking "mental health" days to relax at home. Over the course of a few months, however, she became more aware of the role she was playing in her troubles at work and within her relationships. Treatment initially emphasized problem-solving skills (e.g., learning to avoid revealing her irritability at work, learning to avoid focusing on comments and behaviors that she found annoying, and learning to explore the rationality of her perceptions and responses). As treatment progressed, she began to appreciate the extent to which her difficulties with others, both at work and outside of it, were largely of her own making. She had always recognized that she was more irritable and critical than others, but she had not really appreciated how she drove others away. She had always felt that she was obviously the more vulnerable person and that this would result in sympathy, patience, and tolerance from others. She assumed that other people would approach her and draw her out of her shell. It was some time before she realized that she presented herself as lacking much interest in others (low warmth and low gregariousness) as well as lacking a cheerful or pleasant disposition (low positive emotions) and being rather antagonistic. Although she may have

had good reason to feel embittered over her past relationships, those around her were not at fault and yet were the recipients of her antagonism. They did not approach or appreciate her because she presented herself as being indifferent and even rejecting.

Progress was slow. She remained resentful of her boss and finally found another job where she repeated this same pattern of behavior, although to a much lesser extent. Repeating the same pattern of relationships with a new employer and new colleagues, however, was a significant factor in helping her recognize that it was her personality and not others that was largely the problem.

With the recognition that she was perhaps her own worst enemy, she became increasingly interested in exploring the historical roots of her personality style. It was not at all difficult for her to recognize why she became embittered, withdrawn, and vulnerable. These insights further supported an appreciation of how she brought to her current relationships the wounds and debts from her past. An exploration of her past was also helpful in realizing how some of her introversion and self-consciousness were attributable to a lack of experience and training in social skills. Her parents were poor role models for interpersonal popularity. Her current withdrawal was motivated by a sense of vulnerability and bitterness, but it also reflected in part an inadequacy in social skills. She felt awkward and self-conscious around others because she had never really learned how to approach, relate to, and get involved with others. Treatment, therefore, continued to include a variety of efforts to help her develop more comfortable, relaxed, and agreeable ways of approaching, interacting, and relating to others.

Sarah remained in treatment, but she was working much more effectively at her job and was beginning to develop at least some casual friendships. She was approaching these relationships cautiously and carefully so that they were not experienced as being so overwhelming and was working to minimize the costs of her occasional expressions of antagonism. Her current job was significantly below her level of skills and capacities, but she recognized that she had a ledger of debts from past troubles at work that was her responsibility to overcome.

References

American Psychiatric Association. (1987). *Diagnostic and statistical manual of mental disorders* (3rd ed., rev.). Washington, DC: Author.

American Psychiatric Association. (in press). *Diagnostic and statistical manual of mental disorders* (4th ed.). Washington, DC: Author.

Keller, M. (1989). Current concepts in affective disorders. *Journal of Clinical Psychiatry, 50,* 157–162.

Task Force on DSM-IV. (1991). *DSM-IV options book: Work in progress.* Washington, DC: American Psychiatric Association.

PART IV

TREATMENT OF PERSONALITY-DISORDERED PATIENTS

CHAPTER 15

USE OF THE NEO-PI PERSONALITY DIMENSIONS IN DIFFERENTIAL TREATMENT PLANNING

Cynthia Sanderson and John F. Clarkin

In this chapter, we examine the potential contribution of a dimensional model of personality (i.e., the five-factor model [FFM]) to the planning and application of psychological interventions. Unfortunately, most of this chapter is based on clinical experience and is without the supporting evidence from multiple empirical investigations. To our knowledge, there is little data on the psychosocial or medication treatment of maladaptive traits or personality disorders. We hope that this situation will change in the near future. In any case, the recommendation of a particular treatment for an individual must be seen in the whole context of differential treatment planning. There is growing interest, both in clinical practice (American Psychiatric Association, 1989; Beutler & Clarkin, 1990; Frances, Clarkin, & Perry, 1984) and research (Beutler & Clarkin, 1991; Shoham-Salomon, 1991), in matching the patient with a treatment that is tailored to the specific needs of the individual.

Although there is growing recognition that Axis II personality disorders will modify treatment outcome of Axis I disorders (e.g., the National Institute of Mental Health's treatment of depression), we are making a more general point. We suggest that broad personality dimensions—whether abnormal or not—contribute to and influence both the choice and process of treatment intervention. Rather than of academic interest alone, we suggest that the power of the personality dimensions is substantial and that therapy focus, alliance, and outcome all relate to personality dimensions.

A major stimulus for the examination of the contribution of the FFM, and in particular the NEO Personality Inventory (NEO-PI; Costa & McCrae, 1985) as a measure of FFM, to treatment planning is the incompleteness of the third, revised edition of the *Diagnostic and Statistical Manual for Mental Disorders* (*DSM-III-R*; American Psychiatric Association, 1987) in reference to this clinical task. Of course, the *DSM* system was not meant to be a treatment-planning document but simply an organizing schema for the acquisition for such a process (American Psychiatric Association, 1989). However, it is used as such, and the inadequacies of the *DSM* for differential treatment planning are related to the following considerations.

First, a total picture of personality strengths, excesses, deficits, and dysfunction is needed to plan treatment intervention for the individual patient, regardless of whether he or she complains of Axis I symptomatic syndromes or Axis II disturbed interpersonal relations. Although the Axis I disorders describe common symptomatic patterns, the treatment of these conditions is always modified by the personality characteristics of the individual, none of which are noted in the Axis I diagnostic criteria themselves. Treatment efforts that focus only on the deficits without attention to the assets of the individual's personality are shortsighted. The third edition of the *DSM* (*DSM-III*; American Psychiatric Association, 1980) suggests that one does not treat the person but rather the disorder that the person is manifesting. Although this statement may have some validity when dealing with syndromal symptom patterns on Axis I that have a clear onset and course, this is not so with the personality disorders on Axis II. Personality disorders concern traits that form the very fabric of the individual. When treating personality disorders, one is addressing the "whole" individual and must consider both the pathological and the nonpathological attributes.

Second, both medical and social treatments are focused on particular constellations of behavior, attitudes, moods, and traits but not on diagnostic categories. We argue in this chapter that psychosocial treatment is focused on the trait level. It is also at the construct/trait level that one plans medical treatment. For example, in the medical treatment of borderline personality disorder (BDL) patients, the targets are impulsivity, mood dyscontrol, and thought disorder that have been characteristic of long-term functioning (Cowdry, 1987; Soloff, 1987).

Third, personality disorders as defined in *DSM-III-R* Axis II have very little evidence concerning construct validity. Empirical data so far suggest that internal consistency of the disorders is often poor (Morey, 1988), and many of the disorders include several different constructs (Livesley & Jackson, 1986; Livesley, Jackson, & Schroeder, 1989). In addition, because the Axis II disorders are polythetic, the group of patients who meet the diagnosis are not homogeneous even in the defining characteristics (Clarkin, Widiger, Frances, Hurt, & Gilmore, 1983; Widiger et al., 1990). Furthermore, Axis II does not cover the total universe of personality problems. It has been pointed out, for example, that only half of the interpersonal circle is covered by Axis II (Kiesler, 1986).

Fourth, the categorical nature of Axis I and Axis II is inadequate if not misleading in regard to treatment planning. In the clinical situation, many patients who come for therapy do not meet criteria for the categorization of any one personality disorder but still seek treatment for troubling and disruptive personality traits or patterns. Diagnostically, these individuals may be accurately put into the category of *personality disorder, not otherwise specified* (NOS), or diagnosed as manifesting mixed personality disorder traits. In many settings, NOS is the most prevalent Axis II condition. Alternately, many patients meet criteria for more than one personality disorder, so the clinician does not plan treatment intervention around each disorder independently but rather conceptualizes the person and the multiple foci of inter-

vention in some organized and hierarchical pattern tailored to the individual.

DIFFERENTIAL TREATMENT DECISIONS

For each patient, many different kinds of treatment decisions must be made. In this chapter, we present some important dimensions of treatment and suggest ways in which insights that are gained from a patient's NEO-PI profile can help the therapist tailor the components of treatment to the individual's needs. First, we discuss four fundamental or *macrotreatment* decisions that are made at the initial evaluation stage. These are the selection of (a) *treatment setting* (e.g., inpatient, day hospital, outpatient), (b) *treatment format* (e.g., family, marital, group, individual), (c) *strategies and techniques* (e.g., psychodynamic, cognitive, behavioral), and (d) *duration of treatment* (brief or longer term treatment). A fifth and equally important macrotreatment decision is the potential use of medications; this topic is beyond the scope of this chapter, however. In the second half of the chapter, we discuss important *microtreatment* decisions that are relevant to in-session and between-sessions decisions, such as the breadth of the treatment goals, the depth of the patient's therapy experience, and the degree of the therapist's directiveness (see Beutler & Clarkin, 1990). Several clinical vignettes illustrate our observations. Although there is much interdependence between the various dimensions of treatment planning, we have found it pedagogically helpful to separate them for illustrative purposes (Figure 1).

Macrotreatment Decisions

Setting The settings of treatment have remained somewhat constant in the last several decades: inpatient, day hospital, outpatient clinic, private office, treatment in the family home, and sessions at the site of disorder (e.g., systematic desensitization in vivo). The accessibility of these treatment settings has changed dramatically in the current era of cost containment. Inpatient care has become much more restricted in terms of who obtains it (the most severely disturbed patients in acute distress) and for how long a period of time (the length of stay is becoming much shorter). This constric-

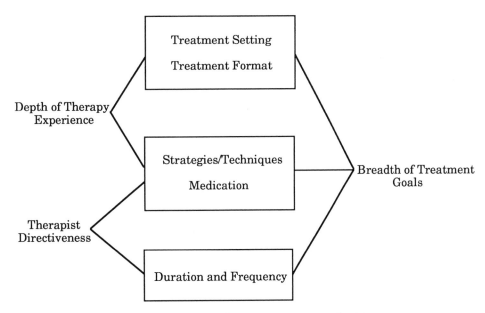

FIGURE 1. Relation of evaluation and ongoing treatment decisions.

tion of resources has forced clinicians to be more creative in using alternatives to hospitalization in crisis situations, such as day hospital settings and crisis intervention.

Format The treatment format is the interpersonal context within which the intervention is conducted. The choice of a particular treatment format (i.e., individual, group, family/marital) is determined by the perspective from which a presenting problem is initially defined, by the patient/family, the clinician, or both. For example, from the clinician's point of view, the treatment of the spouse with depression can vary depending on whether it is viewed as a current adaptation to a larger problem involving the family unit (suggesting a need for family intervention) or as the patient's personal symptomatic adaptation to a unique biological, social, and historical situation (in which case individual or group treatment is more likely indicated). The mediating and final goals of treatment will vary accordingly.

The individual treatment format, with its focus on the individual as the locus of difficulty, has advantages in addressing problems achieving intimacy, the striving for autonomy in adolescents and young adults, or issues that are of such private or embarrassing nature that the confidentiality of the individ-

ual format is required at least for the beginning phase.

The group treatment format provides an economic mode of treatment delivery, an effective means of reducing or circumventing the resistances expressed in individual therapy, and adjunctive support or ancillary therapists in the form of other patients and creates a setting in which interactional forces can be manifested and examined.

Group treatments can be classified as *heterogeneous* or *homogeneous* in membership. Although this distinction is not supported by controlled research, it has been used extensively in clinical practice. In heterogeneous groups, individual patients differ widely in their problems, strengths, ages, socioeconomic backgrounds, and personality traits. Treatment in heterogeneous groups fosters self-revelation of one's inner world in an interpersonal setting where sharing and feedback are encouraged.

There are two general indications for heterogeneous group therapy: First, the patient's most pressing and salient problems occur in current interpersonal relationships, and second, prior individual therapy formats have failed for various reasons (e.g., the patient has a strong tendency to actualize interpersonal distortions in individual therapy formats, or the patient is excessively intellectualized).

The enabling factors for heterogeneous group therapy include an openness to influence from others, willingness to participate in the group process, and willingness and ability to protect group norms. The patient's motivation for group treatment must be sufficiently adequate to foster participation.

Homogeneous groups are self-help or professionally led groups in which all members share the same symptom or set of symptoms. These are the primary (if not sole) focus of the intervention and change. The sense of commonality in jointly combating a common problem provides support and self-validation. Homogeneous groups tend to avoid techniques of psychological interpretations and use group inspiration, didactics, modeling, and advice as the source for behavioral change.

The indication for homogeneous group treatment is that the patient's most salient problem or chief complaint involves a specific disorder for which a homogeneous group is available. These problems fall into four general categories: (a) specific impulse disorders (e.g., obesity, alcoholism, drug addiction, gambling, violence); (b) problems adjusting to and coping with medical disorders such as cardiac ailments, ileostomy, terminal illness, chronic pain, and others; (c) problems of a particular developmental phase such as childhood and adolescence, child-rearing, and aging; and (d) specific mental disorders or symptom constellations such as agoraphobia, somatoform disorders, and schizophrenia.

The family treatment format, in which various subgroups of a family (a nuclear family, a couple, or a couple with family of origin) meet on a regular basis with a therapist, was derived in large part from an emphasis on the contextual origins of the presenting problems. Family and marital treatments have recently been applied more broadly, with greater emphasis on their practical utility rather than solely or primarily on the hypothesized role of family/dyad in the generation and/or maintenance of the problem. Hence, family- and marital-based treatments are used for various medical (e.g., hypertension) and psychiatric disorders (e.g., agoraphobia, schizophrenia), wherein the spouse or family member is enlisted to provide social support to the patient.

The mediating goals of family and marital treatments are to change the repetitive and often rigid interpersonal interchanges by family members that are in themselves the focus of complaint or are hypothesized to be related to the symptoms of one or more individuals. In addition to the use of the usual range of strategies and techniques, the use of the family format allows direct therapeutic assessment and impact on these behaviors as they operate in predictable sequences in the family setting.

The relative indications for family/marital formats might include, for example, (a) family/marital problems presented as such without any one family member designated as the identified patient; (b) family presents with current structured difficulties in intrafamilial relationships, with each person contributing collusively or openly to the reciprocal interaction problems; or (c) family is unable to cope adequately with the chronic mental illness of one family member.

The NEO-PI, in combination with the clinical interview, can help in choosing the treatment format in two ways. First, the NEO-PI helps describe the predominant interpersonal patterns of the patient and suggests areas of difficulty needing treatment regardless of whether these interpersonal problem areas can be addressed in individual, family, or group formats. For example, although the NEO-PI profile is not directly related to the choice of family/marital treatment format (because it is an instrument that is concerned with characteristics of the individual as a self-contained unit), the NEO-PI profile can suggest how that individual relates to others, including family members.

Second, the NEO-PI can help identify those individuals who could effectively use a particular format. For example, the NEO-PI can indicate which individual could use a group format, or alternately, those who would likely need the privacy of individual treatment. Those who are particularly antagonistic (e.g., suspicious, critical, or unempathic) or introverted (low warmth or low gregariousness) may not be suitable for group therapy. The NEO-PI can in any case be useful in anticipating conflicts and problems among the group members (e.g., antagonistic persons may take advantage of the excessively trusting or passive patient; see also chapter 16 in this book for a discussion of choice of treatment format.)

Strategies and Techniques There seems to be a consensus in the clinical literature that the differences between treatments—differences seen as crucial for outcome—are captured at the level of treatment strategies and techniques. We question this assumption as far from complete and suggest rather that psychotherapy has advanced in its specificity not through investigation of techniques but through research on the patient disorders themselves. As the disorders have become specified, the treatments have become more focused. For example, the family treatment of schizophrenia has flourished since the concept of expressed emotion and its influence on the course of the disorder was explicated. Treatments were formulated with the explicit focus of reducing expressed emotion through the use of various strategies and techniques. The implication is that no treatment strategy or technique can be considered in isolation but that its value lies in its usefulness in achieving the mediating goals of treatment for the specific problem diagnosis.

Treatment manuals are now being written to guide research and training in the techniques of the various schools (dynamic, behavior, cognitive) for diverse patient populations, for example, those with anxiety (Beck & Emery, 1985), depression (Beck, Rush, Shaw, & Emery, 1979), schizophrenia (Falloon, Boyd, & McGill, 1984), interpersonal problems (Luborsky, 1984; Strupp & Binder, 1984), and suicidal behaviors (Linehan, 1987). Clinical research has indicated which strategies and techniques are effective with specific patient problem areas.

Paradoxically, although treatment manuals that define treatment packages for all individuals with a common diagnosis or syndrome are growing in number, at the same time there is a concerted effort to assign the individual patient to the most optimal treatment. In this chapter, we suggest that the NEO-PI has the potential for utility at the very intersection of manuals for specific disorders as applied to the individual.

In addition to using the strategies and techniques common to the various schools of therapy, the clinician must consider the use of more specific approaches that might be appropriate for the particular case. In this process, the clinician considers most carefully the mediating goals of treatment and those strategies and techniques that might be instrumental in reaching those goals. The selection of specific

techniques is related to (a) the nature of the problem/disorder (etiology, causes, stressors), (b) the breadth of treatment goals, (c) the depth of therapy experience, and (d) the reactance level of the patient. In rare instances, specific strategies and techniques have shown superiority over competing ones in comparison studies. The clinician must determine individual mediating goals for each patient, given his or her unique diagnosis, social environmental situation, and personality assets and liabilities. For example, psychodynamic techniques have the mediating goal of insight and conflict resolution; behavioral techniques have the mediating goals of specific behavioral changes; cognitive techniques have the mediating goals of change in conscious thought processes; and experiential–humanistic techniques have the mediating goals of increased awareness that is more fully integrated into the patient's personality.

Although the NEO-PI does not relate directly to the mediating goals of the treatment of the individual case, data from this instrument can assist in choosing strategies and techniques for the treatment of the individual. This will come about mainly through the consideration of the patient's problem complexity, coping styles, and reactance level, which is considered in detail later in this chapter.

Duration of Treatment Treatment duration is multifaceted. The concept can refer to (a) the duration of a treatment episode, (b) the duration of a treatment element (e.g., hospitalization within a single treatment episode), or (c) the succession of treatment episodes in a virtually lifetime treatment of a chronic disorder such as schizophrenia. The major reference is to the duration of the *treatment episode*, that is, the time from evaluation to termination of a particular treatment period.

A number of factors make the relationship between duration of a treatment episode and outcome relatively unpredictable. The duration of the treatment episode is related to the amount of effort and length of time needed to achieve the mediating and final goals of the intervention, which in turn are related to the nature of the disorder and symptoms under treatment. In general, the greater the breadth of goals and depth of experience of the treatment, the longer the treatment. Alternatively, when the goals of treatment are circumscribed, treatment can be brief. Setting the duration for a brief treatment can assist in ensuring that the goals will be reached more quickly than leaving the duration open-ended.

Brief Therapy We may well be in an era in which the brief psychotherapies are the predominant form of treatment for many patients. Whether it is planned in advance or not, most patients engage in psychotherapy for only a short period of time. Patients who seek clinical outpatient psychotherapy generally expect it to last no more than 3 months, and a very high percentage of patients actually remain in treatment for fewer than 12 sessions. Most therapy has always been brief; what is new is the notion of *time-limited therapy by design.*

The first step in planning for treatment duration is to decide whether to recommend a brief or longer term outpatient intervention. Some clinicians offer brief therapy as the initial treatment for all patients, except those few who have already had an unsuccessful experience with it, or those who present with clear motivation and indications for long-term treatment. Because it is difficult to predict from one or two interviews which patients require and can benefit from longer interventions, a trial of brief therapy is often useful as an extended evaluation and/or role induction.

The brief psychotherapies differ among themselves in goals, treatment techniques, strategies, format (group, family, or individual), setting (inpatient, day hospital, outpatient), and selection criteria. In fact, the different models of brief therapy are as diverse as those applied in longer treatments. However, certain essential features characterize the brief therapies: establishing a time limit, achieving a focus with clear and limited goals, achieving a workable patient–therapist alliance rapidly, and having an active therapist.

The indications for brief therapy, of whatever model, include the following: (a) A definite focus, precipitating event, or target for intervention must be present; (b) the patient's overall motivation and goals may be limited but must be sufficient for cooperation with the brief treatment; (c) the patient must be judged to be capable of separation from treatment; (d) the patient's usual level of functioning is adequate and does not require the level of change usually

brought about only by long-term or maintenance treatment; (e) limited financial and/or time resources on the part of the patient or the delivery system may incline toward brief treatment; and (f) brief treatment may be chosen in preference to longer treatment to avoid secondary gain, negative therapeutic reactions, unmanageable therapeutic attachments, or other iatrogenic effects.

An important consideration in making the decision for brief treatment is the potential usefulness of one of the brief therapies for a specific patient problem area. Difficulties brought by patients can be broadly conceptualized as either symptomatic or conflictual in nature (Beutler & Clarkin, 1990). Brief treatments have been articulated for symptoms (depression, anxiety), unrecognized feelings, behaviors (phobias), and interpersonal conflicts (Clarkin & Hull, 1991; Hollon & Beck, 1986; Koss & Butcher, 1986).

The NEO-PI can help the clinician choose which brief-focused treatment may be the most beneficial in two ways: (a) by indicating the breadth of problem and (b) by indicating the interpersonal assets that would foster a rapid alliance with the therapist and the acceptance of therapist assistance. Thus, the NEO-PI profile for the ideal patient for planned brief treatment would show isolated but significant elevations on Neuroticism, high Openness to Activities and Ideas, high Warmth (for rapport), and high Agreeableness.

Long-Term Therapy Regardless of technique, the rationale for treatment of long-term duration is that some problems are so ingrained, complex, and extensive that an extended period of time is necessary for their dissection and resolution and for the patient to assimilate and apply new solutions to daily life. Because regularly scheduled long-term psychotherapy is expensive and is minimally supported by available research, the prescription of this duration requires the most thoughtful assessment of indications, contraindications, and enabling factors.

A poor or insufficient response to brief treatment is an empirical demonstration of the need for further intervention. Although most psychotherapy research studies have dealt with brief therapy, these studies are impressive in the number of patients who do not respond to the brief intervention. The overuse and limitations of brief therapies have been previously described (Clarkin & Hull, 1991).

Patient factors that tend to lengthen the treatment include the diagnosis of chronic mental disorders (e.g., schizophrenia, bipolar disorder), multiple problem areas, poor patient enabling factors for treatment, and relatively poor premorbid functioning and adjustment.

Prescription for No Treatment Evaluation only, or the prescription of no treatment for the individual following evaluation, is the briefest intervention. Clinicians are not inclined to recommend no treatment and rarely do so for patients applying for help in a clinical setting (Frances & Clarkin, 1981). For treatment planning purposes, we have found it helpful to distinguish (a) patients who are likely to improve without treatment (spontaneous remission: i.e., healthy individuals in crisis), (b) patients who are likely not to respond (nonresponders: i.e., antisocial, malingering or factitious illness, iatrogenically infantilized patients, poorly motivated patients without incapacitating symptoms), (c) those who are at risk for a negative response to treatment (i.e., severe masochistic, narcissistic, and oppositional patients; patients who enter treatment wanting to justify a legal claim or disability), and (d) those for whom the recommendation of no treatment is an intervention in itself aimed at their resistance (i.e., oppositional patients refusing treatment; Frances et al., 1984).

Combined with a careful history, the NEO-PI may be of assistance in isolating those patients for whom treatment is contraindicated or for whom engagement and/or change in treatment is unlikely. A conceptualization of this parameter early in assessment enables the clinician to save valuable time and effort from a foredoomed treatment or provides information to be used in confronting the patient with the potential roadblocks to effective treatment right from the first evaluation.

Spontaneous Remission A relatively healthy individual who is caught in the throes of a crisis is a likely candidate for spontaneous remission. The NEO-PI profile for such an individual would show strengths in terms of, at most, an isolated and only moderate elevation in Neuroticism and good contact with others (Agreeableness and Extraversion). The

profile would emphasize, in particular, strengths in the area of Conscientiousness. The individual might present with a profile that is not substantially problematic, for example, moderate on Neuroticism and at worst high or low on Extraversion. The patient's problems may be situational and transient, and the patient may have the personality strengths to overcome these problems on his or her own (e.g., high in Conscientiousness and Openness to Ideas and Activity). The best approach might then be to recommend no treatment because the patient can call on his or her own resources.

Clinical Vignette: A Likely Case for Spontaneous Remission Christine was a 29-year-old single female who presented to a hospital outpatient clinic complaining of problems in relationships with men. In this clinical setting, a screening battery was designed to provide suggestions for treatment planning, with data on functioning (Social Adjustment Schedule [SAS-SR]), symptom distress (revised Symptom Checklist [SCL-90]; Beck Depression Inventory [BDI]), and personality traits (NEO-PI). The relative elevation of symptoms (SCL-90) to interpersonal difficulties (scales of the NEO-PI) provides information on treatment focus.

Christine's SCL-90 was quite low; her scaled scores were in the 20–30 range ($M = 50$), which indicates little symptom distress. Likewise, the BDI was below average. The SAS-SR indicated adaptive functioning in all areas, with some minor difficulties in finances and social functioning. Her NEO-PI profile was average for Neuroticism; very high for Extraversion, Openness, and Agreeableness; and high for Conscientiousness. She appeared to be an extravert, quite open to experience, agreeable in her relationships, and conscientious in her behavior. Her distress level, on both the SCL-90 (more of a state measure) and the NEO-PI Neuroticism scale (more of a trait measure), was not significantly elevated.

In the clinical setting, Christine was assigned to brief individual therapy. The patient discontinued treatment after a few sessions in which she discussed some difficulties with a current boyfriend. On hindsight, this patient probably could have been assigned by the clinical team for evaluation only, or she could have been seen for a limit of several sessions. Because she was not substantially symptomatic and because she presented with many strengths, the assessment could have been presented to her in an optimistic way. With the clinician relating to her many strengths, she could have been advised in a positive way that she did not need therapy.

Nonresponders These are individuals who are not likely to benefit from treatment. There are two subgroups of nonresponders that are important to note. One group is composed of individuals low on Conscientiousness but who are also very high on Neuroticism. They are in tremendous pain, but they drop out of treatment quickly. An individual in this group may have a history of being in and out of psychotherapy. A second group is composed of individuals who are low on Conscientiousness and very low on Neuroticism. Individuals in this group may bother other people with their behavior but may not be particularly bothered by it themselves. As a consequence, they have little motivation to change. These individuals may express mild interest but may find various reasons why they cannot continue treatment.

Patients at Risk for a Negative Response to Treatment We are concerned here with individuals who develop a hostile, possibly psychotic transference. In psychodynamic terms, some of these patients manifest a negative therapeutic reaction, which may be due to self-defeating or oppositional personality traits.

On the NEO-PI, these would be patients who are very low on Openness to Actions; if the therapist tries to encourage them to do something that may improve their life even slightly, they will not do it, or will do so in a cursory manner without persistence. The therapist assigns them homework or practice, but the patient always finds a reason to not do it. These are patients also likely to be low on Conscientiousness. They will not be diligent or responsible in their efforts. Low scores on Agreeableness will suggest that they are suspicious, oppositional, and resistant. Nothing that the therapist offers will be valuable. Whatever the therapist recommends is perceived as deficient or as having been tried before with no success. Such individuals will be unlikely to make use of any format, even though they may be very high on Neuroticism, which indicates a high degree of suffering.

No Treatment as an Intervention for Resistance Some patients who apply for treatment are, at the same time, motivated to escape treatment at any possible turn. For example, individuals who are sent to treatment by others (e.g., mates sent by spouses, adolescents and early adults sent to treatment by parents, employees sent by employers, or those sent by the courts) fall into this category. They may be experiencing little dysphoria or distress (e.g., average on Neuroticism). If they are really in trouble (i.e., they are treatment resisters and yet they need treatment, which they impulsively reject), then one might expect high scores on Impulsiveness and Hostility. However, the particularly resistant persons will be low on Openness and low on Agreeableness. They will reject anyone "telling them what to do" because they are not open to change and because they are antagonistic to the suggestions of others.

Evaluation The various just-described macrotreatment decisions are all part of the initial evaluation process. The following vignette illustrates the kinds of issues that may emerge during this process.

Clinical Vignette The patient was a 25-year-old woman, Abigail, who was an executive with a major telecommunication corporation. She had never been in psychotherapy before. She was evaluated and referred by an employee assistance program professional at work because she had been engaged in promiscuous relationships. She presented with the complaint that she had very few friends, despite appearing as an engaging and friendly person. On the NEO-PI, Abigail came out as fairly well adjusted in most areas. She was average on Extraversion, very high on Conscientiousness (a high-achieving woman), high on Agreeableness, and high on Openness to Experience. On Neuroticism, however, Abigail was very high on the Hostility facet scale.

The patient's difficulties were seen as conflict-focused rather than simple, habitual symptoms. Therefore, the treatment goals included conflict resolution, especially as those conflicts were played out in her interpersonal behavior.

Abigail's coping style was somewhat repressive, although still maintaining an active internal life. In many ways, she had some qualities of internalization in that she was open to ideas. She was very intellectual, thought about things, read, and was open to considering other people's points of view. By relating to her repressive and internalized coping style, it seemed possible to plan a therapy experience with depth that included exploration of thoughts, feelings, motives, and drives.

Her reactance potential was high, as manifested by her very high Hostility score on the Neuroticism domain. However, she was also high on Agreeableness and very high on Conscientiousness. The high hostility on the NEO-PI immediately suggested to the therapist a cautious approach. Because of the characteristic hostility, the therapist assumed that it would not be a good idea to confront her. Rather, the therapist would take a slower course, speculating with the patient about the reasons behind the events taking place in her life and slowly introducing the idea that Abigail had a part in it (i.e., appeal to her openness to ideas). Thus, a confrontational brief therapy was not deemed as promising. The patient's level of conscientiousness, however, boded well for an ability to remain involved in a more long-term treatment.

Abigail was assigned to open-ended individual psychodynamic treatment. What emerged over the course of the psychotherapy, however, was that despite this woman's initial friendly, agreeable presentation she had a troubling high degree of hostility. She was oriented toward other people and was generally agreeable, but she had difficulties controlling her temper and anger. Invariably this anger led to a number of interpersonal conflicts. The NEO-PI had uncovered this information immediately, although the interview did not. The initial interviewer was struck more by her strengths (i.e., her conscientiousness and agreeableness). Her difficulties with anger, temper, and hostility were hidden by her ability to be agreeable and conscientious.

As treatment progressed, when the therapist pointed out to Abigail her qualities that lead to problem behaviors (such as that she pushes people away by her hostility), Abigail would react with impulsive anger. Over the course of time, however, Abigail was able to integrate these interventions. She would leave sessions and think for hours about the content of her therapy session (i.e., high Openness) and, in doing

so, she slowly shifted her self-concept and began to change her behavior.

Hostility was exhibited in the transference as Abigail would state how much she liked the therapist, that the therapist was wonderful, and that she was so lucky to have the therapist; but if the therapist was late by a minute or the therapist was momentarily unavailable (e.g., one time the therapist had to answer the phone during the session because someone who was in crisis was calling), Abigail became extremely angry. Abigail was conscientious and agreeable enough to keep the angry reaction to herself until the next session when she would criticize or verbally attack the therapist. After several months, she was able to see this pattern and reflect on it. Because she was high on Openness, Abigail was able to make real gains, including the cessation of promiscuity and the development of a committed relationship. She subsequently married and has recently begun to establish several meaningful friendships. She continues to be very open and interested in how her occasional outbursts of anger affect her life.

Microtreatment Decisions

In contrast to the macrotreatment decisions that are made at evaluation and set the course for the major parameters of treatment, there are a number of microtreatment decisions that are made by the therapist over and over again from the beginning and throughout the treatment. Beutler and Clarkin (1991) postulated that key patient characteristics help the clinician decide about moment-to-moment decisions regarding breadth of treatment goals, depth of therapy experience, and degree of directiveness in the treatment assumed by the patient (see Table 1). We suggest that decisions around these parameters of treatment should be based on patient characteristics of (a) problem complexity, (b) characteristic coping styles, and (c) reactance level.

Problem Complexity and Breadth of Treatment Goals It is therapeutically useful to distinguish between simple or habitual symptoms and complex symptom patterns. Habitual or simple symptoms are isolated, environmentally specific, currently supported by reinforcing environments, and bear a

TABLE 1

Patient Dimensions as Related to Choice of Therapy Procedures

Patient dimension	Therapy procedure
Problem complexity	Breadth of treatment goals
Coping style	Depth of therapy experience
Reactance level	Degree of therapist's directiveness

clearly discernible relationship to their original adaptive form and etiology (Beutler & Clarkin, 1990). In contrast, underlying conflicts can be inferred when the symptoms have departed from their original and adaptive form and are subsequently elicited in environments that bear little relationship to the originally evoking situations.

Matched with the patient's problem complexity is the breadth of treatment goals. We distinguish between conflict-focused goals and simple, symptom-focused goals. Somatic treatments by definition are symptom-focused; likewise, behavioral and cognitive psychotherapies are directed most specifically at altering simple symptom presentations. In contrast, interpersonal, experiential, and psychodynamic therapies are more broadly focused on symptomatic change as related to change in internal characteristics of the patient. Manuals for the cognitive treatment of anxiety (Beck & Emery, 1985) and depression (Beck et al., 1979; Klerman, Weissman, Rounsaville, & Chevron, 1984) are useful for guiding an individual treatment that is focused on the cognitive and interpersonal underpinnings of both of these troubling affects. Manuals for conflict-focused psychotherapies are illustrative by defining conflict-oriented therapeutic focus. Experiential (Daldrup, Beutler, Engle, & Greenberg, 1988), interpersonal (Klerman et al., 1984), psychodynamic (Strupp & Binder, 1984), and family (Minuchin & Fishman, 1981) therapies all formulate treatment foci and mediating goals that are beyond the simple symptom focus itself.

The NEO-PI measures neither the acuteness of symptoms nor conflicts directly. Rather, "trait" symptoms such as depression and anxiety are measured on the Neuroticism scale. The NEO-PI is useful in detecting the presence of single or multiple symptom

patterns (e.g., one facet elevated in Neuroticism or many). The clinical interview is useful in ascertaining whether the symptom is simple or complex and of conflict organization. The dimensions of Neuroticism and Extraversion and their facets provide some indication of the breadth of symptoms that the individual typically experiences. Conflicts might be indicated or have fertile ground in those individuals with high Self-Consciousness and high Vulnerability facet scores in combination with signs of distress (e.g., high scores on Hostility, Depression, and Anxiety).

The breadth of goals (e.g., change that is behavioral and conflict resolving) may not always coincide with the depth of therapy experience. For example, underlying conflicts do not have to be addressed directly in therapy to be resolved. Behavioral change may result in conflict change without directly addressing the conflicts in the treatment. This may be especially true in patients with real strengths (Global Assessment of Functioning Scale score = 90–70).

Thus, the depth of therapy experience does not have a one-to-one relationship with the breadth of therapy goals—at least from an outcome perspective. The depth of therapy experience is limited by (a) the coping styles of the patient (i.e., as defensiveness goes up, depth goes down) and (b) the capability of the patient to handle disturbing material (e.g., exploring conflicts with schizophrenia patients can be counterproductive).

Coping Style and Depth of Therapy Experience

The coping style of the patient, in addition to the focus of difficulty, is central to treatment planning. There is no definitive method of categorizing patient coping styles. We have summarized existing empirical information and reduced the coping styles to four: internalizing, repressive, cyclic, and externalizing (Beutler & Clarkin, 1990).

Internalizing An internalized coping style involves preferential use of defenses such as undoing, self-punishment, intellectualization, isolation of affect, and emotional overcontrol and/or constriction. Individuals with this coping style often present with blunted or constricted affect (low Positive Emotions) and with constrained interpersonal relationships (low Extraversion).

A patient who is using internalization as a coping style, however, probably has a very active inner life.

This would appear on NEO-PI Openness, with Openness to Ideas and Fantasy and possibly Openness to Aesthetics. The individual may be low on Openness to Feelings. This is someone who engages in excessive ideation to control conflict or painful feelings. An individual who uses internalization will present with symptoms—they will be aware of intrapsychic conflict that causes anxiety and depression that they might intellectualize in therapy. Thus, some elevation on the Neuroticism score is to be expected. But the scores on Openness, especially relatively high scores on Openness to Ideas combined with low scores on Openness to Feelings, and low Extraversion might identify the internalizer.

Externalizing In contrast to internalizers, externalizers present with defensive acting-out and projection. They limit and curtail anxiety by assigning responsibility for their behavior to external sources and/or by discharging anxiety through action rather than thought. Interpersonally, these individuals move against others and act against the environment. They keep intense feelings at a distance. Symptoms are ego syntonic.

Those who use externalization would be high on Extraversion, low on Neuroticism, and low on Conscientiousness. These individuals do not internalize or experience much psychological discomfort. Hostility may be their one spike. These individuals will not have much anxiety or depression. Impulsivity may be slightly elevated, which indicates that they act rather than reflect. Again, as they externalize blame, they may indicate some elevations on Hostility. It is unlikely that they would be high scorers on Openness because they do not reflect much or consider widely diverse opinions. They may feel free to criticize others (high antagonism), but as low scorers on Neuroticism, they deny any pain of their own.

Repressive Reliance on repression and denial, such as denial of negative feelings, reaction formation, repression of the content that arouses uncomfortable experiences, negation of the meaning of negative social stimuli, and insensitivity to one's impact on others, are characteristic of a repressive coping style.

On the NEO-PI, such a person could report some degree of intrapsychic pain on Neuroticism, but they would be particularly low on Openness to Ideas and Fantasy. This is a person who does not want to think

about things very much. In fact, he or she may repress feelings as well as thoughts. However, this person may also be very low on Neuroticism because he or she does not want to admit that anything is wrong. In summary, if the individual is low on Neuroticism and very low on Openness (especially Ideas, Fantasy, and Feelings), then the individual may not be interested in opening up or reflecting on any psychological issues. His or her score on Agreeableness could also be moderate to high. This is the kind of individual who goes along with others' suggestions and directions, thereby avoiding conflicts because they repress and deny uncomfortable feelings like anger. Such an individual joins in, does what is expected, and does not address conflict. This makes treatment quite difficult because there is a willingness to agree and join with the therapist in confluence with a lack of openness to thinking about one's life or one's experience.

Cyclic Change and instability characterize individuals with cyclic coping styles. They tend to demonstrate ambivalence about the therapeutic process by acting-out and somatizing. Becoming blameful and vengeful, or alternately becoming withdrawn, guilt-ridden, and self-blaming, is typical of cyclic defenses.

Depth of Experience Addressed in the Treatment

The foci or targets for treatment intervention can be conceptualized as involving four areas of functioning on a dimension of levels of experience (Beutler & Clarkin, 1990): (a) behaviors of excess and insufficiency, (b) dysfunctional cognitive patterns, (c) unidentified feelings and sensory experiences, and (d) unconscious conflicts. There is a progression in this conceptualization from behaviors to cognitions to feelings and motivations, both recognized and unrecognized. Although most treatments probably touch on all these areas, either inadvertently or by design, emphasis on one or more areas of experience can vary considerably depending on the patient and his or her concerns and on the therapist's orientation and focus of treatment intervention.

It is important to match the dominant coping style of the patient with the depth of experience addressed by the treatment procedures. Most specifically, patients who are prone to externalize their distress are probably best matched with behaviorally oriented therapies that are targeted to external behavior rather than being focused on unconscious processes. The externalizing patient will resist nondirective, exploratory psychotherapy. If the externalizing individual comes for therapy, then it may be because of some circumscribed complaint or because a significant other (spouse or boss) insists on behavioral change. Thus, in treatment, the therapist would want to work with strict contingencies for changes in behavior. In extreme cases in which the patient is very low on Neuroticism (lacking much internal motivation for change) but is high on Extraversion and Agreeableness, the therapist might work at a hierarchy of concrete rewards that have intrinsic meaning to the patient.

The externalizing patient's social acting-out and avoidance of responsibility would be reflected in a low score on Conscientiousness. The lower the patient's score on Conscientiousness, the more difficult the therapist's task. This is especially true if the patient is relatively high on Extraversion and average on Agreeableness; the patient will present as a "hail fellow, well met" who may tend to give superficial and affable agreement in sessions, without having the slightest intention of following through in the treatment contract. Likewise, patients who internalize should be matched with therapies that address the level of their unrecognized/unconscious motives and fears.

Reactance Level and Degree of Therapist's Directiveness Reactance is defined as the individual's likelihood of resisting threatened loss of interpersonal control (Beutler & Clarkin, 1990). The high-reactance person is someone who seeks direction from within rather than looking to resources from the outside for solutions or answers. High reactivity would be reflected on the NEO-PI by moderate to high levels of Openness to Ideas and Fantasy. It might also be reflected in average to high Conscientiousness because the high-reactance individual feels in control and takes responsibility for outcomes. The high-reactance person would probably be seen as moderate to low on Agreeableness. This individual would not want other people to make decisions for them. On the other hand, evidence of inner resources would be reflected in Openness to Ideas. We might

think of the high-reactance person as fairly introverted, scoring low on Extraversion. By contrast, the low-reactance person accepts and possibly gravitates to direction from other people, as reflected in higher scores on Agreeableness and Extraversion, and is viewed as a real joiner who likes to be part of groups. He or she would prefer being part of groups, as members of cooperative efforts. Consensus with others is valued. However, the individual who is low in reactance might not have a particular openness to ideas or be high in openness to a fantasy life and one's internal world. On the other hand, there might be openness to action such as one would undertake in a cognitive–behavior treatment (Linehan, 1989).

In general, the reactance level of the patient should be useful in titrating the relative directiveness of the therapy procedure. It is hypothesized that the high-reactance patient would prefer and do better with a nondirective kind of psychotherapy, whereas the low-reactance patient is more available for either. Procedures that tend to reduce immediate distress include ventilation, reassurance, reflection, advice and teaching, hypnosis, breath control, and focus on sensations. In contrast, those procedures that increase arousal levels include confrontation and interpretation, analysis of transference and defense, and clarifications.

Individuals who are high on Extraversion, Agreeableness, and Openness to Ideas probably are ideal candidates for both individual and group cognitive–behavioral treatment. High reactance and low reactance would have not only to do with the modality of the treatment but whether or not it would be supportive or exploratory. The NEO-PI can be used to evaluate high reactance versus low reactance to make decisions about group versus individual psychotherapy as well. The high-reactance person would be screened away from those treatments in which there is direct advice-giving. The NEO-PI can also help select group members. It is very helpful in matching the members of a group together in some way, so that there would be a balance of extraversion–introversion, agreeableness, and reactance levels.

The more introverted (low Extraversion) and the less agreeable (low Agreeableness) the individual, the more the therapist would want to be extremely careful about forming a treatment alliance. The patient who is quite introverted will be careful about him- or herself and may shy away if confronted with too much warmth or friendliness from the therapist.

Clinical Vignette: A High-Reactance Patient A 32-year-old single, male tax attorney appeared for treatment complaining of anxiety. Constant irritability and hostility were manifested in interpersonal relationships. In the initial evaluation, he reported just recently realizing he had many psychological difficulties, as exemplified by his anger and explosive temper on the job, especially at women. He was dating a young woman and felt anxious about how the relationship was proceeding. The woman, he feared, might be getting serious about him. The clinical diagnosis was depression in the context of NOS (with features of paranoid and self-defeating personality disorder traits).

He was given the NEO-PI as part of the evaluation. He obtained clinically significant (T score > 65) elevations on Neuroticism (including the Hostility and Vulnerability facets) and a very low score on Agreeableness. Extraversion was in the average range, and Conscientiousness was in the high-average range. At the macro level of treatment planning, it was decided to recommend individual therapy for the patient with treatment duration undetermined at the initiation of treatment.

The patient's current difficulties stemmed from a long history of troubled relationships with a contradictory mother and a brutal stepfather. This man carried a history of conflict with a marked tendency to see others as hostile, stupid, and difficult to deal with. Theoretically, this patient needed a treatment that had a breadth of treatment goals, including conflict resolution.

This man's rigid defenses—which included projection, rationalization, splitting, and devaluation—were aligned in such a way as to make treatment slow and to limit the depth of experience available to the treatment. Although conflict that stemmed from the past seemed to control his present behavior, the patient was little inclined to even discuss the past. At times he could relate his present fear of women to hatred of his mother, but more generally, he wanted to focus on his present behavior. He asked the therapist for key phrases he could use to control his

impulsive, angry responses to clients. He talked of himself as damaged with little hope of change through therapy but sought a change of his environment. The depth of the therapy experience and breadth of treatment goals were clearly limited by the patient's coping style.

This patient was highly reactant, as evidenced by his high scores on the Hostility and Vulnerability facets of Neuroticism and by his high Conscientiousness and low Agreeableness scores as measured by the NEO-PI. Although he recognized the need for help, the patient feared any loss of control and did not want to place himself in the hands of another. Aware of his dilemma, the therapist let the patient guide the discussion for the most part. Only tentatively did the therapist suggest connections (e.g., his intense reaction to a minor incident in the present as related to his past). Only when the patient directly asked for advice and suggestion did the therapist provide it.

Feedback on his NEO-PI profile was introduced early in the treatment (he was in a managed care plan and the clinician had to talk to the case manager every eight sessions) to focus the intervention, educate the patient about his difficulties, and anticipate possible treatment alliance snags. In addition, the patient was convinced that he was "crazy," but the test results with its norms was reassuring to the patient. The particular combination of high Vulnerability and Hostility was reviewed carefully with the patient, and a focus of treatment was how feelings of vulnerability (related to a past that included harsh treatment by his stepfather and neglect from his mother) in current interpersonal relationships led repetitively to hostile attacks on the patient's part.

The treatment provided to the patient was similar to interpersonal psychotherapy for depression. It involved focusing on his symptoms of anger and depression and their relationship to interpersonal conflict at work and in his intimate relationships. There were several episodes of brief treatment—the patient saw the need for therapy only under acute distress.

ASSESSMENT

A practical question concerns the choice of procedures to use in the initial assessment of patients to foster differential treatment. The clinical interview is the most direct method in assessing the chief complaint, diagnosis, information concerning explicit behavioral dysfunctions, and environmental stressors and supports.

The self-report NEO-PI, inexpensive in clinician time, is useful primarily in providing data on patient personality variables that are relevant to treatment selection and secondarily in providing related diagnostic and problem area information. The NEO-PI alone, however, cannot totally inform the clinician on the foci for intervention. Acute distress—both acute symptomatic distress (Axis I disorders) and environmental stressors (marital disputes, loss of job, etc.)—is not assessed, of course, in the inventory. Rather, the NEO-PI provides the background to the figure created by current distress. This framework of the individual's more enduring orientation and proclivities will inform the focus of intervention but not totally predict or pinpoint it.

We propose that the NEO-PI, combined with the standard clinical evaluation interview, can be of great assistance in making decisions in this therapeutic selection process. The NEO-PI provides vital information on patient dimensions that are central for treatment planning. We also suggest that a small battery of screening tests, as used in one of our clinical cases (case of Christine), might be of assistance in furthering the treatment assignment task. A screening battery that gathers data on current functioning (SAS-SR), symptom distress (SCL-90 and BDI), and personality traits (NEO-PI) provides a three-pronged approach for treatment planning. High functioning, moderate to low symptom distress, and interpersonal difficulties bodes well for brief individual therapy. Poor functioning, high symptom distress, and difficulties in relating would indicate a more symptom-focused, supportive, longer term intervention.

It remains to be seen what will be the most frequent and characteristic profiles of individuals who apply for intervention. The manner in which the profiles relate to *DSM-III-R* diagnoses will provide the clinician with two coordinates in an attempt to locate the individual in treatment-planning space. The NEO-PI can provide data on the typical personality traits, and the *DSM* can provide behavioral and symptomatic information in terms of the diagnostic categories.

CLINICAL ILLUSTRATION

To amplify on several major themes of this chapter, we provide a clinical example with background data on the NEO-PI that relates to the patient's primary diagnosis of BDL. As with other Axis II disorders, BDL describes a group of patients who are homogeneous for the criteria of that disorder but who are quite disparate in other ways. We think that the other sources of heterogeneity are evaluated most effectively for treatment planning using the NEO-PI.

NEO-PI Profile for BDL

We have collected NEO-PI data on carefully diagnosed female BDL patients with other comorbid Axis II conditions. These are individuals with impulsive acting-out, which usually involves food, sex, drugs, and more direct suicidal behavior. The mean NEO-PI profiles across female BDL patients (*n* = 64) are presented in Figure 2. In the spirit of this chapter, we are less interested in whether BDL patients have profiles that are distinct from those of other Axis II groups but more interested in how the profiles, in conjunction with the Axis II diagnosis, can be helpful for treatment planning.

As expected (see Widiger et al., chapter 3 in this book), the BDL patients as a group are extremely high on Neuroticism. All facets of Neuroticism—Anxiety, Depression, Vulnerability, Self-Consciousness, and especially Impulsiveness—are high in the BDL group. The BDL patients are also characterized by extremely low Conscientiousness (aimless lack of goal direction, a lax and negligent orientation) and low Agreeableness (cynical, suspicious, uncooperative, vengeful, irritable, manipulative). Major treatment foci would be the elevated levels of neuroticism and the uncooperative interpersonal behavior. Within these general parameters, however, the individual patient's treatment would be tailored according to specific dimensions and severity.

NEO-PI of an Individual BDL Patient

Consider, for example, treatment planning for Ruth, a 26-year-old, single White female who met criteria for Axis II BDL. Ruth had numerous hospitalizations for suicidal behavior, alcohol abuse, eating dyscontrol, and mood lability; and several times she had

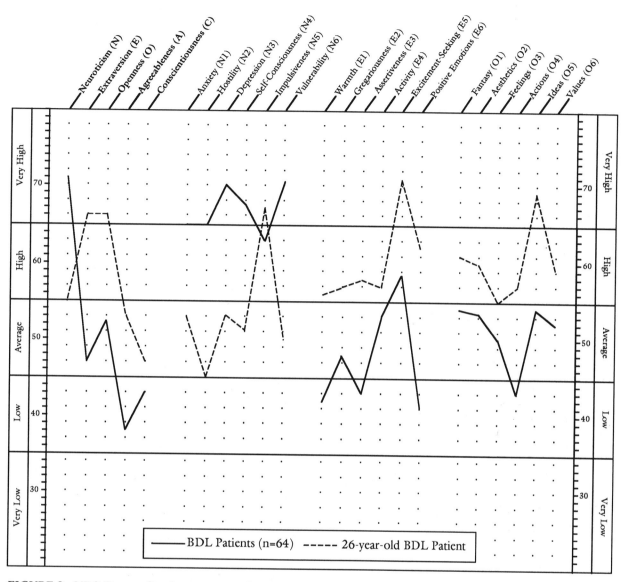

FIGURE 2. NEO Personality Inventory profiles of a group of female borderline personality disorder (BDL) patients (solid line; *n* = 64) and a 26-year-old female BDL patient (broken line). Profile form adapted from the *The NEO Personality Inventory Manual* by P. T. Costa, Jr. and R. R. McCrae, 1985, Odessa, FL: Psychological Assessment Resources. Copyright 1985 by Psychological Assessment Resources.

received the Axis I diagnosis of major depression. She was a social worker by training and had worked for periods between hospitalizations. However, in many respects she was not a typical BDL patient, and this became evident in her NEO-PI profile.

During a course of outpatient individual treatment, Ruth completed the NEO-PI (broken line on Figure 2). She was much lower on Neuroticism than other BDL patients. In terms of facet scores of the Neuroticism domain, she was impulsive but less anxious, hostile, depressed, and vulnerable. She was not

an antagonistic BDL patient. She did at times suffer from mood disorders, but she was not characteristically anxious or depressed. Ruth's BDL pathology was confined largely to her impulse dyscontrol. She also showed relative strengths on the Extraversion, Openness, Agreeableness, and Conscientiousness domains. Using normative data from this test, these scaled scores indicated that she would approach psychotherapy with enthusiasm and approach the therapist with openness and cooperation (Miller, 1991; Waldinger, 1987; Waldinger & Gunderson, 1987).

She would be conscientious in carrying out the tasks of the treatment in a serious way. It is clinical wisdom that BDL patients with antisocial characteristics (low Conscientiousness) have poor treatment prognosis (Kernberg, 1984; Kernberg, Selzer, Koenigsberg, Carr, & Applebaum, 1989; Robins, 1986). Ruth's relatively high levels of Conscientiousness and Agreeableness (average but high compared with the other BDL patients) bode well for therapeutic involvement that was responsible and not corrupted by manipulation and deceit.

Ruth's NEO-PI profile suggested a conflict-focused treatment with emphasis on multiple symptoms that carried across situations and people. Thus, the treatment goals would of necessity include not only behaviors and cognitions but also conflicts that carry across the environmental specifics.

Ruth tended toward externalization and acting-out. On the NEO-PI, this was manifested on the Extraversion domain scale and the Excitement-Seeking facet scale. However, this extraverted orientation was moderated by her openness.

The reactance level of Ruth seemed relatively low, which was manifested on her NEO-PI profile by high Agreeableness and high Warmth. It appeared that she might enter into a productive therapeutic relationship in which she could accept guidance from another. At first she mistrusted the therapist but quickly overcame her doubts and uncertainty.

In 1½ years of individual psychodynamic psychotherapy, Ruth responded remarkably well, and treatment was ended by mutual agreement. Of some 31 BDL patients that we have followed in outpatient psychodynamic treatment, this patient has shown one of the most successful responses (Clarkin et al., 1992). All behavioral impulsivity and self-destructive behavior that the patient had shown previously (eating binges, alcohol abuse, sexual promiscuity, and suicidal behavior) had ceased for over a year. She also became engaged in full-time productive work. Most important, she had a new male friend who, contrary to former mates, was not abusive and destructive toward her. Her enthusiasm in treatment and her ability to work in and out of sessions all seem correlated with her NEO-PI profile. Her responsivity to treatment and her disposition to become successfully involved in a satisfying relationship and productive employment were not suggested by her BDL diagnosis but were suggested by her level of conscientiousness and agreeableness on her NEO-PI profile.

References

American Psychiatric Association. (1980). *Diagnostic and statistical manual of mental disorders* (3rd ed.). Washington, DC: Author.

American Psychiatric Association. (1987). *Diagnostic and statistical manual of mental disorders* (3rd ed., rev.). Washington, DC: Author.

American Psychiatric Association. (1989). *Treatments of psychiatric disorders: A task force report of the American Psychiatric Association.* Washington, DC: Author.

Beck, A. T., & Emery, G. (1985). *Anxiety disorders and phobias: A cognitive perspective.* New York: Basic Books.

Beck, A. T., Rush, A. J., Shaw, B. F., & Emery, G. (1979). *Cognitive therapy of depression.* New York: Guilford Press.

Beutler, L. E., & Clarkin, J. F. (1990). *Systematic treatment selection: Toward targeted therapeutic interventions.* New York: Brunner/Mazel.

Beutler, L. E., & Clarkin, J. F. (1991). Future research directions. In L. E. Beutler & M. Crago (Eds.), *Psychotherapy research: International review of programmatic studies* (pp. 329–334). Washington, DC: American Psychological Association.

Clarkin, J. F., & Hull, J. (1991). Brief therapies. In M. Hersen, A. E. Kazdin, & A. S. Bellack (Eds.), *The clinical psychology handbook* (3rd. ed., pp. 780–796). Elmsford, NY: Pergamon Press.

Clarkin, J. F., Koenigsberg, H., Yeomans, F., Selzer, M., Kernberg, P., & Kernberg, O. (1992). Psychodynamic psychotherapy of the borderline patient. In J. F. Clarkin, E. Marziali, & H. Munroe-Blum (Eds.), *Borderline personality disorder: Clinical and empirical perspectives* (pp. 268–287). New York: Guilford Press.

Clarkin, J. F., Widiger, T., Frances, A., Hurt, S. W., & Gilmore, M. (1983). Prototypic typology and the borderline personality disorder. *Journal of Abnormal Psychology, 92,* 263–275.

Costa, P. T., Jr., & McCrae, R. R. (1985). *The NEO Personality Inventory manual.* Odessa, FL: Psychological Assessment Resources.

Cowdry, R. W. (1987). Psychopharmacology of borderline personality disorder: A review. *Journal of Clinical Psychiatry, 48,* 15–22.

Daldrup, R. J., Beutler, L. E., Engle, D., & Greenberg, L. S. (1988). *Focused expressive psychotherapy: Freeing the overcontrolled patient.* New York: Guilford Press.

Falloon, I. R. H., Boyd, J. L., & McGill, C. W. (1984). *Family care of schizophrenia.* New York: Guilford Press.

Frances, A., & Clarkin, J. F. (1981). No treatment as the prescription of choice. *Archives of General Psychiatry, 38,* 542–545.

Frances, A., Clarkin, J. F., & Perry, S. (1984). *Differential therapeutics in psychiatry: The art and science of treatment selection.* New York: Brunner/Mazel.

Hollon, S. D., & Beck, A. T. (1986). Cognitive and cognitive–behavioral therapies. In S. L. Garfield & A. E. Bergin (Eds.), *Handbook of psychotherapy and behavior change* (3rd. ed., pp. 443–482). New York: Wiley.

Kernberg, O. F. (1984). *Severe personality disorders: Psychotherapeutic strategies.* New Haven, CT: Yale University Press.

Kernberg, O. F., Selzer, M. A., Koenigsberg, H. W., Carr, A. C., & Applebaum, A. H. (1989). *Psychodynamic psychotherapy of borderline patients.* New York: Basic Books.

Kiesler, D. J. (1986). The 1982 interpersonal circle: An analysis of DSM-III personality disorders. In T. Millon & G. L. Klerman (Eds.), *Contemporary directions in psychopathology: Toward the DSM-IV* (pp. 571–598). New York: Guilford Press.

Klerman, G. L., Weissman, M. M., Rounsaville, B., & Chevron, E. (1984). *Interpersonal psychotherapy of depression.* New York: Basic Books.

Koss, M. P., & Butcher, J. N. (1986). Research on brief psychotherapy. In S. L. Garfield & A. E. Bergin (Eds.), *Handbook of psychotherapy and behavior change* (3rd. ed., pp. 627–670). New York: Wiley.

Linehan, M. M. (1987). Dialectical behavior therapy: A cognitive approach to parasuicide. *Journal of Personality Disorders, 1,* 328–333.

Linehan, M. M. (1989). Cognitive and behavior therapy for borderline personality disorder. In R. E. Hales & A. J. Frances (Eds.), *American Psychiatric Association: Annual review* (Vol. 8, pp. 84–102). Washington, DC: American Psychiatric Press.

Livesley, W. J., & Jackson, D. N. (1986). The internal consistency and factorial structure of behaviors judged to be associated with DSM-III personality disorders. *American Journal of Psychiatry, 143,* 1473–1474.

Livesley, W. J., Jackson, D. N., & Schroeder, M. L. (1989). A study of the factorial structure of personality pathology. *Journal of Personality Disorders, 3,* 292–306.

Luborsky, L. (1984). *Principles of psychoanalytic psychotherapy: A manual for supportive–expressive treatment.* New York: Basic Books.

Miller, T. R. (1991). The psychotherapeutic utility of the five-factor model of personality: A clinician's experience. *Journal of Personality Assessment, 57,* 415–433.

Minuchin, S., & Fishman, H. C. (1981). *Family therapy techniques.* Cambridge, MA: Harvard University Press.

Morey, L. (1988). The categorical representation of personality disorder: A cluster analysis of DSM-III-R personality features. *Journal of Abnormal Psychology, 97,* 314–321.

Robins, L. (1986). Epidemiology of antisocial personality disorder. In R. Michels & J. Cavenar (Eds.), *Psychiatry* (Vol. 3., pp. 1–14). Philadelphia: Lippincott.

Shoham-Salomon, V. (1991). Special section: Client–therapy interaction research. *Journal of Consulting and Clinical Psychology, 59,* 203–244.

Soloff, P. H. (1987). Neuroleptic treatment in the borderline patient: Advantages and techniques. *Journal of Clinical Psychiatry, 48,* 26–35.

Strupp, H. H., & Binder, J. L. (1984). *Psychotherapy in a new key.* New York: Basic Books.

Waldinger, R. J. (1987). Intensive psychodynamic therapy with borderline patients: An overview. *American Journal of Psychiatry, 144,* 267–274.

Waldinger, R. J., & Gunderson, J. (1987). *Effective psychotherapy with borderline patients: Case studies.* Washington, DC: American Psychiatric Press.

Widiger, T. A., Frances, A. J., Harris, M., Jacobsberg, L. B., Fyer, M., & Manning, D. (1990). Comorbidity among axis II disorders. In J. Oldham (Ed.), *Axis II: New perspectives on validity* (pp. 163–194). Washington, DC: American Psychiatric Press.

CHAPTER 16

USING PERSONALITY MEASUREMENTS IN CLINICAL PRACTICE

K. Roy MacKenzie

This chapter describes the use of structured instruments for assessing psychotherapy candidates. Two clinical applications are discussed: feedback procedures that help to prepare patients for psychotherapy and intervention strategies chosen on the basis of test results. One goal of this chapter is to encourage ways by which clinicians can integrate diverse theoretical approaches in a planned manner to maximize therapeutic effect. Most of the described measures are also well suited to measuring change over time, so they can also be used for clinical outcome trials or service delivery evaluation studies.

The perspective of this chapter is from experience in a general hospital outpatient setting; however, the principles apply to most clinical services. The program offers the usual spectrum of services: crisis intervention of up to 6 sessions, time-limited therapy falling into the range of 12–25 sessions, and longer term approaches lasting up to a year or more. The detailed assessment approach described in this chapter is used only for those patients who need more than crisis intervention.

The assessment techniques are equally applicable to psychodynamic, interpersonal, and cognitive therapies. They are also suitable for patients entering either individual or group modalities. The study of outcome in randomized clinical trials indicates that the results of group therapy are equivalent to those of individual treatment that uses the same theoretical model (Budman et al., 1988; Pilkonis, Imber, Lewis, & Rubinsky, 1984; Piper, Debanne, Bienvenu, & Garant, 1984). The pressures of cost containment are likely to promote group over individual approaches in the future. As is described later, the use of more sophisticated assessment techniques has some unique advantages for patients entering group therapy.

There is a long history of the use of psychological testing in the assessment of patients for psychotherapy. However, in recent years this type of formal assessment seems to have fallen somewhat out of favor. Although no hard figures are available, it is probably safe to say that most patients who enter psychotherapy receive only a general clinical assessment without augmentation by formal structured assessment procedures. A number of factors may be at work in clinical situations to explain this.

Clinicians tend to make global assessment decisions and often speak of their intuitive sense of understanding the nature of the patient's pathology. They resist the restrictions of formal diagnostic procedures. Indeed, most clinicians probably use categories of the third, revised edition of the *Diagnostic and Statistical Manual of Mental Disorders* (*DSM-III-R*; American Psychiatric Association, 1987) in a nonprecise manner. There is widespread and understandable skepticism with the specific diagnostic criteria listed for each condition. Clinicians have to face situations on a daily basis in which patients do not neatly fit into a specific category, even though a clinical diagnosis is warranted on the basis of significant dysfunction. Often a patient will meet criteria for several categories simultaneously. This is particularly true in the anxiety and mood disorder areas. This diagnostic fragmentation often seems to the clinician to obscure rather than clarify the problems of the individual. A formal diagnostic decision may be useful in ruling out particular treatments but often is of limited use in prescribing the optimum approach. For example, most comparative treatment studies of the depressive and anxiety disorders indicate limited differential effect between psychopharmacological, psychodynamic, and cognitive approaches (Elkin et al., 1989).

These problems with the official nomenclature are multiplied when the focus shifts to Axis II of the *DSM-III-R*. Numerous studies have indicated high rates of overlap between Axis II categorical diagnoses. Although this is most evident among the conditions in a given cluster, overlap also occurs even between diagnoses from different clusters. For the clinician, this induces a degree of doubt as to the validity and usefulness of the concepts being assessed. The idea of neurotic problems is still widely used, even though the word is not officially sanctioned. This diagnostic language uses intrapsychic rather than interpersonal terminology and therefore is subject to even more complex diagnostic dilemmas. It is common to find not only divergence of opinions but directly contradictory conclusions about the same patient. There appears to be a general trend to integrate what used to be the terrain of psychodynamic conceptualization into a broader approach of personality description. The distinction between conflict-based psychodynamic diagnostic terms and description-based personality features has become increasingly blurred.

Psychological testing has tended to be concerned primarily with formal diagnostic issues that often add only marginally to a clinical diagnostic evaluation. Such measures may be of interest to the clinician but are of limited value in providing guidance for the actual therapeutic approach. The traditional tests have usually used a variety of scales, often with esoteric names that needed to be translated into meaningful concepts for the clinician. Few clinicians are cognizant of the theoretical background from which test scales are derived. They therefore feel unprepared to interpret the results to their patients. These factors have made clinicians reluctant to use formal testing results and have often bred outright antagonism to the very idea. This may take the form of concern that the individuality of the patient, the patient's sense of self, may be lost by applying predetermined concepts. This conveniently ignores the fact that all clinicians operate on theoretical assumptions whether or not they are easily described or are understood in the same manner by one's professional peers.

The results of psychological testing have been seen to be of value primarily to the professional. There has not been an emphasis on translating such information into a form that is readily understandable to the average patient. This reinforces the role of the clinician as the director of therapy, operating on the basis of privileged information. This chapter describes an approach to the use of psychological testing that actively incorporates the patient into the application of test results. It also shows how a small number of basic dimensions can be effectively used by the clinician in helping to determine therapeutic choices. This material is based on an underlying belief in the importance of active collaboration between clinician and patient in designing treatment conditions.

PERSONALITY TRAITS IN PERSPECTIVE

The concept of personality represented by the five-factor (referred to as the "Big Five") model (FFM) of personality offers one hopeful alternative to some of the problems just mentioned. In order to apply it, the clinician must first come to grips with the need for a major paradigm shift. The five-factor approach is based on dimensions, that is, taxonomic traits that are descriptive, not etiological, in nature. Most clinicians have been trained to think of dysfunctional patterns as stemming from unfortunate early learning experiences. The psychodynamic clinician conceptualizes these as centering around conflictual issues or failure to master developmental tasks. The cognitive clinician thinks in terms of learned patterns of thinking about self and others. It is somewhat of a culture shock to consider personality as something that one simply has and must live with, like being excessively tall.

For a given personality trait, there is as much likelihood of dysfunction with too much of a given trait as with too little. That is, traits tend to have a normal distribution in the population, and pathology lies at both extremes, like blood pressure. This contrasts with usual diagnostic methods that assume if one has a diagnosis, then one is ill, and if not, then one is healthy. Similarly, many of our therapeutic approaches tend to assume that better function lies only in one direction. For example, it might be thought that the ability to use fantasy and dream material is more "healthy" than a more prosaic attention to pragmatic issues. Thus, a low score on Openness to Fantasy would be taken to mean a failure to come to grips with understanding one's inner self. Such a position ignores the dysfunctional effects of disorganization and scatter that accompanies high Openness scores. An extraverted, engaging interpersonal style might be assumed to be "better" than a quiet and reserved pattern, which might be seen as defensive and reflective of low self-esteem. However, a patient with extraverted characteristics tends to have difficulty with intimate relationships and may so need stimulation that self-destructive patterns emerge.

There is a danger that the clinician may experience a strong pull to select patients who meet the therapist's concept of the ideal psychotherapy candidate. This commonly means patients with evident features of Extraversion, Openness, Agreeableness, and Conscientiousness. The treatments applied are usually based on the theory or technique of the therapist's favored treatment method. Unfortunately, this results in a patient receiving that which the clinician is prepared to offer, more so than what the patient might most need. The use of personality trait concepts may bring some helpful perspectives to the clinical setting (Miller, 1991).

First, the use of personality trait language encourages the clinician to be a neutral observer. The trait approach considers the individual to have a particular predisposition that goes back into earliest childhood and probably has genetic origins. It is not seen to be the result of learning experiences per se. What is of greater interest is how such characteristics have interacted with both the patient's rearing environment and current interpersonal world to produce more-or-less effective functional adaptation. The emphasis is on how the patient can learn to adapt more successfully. This can be helpful in allowing the clinician to differentiate between the long-standing style and the person underneath who must mediate between the style and the particular circumstances. This way of conceptualizing psychopathology is not

exclusive of other theoretical positions. The value of the addition of a personality style viewpoint is to encourage therapeutic efforts to manage a style as well as to resolve a conflict.

Second, an understanding of how the patient "is" in terms of trait terminology helps the clinician to understand the individual's inner reality. Trait descriptions provide a model of how the patient is internally influenced to interact with others. This approach falls into the original meaning of *phenomenological*, that is, how the patient experiences his or her personal psychological world. Such an understanding is likely to enhance empathy as the patient recognizes that the view of self is understood by the clinician. This idea of understanding the patient's perspective is closely aligned with personal construct theory (Kelly, 1955). Constructs are seen as the criteria by which individuals assess their interpersonal worlds. This orientation provides a bridge linking personality dimensions with the use of cognitive strategies as well as interpersonal theory.

Third, the application of trait theory provides the clinician with another vantage point from which to conceptualize how the present circumstances have produced distress or dysfunction. The interface between personal patterns or styles and specific types of people or circumstances can be seen in descriptive terms rather than with an evaluation of personal pathology.

Fourth, the recognition of trait qualities may contribute to the choice of therapeutic strategies. In particular, it may be of considerable value in determining the mix of the less structured approaches that fall under the psychodynamic/interpersonal label and the cognitive or behavioral self-control techniques that use a more structured approach. This is not to say that various techniques cannot be used in a combined manner, but the trait perspective may be illuminating on how to balance the mix.

Fifth, trait theory offers a useful way of predicting various aspects of the therapeutic alliance. This may alert the therapist to issues likely to arise in treatment so that preventive measures can be considered at an early point. To be forewarned is to be forearmed.

Sixth, the trait perspective also may temper the clinician's judgment as to what is likely to change during the course of therapy. Traits are not going to disappear or turn into their opposites, however much the clinician and the patient may want this to happen. In practice, patients usually find it helpful to know that they are not going to have to stop being themselves. The task, rather, is how to come to grips with being more adaptive with what they have to work with.

A BASIC CHANGE–MEASURES PACKAGE

This section describes a systematic application of psychological assessment that is compatible with most service settings. In introducing this, the principles outlined by Pfeiffer, Heslin, and Jones (1976) have been kept in mind. These investigators identified 10 benefits of structured assessment:

1. Encourages client involvement in the treatment process.
2. Fosters open reaction to personal feedback.
3. Clarifies client goals and facilitates contracting for new behavior.
4. Increases objectivity of measuring client change.
5. Provides for comparisons of individual clients with normative groups.
6. Facilitates longitudinal assessment of therapeutic change (i.e., before, after, follow-up).
7. Sensitizes clients and therapists to the multifaceted nature of therapeutic change.
8. Gives clients the sense that their therapist is committed to effective treatment.
9. Improves communication between clients and therapists.
10. Allows the therapist to focus and control therapy more effectively.

The procedure requires a minimum of two assessment interviews. This is not an unreasonable time expectation for most service settings, especially when the outcome is a decision to enter the patient into a treatment program that entails a significant expenditure of time and energy, to say nothing of expense. The patient is first assessed in a standard diagnostic interview that is approximately 1 hour long. From this, a *DSM-III-R* diagnosis is established and a general formulation is developed, thereby pulling together past development, current stress, and relevant psychological issues. On the basis of this interview, the patient is accepted into the treatment program.

The second meeting is also approximately 1 hour long and consists of a detailed feedback session based on a series of questionnaires completed between the two interviews. This basic change–measures package was developed in accord with the principles of multiple measures, multiple areas, and multiple perspectives (MacKenzie & Livesley, 1986). It provides an evaluation of symptoms and interpersonal behaviors in general and in relation to specific significant others, the FFM, and a general assessment of psychosocial functioning. Perspectives are obtained from the patient, the clinician, and a significant other (see Table 1). The package presently consists of the following instruments:

1. Symptom Checklist (SCL-90-R)
2. Inventory of Interpersonal Problems (IIP-B5)
3. Dimensional Assessment of Personality Pathology (DAPP)
4. NEO Personality Inventory (NEO-PI)
5. Structural Analysis of Social Behavior (SASB)
6. Global Assessment of Functioning Scale (GAFS)
7. Target Goals

This list has some redundancy in regard to the FFM, particularly between the IIP-B5 and the NEO-PI. The DAPP adds several scales not found in either of these instruments.

SCL-90-R

This 90-item self-report symptom inventory is the latest version of the original psychological symptom portion of the Cornell Medical Index (Derogatis, 1977). There is a high degree of correlation between the SCL-90-R subscale scores and comparable Minnesota Multiphasic Personality Inventory dimensions. Results are expressed on nine symptom dimensions: somatization, obsessive–compulsive, interpersonal sensitivity, depression, anxiety, hostility, phobic anxiety, paranoid ideation, and psychoticism. A Global Severity Index gives an overall measure of symptom status. This is the most widely used standard measure of general psychopathology.

TABLE 1

A Model for Developing a Change Measures Battery With Examples

Type of information	Source of information			
	Patient	**Clinician**	**Significant other**	**Clinical record**
Demographic/statistics				Data sheet
				Service utilization
Symptoms	SCL-90-R			
Interpersonal	IIP, SASB		SASB	
Personality	DAPP, NEO-PI		DAPP	
Target goals	Target goals	Target goals		
Global functioning		GAFS		

Note. SCL-90-R = Symptom Checklist; IIP = Inventory of Interpersonal Problems; SASB = Structural Analysis of Social Behavior; DAPP = Dimensional Assessment of Personality Pathology; NEO-PI = NEO Personality Inventory; GAFS = Global Assessment of Functioning Scale.

IIP-B5

This is an adaptation of the original instrument developed by Horowitz, Rosenberg, Baer, Ureno, and Villasenor (1988). The wording of the questions is particularly well suited to a clinical population. The question stems are either "It is hard for me to. . .(be assertive)" or "I am too. . .(controlling)." It contains 148 items of which 64 are taken from the original IIP. These items measure eight problem clusters that form a circumplex pattern based on the two major axes of Dominance and Nurturance (Alden, Wiggins, & Pincus, 1990). A vector is calculated that offers the best representation of the two-dimensional space. In addition, conflict scores are calculated for each of the four pairs of opposite segments. A positive conflict score indicates that the patient has an elevated score on conceptually opposite qualities such as Dominance and Submission. The instrument has been expanded by adding items that tap into the domains of Neuroticism, Openness, and Conscientiousness (Pincus, 1991). The Dominance score is taken to represent Extraversion, and the Nurturance score is taken to represent Agreeableness. Thus, the IIP-B5 results in scores representing the Big Five personality traits as well as a circumplex model.

DAPP

The DAPP is a new instrument consisting of 290 items developed from a systematic study of the

dimensions in the personality literature (Livesley, Jackson, & Schroeder, 1989; Schroeder, Wormworth, & Livesley, 1992). Each dimension has been operationalized into specific behavior expressions. Eighteen dimensions are rated by the DAPP, most of which can also be clustered into five principle areas that generally correspond to the FFM. Further information regarding this instrument is found in chapter 7 of this book.

NEO-PI

This 181-item instrument is the original measure of the FFM (Costa & McCrae, 1985), plus an addendum of an additional 74 items for further facet scales of Agreeableness and Conscientiousness (Costa, McCrae, & Dye, 1991). Each dimension has several facets based on item subsets.

SASB

This instrument is based on a unique circumplex model of interpersonal functioning (Benjamin, 1987) and comprises two axes. The first axis runs from positive Affiliation (loving, approaching) to negative Affiliation (attacking, rejecting), whereas the other goes from high Independence (autonomy) to high Interdependence (enmeshment). This conceptual space may be applied to relationships (how one acts on the other, and how one reacts to the other) or to a view of one's self (introject). The measure is applied to Best/Worst/Ideal views of Self and to eight intimate relationships drawn from the patient's life over time. These include mother, father, and the parental relationship itself as seen during preadolescent years. The measure that was used in this study was the SASB INTREX questionnaire, a 16-item form that is used to rate each relationship in each direction: the Other to Me, Me to the Other. The results of the 288-item SASB provide a view of specific relationship patterns rather than a global description of personality dimensions.

GAFS

This is Axis V of the *DSM-III-R* (American Psychiatric Association, 1987), which was developed from the original Health–Sickness Rating Scale as a general measure of psychosocial functioning (Luborsky, 1975).

Target Goals

Three target goals are developed by the initial assessment clinician in collaboration with the patient (Battle et al., 1966). They are based on the combined information from the clinical assessment interview and the results of the questionnaires. When possible, target goals are connected with specific scores from the assessment battery. Each target goal is rated for severity by the patient before treatment begins. At later administrations, the goals are rated for severity, relevance to what has been worked on in therapy, and improvement. The same goals are also rated by the clinician. Goals may be altered as treatment progresses and thus form a record of deepening self-understanding.

Demographics/Statistics

Basic patient demographic information is collected on the registration sheet including age, sex, marital status, education, and employment status. When possible, data concerning use of both health and mental health services before and after treatment provide a powerful measure of effectiveness.

INTRODUCING STRUCTURED ASSESSMENTS IN A CLINICAL SETTING

The manner in which questionnaires are introduced to the patient is crucial for ensuring compliance and reliable results. A systematic attempt is made to legitimize the use of the measurement instruments. The relevance of each measure to the therapeutic experience itself is emphasized. This is done by briefly introducing each measure and explaining the target area it is focusing on: for example, psychological symptoms such as anxiety (SCL-90-R), how one sees one's self (SASB), interpersonal problems such as trouble being intimate (IIP-B5), personality qualities such as extraversion/introversion that may lead to problems (DAPP, NEO-PI), and the nature of specific relationships that have been important to the patient (SASB). This information is given in as direct and open a manner as possible, with the patient's questions and/or concerns being addressed throughout the process. This serves a double purpose: to motivate the patient to answer the questionnaire carefully and thoughtfully and to decrease response anxiety.

The words *research* or *test* are not used. The structured assessments are properly referred to as part of the clinical assessment procedure and as being of value in program evaluation. Patients are encouraged to view the completion of the questionnaire as the beginning of their therapy and as an opportunity to think seriously about themselves and their relationships. With this simple but systematic approach, patient compliance has been extremely high.

The second clinical interview to review the results takes place before the patient begins therapy. This interview is also carefully constructed (Dies, 1983). The patient is reassured that there is no magic to the scoring process of the questions that they have answered. The results are described as being simply "their own words" coming back to them in a different form. Emphasis is placed on their role in defining the issues of importance. The patient receives a handout with his or her personal scores rated from very low to average to very high. He or she also receives a sheet of "scale descriptions" that briefly define what qualities the various dimensions are trying to capture. All results are presented in a tentative manner, inviting discussion, elaboration, and examples. Most patients are able to quickly move into a more in-depth discussion of the issues raised by the results.

For example, one woman responded to her high Agreeableness score by acknowledging that she was forever getting into relationships in which she felt used. She could never drop her smiling acquiescent behavior until the situation got so bad that she had to flee it impulsively. These problematic issues were never directly discussed with her partner. She then went on to identify a recent situation in which she found herself going out of her way specifically to find a man whom she identified as a low-Agreeableness person. The clinician commented aloud that it sounded as if she were trying to complement an area of problem for herself by finding someone who had just the opposite set of qualities. She elaborated with further thoughts about how comfortable and "right" it always seems at the start of such relationships until the control imbalance, a component of the Agreeableness dimension, begins to emerge.

Patients are deeply interested in how they describe important relationships on the SASB questions. Generally, there is prompt acknowledgment and elaboration on the patterns revealed. It is of particular interest to find identical patterns in the descriptions of parental relationships as seen in childhood and current adult relationships. The SASB ratings are unique in that they probe actual relationships, not generalized descriptions of self. This specificity regarding person complements the specificity regarding interpersonal behavioral style that comes from the other personality instruments.

For example, a man with difficulties in a series of relationships with women was shocked to the point of being upset at his results. He described his relationships with these partners as one of outward pleasant passivity accompanied by inner rage at what he saw as their controlling behavior. Eventually, the anger would build up to the point where he would either precipitate a fight (sometimes with a physical attack) or abruptly terminate the relationship. He had always harbored strong negative reactions to his controlling and critical father in

childhood. What shocked him was that his own adult response patterns were modeled on those of his mother toward his father. He had always felt that she had not protected him adequately from his father's attacks and left when he needed her most. This realization stimulated a gradual reassessment of the nature of his parental images.

The clinician must be careful not to make absolute interpretive statements. All results are described in bland and somewhat technical language that encourages a cognitive exploration of the issues raised. The onus is placed on the patient to take the self-generated information and apply it to attitudes or patterns regarding self or others. The feedback material is couched in terms of raising ideas or perspectives that should not be accepted immediately but might be pursued further within the context of therapy.

The clinician might also use the scores to highlight for the patient some aspects of the treatment program that would match issues generated from the questionnaires. For example, patients with very high Neuroticism scores are encouraged to use the stress management and relaxation portions of the day program. Extraverts will be alerted to the value of sitting with their reactions and experiencing them rather than translating them immediately into impulsive action. Patients with very low Openness scores are reassured that they will find the cognitive therapy sessions helpful but that they will have to work hard at making sense of the interpersonal groups. High-Agreeableness patients are forewarned that they don't have to believe everything they hear and will need to concentrate on thinking through and discussing their personal opinions. For patients with low Conscientiousness scores, discussion centers on their struggle to allow themselves to follow through on treatment programs. Such people are usually quite aware of their tendency to drop out of therapy prematurely and recognize this as a pervasive pattern that interferes with how they can find more satisfaction in their lives. The likelihood of finding themselves experiencing a desire to terminate therapy before it is finished is therefore explicitly reviewed along with their ideas about how they might try to counteract this tendency. Most patients talk of revealing their concerns early in the sessions and making a commitment to put such ideas into words as soon as they arise later.

Most patients welcome this direct and candid discussion of core issues that are related to their dysfunctional patterns. The fact that it is generated directly from their own responses to the questionnaires makes the information even more acceptable. Most express relief that key issues are not going to be skirted. They acknowledge that they have known for a long time that they would have to tackle the sorts of concerns that they themselves have identified. Sometimes new, or at least unacknowledged, perspectives are opened up by this process. It seems that patients often have an awareness, perhaps only a hunch, about what needs to be changed but have never actually put it into words before. The assessment procedures help to make these implicit understandings more explicit. By the end of the feedback interview, areas of concern are transformed into target goals.

The feedback process appears to be an effective mechanism for promoting the rapid development of a therapeutic alliance between patient and therapist. To some extent, this undercuts the power imbalance that is inevitable in the clinical context. The process of rapid engagement is particularly important in the use of time-limited approaches for which a fast start leaves more time for working on the most salient material. For example, in a time-limited group psychotherapy program, patients are encouraged to introduce themselves to the group in the first session by recounting what they have just found out about themselves during the preceding feedback session. This process stimulates rapid universalization mechanisms in the group as patients hear each other describing recognizable issues. It also provides a psychological language for discussing interpersonal matters. There is no time lost in general unfocused introductions.

The early disclosure, even if handled relatively superficially, puts the issues on the table. They can then be legitimately reintroduced by the therapist, or by other patients if in a group. Thus, when a patient starts to stray from a focus on core issues or begins to enact the very patterns that had been discussed earlier, a prompt identification can be made. Such focusing or reflective interventions are accepted with less resistance because of their correspondence to what the patient has already said about themselves. Hearing such feedback from other group members draws the focus of psychological work directly into the here-and-now of group interaction and thereby promotes a powerful correctional emotional experience. This process applies not only to the recipient of feedback but also to the person giving it, which lends additional therapeutic power from group work compared with that available in the traditional dyadic therapy context (MacKenzie, 1990).

USING STRUCTURED ASSESSMENTS TO SELECT INTERVENTION STRATEGIES

The approach to administering psychotherapy varies greatly among practitioners. A great deal of this divergence is related to the unidimensional nature of many training programs. The most basic divide is between structured approaches based on cognitive or behavioral techniques and relatively unstructured exploratory techniques of psychodynamic or interpersonal methods. Within each of these traditions are many variations, but there is general agreement about the basics. Between them, however, there is a vast gulf of misunderstanding and antagonism. The discussion that follows concerning intervention strategies implies that every clinician should be competent to provide a diversity of theoretical approaches, or at least to be sympathetically knowledgeable about them.

Outcome studies clearly show that careful application of a treatment regimen results in a large common therapeutic effect. The more stringent the study in terms of suitable control conditions, randomization, and monitoring of the treatment process, the less differential in outcome. The field has not yet come to grips with methods to effectively select patients for specific types of treatment. However, inherent in the dimensional trait literature are some important clues as to how this might be accomplished. Some examples follow—all given in the acknowledged absence of substantial direct empirical evidence at this time.

Example 1

Patients with high Neuroticism scores seem likely to benefit from management strategies that will help them establish some control over their emotional reactivity. Such patients very often respond to stress with an escalating spiral of anxiety and disorganization that becomes self-sustaining. Trying to deal with conflictual issues or interpersonal misperceptions while in such a highly aroused state is difficult. Affect control methods and relaxation exercises may help to interrupt this sequence. These procedures may allow the level of anxiety to drop down into a range where the patient can use other therapeutic components more effectively.

A young man found himself paralyzed with doubts when faced with situations he interpreted as demanding a high level of performance. The more he tried to think of ways to calm himself and not appear tremulous, the more his anxiety escalated. He learned the effective use of deep breathing relaxation techniques that gave him an opportunity to reassess the true nature of the situation. Getting some sense of mastery over his reactivity allowed him to begin to address psychological issues connected with the roots of his low self-esteem.

Example 2

Patients with low Neuroticism scores respond positively if the clinician pays attention to their pragmatic problems and physical symptoms. They see little point in addressing psychological issues if their symptoms are not acknowledged. I have found that group methods are particularly useful in helping such patients make the transition from a symptom/problem-based orientation to a psychological/interpersonal perspective. A group can provide powerful interpersonal support while exerting pressure to reconceptualize the locus of difficulty.

A 40-year-old man was asked to describe his relationship with his parents as a child using the SASB questions, but he stated that he had no recall of any childhood memories before the age of 18. His descriptions of his reaction to a variety of significant people all showed no directionality. His Neuroticism and Openness scores were very low, with the exception of the Openness to Ideas facet scale, which was quite high. Conscientiousness was also very high. Review of these patterns led to a discussion of his almost total lack of contact with emotionality. Everything was handled in a purely cognitive mode, including the discussion of this material. He was surprised to see that he described himself in these terms. He had always been puzzled when others told him he needed to loosen up. He considered himself the successful professional, which he was. He began to acknowledge that he led an extremely lonely personal life but had never wondered why and thought that was something he might ponder. This intellectual approach allowed him to countenance the idea of looking at relationship issues. By the 4th week in an intensive psychotherapy day program, he was becoming able to detect emotional reactions in himself and to have fragmentary memories of childhood events including the ability to visualize his parents.

Example 3

Patients with high Extraversion scores may need help to refrain from translating arousal or anxiety into direct action. For them, the ability to delay responding for long enough to appreciate the issues they are experiencing is important. Many patients with components of the borderline syndrome find it quite helpful to understand that they can tolerate their inner states without having to do something about it. Intervention techniques taken from a self-psychology orientation are often helpful. The therapist carefully does not react to the intrusive demands that something be done. By calmly tolerating these expectations and not feeling the need to respond, the therapist is sending a transactional message that the patient's inner state can be lived with. This promotes a more consolidated sense of self that is independent from the interaction with others.

A 27-year-old woman presented with high Neuroticism, Extraversion, and Openness scores. Her SASB relationship patterns were replete with conflict scores of both a control double-bind nature and ambivalent attachment. She had a history of tumultuous relationships of a highly enmeshed nature. In therapy, she was alternatively angrily critical and tearfully demanding. Her intrusive behaviors were handled in an accepting but noncontrolling manner. They were reflected back to her as dilemmas that she must experience as being quite upsetting. The various facets of her reactions were gently explored for clarification. With time, she became able to tolerate her extremes by saying in effect: "There I go again. I'm angry for no good reason. With time I'll cool down."

Example 4

Patients falling into the introversion spectrum usually have control, perhaps too much control, over their reactions. Structured cognitive approaches may only reinforce this tendency. Interpersonal approaches that focus on acceptance of self and the establishment of relationships are likely to be of greater benefit.

A 35-year-old librarian presented with a major depression triggered by apprehension over concerns that her common-law partner was paying little attention to her and seemed attracted to another. She had tried many methods of trying to accommodate her partner's expressed needs without success. Now she felt hopeless and at an impasse. Her only positive coping method was to take long walks by herself where she could commune with nature. She had a small group of like-minded friends but did not feel she should burden them with her misery. She paid close attention in her feedback session to her self-descriptions, partic-

ularly how she avoided others and exerted tight control over her own reactions. She actively applied this information to her work in an outpatient group and in conversations with her partner. By the end of a 16-week time-limited group, she reported an improvement in mood and self-esteem and emerged as more spontaneous in the group. She had clarified the issues with her partner and was considering a more stimulating job. In the final session of the group, she volunteered her belief that the most important therapeutic effect was connected to the process of being accepted in the group. This had alerted her to the damaging effects of her reclusive style and strengthened her belief in herself.

Example 5

Patients with high openness tend to become overloaded with ideas or fantasies to the point where they become quite disorganized or scattered. They often respond to cognitive techniques that help them master this scattering effect. This can often be accomplished by a soothing approach and the encouragement to restate the issues and look realistically at the options. These patients find themselves taking on too many responsibilities simultaneously and then descending into a frantic whirl trying to keep up with them all. Planned efforts to structure their lives with more control are helpful.

A 42-year-old teacher scored very high on Openness. She described becoming overly stimulated in new situations and feeling overwhelmed with creative ideas. She would begin many projects at the start of each school year that positively engaged her students. But shortly into the year, she found herself feeling burnt out and unable to keep on top of them all. This cycled into a self-critical mode and a sense of disengagement from her class that was severe enough to put her job into jeopardy. She was encouraged to place particular emphasis on the cognitive therapy groups. At 1-year follow-up, she reported that her patterns were much improved and that she regularly repeated the cognitive structured organizing exercises she had developed in the program.

Example 6

Low scores on Openness suggest the patient will be able to use structured approaches more easily. Such patients may need to have special preparation and support if they are to adapt successfully to unstructured therapeutic settings. Piper, McCallum, and Azim (1992) found that patients who score low on Psychological Mindedness, a concept closely related to Openness, tend to drop out of time-limited groups at a high rate. However, those who remain do just as well as high–Psychological Mindedness patients on outcome measures. Others have reported that low-Openness patients do better with biofeedback than imagery techniques for relaxation training (Kelso, Anchor, & McElroy, 1988).

Example 7

The Agreeableness trait is related to control/submission issues that are central to autonomy/enmeshment problems. Patients who fall at either extreme on the Agreeableness dimension are appropriate candidates for dynamic therapies that focus on interpersonal issues. At the high end, the patient's vulnerable predisposition to interpersonal abuse must be addressed directly. This generally involves poor self-esteem and associated difficulty in personal assertion. The example earlier in this chapter exemplified some of these issues.

Example 8

Patients at the low end of Agreeableness must address the issues of suspiciousness and lack of trust that generally underlie their sarcastic, distancing interpersonal style. It has been my impression that dyadic therapy is likely to inflame this quality. The leadership dilution found in therapy groups gives the patient more room to try out a more positive approach to others without losing face to an authority figure.

A 42-year-old man described a childhood of high achievement in academic and sports activities. He felt this was in response to

continual criticism from his father and being ignored by his mother. In his late teens, he realized that his efforts were to no avail. This precipitated a dysthymic state that had persisted ever since. He viewed the world as an unforgiving place where effort was not rewarded and success was futile. His attitude and tone of voice were bitter and sarcastic, and his demeanor had an adolescent quality. His participation in an intensive psychotherapy group was minimal, but he attended regularly. After several months, it became apparent that he was quite involved with some of the members outside of the group. This was an unusual level of socialization for him, even though it involved primarily only meeting for coffee. He remained suspicious of the male group leader, although he clearly attended very closely to him. Efforts at an empathic connection were repeatedly rebuffed. Finally, one of the female members with whom he would socialize, blurted out with tears that she "could not stand to see him gradually dying within himself." This was echoed by other group members and slowly led to his increased participation. At about the 12-month point, he was able to begin to deal with his fear of rejection if he allowed himself to feel positively toward the leader.

Example 9

The patient who scores low on Conscientiousness finds it hard to consistently address the tasks of therapy. Modest goals are best established at the beginning of treatment so that the patient is not set up for an experience of recurrent failure. As mentioned earlier in this chapter, attention to motivational issues should form a continuing theme in treatment.

A 35-year-old man was referred for outpatient treatment because of a sense of being stuck in his life. He had a graduate degree, acquired after a decade of intermittent studies, but he had never put it to use. He worked itinerant construction jobs to make ends meet. He considered himself a musician but worked only sporadic gigs and resolutely refused to learn how to read music. He had started many relationships, but they all dwindled away as he became involved in other interests. He stated that he was now ready to make changes in his life. The assessment interviewer pressed him on motivational issues. This led to an acknowledgment of concern about starting now because it was spring, and he felt that getting a summer job would do him good. He was repeatedly offered the opportunity to make a commitment to the program and finally agreed to do so, saying he realized he had no alternative, that his life was going nowhere. The next week he phoned to say that he had found a job and knew that would be best for him right now.

Example 10

Highly conscientious patients tend to be reliable and consistent in their therapeutic involvement. They often win the admiration of their therapist for their efforts in the session and in following through on homework. However, these features may mask underlying difficulties. The hard work may be approached with a sense of duty and compulsiveness that translates the potential achievements into earnest and perhaps restrictive routines. If anything, these people need an experience in spontaneously not following through. Providing detailed structure to the therapeutic task must therefore be regarded with caution.

A woman in her early 30s, who was married to a professional and was finishing a graduate-level course, was seen as a leader in an intensive day program. She edited an information bulletin, organized activities, and was helpful in interpreting issues for others. Despite this involvement, she reported continuing hopelessness and intermittent active suicidal ideation. It was only after the level of her helpfulness was challenged by the group that she began to reveal her internal sense of desperate futil-

ity if she had nothing to do. This highly charged response allowed her to begin effective personal introspection.

Some general trends are evident in the just-mentioned discussion regarding the decision to use high versus low structure. Patients who are low on Neuroticism, Extraversion (or Introversion), Openness, and Conscientiousness will take to structured approaches more readily. Conversely, high scores on all four suggest that the patient will feel comfortable with unstructured and more novel techniques. In short, with an accumulation of these predictors, an increasingly strong warning is being issued about the type of treatment to which the patient is likely to be receptive. This is not the same thing as predicting what type of treatment will be more effective. As Piper et al. (1992) found out, the low–Psychological Mindedness patients did well if they completed therapy. The problem was that they did not take to it very well and therefore terminated before they had a dose sufficient to produce an effect.

It appears reasonable, at the very least, for the clinician to use these indicators to be forewarned and to institute appropriate pretherapy preparation procedures. Most dropouts tend to occur within the first six sessions. The group literature has demonstrated the effectiveness of pretherapy "role induction" techniques in lowering the rate of these early dropouts (Piper & Perrault, 1989). The preparation, done with handouts and discussion, concentrates on giving patients an appreciation of how the therapy works and how they can get the most out of it. This is a practice that could well be emulated by therapists seeing patients individually. Such systematic preparation material can be unobtrusively inserted into early sessions.

These ideas of low and high structure may also be incorporated into the sequencing of treatment components. In general, the more unstructured dynamic/interpersonal techniques emphasize personal disclosure and expect a degree of spontaneity and initiative from the patient. They involve a greater attention to the process of psychotherapy rather than the overt content. This produces a more interpersonally threatening environment that will be seen as particularly dangerous to patients who are low on Neuroticism,

Extraversion, and Openness. Many treatment programs begin with structured psychoeducational techniques to engage these patients. For example, inpatient units focus on education about how to recognize an emerging relapse, how to stay out of the hospital, medication information, community resources, and so on. Eating disorder programs routinely begin with psychoeducational material and anticipate that a significant number of patients will find this adequate to master their symptoms. Many self-help groups provide a structured approach that fits the needs of the target population they are serving (Lieberman, 1990). In all of these examples, the structured initial approach also acquaints the patient with the idea of talking about his or her problems and indirectly lays the groundwork for more exploratory psychotherapy for those still in need. Because most of the structured programs tend to be quite brief in nature, they are able to retain the low-Neuroticism, -Extraversion, and -Openness people while not turning off the high-Neuroticism, -Extraversion, and -Openness people.

In more complex therapeutic milieu settings such as day programs, two therapeutic tracks might be considered: one that focuses on control and mastery and one that focuses on self-exploration. I have found it important to clarify for patients that these two approaches are complementary, not in competition. By dampening reactivity through self-mastery techniques, the patient is able to deal constructively with internal and interpersonal issues. On the other hand, interpersonal therapy helps to explore the roots of the issues that trigger reactive responses. Clearly, such a dual-track program is only possible when there is goodwill and respect among the clinicians providing each modality.

Many of the examples used in this chapter have referred to group psychotherapy. Almost by definition, personality pathology is manifested in disturbed interpersonal relationships. Such problems seem particularly well suited to a group approach. Indeed, a case can be made that a well-functioning therapy group is more likely to provide an arena in which entrenched patterns can be effectively challenged. The power of group engagement and the resulting collective normative expectations for change can be used to augment technical therapeutic interventions.

Given the equivalency of outcome, it would seem appropriate to expect that clinicians might be called upon to justify the use of individual therapy for patients with major personality disorders.

References

Alden, L. E., Wiggins, J. S., & Pincus, A. L. (1990). Construction of circumplex scales for the Inventory of Interpersonal Problems. *Journal of Personality Assessment, 55*, 521–536.

American Psychiatric Association. (1987). *Diagnostic and statistical manual of mental disorders* (3rd ed., rev.). Washington, DC: Author.

Battle, C. C., Imber, S. D., Hoehn-Saric, R., Stone, A. R., Nash, E. H., & Frank, J. (1966). Target complaints as a criteria of improvement. *American Journal of Psychotherapy, 20*, 184–192.

Benjamin, L. S. (1987). Use of the SASB dimensional model to develop treatment plans for personality disorders: I. Narcissism. *Journal of Personality Disorders, 1*, 43–70.

Budman, S. H., Demby, A., Redondo, J. P., Hannan, M., Feldstein, M., Ring, J., & Springer, T. (1988). Comparative outcome in time-limited individual and group psychotherapy. *International Journal of Group Psychotherapy, 38*, 63–86.

Costa, P. T., Jr., & McCrae, R. R. (1985). *The NEO Personality Inventory manual.* Odessa, FL: Psychological Assessment Resources.

Costa, P. T., Jr., McCrae, R. R., & Dye, D. A. (1991). Facet scales for Agreeableness and Conscientiousness: A revision of the NEO Personality Inventory. *Personality and Individual Differences, 12*, 887–898.

Derogatis, L. R. (1977). *SCL-90 administration, scoring and procedures manual: 1.* Baltimore: Johns Hopkins University Press.

Dies, R. R. (1983). Bridging the gap between research and practice in group psychotherapy. In R. R. Dies & K. R. MacKenzie (Eds.), *Advances in group psychotherapy* (pp. 1–26). New York: International Universities Press.

Elkin, I., Shea, M. T., Watkins, J. T., Imber, S. D., Sotsky, S. M., Collins, J. F., Glass, D. R., Pilkonis, P. A., Leber, W. R., Docherty, J. P., Fiester, S. J., & Parloff, M. B. (1989). National Institute of Mental Health Treatment of Depression Collaborative Research Program: General effectiveness of treatments. *Archives of General Psychiatry, 46*, 971–982.

Horowitz, L. M., Rosenberg, S. E., Baer, B. A., Ureno, G., & Villasenor, V. S. (1988). Inventory of Interpersonal Problems: Psychometric properties and clinical applications. *Journal of Consulting and Clinical Psychology, 56*, 885–892.

Kelly, G. A. (1955). *The psychology of personal constructs.* New York: Norton.

Kelso, H., Anchor, K., & McElroy, M. (1988). The relationship between absorption capacity and electromyographic biofeedback relaxation training with a male clinical sample. *Medical Psychotherapy, 1,* 51–63.

Lieberman, M. A. (1990). A group therapist perspect on self-help groups. *International Journal of Group Psychotherapy, 40,* 251–278.

Livesley, W. J., Jackson, D. N., & Schroeder, M. L. (1989). A study of the factorial structure of personality pathology. *Journal of Personality Disorders, 3,* 292–306.

Luborsky, L. (1975). Clinician's judgments of mental health: Specimen case descriptions and forms for the Health–Sickness Rating Scale. *Bulletin of the Menninger Clinic, 39,* 448–480.

MacKenzie, K. R. (1990). *Introduction to time-limited group psychotherapy.* Washington, DC: American Psychiatric Press.

MacKenzie, K. R., & Livesley, W. J. (1986). Outcome and process measures in brief group psychotherapy. *Psychiatric Annals, 16,* 715–720.

Miller, T. R. (1991). The psychotherapeutic utility of the five-factor model of personality: A clinician's experience. *Journal of Personality Assessment, 57,* 415–433.

Pfeiffer, J. W., Heslin, R., & Jones, J. E. (1976). *Instrumentation in human relations training* (2nd ed.). La Jolla, CA: University Associates.

Pilkonis, P. A., Imber, S. D., Lewis, P., & Rubinsky, P. (1984). A comparative study of individual, group, and conjoint psychotherapy. *Archives of General Psychiatry, 41,* 431–437.

Pincus, A. L. (1991, August). *Extending interpersonal problems to include the "Big Five" personality dimensions.* In L. E. Alden (Chair), *Assessment of interpersonal problems: Implications for treatment and research.* Symposium conducted at the 99th annual meeting of the American Psychological Association, San Francisco, CA.

Piper, W. E., Debanne, E. G., Bienvenu, J. P., & Garant, J. (1984). A comparative study of four forms of psychotherapy. *Journal of Consulting and Clinical Psychology, 52,* 268–279.

Piper, W. E., McCallum, M., & Azim, H. F. A. (1992). *Adaptation to loss through short-term group psychotherapy.* New York: Guilford Press.

Piper, W. E., & Perrault, E. L. (1989). Pretherapy preparation for group members. *International Journal of Group Psychotherapy, 39,* 17–34.

Schroeder, M. L., Wormworth, J. A., & Livesley, W. J. (1992). Dimensions of personality disorder and their relationships to the Big Five dimensions of personality. *Psychological Assessment: A Journal of Consulting and Clinical Psychology, 4,* 47–53.

CHAPTER 17

TREATMENT CASE: A COUPLE WITH SEXUAL DYSFUNCTION AND PARAPHILIA

Peter J. Fagan

James and Mary, 55 and 54 years old, respectively, had been married for 36 years and were referred to the Sexual Behaviors Consultation Unit (John Hopkins Medical Institutions, Baltimore, MD) by James's internist for treatment of impotence. James was dependent on alcohol but was able to obtain full erections daily through paraphiliac arousal patterns. The couple had not had intercourse in decades. The NEO Personality Inventory (NEO-PI; Costa & McCrae, 1985) profiles of the couple suggested interpersonal avoidance on the part of James and emotionally restrictive and obediently compliant traits in Mary. The treatment modality was sensate focus sexual therapy with minimal addressing of interpersonal issues. There were 25 sessions over a 9-month period, and the couple terminated with full sexual functioning. At the 6-month follow-up, James and Mary reported having intercourse, on average, three times per week and being quite sexually satisfied.

HISTORY OF JAMES

Family and Personal History

James was the only child of a middle-class family in an urban eastern U.S. city. He described his father as being strict and overbearing but never physically abusive to him. His mother was easygoing, quiet, and emotionally distant. James described his home environment as cold with little exchange of affection. He added, however, that he was comfortable with this and had many fond memories of the household.

There was no report of family psychiatric illness or substance abuse.

James reported that he had no unusual childhood illnesses or behaviors. From the beginning of his formal education, he found school frightening and withdrew from his classmates. James was academically gifted, but he was socially quite intimidated, especially after he skipped a grade. James completed college and had been employed by the same firm for the past 23 years. His work was largely done at his desk with minimal interpersonal contact. James reported very little job satisfaction and was "counting the days" until his retirement.

James's medical condition was significant for alcohol dependence for the past 20 years. He ingested about 8 ounces of alcohol daily and had never been treated for alcoholism. He had mild prostatic hypertrophy but was otherwise in good health and taking no regular medication. James's past psychiatric history consisted of one consultation in his 20s for impotence. At that time he was diagnosed as having a psychoneurotic reaction and did not enter treatment.

Sexual/Marital History

James's earliest and strongest sexual memories were of being taken to a private institutional swimming pool when he was 10 years old. At the time there were many women swimming in the pool. He had no bathing suit, and his mother permitted him to swim nude. He found this very exciting and wanted to make physical contact with the women. This episode served throughout his life as the basis for many masturbatory fantasies that centered around his exposing himself to women. James recalled seeing his parents nude about the house on many occasions. On occasion, he "accidentally" exposed himself to teenage girls who were visiting his home.

He had in his early adolescence two contacts with an older man who fondled his genitals, but there were no orgasms. There were no homosexual behaviors with others.

James and Mary met as teenagers and dated for 3 years before marrying. On the wedding night, James was quite anxious about his sexual performance because the couple had not had either intercourse or experienced mutual orgasm. He was unable to develop an erection. He continued to have problems with impotence throughout his marriage. He reported that intercourse did not seem instinctive to him, and it was not clear how he was expected to perform it. He recalled on one occasion after a particularly successful day at work that he went home with a strong sense of self-confidence and had a firm erection and intercourse with his wife. Over the years he was only able to recall a few times on which they had sexual intercourse. They were the three acts that led to the birth of their two children. Throughout the marriage, their sexual life together had consisted of mutual manual and/or oral stimulation approximately once every 3 months and no intercourse.

Concurrent with his history of erectile dysfunction and avoidance of sexual intercourse, James developed a paraphiliac ritual of watching erotic videos and writing erotica. Both of these practices would occur during the night hours and would involve drinking 8 ounces of alcohol, eating a meal that would not vary in content, and achieving sexual arousal and masturbation with full erection. The narrative texts that he would compose involved exhibitionism, voyeurism, and gender transpositions. The gender transposition involved writing in the first person as women with sexual problems.

James stated that his wife tolerated the sexual behavior established over the years and, in fact, corrected the spelling and grammar of the erotic texts he wrote. The writing was for personal gratification, not for publication.

At evaluation, James and Mary were not sleeping in the same room because of James's wish to engage in video and writing erotica throughout the hours of the night.

HISTORY OF MARY

Family and Personal History

Mary was the middle of three children in an upper middle-class urban family. She reported no remarkable characteristics about her parents or her early childhood. Her family psychiatric history included presenile dementia in a maternal grandmother and alcoholism in a paternal grandfather.

Mary was a quiet, studious young girl, who was liked by both peers and teachers. She eventually received an advanced degree in biology. Mary did not use tobacco, drugs, or alcohol. She had no remarkable medical history. She was in psychotherapy for 1 year after marrying her husband because she had difficulties with marital communications. She felt she got "nothing out of this therapy."

Sexual/Marital History

Mary met her husband when she was 15. At the time she felt that she was a homely person with eyeglasses, acne, and obesity. She felt that other boys would not be attracted to her and was quite grateful for his attention. They dated for 3 years and were married. She described the marriage as being a somewhat distant one in which they both developed a pattern of parallel activities. She felt that James was withdrawn, and she allowed him to "go off and do his own thing."

Mary was aware that her husband preferred to masturbate alone while involved with his erotica. She added that he would approach her every 2–3 months to perform cunnilingus on her. She achieved orgasms from this, but this was her only sexual contact with her husband. She masturbated about once or twice a month.

Mary noted that in the last several months before evaluation James was interested in trying to have regular sex with her but was unsuccessful in having an erection. Mary stated that she tried to get more information about sex and had purchased marriage manuals but that her husband was not interested in looking at them.

HISTORY OF THE PRESENTING PROBLEM

Although his coital impotence was chronic, James stated that about 6 months before seeking consultation he developed an interest in country and western music. The sentimentality of this music touched him and generated an interest in reviving his sexual relationship with his wife. They made efforts to become more affectionate physically. They set aside one morning each weekend for attempts at intercourse, which failed except for one brief episode of vaginal penetration without ejaculation. James complained that his wife seemed to have very little interest in stimulating him sexually and that she reacted poorly to any attempt on his part to introduce variety to their sexual activity. Neither expressed concern about the paraphiliac activities. They sought therapy to "learn how to do it," referring to vaginal intercourse.

MENTAL STATUS EXAMINATIONS

The mental status examinations of James and Mary were unremarkable for any affective or cognitive disorders. No diagnosis was given to Mary. James was given the diagnoses of male erectile disorder, alcohol abuse (alcohol dependence), and paraphilia, not otherwise specified. Third, revised edition of the *Diagnostic and Statistical Manual of Mental Disorders* (American Psychiatric Association, 1987) Axis II diagnoses were deferred for both.

THE NEO PERSONALITY INVENTORY AND TREATMENT STRATEGY

James and Mary's NEO Personality Inventory (NEO-PI; Costa & McCrae, 1985) profiles (Figures 1 and 2) indicated that they were, with the exception of James's very high self-consciousness and Mary's high anxiety, a couple who were generally stable and not subject to intrapsychic distress. They reported average levels of Neuroticism. Thus, their NEO-PI profiles corroborated the clinical impression that they were not in either acute crisis or great psychological distress.

The questions of motivation for treatment and "why seek treatment now?" were important to clarify. Was this an avoidant man who was daring to come closer to his wife as he aged or a schizoid man who would not sustain further work in therapy with me or "in vivo" with his wife?

I felt that an answer to this treatment prognosis question lay in James's very high self-consciousness. One of the main differences between avoidant and schizoid personalities is that although both are generally low on Extraversion (especially low Warmth and low Gregariousness), an avoidant person is generally high on Neuroticism. Although five of the six facets of Neuroticism of James's profile were within the average range, the very high self-consciousness indicated that his interpersonally avoidant behaviors (very low Extraversion) were associated with high levels of distress when in interaction with others.

I hypothesized that James's avoidant behaviors were defensive against further embarrassment. I hoped that, given a sufficiently "safe" environment in both therapy and his home, he would find interpersonal behavior tolerable and, perhaps, sexual behavior enjoyable. My task as therapist was to establish this safe environment for James, an avoidant and aging man who was becoming more dependent on his wife. In his words, he wanted to experience for himself the feelings of love and romance that were sparked on the occasions of hearing country and western music.

Mary reported high levels of anxiety, but in general, her average level of overall Neuroticism on the NEO-PI indicated that she was quite resilient, hardy (low vulnerability), and not given to any quick frustrations or angry outbursts (very low hostility). Her Neuroticism scales described a woman who was, albeit somewhat anxious, nonetheless a patient, long-suffering, and stolid person. In terms of tolerating a therapeutic course dictated by the limits of her husband's motivation and direction, she seemed to be a promising partner.

In the Extraversion domain, neither James nor Mary was highly extraverted. Indeed, as noted earlier, James was highly introverted (very low warmth and gregariousness). Mary's high warmth showed considerable scatter from the other Extraversion facets. There was an outgoing quality to her in that she liked to be talkative and to bond or attach with other people. I suspected that this trait had expressed itself with her children or, perhaps, with colleagues at work; however, it was not tendered in the marital relationship. She reported low gregariousness, and

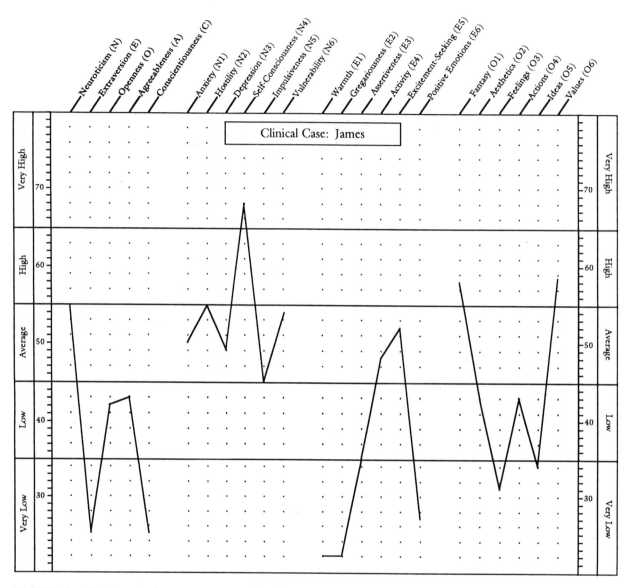

FIGURE 1. NEO Personality Inventory profile of James. Profile form adapted from *The NEO Personality Inventory Manual* by P. T. Costa, Jr. and R. R. McCrae, 1985, Odessa, FL: Psychological Assessment Resources. Copyright 1985 by Psychological Assessment Resources.

her generally low Extraversion provided the basis for compatibility with a man who warily avoided social contact.

Both James and Mary had low assertiveness, which in this couple, appeared to be presenting itself as a mutually passive dependency on and also avoidance of one another. James also had very low positive emotions, an indication that is highly suggestive of chronic dysthymia. I speculated whether the alcohol abuse was an attempt at self-medicating James's chronically negative affective state.

James and Mary showed a considerable amount of variability in their Openness facet scores. Most important, both had very low Openness to Feelings. They indicated an extremely narrow range of emotions and, in general, were insensitive to both their own feelings and the feelings of their partner. The emotional distance of the marriage did not evoke feelings of abandonment or rejection in Mary despite her high Warmth. She did not feel any estrangement from her husband. He was quite comfortable with the distance in any case. The couple's joint very low

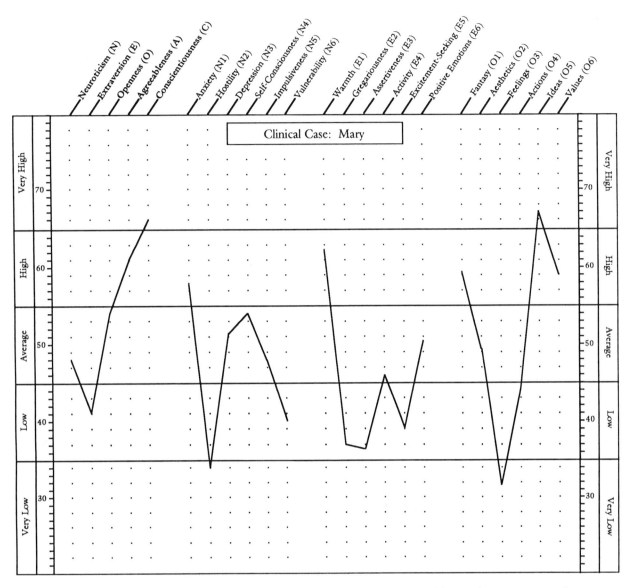

FIGURE 2. NEO Personality Inventory profile of Mary. Profile form adapted from *The NEO Personality Inventory Manual* by P. T. Costa, Jr. and R. R. McCrae, 1985, Odessa, FL: Psychological Assessment Resources. Copyright 1985 by Psychological Assessment Resources.

Openness to Feelings probably had a positive effect in preserving the homeostasis of the emotional distance in the marriage over the years.

In the remaining Openness facets, James had quite rich imagination (high fantasy), which is typical among our paraphiliac patients. Mary also had high fantasy, which coupled with her high openness to values, contributed to her toleration of his erotic activities. They both indicated that they preferred to follow strict routines or were set in their ways (i.e., low actions). I knew that it would be very important

therefore not to impose any behavioral assignments "from on high" but to make sure that in their sessions they expressed an unpressured willingness to collaborate in the behavioral suggestions that I would make.

James's low level of Agreeableness indicated that he would work for his own self-interest. The fact that he had initiated this consultation gave some indication that, at this point in his life, he felt it was in his self-interest to have increased sexual contact and, hopefully, intercourse with his wife. The fact that the low Agreeableness was approximately a *T* score of 43 suggested that there were not going to be insurmountable difficulties in evoking his self-interest. He was only seven *T*-score units from the mean and would not be exceptionally antagonistic. But his low Agreeableness and very low openness to feelings suggested to me that it would be pointless during therapy to appeal to a sense of empathy for his wife or to attempt to probe his awareness of his own feelings or those of others.

Mary's compensatory high level of Agreeableness indicated that she would behave in ways that would attempt to please and satisfy her husband. If he wanted a vigorous sexual life together, she would cooperate in trying to achieve this goal. He would decide what was in his interest, and she would go along with this in order to keep the peace and to please him.

The greatest difference between James's and Mary's NEO-PI profiles lay in the four standard-deviation spread in their Conscientiousness scores. Clearly, James had no real organization in his life. His drinking, avoidant behavior, and general eroticization of life's tensions were clearly being reflected in his low level of Conscientiousness. Mary, on the other hand, was very goal-oriented and organized. Her high level of conscientiousness was a good prognostic indicator that, given his sustained interest in making the behavioral sexual changes, she would be a willing collaborator and would provide him with the goal-seeking support that she had consistently brought to the marriage.

The challenge of working therapeutically with this couple lay in not "pushing" them together physically and emotionally beyond what James could tolerate. Mary was both quite tolerant of her husband's distance and welcoming of his coming closer to her, as her high warmth would suggest.

I chose to "take the patients as they were" in terms of both their presenting complaint and the limitations and strengths of their personality profiles. I did not attempt major character restructuring or forays into behavioral changes (except drinking patterns) other than the one change that they requested: to have more frequent sex and, hopefully, intercourse. The following treatment goals were set for James: (a) to maintain an erection for intercourse, (b) to have orgasm with Mary by any means, and (c) to increase her desire to want to have sexual interaction with him. We also agreed that we would set a limit to the number of sessions after five sessions.

COURSE OF TREATMENT

James and Mary eagerly began a regimen of sensate focus sexual therapy. It was clear from the onset of the therapy that James had a great investment in the progress of the therapy. Although throughout his marital life he had been quite content to have his principal sexual outlet be the paraphiliac masturbatory activities, at this particular point in his life, he wished to have regular intercourse and sleep with his wife.

No efforts were made to remove the paraphiliac behaviors. Obviously, changes in James's sexual patterns had to be made to permit the couple to spend more time together during the night or during times when both would be physically and emotionally ready for the sexual exercises. The result was that the paraphiliac behaviors became less frequent and less salient to James. The paraphilia were not "taken away" by me but seen as less important to James.

James was evaluated for alcoholism as recommended. He was diagnosed by the psychiatrist–evaluator as alcohol dependent but refused an inpatient detoxification program. However, James did gradually cut back on his alcohol consumption, reducing it to approximately 1 ounce per day. He experienced no withdrawal symptoms.

In the initial sessions of sensate focus therapy, James and Mary concentrated on their physiological responses of relaxation and some sexual arousal. After 5 sessions, a session limit was set at 20 more sessions. For the first 2 months, they made gradual progress in terms of increasing sexual response. They slowly began to talk more and more about nonsexual issues in their life (e.g., family and work). They even spoke briefly about their emotions and feelings of increasing intimacy. When this occurred, the treatment modality became cognitive. This was tolerated much better by Mary. James was very concrete (very low openness to ideas) and more interested in achieving behavioral gains.

By the 4th month of therapy, penile–vaginal penetration was achieved successfully. In the 5th month, they had intravaginal ejaculation. Later that month Mary manually brought James to ejaculation. This was the first time this had occurred in the life of the couple. By the next month, they were having intercourse regularly, and one week they reported having intercourse successfully four times. Mary was enjoying both the sexual pleasure and the increased emotional and physical contact with her husband.

The final 3 months of therapy were involved in generalizing the behavior from a compulsive following of doctor's directions to integrating the sexual behaviors within their own marital relationship. There were subtle allusions to feelings of dependency on me. These were not able to be processed in any depth (low openness to feelings).

At the 6-month follow-up, James and Mary reported that they were sleeping together and having intercourse regularly with no remarkable problems. Although James was experiencing increased stress at work, this was not affecting the sexual life of the couple. The alcohol dependence had been modified, but I felt that there was still a likelihood of alcohol abuse on James's part.

SUMMARY

Avoidant traits (high self-consciousness and very low Extraversion), sexual paraphilia, and alcohol depend-

ence are not a triad that inspires therapeutic optimism in the treatment of sexual dysfunction. In the case of James and Mary, optimism was tempered with the realism of the personality data that were provided by the NEO-PI. The NEO-PI profiles guided the setting of general limitations on what change could be sought in the therapy with James and Mary. Clear behavioral goals were identified and approached in a behavioral treatment modality. Major personality changes were not attempted. James's very low Extraversion and self-interest (low Agreeableness) and Mary's high Agreeableness and very high Conscientiousness were the salient personality traits in the treatment design. The couple worked diligently in treatment and on their in vivo assignments. The continued robust frequency of sexual intercourse by James and Mary at the 6-month follow-up was a reminder to me that limited treatment goals are frequently the best means to successful treatment outcome.

References

American Psychiatric Association. (1987). *Diagnostic and statistical manual of mental disorders* (3rd ed., rev.). Washington, DC: Author.

Costa, P. T., Jr, & McCrae, R. R. (1985). *The NEO Personality Inventory manual.* Odessa, FL: Psychological Assessment Resources.

PART V

RECONCEPTUALIZATION

TWO APPROACHES TO IDENTIFYING THE DIMENSIONS OF PERSONALITY DISORDER: CONVERGENCE ON THE FIVE-FACTOR MODEL

Lee Anna Clark and W. John Livesley

Since the introduction of a separate axis for personality disorders in the third edition of the *Diagnostic and Statistical Manual of Mental Disorders* (*DSM-III*; American Psychiatric Association, 1980), debate has continued regarding the most valid approach to their description and diagnosis. From the beginning, these disorders have been conceptualized as personality traits that are inflexible and maladaptive and that cause either significant functional impairment or subjective distress (American Psychiatric Association, 1980, 1987). Delineation of the specific traits constituting the personality disorders, however, has been unsystematic and imprecise. Moreover, the *DSM* Axis II criteria, which are intended as manifestations of the component traits, were developed informally on the basis of expert consensus. This approach was necessitated in part by the lack of empirical research into the structure of maladaptive personality traits. Prior to 1980, research in normal-range personality was abundant, and although thousands of studies used the Minnesota Multiphasic Personality Inventory (Hathaway & McKinley, 1967) to examine personality pathology in various settings and diagnostic groups, research specifically investigating the traits of personality-disordered individuals was limited (notable exceptions include Presley & Walton, 1973; Tyrer & Alexander, 1979). Over the past decade, however, interest in the trait dimensions of personality disorder has increased markedly, with a corresponding increase in relevant research activity.

As is typical of relatively new areas of research, investigators have approached the study of maladap-tive personality traits in a variety of ways. For example, personality disorder has been studied in relation to the interpersonal circumplex (Kiesler, 1986; Trapnell & Wiggins, 1990; Wiggins, 1982; Wiggins & Pincus, 1989) and, as the chapters in this book attest, the five-factor model (FFM) of personality. Moreover, Cloninger (1987) developed a three-factor model of personality disorder (which he later expanded to include four "temperament" and three "character" dimensions; Cloninger, Svrakic, & Przybeck, in press). In each of these cases, an existing theoretical and/or empirical model of personality was used, either directly or with adaptation, to conceptualize personality disorder. These may be termed *top-down* approaches.

In contrast, we (Clark, 1990, 1993; Livesley, 1986, 1987; Livesley, Jackson, & Schroeder, 1989) independently adopted *bottom-up* strategies, in which the research begins with an examination of lower order components and builds gradually toward a final structure. For the Axis II disorders, this meant beginning with the symptomatic traits and behaviors of personality disorder. Then, by combining traits and behaviors that were conceptually related and/or empirically correlated, we each developed dimensional structures to represent the domain. We are not the only investigators to have used a bottom-up strategy. For example, Morey (1988) used cluster analysis to examine the covariance of clinician-rated personality features, whereas Hyler et al. (1990) reported an item–level factor analysis of a self-report questionnaire that assesses each of the *DSM-III* Axis II criteria. In neither case, however, was the research goal per se to develop a structure that characterized the domain of personality disorders, whereas that was a primary goal of each of our research programs. Therefore, this chapter's focus is a comparison of the structures that emerged from our respective research efforts.

To the extent that a phenomenon is robust, different methods will lead to similar conclusions about its nature. For example, although they have gone by many different names, the traits of neuroticism and extraversion have emerged repeatedly in diverse analyses of personality (e.g., Cloninger, 1987; Tellegen, 1985; Zuckerman, Kuhlman, & Camac, 1988). Similarly, we were motivated to write this chapter because we were impressed with the high degree of convergence between our dimensional structures, despite the fact that they had been developed using rather different methods. Given the many difficulties one encounters in attempting to conceptualize and assess personality pathology, it was gratifying to find that the core dimensions of this domain are sufficiently robust to emerge under diverse conditions. Detailed descriptions of the developmental processes followed by each of us are available elsewhere (Clark, 1990, 1993; Livesley, 1986; Livesley et al., 1989), so we only summarize them briefly in this chapter. Because specific comparisons of each dimensional structure to the FFM also can be found elsewhere in this book (Clark, Vorhies, & McEwen, chapter 6 in this book; Schroeder, Wormworth, & Livesley, chapter 7 in this book), we focus here more broadly on how the two trait systems converge on a higher order structure.

LIVESLEY'S STRUCTURE AND ITS DEVELOPMENT

Livesley began his investigation by compiling a comprehensive list of trait descriptors and behavioral acts that were considered to be characteristic of each of the *DSM-III* Axis II categories by a content analysis of the personality disorder literature (Livesley, 1986). These characteristics, which included all *DSM-III* and *DSM-III-R* criteria, were sent to a large number of clinicians who rated the prototypicality of the items for

the relevant diagnosis. The results, and those of a follow-up study (Livesley, 1987), indicated good agreement regarding the prototypical characteristics of each diagnosis. Highly prototypical items for each disorder often referred to the same dimension, so that it was possible to characterize each diagnosis using a relatively small number of dimensions, each consisting of conceptually related items (Livesley, 1987; Livesley et al., 1989). For example, *mistrustful*, *searches for hidden meanings*, and *sees the world as hostile and opposed to him/her* were all prototypical of paranoid personality disorder, and all represented the dimension of *suspiciousness*. Altogether, 79 dimensions were identified, and self-report items were written to assess each dimension. This initial questionnaire was completed by two samples of normal subjects, and psychometric analyses led to refinement of the scales, including the splitting of some dimensions into subcomponents.

The result was an instrument with 100 dimensions represented by 16 items per dimension, which was administered to a sample of normal subjects and a sample of patients with a primary diagnosis of personality disorder. The data were submitted independently to principal components analysis and, initially, 15 factors were identified from each data set (Livesley et al., 1989). These factors provided the basic structure, and subsequent modification led to the development of 18 dimensions that are the focus of comparison in this chapter (Livesley, 1991; Schroeder, Wormworth, & Livesley, 1992, chapter 7 in this book). Specifically, rational considerations led to 1 of the 15 factors being divided into two dimensions. In addition, traits related to suspiciousness did not form a separate factor but nevertheless were used to construct a scale because of the clinical importance of these behaviors. Similar considerations led to the decision to establish a scale for self-harm. Finally, items were chosen to represent these 18 factors. When selecting items from the original pool, steps were taken to ensure that adequate sampling of the domain was retained. The result was a 290-item questionnaire, the Dimensional Assessment of Personality Pathology—Basic Questionnaire (DAPP-BQ; Livesley, 1990). More information about the DAPP-BQ, including its relation to the FFM, is available in chapter 7 of this book.

CLARK'S STRUCTURE AND ITS DEVELOPMENT

Rather than using characteristic traits and behaviors as Livesley did, Clark (1990) began her investigation with the criterial symptoms of personality disorder. All of the *DSM* personality disorder criteria were included, plus criteria from various non-*DSM* conceptualizations of personality disorder (e.g., Cleckley, 1964; Liebowitz & Klein, 1981; Perry & Klerman, 1978) and from selected Axis I disorders (dysthymia, cyclothymia, and generalized anxiety disorder) that resemble personality disorders in important respects; that is, they have relatively chronic, traitlike manifestations (Akiskal, Hirschfeld, & Yerevanian, 1983; Frances, 1980). Complex criteria were divided into subcomponents (e.g., *unduly conventional, serious and formal,* and *stingy* were considered as four separate criteria). Clinicians sorted these criteria into synonym groups, and a consensual set of 22 symptom clusters was identified through a factor analysis of the resulting co-occurrence matrix (Clark, 1990).

Because this initial research was completed before the *DSM-III-R* appeared, each Axis II symptom in the *DSM-III-R* was examined to determine whether it represented a new criterion that had not appeared in the *DSM-III.* All new criteria were given to a set of clinicians, who were asked to judge whether each could be placed into one of the 22 previously identified symptom clusters. Only criteria from the two provisional diagnoses (the sadistic and self-defeating personality disorders) were viewed as not categorizable into the 22 clusters. Therefore, it appeared that the basic structures of the primary criterion sets of the *DSM-III* and *DSM-III-R* were essentially the same.

It is this 22-factor structure that is the focus of comparison in this chapter. Examples and a list of these clusters are shown elsewhere in this book (see Clark et al., chapter 6 in this book, Tables 1 and 2). Ratings on a sample of hospitalized psychiatric patients indicated that the clusters have good interrater reliability (Clark, McEwen, Collard, & Hickok, 1993). Moreover, preliminary analyses of their internal consistency using clinical ratings from a structured interview suggest that they represent homogeneous symptom clusters (Clark, Pfohl, &

Blashfield, 1991). Self-report data based on the clusters is reported later.

COMPARISONS OF THE TWO STRUCTURES

Conceptual Considerations

Before examining the structures directly, it is interesting to consider the methodological and theoretical implications of these two research strategies and whether there are reasons for why they might be expected to produce convergent or divergent results. The first and most obvious constraint is that both investigators were attempting to identify traits relevant to personality disorder, so that each was broadly addressing the same content domain. However, their methods for defining this domain were quite different. First, neither limited their investigation to the *DSM* but used a broader literature to help define the domain of personality disorder. Although the literature reviews most likely overlapped somewhat, many writings were surely unique to one or the other researcher. For example, Clark (1990) included chronic affective trait symptoms from selected Axis I disorders, whereas Livesley did not.

Second, if one considers that various manifestations or characterizations of personality disorder fall along a continuum ranging from the highly abstract and general to the very concrete and specific, it appears that the two investigators sampled from different parts of this continuum. Livesley (1986) selected many terms from the extremes of the continuum, including both general trait terms (e.g., *introverted, manipulative, perfectionistic*) and specific behavioral items (e.g., *wore eye-catching, revealing clothing; rechecked timetable several times*). In contrast, Clark's investigation began with symptom criteria, which tend to vary around the middle of the generality/specificity continuum (e.g., *easily hurt by criticism or disapproval; overly concerned with hidden motives*). Thus, these criteria tend to be more specific than general trait terms but less narrow than specific behavioral items. Clearly, if the trait structure of personality disorder is robust, one would expect congruence across the range of items from highly general to very specific, but such a result is not determined in advance. Thus, in terms of the items with which the investigations were begun, there was ample opportunity for the structures to diverge, despite the fact that they broadly addressed the same content domain.

A third major difference in the methodologies of the two investigators was in how they pursued identification of the trait dimensions. Clark used a conceptual free-sort task, in which raters grouped semantically similar symptoms regardless of their diagnostic origin; the question of which symptoms combined to form dimensions was then determined by factor analysis. In contrast, Livesley's initial research was tied conceptually to the Axis II diagnoses, with raters judging the prototypicality of the traits or behaviors for a given disorder. Furthermore, whereas Livesley used both judgments of semantic similarity and factor analysis as data reduction techniques, the basis for evaluating these procedures was self-ratings of the most highly prototypical items, rather than clinical judgments as used by Clark. Therefore, we again see ample opportunity for the emergence of rather diverse trait structures in these different procedures.

Content Comparisons

The first step in comparing the two trait structures was to match each of the factors in one structure with one (or more) factors in the other on the basis of similar content. The factor labels used by the investigators provided an initial indication of corresponding factors (e.g., Livesley's social avoidance was expected to correspond to Clark's social isolation), but the greatest weight was placed on the specific component dimensions (Livesley) or criteria (Clark) composing the factors. Table 1 shows the results of this content-based matching.

As can been seen in Table 1, a clear correspondence emerged across the two structures, with about one third of the factors showing a one-to-one match. Inevitably, differences in degree of differentiation occurred, such that one structure or the other elaborated or simplified certain content areas. Nevertheless, in the remaining cases, two factors from one structure (or three, in one instance only) corresponded to a single factor in the other, and in no case did the content of a factor in one structure split so much as to map onto more than two factors in the

other. Because Clark's 22-cluster structure is slightly more differentiated than Livesley's 18-factor structure, it was more often the case that multiple-symptom clusters represented content tapped by a single Livesley factor, but both types of asymmetry were seen. For example, Livesley's anxiousness factor overlapped with content in Clark's pessimism and negative affect clusters. Conversely, Clark's self-centered exploitation matched Livesley's rejection and interpersonal disesteem factors. Moreover, one symptom cluster—hypersexuality—failed to emerge in Livesley's analyses.

It is noteworthy that the two-dimensional systems were similar not just at the factor level but at the level of more detailed structures as well. For example, between Livesley's compulsivity and Clark's conventionality/rigidity, three components of the former—orderliness, precision, and conscientiousness—could be matched directly with the latter's symptoms of preoccupation with detail, perfectionism, and overconscientiousness, respectively. Although such exact matching was not seen uniformly, overall the structures were surprisingly congruent at this lower level, given their rather different origins.

A few discrepancies should also be noted. One divergence occured between the social avoidance and social isolation factors, the former involving a desire for improved affiliative relationships and the latter including the symptom "neither desires nor enjoys close relationships." An examination of the other components of these factors suggests that the former factor leans conceptually toward the avoidant personality disorder, which is said to include desire but fear of interpersonal relationships, whereas the latter represents the more classical schizoid temperament that rejects interpersonal involvement more completely. It is noteworthy that empirical differentiation of these two types has been difficult; perhaps an investigation of the relation between these two factors will shed some light on this problem.

Another point of discrepancy occurred with the trait of pessimism. In Clark's structure, pessimism emerged as a dimension, characterized by such symptoms as guilt, brooding, and exaggeration of difficulties. Together with negative affect, this dimension corresponded to Livesley's anxiousness factor.

TABLE 1

Content-Based Comparison of Two Structures of the Traits of Personality Disorder

Livesley's 18 factor scales	Clark's 22 symptom clusters

Self-harm
    Ideas of self-harm
    Self-damaging acts
	Suicide proneness
	        Recurrently thinks of death or suicide
	        Self-mutilating behavior
	        Recurrent suicidal threats, gestures, or behavior

Identity problems
    Labile self-concept
	Self-derogation
	        Identity disturbance
	        Low self-esteem

Anhedonia
Chronic feelings of emptiness
Pessimism
	Anhedonia
	        Low energy
	        Emptiness; boredom
	        Little interest in enjoyment or pleasurable activities

Affective lability
    Affective instability
    Affective overreactivity
	Instability
	        Shifting, shallow emotional expression
	        Reacts to criticism with feelings of rage or shame
	        Unstable interpersonal relationships

Generalized hypersensitivity	Hypersensitivity
	        Easily hurt by criticism or disapproval
	        Reacts to criticism with feelings of rage or shame
	        Bears grudges or is unforgiving of slights and insults

Labile anger
Irritability
	Anger/Aggression
	        Inappropriate, intense anger; lack of anger control
	        Irritability

Anxiousness
    Guilt proneness
    Indecisiveness
    Rumination
	Pessimism
	        Feels guilty concerning past activities
	        Exaggeration of difficulties
	        Broods over past events

Trait anxiety	Negative affect
	        Anxious, worried, on edge
	        Excessive social anxiety
	        Restlessness, unable to relax

Suspiciousness
    Hypervigilance
 	
    Suspiciousness
	Suspiciousness
	        Expects to be exploited or harmed
	        Overly concerned with hidden motives
	
	        Suspiciousness; paranoid ideation
	        Reluctant to confide in others
	        Questions the loyalty or trustworthiness of friends

Rejection
    Judgmental
    Rigid cognitive style
    Interpersonal hostility
    Dominance
	Self-centered exploitation
	        Inconsiderate of others
	        Lack of generosity when no personal gain will result
	        Disregards the personal integrity and rights of others
	        Treats those under his/her control unusually harshly

Interpersonal disesteem
    Interpersonal irresponsibility
    Exploitation
    Contemptuousness
    Remorseless
    Lack of empathy
    Egocentrism
	Self-centered exploitation
	        Takes advantage of others for his/her own ends
	        Interpersonally exploitative
	        Humiliates or demeans people in front of others
	        Treats those under his/her control unusually harshly
	        Lacks empathy
	        Indifferent to the feelings of others

Continued on next page

265

TABLE 1 (*continued*)

Livesley's 18 factor scales	Clark's 22 symptom clusters

Sadism	Anger/aggression
	  Aggressive
	  Uses cruelty or violence to establish dominance

Passive oppositionality
  Passivity
 	
  Oppositional
 	
  Lack of organization
	Passive–aggressiveness
	  Inefficient, ineffective or unproductive
	  Fails to accomplish tasks crucial to personal objectives
	  Obstructs efforts of others by failing to do his/her work
	  Resents useful suggestions from others
	  Indecisive
	  Has difficulty initiating projects

Narcissism
  Need for adulation
  Attention seeking
 	
  Grandiosity
 	
  Need for approval
	Dramatic exhibitionism
	  Requires constant admiration
	  Uncomfortable when not the center of attention
	
	Grandiose egocentrism
	  Grandiose sense of self-importance
	  Sense of entitlement
	  Egocentric, vain, demanding
	  Insists that others submit to his/her way of doing things

Social avoidance
  Defective social skills
  Low affiliation
  Social apprehension
  Fearful of interpersonal hurt
  Desire for improved affiliative relationships
	Social isolation
	  Engages in peripheral social and vocational roles
	  Has no close friends or confidants
	  Chooses solitary activities
	  Distances oneself from close personal attachments
	  [Neither desires nor enjoys close relationships]

Intimacy problems
  Inhibited sexuality
  Avoidant attachment
  Desire for improved attachment
	Emotional coldness
	  Restricted ability to express warm and tender feelings
	  Unresponsive in interpersonal relationships

Restricted expression
  Restricted affective expression
  Restricted expression of anger and of positive
    sentiments
  Reluctant self-disclosure
  Self-reliance
	Emotional coldness
	  Displays constricted affect
	  Rarely experiences strong emotions such as anger or joy
	
	  Rarely makes reciprocal gestures or facial expressions

Insecure attachment
  Separation protest
  Feared loss
  Intolerant of aloneness
  Proximity seeking
  Secure base
	Dependency
	  Preoccupied with fears of being abandoned
	  Agrees with people for fear of rejection
	  Feels uncomfortable or helpless when alone
	  Goes to great lengths to avoid being alone
	  Feels devastated when close relationships end

Diffidence
  Submissiveness
  Suggestibility
  Need for advice
	Dependency
	  Subordinates own needs to those of others
	  Allows others to make decisions for him/her
	  Constantly seeks reassurance

Compulsivity
  Orderliness
  Precision
  Conscientiousness
	Conventionality/rigidity
	  Preoccupation with details, order, organization
	  Perfectionism that interferes with task completion
	  Overconscientiousness, scrupulousness

Continued on next page

TABLE 1 (*continued*)	
Livesley's 18 factor scales	**Clark's 22 symptom clusters**
Stimulus seeking	Impulsivity
Impulsivity	Impulsive, fails to plan ahead
Recklessness	Recklessness
	High energy
Sensation seeking	Craves activity and excitement
	Excessive involvement in pleasurable activities
	Elevated or expansive mood; overoptimistic
Conduct problems	Antisocial behavior
Interpersonal violence	Lies for the purpose of harming others
Fails to adopt social norms	Fails to conform to social norms
Addictive behaviors	Fails to honor financial obligations
Juvenile antisocial	
Cognitive distortion	Schizotypal thought
Depersonalization	Depersonalization/derealization
Schizotypal cognition	Magical thinking, ideas of reference, illusions
Brief stress psychosis	

However, in Livesley's structure, pessimism emerged as a (lower level) aspect of identity problems, along with anhedonia, chronic feelings of emptiness, and labile self-concept, which were represented by the symptom clusters of self-derogation and anhedonia in Clark's structure. It is possible that these discrepancies result from differences in the way that the specific terms were used in the different research protocols. A related possibility is that all of these dimensions actually are facets of a broader higher order trait such as neuroticism and that the noted discrepancies represent methodological artifacts. We hope that further investigation into these structures will clarify the various points of divergence.

Although a few discrepancies were noted, when taken as a whole, the two independently derived structures represent a striking congruence in the identified traits of personality disorder. Given their rather diverse theoretical and methodological origins, this remarkable structural convergence suggests that there are a number of robust traits in the domain of personality disorder. Moreover, given that neither investigator limited his or her research to the traits, symptoms, or behaviors defined by the *DSM*, it is likely that these structures have a high degree of generality. That is, although it is possible that additional traits may be identified if new personality disorders were defined, the likelihood is small that these traits

would fall totally outside these structures. Rather, they would probably represent variations on one of the basic themes already identified.

A final noteworthy point is that a comparable number of factors emerged in each of these structures. However, examination of the content of either set of factors suggests that there will be significant intercorrelations among some of the dimensions. Thus, further questions remain regarding (a) whether a consistent higher order level of structure will emerge based on these two sets of dimensions and (b) whether a lower order structure (such as those of Livesley or Clark) or a higher order one (such as the FFM) is more optimal for characterizing the domain of personality-disordered traits. Although a complete answer to these questions awaits more research, it is possible to begin to answer the former on the basis of existing data. We turn now to this question.

Conceptual Convergence With the FFM

In attempting to match the factors across the two solutions, it was helpful initially to group the dimensions into several very broad categories. Because a number of the dimensions (e.g., affective lability and anxiousness, which corresponded to instability–hypersensitivity–anger/aggression and pessimism–negative affect, respectively) had various negative affective states as one of their main components, they were seen as forming a large general category. Similarly, because several factors (e.g., self-centered exploitation, which corresponded to rejection and interpersonal disesteem and passive oppositionality/passive–aggressiveness) suggested antagonistic interpersonal relationships, they were placed together in a larger group.

Next, as described earlier, we used the descriptive facets of each factor to match specific dimensions across the two structures. When this was completed, we reconsidered the issue of broad higher order dimensions. Somewhat to our surprise, the dimensions of the FFM appeared to emerge in broad outline. For example, the factors having negative affective component states seemed to represent the broad dimension of Neuroticism. Similarly, the factors tapping hostile and exploitative interpersonal relationships were characteristic of the higher order dimension of (dis)agreeableness. Extraversion appeared to be represented by factors such as social avoidance (social isolation) and emotional coldness (intimacy problems, restricted expression), whereas compulsivity (conventionality/rigidity) undoubtedly tapped conscientiousness. Finally, cognitive distortion (schizotypal thought) was thought to represent extreme openness.

Although the basic dimensions of the FFM generally appeared to be represented by these traits of personality disorder, several dimensions seemed to be related to more than one of the five factors. For example, suspiciousness was thought perhaps to represent aspects of both neuroticism and (dis)agreeableness, and dependency (insecure attachment, diffidence) was thought to represent a facet of neuroticism, introversion, or both. Furthermore, it was not clear whether conduct problems (antisocial behavior) was better characterized as low conscientiousness (conventionality/rigidity) or (dis)agreeableness.

Fortunately, however, it was not necessary to depend only on content considerations to determine the most optimal categorization of the disordered personality dimensions into the five factors. That is, each of us had collected data investigating our structures in relation to the FFM. Therefore, we turn now to an examination of these empirical data.

Empirical Evidence

We can use the common metric of the FFM to compare the two trait structures of personality disorder to examine three interrelated questions. First, how accurate are our conceptual matches of specific dimensions? If two factors for which we had hypothesized a correspondence were both related to the same FFM domain(s), this would provide evidence regarding the validity of the match. Conversely, if corresponding factors were related to different FFM domains, our hypothesis about their conceptual identity would be called into question. At the very least, the operational measurement of the factors would be shown to be discrepant.

Second, we can use these same data to examine our hypotheses regarding the higher order arrangement of the personality disorder factors. It is conceivable that a pair of factors were accurately matched but that their placement in the FFM was incorrectly hypothesized. Thus, we can ask if the matched dimensions are in fact correlated with the hypothesized FFM domain. Finally, the empirical relations between the five factors and the dimensions of personality disorder will provide evidence regarding those dimensions that were not clearly or easily classified conceptually in terms of the FFM. For example, is the characterization of certain matched factors unclear because they are correlated with more than one FFM domain?

In this section, we describe the results of comparative analyses using three samples. For Sample 1—from which the data on Livesley's 18-factor structure were obtained—the subjects, measures, and procedures are described in chapter 7 of this book. Briefly, 300 general population subjects (150 men, 150 women) completed the DAPP-BQ (Livesley, 1990) and the NEO Personality Inventory (NEO-PI; Costa & McCrae, 1985, 1989).

For Sample 2, the subjects and procedures are described in chapter 6 of this book. In brief, 225 university students (140 women, 85 men) completed the Schedule for Nonadaptive and Adaptive Personality (SNAP; Clark, 1993) and the NEO-PI. Sample 3 consisted of 76 psychiatric patients who participated in an ongoing project comparing interview-based and self-report assessment of personality disorders. These patients completed the SNAP and the Five-Factor

Inventory (FFI; Costa & McCrae, 1989), a short form of the NEO-PI. The FFI scales can be scored from the full NEO-PI completed by the students in Sample 2; therefore, to equate the data derived from Samples 2 and 3, we use FFI scale scores for both samples.

Demographics of Sample 3

The patients (38 women and 38 men) ranged from 18 to 53 years of age ($M = 32.1$, $SD = 8.6$). Most (80%) were White, and 70% of the remainder were Black. The average patient had a high school education (43%), with education levels ranging from seventh grade to postgraduate study. Approximately half (49%) were single, 21% were married, 14% were divorced, and 16% were separated. The majority (59%) were inpatients on one of three units at a state hospital (32% from a substance abuse unit, 14% from a personality disorders unit, and 13% from an acute care unit). The remainder were outpatients from a variety of private and community agencies.

Measures

Symptom Clusters The SNAP is a 375-item self-report inventory in a true–false format that was designed primarily to provide 15 personality trait scale scores (see Appendix E). However, the item pool is constituted so that it also can provide an assessment of the various personality disorder symptoms that constitute the 22 identified clusters. In most cases, two items are provided for each symptom criterion, although in some cases only one or as many as six items represent the criterion. For example, the schizoid personality disorder criterion *rarely, if ever, claims or appears to experience strong emotions, such as anger or joy* is represented by the two items: *It often seems that I simply have no feelings* and *I rarely feel strong emotions such as anger or joy.*

Preliminary scales were constructed for each of the 22 symptom clusters by compiling the SNAP items that represented each of the component symptoms.[1] Scores were derived for each symptom cluster by summing the total number of items endorsed. Internal consistency analyses were then conducted using both Samples 2 and 3. Items with low item–total correlations in both samples were eliminated. Because of limitations in the item pool, one cluster (hypersexuality) was represented by only 4 items, too few to permit the development of a reliable scale. For the other 21 scales, the number of items ranged from 6 (suicide proneness and self-derogation) to 25 (grandiose egocentrism), with an average of 13 items per cluster. Internal consistency reliabilities averaged 0.71 (range = 0.50 for suicide proneness to 0.79 for negative affect and social isolation) in Sample 2 (students) and 0.75 (range = 0.55 for emotional coldness to 0.86 for suspiciousness) in Sample 3 (patients).

Five-Factor Inventory The FFI (Costa & McCrae, 1989) is a 60-item questionnaire developed from the item pool of the NEO-PI using factor analytic methods. Each scale consists of 12 items that most strongly and consistently represent one of the five domains assessed by the NEO-PI. Internal consistency reliabilities in Sample 2 were 0.85 (Neuroticism), 0.80 (Extraversion), 0.67 (Openness), 0.77 (Agreeableness), and 0.82 (Conscienciousness). In Sample 3, the corresponding values were 0.82 (Neuroticism), 0.80 (Extraversion), 0.65 (Openness), 0.81 (Agreeableness), and 0.83 (Conscienciousness).

Empirical Comparison of Two Sets of Personality-Disordered Traits

In each of the three samples, correlations were computed between a measure of the FFM (the NEO-PI in Sample 1 and the FFI in Samples 2 and 3) and either the 18 DAPP-BQ factor scales (Sample 1) or the 21 SNAP-based symptom clusters (Samples 2 and 3). Even in the smallest group, Sample 3 ($n = 76$), correlations of 0.22 or greater were significant at the $p = .05$ level, so it was decided to use a higher cutoff point to represent a conceptually significant correlation, rather than to use statistical significance as an index. Therefore, any DAPP-BQ factor or SNAP cluster that correlated |0.35| or stronger with any FFM scale was identified, as were scales whose highest correlation with any FFM scale was less than |0.35|. The correlations of conceptually matched traits (shown in Table 1) were then examined for the com-

---

[1] An earlier version of the SNAP diagnostic criterion scales was used in these samples.

parability of their correlational patterns with the FFM scales.

The results are shown in Table 2. A scale—and its counterpart(s) in the other structure—was included if it met the conditions just described. Openness was not included because no scales correlated consistently with this domain. To highlight the most salient correlations with the FFM scales, factor or cluster scale names and correlations are shown in boldface type if they represent the strongest correlation with a given FFM scale. For example, Identity Problems correlated +0.67 with Neuroticism and −0.43 with Extraversion. Therefore, it is shown in boldface under Neuroticism and in plain type under Extraversion because its correlation with Neuroticism was its strongest. For the SNAP symptom clusters, scale names are shown in boldface type only if the correlation with a particular FFM scale was the highest in both Samples 2 and 3. Thus, negative affect and pessimism (and their correlations) are shown in boldface under Neuroticism because those were their highest correlations in both the student and patient samples. However, for suspiciousness, the strongest correlation in Sample 3 (patients) was with agreeableness, whereas it was with Neuroticism in Sample 2 (students). Therefore, only the individual correlations (and not the cluster name) are shown in boldface type.

As can be seen in the table, the empirical correspondence of the matched scales was generally quite good. Of the 16 DAPP-BQ scales assessed (self-harm and cognitive distortion were not included in Sample 1), 14 shared their highest correlation with at least one of their SNAP-based counterparts, and 8 showed exactly the same correlational pattern across the two structures in all three samples. Of the six conceptual sets that showed some correlational differences, there were two notable patterns. In three cases, a single Livesley scale had two or more counterparts in Clark's structure, and not all of the counterparts had the same correlational pattern with the five factors as did Livesley's scale. For example, DAPP-BQ stimulus seeking matched with SNAP high energy and impulsivity; and stimulus seeking and high energy were both strongly correlated with Extraversion, whereas impulsivity was not. Impulsivity's highest correlation was with (low) Conscientiousness, which was uncor-

related with stimulus seeking. In other cases, the matched scales showed the same correlation with one FFM scale but not another. For example, DAPP-BQ passive oppositionality and SNAP passive aggressiveness were both strongly (negatively) correlated with Conscientiousness; however, only passive oppositionality showed a strong secondary correlation with Neuroticism.

Of the two sets of matched scales that showed somewhat different patterns, one pair differed only in emphasis. Specifically, DAPP-BQ social avoidance and SNAP social isolation each correlated both with Neuroticism and (negatively) with Extraversion; however, social avoidance correlated more highly with Neuroticism, whereas social isolation correlated more strongly with Extraversion. Thus, of 16 conceptual matches, only one set—narcissism and its counterparts dramatic exhibitionism and grandiose egocentrism—showed markedly different patterns. This and other differences are discussed further subsequently, but first we examine the similarities between the structures in more detail.

Similarities Between the Two Structures in Relation to the FFM

Table 3 summarizes the empirically validated correspondences between conceptually matched scales in Clark's and Livesley's structures. Congruent with previous formulations of this higher order dimension, Neuroticism was characterized by scales assessing negative affects and affective instability; by problems with identity and self-esteem; and by insecurity, dependency, and mistrust in interpersonal relationships. Similarly, the correlates of the domain of Extraversion were consistent with current conceptions of this dimension. Specifically, the low end was characterized by social avoidance and isolation, difficulties in forming close interpersonal relationships, and restricted expression of emotions including anhedonia. In contrast, the high end of the dimension reflected the active and energetic seeking out of arousing stimuli.

Agreeableness was entirely represented by scales tapping the low end of the dimension. Specifically, disagreeableness was characterized by a variety of interpersonal difficulties, including angry, rejecting, unstable, and exploitative relationships; suspicious-

TABLE 2

Correlations Between the NEO Personality Inventory (NEO-PI)/NEO Five-Factor Inventory (FFI) Scales and Two Sets of Personality Disordered Traits

DAPP-BQ factor scales	r^a	SNAP symptom clusters	r^b	r^c
		Neuroticism		
Anxiousness	**0.82**	**Negative affect**	**0.73**	**0.64**
		Pessimism	**0.72**	**0.67**
Affective lability	**0.69**	**Instability**	**0.50**	**0.63**
		Hypersensitivity	0.53	**0.50**
		Anger/aggression	0.17	0.31
Identity problems	**0.67**	**Self-derogation**	**0.32**	**0.38**
		Anhedonia	0.34	0.21
Social avoidance	**0.62**	Social isolation	0.47	0.27
Diffidence	**0.57**	**Dependency**	**0.47**	**0.56**
Insecure attachment	**0.46**			
Passive oppositionality	0.54	Passive–aggressiveness	0.32	0.26
Narcissism	**0.52**	Dramatic exhibitionism	0.00	0.03
		Grandiose egocentrism	0.34	0.25
Self-harm	—[d]	**Suicide proneness**	**0.46**	**0.36**
Suspiciousness	0.36	Suspiciousness	0.41	**0.51**
		Extraversion		
Social avoidance	−0.57	**Social isolation**	**−0.60**	**−0.69**
Stimulus seeking	**0.56**	**High energy**	**0.57**	**0.56**
		Impulsivity	0.10	0.07
Restricted expression	**−0.45**	**Emotional coldness**	**−0.52**	**−0.60**
Intimacy problems	**−0.35**			
Identity problems	−0.43	Anhedonia	−0.54	−0.51
		Self-derogation	−0.26	−0.22
Narcissism	0.14	**Dramatic exhibitionism**	**0.38**	**0.59**
		Agreeableness		
Interpersonal disesteem	**−0.73**	**Self-centered exploitation**	**−0.65**	**−0.69**
Rejection	**−0.52**	**Anger/aggression**	**−0.56**	**−0.55**
Suspiciousness	**−0.59**	Suspiciousness	**−0.60**	−0.50
Conduct problems	**−0.41**	**Antisocial behavior**	**−0.50**	**−0.51**
Narcissism	−0.32	**Grandiose egocentrism**	**−0.47**	**−0.30**
Affective lability	−0.35	Hypersensitivity	**−0.55**	−0.38
		Instability	−0.42	−0.40
		Conscientiousness		
Passive oppositionality	**−0.71**	**Passive–aggressiveness**	**−0.60**	**−0.61**
Compulsivity	**0.63**	**Conventionality/rigidity**	**0.32**	**0.39**
Stimulus seeking	0.02	Impulsivity	−0.38	**−0.45**
Conduct problems	−0.18	Antisocial behavior	−0.44	**−0.44**

Note. DAPP-BQ = Dimensional Assessment of Personality Pathology–Basic Questionnaire. SNAP = Schedule for Nonadaptive and Adaptive Personality. A correlation that is shown in **boldface** indicates the strongest correlation between a factor or cluster and a five-factor measure in a given sample.
[a]Correlation with NEO-PI domain scales; $N = 300$ normal adults.   [b]Correlation with FFI scales; $N = 76$ patients.   [c]Correlation with FFI scales; $N = 225$ university students.   [d]DAPP-BQ self-harm and cognitive distortion factors were unavailable in this sample.

TABLE 3

Similarities Between Two Sets of Personality-Disordered Traits in Terms of the Five-Factor Model (FFM)

FFM scale	DAPP-BQ factor scales	SNAP symptom clusters
Neuroticism	Anxiousness	Negative affect
		Pessimism
	Affective lability	Instability
		Hypersensitivity
	Identity problems	Self-derogation
	Insecure attachment	Dependency
	Diffidence	
	Suspiciousness	Suspiciousness
Extraversion (Introversion)	Social avoidance	Social isolation
	Stimulus seeking	High energy
	Intimacy problems	Emotional coldness
	Restricted expression	
	Identity problems	Anhedonia
(Dis)Agreeableness	Rejection	Self-centered exploitation
	Interpersonal disesteem	Self-centered exploitation
		Anger/aggression
	Suspiciousness	Suspiciousness
	Conduct problems	Antisocial behavior
	Affectivity lability	Instability
		Hypersensitivity
(Low) Conscientiousness	Passive oppositionality	Passive–aggressiveness
	Compulsivity	Conventionality/rigidity

Note. DAPP-BQ = Dimensional Assessment of Personality Pathology–Basic Questionnnaire. SNAP = Schedule for Nonadaptive and Adaptive Personality. Traits are included if they correlated |0.35| or stronger with the same five-factor domain scale in all three samples examined or, if $r < |0.35|$, the correlation was the strongest for that factor or cluster. All scales meeting these conditions had been matched conceptually.

---

ness and hypersensitivity toward others; and overt antisocial behaviors or conduct problems. Finally, the domain of Conscientiousness was readily recognizable in its correlates of passive opposition to cooperation or conformity versus rigid compulsivity and conventionality.

In sum, the factor scales of the DAPP-BQ and the SNAP-based personality disorder symptom clusters are themselves highly convergent and yield an elaborated picture of the FFM that is quite consistent with previous descriptions of these domains. It must be noted, however, that the Openness domain was not represented in these structures of personality-disordered traits and symptoms. It is possible that cognitive distortion, which was not assessed in Sample 1, would be related to Openness, but its SNAP-based conceptual counterpart, eccentric thought, was not consistently related to this domain. Therefore, the importance of Openness in the structure of the traits of personality disorder remains unknown.

Differences Between the Two Structures in Relation to the FFM

An examination of points of divergence between the two structures in relation to the FFM can shed light on the different ways that what is nominally the same trait can be assessed. Conceptual matches between Clark's and Livesley's structures that were not completely confirmed empirically are summarized in Table 4. As mentioned earlier, many of the differences were only partial or reflect complementary differences in the way the scales divided across two higher order dimensions. It is noteworthy that no simple pattern of divergence emerged. That is, of the seven matches that showed some empirical differences in their correlational patterns with the FFM measures, no pattern appeared exactly the same way twice. Therefore, each one is discussed briefly.

Differences in the relations of DAPP-BQ stimulus seeking to its conceptual matches, SNAP-based high energy and impulsivity, have already been mentioned. Specifically, stimulus seeking and high energy both correlated with Extraversion (and impulsivity did not), whereas impulsivity correlated (negatively) with Conscientiousness (and stimulus seeking did not). This suggests that, although stimulus seeking includes items tapping impulsivity and recklessness, they are phrased so that they carry an active, positive emotional tone, whereas SNAP-based impulsivity items more strongly reflect the nonconscientious, irresponsible aspect of recklessness. For example, contrast the stimulus seeking scale item "I like to flirt with danger" with the impulsivity cluster item "I've gotten a lot of speeding tickets." It is noteworthy that the proper placement of impulsivity in the higher order structure of personality traits has been the subject of some debate (Watson & Clark, 1993), with some writers viewing it as a facet of Extraversion (e.g., Eysenck & Eysenck, 1969), some as a facet of Neuroticism (Costa & McCrae, 1985), and still others as a facet of Conscientiousness (Tellegen, 1985). Thus, this discrepancy is not at all unique to personality disorder and may reflect the fact that impulsivity is not a homogeneous dimension but has several different facets.

In a related vein, both DAPP-BQ conduct problems and SNAP antisocial behavior were related to (low) Agreeableness. Only antisocial behavior, however, was correlated also with (low) Conscientiousness. Both scales contain items reflecting irresponsible behavior, so this commonality apparently reflects (low) Agreeableness rather than (low) Conscientiousness. The different correlational patterns suggest that the SNAP antisocial behavior items also imply the rejection of a well-ordered and organized life, whereas the DAPP-BQ conduct problems items do not, although this conclusion is not immediately obvious from an inspection of the item content. Thus, more research is needed to clarify the meaning of the discrepant patterns.

Although it was stated earlier that no two correlational patterns of divergence were exactly the same, there did appear to be one systematic difference between the two structures. That is, in several cases, a DAPP-BQ scale was correlated with both Neuroticism and another of the five-factor dimensions, whereas the corresponding SNAP scale was correlated only with the second dimension and not also with Neuroticism. We mentioned two of these cases earlier. DAPP-BQ social avoidance correlated most strongly with Neuroticism but had a strong secondary (negative) correlation with Extraversion. Its SNAP-based counterpart, social isolation, correlated most highly with Extraversion and correlated strongly with Neuroticism only in Sample 2. This difference appears to correspond to the *DSM*-based distinction between the interpersonal relations of people with avoidant personality disorder and those with schizoid personality disorder. That is, the former are said to both desire and fear social contact, suggesting a negative emotional component to their social avoidance that would link it with the domain of neuroticism. The latter, however, are more affectively disengaged from other people, which suggests introversion more than neuroticism. It is interesting to note that the names provided by Livesley and Clark for their respective dimensions appear to capture the distinction that is represented in their empirical correlations.

DAPP-BQ passive oppositionality and SNAP-based passive aggressiveness represent the second pair of scales in which the DAPP-BQ scale was correlated with Neuroticism and the SNAP-based scale was not. The strongest correlation of both scales was (negatively) with Conscientiousness; however, only passive

---

TABLE 4

Differences Between Two Sets of Personality Disordered Traits in Terms of the Five-Factor Model (FFM)

DAPP-BQ factor	FFM scale	SNAP symptom cluster	FFM scale
Stimulus seeking	Extraversion	Impulsivity	(−) Conscientiousness
Conduct Problems	(−) Agreeableness only	Antisocial behavior	(−) Agreeableness and (−) Conscientiousness
Social avoidance	(−) Extraversion and Neuroticism	Social isolation	(−) Extraversion only
Passive oppositionality	(−) Conscientiousness and Neuroticism	Passive–aggressiveness	(−) Conscientiousness only
Affective lability	(−) Agreeableness and Neuroticism	Anger/aggression	(−) Agreeableness only
Identity problems	Neuroticism and (−) Extraversion	Self-derogation	Neuroticism only
		Anhedonia	(−) Extraversion only
Narcissism	Neuroticism	Dramatic exhibitionism	Extraversion
		Grandiose egocentrism	(−) Agreeableness

Note. DAPP-BQ = Dimensional Assessment of Personality Pathology–Basic Questionnaire. SNAP = Schedule for Nonadaptive and Adaptive Personality. Traits are included if: (a) they were matched conceptually and (b) the factor or cluster from one structure correlated |0.35| or stronger with a particular five-factor domain scale or, if $r < |0.35|$, the scale was the strongest correlate of the factor or cluster, and the corresponding scale from the other structure did not meet either of these empirical conditions.

---

oppositionality was correlated also with Neuroticism. The reason for this phenomenon may lie partly in the history of the development of the SNAP. Because of the overabundance of scales measuring neuroticism (see Watson & Clark, 1984), Clark (1993) was concerned with minimizing the role of this dimension in the SNAP item pool, except for a few scales explicitly designed to tap this domain. Therefore, in developing the SNAP scales, items that correlated |0.35| or higher with a measure of neuroticism were systematically eliminated. Although a number of SNAP scales, nevertheless, still had substantial neuroticism-related variance, this process had the effect of reducing the influence of this highly pervasive dimension. Most likely, the differential pattern of DAPP-BQ and SNAP correlations with five-factor Neuroticism reflects this fact.

The two other cases of differential correlations with Neuroticism both involved one DAPP-BQ scale being matched to more than one SNAP-based cluster. First, affective lability matched SNAP-based instability, hypersensitivity, and anger/aggression. All of these scales correlated (negatively) with Agreeableness; moreover, all but anger/aggression were also correlated with Neuroticism (indeed, this was the stronger correlation in most cases). Thus, the lack of convergence simply reflects the fact that anger/aggression reflects only Agreeableness. This suggests that this cluster emphasizes the overt behavioral aspects of anger/aggression rather than the more subjective affective experience that underlies them, which is consistent with the explanation of the SNAP item pool offered previously.

Second, DAPP-BQ identity problems, which correlated strongly with both Neuroticism and (low) Extraversion, was matched with SNAP-based self-derogation and anhedonia. These scales, rather than both correlating with the two FFM domains, showed relatively independent correlational patterns. That is, self-derogation was related to Neuroticism but not to Extraversion, whereas anhedonia was related to (low) Extraversion but not to Neuroticism. Thus, in this case, two aspects of DAPP-BQ identity problems were tapped separately by the two SNAP-based cluster scales.

Finally, the only match to show a clear and complete divergence in its empirical relations was that between DAPP-BQ narcissism and SNAP-based dramatic exhibitionism and grandiose egocentrism. Interestingly, narcissism was again correlated with Neuroticism, whereas dramatic exhibitionism and grandiose egocentrism were correlated with Extraversion and (low) Agreeableness, respectively. Inspection of the items of each scale suggests reasons for this divergence. Many of the narcissism items concerning attention seeking have a quality of overt neediness and dissatisfaction when these needs are not met. Items include *I need people to reassure me that they think well of me* and *I am only really satisfied when people acknowledge how good I am.* Thus, the items have a negative affective tone that appears to tap the domain of Neuroticism. In contrast, dramatic exhibitionism assesses this need through items that reflect attention-seeking behaviors (e.g., *I wear clothes that draw attention*) and that express positive emotions in connection with receiving attention (e.g., *I like being the topic of conversation*), which may serve to link the scale with Extraversion. In contrast, the grandiose egocentrism items express a haughty sense of being entitled to others' attention (e.g., *I deserve special recognition*) and a sense of indignation when admiration is not forthcoming (e.g., *People don't give me enough credit for my work*), which seem to tap the interpersonal antagonism of (dis)agreeableness.

It should be noted, however, that the narcissism scale is not devoid of positive or grandiose content (e.g., *I like to dramatize things* and *I am destined for greatness*); similarly, both of the SNAP-based scales contain items expressing neediness and/or negative affect (e.g., *I feel a strong need to have others approve of me* and *It irritates me greatly when I am asked to do something I don't want to do*). Thus, the marked lack of convergence in the scales' correlational patterns with the FFM measures remains a bit puzzling. We

hope to shed light on this issue using data currently being collected that will permit a direct examination of the intercorrelations of the SNAP and DAPP-BQ scales, as well as provide additional evidence regarding their correlations with measures of the FFM.

CONCLUSIONS

We have described two rather different approaches to identifying and assessing the basic traits of personality disorder, one of which focused on prototypical traits and behaviors for the various personality disorders, the other of which was based more directly on the criterion symptoms of personality disorder. In addition, we have shown that these diverse strategies nevertheless yielded personality trait structures that were highly comparable in terms of their overt content. Finally, we have demonstrated that measures developed independently to assess these two sets of identified trait dimensions show strongly convergent correlational patterns with measures of the FFM. Moreover, the traits that correlated with each FFM domain clearly represented content consistent with previous interpretation of these higher order dimensions. (It should be noted, however, that Openness was not represented strongly or consistently in the structures.)

Differences in emphasis or focus did emerge for some scales, but most of these were minor, and it is noteworthy that only one pair of scales that were conceptually matched showed no empirical convergence. In general, the DAPP-BQ scales seemed to be more saturated with Neuroticism, and this likely reflects the systematic removal of this variance in the development of the SNAP.

These data thus provide further support for the notion that the personality trait dimensional structure defined by the FFM is very robust and will emerge reliably as long as a broad range of personality traits are assessed. Further research into the observed differences will shed light on the alternative ways that nominally similar constructs of personality disorder can be construed, which will serve to increase understanding of this domain. Finally, more research is needed to determine the role of Openness in personality disorder.

References

Akiskal, H. S., Hirschfeld, R. M., & Yerevanian, B. I. (1983). The relationship of personality to affective disorder. *Archives of General Psychiatry, 40,* 801–810.

American Psychiatric Association. (1980). *Diagnostic and statistical manual of mental disorders* (3rd ed.). Washington, DC: Author.

American Psychiatric Association. (1987). *Diagnostic and statistical manual of mental disorders* (3rd ed., rev.). Washington, DC: Author.

Clark, L. A. (1990). Toward a consensual set of symptom clusters for assessment of personality disorder. In J. N. Butcher & C. D. Spielberger (Eds.), *Advances in personality assessment* (Vol. 8, pp. 243–266). Hillsdale, NJ: Erlbaum.

Clark, L. A. (1993). *Manual for the Schedule for Nonadaptive and Adaptive Personality (SNAP)*. Minneapolis: University of Minnesota Press.

Clark, L. A., McEwen, J. L., Collard, L., & Hickok, L. G. (1991). Symptoms and traits of personality disorder: Two new methods for their assessment. *Psychological Assessment, 5,* 81–91.

Clark, L. A., Pfohl, B., & Blashfield, R. (1991). [Internal consistency analyses of conceptually derived clusters of personality disorder symptoms]. Unpublished raw data.

Cleckley, H. (1964). *The mask of sanity* (4th ed.). St. Louis, MO: Mosby.

Cloninger, C. R. (1987). Neurogenetic adaptive mechanism in alcoholism. *Science, 236,* 410–416.

Cloninger, C. R., Svrakic, D. M., & Przybeck, T. R. (in press). A psychobiological model of temperament and character. *Archives of General Psychiatry.*

Costa, P. T., Jr., & McCrae, R. R. (1985). *The NEO Personality Inventory manual.* Odessa, FL: Psychological Assessment Resources.

Costa, P. T., Jr., & McCrae, R. R. (1989). *The NEO Personality Inventory/NEO Five-Factor Inventory manual supplement.* Odessa, FL: Psychological Assessment Resources.

Eysenck, H. J., & Eysenck, S. B. G. (1969). *Eysenck Personality Inventory manual.* San Diego, CA: EdITS.

Frances, A. J. (1980). The DSM-III personality disorders section: A commentary. *American Journal of Psychiatry, 137,* 1050–1054.

Hathaway, S. R., & McKinley, J. C. (1967). *Minnesota Multiphasic Personality Inventory manual.* New York: Psychological Corporation.

Hyler, S. E., Lyons, M., Rieder, R. O., Young, L., Williams, J. B. W., & Spitzer, R. L. (1990). The factor structure of self-report DSM-III Axis I symptoms and their relationship to clinicians' ratings. *American Journal of Psychiatry, 147,* 751–757.

Kiesler, D. J. (1986). The 1982 interpersonal circle: An analysis of DSM-III personality disorders. In T. Millon & G. L. Klerman (Eds.), *Contemporary directions in psychopathology: Toward the DSM-IV* (pp. 571–597). New York: Guilford Press.

Liebowitz, M. R., & Klein, D. F. (1981). Interrelationship of hysteroid dysphoria and borderline personality disorder. *Psychiatric Clinics of North American, 4,* 67–87.

Livesley, W. J. (1986). Traits and behavioral prototypes of personality disorder. *American Journal of Psychiatry, 143,* 728–732.

Livesley, W. J. (1987). A systematic approach to the delineation of personality disorders. *American Journal of Psychiatry, 144,* 772–777.

Livesley, W. J. (1990). *Dimensional Assessment of Personality Pathology—Basic Questionnaire.* Unpublished manuscript, University of British Columbia, Vancouver, Canada.

Livesley, W. J. (1991). Classifying personality disorders: Ideal types, prototypes, or dimensions? *Journal of Personality Disorders, 5,* 52–59.

Livesley, W. J., Jackson, D., & Schroeder, M. L. (1989). A study of the factorial structure of personality pathology. *Journal of Personality Disorders, 3,* 292–306.

Morey, L. C. (1988). The categorical representation of personality disorders: A cluster analysis of DSM-III-R personality features. *Journal of Abnormal Psychology, 97,* 314–321.

Perry, J. C., & Klerman, G. L. (1978). The borderline patient: A comparative analysis of four sets of diagnostic criteria. *Archives of General Psychiatry, 35,* 141–150.

Presley, A. S., & Walton, H. J. (1973). Dimensions of abnormal personality. *British Journal of Psychiatry, 122,* 269–276.

Schroeder, M. L., Wormworth, J. A., & Livesley, W. J. (1992). Dimensions of personality disorder and their relationship to the Big Five dimensions of personality. *Psychological Assessment, 4,* 47–53.

Tellegen, A. (1985). Structures of mood and personality and their relevance to assessing anxiety, with an emphasis on self-report. In A. H. Tuma & J. D. Maser (Eds.), *Anxiety and anxiety disorders* (pp. 681–706). Hillsdale, NJ: Erlbaum.

Trapnell, P. D., & Wiggins, J. S. (1990). Extension of the Interpersonal Adjective Scales to include the Big Five dimensions of personality. *Journal of Personality and Social Psychology, 59,* 781–790.

Tyrer, P., & Alexander, J. (1979). Classification of personality disorder. *British Journal of Psychiatry, 135,* 163–167.

Watson, D., & Clark, L. A. (1984). Negative affectivity: The disposition to experience unpleasant emotional states. *Psychological Bulletin, 95,* 465–490.

Watson, D., & Clark, L. A. (in press). The positive emotional core of extraversion. In R. Hogan, J. Johnson, &

S. Briggs (Eds.), *Handbook of personality psychology.* San Diego, CA: Academic Press.

Wiggins, J. S. (1982). Circumplex models of interpersonal behavior in clinical psychology. In P. Kendall & J. N. Butcher (Eds.), *Handbook of research methods in clinical psychology* (pp. 183–221). New York: Wiley.

Wiggins, J. S., & Pincus, A. L. (1989). Conceptions of personality disorders and dimensions of personality. *Psychological Assessment: A Journal of Consulting and Clinical Psychology, 1,* 305–316.

Zuckerman, M., Kuhlman, D. M., & Camac, C. (1988). What lies beyond E and N? Factor analyses of scales believed to measure basic dimensions of personality. *Journal of Personality and Social Psychology, 54,* 96–107.

CHAPTER 19

PERSONALITY DISORDERS: CONCEPTUAL DISTINCTIONS AND CLASSIFICATION ISSUES

Theodore Millon

Most of the empirical discoveries and theoretical constructs that have occupied the attention of psychologists and psychiatrists have suffered the fate that General Douglas MacArthur thought unique to old generals, that is, they never die, they just fade away. As Meehl (1978) put it some years ago:

> There is a period of enthusiasm about a new theory, a period of attempted application to several fact domains, a period of disillusionment as the negative data come in, a growing bafflement about inconsistent and unreplicable empirical results, multiple resorts to ad hoc excuses, and then finally people just sort of lose interest in the thing and pursue other endeavors. (p. 807)

Theories, constructs, and findings of such fortune are legion, a sad comment on the "scientific" status of our subject, no less our naive eagerness to follow one evanescent or insubstantial fad after another. Although most conceptual pursuits in the other psychologies have come and gone, justly or otherwise (as others have remained immutably entrenched despite impressive rebuttals or incompatible evidence), there are encouraging signs that cumulative knowledge and a refining process may be under way in the study of personality.

Especially promising is the observation that the essential elements that give substance to personality—the fact that people exhibit distinctive and abiding characteristics—have survived through the ages,

albeit under diverse rubrics and labels. This durability attests, at the very least, either to personality's intuitive consonance with authentic observation, its intrinsic, if naive, human interest, or to its decided and convincing utility. The apparent viability of the concept, as well as its invulnerability in academic circles, is all the more noteworthy when one considers the number of spirited, if misguided, efforts in recent years to undo it. This achievement is even more impressive when one considers the number of recently popular constructs that have faded to a status more consonant with their trivial character or have, under the weight of their scientific inefficacy, succumbed to scholarly weariness or boredom. By contrast, personality and its disorders appear not only to have weathered mettlesome assaults, as witnessed by the position reversals of its most ardent critics (e.g., Mischel, 1973, 1979), but also appear to be undergoing a wide-ranging renaissance in both clinical and scientific circles. This resurgence may be worth elaborating briefly because it signifies the coalescence of powerful, if disparate, trends.

First, from a rather mundane and practical viewpoint, most mental health practitioners use their professional skills today in outpatient rather than inpatient settings. Their "clients" are no longer the severely disturbed "state hospital" psychotics but ambulatory individuals seen in private offices or community clinics; these clients are beset with personal stressors, social inadequacies, or interpersonal conflict, which are typically reported in symptoms such as anxiety, depression, or alcoholism but which signify the outcroppings of long-standing patterns of maladaptive behaving, feeling, thinking, and relating: in other words, their "personality style."

Second, a few words should be said concerning the special role of recent third and third, revised editions of the *Diagnostic and Statistical Manual of Mental Disorders* (*DSM-III* and *DSM-III-R*, respectively; American Psychiatric Association, 1980, 1987) in giving prominence to the personality disorders. With this official system, personality not only gained a place of consequence among syndromal categories but became central to its multiaxial schema. The logic for assigning personality its own axis is more than a matter of differentiating syndromes of a more acute and dramatic form from those that may be overlooked by virtue of their long-standing and prosaic character. More relevant to this partitioning decision was the assertion that personality can serve usefully as a substrate of affective, cognitive, and behavioral dispositions from which clinicians can better grasp the "meaning" of their patients' more transient or florid disorders. In the recent *DSMs*, then, personality disorders have not only attained a nosological status of prominence in their own right, but they have also been assigned a contextual role that makes them fundamental to the understanding of other psychopathologies.

Third, there has been a marked shift in the focus of psychological therapies from that of "surface" symptoms to that of "underlying" personality functions (Beck & Freeman, 1990). This reorientation reflects an intriguing evolution that has been shared among diverse theories since the mid-part of this century. Auchincloss and Michels (1983) describe this progression in an illuminating review of the analytical concept of "character." They wrote, "Today it is generally accepted that character disorders, not neurotic symptoms, are the primary indication for analysis. . . . Psychoanalysis (as a technique) and character analysis have become synonymous" (p. 2). Recent contributions of ego, self, and object-relations theorists have extended the awareness of the highly varied consequences of early psychic difficulties. Today, character structure is seen not only as a system of defensive operations but as a complex organization of structures that are the focus of therapeutic attention and intervention. Similar shifts in emphasis are also evident in the recent writings of cognitive–behavioral and interpersonal therapeutic theorists.

It is not only the changing patient population of clinical practice or the recently evolved role given character in both therapeutic theory and the *DSM* that signifies the growing prominence of the construct. In the realms of "hard science," that of quantitative assessment and psychometrics, psychologists and psychiatrists alike have turned their skills toward the reliable identification and valid measurement of the new "disorders" of personality. This focus may be seen most clearly in the content of recently developed clinical instruments. These assessment tools contrast in scope and intent with both the historically important projective techniques, such as the Rorschach, and well-established, nondynamic objective inventories such as the Minnesota Multiphasic Personality Inventory (Hathaway & McKinley, 1967). Newly minted are a group of impressively constructed clinical interview schedules, such as the diagnostic interview to assess patients for borderline personality disorder (Gunderson, Kolb, & Austin, 1981), which seek to build a composite picture of a single, comprehensive entity, in this case the "borderline personality," or the broadly based self-report inventory, the Millon Clinical Multiaxial Inventory (Millon, 1977, 1987), with its psychometrically validated series of scales designed to identify and describe the dynamics of all 13 *DSM-III-R* and fourth edition *DSM* (*DSM-IV*; American Psychiatric Association, in press) Axis II disorders. As this book attests, an effort is now underway to bridge the traditional focus of psychologists on personality traits and factors with the renewed scientific examination of personality disorders. It is a rapprochement that I very much favor (Millon, 1990), viewing the present volume as an important step in fostering this long overdue reconciliation of methods and perspectives. Although I am not as convinced as are the editors of this book that their specific approach is the most fruitful one available, I have no doubt that it will spark fresh ideas and insights to guide ongoing empirical studies and theoretical analyses.

This chapter is divided into two sections: The first part addresses matters that are related to defining the constructs of personality and personality disorders themselves, and the second part examines issues that are related to alternate conceptions of how the different personality disorders may best be classified.

CONCEPTUAL DISTINCTIONS

Opinions differ concerning how best to define personality, normal or otherwise. There is general agreement, however, that personality is an inferred abstraction, a concept or a construct, rather than a tangible phenomenon with material existence. Problems inevitably arise, however, when professionals reify these conceptual constructs into substantive entities. To paraphrase Kendell (1975), "familiarity leads us to forget their origins in human imagination." The disorders of personality should certainly not be construed as palpable "diseases." They are man-made constructions that have been invented to facilitate scientific understanding and professional communication.

Personality and Personality Disorders
What Should the Constructs of Personality and Personality Disorder Represent? Personality may be conceived as the psychological equivalent of the human body's biological system of structures and functions. The body as a whole comprises a well-organized yet open system of relatively stable structures that interconnect functionally as they process a wide range of both internal and external events in a coherent and efficient manner. The diversity of functions carried out by the body is awesome in its complexity and efficacy, as is the internal organization of structures that are impressively elaborate in their intricacy and articulation. The distinctive configuration of structures and functions that have evolved ensures that the system as a whole remains both viable and stable. This is achieved by processes that maintain internal cohesion and by actions that use, control, or adapt to external forces. A biological disorder arises when one or several of the following occurs: (a) the balance and synchrony among internal components go awry; (b) a particular structure is traumatized or deteriorates, with the result that it repetitively or persistently malfunctions; or (c) foreign entities such as bacteria or viruses intrude themselves, either overwhelming or insidiously undermining the system's integrity.

The construct of personality may be conceived as a psychic system of structures and functions that parallels that of the body. It is not a potpourri of unrelated traits and miscellaneous behaviors but a tightly knit organization of stable structures (e.g., internalized memories and self-images) and coordinated functions (e.g., unconscious mechanisms and cognitive processes). Given continuity in one's constitutional equipment and a narrow band of experiences for learning behavioral alternatives, this psychic system develops an integrated pattern of characteristics and inclinations that are deeply etched, cannot be easily eradicated, and pervade every facet of the life experience. This system is the sum and substance of what the construct of personality would "mean." Mirroring the body's organization, the psychic system is a distinctive configuration of interlocking perceptions, feelings, thoughts, and behaviors that provides a template and disposition for maintaining psychic viability and stability. From this perspective, personality disorders would be best conceived as stemming from failures in the system's dynamic pattern of adaptive competencies. Just as physical ill health is never a simple matter of an intrusive alien virus but reflects also deficiencies in the body's capacity to cope with particular physical environments, so too is psychological ill health not merely a product of psychic stress alone but represents deficiencies in the personality system's capacity to cope with particular psychosocial environments.

Implied in the preceding paragraph is the assertion that adequate clinical analyses of both physical and mental disorders require data beyond those that inhere in the individual alone. In the biological realm, it must encompass knowledge of relevant features of the physical environment; in the psychological domain, it calls for an awareness of the character of the psychosocial environment. Kendell (1975) points to the reciprocal nature of this person–environment field in the following example:

> A characteristic which is a disadvantage in one environment may be beneficial in another. The sickle cell trait is a deviation from the norm which in most environments produces a slight but definite biological disadvantage. In an environ-

*ment in which malaria is endemic, how-
ever, it is positively beneficial. . . . This is
a particularly serious matter where mental illness is concerned because here the
environment, and especially its social
aspects, is often of paramount importance. Qualities like recklessness and
aggressiveness, for example, may lead a
man to be regarded as a psychopath in
one environment and to be admired in
another. (p. 15)*

For the greater part of the history of psychodi-
agnostics, attention has focused on the patient's
internal characteristics alone. When one moves to
an ecological perspective (Millon, 1990), external
social and interpersonal dynamics are given equal
status. As noted in Kendell's illustration, it may be
clinically impossible to disentangle these elements
when appraising the clinical consequences of an
internal characteristic, for example, whether the
sickle cell trait is advantageous or disadvantageous.
For diagnostic purposes, internal and external factors are inextricably linked elements. Intrapsychic
structures and dispositions are essential, but they
will prove functional or dysfunctional depending
on their efficacy in specific interpersonal, familiar,
or social contexts.

The rationale for broadening the notion of a
disorder to include the interplay of both internal
and external systems is especially appropriate when
evaluating personality pathology. Not only does
personality express itself in everyday, routine interactions within group and familiar settings, but the
ordinary characteristics that compose the patient's
personality will elicit reactions that feed back to
shape the future course of whatever impairments
the person may already have. Thus, the behaviors,
mechanisms, and self-attitudes that individuals
exhibit with others will evoke reciprocal responses
that influence whether their problems will
improve, stabilize, or intensify. It is not only how
experiences are processed intrapsychically, therefore, but also how social and familiar dynamics
unfold that will determine whether the patient
functions in an adaptive or maladaptive manner.

Historically, personality disorders have been in
a tangential position among psychopathological
syndromes, never having achieved a significant
measure of recognition in the literature of either
abnormal psychology or clinical psychiatry. Until
recently, they have been categorized in the official
nomenclature with a melange of other, miscellaneous, and essentially secondary syndromes. The
advent of *DSM-III* changed this status radically.
With the *DSM-III* multiaxial format, which was a
significant breakthrough in its own right (Williams,
1985a, 1985b), personality pathologies comprise,
by themselves, one of only two required "mental
disorder" axes. Henceforth, diagnoses assess not
only the patient's current symptom picture, via
Axis I, but in addition, those pervasive features
that characterize the enduring personality pattern,
as recorded on Axis II. In effect, the revised multiaxial format requires that symptom states no
longer be diagnoses as clinical entities isolated
from the broader context of the patient's lifelong
style of relating, coping, behaving, thinking, and
feeling—that is, his or her personality.

This conception of personality breaks the long-
entrenched habit of conceiving syndromes of psychopathology as one or another variant of a disease, that is, some "foreign" entity or lesion that
intrudes insidiously within the person to undermine his or her so-called normal functions. The
archaic notion that all mental disorders represent
external intrusions or internal disease processes is
an offshoot of prescientific ideas such as demons or
spirits that ostensibly "possess" or cast spells on
the person. The role of infectious agents and ana-
tomical lesions in physical medicine reawakened
this archaic view. Of course, personality researchers no longer believe in demons, but many still
hold the conception of some alien or malevolent
force invading or unsettling the patient's otherwise
healthy status.

Such naive notions carry little weight among
modern-day medical and behavioral scientists.
Given the increasing awareness of the complex
nature of both health and disease, modern scientists recognize that most physical disorders result
from a dynamic and changing interplay between
individuals' capacities to cope and the environment

within which they live. It is the patients' overall constitutional makeup—their vitality, stamina, and immune system—that serves as substrate that inclines them to resist or succumb to potentially troublesome environmental forces. Psychopathological disorders should be conceived as reflecting the same interactive pattern. Here, however, it is not the immunological defenses or enzymatic capacities but the patient's personality pattern— that is, coping skills and adaptive flexibilities—that determines whether the person will master or succumb to his or her psychosocial environment. Just as physical ill health is likely to be less a matter of some alien virus than a dysfunction in the body's capacity to deal with infectious agents, so too is psychological ill health likely to be less a product of some intrusive psychic strain than a dysfunction in the personality's capacity to cope with life's difficulties. Viewed this way, the structure and characteristics of personality become the foundation for the individual's capacity to function in a mentally healthy or ill way.

Differentiating Normal From Disordered Personalities

No sharp line divides normal from pathological behavior; they are relative concepts representing arbitrary points on a continuum or gradient. Not only is personality so complex that certain areas of psychological functioning operate normally while others do not, but environmental circumstances change such that behaviors and strategies that prove adaptive at one time fail to do so at another. Moreover, features differentiating normal from abnormal functioning must be extracted from a complex of signs that not only wax and wane but often develop in an insidious and unpredictable manner.

Pathology results from the same forces that are involved in the development of normal functioning. Important differences in the character, timing, and intensity of these influences will lead some individuals to acquire pathological structures and functions, whereas others develop adaptive ones. When an individual displays an ability to cope with the environment in a flexible manner, and when his or her typical perceptions and behaviors foster increments in personal satisfaction, then the person may be said

to possess a normal or healthy personality. Conversely, when average or everyday responsibilities are responded to inflexibly or defectively, or when the individual's perceptions and behaviors result in increments of personal discomfort or curtail opportunities to learn and to grow, then we may speak of a pathological or maladaptive pattern.

Numerous attempts have been made to develop definitive criteria for distinguishing psychological normality from abnormality. Some of these criteria focus on features that characterize the so-called normal, or ideal, state of mental health (e.g., Offer & Sabshin, 1974; others have sought to specify theoretically grounded criteria for concepts such as normality or abnormality; see Millon, 1991b). The most common criterion used is a statistical one in which normality is determined by those behaviors that are found most frequently in a social group; and pathology or abnormality, by features that are uncommon in that population. Among diverse criteria used to signify normality are a capacity to function autonomously and competently, a tendency to adjust to one's environment effectively and efficiently, a subjective sense of contentment and satisfaction, and the ability to self-actualize or to fulfill one's potentials. Psychopathology would be noted by deficits among the preceding.

Differentiating Personality Disorders From Other Psychopathologies

Although the term *disorder* is used as a label for all of the major syndromes of the official nosology, current classification systems can go awry if their categories encompass too wide a range of clinical conditions. There is a need to subdivide the subject of psychopathology along useful points of distinction. As discussed in Millon (1987, 1990), a logical framework for a taxonomy of mental disorders would be one based on several theoretically grounded dimensions and bipolarities that lend themselves to quantitative distinctions. At the simplest level, they would be differentiated by the degree to which manifest pathological processes fall on a continuum from "circumscribed" (focal) to "pervasive" (systemic) and on a continuum from "transient" (acute) to "enduring" (chronic). It is largely on the basis of these two simple distinctions that differentiations may be made among personality disorders, clinical syndromes, and adjustment reactions.

Differentiating Personality Disorders, Clinical Syndromes, and Adjustment Reactions

Reflecting the two polarities of circumscribed–pervasive and transient–enduring is the extent to which observed pathologies can be attributed to ingrained traits or internal characteristics versus recent stressors or external precipitants. As previously discussed, pathology always reflects a person–environment interaction. Nevertheless, it is useful to distinguish types of pathology in terms of the extent to which their determinants derive from personological versus situational forces, an issue that evoked considerable debate in the field of personality research during the past 2 decades.

Personality disorders (Axis II) are best conceived as those conditions that are "activated" primarily by internally embedded structures and pervasive ways of functioning. At the opposite end of this person–situation or internal–external continuum are the adjustment reactions, which are best construed as specific pathological responses attributable largely to circumscribed environmental precipitants. Between these polar extremes lie what have been termed *clinical syndromes* (Axis I), that is, categories of psychopathology that are anchored more or less equally and simultaneously to internal personal attributes and external situational events. Exhibited as intensifications of a patient's characteristic style of functioning or as disruptions in his or her underlying psychic make-up, clinical syndromes are conceived as responses to situations for which the individual's personality structure is notably vulnerable.

Viewed from a different perspective, the attributes that compose personality have an inner momentum and autonomy; they are expressed with minimal inducement or external provocation. In contrast, the responses that compose adjustment reactions are conceived as stimulus-specific. They not only operate independently from the individual's personality but are elicited by events that are apt to be judged consensually as "objectively" troublesome. Clinical syndromes are similar to adjustment reactions (both compose Axis I of the *DSM*) in that they are prompted also by external events, but their close connection to inner personality traits results in the intrusion of memories and affects that complicate what might otherwise be a simple response to the environment. Hence, these syndromes often fail to "make objective sense," often appearing irrational and strangely complicated. To the knowledgeable clinician, however, these syndromes signify the presence of an unusual vulnerability on the part of the patient; in effect, a seemingly neutral stimulus has reactivated a painful hidden memory or emotion. Viewed in this manner, clinical syndromes arise in individuals who are encumbered with notably adverse biological dysfunctions or early experiences.

Unfortunately, the rather neat conceptual distinctions that I have just made are not readily observed in the "real" world of clinical conditions. Interaction and overlap will almost always blur the boundaries that have been drawn given that psychopathologies are rarely qualitatively distinct "disease entities."

Interrelationships Among Personality Disorders and Clinical Syndromes

The view that mental disorders are composed of distinct entities reflects the personality research field's level of scientific development rather than the intrinsic nature of psychopathological phenomena. Hempel (1961), for example, noted that in their early stages all sciences tend to order their variables into separate or discrete classes. As progress occurs, advanced methods of analysis become available to enable scientists to deal with the interplay of elements comprising their field and, thereby, specify how formerly unconnected characteristics overlap and interrelate. It would appear, then, that as personological and psychopathological sciences progress, syndromes are likely to be conceived less as discrete independent entities but more as converging and reciprocal entities that exhibit both interconnected and distinct features (Grove & Tellegen, 1991).

A step toward the twin goals of differentiation and coordination was taken in *DSM-III*, in which the two major axes are separate yet interrelated. Axis I consists of the clinical syndromes—those symptom states that wax and wane in their severity over time and that display themselves as the more acute and dramatic forms of psychopathology. On Axis II are found the personality disorders, which represent the more enduring and pervasive characteristics that often underlie, and provide a context for understanding, the more florid and transient Axis I symptomatologies. Each axis is recorded separately, yet they are conceived as representing interrelated clinical features. In its multiaxial construction, *DSM-III* sought to encourage clinicians to explore relationships among diagnostic categories. It was hoped that clinical syndromes would no longer be seen as standing on their own as discrete entities; rather, they would be viewed as precursors, extensions, or substrates for one another. More specifically, the clinical syndromes would be understood, at least in part, to be disruptions of functioning among the personality disorders, springing forth, so to speak, to dominate the clinical picture under stressful or otherwise vulnerable circumstances. Envisioned in this fashion, clinical syndromes are not distinct diagnostic entities but are interrelated with complex personality characteristics.

How are these two elements of clinical psychopathology likely to be related (Docherty, Feister, & Shea, 1986)? Of the numerous explanations offered to account for these relationships, the most widely held possibility is that personality is etiological, that is, that personality disorders precede the onset of the clinical syndrome and therefore establish a vulnerability to symptom formation (Klerman, 1973). This viewpoint, which is most heavily supported by psychoanalytic theorists, emphasizes the developmental history and early family environment as factors that shape individuals and predispose them to the clinical states of anxiety, worthlessness, or dejection (McCranie, 1971).

A related explanation of the connection between the two axes is that certain personalities may repeatedly create stressful life circumstances that precipitate development of clinical episodes (Akiskal, Khani, & Scott-Strauss, 1979). Illustrative of this are borderline personalities with their erratic lifestyle and propensity toward tumultuous relationships and self-destructive behaviors.

In a related hypothesis, characterological features may render an individual vulnerable to certain psychosocial stressors. The growing body of research on stress events, anxiety, and depression reflects the mounting interest in this theory. Studies have shown that depressions are frequently preceded by stressful

events that are often associated with separation or loss (Paykel, Myers, & Dienelt, 1970). Because not all people who experience stress become anxious or depressed, it is felt that a genetic predisposition and/or life history factors (e.g., personality style, effectiveness of coping mechanisms, or available supports) may predispose certain individuals toward a clinical outcome (Becker, 1977). The dependent individual, for example, tends to be quite susceptible to feelings of anxiety and depression under the conditions of interpersonal loss, abandonment, or rejection.

Another explanatory approach suggests that many personality disorders may actually represent subclinical manifestations of major clinical syndromes (Akiskal, Hirschfeld, & Yerevanian, 1983; Akiskal et al., 1979). From this perspective, lifelong affective traits or "affective personalities" (e.g., the cyclothymic personality) may represent gradual stages of transition to full syndromic affective episodes (e.g., manic–depressive illness). Similarly, the schizotypal personality disorder may be a dilute form of schizophrenia, and the avoidant personality disorder may be a chronic and pervasive variant of clinical anxiety or social phobia.

It has also been argued that rather than increasing vulnerability to a clinical state such as depression, personality may exert a pathoplastic effect, that is, it colors and molds the particular expression of the clinical symptoms (Paykel, Klerman, & Prusoff, 1976). Depending on the premorbid personality, symptoms such as hopelessness, anxiety, or self-deprecation may serve a variety of goals. In this hypothesis, the secondary gains of certain clinical states may elicit nurturance from others, excuse the avoidance of unwanted responsibilities, rationalize poor performance, or safely permit the expression of anger toward others. Partly determined by the gains received, clinical syndromes may take the form of dramatic gestures, irritable negativism, passive loneliness, or philosophical intellectualization.

Docherty et al. (1986) offered another possible basis for the comorbidity of certain Axis I and Axis II disorders, one they termed the *coeffect thesis*. As they state it:

> *This model proposes that the personality disorder and the syndrome disorder are*

*separate psychobiological structures. How-
ever, it is proposed that they both arise
from a common cause or third factor, a
single disease process that generates both
entities. In this model, neither the personality disorder nor the syndrome disorder is
causative of the other. They are simply correlates. Each is caused by a common third
variable. For example, a particular form of
child-raising experience may give rise to
dependent personality and also, independently, to vulnerability to depressive episodes. (p. 317)*

Not to be overlooked in these patterns of relationship
is the evidence that personality characteristics may
influence a clinically disturbed individual's response
to both psychopharmacological and psychotherapeutic treatment (Akiskal et al., 1980; Charney, Nelson,
& Quinlan, 1981).

CLASSIFICATION ISSUES

Whatever data are included to provide the substantive body of a classification, personological or otherwise, decisions must be made concerning the
framework into which the nosology will be cast, the
rules that will govern the classes into which the clinical attributes and defining features will be placed,
and the compositional properties that will characterize these attributes and features (Millon, 1991a).
These issues deal with the overall architecture of the
nosology, regardless of whether it is organized hori-
zontally, vertically, or circularly; regardless of
whether all or only a limited and fixed subset of features should be required for class membership;
regardless of whether its constituents should be conceived as categories or dimensions; and regardless of
whether they should be based on manifest observables or latent features, as well as a host of other differentiating characteristics from which one may
choose. A few of the more significant of these elements and the choices to be made among them are
discussed in this section, a task of no simple proportions because there is nothing logically self-evident,
nor is there a traditional format or contemporary
consensus to guide selections among these alterna-

tives (Grove & Tellegen, 1991; Gunderson, Links, &
Reich, 1991; Livesley, 1991).

Because reliable and useful classifications were
developed long before the advent of modern scientific thought and methods acquired by intelligent
observation and common sense alone, what special
values are derived by applying the complicated and
rigorous procedures required in developing explicit
criteria, categorical homogeneity, and diagnostic efficiency? Is rigor, clarity, precision, and experimenta-
tion more than a compulsive and picayunish concern
for details, more than the pursuit for the honorific
title of "science"? Are the labors of differentiating
clinical attributes or exploring categorical cutting
scores in a systematic fashion worth the time and
effort involved?

There is little question in this "age of science" that
the answer would be yes. But why? What are the distinguishing virtues of precision in one's terminology,
the specification of observable conceptual referents,
and the analysis of covariant attribute clusters? What
sets these procedures apart from everyday methods
of categorizing knowledge? Most relevant, is conceptual definition and classification possible in the
domain of personological disorders? Can these most
fundamental of scientific activities be achieved in a
subject that is inherently inexact and of only modest
levels of intrinsic order, that is, a subject in which
even the very slightest variations in context or ante-
cedent conditions—often of a minor or random character—produce highly divergent consequences
(Bandura, 1982)? Because this "looseness" within the
network of variables in psychic pathology is unavoidable, are there any grounds for believing that such
endeavors could prove more than illusory? Persuasive
answers to these questions that are of a more philosophical nature must be bypassed in this all-too-con-
cise chapter; those who wish to pursue this line of
analysis would gain much by reading, among others,
Pap (1953), Hempel (1965), and Meehl (1978). In
the following section I discuss, albeit briefly, a more
tangible and psychologically based rationale for
believing that formal classification in personality
pathology may prove to be at least a moderately
fruitful venture.

Can Personality Disorders Be Classified?

There is a clear logic to classifying "syndromes" in
medical disorders. Bodily changes wrought by infec-

tious diseases and structural deteriorations repeatedly display themselves in a reasonably uniform pattern of signs and symptoms that "make sense" in terms of how anatomic structures and physiological processes are altered and then dysfunction. Moreover, these biological changes provide a foundation not only for identifying the etiology and pathogenesis of these disorders but also for anticipating their course and prognosis. Logic and fact together enable one to construct a rationale to explain why most medical syndromes express themselves in the signs and symptoms they do, as well as the sequences through which they unfold.

Can the same be said for personological and psychopathological classifications? Is there logic, or perhaps evidence, for believing that certain forms of clinical expression (e.g., behaviors, cognitions, affects, mechanisms) cluster together as do medical syndromes; that is, not only covary frequently but make sense as a coherently organized and reasonably distinctive group of characteristics? Are there theoretical and empirical justifications for believing that the varied features of personality display a configurational unity and expressive consistency over time? Will the careful study of individuals reveal congruency among attributes such as overt behavior, intrapsychic functioning, and biophysical disposition? Is this coherence and stability of psychological functioning a valid phenomenon, that is, not merely imposed on observed data by virtue of clinical expectation or theoretical bias?

There are reasons to believe that the answer to each of the preceding questions is yes. Stated briefly and simply, the observations of covariant patterns of signs, symptoms, and traits may be traced to the fact that people possess relatively enduring biophysical dispositions, which give a consistent coloration to their experience, and that the range of experiences to which people are exposed throughout their lives is both limited and repetitive (Millon, 1969, 1981). Given the limiting and shaping character of these biogenic and psychogenic factors, it should not be surprising that individuals develop clusters of prepotent and deeply ingrained behaviors, cognitions, and affects that clearly distinguish them from others of dissimilar backgrounds. Moreover, once a number of the components of a particular personality pattern

are identified, knowledgeable clinicians can trace the presence of other, unobserved but frequently correlated features comprising that pattern.

If one accepts the assumption that most people do display a pattern of internally consistent characteristics, then one is led next to the question of whether groups of patients evidence commonality in the patterns that they display. The notion of clinical categories rests on the assumption that there are a limited number of such shared covariances, for example, regular groups of diagnostic signs and symptoms that can confidently be used to distinguish certain classes of patients. (It should be noted that because patients can profitably be classified into categories does not negate the fact that patients, so classified, display considerable differences as well, differences that are routinely observed with medical diseases.)

Another question that must be addressed concerning the nature of personological categories may be phrased best as follows: Why does the possession of characteristic A increase the probability, appreciably beyond chance, of also possessing characteristics B, C, and so on? Put in a less abstract way, why do particular behaviors, attitudes, mechanisms, and so on, covary in repetitive and recognizable ways rather than exhibit themselves in a more-or-less haphazard fashion? Put in an even more concrete way, why do behavioral defensiveness, interpersonal provocativeness, cognitive suspicion, affective irascibility, and excessive use of the projection mechanism co-occur in the same individual rather than be uncorrelated and randomly distributed among different individuals?

The "answers" are, first, that temperament and early experience simultaneously effect the development and nature of several emerging psychological structures and functions; that is, a wide range of behaviors, attitudes, affects, and mechanisms can be traced to the same origins, which thereby leads to their frequently observed covariance. Second, once an individual possesses these initial characteristics, they set in motion a series of derivative life experiences that shape the acquisition of new psychological attributes that are causally related to the characteristics that preceded them in the sequential chain. Common origins and successive linkages increase the probability that certain psychological characteristics will frequently be found to pair with specific others, which thereby results in repetitively observed symptom or trait clusters. Illustrations of these reciprocal covariances and serially unfolding concatenations among longitudinal influences (e.g., etiology) and concurrent attributes (e.g., signs, traits) may be found in Millon (1969, 1981, 1990).

Although grievances itemizing the inadequacies of both current and historical systems of classification have been voiced for years, as are suggestions that endeavors to refine these efforts are fussy and misdirected, if not futile and senseless pretensions that should be abandoned, the presence of such systems is both unavoidable—owing to humankinds's linguistic and attribution habits—as well as inevitable—owing to humankind's need to differentiate and record, at the very least, the most obvious of dissimilarities among the psychologically impaired. Given the fact that one or another set of classes is inevitable, or as Kaplan (1964, p. 279) once phrased it, "it is impossible to wear clothing of no style at all," it would appear both sensible and fitting that one should know the explicit basis upon which such distinctions are to be made, rather than have them occur helter-skelter in nonpublic and nonverifiable ways. Furthermore, if personality pathology is to evolve into a true science, then its diverse phenomena must be subject to formal identification, differentiation, and quantification procedures. Acts such as diagnosis and assessment presuppose the existence of discernable phenomena that can be recognized and measured. Logic necessitates, therefore, that psychopathological states and processes be distinguished from one another, being thereby classified or grouped in some manner before they can be subjected to identification and quantification.

Whatever data are included to provide the substantive body of a classification system, decisions must be made concerning the structural framework into which the groupings will be fit, the rules that will govern the clinical attributes and defining features selected, and the compositional properties that will characterize these attributes. These issues deal with the overall architecture of the classification, regardless of whether its constituents should be conceived as categories or dimensions, as well as a host of other differentiating characteristics from which one

may choose. A number of the more significant of these structural elements, and the choices to be made among them, have been discussed in this section, a task of no simple proportions because there is nothing logically self-evident, nor is there a traditional format or contemporary consensus to guide selections among these alternatives (for a fuller discussion of this topic see Millon, 1987; Frances & Widiger, 1986).

Categorical Types, Dimensional Traits, and Prototypal Models

Important differences separate medical from psychological traditions in their approach to classifying their primary subject domains. Psychology's substantive realms have been approached with considerable success by using methods of dimensional analysis and quantitative differentiation (e.g., intelligence measures, aptitude levels, trait magnitudes, etc.). By contrast, medicine has made its greatest progress by increasing its accuracy in identifying and categorizing discrete disease entities. The issue separating these two historical approaches as it relates to the subject domain of personality disorders may best be examined by posing the following: Should personality pathology be conceived and organized as a series of dimensional traits that combine to form a unique profile for each individual, or should certain central characteristics be selected to exemplify and categorize personality types found commonly in clinical populations?

The view that personality pathology might best be conceived as dimensional traits has only recently begun to be taken as a serious alternative to the more classic categorical approach. Certain trait dimensions have been proposed in the past as relevant to these disorders (e.g., dominance–submission, extraversion–introversion, and rigidity–flexibility), but these have not been translated into the full range of personality syndromes. Some traits have been formulated such that one extreme of a dimension differs significantly from the other in terms of their clinical implications; an example would be emotional stability versus emotional vulnerability. Other traits are psychologically curvilinear such that both extremes have negative implications; an example of this would be found in an activity dimension such as listlessness versus restlessness.

There are several advantages to dimensional models that should be noted. Most important is that they combine several clinical features or personality traits into a single profile. By their comprehensiveness, little information of potential significance is lost, nor is any single trait given special attention, such as when only one distinctive characteristic is brought to the foreground in a categorical typology. Furthermore, a trait profile permits the inclusion of unusual or atypical cases; in typologies, odd, infrequent, or "mixed" conditions often are excluded because they do not fit the prescribed categories. Given the diversity and idiosyncratic character of many clinical personalities, a dimensional system encourages the representation of individuality and uniqueness rather than "forcing" patients into categories for which they are ill-suited. Another advantage of a dimensional format is that the strength of traits is gauged quantitatively, and therefore, each characteristic extends into the normal range; as a consequence, normality and abnormality are merely arranged as points on a continuum rather than as distinct and separable phenomena.

Despite their seeming advantages, dimensional systems have not taken strong root in the formal diagnosis of personality pathology. Numerous complications and limitations have been noted in the literature, and these are briefly noted.

First is the fact that there is little agreement among dimensional theorists concerning the number of traits necessary to represent personality. Historically, for example, Menninger (1963) contended that a single dimension would suffice; Eysenck (1960) asserted that three are needed; whereas Cattell (1965) claimed to have identified as many as 33 and believes there are many more. However, recent models, most notably the five-factor model (FFM; Costa & McCrae, 1990; Goldberg, 1990; Norman, 1963), have begun to achieve a modest level of consensus. The problem here is that theorists may "invent" dimensions that are in accord with their expectations rather than "discovering" them as if they were intrinsic to nature, merely awaiting scientific detection. The number of traits or factors required to assess personality may not be determined by the ability of research to disclose some inherent truth but rather by predilections for conceiving studies and organizing the data they generate (Kline & Barrett, 1983; Millon, 1990).

Second, describing personality with more than a few trait or factor dimensions may produce complex profiles or intricate configurations that require algebraic or otherwise resourceful representation. There is nothing intrinsically wrong with such quantitative and original schemata, but they may pose considerable difficulty in comprehension, as well as require inventive syntheses among clinicians. Not only are most mental health workers hesitant about working with multivariate statistics or innovative configurations, but the consequent feeling that one is lost in one's own professional discipline is not likely to make such schemata attractive, much less practical for everyday use. Apart from matters of convenience and comfort, innovative representations are likely themselves to be grouped into categories before their commonalities and differences can be communicated. In effect, once a population has been identified as possessing a similar profile or dimensional pattern, it will likely become a category. Thus, although the original format may have been a factorial or dimensional pattern, it will likely become a category, and those who are grouped within a particular category will invariably be spoken of as a "type."

Categorical models have been the preferred schema for representing both clinical syndromes and personality disorders. It should be noted, however, that most contemporary categories neither imply nor are constructed to be all-or-none typologies. Although categorical models single out and give prominence to certain features of behavior, they do not overlook the other features but merely assign them lesser significance. It is this process of assigning centrality or relative dominance to particular characteristics that distinguishes a schema of categories from one composed of trait dimensions. Conceived in this manner, a type simply becomes a superordinate category that subsumes and integrates psychologically covariant traits that, in turn, represent a set of correlated habits that, in their turn, stand for a response displayed in a variety of situations. When this superordinate type is found with some frequency in clinical populations, there is reason to conclude that it may be useful as a concept that gives coherence to seemingly diverse symptoms.

Among the advantages of categorical typologies is their ease of use by clinicians who must make relatively rapid diagnoses with large numbers of patients whom they see briefly. Although clinical attention in these cases is drawn to only the most salient features of the patient, a broad range of traits that have not been directly observed are strongly suggested. It is this capacity to suggest characteristics beyond those immediately observed that adds special value to an established system of types. For example, if one assumes that an individual is diagnosed as a histrionic personality following the observation that his or her behaviors were seductive and dramatic, then, although the database is limited, there is reason to believe that this individual is also likely to be characterized as stimulus-seeking, needful of attention, interpersonally·capricious, emotionally labile, and so on. In effect, assignment to a particular type or category often proves useful by alerting the clinician to a range of unobserved but frequently correlated behaviors. This process of extending the scope of associated characteristics contrasts with the tendency of dimensional schemata to fractionate personality into separate and uncoordinated traits. Typologies restore and recompose the unity of personality by integrating seemingly diverse elements into a single coordinated syndrome. Moreover, the availability of well-established syndromes provides standard references for clinicians who would otherwise be faced with repeated analyses and de novo personality constructions.

There are, of course, objections to the use of categorical typologies in personality. They contribute to the fallacious belief that psychopathological syndromes are discrete entities, even medical diseases, when, in fact, they are merely concepts that help focus and coordinate observations. Furthermore, categories often fail to identify and include important aspects of behavior because they reflect a decision to narrow the list of characteristics that are considered primary. Of course, the discarding of information is not limited to categories; dimensional schemata also choose certain traits or factors to the exclusion of others. The problem, however, is that categorical types tend to give primacy to only a single characteristic. Another criticism is that the number and diversity of types are far less than the individual

differences observed in clinical work. Not only are there problems in assigning many patients to the limited categories available, but clinicians often claim that the more they know a patient, the greater the difficulty they have in fitting him or her into a single category. A final criticism reflects the diversity of competing systems available; numerous classifications have been formulated in the past century, and one may question whether any system is worth using if there is so little consensus among categorists themselves. Is it possible to conclude from this review that categorical or dimensional schemata are potentially the more useful for personality classifications? An illuminating answer may have been provided by Cattell, who wrote:

> *The description by attributes [traits] and the description by types must . . . be considered face and obverse of the same descriptive system. Any object whatever can be defined either by listing measurements for it on a set of [trait] attributes or by sequestering it to a particular named [type] category. (1970, p. 40)*

In effect, Cattell concluded that the issue of choosing between dimensional traits and categorical types is both naive and specious because they are two sides of the same coin. The essential distinction to be made between these models is that of comprehensiveness. Types are higher order syntheses of lower order dimensional traits; they encompass a wider scope of generality. For certain purposes it may be useful to narrow attention to specific traits; in other circumstances a more inclusive level of integration may be appropriate (Grove & Tellegen, 1991).

There is another, more recent, solution to the question of how the data of personality pathology might best be organized. The construct "prototype" has a long history, but only recently has it been introduced as a potentially useful option for classifying psychopathology. As presently formulated it appears to meld several attributes of both categorical and dimensional schemata. It may prove especially apt as personality researchers seek to develop a format for representing both the composite of diverse elements that comprise personality (the dimensional aspect) as well as the features that distinguish personality from other forms of psychopathology, namely, its durability and pervasiveness (the categorical aspect).

Cantor, Smith, French, and Mezzich (1980) noted that the "classical" approach to diagnosis depends on the identification of singly necessary or jointly sufficient features. By contrast, the prototypal view merely requires that sets be composed of correlated features. As a result of this conceptual openness,

> *prototypes permit extensive heterogeneity of category instances. Thus, one instance may contain most of the correlated features of the prototype and another may contain hardly any at all. . . . Prototypes make sense out of variations in typicality, where typical instances are simply those that share many correlated features with the category prototype. . . . The higher the overlap, the faster, more accurately, and more confidently the instance can be classified. An immediate consequence of this prototype-matching process is that typical instances will be categorized more efficiently than atypical ones, because typical instances have greater featural overlap with their prototypes. . . . To the degree that the prototypes for two categories have many common features and few distinctive ones, the categorizer may have difficulty distinguishing between members of these categories. . . . There is one more factor that must be considered in a prototype-matching process. This factor reflects the degree of richness of a category prototype (as measured by the total number of its features) as well as the distinctiveness of the prototype (as measured by the number of its features that are not shared by rival categories). (Cantor et al., 1980, pp. 184–185)*

It is evident that the prototype approach shares many of the attributes associated with the dimensional approach, notably the diversity of the correlated traits and symptoms involved and, hence, the heterogeneity found among similarly diagnosed patients. Albeit

implicitly, the prototype model guided the thinking of several *DSM* Task Force members who formulated both the rules and diagnostic criteria of the manual, for example, the opportunity to select only a subset of the criteria that composed a category, the presence of "mixed" syndromes, and even the encouragement of multiple diagnoses. Cantor et al. (1980) observed that these *DSM* changes

> *help to emphasize, rather than obscure, the probabilistic nature of diagnostic categorizations. On the basis of the new manual, clinicians can now be trained to expect heterogeneity among patients and to recognize the probabilistic nature of diagnostic categorization. Also, utilization of confidence/typicality ratings in diagnosis can be encouraged, and diagnoses can be made on the basis of degree of fit between the patient's clusters of symptoms and the prototypes for various different categories. (p. 192)*

Diverging from a single, overarching attribute that characterizes a categorical typology, the prototype concept appears well suited to represent the pervasive and durable features that distinguish personality disorders from the frequently transient and narrowly circumscribed expressive sphere of the clinical syndromes.

The fact that some diagnostic classes in contemporary nosologies (e.g., *DSM-III, International Classification of Diseases–9th Revision* [World Health Organization, 1991]) are composed essentially of a single clinical feature (e.g., depression), whereas others encompass several mixed features (e.g., histrionic personality), has not only confounded discussions of categoricality versus dimensionality but has contributed a share of confusion to theory, research, and practice, as well.

Skinner (1986) has elaborated several "hybrid models" in an effort to integrate elements of a number of divergent schemata. In what he termed the *class-quantitative* approach, efforts are made to synthesize quantitative dimensions and discrete categories. Likewise, Livesley (1986a, 1986b) has formulated a schema to bridge both conceptual models.

I previously described an endeavor of a similar nature (Millon, 1984, 1986, 1990). Termed the *prototypal domain model*, this schema mixes categorical and dimensional elements in a personological classification. As in the official *DSM* schema, several criteria are specified for each disorder, but these criteria encompass a large set of clinical domains (e.g., mood/temperament, cognitive style). It is the diagnostic criterion that is conceived to be prototypal, not the personality as a whole. Each specific domain is given a prototypal standard for each personality. To illustrate: If the clinical attribute "interpersonal conduct" was deemed of diagnostic value in assessing personality disorders, then a specific prototypal criterion would be identified to represent the characteristic or distinctive manner in which each personality disorder ostensibly conducts its interpersonal life.

By composing a classification schema that includes all relevant clinical domains (e.g., self-image, expressive acts, interpersonal conduct, cognitive style) and that specifies a prototypal feature for every domain for each of the personality disorders, the proposed format would then be fully comprehensive in its clinical scope and possess directly comparable prototypal features for its parallel diagnostic categories. A schema of this nature would furnish both detailed substance and clinical symmetry to its taxonomy.

To enrich this schema's qualitative categories (the several prototypal features comprising the clinical range seen in each domain) with quantitative discriminations (numerical intensity ratings), clinicians would not only identify which prototypal features (e.g., distraught, hostile, labile) in a clinical domain (e.g., mood/temperament) best characterizes a patient, but they would record a rating or number (e.g., from 1 to 10) to represent the degree of prominence or pervasiveness of the chosen feature(s). Clinicians would be encouraged in such a prototypal schema to record and quantify more than one feature per clinical domain (e.g., if suitable, to note both "distraught" and "labile" moods, should their observations lead them to infer the presence of two prototypal characteristics in that domain).

The prototypal domain model illustrates that categorical (qualitative distinction) and dimensional (quantitative distinction) approaches need not be framed in opposition, much less be considered mutually exclusive. Assessments can be formulated to (a) recognize qualitative (categorical) distinctions in what prototypal features best characterize a patient, which thereby permits the multiple listing of several such features, and (b) differentiate these features quantitatively (dimensionally) so as to represent their relative degrees of clinical prominence or pervasiveness. The prototypal domain approach includes the specification and use of categorical attributes in the form of distinct prototypal characteristics, yet this approach allows for a result that permits the diversity and heterogeneity of a dimensional schema.

Manifest and Latent Taxa

The major classes of nosological systems are called *taxa* (singular: *taxon*); they may be differentiated in a number of ways. What may be labeled as *manifest taxa* involve classes that are based on observable or phenotypic commonalities (e.g., overt behaviors). *Latent taxa* pertain to groupings formed on the basis of abstract mathematical derivations (factor or cluster analysis) or the propositional deductions of a theory, each of which ostensibly represents the presence of genotypic commonalities (e.g., etiologic origins or trait similarities).

The polar distinction between manifest taxa, at the one end, and latent taxa, at the other, represents in part a broader epistemological dichotomy that exists between those who prefer to use data derived from observational contexts versus those who prefer to draw their ideas from more theoretical or mathematically deduced sources. A parallel distinction was first drawn by Aristotle when he sought to contrast the understanding of disease with reference to knowledge of latent principles—which ostensibly deals with all instances of a disease, however diverse, versus direct observational knowledge, which deals presumably only with specific and individual instances. To Aristotle, knowledge that is based on direct experience alone represented a more primitive type of knowledge than that informed by mathematics or conceptual theory which could, through the application of principles, explain not only why a particular disease occurs but illuminate commonalities among seemingly diverse ailments. This same theme was raised in the writings of the distinguished 19th century neurologist, Hughlings Jackson. For example, Jackson drew a distinction between two kinds of disease classifications: The first, termed *theoretical*, was designed to advance the state of knowledge; the second, termed *clinical*, was organized for routine or daily practice. Both were seen as necessary, but Jackson asserted that with each elucidation of a contemporary disease there would be an accretion of theory, which would result in the ultimate supplanting of "mere" clinical knowledge.

Manifest Clinical Taxa For the greater part of history (Zilboorg & Henry, 1941; Menninger, 1963), psychiatric taxonomies were formed on the basis of clinical observation, that is, the witnessing of repetitive patterns of behavior and emotion among a small number of carefully studied mental patients. Etiologic hypotheses were generated to give meaning to these patterns of covariance (e.g., Hippocrates anchored differences in observed temperament to his humoral theory, and Kraepelin distinguished two major categories of severe pathology—dementia praecox and manic–depressive disease—in terms of their ostensive divergent prognostic course). The elements comprising these theoretic notions were post hoc, however; they were imposed after the fact on prior observational data, rather than serving as a generative source for taxonomic categories. The most recent example of a clinical taxonomy—one tied explicitly to phenomenological observation and constructed by intention to both atheoretical and nonquantitative elements—is, of course, the *DSM-III*. Spitzer, chairperson of the *DSM* Task Force, stated in *DSM-III* (American Psychiatric Association, 1980) that "clinicians can agree on the identification of mental disorders on the basis of their clinical manifestations without agreeing on how the disturbances came about" (p. 7).

Albeit implicitly, *DSM-III* is a product of speculation regarding latent causes or structures. Nevertheless, a major goal of the *DSM* Task Force was to eschew theoretic notions, while adhering to as strict an observational philosophy as possible. In doing so, only those attributes that could be readily seen or consensually validated were to be permitted as diagnostic criteria. Numerous derelictions from this epistemology are notable, nevertheless, especially among the personality disorders, for which trait ascriptions call for inferences beyond direct sensory inspection.

Not all who seek to render taxa on the basis of observational clinical data insist on keeping latent inferences to a minimum (Tversky, 1977); and by no means do those who draw their philosophical inspiration from a manifest mindset restrict themselves to the mere specification of surface similarities (Medin, Altom, Edelson, & Freko, 1982). It is not only those who use mathematical procedures and who formulate theoretically generated nosologies who "succumb" to the explanatory power and heuristic value of pathogenic or structural inferences. Feinstein (1977), a distinguished internist, provides an apt illustration of how one person's "factual" observations may be another's latent inference. As Feinstein put it:

> *In choosing an anchor or focus for taxonomy, we can engage in two distinctly different types of nosologic reasoning. The first is to form names, designations or denominations for the observed evidence, and to confine ourselves exclusively to what has actually been observed. The second is to draw inferences from the observed evidence, arriving at inferential titles representing entities that have not actually been observed. For example, if a patient says "I have substantial chest pain, provoked by exertion, and relieved by rest," I, as an internist, perform a denomination if I designate this observed entity as angina pectoris. If I call it coronary artery disease, however, I perform an inference, because I have not actually observed coronary artery disease. If a radiologist looking at a coronary arteriogram or a pathologist cutting open the coronary vasculature uses the diagnosis coronary artery disease, the decision is a denomination. If the radiologist or pathologist decides that the coronary disease was caused by cigarette smoking or by a high fat diet, the etiologic diagnosis is an inference unless simultaneous evidence exists that the patient did indeed smoke or use a high fat diet. (p. 192)*

In large measure, clinically based taxa gain their importance and prominence by virtue of consensus and authority. Cumulative experience and habit are crystallized and subsequently confirmed by official bodies such as the various *DSM* committees (Millon, 1986). Specified criteria are denoted and articulated; these criteria then acquire definitional, if not stipulative, powers—at least in the eyes of those who come to accept the selected manifest clinical attributes as infallible taxonomic indicators.

Latent Mathematical Taxa   Inasmuch as manifest clinical taxa stem from the observations and inferences of diagnosticians, they comprise, in circular fashion, the very qualities that clinicians are likely to see and deduce. Classes so constructed will not only direct future clinicians to focus on and mirror these same taxa in their patients, but they may lead future nosologists away from potentially more useful constructs with which to fathom less obvious patterns of attribute covariation. As noted earlier, it is toward the end of penetrating beneath the sensory domain to more latent commonalities that taxonomists have turned to either numerical methods or to theoretical principles. It is the former that will be examined in this section.

Andreasen and Grove (1982) summarized the advantages of what they variously term empirical or numerical methods of computing patient similarities as follows:

> First, the empirical method gives an opportunity for the observed characteristics of the subjects to determine the classification and perhaps to lead to a classification that the clinician was unable to perceive using clinical judgment alone. Second, the empirical method allows a great deal of information on the subjects to enter into the genesis of the classifications; human beings can keep in mind only a relatively small number of details concerning a case at any given time, but the empirical approach can process very large sets of measurements. Third, empirical or numerical approaches can combine cases in more subtle ways than can clinicians; combinations of features too complex to grasp intuitively may yield bet-

ter classifications than simple combinations. (p. 45)

There has been a rapid proliferation of new and powerful mathematical techniques for both analyzing and synthesizing vast bodies of clinical data. This expansion has been accelerated by the ready availability of inexpensive computer hardware and software programs. Unfortunately, such mushrooming has progressed more rapidly than its fruits can be digested. As a consequence, to quote Kendell (1975), who commented early in this technological development, "most clinicians . . . have tended to oscillate uneasily between two equally unsatisfactory postures of ignoring investigations based on these techniques, or accepting their confident conclusions at face value" (p. 106).

There are numerous purposes to which this growing and diverse body of quantitative methods can be put, of which only a small number are relevant to the goal of aiding in taxonomic construction. Other statistical techniques relate to the validation of existent nosologies (e.g., discriminant analyses) rather than to their creation. Among those used to facilitate taxonomic development, some focus on clinical attributes as their basic units, whereas patients themselves are the point of attention of others. For example, factor analysis condenses sets of clinical attributes and organizes them into syndromic taxa. Cluster analysis, by contrast, is most suitable for sorting the characteristics of patients on the basis of their similarities into personological taxa. A brief review of the former technique is appropriate in this chapter; other mathematical procedures that may usefully be used in taxonomic construction and evaluation, such as latent class, log-linear, and discriminant analysis, as well as multivariate analysis of variance, may be examined in a number of relevant texts.

Factorial techniques represent relationships among attributes (signs, symptoms) and have their primary value in identifying core dimensions. Although subsequent research suggests the contrary, early reviewers concluded that their statistical properties render them unsuitable to the task of uncovering personal similarities or to optimally classify individuals (Torgerson, 1968; Zubin, 1968).

The notion that the presence of covarying symptoms might signify underlying disease entities can be traced to the 17th-century writings of Thomas Synchenham. In connecting this notion to factor analytic techniques, Blashfield (1984) commented:

> *Sydenham, who promoted the concept of syndrome ... argued that a careful observer of patients could note that certain sets of symptoms tended to co-occur. If these co-occurring sets of symptoms were seen repeatedly across a number of patients, this observance would suggest that the syndrome may represent more than a chance collection of symptoms. Instead, the consistent appearance of a syndrome would suggest a disease with a common etiology and a common treatment. Factor analysis ... can be thought of as a statistical tool used to isolate syndromes of co-occurring symptoms. ... In addition, factor analysis provides a statistical estimate of the "underlying factor" that explains the association among a collection of related symptoms. (pp. 169–170)*

The designation *factor analysis* is a generic term encompassing a variety of numerical procedures that serve to achieve different goals, the details of which are not relevant to this chapter. In essence, it seeks to reveal the underlying structure of its attributes by identifying factors that account for the covariation of the attributes. Toward this end, linear combinations of the attributes are sequentially chosen to cumulate as much variance as possible. Factors that are derived in this manner are often "rotated" after their initial mathematical solution to increase their psychological meaning.

Despite the ostensively productive lines of investigation that factorial techniques have demonstrated (a book such as this is clear evidence for its utility), several problems continue to be raised concerning its applicability as an instrument of classification construction. Thus, early in the application of factorial techniques, Kendell (1975) reported that skepticism in the field remains high,

largely because of the variety of different factor solutions that can be obtained from a single set of data and the lack of any satisfactory objective criterion for preferring one of these to the others. The number of factors obtained and their loadings are often affected considerably by relatively small changes in the size or composition of the subject sample, or in the range of test employed. (p. 108)

Furthermore, Sprock and Blashfield (1984) concluded that

> *deciding when to stop the process of selecting the number of factors, rotating the solutions, and interpreting the factors are all highly subjective and at the discretion of the user. Therefore, many distrust the results. (p. 108)*

In addition to these methodological caveats, a number of conceptual forewarnings must be kept in mind regarding the structural implications of a factorial approach. As is known among those involved in the development of psychometric instruments (Loevinger, 1957; Millon, 1977, 1986), a reasonable degree of "fidelity" should exist between the pattern of relationships among the scales of a test and its structural model of psychopathology. For the same reasons, taxa should conform in their pattern of relationships to their taxonomy's structural conception (Smith & Medin, 1981). For example, assume that a model of psychopathology posits its taxa as both monothetic and independent, that is, each containing exclusive and uncorrelated attributes. If that is how psychopathology has been conceived, then a factorial structure would fit it handsomely: The attributes comprising each taxa would not only intercorrelate positively, but they correlate negatively with all of the other taxa comprising the nosology. Factors would exhibit fidelity to such a psychopathological model.

However, and despite the popularity of factor analysis with many a distinguished psychometrician, the psychological composition of factorial structures is far from universally accepted. Not only do few psychopathological entities give evidence of factorial "purity" or attribute independence, but factorial solutions tend to be antithetical to the predominant polythetic structure and overlapping relationships that exist among clinical conditions. Neither personological nor syndromic taxa consist of entirely homogeneous and discrete clinical attributes. Rather, taxa are composed of diffuse and complex characteristics that share many attributes in common, factorially derived or otherwise.

Nevertheless, the existence of this book demonstrates the growing literature and impressive findings that support one such model, the FFM (Costa & McCrae, 1990; Digman, 1990; Goldberg, 1990; McCrae & Costa, 1985; Norman, 1963). Costa and McCrae have provided strong evidence for the power of the "Big Five" as a latent mathematical framework for unraveling diverse and more complex structures of numerous other personality instruments. In their recent writings they have extended the applicability of these five factors as descriptive underpinnings for the *DSM-III* personality disorders. It is this view that comprises both the intent and substance of the present book. This is not the chapter or setting for such purposes, but it should be noted in passing that other equally astute and productive investigators have registered a measure of dissent from both the sufficiency of scope of the FFM or its adequacy as a latent explicator of the personality disorders (Grove & Tellegen, 1991; Livesley, 1991; Tellegen & Waller, 1987; Waller & Ben-Porath, 1987). Beyond these skeptics of the fruitfulness of the FFM are those who question the wisdom of using latent mathematical methods at all. In his usual perspicacious manner, Kendell's comment of more than a decade ago (1975), upon reviewing the preceding 20-year period, may be judged by some as no less apt today as then:

> *Looking back on the various studies published in the last twenty years it is clear that many investigators, clinicians and statisticians, have had a naive, almost Baconian, attitude to the statistical techniques they were employing, putting in all data at their disposal on the assumption that the computer would sort out the relevant from the irrelevant and expose the underlying*

> *principles and regularities, and assuming all that was required of them was to collect the data assiduously beforehand. Moreover, any statistician worth his salt is likely to be able, by judicious choice of patients and items, and of factoring or clustering procedures, to produce more or less what he wants to. (p. 118)*

To summarize, factorial methods of taxonomic construction may rest on a model that does not automatically accord with the combinations and covariations that characterize the intrinsic structure of pathology. Despite these caveats, factor analytic methods may yet prove helpful as a tool to identify and clarify certain of the more central attributes that comprise these complex taxa. The task of combining factor attributes into patterns and configurations that correspond to the personality disorders is one that transcends the powers of mathematical technique. To achieve this task one must still depend on clinical "artistry" or the deductive powers of a theory-based model, which is another approach to uncovering latent principles for constructing a nosology, and one that is addressed in the following section.

Latent Theoretical Approaches The biases of statisticians in shaping data are likely to be implicit or arcane, whereas those of taxonomic theorists are explicit and straightforward. For the most part, the concepts and orientations of theorists are stated as plainly as their subject permits, although the propositions and deductions they derive therefrom rarely are as empirically clear as one might wish.

Nevertheless, distinguished philosophers such as Hempel (1965) and Quine (1977) considered that mature sciences must progress from an observationally based stage to one that is characterized by abstract concepts, or theoretical systemizations. It is the judgment of these philosophers that classification alone does not make a true scientific taxonomy and that overt similarity among attributes does not necessarily comprise a scientific category (Smith & Medin, 1981). The card catalog of the library or an accountant's ledger sheet, for example, are well-organized classifications but can hardly be viewed as a taxonomy or a science.

The characteristic that distinguishes *latent theoretical taxonomy* from latent mathematical taxonomy is its success in grouping its elements according to logically consonant explanatory propositions. These propositions are formed when certain attributes that have been isolated or categorized have been shown or have been hypothesized to be dynamically or causally related to other attributes or categories. The latent taxa comprising a theoretical nosology are not, therefore, mere collections of overtly similar factors or categories but are linked or unified into a pattern of known or presumed relationships among them. This theoretically grounded configuration of relationships would be the foundation and essence of a heuristic taxonomy.

Certain benefits can be derived from systematizing data in a theoretical fashion that are not readily available either from clinical or numerical procedures (Wright & Murphy, 1984). Given the countless ways of observing and analyzing a set of data, a system of explanatory propositions becomes a useful guide to clinicians as they sort through and seek to comprehend the stream of amorphous signs and chaotic symptoms they normally encounter. Rather than shifting from one aspect of behavior, thought, or emotion to another, according to momentary and uncertain impressions of importance, theoretically guided clinicians may be led to pursue in a logical and perhaps more penetrating manner only those aspects that are likely to be related and to experience thereby a sense of meaningful order (Dougherty, 1978). In addition to furnishing this guidance, a theoretically anchored taxonomy provides diagnosticians with a consistent set of hypotheses concerning clinical relationships that they may not have observed before. It enlarges the sensitivity and scope of knowledge of observers by alerting them to previously unnoticed relationships among attributes and then guides these new observations into a theoretically coherent body of knowledge.

Before concluding this chapter, I ask: What is it that distinguishes a theoretically grounded taxonomy from one that provides a mere explanatory summary of known observations and inferences?

Simply stated, the answer lies in its power to generate observations and relationships other than those used to construct it. This generative power is what

Hempel (1965) termed the "systematic import" of a scientific classification. In contrasting what are familiarly known as "natural" (theoretically guided, deductively based) and "artificial" (conceptually barren, similarity-based) classifications, Hempel wrote (1965):

> *Distinctions between "natural" and "artificial" classifications may well be explicated as referring to the difference between classifications that are scientifically fruitful and those that are not; in a classification of the former kind, those characteristics of the elements that serve as criteria of membership in a given class are associated, universally or with high probability, with more or less extensive clusters of other characteristics. (p. 116)*
>
> *Classification of this sort should be viewed as somehow having objective existence in nature, as "carving nature at the joints" in contradistinction of "artificial" classifications, in which the defining characteristics have few explanatory or predictive connections with other traits. In the course of scientific development, classifications defined by reference to manifest, observable characteristics will tend to give way to systems based on theoretical concepts. (p. 148)*

DSM-III and *DSM-III-R* were developed intentionally and explicitly to be atheoretical. This stance was taken not from an antipathy to theory per se but rather to maximize acceptance of the document by clinicians of diverse viewpoints. Extolling the tenets in the *DSM* of one or another theoretical school would, it was believed, alienate those holding dissimilar perspectives and thereby disincline them from adopting and using the manual.

It is unfortunate that the number of theories that have been advanced to "explain" personality and psychopathology is directly proportional to the internecine squabbling found in the literature. Paroxysms of "scientific virtue" and pieties of "methodological purity" rarely are exclaimed by theorists themselves but are by their less creative disciples. As I have previously commented (Millon, 1969):

Theories arise typically from the perceptive observation and imaginative speculation of creative scientists. This innovator is usually quite aware of the limits and deficiencies of his "invention" and is disposed in the early stages of his speculation to modify it as he develops new observations and insights. Unfortunately, after its utility has been proven in a modest and limited way, the theory frequently acquires a specious stature. Having clarified certain ambiguities and survived initial criticisms, it begins to accumulate a coterie of disciples. These less creative thinkers tend to accept the theory wholeheartedly and espouse its superior explanatory powers and terminology throughout the scientific market place. They hold to its propositions tenaciously and defend it blindly and unequivocally against opposition. In time it becomes a rigid and sacred dogma and, as a result, authority replaces the test of utility and empirical validity. Intelligent men become religious disciples; their theory is a doctrine of "truth," not a guide to the unknown. (p. 41)

Ostensibly toward the end of pragmatic sobriety, those of an antitheory bias have sought to persuade the profession of the failings of premature formalization, warning that one cannot arrive at the future yearned for by lifting the science of psychology by its own bootstraps. To these individuals, there is no way to traverse the road other sciences have traveled without paying the dues of an arduous program of empirical research. Formalized axiomatics, they say, must await the accumulation of "hard" evidence that is simply not yet in. Shortcutting the route with ill-timed theoretical systematics, such as a latent taxonomy, will lead the profession down primrose paths, preoccupying its attentions as it winds fruitlessly through endless detours, each of which could be averted by holding fast to an empirical philosophy or a clinical methodology.

No one argues against the view that theories that float, so to speak, on their own, unconcerned with the empirical domain or clinical knowledge, should

be seen as the fatuous achievements they are, and the travesty that these theories may make of the virtues of a truly coherent nosological system should not be overlooked. Formal theory should not be "pushed" far beyond the data, and its derivations should be linked at all points to established clinical observations. Given the vast scope of personalities as well as the extent of knowledge still to be gathered, nosological theories are best kept limited today in both their focus and their specificity. As I have stated previously (Millon, 1987), structurally weak theories make it impossible to derive systematic and logical nosologies; this results in conflicting derivations and circular reasoning. Most nosological theories of psychopathology have generated brilliant deductions and insights, but few of these ideas can be attributed to their structure, the precision of their concepts, or their formal procedures for hypothesis derivation.

Nevertheless, impressive theoretical concepts with taxonomic implications continue to be generated by contemporary thinkers in the field of personality disorders; a forthcoming book composed of chapters authored by a group of such theorists attests to the maturity of this model of taxonomic construction (Kernberg et al., in press).

In conclusion, and despite the shortcomings of historical concepts of personality pathology, latent mathematic models and latent theories may "facilitate a deeper seeing, a more penetrating vision that goes beyond superficial appearances to the order underlying them" (Bowers, 1977). The present volume should contribute substantively to this "deeper and more penetrating vision."

References

Akiskal, H. S., Hirschfeld, R., & Yerevanian, B. (1983). The relationship of personality to affective disorders. *Archives of General Psychiatry, 40*, 801–810.

Akiskal, H. S., Khani, M. K., & Scott-Strauss, A. (1979). Cyclothymic temperamental disorders. *Psychiatric Clinics of North America, 2*, 527–554.

Akiskal, H. S., Rosenthal, T. L., Paykal, R. F., Lemmi, H., Rosenthal, R. H., & Scott-Strauss, A. (1980). Characterological depressions: Clinical and sleep EEG findings separating "subaffective dysthymias" from "character-spectrum disorders." *Archives of General Psychiatry, 37*, 777–783.

American Psychiatric Association. (1980). *Diagnostic and statistical manual of mental disorders* (3rd ed.). Washington, DC: Author.

American Psychiatric Association. (1987). *Diagnostic and statistical manual of mental disorders* (3rd ed., rev.). Washington, DC: Author.

American Psychiatric Association. (in press). *Diagnostic and statistical manual of mental disorders* (4th ed.). Washington, DC: Author.

Andreasen, N., & Grove, W. (1982). The classification of depression: A comparison of traditional and mathematically derived approaches. *American Journal of Psychiatry, 139,* 45–52.

Auchincloss, E. L., & Michels, R. (1983). Psychoanalytic theory of character. In J. P. Frosch (Ed.), *Current perspectives in personality disorders* (pp. 3–19). Washington, DC: American Psychiatric Press.

Bandura, A. (1982). The psychology of chance encounters and life paths. *American Psychologist, 37,* 747–755.

Beck, A. T., & Freeman, A. (1990). *Cognitive therapy of personality disorders.* New York: Guilford Press.

Becker, J. (1977). *Affective disorders.* New York: General Learning Press.

Blashfield, R. K. (1984). *The classification of psychopathology.* New York: Plenum.

Bowers, K. S. (1977). There's more to Iago than meets the eye. In D. Magnusson & N. S. Endler (Eds.), *Personality at the crossroads* (pp. 112–131). Hillsdale, NJ: Erlbaum.

Cantor, N., Smith, E. E., French, R. D., & Mezzich, J. (1980). Psychiatric diagnosis as prototype categorization. *Journal of Abnormal Psychology, 89,* 181–193.

Cattell, R. B. (1965). *The scientific analysis of personality.* Chicago: Aldine.

Cattell, R. B. (1970). The integration of functional and psychometric requirements in a quantitative and computerized diagnostic system. In A. R. Mahrer (Ed.), *New approaches to personality classification* (pp. 9–52). New York: Columbia University Press.

Charney, D. S., Nelson, J. C., & Quinlan, D. M. (1981). Personality traits and disorder in depression. *American Journal of Psychiatry, 138,* 1601–1604.

Costa, P. T., Jr., & McCrae, R. R. (1990). Personality disorders and the five-factor model of personality. *Journal of Personality Disorders, 4,* 362–371.

Digman, J. M. (1990). Personality structure: Emergence of the five-factor model. *Annual Review of Psychology, 41,* 417–440.

Docherty, J. P., Feister, S. J., & Shea, T. (1986). Syndrome diagnosis and personality disorder. In A. Frances & R. E. Hale (Eds.), *American Psychiatric Association Annual Review* (Vol. 5, pp. 315–355). Washington, DC: American Psychiatric Association.

Dougherty, J. W. D. (1978). Salience and relativity in classification. *American Ethnologist, 5,* 66–80.

Eysenck, H. J. (1960). *The structure of human personality.* London: Routledge & Kegan Paul.

Feinstein, A. R. (1977). A critical overview of diagnosis in psychiatry. In V. M. Rakoff, H. C. Stancer, & H. B. Kedward (Eds.), *Psychiatric diagnosis* (pp. 189–206). New York: Brunner/Mazel.

Frances, A., & Widiger, T. (1986). The classification of personality disorders: An overview of problems and solutions. In A. Frances & R. E. Hale (Eds.), *American Psychiatric Association Annual Review* (Vol. 5, pp. 240–257). Washington, DC: American Psychiatric Association.

Goldberg, L. R. (1990). An alternative "description of personality": The Big-Five factor structure. *Journal of Personality and Social Psychology, 59,* 1216–1229.

Grove, W. M., & Tellegen, A. (1991). Problems in the classification of personality disorders. *Journal of Personality Disorders, 5,* 31–41.

Gunderson, J. G., Kolb, J. E., & Austin, V. (1981). The diagnostic interview for borderline patients. *American Journal of Psychiatry, 138,* 896–903.

Gunderson, J. G., Links, P. S., & Reich, J. H. (1991). Competing models of personality disorders. *Journal of Personality Disorders, 5,* 60–68.

Hathaway, S. R., & McKinley, J. C. (1967). *Minnesota Multiphasic Personality Inventory manual.* NY: Psychological Corporation.

Hempel, C. G. (1961). Introduction to problems of taxonomy. In J. Zubin (Ed.), *Field studies in the mental disorders* (pp. 3–22). New York: Grune & Stratton.

Hempel, C. G. (1965). *Aspects of scientific explanation.* New York: Free Press.

Kaplan, A. (1964). *The conduct of inquiry.* San Francisco: Chandler.

Kendell, R. E. (1975). *The role of diagnosis in psychiatry.* Oxford, UK: Blackwell Scientific.

Kernberg, O., Millon, T., Cloninger, R., Beck, A. T., Benjamin, L., & Clarkin, J. (in press). *Modern theories of personality disorder.* New York: Guilford Press.

Klerman, G. L. (1973). The relationship between personality and clinical depressions: Overcoming the obstacles to verifying psychodynamic theories. *International Journal of Psychiatry, 11,* 227–233.

Kline, P., & Barrett, P. (1983). The factors in personality disorders: Ideal types, prototypes, or dimensions? *Journal of Personality Disorders, 5,* 52–59.

Livesley, W. J. (1986a). Theoretical and empirical issues in the selection of criteria to diagnose personality disorders. *Journal of Personality Disorders, 1,* 88–94.

Livesley, W. J. (1986b). Trait and behavior prototypes of personality disorder. *American Journal of Psychiatry, 43,* 1018–1022.

Livesley, W. J. (1991). Classifying personality disorders: Ideal types, prototypes or dimensions. *Journal of Personality Disorders, 5,* 52–69.

Loevinger, J. (1957). Objective tests as measurements of psychological theory. *Psychological Reports, 3,* 635–694.

McCrae, R. R., & Costa, P. T., Jr. (1985). Updating Norman's "adequate taxonomy": Intelligence and personality dimensions in natural language and in questionnaires. *Journal of Personality and Social Psychology, 49,* 710–721.

McCranie, E. J. (1971). Depression, anxiety and hostility. *Psychiatric Quarterly, 45,* 117–133.

Medin, D. L., Altom, M. W., Edelson, S. M., & Freko, D. (1982). Correlated symptoms and simulated medical classification. *Journal of Experimental Psychology: Learning and Memory and Cognition, 8,* 37–50.

Meehl, P. (1978). Theoretical risks and tabular asterisks: Sir Karl, Sir Ronald, and the slow progress of soft psychology. *Journal of Consulting and Clinical Psychology, 46,* 806–834.

Menninger, K. (1963). *The vital balance.* New York: Viking.

Millon, T. (1969). *Modern psychopathology: A biosocial approach to maladaptive learning and functioning.* Philadelphia: W. B. Saunders.

Millon, T. (1977). *Millon Clinical Multiaxial Inventory manual.* Minneapolis, MN: National Computer Systems.

Millon, T. (1981). *Disorders of personality: DSM-III, Axis II.* New York: Wiley-Interscience.

Millon, T. (1984). On the renaissance of personality assessment and personality theory. *Journal of Personality Assessment, 48,* 450–466.

Millon, T. (1986). Personality prototypes and their diagnostic criteria. In T. Millon & G. L. Klerman (Eds.), *Contemporary directions in psychopathology: Towards the DSM-IV* (pp. 671–712). New York: Guilford Press.

Millon, T. (1987). On the nature of taxonomy in psychopathology. In C. Last & M. Hersen (Eds.), *Issues in diagnostic research* (pp. 3–83). New York: Plenum.

Millon, T. (1990). *Toward a new personality: An evolutionary model.* New York: Wiley-Interscience.

Millon, T. (1991a). Classification in psychopathology: Issues, alternatives, standards. *Journal of Abnormal Psychology, 100,* 245–261.

Millon, T. (1991b). Normality: What can we learn from evolutionary theory. In D. Offer & M. Sabshin (Eds.), *The diversity of normal behavior* (pp. 356–404). New York: Basic Books.

Mischel, W. (1973). On the empirical dilemmas of psychodynamic approaches: Issues and alternatives. *Journal of Abnormal Psychology, 82,* 335–344.

Mischel, W. (1979). On the interface of cognition and personality. *American Psychologist, 34,* 740–754.

Norman, W. T. (1963). Toward an adequate taxonomy of personality attributes: Replicated factor structure in peer nomination personality ratings. *Journal of Abnormal and Social Psychology, 66,* 574–583.

Offer, D., & Sabshin, M. (1974). *Normality: Theoretical and clinical concepts of mental health* (rev. ed.). New York: Basic Books.

Pap, A. (1953). Reduction-sentences and open concepts. *Methods, 5,* 3–30.

Paykel, E. S., Klerman, G. L., & Prusoff, B. A. (1976). Personality and symptom pattern in depression. *British Journal of Psychiatry, 129,* 327–334.

Paykel, E. S., Myers, J. K., & Dienelt, M. N. (1970). Life events and depression. *Archives of General Psychiatry, 221,* 753–760.

Quine, W. V. O. (1977). Natural kinds. In S. P. Schwartz (Ed.), *Naming, necessity and natural groups* (pp. 22–39). Ithaca, NY: Cornell University Press.

Skinner, H. (1986). Construct validation approach to psychiatric classification. In T. Millon & G. L. Klerman (Eds.), *Contemporary directions in psychopathology: Towards the DSM-IV.* New York: Guilford Press.

Smith, E. E., & Medin, D. L. (1981). *Categories and concepts.* Cambridge, MA; Harvard University Press.

Sprock, J., & Blashfield, R. K. (1984). Classification and nosology. In M. Hersen, A. Kazdin, & A. Bellack (Eds.), *The clinical psychology handbook.* Elmsford, NY: Pergamon Press.

Tellegen, A., & Waller, N. G. (1987, August). *Reexamining basic dimension natural language trait descriptions.* Paper presented at the 95th annual meeting of the American Psychological Association, New York.

Torgerson, W. T. (1968). Multidimensional representation of similarity structures. In M. M. Katz, J. O. Cole, & W. E. Barton (Eds.), *Classification in psychiatry and psychopathology* (pp. 212–220). Washington, DC: Public Health Service Publications.

Tversky, A. (1977). Features of similarity. *Psychological Review, 84,* 327–352.

Waller, N. G., & Ben-Porath, Y. S. (1987). Is it time for clinical psychology to embrace the five-factor model of personality? *American Psychologist, 42,* 887–889.

Williams, J. B. W. (1985a). The multiaxial system of the DSM-III: Where did it come from and where should it go? I. Its origins and critiques. *Archives of General Psychiatry, 42,* 175–180.

Williams, J. B. W. (1985b). The multiaxial system of the DSM-III: Where did it come from and where should it go? II. Empirical studies, innovations, and recommendations. *Archives of General Psychiatry, 42*, 181–186.

World Health Organization. (1991). *International classification of diseases* (Vols. 1–3; 9th ed., rev.). Geneva, Switzerland: Author.

Wright, J. C., & Murphy, G. L. (1984). The utility of theories in intuitive statistics: The robustness of theory-based judgments. *Journal of Experimental Psychology: General, 113*, 301–322.

Zilboorg, G., & Henry, G. W. (1941). *A history of medical psychology*. New York: Norton.

Zubin, J. (1968). Biometric assessment of mental patients. In M. M. Katz, J. O. Cole, & W. E. Barton (Eds.), *Classification of psychiatry and psychopathology* (pp. 353–377). Washington, DC: Public Health Service Publications.

CHAPTER 20

A REFORMULATION OF AXIS II: PERSONALITY AND PERSONALITY-RELATED PROBLEMS

Robert R. McCrae

The intention of this book is to examine relations between personality disorders and the dimensions of personality identified in the five-factor model (FFM) of personality. Are the same or related constructs common to both? How can specific disorders be characterized in terms of personality factors? Can comorbidity among disorders be attributed to covariation of underlying personality traits? What distinguishes normal from pathological personality?

All of these questions are in one sense naive. They all begin with the assumption that there is in fact a class of disorders, more or less accurately identified by the revised third edition of the *Diagnostic and Statistical Manual of Mental Disorders* (*DSM-III-R*; American Psychiatric Association, 1987), that are characterized by maladaptive personality traits. In addressing these questions, we have tacitly reified personality disorders, granting them the scientific status that we would accord such conditions as Alzheimer's disease or opioid withdrawal. I believe that this basic assumption can be challenged and that there are alternative formulations of Axis II that are both more consistent with the facts and more heuristic for treatment implications.

In questioning the existence of personality disorders, I am not joining those like Szasz (1960) who deny the applicability of the medical model itself to psychiatric conditions nor am I making a trivial philosophical point about the limitations of scientific constructs as representations of reality. I am perfectly willing to admit that there are mental disorders, just as I am ready to defend the veridicality of personality traits (McCrae, 1982). And certainly, I do not deny

that there are many individuals, currently diagnosable as having a personality disorder, who are deeply maladjusted and in need of therapy. I am simply suggesting that the medical model has perhaps been misapplied in this case.

Any psychiatric disorder ought to be defined by a syndrome of covarying symptoms that more or less sharply differentiate those who have the disorder from those who do not; different disorders should be independent, with comorbidity not exceeding chance. This state of affairs does not describe the personality disorders at all. Experts often disagree sharply over what features characterize the disorders (e.g., Gunderson & Zanarini, 1987). There is substantial heterogeneity within diagnostic groups (e.g., Clarkin, Widiger, Frances, Hurt, & Gilmore, 1983). The diagnosis of individual patients is often unreliable (Standage, 1989), and different instruments intended to assess the same disorders often show low convergent validity (Trull, 1993). Elegant statistical analyses have shown that the symptoms of some diagnoses covary not as elements of a discrete type but as definers of a continuous dimension (Trull, Widiger, & Guthrie, 1990). The problem of comorbidity is so severe that *DSM-III-R* specifically warns against the traditional practice of seeking a "single, specific personality disorder" (p. 336) diagnosis.

If the individual personality disorders suffer these limitations, the set of disorders recognized in *DSM-III-R* has other problems. Without minimizing the thought, research, and scholarship that has gone into the *DSM* classification, the fact remains that the collection of disorders that it recognizes is essentially arbitrary. The inclusion of two disorders (sadistic and self-defeating) as provisional diagnoses and continuing debates on the inclusion or exclusion of other diagnoses (American Psychiatric Association, 1991) indicate that the system is at best unfinished, and discrepancies with other systems show the prevailing lack of scientific consensus (Kato, 1988). More important, as both Clark (1990) and Livesley, Jackson, and Schroeder (1989) have shown, the empirical structure of personality disorder symptoms does not reproduce the theoretical structure suggested by *DSM-III-R*.

Personality disorder researchers are well aware of these problems but tend to view them as indicating the need for refinement of a basically sound system: Delete this diagnosis, add that one; change the required number of criterial elements; allow distinctions between "mild," "moderate," and "severe"; improve the reliability of ratings or the validity of self-report instruments and the problems will be resolved. In my view, these are but many epicycles added to a Ptolemaic system, and the time has come to try a new approach. The purpose of this chapter is to sketch out an alternative (cf. Costa & McCrae, 1992a).

PERSONALITY ASSESSMENT ON AXIS II

Axis II was included in *DSM-III* (American Psychiatric Association, 1980) because psychiatrists recognized that there are important and enduring individual differences in personality that may have implications for psychopathology. As the Task Force on *DSM-IV* noted,

> the multiaxial system helps to ensure that a complete evaluation is conducted so that important personality, developmental, and medical information is assessed. It encourages the clinician to move beyond the assessment of diagnosis to the consideration of other factors . . . that are important in treatment planning and prognosis." (American Psychiatric Association, 1991, p. W:1)

These goals would be facilitated by substituting a dimensional model of personality for the present cat-

egorical model of personality disorders. Every complete psychiatric diagnosis should include an assessment of the standing of the patient on each of the five basic personality factors.

As a description of personality, the FFM has many advantages over the present Axis II system. The factors provide the framework for a widely accepted, empirically based, comprehensive taxonomy of personality traits. Although there remain some differences among five-factor theorists about the interpretation of the factors, there is substantial cross-instrument validity for alternative measures (Trapnell & Wiggins, 1990). All of the factors appear to be heritable to some extent (Costa & McCrae, 1992a), which should make them of particular interest to biologically oriented psychiatrists and psychologists. Moreover, they are cross-culturally replicable (Yang & Bond, 1990), making them suitable for inclusion in the *International Classification of Diseases* (World Health Organization, 1992). All five are known to be very stable in adulthood (Costa & McCrae, 1992b), which may help differentiate them from the transient or intermittent disorders of Axis I. Finally, as several chapters in this book attest, the factors have been shown to have meaningful links to a number of measures of the current personality disorders, and—with the possible exception of cognitive aberration—the personality disorders appear to add no new dimension of personality. This suggests that the information about personality currently registered in Axis II would be retained in the new format.

In its simplest form, Axis II personality assessment using the FFM would require global judgments of each of the five factors. A somewhat more elaborate version might include separate assessments of more specific traits defining each of the five factors. For example, global extraversion might be subdivided into sociability, activity level, and positive emotionality. Because they are conceived as continuous dimensions, a minimally adequate assessment would make distinctions along a 5-point scale, from *very low* to *very high*; alternatively, a 90-point format like that used for the Global Assessment of Functioning scale might be developed for each factor.

The ratings would reflect the professional judgment of the psychologist or psychiatrist, based on many different sources of evidence. Clinical judgments of standing on the five factors based on psychological history and interview might be used, particularly if the clinician has been specifically trained to assess these aspects of personality (M. J. Miller, 1990). In general, however, personality assessment is usually best accomplished by the use of standardized instruments. There are several validated self-report measures of the full FFM (Briggs, 1992) and many scales that measure one or more of the basic factors. In addition, there are validated observer rating forms that can be completed by family members or other informants (Mutén, 1991). Self-reports and observer ratings would provide quantified information relative to appropriate normative groups and, in the context of other relevant information (e.g., the presence of a concurrent Axis I disorder that might distort self-reports), could provide the basis for final clinical judgments.

DIAGNOSIS OF PERSONALITY-RELATED PROBLEMS

Although information on personality is not in itself a diagnosis, it could become the basis for diagnoses of personality-related problems. Individuals with particular personality traits are predisposed to have particular kinds of difficulties in living. For example, individuals high in Conscientiousness may be workaholics whose devotion to work interferes with marriage and family; individuals low in Conscientiousness may be so lacking in drive that they find it difficult to hold a job. Faced with a high-Conscientiousness patient, the clinician should consider whether there is an excessive and maladaptive absorption in work; if so, the clinician would give a diagnosis of "high Conscientiousness–related problems."

The association between personality and problems is probabilistic; not all high-Conscientiousness individuals are workaholics, and an individual might spend too much time at work even though he or she is not particularly conscientious. In the former case, there might be no grounds for a diagnosis; in the latter, there is evidence of a problem, but it is probably not a personality-related problem. Perhaps the individual spends so much time at work because there is too much tension in the marriage.

A diagnostic system for personality-related problems would require a catalog of symptoms or prob-

lems related to each pole of each of the five factors. Table 1 gives a sample of how this might appear. The personality profile of the individual would alert the clinician to the relevant sections of the catalog, and the problems indicated there would become the focus of diagnostic inquiry. Patients who are assessed as being very high or very low on a factor would be more likely to qualify for a diagnosis than would those who are merely high or low; patients with average scores would be precluded from receiving a diagnosis of problems related to that factor. In principle, an individual could receive from zero to five personality-related problems diagnoses.

The symptoms listed in Table 1 are only illustrative. The actual lists would be based on the research literature linking personality traits to problems. The work of Livesley (1991), Clark (1990), and Pincus and Wiggins (1990) provides a good start; presumably, the task would ultimately fall to a *DSM* task force. It would be possible to adopt more sophisticated approaches, linking symptoms to more specific traits within the five factors or to additive or interactive combinations of factors. Perhaps this level of diagnosis should be left to computer interpretive reports; *DSM* diagnoses are, after all, only a global indication of the patient's status.

A more difficult question concerns the criterion of impairment. Everyone high in Neuroticism has chronic negative affects, but most high-Neuroticism individuals manage to live reasonably rewarding lives despite low spirits. Which of these people are impaired? The dimensional model advocated here explicitly denies that there are qualitative differences between "pathological" and "normal" levels of personality traits, and something similar might be said about the problems associated with personality traits. At what point are problems so severe that they warrant a diagnosis? The *DSM-III-R* criterion of "significant impairment in social or occupational functioning or subjective distress" is appropriate but vague.

Perhaps the answer is social rather than medical. That is, problems warrant a diagnosis when they become severe enough to lead an individual to come for help or to be referred for therapy by family, associates, or social institutions. As long as no one— including the individual—objects to an individual's social isolation, conformity to authority, or fastidi-

---

TABLE 1

Symptoms and Problems Associated With Personality Factors

High Neuroticism

Chronic negative affects, including anxiety, fearfulness, tension, irritability, anger, dejection, hopelessness, guilt, shame; difficulty in inhibiting impulses: for example, to eat, drink, smoke, or spend money; irrational beliefs: for example, unrealistic expectations, perfectionistic demands on self, unwarranted pessimism; unfounded somatic concerns; helplessness and dependence on others for emotional support and decision making.

Low Neuroticism

Lack of appropriate concern for potential problems in health or social adjustment; emotional blandness.

High Extraversion

Excessive talking, leading to inappropriate self-disclosure and social friction; inability to spend time alone; attention seeking and overly dramatic expression of emotions; reckless excitement seeking; inappropriate attempts to dominate and control others.

Low Extraversion

Social isolation, interpersonal detachment, and lack of support networks; flattened affect; lack of joy and zest for life; reluctance to assert self or assume leadership roles, even when qualified; social inhibition and shyness.

High Openness

Preoccupation with fantasy and daydreaming; lack of practicality; eccentric thinking (e.g., belief in ghosts, reincarnation, UFOs); diffuse identity and changing goals: for example, joining religious cult; susceptibility to nightmares and states of altered consciousness; social rebelliousness and nonconformity that can interfere with social or vocational advancement.

Low Openness

Difficulty adapting to social or personal change; low tolerance or understanding of different points of view or lifestyles; emotional blandness and inability to understand and verbalize own feelings; alexythymia; constricted range of interests; insensitivity to art and beauty; excessive conformity to authority.

High Agreeableness

Gullibility: indiscriminate trust of others; excessive candor and generosity, to detriment of self-interest; inability to stand up to others and fight back; easily taken advantage of.

Low Agreeableness

Cynicism and paranoid thinking; inability to trust even friends or family; quarrelsomeness; too ready to pick fights; exploitative and manipulative; lying; rude and inconsiderate manner alienates friends, limits social support; lack of respect for social conventions can lead to troubles with the law; inflated and grandiose sense of self; arrogance.

High Conscientiousness

Overachievement: workaholic absorption in job or cause to the exclusion of family, social, and personal interests; compulsiveness, including excessive cleanliness, tidiness, and attention to detail; rigid self-discipline and an inability to set tasks aside and relax; lack of spontaneity; overscrupulousness in moral behavior.

Low Conscientiousness

Underachievement: not fulfilling intellectual or artistic potential; poor academic performance relative to ability; disregard of rules and responsibilities can lead to trouble with the law; unable to discipline self (e.g., stick to diet, exercise plan) even when required for medical reasons; personal and occupational aimlessness.

---

ousness, there is no basis for calling the behavior an impairment. This criterion would prove disagreeable to epidemiologists, who would point out that the prevalence of a disorder would vary widely with the availability of services, the acceptance of psychotherapy as a way of improving one's life, and the policies of courts and social services agencies. But *prevalence* is a medical term, presupposing that there are real cases of a disorder out there to be counted. My argument is that this model does not apply to personality disorders. In this context, a diagnosis is not the certification that a discrete disorder exists but the identification of a set of problems that require the intervention of a mental health professional.

IMPLICATIONS FOR TREATMENT

Coding both personality assessment and personality-related problems on Axis II can be particularly useful for treatment. In the first place, it focuses attention on the patient's difficulties in living. Personality assessment guides the clinician to particular sets of issues that are likely to be problematic, and these become the object of treatment. Because the full range of personality traits is covered, problems may be noted that would otherwise have gone unnoticed. There is no requirement that some minimum number or particular configuration of personality-related problems be noted to justify a diagnosis, as is currently the case with personality disorder diagnosis. If there are problems requiring treatment, a diagnosis would be justified.

Conceptually, the system embodies a distinction between the underlying personality traits and the associated symptoms and problems. In principle, therapy might be directed either at the traits or at the resulting symptoms, but in practice it is likely that treatment will focus on the problems themselves. Personality traits are enduring dispositions that are resistant to change in the course of normal experience, and it seems unlikely that psychotherapeutic interventions would make dramatic changes in basic dispositions (Costa & McCrae, 1986). Usually, however, people are able to adapt to their own personalities, finding ways to manage their lives and

relationships that are consistent with their own traits. It is only when external pressures or circumstances overwhelm the adaptive capacity of the individual that help is sought. Psychotherapy in these cases might have the much more limited and realistic goal of relieving symptoms.

Finally, the explicit assessment of all five factors would call attention to features of personality that may have implications for prognosis and treatment, even if they are unrelated to diagnosis. There is some evidence that individuals with different personality traits respond differently to various kinds of therapy. Shea (1988) reported that depressed patients who were high in interpersonal involvement (i.e., Extraversion) responded better to interpersonal therapy, whereas those who were low in Extraversion responded better to medication. DiLoreto (1971) found that introverts profited more from rational–emotive therapy, whereas extroverts profited more from client-centered therapy. T. Miller (1991) suggested that Openness to Experience may also be relevant to the choice of treatments—a view supported by the research of Qualls and Sheehan (1979). Systematic research on interactions between forms of therapy and the five personality factors would provide a basis for matching treatments to patients.

TOWARD A *DSM-V* FACTOR MODEL

The reformulation of Axis II in terms of personality assessment and the diagnosis of personality-related problems would require a radical, but not impossible, shift in conceptualization. Indeed, such a change would simply carry to its logical conclusion the decision in *DSM-III* to separate personality disorders from other, usually more florid and transient, mental disorders. Criticisms of the categorical medical model are decades old; what is relatively new is the widespread acceptance among personality psychologists of a model of personality structure that could be the basis of a new Axis II. The FFM provides that needed consensus.

Clinicians often lag behind researchers in accepting new ideas. In this case, however, the reverse may well prove true. As Wong (1987) noted, "a discrepancy exists between what the clinicians intuitively feel they are treating and what they eventually record as the *DSM-III* diagnosis" (p. 328). Clinicians make the mandatory diagnoses to justify third-party payments and then proceed to the process of therapy, a process that typically centers on learning what the patient is like, identifying specific problems in living, and seeking solutions for them. Surely the *DSM* should provide them with guidance in assessing personality and identifying associated problems and solutions. The plan proposed here would rectify many of the scientific problems of Axis II and at the same time be more relevant to clinical practice. *DSM-V* is not too soon to implement it.

References

American Psychiatric Association. (1980). *Diagnostic and statistical manual of mental disorders* (3rd ed.). Washington, DC: Author.

American Psychiatric Association. (1987). *Diagnostic and statistical manual of mental disorders* (3rd ed., rev.). Washington, DC: Author.

American Psychiatric Association. (1991). *DSM-IV options book: Work in progress (9/1/91)*. Washington, DC: Author.

Briggs, S. R. (1992). Assessing the five-factor model of personality description. In R. R. McCrae (Ed.), The five-factor model: Issues and applications [Special issue]. *Journal of Personality, 60,* 253–293.

Clark, L. A. (1990). Toward a consensual set of symptom clusters for assessment of personality disorder. In J. N. Butcher & C. D. Spielberger (Eds.), *Advances in personality assessment* (Vol. 8, pp. 243–266). Hillsdale, NJ: Erlbaum.

Clarkin, J. F., Widiger, T. A., Frances, A., Hurt, S. W., & Gilmore, M. (1983). Prototypic typology and the borderline personality disorder. *Journal of Abnormal Psychology, 92,* 263–275.

Costa, P. T., Jr., & McCrae, R. R. (1986). Personality stability and its implications for clinical psychology. *Clinical Psychology Review, 6,* 407–423.

Costa, P. T., Jr., & McCrae, R. R. (1992a). The five-factor model and its relevance to personality disorders. *Journal of Personality Disorders, 6,* 343–359.

Costa, P. T., Jr., & McCrae, R. R. (1992b). Trait psychology comes of age. In T. B. Sonderegger (Ed.), *Nebraska Symposium on Motivation: Psychology and aging* (pp. 169–204). Lincoln: University of Nebraska Press.

DiLoreto, A. O. (1971). *Comparative psychotherapy: An experimental analysis.* Chicago: Aldine-Atherton.

Gunderson, J. G., & Zanarini, M. C. (1987). Current overview of the borderline diagnosis. *Journal of Clinical Psychiatry, 48*(Suppl. 8), 5–11.

Kato, M. (1988). Issues on diagnosing and classifying personality disorders. In J. E. Mezzich & M. von Cranach (Eds.), *International classification in psychiatry: Unity and diversity* (pp. 166–174). New York: Cambridge University Press.

Livesley, W. J. (1991). Classifying personality disorders: Ideal types, prototypes, or dimensions? *Journal of Personality Disorders, 5,* 52–59.

Livesley, W. J., Jackson, D. N., & Schroeder, M. L. (1989). A study of the factorial structure of personality pathology. *Journal of Personality Disorders, 3,* 292–306.

McCrae, R. R. (1982). Consensual validation of personality traits: Evidence from self-reports and ratings. *Journal of Personality and Social Psychology, 43,* 293–303.

Miller, M. J. (1990). The power of the "OCEAN": Another way to diagnose clients. *Counselor Education and Supervision, 29,* 283–290.

Miller, T. (1991). The psychotherapeutic utility of the five-factor model of personality: A clinician's experience. *Journal of Personality Assessment, 57,* 415–433.

Mutén, E. (1991). Self-reports, spouse ratings, and psychophysiological assessment in a behavioral medicine program: An application of the five-factor model. *Journal of Personality Assessment, 57,* 449–464.

Pincus, A. L., & Wiggins, J. S. (1990). Interpersonal problems and conceptions of personality disorders. *Journal of Personality Disorders, 4,* 342–352.

Qualls, P. J., & Sheehan, P. W. (1979). Capacity for absorption and relaxation during electromyograph biofeedback and no-feedback conditions. *Journal of Abnormal Psychology, 88,* 652–662.

Shea, M. T. (1988, August). *Interpersonal styles and short-term psychotherapy for depression.* Paper presented at the 96th annual meeting of the American Psychological Association, Atlanta, GA.

Standage, K. (1989). Structured interviews and the diagnosis of personality disorders. *Canadian Journal of Psychiatry, 34,* 906–912.

Szasz, T. S. (1960). The myth of mental illness. *American Psychologist, 15,* 113–118.

Trapnell, P. D., & Wiggins, J. S. (1990). Extension of the Interpersonal Adjective Scales to include the Big Five dimensions of personality. *Journal of Personality and Social Psychology, 59,* 781–790.

Trull, T. J. (1993). Temporal stability and validity of two personality disorder inventories. *Psychological Assessment, 5,* 11–18.

Trull, T. J., Widiger, T. A., & Guthrie, P. (1990). The categorical versus dimensional status of borderline personality disorder. *Journal of Abnormal Psychology, 99,* 40–48.

Wong, N. (1987). Overview. In G. L. Tischler (Ed.), *Diagnosis and classification in psychiatry: A critical appraisal of DSM-III* (pp. 321–332). New York: Cambridge University Press.

World Health Organization. (1992). *Manual of the international classification of diseases, injuries, and causes of death* (10th ed.). Geneva, Switzerland: Author.

Yang, K., & Bond, M. H. (1990). Exploring implicit personality theories with indigenous or imported constructs: The Chinese case. *Journal of Personality and Social Psychology, 58,* 1087–1095.

CHAPTER 21

CONCEPTUALIZING A DISORDER OF PERSONALITY FROM THE FIVE-FACTOR MODEL

Thomas A. Widiger

Chapter 3 of this book provided a description of each of the revised third edition and fourth edition of the *Diagnostic and Statistical Manual of Mental Disorders* (*DSM-III-R* and *DSM-IV*, respectively; American Psychiatric Association, 1987, in press) personality disorders from the perspective of the five-factor model (FFM) of personality. This translation is helpful to those who are familiar with the *DSM* constructs and wish to understand how a person with one or more of these diagnoses would be described using the five-factor constructs. However, chapter 3 did not indicate how one would diagnose a disorder of personality on the basis of a FFM description without any reference to the *DSM-III-R* or *DSM-IV*. If the FFM is to provide a viable alternative to Axis II of *DSM-III-R* (or *DSM-IV*), then one should be able to diagnose a personality disorder using the five factors. The purpose of this chapter is to indicate how this might be done. I begin with a discussion of the general concept of a mental disorder, followed by a discussion of the concept of a personality disorder and how a diagnosis of a personality disorder would be made using the revised NEO Personality Inventory (NEO-PI-R; Costa & McCrae, 1990).

MENTAL DISORDER

It is stated in *DSM-III-R* that it is "when personality traits are inflexible and maladaptive and cause either significant functional impairment or subjective distress that they constitute Personality Disorders" (American Psychiatric Association, 1987, p. 335). "The constellation of behaviors or traits causes either significant impairment in social or occupational functioning or subjective distress" (p. 335). This is a reasonable description of what is meant by a personality disorder that is also consistent with the broader definition of mental disorder provided in the introduction to the manual. "In *DSM-III-R* each of the mental disorders is conceptualized as a clinically significant behavioral or psychological syndrome or pattern that occurs in a person and that is associated with present distress (a painful symptom) or disability (impairment in one or more important areas of functioning) or with a significantly increased risk of suffering death, pain, disability, or an important loss of freedom" (p. xxii).

It should be emphasized, however, that no infallible operational definition of a mental or personality disorder can be provided (Frances, Widiger, & Sabshin, 1991; Meehl, 1986). Scientific constructs can rarely be reduced to an explicit, specific set of observables without losing their explanatory power and their theoretical meaning. Observable manifestations can contribute to an understanding of what is meant by a concept and to its measurement, but they will be insufficient in providing a definition of the concept (Hempel, 1965; Leahey, 1980). For example, intelligence is a valid scientific construct, but it cannot be so explicitly defined that its presence or degree can be assessed unambiguously. Intelligence tests provide valid assessments of the construct, but intelligence is not confined to the skills, abilities, or functions measured by any particular intelligence test. It would be nice if a precise operational definition of a personality disorder or a mental disorder could be provided, such that no ambiguous cases would occur, but this is not realistic for most scientific constructs, particularly those within the life sciences (Meehl & Golden, 1982; Rorer, 1990; Wakefield, 1992).

Widiger and Trull (1991) defined a mental disorder as "an involuntary, organismic impairment in psychological functioning (i.e., cognitive, affective, and/or behavioral)" (p. 112). This is a fairly broad definition, but it does capture the fundamental, defining features of a mental disorder. The more specific characteristics or manifestations of a personality disorder—such as distress, disability, irrationality, deviation from a social norm, "a tendency to foster vicious or self-defeating circles, and a tenuous stability under conditions of stress" (Millon, 1990, p. 342)—are best considered as providing fallible indication of the presence or degree of a mental disorder rather than as providing an operational definition. They are useful in indicating the likelihood that and the extent to which a person is suffering from a mental disorder, but they are not infallible in its assessment. For example, distress (dysphoria) is a useful and valid indicator of the presence and degree of disorder. The presence of dysphoria does suggest that there is something wrong within the organism (i.e., organismic impairment). It can also suggest the extent or degree to which the person is disordered (e.g., degree of dysphoria will correlate highly with the severity of a depression). However, distress is not an infallible indicator. Distress is at times normal and adaptive. The absence of distress in response to a loss would be more suggestive of a mental disorder than it would of the presence of distress (e.g., reflecting perhaps a schizoid, narcissistic, or psychopathic indifference toward others).

PERSONALITY DISORDER

The most useful (but still fallible) indicators of a personality disorder are social dysfunction, occupational dysfunction, and, to a lesser extent, distress, as suggested by the definition of a personality disorder provided in the *DSM-III-R*. Personality traits are maladaptive (disordered) to the extent to which they result in an impairment in social functioning, occupational functioning, or personal distress. Some personality traits are maladaptive across most situations (e.g., a high level of trait depression is unlikely to be adaptive in any situation). However, the maladaptivity of many personality traits may also be a direct result of the inflexibility of a person to a situational demand, option, or stressor. It is inherent to the concept of personality that people exhibit a characteristic manner of thinking, feeling, behaving, or relating to others across time and situations (Epstein & O'Brien, 1985). To the extent that a person is entirely flexible (i.e., adaptive) to whatever situations arise, this person could be said to lack characteristic personality traits. All people, at least to some extent, will be hindered in their ability to adapt flexibly to stress; to make optimal life decisions; to fulfill desired potentials; or to sustain satisfying, progressive, and meaningful relationships as a result of one or more of their personality traits. Each personality style will have its own Achilles' heel and limitations. In this respect, all people can be said to have some degree of personality disorder.

The *DSM-III-R* attempts to distinguish between disorder and normality in part by emphasizing that the impairment in social or occupational functioning is clinically significant. However, clinical significance is itself a poorly defined and arbitrary demarcation. Clinical significance could mean that the extent of maladaptivity is of sufficient concern to cause the individual to seek treatment or is of sufficient concern to those with whom the individual interacts to cause them to request, demand, or pressure for a change in the individual (Frances et al., 1991). However, that point at which a personality trait becomes sufficiently problematic to an individual or to those around him or her such that treatment is desired or recommended will vary considerably across individuals and those with whom they interact. Dysfunction will at times be so substantial that treatment is clearly desirable and perhaps even necessary for continued survival (e.g., suicidality), but there is no absolute level of dysfunction at which treatment becomes desirable. A useful analogy is the physical impairment of myopia. People will vary considerably with respect to the extent of myopia that they will accept and tolerate before they seek treatment (e.g., variability in concerns regarding physical appearance, financial limitations, awareness of the benefits of treatment, and the relative importance of accurate vision to the occupational and social role functioning of the particular individual). Clinical significance could mean that the maladaptivity is to the point at which the person would benefit from some form of treatment (regardless of the motivation). However, it would be difficult to find a person whose personality does not result in any problems, inhibitions, impairments, or limitations that would not benefit from some form of psychotherapy.

The notion that all people have some degree of personality disorder may appear to contradict the suggestion of McCrae in chapter 20 of this book that there are no disorders of personality, only problems of living that are secondary to personality traits. However, McCrae disagrees primarily with a "medical" model that suggests that there is a categorical distinction between normal and abnormal personality (e.g., Guze & Helzer, 1987). The concept of disorder, however, need not be qualitative or categorical. Many "medical" (physical) disorders exist along a continuum (e.g., hypertension and myopia). Each level along the continuum is associated with different degrees of maladaptivity. The continuum or dimensional model of disorder proposed in this chapter is not inconsistent with a medical model that recognizes the existence of degrees of maladaptivity.

Personality health, like physical health, is an ideal achieved by no one (Frances et al., 1991; Freud, 1937/1963; Kendell, 1975). Everybody will suffer from a variety of physical disorders throughout their lives (e.g., influenzas, colds, wounds, and infections). Most, if not all, people will suffer from at least one chronic physical impairment throughout most of their lives (e.g., myopia). The average person lacks an entirely healthy body, and the average person lacks an entirely flexible or optimally functioning personality.

On the other hand, each person will also have many adaptive personality traits. The *DSM-III-R* categorical distinctions between the presence and the absence of a personality disorder imply that people who fail to meet the diagnostic criteria for any personality disorder lack maladaptive traits and that people who do meet the diagnostic criteria lack any adaptive personality traits. The dimensional model proposed in this book suggests not only that all

people have some degree of maladaptive personality traits but also that all people have some degree of adaptive personality traits. Even the more dysfunctional borderline and schizotypal patients will have adaptive personality traits.

A borderline patient will be characterized for the most part by extreme neuroticism (see chapter 3 in this book), but any particular borderline patient may also be characterized by high Conscientiousness that will be helpful for stable employment and sustained effort in psychotherapy (e.g., see chapter 11 in this book). Even the personality traits that are maladaptive in any particular person can be adaptive in some contexts or at some times. Excessive achievement striving ("workaholism") can be maladaptive to social functioning (e.g., sacrificing valuable and important time with one's spouse or children) but may contribute to career success. An excessive fantasy life can contribute to a detachment and withdrawal from the world, but it may also facilitate a responsivity to certain therapeutic techniques (e.g., see chapter 15 in this book). Toughmindedness can be problematic in developing and maintaining a love relationship (e.g., low empathy), but it may be useful in certain occupations and roles (e.g., police officer or soldier). Very high levels of trust and altruism are clearly admirable and valuable traits, but they may result in a vulnerability to exploitation and abuse by others.

In sum, the dimensional model proposed herein emphasizes that personality should not be classified as disordered versus normal. An assessment of personality should be comprehensive and individualized. Each person is characterized by a particular constellation of traits that will have different degrees of adaptivity and maladaptivity across various situations and roles.

DIAGNOSIS WITH THE NEO-PI-R

To the extent that maladaptive personality traits are extreme variants of normal personality traits (Kiesler, 1991; Widiger & Frances, 1985; Wiggins, Phillips, & Trapnell, 1989), the degree of deviation on any particular NEO-PI-R domain or facet scale would suggest maladaptivity. For the most part, this will, in fact, be the case (Costa & McCrae, 1990; Schroeder, Wormworth, & Livesley, 1992; Trull, 1992; Wiggins

& Pincus, 1989). The extent to which a person is elevated on Neuroticism and any one of its facets will be highly correlated with maladaptivity. The extent to which a person is excessively introverted or closed to experience or is characterized by low Conscientiousness will also be highly correlated with maladaptivity.

However, each domain of personality functioning will not have equivalent implications with respect to maladaptivity. Elevations on Neuroticism are clearly more suggestive of dysfunction than are elevations on Extraversion or Conscientiousness and are perhaps more suggestive of dysfunction than are comparable elevations on antagonism or introversion. Elevations on introversion are perhaps more suggestive of dysfunction than are comparable elevations on Extraversion, and low Conscientiousness is perhaps more suggestive of dysfunction than is a comparable degree of high Conscientiousness. There will also be variability across facets within any particular domain of personality functioning. Excessive openness to fantasy may be more suggestive of dysfunction than excessive openness to aesthetics, very low positive emotions may be more suggestive of dysfunction than very low activity, and excessive trait depression may be more strongly related to higher levels of dysfunction than excessive self-consciousness. In sum, if one were to use a cutoff point along a domain or facet scale to identify a point at which clinically significant maladaptivity is likely to be present, the cutoff point would vary across the domains and their facets (one would also need to use different cutoff points within any facet for different types or meanings of "clinical significance").

The different domains of personality also have different implications with respect to which aspect of personality dysfunction is most heavily involved (i.e., personal distress, social dysfunction, or occupational dysfunction). For example, Neuroticism may be more closely associated with personal distress than with social or occupational dysfunction, and Neuroticism may be more closely associated with distress than may introversion or antagonism. Neuroticism is the disposition to experience negative affects (Watson & Clark, 1984). It is likely that people who are very high on Neuroticism will also experience impairment in social and/or occupational functioning secondary

to their neuroticism (e.g., impulsivity and depression could impair occupational functioning), although Neuroticism is more closely associated with distress than with social or occupational dysfunction. Likewise, it is possible that introversion and antagonism are more suggestive of social dysfunction than is Neuroticism, Conscientiousness, or Openness, given that much of the variance in interpersonal functioning is defined by these two domains of personality (McCrae & Costa, 1989; Wiggins & Pincus, 1989). It is also possible that low Conscientiousness has more implications for occupational dysfunction than for personal distress or social dysfunction, given that achievement striving, competence, and dutifulness are relatively more important for occupational success than for personal distress or social dysfunction.

In any case, as just indicated, it would be inconsistent with the continuum and complexity of personality dysfunction to simply provide cutoff scores at various points across NEO-PI-R domain and facet scales. People below any particular cutoff point will have maladaptive personality traits, and people above any particular cutoff point will vary in the extent of their maladaptivity. Even a person at the average level across all of the domains and facets of the NEO-PI-R will have some degree of maladaptivity. An average score on a NEO-PI-R scale does not indicate ideal or optimal functioning with respect to that dimension. It is a normative or statistical normality, not an absolute normality that suggests an absence of dysfunction. An average score only indicates that the person is at the average level relative to a particular population. For example, the average (normative) level of Neuroticism does not imply that the person lacks any problematic vulnerability, self-consciousness, or anxiety. It just means that the person's level of self-consciousness is no worse than the average person's level of self-consciousness. Normality in this sense does not imply the absence of maladaptive personality traits; it implies only that the person is no worse off than the average person. Just as the average person has mild physical impairments, so too will the average person have mild impairments in personality functioning.

Increased elevations on an NEO-PI-R scale do indicate an increased likelihood for the presence of maladaptive personality traits, but it is important in any particular instance to assess this maladaptivity directly. For example, a very high score on the anxiety facet of Neuroticism indicates a high likelihood of personal distress, but it is still important to assess whether there is any associated social or occupational dysfunction. Likewise, a very low score on Conscientiousness indicates a high likelihood of occupational dysfunction, but there may be social dysfunction as well. A very high score on Conscientiousness may be ambiguous because it may suggest an overly compulsive devotion to duty, achievement, and perfection, but this devotion may contribute to at least some occupational success while at the same time providing stress or conflicts within a marital relationship.

In all cases, it is important to assess the environmental context in which the person is functioning. High antagonism may be adaptive for a police officer or a soldier but maladaptive for a nun, nurse, therapist, or pastoral counselor (Widiger, 1993). The failure to consider the environmental context was one of the major criticisms of the *DSM-III-R* proposal for a self-defeating personality disorder diagnosis (Widiger & Frances, 1989). Many of the apparent self-defeating personality traits (e.g., inciting angry or rejecting responses in others, engagement in excessive self-sacrifice, and failure to accomplish tasks crucial to personal objectives; American Psychiatric Association, 1987) could represent a situational response of a woman to an abusive marital relationship (Walker, 1987).

The optimal approach to the diagnosis of a personality disorder is to conduct both an NEO-PI-R assessment and an assessment of the exact nature of the personal distress, social dysfunction, and occupational dysfunction that is presently occurring in that person's life. The latter assessment could consist simply of an unstructured clinical interview guided by the scores obtained from the NEO-PI-R. One would inquire as to (a) dysfunctions that are likely to be associated with particular scale elevations (e.g., identify the specific nature of the vulnerabilities given a very high score on the vulnerability facet of Neuroticism), (b) adaptive strengths that are likely to be associated with particular scale elevations (e.g., openness to ideas, Conscientiousness, and Agreeableness), and (c) whether an elevation was secondary to or even adaptive for a particular situation or social role

(e.g., compliance that is secondary to abuse or tough-mindedness in a soldier).

It might also be constructive to use a structured assessment of distress, social dysfunction, and occupational dysfunction to systematically and comprehensively assess specific areas of dysfunction within these broad domains. One such instrument is the Psychiatric Epidemiology Research Interview (PERI; B. P. Dohrenwend, Shrout, Egri, & Mendelsohn, 1980; B. S. Dohrenwend, Dohrenwend, Link, & Levav, 1983). PERI was developed to assess important areas of dysfunction independent of any particular mental disorder. The instrument includes 38 scales, such as demoralization, suicidality, insomnia, drinking problems, job satisfaction, sexual problems, marital attainment, marital performance, job attainment, job performance, and housework. The current version of PERI was not entirely successful in providing assessments that were independent of any particular mental disorder, given that some of the scales are confounded with personality disorders (e.g., one scale is explicitly concerned with schizoid personality traits), but Funtowicz and Widiger (1992) developed a self-report version of PERI that emphasizes dysfunctions that most likely occur in a personality disorder and that are not explicitly confounded with a personality disorder diagnosis.

CONCLUSIONS

In sum, a diagnosis of personality disorder should include a comprehensive and systematic assessment of all domains of personality functioning, considering both the adaptive strengths and the maladaptive weaknesses (Costa & McCrae, 1992). No personality will be without some adaptive strengths or without some adaptive weaknesses, and some personality traits that are maladaptive within one environmental context may be adaptive within another. An assessment of personality disorder should then be specific to the role and situational context in which the person must function. I recommend using the NEO-PI-R (or any comparable instrument) to provide a comprehensive description of the subject's personality and then assessing the extent to which the respective traits are maladaptive with respect to that person's social relationships, occupational functioning, and personal well-being.

References

American Psychiatric Association. (1987). *Diagnostic and statistical manual of mental disorders* (3rd ed., rev.). Washington, DC: Author.

American Psychiatric Association. (in press). *Diagnostic and statistical manual of mental disorders* (4th ed.). Washington, DC: Author.

Costa, P. T., Jr., & McCrae, R. R. (1990). Personality disorders and the five-factor model of personality. *Journal of Personality Disorders, 4,* 362–371.

Costa, P. T., Jr., & McCrae, R. R. (1992). Normal personality assessment in clinical practice: The NEO Personality Inventory. *Psychological Assessment, 4,* 5–13.

Dohrenwend, B. P., Shrout, P. E., Egri, G., & Mendelsohn, F. S. (1980). Nonspecific psychological distress and other dimensions of psychopathology: Measures for use in the general population. *Archives of General Psychiatry, 37,* 1229–1236.

Dohrenwend, B. S., Dohrenwend, B. P., Link, B., & Levav, I. (1983). Social functioning of psychiatric patients in contrast with community cases in the general population. *Archives of General Psychiatry, 40,* 1174–1182.

Epstein, S., & O'Brien, E. (1985). The person–situational debate in historical and current perspective. *Psychological Bulletin, 98,* 513–537.

Frances, A. J., Widiger, T. A., & Sabshin, M. (1991). Psychiatric diagnosis and normality. In D. Offer & M. Sabshin (Eds.), *The diversity of normal behavior* (pp. 3–38). New York: Basic Books.

Freud, S. (1963). *Therapy and technique.* New York: Collier. (Original work published 1937)

Funtowicz, M., & Widiger, T. A. (1992). *Sex bias in the DSM-III-R classification of personality disorder.* Unpublished manuscript, University of Kentucky, Lexington.

Guze, S. B., & Helzer, J. E. (1987). The medical model and psychiatric disorders. In R. Michels & J. Cavenar (Eds.), *Psychiatry* (Vol. 1, Chap. 51, pp. 1–8). Philadelphia: Lippincott.

Hempel, C. (1965). *Aspects of scientific explanation and other essays in the philosophy of science.* New York: Free Press.

Kendell, R. E. (1975). *The role of diagnosis in psychiatry.* Oxford, UK: Blackwell Scientific.

Kiesler, D. J. (1991). Interpersonal methods of assessment and diagnosis. In C. R. Snyder & D. R. Forsyth (Eds.), *Handbook of social and clinical psychology: The health perspective* (pp. 438–468). Elmsford, NY: Pergamon Press.

Leahey, T. H. (1980). The myth of operationism. *Journal of Mind and Behavior, 1,* 127–143.

McCrae, R. R., & Costa, P. T., Jr. (1989). The structure of interpersonal traits: Wiggins's circumplex and the five-factor model. *Journal of Personality and Social Psychology, 56,* 586–595.

Meehl, P. E. (1986). Diagnostic taxa as open concepts: Metatheoretical and statistical questions about reliability and construct validity in the grand strategy of nosological revision. In T. Millon & G. Klerman (Eds.), *Contemporary directions in psychopathology* (pp. 215–213). New York: Guilford Press.

Meehl, P. E., & Golden, R. R. (1982). Taxometric methods. In P. Kendall & J. Butcher (Eds.), *Handbook of research methods in clinical psychology* (pp. 127–181). New York: Wiley.

Millon, T. (1990). The disorders of personality. In L. A. Pervin (Ed.), *Handbook of personality theory and research* (pp. 339–370). New York: Guilford Press.

Rorer, L. G. (1990). Personality assessment: A conceptual survey. In L. A. Pervin (Ed.), *Handbook of personality theory and research* (pp. 693–720). New York: Guilford Press.

Schroeder, M. A., Wormworth, J. A., & Livesley, W. J. (1992). Dimensions of personality disorder and their relationships to the Big Five dimensions of personality. *Psychological Assessment, 4,* 47–53.

Trull, T. J. (1992). DSM-III-R personality disorders and the five-factor model of personality: An empirical comparison. *Journal of Abnormal Psychology, 101,* 553–560.

Wakefield, J. C. (1992). Disorder as harmful dysfunction: A conceptual critique of DSM-III-R's definition of mental disorder. *Psychological Review, 99,* 232–247.

Walker, L. (1987). Inadequacies of the masochistic personality disorder diagnosis for women. *Journal of Personality Disorders, 1,* 183–189.

Watson, D., & Clark, L. A. (1984). Negative affectivity: The disposition to experience aversive emotional states. *Psychological Bulletin, 96,* 465–490.

Widiger, T. A. (1993). The DSM-III-R categorical personality disorder diagnoses: A critique and an alternative. *Psychological Inquiry, 4,* 75–90.

Widiger, T. A., & Frances, A. J. (1985). The DSM-III personality disorders: Perspectives from psychology. *Archives of General Psychiatry, 42,* 615–623.

Widiger, T. A., & Frances, A. J. (1989). Controversies concerning the self-defeating personality disorder. In R. Curtis (Ed.), *Self-defeating behaviors: Experimental research, clinical impressions, and practical implications* (pp. 289–309). New York: Plenum.

Widiger, T. A., & Trull, T. J. (1991). Diagnosis and clinical assessment. *Annual Review of Psychology, 42,* 109–133.

Wiggins, J. S., Phillips, N., & Trapnell, P. (1989). Circular reasoning about interpersonal behavior: Evidence concerning some untested assumptions underlying diagnostic classification. *Journal of Personality and Social Psychology, 56,* 296–305.

Wiggins, J. S., & Pincus, A. L. (1989). Conceptions of personality disorders and dimensions of personality. *Psychological Assessment: A Journal of Consulting and Clinical Psychology, 1,* 305–316.

SUMMARY AND UNRESOLVED ISSUES

Paul T. Costa, Jr. and Thomas A. Widiger

The preceding 21 chapters of this book have provided a psychologically based approach to understanding disorders of personality. In the introduction, we began with a critique of the revised third edition of the *Diagnostic and Statistical Manual of Mental Disorders* (*DSM-III-R*; American Psychiatric Association, 1987) personality disorder diagnoses. The authors of Part I indicated conceptually how the *DSM-III-R* (and the fourth edition of the *DSM* [*DSM-IV*]; American Psychiatric Association, in press) personality disorders represent maladaptive variants of the personality traits that are present in all individuals to varying degrees. In Part II, the authors presented a variety of empirical studies and research findings using the five-factor model (FFM; Costa & McCrae, 1992a) of personality with various patient populations, and in Part III, clinical case studies illustrated the power of the FFM to capture the essence of major features of several personality disorder types including the borderline, narcissistic, and passive–aggressive types. Treatment of personality-disordered patients was addressed in Part IV, and in Part V, the authors reconceptualized personality disorders by identifying dimensions and analyzing the conceptual distinctions and classification issues. The focus of the book has been centered around the FFM, which has substantial and growing empirical support as a comprehensive model of personality functioning, and the discussions of the FFM indicated how clinicians can use this model to guide diagnosis and treatment of personality disorders.

Since the chapters in this book were written, there have been other research findings, too numerous to summarize in these remaining pages, that support, extend, and amplify the hypotheses specified (Soldz, Budman, Demby, & Merry, 1993; Trull, 1992). A particularly important exchange occurred recently in the pages of *Psychological Inquiry*: A lead article by Widiger (1993) highlighted many of the issues examined in this book dealing with the applicability of the FFM to the personality disorder categories. Many of the commentators to Widiger's article raised critical questions and objections to his advocacy of the FFM as a useful guide to advancing the understanding of personality and disorders of personality. For example, some commentators suggested alternative dimensional models, including the interpersonal circumplex dimensions of affiliation and dominance; models that are based on neurobiological mechanisms in learning and motivation; and models that are based on evolutionary functions of survival, adaptation, and replication. Vigorous programs of comparative research will help provide information relevant to deciding on the optimal dimensional model.

Compared with the FFM, the *DSM* categories are no less controversial, as demonstrated by the numerous changes the diagnostic categories have undergone in the last decade. The third edition of the *DSM* (*DSM-III*; American Psychiatric Association, 1980) provided four new personality disorder diagnoses (avoidant, narcissistic, borderline, and schizotypal), two more were added in an appendix to *DSM-III-R* (self-defeating and sadistic), one more has been added in an appendix to *DSM-IV* (depressive), two have been deleted from this appendix in *DSM-IV* (self-defeating and sadistic), and one has been moved from the body of the manual to the appendix in *DSM-IV* (passive–aggressive). None of these decisions were without considerable controversy. Substantial objections were raised with respect to decisions to include the avoidant (Gunderson, 1983; Kernberg, 1984; Livesley, West, & Tanney, 1985; Michels, 1984), schizotypal (Gunderson, 1983; Siever & Gunderson, 1979), and self-defeating (Caplan, 1987; Walker, 1987) personality disorders. It is likely that the *DSM-IV* decisions to include the depressive and demote the self-defeating and passive–aggressive diagnoses will also generate controversy. Compelling arguments have also been made for alternative proposals, such as the hyperthymic (Akiskal & Akiskal, 1992) and racist (Hamlin, 1990) diagnoses.

One interpretation of these controversies is that psychiatrists and other clinicians have now begun to appreciate the importance of personality pathology. There is a wide range of contexts and functioning in which personality leads to problems in living and adaptation. The premise of this book is that the best guide to personality pathology is an understanding of personality itself, which at present is best provided by the FFM.

STATUS OF THE HYPOTHESIS

How well can personality pathology be described by the FFM? We can not review all of the evidence for the hypotheses linking the FFM's domains and facets to each of the personality disorder categories presented in the pages of this book and in the recent literature. But we present two examples: the category of borderline personality disorder and the dimension of Openness to Experience.

Borderline Personality Disorder

Is it true that studies of the FFM reveal something useful about personality disorder categories? The borderline personality diagnosis is of great interest to psychiatrists, psychologists, and other clinicians who are interested in Axis II disorders. In chapter 3 of this book, Widiger, Trull, Clarkin, Sanderson, and Costa hypothesized that major diagnostic features of the borderline personality disorder correspond to the five Neuroticism facets of hostility, impulsivity, vul-

nerability, depression, and anxiety; low standing on the dimensions of Agreeableness and Conscientiousness are also hypothesized to be characteristic of the borderline personality disorder.

Benjamin (1993) has nevertheless suggested that the FFM dimension of Neuroticism does not capture well the pathology of borderline personality disorder: "the five-factor NEO does not convey the intensity of [the borderline's] turmoil, the threat of suicide, or the ritualistic-like painful carving on her own body" (p. 92). However, it is important not to confuse the FFM dimensions with their assessment by the revised NEO Personality Inventory (NEO-PI-R). The NEO-PI-R is the most established and validated measure of the FFM (Costa & McCrae, 1992b), but it does not provide an operational definition of the full range of the FFM dimensions. The binge-eating impulsivity of the borderline personality disorder is represented well within the NEO-PI-R but not the impulsive spending, sexual promiscuity, substance abuse, shoplifting, reckless driving, and self-mutilative behaviors that are often seen in borderline patients (Widiger, 1993). These behaviors are within the domain of Neuroticism, but they were not included within the NEO-PI-R because they were rare within the normal population for which the NEO-PI was originally developed. It is readily apparent that the typical borderline symptomatology does represent a more extreme variant of (statistically) normal impulsivity, angry hostility, depression, and vulnerability. This has been demonstrated empirically in chapters 5, 8, 10, and 18 and has been illustrated nicely with the clinical cases in chapters 11 and 15.

In chapter 5, Wiggins and Pincus showed that the Minnesota Multiphasic Personality Inventory (Hathaway & McKinley, 1967) Borderline scale loads highly on a factor marked by Neuroticism scores from three different measures of the FFM: the NEO-PI (Costa & McCrae, 1985), the extended, revised Interpersonal Adjective Scales (IASR-B5; Trapnell & Wiggins, 1990; see also Goldberg, 1981), and the Hogan Personality Inventory (Hogan, 1986).

Lehne (in chapter 10) reported that the Millon Clinical Multiaxial Inventory (Millon, 1977) Borderline scale, as predicted, correlates significantly with NEO-PI domain Neuroticism scores in a large sample of forensic patients.

In chapter 18, Clark and Livesley showed strong correlations between *DSM-III-R* borderline criterial symptoms from both the Dimensional Assessment of Personality Pathology–Basic Questionnaire (DAPP-BQ; Livesley, 1990) factor scales (anxiousness, affective lability, identity problems, insecure attachment) and the Schedule for Nonadaptive and Adaptive Personality (SNAP; Clark, 1993) borderline personality symptom clusters (instability, hypersensitivity, self-derogation, and suicide proneness) and Neuroticism scores from two measures of the FFM in samples of university students, community adults, and patients.

Brooner, Schmidt, and Herbst (in chapter 8) demonstrated in a subgroup of opioid-abusing outpatients with borderline diagnoses that these individuals have a distinctive personality profile consisting of elevations on four of the five hypothesized facets of Neuroticism (i.e., angry hostility, depression, impulsivity, and vulnerability) as well as low Agreeableness and Conscientiousness scores. Studying an even larger group of carefully diagnosed female borderline personality disorder patients, Sanderson and Clarkin (in chapter 15) showed the hypothesized distinctive personality profile of extreme Neuroticism scores on all six Neuroticism facets. Their 64 borderline patients were also characterized by low Agreeableness and extremely low Conscientiousness. Finally, in his case study of the borderline personality disorder (chapter 11), Bruehl illustrated how excessive elevations of the facets of Neuroticism captured not only the clinician's experience of most borderline patients but the major features of this disorder as well.

Openness to Experience

Most personality disorders clearly have predictable personality correlates from the FFM. Conversely, one can ask whether all the personality dimensions of the FFM are relevant to personality pathology. It is clear from the example of borderline personality disorder that Neuroticism is an exceedingly important dimension. Extraversion and Agreeableness–Antagonism, the two axes of the interpersonal circumplex, have long been linked to interpersonal disorders (Carson, 1991; McLemore & Benjamin, 1979; Wiggins, Phillips, & Trapnell, 1989). Perhaps the most controversial case is that of Openness to Experience. Some

investigators have argued that only four of the five dimensions are related to personality pathology (e.g., Clark, 1993; Clark & Livesley, chapter 18 in this book; Hyler & Lyons, 1988; Kass, Skodol, Charles, Spitzer, & Williams, 1985). It is certainly the case that Openness to Experience is not directly linked to any single disorder in the same way that borderline personality disorder is to Neuroticism or that histrionic and schizoid personality disorders are to Extraversion–Introversion. But Widiger et al. (see Table 1 in chapter 3) hypothesized conceptual links to several of the personality disorders: for example, high openness to fantasy in schizotypal and narcissistic disorders; constricted or restricted affect (low openness to feelings) in schizoid, schizotypal, and obsessive–compulsive disorders; and high openness to feelings in histrionic personality disorder. There is some support for these hypotheses (e.g., Trull, 1992).

There is also a considerable amount of data showing that Openness to Experience is relevant to aspects of personality psychopathology. "Open" people are characterized by high scores on measures of dissociative tendencies, eccentric perceptions, and magical ideation (McCrae & Costa, in press). Individuals who are low scorers on Openness to Experience have rigid sex roles, more conservative sex attitudes, and sexual repression (Costa, Fagan, Piedmont, Ponticas, & Wise, 1992). Low Openness scores are also associated with DAPP-BQ Restricted Expression scale scores (Schroeder et al., chapter 7 in this book).

Stronger correlations are generally seen when individual facets of Openness to Experience are examined. Dissociative tendencies are most strongly related to openness to fantasy. On the other hand, more conservative sexual attitudes and rigid sex roles are correlated chiefly with low openness to values. Some disorders (e.g., schizotypal) combine open characteristics like eccentric thinking with closed characteristics such as restricted affect and anhedonia. Such combinations mean that overall openness may not be related to the disorder.

The problematic comorbidity of schizoid and schizotypal personality disorders may be due, in part, to the failure to distinguish the aspects of Openness to Experience that prototypical schizoid and schizotypal individuals display. Both disorders would be expected to appear low in openness to feelings, as indicated by the constricted affect and anhedonic criterial items. But the prototypical schizotypal individual may be readily distinguished from the prototypical schizoid individual by the relative standing on the Openness to Experience facets of excessive openness to fantasy and aesthetics. Odd beliefs and magical thinking are likely outcomes of extremely high openness to fantasy, whereas unusual perceptual experiences are reflections of a maladaptively high openness to fantasy (for an alternative view of schizotypal thinking as pseudo-openness see Tien, Costa, & Eaton, 1992).

To summarize, aspects of Openness to Experience are clearly relevant to personality pathology, but future research in this area needs to be conducted at the level of individual facets within each of the "Big Five" domains, a point of view cogently expressed by others (Clark, 1993; Harkness, 1992; Tellegen, 1985).

It appears that the links between personality disorders and normal personality dimensions first described by Wiggins and Pincus (1989) are robust in both normal and clinical populations and that the FFM can illuminate the *DSM-III-R* (and *DSM-IV*) disorders of personality and personality pathology more generally.

FUTURE DIRECTIONS: TWO APPROACHES TO PERSONALITY PATHOLOGY

As discussed in the last part of this book (Reconceptualization), future research on personality disorders can take one of two quite different approaches. Most of this book's contributors have argued for alternative dimensional approaches to replace the current *DSM* categorical approaches to diagnosing and treating personality pathology. Millon (chapter 19) provided a scholarly consideration and defense of attempts, like the *DSM*, to develop formal classifications of personality pathology. His position (and related ones that argue for retaining a set of personality disorder categories), although a minority one in this book, is, in fact, the prevailing one in the official, or real, world of diagnostic decision-making. For many years to come, people will be using the *DSM-IV*, and a

major question is how one can most effectively use the FFM to understand and treat the disorders defined in the *DSM* manual. Regardless of whether the personality disorder categories are retained or replaced, the FFM is surely going to be central to future research on personality pathology.

Staying the Categorical Course

As just stated, there will be 10 categories of personality disorder in the *DSM-IV*. We address three important issues that we feel need to be addressed if clinicians are to stay the categorical course. First, how can personality assessment be used to diagnose personality disorders? *DSM-III-R* states that "it is only when personality traits are inflexible and maladaptive and cause either significant functional impairment or subjective distress that they constitute Personality Disorders" (American Psychiatric Association, 1987, p. 335), but the *DSM* does not provide an operational definition or a clear-cut way to determine the significant level of inflexibility, maladaptivity, impairment, or distress—or even how to assess a trait. This problem could be resolved empirically by administering measures of the FFM to many personality-disordered groups and developing cutoff points and prediction equations to indicate the probability of associated personality disorder diagnoses. Even before cutoff points are developed, clinicians can use scores on the FFM's domains and facets to suggest possible diagnoses (to be confirmed by further clinical interviews or other personality disorder instruments). For example, high self-consciousness and anxiety scores, along with very low openness to actions scores might suggest diagnoses of avoidant personality disorder.

If the dimensions of the FFM are to be used in diagnosing *DSM* personality disorders, then alternative methods of assessing the dimensions need to be considered. Personality disorder research has traditionally emphasized the structured interview, and a comparable approach would be to obtain clinician ratings on the dimensions of the FFM (Miller, 1990), as illustrated in the case studies in this book. Self-report measures of personality disorders have also been widely used, and there are several standardized instruments for measuring the FFM through self-reports. A third alternative, which is not yet widely

used, would be ratings of personality from knowledgeable informants (e.g., spouses, peers). Research
in normal populations has shown that there is a considerable convergence among these different data
sources. Arguably, however, the presence of personality pathology might distort self-reports. Research on
the convergence of expert ratings, self-reports, and
informant ratings of personality in clinical populations will be valuable, as will studies that compare
these alternatives, alone and in combination, as predictors of clinical diagnoses.

A second question concerns the features that distinguish individuals with personality disorders from
individuals with similar personality profiles but no
personality disorders. Do more pathological or maladaptive variants of the normal dimensions of personality need to be defined (Widiger & Costa, in press)?
Is there a need for some dimensions beyond the FFM
to distinguish disordered personality from normal
personality?

Cognitive perceptual aberrations have been suggested as a leading candidate dimension to distinguish normal from abnormal personalities (Costa &
McCrae, 1990). Disturbances in thinking, and disordered cognition more broadly considered, might be a
pervasive feature of many forms of personality
pathology. Misperceptions of reality may be at the
root of the odd beliefs and magical thinking that
characterize the schizotypal personality disorder.
Ideas of reference and unusual perceptual experiences (bodily illusions) signify that schizotypal individuals have a different relation to conventional
reality than do most other individuals. More subtle
aspects of disordered cognition that are found in several other personality disorder categories (histrionic,
schizoid) include odd thinking and speech, as exemplified by vague, circumstantial, metaphorical, or
stereotyped speech.

Research in this area certainly needs to look carefully at the incremental contribution of these alternatives. Clark, Vorhies, and McEwen (chapter 6 of this
book) have taken an important first step in this
direction through the use of hierarchical multiple
regression analyses in which they first entered the
five dimensions of the FFM and then entered SNAP
personality disorder scales to determine the variance
accounted for by normal personality dimensions and

the explanatory power of dimensions beyond the
FFM.

Third, are new personality disorder categories
needed? The history of the *DSM* shows that the number and nature of the personality disorders is not
fixed. There may be other useful personality disorder
categories to consider. The FFM provides a comprehensive, logical, and systematic method of looking
for aspects of personality that might be pathological.
In this regard, the most obvious gap in the current
DSM taxonomy are disorders distinctly or uniquely
related to Openness to Experience.

If *DSM-IV* had been developed in the 1950s, an
important new candidate for consideration as a personality disorder might have been authoritarianism.
In the 1950s, psychologists and psychoanalytically
oriented psychiatrists were deeply concerned with
psychopathology related to dogmatic and absolutist
thinking, blind obedience to political and legal
authority, and hostile aggression toward outgroups—
minorities and deviants. The concept of authoritarianism grew out of studies of sociopolitical and economic attitudes and ideological individual difference
variables, which were vigorously pursued in the
1930s. As summarized by Christie (1991), the key
conceptual elements of this multifaceted syndrome
included emphasis on harsh discipline and conventionality in child rearing, submission to authority figures and institutions, and suspiciousness and
hostility toward outgroups.

Authoritarianism is not popular today because it
appears to make cultural, political, economic, and
religious judgments instead of psychological judgments. But low Openness to Experience (i.e., closed
to experience) may well be associated with certain
forms of psychopathology. The prototypically
"closed" person would resist technological innovation
and social change. Problems related to low Openness
to Experience might be seen in terms of dogmatism,
racism, sexism, and other ideological "isms." Several
nonideological variables related to authoritarian personality structure are of interest as well, including
rigidity of cognitive and emotional style, intolerance
of ambiguity, extreme needs for cognitive closure,
and preference for simplicity. It is plain that these
cognitive mechanisms and styles could lead to distinctive adaptive problems in complex societies with
shifting social mores and often sweeping technologi-

cal changes. Individuals with extremely low scores on Openness to Experience would doubtlessly be challenged to deal with each of these issues. Under such circumstances, the extremely closed person might be especially susceptible to the influence of cults and other organizations that seem to provide solutions to these challenges of cognitive assimilation/accommodation.

This condition might be recognized as a personality disorder in the next revision of the *DSM*. Other conditions (including perhaps excessive Openness to Experience) might also be identified by systematically examining the potential pathological expression of the traits that define the FFM.

Daring to Be Dimensional

A number of the contributors to this book have suggested that the current categorical model is at best a crude approximation to an adequate description of personality pathology. Rather than create new categories, they have argued that personality researchers should move to a dimensional approach. Although it has much to recommend it, the dimensional approach has a great deal of catching up to do with the categorical model in terms of clinical experience and application.

If, by using a dimensional approach to personality pathology, personality researchers abolish the distinctions between normal and abnormal personality traits, then they need to have coherent theories of psychopathology to indicate when it is appropriate to make clinical interventions to help people with personality-related pathology or problems. An upcoming volume titled *Differentiating Normal From Abnormal Personality* (Strack & Lorr, in press) gives a more comprehensive treatment to these issues than can be done here.

From the dimensional perspective, the distinction between normal and abnormal is not found in the nature of the personality dimensions (e.g., it is not that some are abnormal and others are normal), but it is more a matter of the fit between an individual's enduring dispositions and the problems or adaptive tasks that he or she is confronted with and that are central to his or her life. Under this view, the problem of accounting for personality pathology is not completely solved by adding dimensions of personal-

ity pathology, such as a dimension of cognitive–perceptual aberration. More research is needed that relates symptoms or problems in living to the traits in the FFM. Such research would form the basis for the systematic assessment of personality-related problems.

Even more urgent and convincing to clinicians would be research spelling out the treatment implications of FFM-based personality assessment. Sanderson and Clarkin (chapter 15 in this book) have taken an important first step in presenting some ways that personality information might guide treatment strategy and decision making. Much more systematic research along these lines will be important for both patients and the field of personality disorder research.

THE FFM AND THE *DSM*

Should the FFM have official status? This question is prompted by several responses to Widiger's (1993) advocacy of the FFM as an alternative framework for diagnosing personality disorders (Benjamin, 1993; Carson, 1993; Davis & Millon, 1993; Frances, 1993; Nathan, 1993; Schmidt, Wagner, & Kiesler, 1993). We believe that it would be premature to replace Axis II categories by the FFM. But a dual system would stimulate the kind of research and clinical experience that is needed to form the basis for choosing the optimal approach.

When a patient presents with borderline features, the advantage of a categorical system is that it gives a set of clinical expectations about personality traits that dimensional standing may not elicit. When the patient is a prototypical borderline, these expectations are correct. However, when the patient has only some features of borderline personality disorder, the expectations may be incorrect. By directly measuring most of the person's personality traits, the clinician's initial impressions can be corrected, expanded, and refined. Personality information provided by direct assessment will also be of use in managing and treating personality-disordered patients more effectively. Finally, a dual system would retain important personality information that is sometimes lost by the current placement of individuals into distinct categories. People who meet only three of the five *DSM-III-*

R borderline criteria may be described in terms of their standing on the FFM dimensions that are relevant to affective instability and reactivity, style of interpersonal relating, degree of organization and impulse control, and so on, even though they fail to meet the *DSM-III-R* criteria.

DSM-IV includes a statement about various dimensional models but fails to recommend any one of them. The *DSM-IV* Personality Disorder Work Group (Task Force on DSM-IV, 1991) approved a statement recognizing the existence of alternative dimensional models including the odd–eccentric, dramatic–emotional, and anxious–fearful clustering of the personality disorder categories; maladaptive personality dimension models such as the SNAP and the DAPP-BQ; and models underlying the entire domain of personality functioning, including the FFM. However, the work group felt that it would be "premature to give official recognition" to the FFM because there are different interpretations of the five dimensions.

In our view, the body of research on personality structure and the studies described in this book make it clear that the FFM is the best available model of personality structure and that it is undeniably relevant to an understanding of personality disorders. Future research may well improve upon the FFM, but in the meantime, clinicians and researchers would benefit from the official inclusion of the FFM as a supplement to Axis II diagnosis.

But would clinicians use a dimensional approach? Yes, many already do (e.g., Costa & McCrae, 1992a; MacKenzie [chapter 16 in this book]). The *DSM-IV* Personality Disorder Work Group in its statement on dimensional models raised the concern of how to assess the dimensions of personality via a clinical interview and how they would be used to make treatment and other clinical decisions. These are not insurmountable obstacles. The next few years will provide a much better picture about how dimensional approaches can be implemented in clinical practice.

Some observers have said that what is at issue here is the American Psychiatric Association "versus" the American Psychological Association. In other words, the potential conflict between psychiatric/categorical and psychological/dimensional models could

stall progress in this field. It has been suggested that the American Psychological Association should issue a rival *DSM* that uses a dimensional approach. We believe a far better solution would be cooperation between the two approaches, which would lead to more coordinated research and shared clinical experience.

Perhaps by the time that *DSM-V* is published, a better system can be offered that incorporates what is known about personality as the basis for understanding personality pathology. We hope this book advances that goal.

References

Akiskal, H. S., & Akiskal, K. (1992). Cyclothymic, hyperthymic, and depressive temperaments as subaffective variants of mood disorders. In A. Tasman & M. B. Riba (Eds.), *Review of psychiatry* (Vol. 11, pp. 43–62). Washington, DC: American Psychiatric Press.

American Psychiatric Association. (1980). *Diagnostic and statistical manual of mental disorders* (3rd ed.). Washington, DC: Author.

American Psychiatric Association. (1987). *Diagnostic and statistical manual of mental disorders* (3rd ed., rev.). Washington, DC: Author.

American Psychiatric Association. (in press). *Diagnostic and statistical manual of mental disorders* (4th ed.). Washington, DC: Author.

Benjamin, L. S. (1993). Dimensional, categorical, or hybrid analyses of personality: A response to Widiger's proposal. *Psychological Inquiry, 4*, 91–134.

Caplan, P. (1987). The psychiatric association's failure to meet its own standards: The dangers of self-defeating personality disorder as a category. *Journal of Personality Disorders, 1*, 178–182.

Carson, R. C. (1991). Dilemmas in the pathway of the DSM-IV. Special Issue: Diagnosis, dimensions and DSM-IV: The science of classification. *Journal of Abnormal Psychology, 100*, 302–307.

Carson, R. C. (1993). Can the Big Five help salvage the DSM? *Psychological Inquiry, 4*, 98–100.

Christie, R. (1991). Authoritarianism and related constructs. In J. P. Robinson, P. R. Shaver, & L. S. Wrightsman (Eds.), *Measures of personality and social psychological attitudes* (Vol. 1, pp. 501–571). San Diego, CA: Academic Press.

Clark, L. A. (1990). Toward a consensual set of symptom clusters for assessment of personality disorder. In J. Butcher & C. Spielberger (Eds.), *Advances in personality assessment* (Vol. 8, pp. 243–266). Hillsdale, NJ: Erlbaum.

Clark, L. A. (1993). *Manual for the Schedule for Nonadaptive and Adaptive Personality (SNAP)*. Minneapolis: University of Minnesota Press.

Costa, P. T., Jr., Fagan, P. J., Piedmont, R. L., Ponticas, Y., Wise, T. N. (1992). The five-factor model of personality and sexual functioning in outpatient men and women. *Psychiatric Medicine, 10,* 199–215.

Costa, P. T., Jr., & McCrae, R. R. (1985). *The NEO Personality Inventory manual*. Odessa, FL: Psychological Assessment Resources.

Costa, P. T., Jr., & McCrae, R. R. (1990). Personality disorders and the five-factor model of personality. *Journal of Personality Disorders, 4,* 362–371.

Costa, P. T., Jr., & McCrae, R. R. (1992a). The five-factor model of personality and its relevance to personality disorders. *Journal of Personality Disorders, 6,* 343–359.

Costa, P. T., Jr., & McCrae, R. R. (1992b). *Revised NEO Personality Inventory (NEO-PI-R) and NEO Five-Factor Inventory (NEO-FFI) professional manual*. Odessa, FL: Psychological Assessment Resources.

Davis, R. D., & Millon, T. (1993). The five-factor model for personality disorders: Apt or misguided. *Psychological Inquiry, 4,* 104–109.

Frances, A. (1993). Dimensional diagnosis of personality—Not whether, but when and which. *Psychological Inquiry, 4,* 110–111.

Goldberg, L. R. (1981). Language and individual differences: The search for universals in personality lexicons. In L. Wheeler (Ed.), *Review of personality and social psychology* (Vol. 2, pp. 141–165). Beverly Hills, CA: Sage.

Gunderson, J. G. (1983). DSM-III diagnosis of personality disorders. In J. Frosch (Ed.), *Current perspectives on personality disorders* (pp. 20–39). Washington, DC: American Psychiatric Press.

Hamlin, W. T. (1990). *The chains of psychological slavery: The mental illness of racism*. Baltimore: ICFP Inc.

Harkness, A. R. (1992). Fundamental topics in the personality disorders: Candidate trait dimensions from lower regions of the hierarchy. *Psychological Assessment, 4,* 251–259.

Hathaway, S. R., & McKinley, J. C. (1967). *Minnesota Multiphasic Personality Inventory manual*. New York: Psychological Corporation.

Hogan, R. (1986). *Hogan Personality Inventory manual*. Minneapolis, MN: National Computer Systems.

Hyler, S. E., & Lyons, M. (1988). Factor analysis of the DSM-III personality disorder clusters: A replication. *Comprehensive Psychiatry, 29,* 304–308

Kass, F., Skodol, A. E., Charles, E., Spitzer, R. L., & Williams, J. B. W. (1985). Scaled ratings of DSM-III personality disorders. *American Journal of Psychiatry, 142,* 627–630.

Kernberg, O. F. (1984). *Severe personality disorders*. New Haven, CT: Yale University Press.

Livesley, W. J. (1990). *Dimensional Assessment of Personality Pathology–Basic Questionnaire*. Unpublished manuscript, University of British Columbia, Vancouver, Canada.

Livesley, W. J., Jackson, D. N., & Schroeder, M. L. (1992). Factorial structure of traits delineating personality disorders in clinical and general population samples. *Journal of Abnormal Psychology, 101,* 432–440.

Livesley, W. J., West, M., & Tanney, A. (1985). Historical comment on the DSM-III schizoid and avoidant personality disorders. *American Journal of Psychiatry, 142,* 1344–1347.

McCrae, R. R. (in press). Psychopathology from the perspective of the five-factor model. In S. Strack & M. Lorr (Eds.), *Differentiating normal from abnormal psychology*. New York: Springer.

McCrae, R. R., & Costa, P. T., Jr. (in press). Conceptions and correlates of openness to experience. In R. Hogan, J. A. Hogan, & S. R. Briggs (Eds.), *Handbook of personality psychology*. San Diego, CA: Academic Press.

McLemore, C. W., & Benjamin, L. S. (1979). Whatever happened to interpersonal diagnosis? A psychosocial alternative to DSM-III. *American Psychologist, 34,* 17–34.

Michels, R. (1984). First rebuttal. *American Journal of Psychiatry, 141,* 548–551.

Miller, M. (1990). The power of the "OCEAN": Another way to diagnose clients. *Counselor-Education-and-Supervision, 29,* 283–290.

Millon, T. (1977). *Millon Clinical Multiaxial Inventory manual*. Minneapolis, MN: National Computer Systems.

Nathan, P. E. (1993). Can alcohol abuse and dependence be dimensionalized—and should they be? *Psychological Inquiry, 4,* 113–115.

Schmidt, J. A., Wagner, C. C., & Kiesler, D. J. (1993). DSM-IV Axis II: Dimensionality ratings? "Yes"; Big Five? "Perhaps later." *Psychological Inquiry, 4,* 119–121.

Siever, L. J., & Gunderson, J. G. (1979). Genetic determinants of borderline conditions. *Schizophrenia Bulletin, 5,* 59–86.

Soldz, S., Budman, S., Demby, A., & Merry, J. (1993). Representation of personality disorders in circumplex and five-factor space: Explorations with a clinical sample. *Psychological Assessment, 5,* 41–52.

Strack, S., & Lorr, M. (Eds.). (in press). *Differentiating normal from abnormal psychology*. New York: Springer.

Task Force on DSM-IV. (1991). *DSM-IV options book: Work in progress (9/1/91)*. Washington, DC: American Psychiatric Association.

Tellegen, A. (1985). Structures of mood and personality and their relevance to assessing anxiety, with an emphasis on self-report. In H. Tuma & J. D. Maser (Eds.), *Anxiety and the anxiety disorders* (pp. 681–706). Hillsdale, NJ: Erlbaum.

Tien, A. Y., Costa, P. T., Jr., & Eaton, W. W. (1992). Covariance of personality, neurocognition, and schizophrenia spectrum traits in the community. *Schizophrenia Research, 7,* 149–158.

Trapnell, P. D., & Wiggins, J. S. (1990). Extension of the Interpersonal Adjective Scales to include the Big Five dimensions of personality. *Journal of Personality and Social Psychology, 59,* 781–790.

Trull, T. J. (1992). DSM-III-R personality disorders and the five-factor model of personality: An empirical comparison. *Journal of Abnormal Psychology, 101,* 553–560.

Walker, L. (1987). Inadequacies of the masochistic personality disorder diagnosis for women. *Journal of Personality Disorders, 1,* 183–189.

West, K. (1993). *The placement of cognitive and perceptual aberrations within the five-factor model.* Unpublished manuscript, University of Kentucky, Lexington.

Widiger, T. A. (1992). Categorical versus dimensional classification: Implications from and for research. *Journal of Personality Disorders, 6,* 287–300.

Widiger, T. A. (1993). The DSM-III-R categorical personality disorder diagnoses: A critique and an alternative. *Psychological Inquiry, 4,* 75–90.

Widiger, T. A., & Costa, P. T. Jr. (in press). Personality and personality disorders. *Journal of Abnormal Psychology.*

Widiger, T. A., & Sanderson, C. J. (in press). Towards a dimensional model of personality disorder in DSM-IV and DSM-V. In W. J. Livesley (Ed.), *DSM-IV personality disorders.* New York: Guilford Press.

Widiger, T. A., & Trull, T. J. (1992). Personality and psychopathology: An application of the five-factor model. *Journal of Personality, 60,* 363–393.

Wiggins, J. S., Phillips, N., & Trapnell, P. (1989). Circular reasoning about interpersonal behavior: Evidence concerning some untested assumptions underlying diagnostic classification. *Journal of Personality and Social Psychology, 56,* 296–305.

Wiggins, J. S., & Pincus, A. L. (1989). Conceptions of personality disorders and dimensions of personality. *Psychological Assessment: A Journal of Consulting and Clinical Psychology, 3,* 305–316.

DSM-III-R Personality Disorders and the Five-Factor Model

Diagnostic criteria	PAR	SZD	SZT	ATS	BDL	HST	NAR	AVD	DEP	OBC	PAG
Neuroticism											
Anxiety	h		h	h/**L**	H			H	H		
Hostility	H	L		H	H	H	H			h	H
Depression			h	h	H		h/L	h	H	h	
Self-Consciousness		L	H	**L**	**H**	H	H	H	h	h	
Impulsiveness				H	H						
Vulnerability			h		H	h	**H**	H	H		
Extraversion											
Warmth	l	L	L	l		H		L/H	**h**	L	
Gregariousness	l	L	L		**h**	h		L			
Assertiveness					**h**		H	L	L	H	
Activity						h		L			
Excitement Seeking		**L**		H		h		L		**l**	
Positive Emotions	l	L			**h**	H					l
Openness											
Fantasy			H			h	H				
Aesthetics	l										
Feelings	l	L	L			H				L	
Actions	**L**					h		L			
Ideas			H			l					
Values			h							L	
Agreeableness											
Trust	L		L			h					
Straightforwardness	L			L	**L**	l	l				L
Altruism				L		L	L		H	L	
Compliance	L	h		L	L				H	L	L
Modesty	l			**L**			L		H		
Tendermindedness	l			L			L		**h**		
Conscientiousness											
Competence	h					l	**h**				L
Order										H	
Dutifulness				L						H	L
Achievement Striving		l			L		**h**		L	H	
Self-Discipline				L	L						L
Deliberation				L						H	

Note. H, L = high, low, respectively, based on *DSM-III-R* (American Psychiatric Association, 1987) diagnostic criteria; h, l = high, low, respectively, based on associated features provided in *DSM-III-R* (American Psychiatric Association, 1987); **H/h, L/l** = high, low, respectively, based on clinical literature. Personality disorders: PAR = paranoid; SZD = schizoid; SZT = schizotypal; ATS = antisocial; BDL = borderline; HST = histrionic; NAR = narcissistic; AVD = avoidant; DEP = dependent; OBC = obsessive–compulsive; PAG = passive–aggressive.

Personality Disorders Proposed for *DSM-IV*

Diagnostic criteria	NEG	SDF	DPS	SDS
Neuroticism				
Anxiety			H	
Hostility	H			h
Depression		H	H	l
Self-Consciousness			H	
Impulsiveness				
Vulnerability		H		
Extraversion				
Warmth				
Gregariousness				
Assertiveness	H			H
Activity				
Excitement Seeking				
Positive Emotions		L		
Openness				
Fantasy				
Aesthetics				
Feelings				
Actions				
Ideas				
Values				
Agreeableness				
Trust				
Straightforwardness		L		
Altruism		H		**L**
Compliance	L	L		L
Modesty				
Tendermindedness			L	L
Conscientiousness				
Competence	L			
Order				
Dutifulness				
Achievement Striving		L		
Self-Discipline		L		
Deliberation				

Note. H/h, L/l = high, low, respectively, based on proposed *DSM-IV* diagnostic criteria (Task Force on DSM-IV, 1991); **H, L** = high, low, based on clinical literature. Personality disorders: NEG = negativistic; SDF = self-defeating; DPS = depressive; SDS = sadistic.

Diagnostic Criteria of *DSM-III-R* Axis II Personality Disorders

CLUSTER A

Paranoid Personality Disorder

A. A pervasive and unwarranted tendency, beginning by early adulthood and present in a variety of contexts, to interpret the actions of people as deliberately demeaning or threatening, as indicated by at least four of the following:

1. expects, without sufficient basis, to be exploited or harmed by others
2. questions, without justification, the loyalty or trustworthiness of friends or associates
3. reads hidden demeaning or threatening meanings into benign remarks or events (e.g., suspects that a neighbor put out trash early to annoy him)
4. bears grudges or is unforgiving of insults or slights
5. is reluctant to confide in others because of unwarranted fear that the information will be used against him or her
6. is easily slighted and quick to react with anger or to counterattack
7. questions, without justification, fidelity of spouse or sexual partner

B. Occurrence not exclusively during the course of schizophrenia or a delusional disorder

Schizoid Personality Disorder

A. A pervasive pattern of indifference to social relationships and a restricted range of emotional experience and expression, beginning by early adulthood and present in a variety of contexts, as indicated by at least four of the following:

1. neither desires nor enjoys close relationships, including being part of a family
2. almost always chooses solitary activities
3. rarely, if ever, claims or appears to experience strong emotions, such as anger and joy
4. indicates little if any desire to have sexual experiences with another person (age being taken into account)
5. is indifferent to the praise and criticism of others

6. has no close friends or confidants (or only one) other than first-degree relatives
7. displays constricted affect (e.g., is aloof, cold, rarely reciprocates gestures or facial expression, such as smiles or nods)

B. Occurrence not exclusively during the course of schizophrenia or a delusional disorder

Schizotypal Personality Disorder

A. A pervasive pattern of deficits in interpersonal relatedness and peculiarities of ideation, appearance, and behavior, beginning by early adulthood and present in a variety of contexts, as indicated by at least five of the following:

1. ideas of reference (excluding delusions of reference)
2. excessive social anxiety (e.g., extreme discomfort in social situations involving unfamiliar people)
3. odd beliefs or magical thinking, influencing behavior and inconsistent with subcultural norms (e.g., superstitiousness, belief in clairvoyance, telepathy, or "sixth sense," "others can feel my feelings"; in children and adolescents, bizarre fantasies or preoccupations)
4. unusual perceptual experiences (e.g., illusions, sensing the presence of a force or person not actually present, e.g., "I felt as if my dead mother were in the room with me")
5. odd or eccentric behavior or appearance (e.g., unkempt, unusual mannerisms, talks to self)
6. no close friends or confidants (or only one) other than first-degree relatives
7. odd speech (without loosening of associations or incoherence, e.g., speech that is impoverished, digressive, vague, or inappropriately abstract)
8. inappropriate or constricted affect (e.g., silly, aloof, rarely reciprocates gestures or facial expressions, such as smiles or nods)
9. suspiciousness or paranoid ideation

B. Occurrence not exclusively during the course of schizophrenia or a delusional disorder

CLUSTER B

Antisocial Personality Disorder

A. Current age of at least 18 years
B. Evidence of conduct disorder with onset before the age of 15 years, as indicated by a history of three or more of the following:

1. was often truant
2. ran away from home overnight at least twice while living in parental or parental surrogate home (or once without returning)
3. often initiated physical fights
4. used a weapon in more than one fight
5. forced someone into sexual activity with him or her
6. was physically cruel to animals
7. was physically cruel to other people
8. deliberately destroyed others' property (other than by fire-setting)
9. deliberately engaged in fire-setting

10. often lied (other than to avoid physical or sexual abuse)
11. has stolen without confrontation of a victim on more than one occasion (including forgery)
12. has stolen with confrontation of a victim (e.g., mugging, purse-snatching, extortion, armed robbery)

C. A pattern of irresponsible and antisocial behavior since the age of 15 years, as indicated by at least four of the following:

1. is unable to sustain consistent work behavior, as indicated by any of the following (including similar behavior in academic settings if the person is a student):

   a. significant unemployment for 6 months or more within 5 years when expected to work and work was available
   b. repeated absences from work unexplained by illness in self or family
   c. abandonment of several jobs without realistic plans for others

2. fails to conform to social norms with respect to lawful behavior, as indicated by repeatedly performing antisocial acts that are grounds for arrest (whether arrested or not, e.g., destroying property, harassing others, stealing, pursuing an illegal occupation)
3. is irritable and aggressive, as indicated by repeated physical fights or assaults (not required by one's job or to defend someone or oneself), including spouse- or child-beating
4. repeatedly fails to honor financial obligations, as indicated by defaulting on debts or failing to provide child support or support for other dependents on a regular basis
5. fails to plan ahead, or is impulsive, as indicated by one or both of the following:

   a. traveling from place to place without a prearranged job or clear goal for the period of travel or clear idea about when the travel will terminate
   b. lack of a fixed address for a month or more

6. has no regard for the truth, as indicated by repeated lying, use of aliases, or "conning" others for personal profit or pleasure
7. is reckless regarding his or her own or others' personal safety, as indicated by driving while intoxicated or recurrent speeding
8. if a parent or guardian, lacks ability to function as a responsible parent, as indicated by one or more of the following:

   a. malnutrition of child
   b. child's illness resulting from lack of minimal hygiene
   c. failure to obtain medical care for a seriously ill child
   d. child's dependence on neighbors or nonresident relatives for food or shelter
   e. failure to arrange for a caretaker for young child when parent is away from home
   f. repeated squandering, on personal items, of money required for household necessities

9. has never sustained a totally monogamous relationship for more than 1 year
10. lacks remorse (feels justified in having hurt, mistreated, or stolen from another)

D. Occurrence of antisocial behavior not exclusively during the course of schizophrenia or manic episodes

Borderline Personality Disorder

A pervasive pattern of instability of mood, interpersonal relationships, and self-image, beginning by early adulthood and present in a variety of contexts, as indicated by at least five of the following:

1. a pattern of unstable and intense interpersonal relationships characterized by alternating between extremes of overidealization and devaluation
2. impulsiveness in at least two areas that are potentially self-damaging (e.g., spending, sex, substance abuse, shoplifting, reckless driving, binge eating; do not include suicidal or self-mutilating behavior covered in 5)
3. affective instability: marked shifts from baseline mood to depression, irritability, or anxiety, usually lasting a few hours and only rarely more than a few days
4. inappropriate, intense anger or lack of control of anger (e.g., frequent displays of temper, constant anger, recurrent physical fights)
5. recurrent suicidal threats, gestures, or behavior, or self-mutilating behavior
6. marked and persistent identity disturbance manifested by uncertainty about at least two of the following: self-image, sexual orientation, long-term goals or career choice, type of friends desired, preferred values
7. chronic feelings of emptiness or boredom
8. frantic efforts to avoid real or imagined abandonment (do not include suicidal or self-mutilating behavior covered in 5)

Histrionic Personality Disorder

A pervasive pattern of excessive emotionality and attention-seeking, beginning by early adulthood and present in a variety of contexts, as indicated by at least four of the following:

1. constantly seeks and demands reassurance, approval, or praise
2. is inappropriately sexually seductive in appearance or behavior
3. is overly concerned with physical attractiveness
4. expresses emotion with inappropriate exaggeration (e.g., embraces casual acquaintances with excessive ardor, uncontrollable sobbing on minor sentimental occasions, has temper tantrums)
5. is uncomfortable in situations in which he or she is not the center of attention
6. displays rapidly shifting and shallow expression of emotions
7. is self-centered, actions being directed toward obtaining immediate satisfaction; has no tolerance for the frustration of delayed gratification
8. has a style of speech that is excessively impressionistic and lacking in detail (e.g., when asked to describe mother, can be no more specific than, "She was a beautiful person")

Narcissistic Personality Disorder

A pervasive pattern of grandiosity (in fantasy or behavior), lack of empathy, and hypersensitivity to the evaluation of others, beginning by early adulthood and present in a variety of contexts, as indicated by at least five of the following:

1. reacts to criticism with feelings of rage, shame, or humiliation (even if not expressed)
2. is interpersonally exploitative: takes advantage of others to achieve his or her own ends
3. has a grandiose sense of self-importance (e.g., exaggerates achievements and talents, expects to be noticed as "special" without appropriate achievement)

4. believes that his or her problems are unique and can be understood only by other special people

5. is preoccupied with fantasies of unlimited success, power, brilliance, beauty, or ideal love

6. has a sense of entitlement: unreasonable expectation of especially favorable treatment (e.g., assumes that he or she does not have to wait in line when others must do so)

7. requires constant attention and admiration (e.g., keeps fishing for compliments)

8. lack of empathy: inability to recognize and experience how others feel (e.g., annoyance and surprise when a friend who is seriously ill cancels a date)

9. is preoccupied with feelings of envy

CLUSTER C

Avoidant Personality Disorder

A pervasive pattern of social discomfort, fear of negative evaluation, and timidity, beginning by early adulthood and present in a variety of contexts, as indicated by at least four of the following:

1. is easily hurt by criticism or disapproval

2. has no close friends or confidants (or only one) other than first-degree relatives

3. is unwilling to get involved with people unless certain of being liked

4. avoids social or occupational activities that involve significant interpersonal contact (e.g., refuses a promotion that will increase social demands)

5. is reticent in social situations because of a fear of saying something inappropriate or foolish, or of being unable to answer a question

6. fears being embarrassed by blushing, crying, or showing signs of anxiety in front of other people

7. exaggerates the potential difficulties, physical dangers, or risks involved in doing something ordinary but outside his or her usual routine (e.g., may cancel social plans because she anticipates being exhausted by the effort of getting there)

Dependent Personality Disorder

A pervasive pattern of dependent and submissive behavior, beginning by early adulthood and present in a variety of contexts, as indicated by at least five of the following:

1. is unable to make everyday decisions without an excessive amount of advice or reassurance from others

2. allows others to make most of his or her important decisions (e.g., where to live, what job to take)

3. agrees with people even when he or she believes they are wrong because of fear of being rejected

4. has difficulty initiating projects or doing things on his or her own

5. volunteers to do things that are unpleasant or demeaning in order to get other people to like him or her

6. feels uncomfortable or helpless when alone or goes to great lengths to avoid being alone

7. feels devastated or helpless when close relationships end

8. is frequently preoccupied with fears of being abandoned
9. is easily hurt by criticism or disapproval

Obsessive–Compulsive Personality Disorder

A pervasive pattern of perfectionism and inflexibility, beginning by early adulthood and present in a variety of contexts, as indicated by at least five of the following:

1. perfectionism that interferes with task completion (e.g., inability to complete a project because own overly strict standards are not met)
2. preoccupation with details, rules, lists, order, organization, or schedules to the extent that the major point of the activity is lost
3. unreasonable insistence that others submit to exactly his or her way of doing things or unreasonable reluctance to allow others to do things because of the conviction that they will not do them correctly
4. excessive devotion to work and productivity to the exclusion of leisure activities and friendships (not accounted for by obvious economic necessity)
5. indecisiveness: decision making is avoided, postponed, or protracted (e.g., the person cannot get assignments done on time because of ruminating about priorities; do not include if indecisiveness is due to excessive need for advice or reassurance from others)
6. overconscientiousness, scrupulousness, and inflexibility about matters of morality, ethics, or values (not accounted for by cultural or religious identification)
7. restricted expression of affection
8. lack of generosity in giving time, money, or gifts when no personal gain is likely to result
9. inability to discard worn-out or worthless objects even when they have no sentimental value

Passive–Aggressive Personality Disorder

A pervasive pattern of passive resistance to demands for adequate social and occupational performance, beginning by early adulthood and present in a variety of contexts, as indicated by at least five of the following:

1. procrastinates (i.e., puts off things that need to be done so that deadlines are not met)
2. becomes sulky, irritable, or argumentative when asked to do something he or she does not want to do
3. seems to work deliberately slowly or to do a bad job on tasks that he or she really does not want to do
4. protests, without justification, that others make unreasonable demands on him or her
5. avoids obligations by claiming to have "forgotten"
6. believes that he or she is doing a much better job than others think he or she is doing
7. resents useful suggestions from others concerning how he or she could be more productive
8. obstructs the efforts of others by failing to do his or her share of the work
9. unreasonably criticizes or scorns people in positions of authority

PROPOSED PERSONALITY DISORDERS

Sadistic Personality Disorder

A. A pervasive pattern of cruel, demeaning, and aggressive behavior, beginning by early adulthood, as indicated by the repeated occurrence of at least four of the following:

1. has used physical cruelty or violence for the purpose of establishing dominance in a relationship (not merely to achieve some noninterpersonal goal, such as striking someone in order to rob him or her)
2. humiliates or demeans people in the presence of others
3. has treated or disciplined someone under his or her control unusually harshly (e.g., a child, student, prisoner, or patient)
4. is amused by, or takes pleasure in, the psychological or physical suffering of others (including animals)
5. has lied for the purpose of harming or inflicting pain on others (not merely to achieve some other goal)
6. gets other people to do what he or she wants by frightening them (through intimidation or even terror)
7. restricts the autonomy of people with whom he or she has a close relationship (e.g., will not let spouse leave the house unaccompanied or permit teen-age daughter to attend social functions)
8. is fascinated by violence, weapons, martial arts, injury, or torture

B. The behavior in A has not been directed toward only one person (e.g., spouse, one child) and has not been solely for the purpose of sexual arousal (as in sexual sadism).

Self-Defeating Personality Disorder

A. A pervasive pattern of self-defeating behavior, beginning by early adulthood and present in a variety of contexts. The person may often avoid or undermine pleasurable experiences, be drawn to situations or relationships in which he or she will suffer, and prevent others from helping him or her, as indicated by at least five of the following:

1. chooses people and situations that lead to disappointment, failure, or mistreatment even when better options are clearly available
2. rejects or renders ineffective the attempts of others to help him or her
3. following positive personal events (e.g., new achievement), responds with depression, guilt, or a behavior that produces pain (e.g., an accident)
4. incites angry or rejecting responses from others and then feels hurt, defeated, or humiliated (e.g., makes fun of spouse in public, provoking an angry retort, then feels devastated)
5. rejects opportunities for pleasure or is reluctant to acknowledge enjoying himself or herself (despite having adequate social skills and the capacity for pleasure)
6. fails to accomplish tasks crucial to his or her personal objectives despite demonstrated ability to do so (e.g., helps fellow students write papers but is unable to write his or her own)
7. is uninterested in or rejects people who consistently treat him or her well (e.g., is unattracted to caring sexual partners)

    8. engages in excessive self-sacrifice that is unsolicited by the intended recipients of the sacrifice

B. The behaviors in A do not occur exclusively in response to, or in anticipation of, being physically, sexually, or psychologically abused.

C. The behaviors in A do not occur only when the person is depressed.

Description of the Revised NEO Personality Inventory (NEO-PI-R) Facet Scales

NEUROTICISM FACETS

N1: Anxiety
Anxious individuals are apprehensive, fearful, prone to worry, nervous, tense, and jittery. The scale does not measure specific fears or phobias, but high scorers are more likely to have such fears, as well as free-floating anxiety. Low scorers are calm and relaxed; they do not dwell on things that might go wrong.

N2: Angry Hostility
Angry hostility represents the tendency to experience anger and related states such as frustration and bitterness. This scale measures the individual's readiness to experience anger; whether the anger is expressed depends on the individual's level of Agreeableness. Note, however, that disagreeable people often score high on this scale. Low scorers are easygoing and slow to anger.

N3: Depression
This scale measures normal individual differences in the tendency to experience depressive affect. High scorers are prone to feelings of guilt, sadness, hopelessness, and loneliness. They are easily discouraged and often dejected. Low scorers rarely experience such emotions, but they are not necessarily cheerful and lighthearted—characteristics that are associated instead with Extraversion.

N4: Self-Consciousness
The emotions of shame and embarrassment form the core of this facet of Neuroticism. Self-conscious individuals are uncomfortable around others, sensitive to ridicule, and prone to feelings of inferiority. Self-consciousness is akin to shyness and social anxiety. Low scorers do not necessarily have poise or good social skills; they are simply less disturbed by awkward social situations.

Adapted from the *Revised NEO Personality Inventory (NEO-PI-R) and NEO Five-Factor Inventory (NEO-FFI) Professional Manual* by P. T. Costa, Jr. and R. R. McCrae, 1992, Odessa, FL: Psychological Assessment Resources. Copyright 1992 by Psychological Assessment Resources.

N5: Impulsiveness

In the NEO-PI-R, impulsiveness refers to the inability to control cravings and urges. Desires (e.g., for food, cigarettes, possessions) are perceived as being so strong that the individual cannot resist them, although he or she may later regret the behavior. Low scorers find it easier to resist such temptations, having a high tolerance for frustration. The term *impulsive* is used by many theorists to refer to many different and unrelated traits. NEO-PI-R impulsiveness should not be confused with spontaneity, risk-taking, or rapid decision time.

N6: Vulnerability

The final facet of Neuroticism is vulnerability to stress. Individuals who score high on this scale feel unable to cope with stress, becoming dependent, hopeless, or panicked when facing emergency situations. Low scorers perceive themselves as capable of handling themselves in difficult situations.

EXTRAVERSION FACETS

E1: Warmth

Warmth is the facet of Extraversion that is most relevant to issues of interpersonal intimacy. Warm people are affectionate and friendly. They genuinely like people and easily form close attachments to others. Low scorers are neither hostile nor necessarily lacking in compassion, but they are more formal, reserved, and distant in manner than are high scorers. Warmth is the facet of Extraversion that is closest to Agreeableness in interpersonal space, but it is distinguished by a cordiality and heartiness that is not part of Agreeableness.

E2: Gregariousness

A second aspect of Extraversion is gregariousness—the preference for other people's company. Gregarious people enjoy the company of others, and the more the merrier. Low scorers on this scale tend to be loners who do not seek—or who even actively avoid—social stimulation.

E3: Assertiveness

High scorers on this scale are dominant, forceful, and socially ascendant. They speak without hesitation and often become group leaders. Low scorers prefer to keep in the background and let others do the talking.

E4: Activity

A high activity score is seen in rapid tempo and vigorous movement, in a sense of energy, and in a need to keep busy. Active people lead fast-paced lives. Low scorers are more leisurely and relaxed in tempo, although they are not necessarily sluggish or lazy.

E5: Excitement Seeking

High scorers on this scale crave excitement and stimulation. They like bright colors and noisy environments. Excitement seeking is akin to some aspects of sensation seeking. Low scorers feel little need for thrills and prefer a life that high scorers might find boring.

E6: Positive Emotions

The last facet of Extraversion assesses the tendency to experience positive emotions such as joy, happiness, love, and excitement. High scorers on the positive emotions scale laugh easily and often. They are cheerful and optimistic. Low scorers are not necessarily unhappy; they are merely less exuberant and high-spirited. Research has shown that happiness and life satisfaction are related to both Neuroticism and Extraversion and that positive emotions is the facet of Extraversion most relevant to the prediction of happiness.

OPENNESS TO EXPERIENCE FACETS

O1: Fantasy

Individuals who are open to fantasy have a vivid imagination and an active fantasy life. They daydream not simply as an escape but as a way of creating for themselves an interesting inner world. They elaborate and develop their fantasies and believe that imagination contributes to a rich and creative life. Low scorers are more prosaic and prefer to keep their minds on the task at hand.

O2: Aesthetics

High scorers on this scale have a deep appreciation for art and beauty. They are moved by poetry, absorbed in music, and intrigued by art. They need not have artistic talent, nor even necessarily what most people would consider good taste; but for many of them, their interest in the arts will lead them to develop a wider knowledge and appreciation than that of the average individual. Low scorers are relatively insensitive to and uninterested in art and beauty.

O3: Feelings

Openness to feelings implies receptivity to one's own inner feelings and emotions and the evaluation of emotion as an important part of life. High scorers experience deeper and more differentiated emotional states and feel both happiness and unhappiness more intensely than do others. Low scorers have somewhat blunted affects and do not believe that feeling states are of much importance.

O4: Actions

Openness is seen behaviorally in the willingness to try different activities, go new places, or eat unusual foods. High scorers on this scale prefer novelty and variety to familiarity and routine. Over time, they may engage in a series of different hobbies. Low scorers find change difficult and prefer to stick with the tried-and-true.

O5: Ideas

Intellectual curiosity is an aspect of Openness that has long been recognized. This trait is seen not only in an active pursuit of intellectual interests for their own sake but also in open-mindedness and a willingness to consider new, perhaps unconventional ideas. High scorers enjoy both philosophical arguments and brain teasers. Openness to ideas does not necessarily imply high intelligence, although it can contribute to the development of intellectual potential. Low scorers on this scale have limited capacity and, if highly intelligent, narrowly focus their resources on limited topics.

O6: Values

Openness to values means the readiness to reexamine social, political, and religious values. Closed individuals tend to accept authority and honor tradition and as a consequence are generally conservative, regardless of political party affiliation. Openness to values may be considered the opposite of dogmatism.

AGREEABLENESS FACETS

A1: Trust

High scorers on this scale have a disposition to believe that others are honest and well-intentioned. Low scorers on this scale tend to be cynical and skeptical and to assume that others may be dishonest or dangerous.

A2: Straightforwardness

Straightforward individuals are frank, sincere, and ingenuous. Low scorers on this scale are more willing to manipulate others through flattery, craftiness, or deception. They view these tactics as necessary social skills and may regard more straightforward people as naive. When interpreting this scale (as well as other Agreeableness and Conscientiousness scales), it is particularly important to recall that scores reflect standing relative to other individuals. A low scorer on this scale is more likely to stretch the truth or to be guarded in expressing his or her true feelings, but this should not be interpreted to mean that he or she is a dishonest or manipulative person. In particular, this scale should not be regarded as a lie scale, either for assessing the validity of the test itself or for making predictions about honesty in employment or other settings.

A3: Altruism

High scorers on this scale have an active concern for others' welfare as shown in generosity, consideration of others, and a willingness to assist others in need of help. Low scorers on this scale are somewhat more self-centered and are reluctant to get involved in the problems of others.

A4: Compliance

This facet of Agreeableness concerns characteristic reactions to interpersonal conflict. The high scorer tends to defer to others, to inhibit aggression, and to forgive and forget. Compliant people are meek and mild. The low scorer is aggressive, prefers to compete rather than cooperate, and has no reluctance to express anger when necessary.

A5: Modesty

High scorers on this scale are humble and self-effacing although they are not necessarily lacking in self-confidence or self-esteem. Low scorers believe they are superior people and may be considered conceited or arrogant by others. A pathological lack of modesty is part of the clinical conception of narcissism.

A6: Tendermindedness

This facet scale measures attitudes of sympathy and concern for others. High scorers are moved by others' needs and emphasize the human side of social policies. Low scorers are more hardheaded and less moved by appeals to pity. They would consider themselves realists who make rational decisions based on cold logic.

CONSCIENTIOUSNESS FACETS

C1: Competence
Competence refers to the sense that one is capable, sensible, prudent, and effective. High scorers on this scale feel well prepared to deal with life. Low scorers have a lower opinion of their abilities and admit that they are often unprepared and inept. Of all the Conscientiousness facets, competence is most highly associated with self-esteem and internal locus of control.

C2: Order
High scorers on this scale are neat, tidy, and well-organized. They keep things in their proper places. Low scorers are unable to get organized and describe themselves as unmethodical. Carried to an extreme, high order might contribute to a compulsive personality disorder.

C3: Dutifulness
In one sense, conscientious means "governed by conscience," and that aspect of Conscientiousness is assessed as dutifulness. High scorers on this scale adhere strictly to their ethical principles and scrupulously fulfill their moral obligations. Low scorers are more casual about such matters and may be somewhat undependable or unreliable.

C4: Achievement Striving
Individuals who score high on this facet have high aspiration levels and work hard to achieve their goals. They are diligent and purposeful and have a sense of direction in life. Very high scorers, however, may invest too much in their careers and become workaholics. Low scorers are lackadaisical and perhaps even lazy. They are not driven to succeed. They lack ambition and may seem aimless, but they are often perfectly content with their low levels of achievement.

C5: Self-Discipline
Self-discipline refers to the ability to begin tasks and carry them through to completion despite boredom and other distractions. High scorers have the ability to motivate themselves to get the job done. Low scorers procrastinate in beginning chores and are easily discouraged and eager to quit. Low self-discipline is easily confused with impulsiveness—both are evident of poor self-control—but empirically they are distinct. People high in impulsiveness cannot resist doing what they do not want themselves to do; people low in self-discipline cannot force themselves to do what they want themselves to do. The former requires an emotional stability; the latter, a degree of motivation that they do not possess.

C6: Deliberation
The final facet of Conscientiousness is deliberation—the tendency to think carefully before acting. High scorers on this facet are cautious and deliberate. Low scorers are hasty and often speak or act without considering the consequences. At best, low scorers are spontaneous and able to make snap decisions when necessary.

Brief Content Descriptions of the SNAP Trait and Temperament Scales

NEGATIVE TEMPERAMENT (NT)

High: prone to negative emotional experiences; moody; feel chronically nervous and stressed; easily annoyed or irritated; worry a great deal; have difficulty concentrating.

Low: not nervous or anxious; take life's difficulties in stride; usually remain calm; not easily upset; recover quickly from negative experiences.

MISTRUST (MST)

High: suspicious; mistrustful; cynical about interpersonal relationships; often feel betrayed or disappointed; self-protective; believe it's best to keep others at a distance.

Low: trustful/naive about interpersonal relationships; feel stable and secure in friendships; do not hide their feelings; feel they are treated fairly.

MANIPULATIVENESS (MAN)

High: manipulate others; enjoy taking advantage of others' weaknesses; little regard for others' rights and feelings; bend rules as far as possible; consider themselves clever and skillful at con games.

Low: do not enjoy "beating the system"; respectful of others; would not hurt others to get things; do not avoid work or bend the truth to advantage.

AGGRESSION (AGG)

High: easily angered; may have violent temper; quarrel frequently; enjoy physical fights; readily provoked by insults; hold grudges; seek revenge.

Low: not readily angered; easily control their temper; do not enjoy fighting; go out of their way to avoid a fight; forgive and forget insults.

SELF-HARM (SFH)

High: very low self-esteem; feel they have made a mess of their lives; do not like themselves; deal

Adapted from the *Manual for the Schedule for Nonadaptive and Adaptive Personality (SNAP)* by L. A. Clark, 1993, Minneapolis: University of Minnesota Press. Copyright 1993 by University of Minnesota Press.

with frustration by hurting themselves; may feel that suicide is the only way out; may have tried to commit suicide.

Low: satisfied with the way they handle their lives; like themselves; not self-abusive; do not consider suicide a solution.

ECCENTRIC PERCEPTIONS (EP)

High: have depersonalization and derealization experiences; feel they have ESP or other special abilities; claim to have unusual or synesthetic experiences (out-of-body episodes, sensing odors as colors).

Low: do not have depersonalization/derealization experiences; do not feel they have unusual abilities; deny any odd perceptual experiences.

DEPENDENCY (DEP)

High: depend on others for direction and approval; have difficulty making up their minds; prefer to have others choose for them; lack confidence in decisions; concerned with pleasing others; check with others for approval.

Low: self-reliant; enjoy handling their own problems and making their own decisions; confident in their choices; decide things easily.

POSITIVE TEMPERAMENT (PT)

High: enjoy active and exciting lives; have a great deal of energy; work hard; undertake projects with enthusiasm; lively; cheerful; alert; interested in may things; optimistic about the future.

Low: do not find their lives interesting or exciting; easily fatigued; rarely feel enthusiastic; have few interests; not excited by new projects.

EXHIBITIONISM (EXH)

High: love the limelight; like to perform; like being the center of attention; dress and act so that people will notice them; enjoy flirting.

Low: do not enjoy being the focus of attention; dress and act so as not to be noticed; avoid public performance; do not try to attract others.

ENTITLEMENT (ENT)

High: view themselves as special and extraordinary; feel they are knowledgeable, talented, and have admirable and enviable qualities; believe they deserve special recognition and privileges beyond their current level.

Low: self-effacing; humble; do not feel they are special, unusually talented, or particularly admirable; do not believe they deserve special privileges or recognition.

DETACHMENT (DET)

High: loners; aloof and distant from others; have few friends; keep to themselves; prefer to spend their time alone; do not have warm feelings towards others; claim not to experience many strong emotions.

Low: "people people"; go out of their way to meet people; enjoy the feeling of being with friends; warm and open with others.

DISINHIBITION (DIS)

High: act spontaneously with little regard for consequences; pursue stimulating experiences without regard to risks or to social/legal norms; disorganized; often fail to honor commitments to others.

Low: not impulsive; do not manipulate others for their own ends; hold conventional, conservative views; serious; do things in order; follow rules.

IMPULSIVITY (IMP)

High: reckless; prefer to do the first thing that comes to mind; do not stop to think things over; live moment-to-moment without plans for the future; like to take chances; spend money and time on impulse.

Low: cautious; live a safe, quiet life; prefer a level-headed, "sensible" approach; think decisions through; plan things slowly and carefully; keep track of money; plan daily activities; prepare for the future.

PROPRIETY (PRO)

High: greatly concerned with proper standards of conduct; value reputation highly; place appearances over personal comfort or convenience; emphasize the importance of following social conventions; offended when others violate social rules.

Low: not concerned with social standards; comfortable with rude or boorish behavior; do not care about protecting their reputation; not strict about "right" and "wrong"; place little importance on rules or conventions.

WORKAHOLISM (WRK)

High: enjoy work more than play; neglect friends/family for work; driven; must finish everything they start; do not consider a job finished until it's perfect; continue to work on problems long after others have given up.

Low: do not enjoy hard work; do not neglect other aspects of life for work; always find time for fun; do not push themselves; do not feel the need to finish everything; will give up on a project if tired.

Author Index

Subject Index

About the Editors

Paul T. Costa, Jr., is chief of the Laboratory of Personality and Cognition at the National Institute on Aging's Gerontology Research Center, Baltimore, Maryland. He received his PhD in human development and clinical psychology from the University of Chicago. He has academic appointments in the Departments of Psychiatry and Behavioral Sciences at the Johns Hopkins University School of Medicine and at the Duke University School of Medicine and is a clinical professor of psychiatry at the Georgetown University School of Medicine. He has also held academic positions at Harvard University and the University of Massachusetts at Boston. With his colleague Robert R. McCrae, Dr. Costa has been studying the structure and stability of personality for the past 15 years. He is coauthor of the Revised NEO Personality Inventory and has published more than 170 journal articles and book chapters. He has served on the editorial boards of numerous journals on aging, health, and personality.

Thomas A. Widiger is a professor of psychology at the University of Kentucky (Lexington). He received his PhD in clinical psychology from Miami University (Ohio) and served his internship at the Cornell University Medical College (Westchester). Dr. Widiger has published over 100 journal articles and book chapters on personality disorder and is on the editorial boards of numerous journals on psychopathology and assessment. He served as the research coordinator for the American Psychiatric Association's 4th edition of the *Diagnostic and Statistical Manual of Mental Disorders (DSM-IV)*; he was also a member of the *DSM-IV* Task Force and the *DSM-IV* Personality Disorders Work Group. His currently active clinical practice focuses particularly on maladaptive personality traits.